CANADA'S URBAN PAST

CANADA'S URBAN PAST

A BIBLIOGRAPHY TO 1980
AND
GUIDE TO CANADIAN URBAN STUDIES

Alan F. J. Artibise and Gilbert A. Stelter

UNIVERSITY OF BRITISH COLUMBIA PRESS
VANCOUVER AND LONDON

CANADA'S URBAN PAST:
A BIBLIOGRAPHY TO 1980 AND GUIDE TO CANADIAN URBAN
STUDIES

© THE UNIVERSITY OF BRITISH COLUMBIA 1981
ALL RIGHTS RESERVED

This book has been published with the assistance of the Canada Council.

Canadian Cataloguing in Publication Data

Artibise, Alan F. J. 1946-
   Canada's urban past

ISBN 0- 7748-0134-4

1. Cities and towns—Canada—Bibliography. 2. Cities and towns—Study and teaching—Canada—Bibliography.
I. Stelter, Gilbert A., date.
II. Title.
Z7164.U7A78   016.3077'6'0971   C81-091085-3

International Standard Book Number 0-7748-0134-4

Printed in Canada

Contents

Acknowledgements   *xii*
Introduction   *xiii*
Directions for Users   *xxxiii*
Abbreviations   *xxxv*

I. General

1. General   1
   a. Bibliographies and Guides to Sources   1
   b. General Works   2
   c. Historiography and Methodology   4
2. Growth and Economic Development   8
   a. Economic Growth in General   8
   b. Factors in Economic Growth   9
   c. Urban Systems, Regionalism, and Metropolitanism   10
   d. Transportation   11
   e. New and Company Towns   12
3. Population   14
   a. The Process of Urbanization   14
   b. Social Characteristics of Population   15
   c. Migration, Immigration, and Ethnicity   16
   d. Native Population   17
   e. Occupation and Class   18
4. Urban Environment   19
   a. Planning   19
   b. Land and Development   24
   c. Building and Architecture   25
   d. Housing   27
   e. Form and Internal Structure   30
   f. Urban Renewal   31
5. Municipal Government   32
   a. General Studies   32
   b. Politics and Political Parties   34
   c. Structure, Administration, and Reform   35
   d. Finance and Taxation   37
   e. Services   39

II. Maritimes
    1. General   42

III. Nova Scotia
    1. General   44
    2. Amherst   46
    3. Annapolis Royal   46
    4. Antigonish   47
    5. Halifax-Dartmouth   47
        a. General   47
        b. Pre-1870   51
        c. Post-1870   53
    6. Louisbourg   54
    7. Pictou   55
    8. Shelburne   56
    9. Springhill   56
    10. Sydney and Cape Breton   56
    11. Windsor   57
    12. Yarmouth   58
    13. Other Centres   58

IV. New Brunswick
    1. General   60
    2. Fredericton   61
    3. Moncton   62
    4. Sackville   63
    5. St. Andrews   63
    6. St. John   63
    7. Other Centres   66

V. Prince Edward Island
    1. General   68
    2. Charlottetown   69

VI. Newfoundland
    1. General   70
    2. Corner Brook   72
    3. Saint John's   73
    4. Other Centres   75

VII. Quebec
   1. General — 76
   2. Arvida — 84
   3. Asbestos — 84
   4. Chicoutimi and the Saguenay Region — 84
   5. Drummondville — 86
   6. Granby — 86
   7. Hull — 86
   8. Joliette — 87
   9. Montreal and Environs — 88
      a. General — 88
      b. French Regime to 1760 — 95
      c. 1760-1850 — 96
      d. 1850-1920 — 99
      e. 1920-Present — 103
   10. Quebec City — 113
      a. General — 113
      b. French Regime to 1760 — 116
      c. 1760-1850 — 118
      d. 1850-1920 — 120
      e. 1920-Present — 121
   11. Rimouski — 123
   12. Rouyn-Noranda — 123
   13. St. Jean D'Iberville — 123
   14. St. Jérôme — 124
   15. St. Hyacinthe — 124
   16. Schefferville — 124
   17. Shawinigan — 125
   18. Sherbrooke — 125
   19. Sorel — 126
   20. Témiskaming (Kipawa) — 126
   21. Thetford Mines — 127
   22. Trois-Rivières — 127
   23. Other Centres — 128

VIII. Ontario
   1. General — 131
   2. Belleville — 140
   3. Brantford — 140

4. Brockville	141
5. Cambridge (formerly Galt, Hespeler, and Preston)	141
6. Cobalt	141
7. Cobourg	142
8. Elliott Lake	142
9. Goderich	142
10. Guelph	143
11. Hamilton	145
a. General	145
b. Pre-1921	146
c. Post-1921	148
12. Kapuskasing	149
13. Kingston	149
a. General	149
b. Pre-1850	152
c. 1850-1921	154
d. Post-1921	154
14. Kirkland Lake	154
15. Kitchener-Waterloo	155
16. London	157
a. General	157
b. Pre-1921	158
c. Post-1921	160
17. North Bay	161
18. Orillia	162
19. Oshawa	162
20. Ottawa	162
a. General	162
b. Pre-1850	164
c. 1850-1921	165
d. Post-1921	166
21. Parry Sound	169
22. Peterborough	169
23. Sarnia	170
24. Sault Ste. Marie	171
25. St. Catharines and the Niagara Region	171
26. Stratford	173
27. St. Thomas	174

28. Sudbury	174
29. Thunder Bay	176
30. Timmins	177
31. Toronto and Environs	177
a. General	177
b. Pre-1850	183
c. 1850-1921	185
d. Post-1921	190
32. Windsor	199
33. Other Centres	200

IX. Western Canada
1. General	203

X. Manitoba
1. General	207
2. Brandon	208
3. Churchill	208
4. Dauphin	209
5. Minnedosa	209
6. Portage la Prairie	209
7. St. Boniface	209
8. The Pas	209
9. Winnipeg	210
a. General	210
b. Pre-1921	213
c. Post-1921	215
10. Other Centres	219

XI. Saskatchewan
1. General	221
2. Battleford and North Battleford	222
3. Lloydminster	223
4. Moose Jaw	223
5. Prince Albert	223
6. Regina	223
7. Saskatoon	225
8. Swift Current	227
9. Other Centres	227

XII. Alberta
    1. General — 229
    2. Calgary — 231
        a. General — 231
        b. Pre-1921 — 232
        c. Post-1921 — 234
    3. Edmonton — 236
        a. General — 236
        b. Pre-1921 — 238
        c. Post-1921 — 238
    4. Lethbridge — 241
    5. Medicine Hat — 241
    6. Red Deer — 242
    7. Other Centres — 242

XIII. British Columbia
    1. General — 244
    2. Esquimalt — 247
    3. Fort Langley — 247
    4. Kamloops — 247
    5. Kitimat — 248
    6. Nanaimo — 248
    7. New Westminster — 249
    8. Penticton — 249
    9. Prince George — 249
    10. Prince Rupert — 249
    11. Vancouver and Environs — 250
        a. General — 250
        b. Pre-1921 — 255
        c. Post-1921 — 257
    12. Vernon — 260
    13. Victoria — 261
    14. Other Centres — 264

XIV. The North
    1. General — 267
    2. Dawson City — 269
    3. Whitehorse — 270
    4. Yellowknife — 271
    5. Other Centres — 272

A Guide to Canadian Urban Studies   273

I.   Introduction   275
II.   Newsletters and Journals   276
III. Canadian Housing Information Centre   278
IV.   Public Archives of Canada   280
V.   Provincial and Territorial Archives   287
VI.   Municipal Archives, Specialized Libraries, and Urban
         Information Centres   303
VII. Audio-Visual Resources   309
VIII. Other Resources   313

Author Index   323

Place Index   370

Subject Index   376

Acknowledgements

This volume could not have been completed without the assistance of many generous people. The following paragraphs attempt to acknowledge them but should any names have been unintentionally omitted, we apologize in advance.

Our first debt is to Dr. Jane C. Fredeman, Senior Editor, University of British Columbia Press. In addition to encouraging this project, she and her staff spent many hours solving numerous problems. Most importantly, all this work was handled in an understanding, cheerful, and efficient manner.

Several research assistants worked on various sections of the bibliography over the past four years. At the University of Victoria, financial support for these assistants came from the University and from the Youth Employment Program of the B.C. Government. Excellent work was done by Emmy Preston, June Bouchard, and especially William Younie. In addition to other duties, Bill prepared the first draft of the author index. At the University of Guelph, financial support for assistants was provided by the Department of History. Special mention must be made of Murray Nicolson, who spent many hours on a first draft of the complex subject index, and of Andy McCammon, who prepared the preliminary draft of the place index.

A number of friends and colleagues read earlier drafts of the bibliography, provided thesis references, and made many useful suggestions about both content and form. Among them are Larry McCann, Paul-André Linteau, Ronald Rudin, Patricia E. Roy, Donald Davis, Judith Fingard, Terry Crowley, James Lemon, John Weaver, John Taylor, Ernest Epp, Larry Kulisek, Elwood Jones, Peter Rider, Gerald Bloomfield, John H. Thompson, P. A. Buckner, and Donald Swainson.

Sincere thanks must also be extended to the staffs of various archives and libraries for their assistance in the preparation of portions of the Guide. Without this help, this section of the volume would not have been possible.

A special thanks is due June Belton of the University of Victoria. She typed two drafts of the bibliography in her usual professional manner. Indeed, June's skills extend far beyond typing and she was responsible for catching many errors and inconsistencies.

While many people contributed to this volume, we accept full responsibility for any errors it may contain. We hasten to add, however, that sins of omission and commission brought to our attention will be rectified in any future editions of this bibliography and guide.

Alan F.J. Artibise, Victoria
Gilbert A. Stelter, Guelph

Introduction

Until recently, it was commonplace for students of the Canadian city to decry the lack of basic work in the field of urban studies and to assert that this void had to be filled before substantial progress could be made. Like all generalizations, this one contains elements of truth. There are important gaps in our knowledge of Canadian urban development. Since this volume identifies the present state of research in urban history, it will help to locate areas of insufficient research and, as a result, facilitate a more comprehensive approach to the study of Canadian urban development.

However, these gaps have often been overemphasized. Much work in the field of urban studies was either "lost" in rarely consulted journals or enclosed within disciplinary boundaries, remaining unknown to all but a few urban specialists. As well, an entire genre—local history—was too hastily dismissed as irrelevant to scholars. Local histories do have certain deficiencies. Often written to commemorate an anniversary, these pleasant volumes rarely go beyond the chronicling of events. Their authors usually do not ask many meaningful questions about urbanization, being content to establish ties with a glorious past through elaborate accounts of the first settlers. But this is not to say that these studies are not useful in the search for historical understanding; they are. The "antiquarian" writers base their work on the assumption that specific towns and cities have distinct personalities, and this tradition still has value. Local histories can also serve as valuable sources. They provide a detailed outline of past events and thus a place to begin study. Any scholar interested in a given community has a marked advantage if he finds one or more accounts prepared by the local anniversary committee or by other groups or individuals.

This bibliography—with its more than 7,000 entries, its extensive guide, and detailed indexes—brings together many kinds of urban and urban-related materials. We undertook the task because of our strong belief that such a volume will for the first time enable those interested in studying Canadian urban development to make full use of virtually all of the material that already exists.

For all its value as a reference tool, this volume cannot by itself dramatically alter the shape or direction of Canadian urban history. Significant progress will be achieved only when students of the city combine the information contained in completed and on-going research with more sophisticated methodologies and clearer conceptual frameworks. Studies of Canadian urban development must not only include the interpretation and analysis of specific historical events, they must also explore the causes of social change and study the relationships among the several dimensions of human experience (political, social, economic, demographic, and spatial). To do so, the relevant tools and concepts developed by the social sciences are essential. In addition, the urban historian has to be concerned with the historical process of urbanization, "a process which envelopes an enormous range of places, not only within one country, but across the face of the globe."[1] The challenge is to relate this complex process to the specific experience of particular places, to use the particularity of the place to illustrate the generalities of the process, and vice-versa. Students of urban development must take a town or city and explain its present condition in terms of the historical forces that have put it there, thus providing a measure of understanding of the way in which people attempt to order their lives and to participate in the decisions that give a particular place a style, form, and direction. In this way urban history becomes an integral part of the larger story of the development of a region or nation.

The balance of this introduction is designed to assist the user in the pursuit of these complex tasks. We first give the reader a rationale for the material we chose to include in this volume, and then we provide a detailed guide to current approaches to urban history, discussing both their weaknesses and their strengths. The main objective of this section will have been achieved if readers gain a new appreciation not only of the challenges facing urban history, but also of its great potential in the on-going search for historical understanding.

PRINCIPLES OF SELECTION

Several principles have guided our choice of material. The first is that urban history is a field of knowledge in which many disciplines converge; it is not a single discipline in any exclusive sense. What urban historians have in common is a special concern for time and place. This concern usually places the urban historian somewhere between the social scientist—primarily concerned with large scale, general patterns—and the local historian—concerned with the unique and particular qualities of a specific community. At the international level, a number of disciplines have brought their specialized expertise to urban history with positive results. In the United States, urban history has often been regarded as an aspect of social history and the related social sciences, while in Canada the influence of geography has been most apparent. Architects, planners, and political scientists have also turned to the urban past with new interest. Research and writing on economic and social development is usually done by geographers and historians, not economists or sociologists, although there are signs that this is changing.[2]

A second principle is that towns and cities must be regarded as nodes or subsystems of a larger society. In other words, the urban unit can be more effectively studied if seen in a regional, a national, or even an international context. For this reason, we have included a large quantity of material which might be regarded as only marginally urban history, but which provides information extremely valuable to those dealing with the urban past. Also, we have carefully selected what we believe to be some of the best non-Canadian material and included it in Section I of the bibliography and in several portions of the guide.

A third principle concerns the relationship of the past and the present. We believe that the past represents a significant dimension of the present.[3] This is not to suggest that the past should be studied in order to take policies designed for another age and apply them to our own. Urban history could not be a policy science, by itself providing directions for the present, even if the state of the field were much more developed than it is. Nevertheless, a firm knowledge of the evolution of a particular city, or of a country's system of cities, is a prerequisite to making some sense out of seemingly chaotic modern cities. In this regard, material listed here could be divided into that which is primarily concerned with description or analysis of change over time and that which is consciously policy-oriented. The first type includes a good deal of literature dealing with the very recent past; and items are included even where their primary aim is not historical. Literature which represents policy proposals has been included only if it was written several decades ago. For example, some of the significant articles advocating changes in the philosophy and practise of planning during the 1920's have been included. On the other hand, most of the numerous recent policy pronouncements have not been, but bibliographies for such policy areas as housing, citizen participation, and heritage conservation are cited.

A GUIDE TO APPROACHES IN URBAN HISTORY

Finding one's way through the great number of studies now available can be a complex task, even with a detailed bibliography at hand. We will therefore offer suggestions about the best guides to urban history and propose our own categorization of the literature in the field. The most useful entry points are probably a series of survey articles. At the international level, articles by H. J. Dyos in Britain and Michael Frisch and Theodore Hershberg in the United States are particularly relevant.[4] The major accounts of Canadian development from the point of view of historians have been provided by Frederick Armstrong, Gilbert Stelter, and John Weaver.[5] James Lemon and John Marshall have written key articles relating geography to urban history.[6] Also useful are Harold Kalman on the history of architecture and Deryck Holdsworth on the preservation movement.[7] Less formal discussions of the nature of urban history and what has been done in the field are found in some of the recent interviews Bruce Stave has published. Stave began by interviewing nine of the major founders of urban history in the United States,[8] but he has branched out to include scholars in Britain and Australia,[9] and most recently, Canada.[10]

Several journals devoted to urban history are essential sources for information on what is being done. At the international level, three publications stand out. The *Urban History Yearbook,* founded by the late H. J. Dyos and published by the Leicester University Press, emphasizes British urban history, but it makes a fairly successful effort to cover developments throughout the world. Canadian books are regularly reviewed, and Canadian publications are included in its impressive annual international bibliography. The *Journal of Urban History* is the major periodical published in the United States. It makes a special effort to include material that deals with new research techniques and methodologies, interdisciplinary approaches, comparative studies, and historiography. The *JUH* also has an excellent review section encompassing review essays on urban history in the international context. Also worthy of note is *Urbanism: Past and Present,* which superseded the Urban History Group *Newsletter* published between 1954 and 1975. A major objective of *UPP* is to establish a dialogue among the social sciences and humanities through a regular commentary on articles by various specialists. For Canadian urban history, the focal point is the *Urban History Review,* edited by Alan Artibise and published by the National Museum of Man. Begun as a newsletter in 1972, the *UHR* has since become a full-fledged journal with major articles, but it also continues to perform its function of providing up-to-date information on publications, conferences, on-going research, and developments in the archives field.

The existence of these and other urban history journals[11] should not be taken as evidence that urban history is clearly defined. In many cases it remains a rubric under which is placed anything and everything that has happened in the past in villages, towns, and cities. Most "urban historians" have failed to distinguish between research treating the city as the unit of study and that using the city merely as a convenient setting for the study of processes that are not exclusively urban in nature. They have also usually failed to make a distinction between the city as a dependent variable and the city as an independent variable. The result, in Canada and elsewhere, has been a good deal of conceptual confusion.

Fortunately, several important attempts have already been made to overcome these problems, most notably by Eric Lampard and Theodore Hershberg.[12] Drawing on the suggestions made by these and other scholars, and on our own experience gained in compiling this volume, we believe that virtually all Canadian urban history can be placed into one of three major categories. The first is *urban as entity,* in which the aim is to explain the formation of the urban environment in terms of both people and place. A variety of independent variables—population movements, technology, economic growth, politics—are assessed for their impact on the final result, the city. The second is *urban as process,* in which the urban environment itself becomes the independent variable, affecting the people and events contained within the boundaries of a particular community. The third is *urban as setting,* in which the city or town is an incidental location for the study of other explanatory categories such as class and social mobility or capitalism and labour relations. We will analyse the kind of literature now available in each of these categories.

1. *Urban as entity.* The studies in this category constitute the bulk of writing on urban history. They involve viewing the city as an entity whose form and structure are determined by large-scale economic, political, and social forces and by thousands of individual decisions. Although most studies do not make it explicit, the city is thus regarded as a "dependent variable," the product of these forces. A key feature is a sense of place, implying a recognition of the particular qualities of a city, including a sensitivity not only to geographic site, but also to its situation—its context locally, regionally, and nationally—and to the complex mix of people which make up its population and the way in which they are organized. The studies in this category are done at both the level of urbanization as a societal process and at the level of the individual place. There are three major types of literature in this category of urban as entity: urban biographies; studies of urban systems; and studies of particular themes such as population growth, economic development, building the physical artifact, and the evolution of municipal government.

The urban biography forms by far the largest body of literature about the urban past. The quality varies greatly, ranging from sophisticated attempts to look at the total experience of a city to local boosterism in which the city is seen as a continuously unfolding success story where all residents, regardless of class, supposedly share common goals. In most biographies the city or town is treated as a personality with distinguishable characteristics. The best urban biographies place the community into a larger context, thereby revealing the extent to which local developments and events relate to regional or national phenomena and how developments in the particular community might be similar to or different from the norm. An example of a successful biography of this kind is *The Rise of Toronto, 1850-1890* (1947) by Donald C. Masters. The particular mix of people and the nature of commercial enterprise are carefully described, as is Toronto's position in Ontario and its competition with Montreal for domination of the national urban scene. In this same tradition, but much less detailed, is John Cooper's *Montreal, A Brief History* (1969), in which the relationship between various aspects of urban life are briefly suggested. Alan Artibise gives evidence of the positive qualities of urban biography in his *Winnipeg: A Social History of Urban Growth, 1874-1914* (1975). This volume provides a rounded narrative of the city's development and particularly of the role of a growth-conscious commercial elite.

A number of more popularly written urban biographies also approach their subject as an entity and are useful to the urban historian. A recent example is Paul O'Neill's two-volume *The Story of St. John's, Newfoundland* (1975 and 1976). Like many local histories, O'Neill's account tends to include virtually everything of interest that went on within the city's boundaries, and his topically organized chapters inhibit any conception of the community's development over time. Yet O'Neill is a masterful storyteller, and the volumes contain carefully assembled information about economic development, politics, and cultural activities. A recent project of the National Museum of Man—the *History of Canadian Cities Series*—attempts to combine the best qualities of the scholarly biography with the readability of the popular form. The series is based on the assumption that a community's history has meaning not discernible by a study of fragmentary portions only and that the totality of the urban experience is usually not present in thematic studies. The authors attempt to see the community as a whole and to relate the parts to a larger context. The series is also based on the belief that, while each city has a distinct personality that deserves to be discovered, the volumes must also provide data and analysis that will lift the narrative of a given city's experience to the level where it will elucidate questions that are of concern to Canadians generally. These include such matters as ethnic relationships, regionalism, provincial-municipal interaction, social mobility, labour-management relationships, urban planning, and general economic development. The series is also visually attractive since each volume contains more than one hundred illustrations. Published to date are volumes on *Winnipeg* (1977), *Calgary* (1978), and *Vancouver* (1980), and many more volumes are in preparation. A significant feature of the series is the inclusion of medium and smaller sized cities and towns such as Fredericton, Whitehorse, and Kitchener/Waterloo.

A second type of literature in which the urban entity is regarded as a dependent variable is that dealing with urban systems at the national and regional levels. The idea that cities form a central component of a national heartland-hinterland relationship has been explored in terms of economic geography by James Simmons and in terms of metropolitanism by historian J. M. S. Careless.[13] Both emphasize the openness of the Canadian system, that is, the extent to which it is influenced by external forces. Because cities play an important role in the export of raw materials abroad, fluctuations in the international demand for these products have an immediate and direct effect on urban growth. At the regional level of systems, economists Harvey Lithwick and Gilles Paquet have regarded an urban system as something like the skeleton or framework of a region, and a good deal of recent research takes this approach.[14] The place of cities in Western Canada has been examined by Careless and Artibise, and in the Maritimes by Careless. Jacob Spelt's study of urban development in South-Central Ontario is still the standard work on the history of urbanization in that province.[15] Some of the best work on the place of a single city in its regional setting has been done by geographer Larry McCann in his analysis of two metropolitan centres, Vancouver and Halifax, and by economist Paul Phillips on Winnipeg.[16]

Perhaps the clearest example of urban places as dependent variables are the resource towns created by companies exploiting a natural resource. The literature on this aspect of Canadian urban development is plentiful and has recently been reviewed in a special issue of *Plan Canada*.[17] Gilbert Stelter has written about

Sudbury, Ontario, as a commercial centre of a group of smaller communities directly based on the mining and smelting of nickel.[18] This group of communities formed something of an urban field, with each performing distinct functions, much like the urban field described by Fred Dahms in his work on the small towns of Wellington County, Ontario.[19]

A third type of literature in this category of urban as entity deals with specific themes such as population, economic growth, building the physical artifact, and municipal government. Population is the starting point for some scholars who study city formation. In the standard monograph on the subject, Leroy Stone's *Urban Development in Canada* (1967), a framework is provided which allows comparison among communities. Stone begins with the general and moves to the particular, from a study of urbanization as a process to a study of the cities themselves. Studies of the ethnic and religious characteristics of a city's population and how this would help determine a city's character are still relatively rare. Exceptions are articles by Norbert MacDonald on Vancouver and by Artibise on Winnipeg.[20] But the degree to which the concentration of population in cities reflected significant structural changes in the society of the Western World, such as the slow conversion of high fertility rate, large family rural populations into lower fertility rate, small family urbanites, has not been studied in any extended way in Canada.[21]

A more popular field of study is the question of city formation and economic growth. Why do cities grow or not grow? What are the most significant factors which promote or inhibit growth? Differences in explanation usually stem from a failure to distinguish between two related sides of urban growth: that which is the product of large-scale forces such as the external demand for staples, population movements, and the process of industrialization; and the city and its residents as a force which stimulates or inhibits development and often determines the direction and location of development. One of the future tasks of urban history is the classification of the differences between, and the relationships of, these two forces. Some progress toward this goal has already been achieved, but a clear conceptual framework, which can be labelled the evolutionary conception of urban systems is only now emerging.[22] Indeed, several researchers have already used this approach in their work and others are in the process of doing so.[23] To date, however, no overview has been attempted.

The evolutionary view of urban development sees a continuous series of individual and collective responses to a changing urban and regional environment. Cities are partially ordered collectivities which, at certain times, draw participants and, at other times, spin them off. In this context, each round of decisions by the participants results in resource exploitation and transformation and, therefore, some greater or lesser modification in the human and natural environment. Clearly, in such a view, no city is exactly like another. Nonetheless, the interactive process of decision-making is subject to some generality.

At the core of this evolutionary process is the concept of density. It is not merely the density of human beings, but of economic activities, social organizations, and urban artifacts. These elements together make up the evolving urban environment. Since it is the density of all these factors which constitute the stuff of urban studies, urban history must analyse the interrelationships among these various densities over time.

In the evolutionary framework, what separates life in a farming village from life in a large metropolitan centre is only incidentally a question of scale. Over time, as cities get larger, more cities become large, while even more cities come into existence. There are a series of thresholds which change the intensity of the densities of people, organizations, activities, and artifacts. These are moving thresholds, not absolutes, but a series of simultaneous relationships between people and their urban environment, between each city and the area it serves, and finally, between the present possibilities and the legacy of past decisions.

The outcomes of different mixtures of densities vary subject to the development context in which the mixtures occur, so that technological development and per capita income serve as constraints on the outcome of each local density mixture. For example, one of the things that distinguishes urban development in North and South America, Australia, and some parts of the Soviet Union from urban development elsewhere is that on these continents the growth of cities, the growth of the national economy, the settlement of low-density areas, and initial utilization of resources in newly settled areas occurs simultaneously. That is, as a newly established area is filled with people, not only do market densities change, but the density of organizations and activities at the core cities change as well. Part of that filling-in process always involves the formation of new settlements. Some of the new settlements are competitive, and some are complementary to existing settlements.[24]

There is strong evidence that the character of city formation in Canada (in the East as well as the West) was determined by the settlement process. Throughout most of our history, each generation of city-builders confronted a major portion of the economic landscape which could be developed relatively free of the residue of earlier decision-makers. The urban system was constantly in the process of restructuring itself with the formation of new commercial and industrial centres, each of which went through its own evolution in a somewhat disjunctive fashion from the evolution of the system as a whole. Furthermore, as the hierarchy was reordered, there was a general westward shift in the resource development sites.[25] What constituted growth advantages and disadvantages in this system of moving thresholds and shifting markets depended on the timing of settlements in newer areas and on how each city's economy meshed with the larger developing regional and national system. Older areas had the major concentrations of population and dominated the distribution of capital, knowledge, and technology. However, the cities with newly established economies were relatively unobstructed by earlier commitments and had a chance to implement new technology and new capital improvements immediately.

This evolutionary framework is less precise than the well-ordered world of central place theory or the empirical precision of modern output models. Yet efforts to form these broad generalizations into more vigorously specified models appears to be a productive avenue. Evolutionary models of urbanization can perhaps account for some of the variance in the historical urban data generated in recent years. This variance suggests that during periods of very rapid growth a basic structure is put in place according to the constraints and possibilities of that day, and subsequently this past continues to influence the specific behaviour of individuals and institutions in the city. Evolutionary models thus require that some sort of age analysis be incorporated into the study of any given city.[26] More importantly, however, some multi-variable accounting system is required so that any city may take shape in response to a variety of interactions with other cities in the regional, national, or international framework. Rates and composition of population migration and growth will vary according to circumstances in other parts of the network, as do occupations and employment, political institutions, and so on.

In addition to studies that deal with population and city formation, there is a growing body of literature that examines the evolution of the physical environment. This is an area where a number of other disciplines, particularly geography, architecture, and planning, can most directly make a contribution to the knowledge of the urban past. Most of the work on the history of city planning is concentrated on the reform movement of the early twentieth century when planning became professionalized and subject to the influences of the city beautiful and garden city movements. The rhetoric and thinking of the planners has been well documented by Paul Rutherford, Walter Van Nus, Peter Smith, and Thomas Gunton.[27] The relationship between planners' ideals and the hard, practical realities of actual city-building is outlined by Elizabeth Bloomfield's analysis of planning in Kitchener/Waterloo and by Max Foran's description of the physical evolution of Calgary.[28] In terms of successive planning styles, several historians and geographers have recently suggested that resource town planning is a useful, accurate reflection of planning styles in vogue at a time when specific resource towns were built, particularly because the company's planners could put their ideas into effect directly without worrying about any existing infrastructure.[29]

If any theme runs through the recent literature on planning, it is the question of who makes planning decisions, and especially the importance of the dominant business elite in determining the shape of the urban landscape. For example, John Bottomley has shown how Vancouver's elite operated through the Vancouver Board of Trade to lobby the city and British Columbia to adopt planning legislation they considered necessary for efficient economic and urban growth.[30] Meena Dahr has interpreted the evolution of land use planning in Toronto in much the same way.[31] Perhaps the most compelling reasons planners forsook a kind of planning that advocated general and comprehensive plans for a relatively powerless managerial role has been suggested by Walter Van Nus's work on the evolution of zoning. Not only were planners severely limited in the funds they had available to draw up by-laws, but also the restricted franchise of most Canadian cities meant that the interests of the property owners dominated municipal politics. The basis of political support for zoning was thus the desire to protect property values.[32]

The relationship between planning and promotion is brought into clear focus in Paul-André Linteau's work on Maisonneuve, an industrial suburb of Montreal. He shows how promoters reaped windfall profits on large tracts of land they owned by controlling the municipal council and bringing about the adoption of an industrial policy favouring population growth.[33] Linteau and his colleague at the Université du Quebec à Montréal, Jean-Claude Robert, have also examined Montreal in the early nineteenth century in terms of land development. One of their interests is the French-Canadian capitalist; they argue that while French-Canadian capitalists were definitely a minority in the fields of finance, commerce, and industry, they nevertheless exercised real power through their domination of land investment in their role as land developers.[34] The nature of land development in nineteenth-century Ontario has been clarified by Michael Doucet's thesis on Hamilton. As in other Victorian cities, Doucet found that the development process in Hamilton was essentially decentralized, uncoordinated, and unregulated, with hundreds of different people involved at various stages of the process. He makes a sharp distinction between speculators and builders. While speculation did not lead to escalating prices, because the premature nature of much sub-division created a surplus of building lots which kept prices down, the small scale of the construction industry and the lack of regulation produced fragmented patterns of development.[35] In a study of a Hamilton suburb during the twentieth century, John Weaver has shown how developers produced their own form of control, employing restrictive covenants to force social or racial conformity in land ownership and stylistic conformity in the construction of buildings.[36]

The patterns of land arrangement partly determined the type of residences constructed on the land, but local traditions—preference for single-detached houses in the West and the Maritimes versus the row house in Montreal, for example—had an effect on what was built. While housing as a subject of historical research remains largely unexplored in Canada, pieces of the story can be seen in scattered materials.[37] The quality and amount of housing available to individuals depended basically on their income, for the provision of housing was usually left to market forces. The "invisible hand" of the competitive market did not allow lower income groups the privilege of decent accommodation, but public concern seldom led to public ameliorative action.[38] More than any other aspect of city-building, housing remained almost totally in the hands of the private sector.[39]

While housing has been neglected as an area of study, internal public transportation is being studied vigorously, particularly by the street railway buffs.[40] The horse-drawn and then the electrically driven streetcar made possible the spatial expansion beyond the compact, walking-distance community. The impact of internal transportation was actually the reverse of that of intercity transportation. Railways led to a centralization of industrial and commercial functions in cities at strategic locations along the rail lines because bulky goods could not be moved easily within cities. But the streetcar encouraged decentralization, especially after electrification. In some cases like Montreal and Vancouver, street cars preceded development and stimulated the subdivision of land;[41] in others, like Toronto and Winnipeg, they were drawn to areas that were being developed.[42]

Perhaps because Toronto's public transportation system has long had a reputation for quality and efficiency, it has come under considerable recent academic scrutiny. Michael Doucet had described Toronto's successful experience in terms of its adoption of a municipally owned system in 1921; through public ownership it was able to avoid the pitfalls and destruction of the privately owned systems in the United States.[43] This interpretation was quickly challenged by Donald Davis in a convincing rejoinder. Davis argued that Toronto's good fortune was largely an accidental by-product of the private company's greed. Refusing to build beyond the heavily built-up parts of the city in order to ensure a good profit from heavy ridership, the company actually forced Toronto to remain a compact city, making possible the later public transportation successes.[44]

Stimulated in part by the struggles in each city to preserve significant buildings, the interest in urban architectural history has grown rapidly. Much of the current literature, however, continues to emphasize the homes and business establishments of the elite to the exclusion of that portion of the cityscape not produced by well-known architects. This applies to the older classic, Eric Arthur's *Toronto, No Mean City* (1964), as well as to William Dendy's more recent *Lost Toronto* (1978) and Martin Segger's, *Victoria: A Primer for Regional History in Architecture* (1979). These volumes, nevertheless, are important efforts in developing a general appreciation of past urban environments. A growing body of literature relates architecture to function and to its community setting.[45] Deryck Holdsworth has shown the relationship between architectural styles and home ownership in early twentieth-century Vancouver. He found two complementary trends: the vehicle for fulfilling the desire for home ownership was usually the California bungalow, while nostalgia for the past was represented by the Tudor Cottage. In a broad sense these styles reflected the social and spatial compartmentalization of the city.[46] A broader perspective is also evident in Harold Kalman's *Exploring Vancouver 2* (1978), for commonplace and anonymous structures (in terms of known architects) are included as well as the famous landmarks. Perhaps the most effective guides to the built form of the past are the series of walking tours published by several local chapters of Institutes of Architects, such as *Exploring Toronto* (1977), *Exploring Montreal* (1975), and *Exploring Halifax* (1976). Each looks at districts as well as individual buildings, at the vernacular as well as the architecturally "significant," spectacular structures.

In a recent important review article, Deryck Holdsworth has pointed to the connection between a sound awareness (on the part of both the general public and academics) of the built environment of the past and current conservation strategies.[47] This connection has been aided by the establishment of the Canadian Inventory of Historic Buildings in 1970 and the setting up of teams of professionals in Ottawa and in regional centres. An important product of this initiative has been the publication of manuals such as Ann Falkner's *Without Our Past?* (1977), a handbook on preservation procedures for local citizens. In Ontario, a provincial heritage act in 1974 gave rise to the creation of some eighty Local Architectural Conservation Advisory Committees (LACACs). Their impressive record was collected in *Conserving Ontario's Main Streets* (1978), a good example of the success which can be achieved if professionals combine with an increasingly aware public and move away from a narrow concern only with great or "pretty" buildings.

The role of municipal government in shaping the form of towns and cities is under active investigation on several points. Most of the interest is centred on the era of reform from 1880 to 1920—roughly parallelling the American Progressive movement—when Canadians experimented with American models of centralized decision-making and scientific management such as boards of control, city managers, and commission government. There has been little agreement on how to regard this period and its accomplishments. According to Paul Rutherford, the middle class reformers who led this movement were agents of positive social change.[48] Most recent commentators argue, however, that the reformers' rhetoric hid their desire to make cities less democratic by expanding bureaucracies and increasing regulatory powers at the expense of newcomers and the poor.[49] One of the traditions stemming from this period was the notion of non-partisanship in municipal politics. In some cases at least, the tradition has been more apparent than real. Ed Rea's analysis of Winnipeg city politics has shown that Winnipeg city council has been the arena for two contending groups which sought political control in order to implement their conflicting ideologies; these can be readily identified as "citizen" and "labour." The citizens have controlled Winnipeg's council for over fifty years, yet responsibility has been evaded by a failure to acknowledge partisan control.[50] The structural change and the accompanying ideology of local government formulated during this reform period—such ideas as non-partisanship and such structures as at-large rather than ward elections and boards of control—are still with us. A system designed for another age remains a significant factor affecting present-day decision-making, for example, by removing many of the key issues from the arena of legislative debate.

The activity of city governments in coping with the problems of growth and providing a variety of services has only recently been studied. One area involves the question of municipal ownership of utilities and the extent to which this was an ideological issue. In their study of the Toronto waterworks system, 1840-1877, Elwood Jones and Douglas McCalla argue that the reasons for delaying municipal ownership did not involve political positions. Debates were couched in practical terms of growth and changing economic, technical and institutional contexts.[51] One of the most significant aspects of municipal government and its services is the powerlessness of municipal governments in relation to other levels of government. Terry Copp has shown how Montreal was hampered in its efforts to handle the crisis of the depression by its lack of financial autonomy and its lack of political clout in a rural-dominated provincial legislature.[52] In some cases, a loss of municipal autonomy was partially self-inflicted. John Taylor has suggested that during the Great Depression western cities were unwilling to face certain social responsibilities and made themselves virtually impotent in the face of federal, provincial, and private control.[53]

2. *Urban as process*. In the previous category attention was directed toward what created the urban environment. In the category of urban as process, the question is: How did the urban environment affect the people and activities within it? Thus, the city is regarded as an independent variable in some way influencing social organization and behaviour. All urban environments share some characteristics, but basic differences based on time, place, and function require a sensitivity to particular contexts. Some of the classic studies of urban history, such as Lewis Mumford's *The City in History* (1961), have suggested a classification of functional community types based on changes in technology and economic function. To this could be added population movements and political change. What emerges are stages in the evolution of Canadian urban environments from that of the colonial mercantile city of the seventeenth and eighteenth centuries to the commercial city of the nineteenth century and the industrial city of the late nineteenth century.

Some of the best clues to understanding urban as process derive from Theodore Hershberg's monumental project on Philadelphia. He takes "*work* and *residence* as the basic building blocks of the physical and social environment"[54] and suggests that major changes in these occur as the environments change. Changes in the modes and means of productive activity affect both the setting in which work takes place and the content of that work. For example, during the move from the commercial to the industrial stage, work and residence are separated, tasks become specialized, and work is reorganized hierarchically. According to Hershberg, these "changes gradually affected identity, roles, values and expectations, social networks, class consciousness, and so on through an almost endless list of human experience."[55] In the same fashion, he argues for a strong relationship between residential patterns and human behaviour. His findings for Philadelphia indicate that the residential fabric was determined to a large extent by the distribution of jobs, and, thus, the changing economic functions of the city have a bearing on the spatial arrangements of the population. An extensive literature is devoted to the many aspects of behaviour tied to residential patterns.

A growing body of historical literature in Canada could be placed in this category, although work here is not nearly as widespread as work on urban as entity.

The first major study of this type was Peter Goheen's *Victorian Toronto, 1850 to 1900: Pattern and Process of Growth* (1970). Goheen regarded Toronto as a special kind of environment with unique patterns of social organization. One of his concerns was the significant shift in the scale of the industrial units of production as many small workshops with a few employees were consolidated into larger factories, each with a considerable number of employees. Another was the improvement in public transportation which changed the nature of time and distance in the city and made it possible to separate place of residence from place of work. The social consequences of the process were similar to those in other large cities on the continent: social differences slowly became translated into spatial segregation by economic rank and, to a lesser extent, religious affiliation.

Another major study of this type is Michael Katz's reconstruction of social and family patterns within Hamilton during the 1850's. His *The People of Hamilton, Canada West* (1975) represented a major advance in terms of a concern for urban context from his earlier work on the subject which resembled most of the American mobility studies and gave no sense of how the particular places people lived in influenced their behaviour. Among his central contentions is that Hamilton represented a distinct city type, the commercial city; thus, the place he was studying was representative of a social system which persisted for several centuries in the Atlantic world. His general conclusion was that the two underlying themes of nineteenth-century urban history were inequality and transiency. He demonstrated the distance between the rich and the poor in several ways and suggested that the degree of inequality increased rather than decreased with the onset of industrialization. Two of Katz's associates who examined Hamilton's mid-nineteenth-century social geography, Ian Davey and Michael Doucet, found that the city had not yet achieved the kind of social and spatial organization associated with industrial cities. While the central area showed a surprising degree of specialization, the residential distribution of the population constituted a more complex pattern, not the clearly segregated pattern of a later period.[56]

A particularly promising area of study in terms of urban as process is that of the immigrant and the city. The Irish immigrants of the mid-nineteenth century greatly increased the populations and affected the character of many Canadian cities. How the urban experience changed them has been examined in detail by Murray Nicolson in an analysis of the Irish Catholics in Victorian Toronto. In order to resist assimilation into the predominantly Protestant milieu of the city, Irish Catholics consciously created a parallel structure of education, health and welfare, and even of employment. Their religion became one of the major bulwarks in maintaining their ethnic identity.[57] The non-English speaking immigrants of the early twentieth century also often settled directly in the largest cities. Lillian Petroff's study of the Macedonian community in Toronto is a useful outline of how the boarding houses—the temporary quarters of men intending to return home—gave way to more permanent residential patterns as sojourners became settlers and adopted a larger view of the city. This often coincided with a transition from bachelorhood to marriage and from an interest only in factory work to the possibilities of shopkeeping, even outside the ethnic neighbourhood.[58]

Another stimulating example of the study of urban as process is Carl Betke's account of Edmonton's early development.[59] In an original and ably argued article, Betke asserts that while individualism was not entirely overcome in the city by the early 1900's, independent behaviour had been sacrificed in many fields as the city and its many agencies—public and private—became the units governing individual conduct. Significantly, however, while Edmonton developed a wide array of social mechanisms which emphasized community, the mechanisms themselves—ethnic societies, churches, labour and sport organizations, and so forth—were usually copies of or affiliated with national or international associations. Related to the paper's discussion of the mechanisms of early Edmonton community, therefore, is the theme of the derivative quality of the new prairie urbanism.

These few examples of studies of urban as process indicate that this category lags far behind that of urban as entity. Yet the study of urban as process is perhaps the most promising area of research since once completed, it will be possible to see the simultaneity, the complex feedback loops, and the unanticipated consequences that issue from change in a given corner of the urban system. Solid, empirically based work in the area of urban as process will put Canadian historians in a position to understand the interplay of personalities, political decisions, major events, institutional behaviour, and impersonal, large-scale, socioeconomic and demographic forces.

3. *Urban as setting.* Much material sometimes classified as urban history deals with things that happened in cities. The city itself is not the central concern; it is merely a backdrop, the arena within which subjects of greater concern to the writer are discussed. The categorization is not meant to denegrate studies of this type, for they can be of considerable importance. However, it is necessary to make explicit the conceptions underlying the vast amount of literature which more or less directly deals with cities or events in cities.

From the substantial number of items in this category, labour history can be used as an example. One of the common threads running through the so-called "second generation" of labour or, as some prefer, working-class historians is a commitment to the community study. Gregory Kealey, Bryan Palmer, and others have argued that labour historians must immerse themselves in studies set in single towns and cities or regional communities since this is the only way that an author can appreciate the real historical experience of workers.[60] This approach, they argue, is far closer to the realities of Canadian social and industrial development than historians concerned with national issues have suggested.

Few urban historians would argue with this commitment by labour historians to the community study. Indeed, several of these studies not only contribute to labour history but also make a significant contribution to our understanding of

Canadian urban development. Included in this group of studies are David Bercuson's *Confrontation at Winnipeg: Labour, Industrial Relations and the General Strike* (1974), Michael Piva's *The Condition of the Working Class in Toronto, 1900-1921* (1979), and Gregory Kealey's *Toronto Workers Respond to Industrial Capitalism, 1867-1892* (1980). All three volumes firmly set their studies of the working class in a particular community and, while they do not go so far as to deal with urban as process, they effectively use the sharp detail of limited chronology and restricted setting to illuminate the complex dimensions of the past.

Some studies that use urban as setting are not so successful. For all its value to labour history, Bryan Palmer's *A Culture in Conflict: Skilled Workers and Industrial Capitalism in Hamilton, Ontario, 1860-1914* (1979) makes little contribution to urban studies. The workers the author deals with are not firmly set in the community of Hamilton; indeed, one is left with the strong impression that the characters of this study could have lived almost anywhere. Details about the city's population (size, ethnic composition, demography), about the general nature of labour organization, about social services and housing, and so on would have made the analysis of skilled workers far more convincing. The point is that all those who use urban as setting must appreciate the need to take considerable care in providing detailed contextual data. It is here, for example, that professional historians can most often call upon the materials of local history to provide the necessary detail.

CONCLUSION

Several conclusions follow from this overview of Canadian urban history. The first and most obvious is that there is much promise in all the new energy evident in historical studies of the Canadian city, particularly in regard to the increased sophistication in methodology, the genuine interest in interdisciplinary communication, and the desire to develop new conceptual frameworks. These related trends will almost certainly continue to exert a powerful influence on students of the Canadian city and will also almost certainly produce a sufficient number of generalizations and hypotheses to force other scholars to see their assumptions and conceptual frameworks in a new light.

At the same time, nothing is more likely to put a researcher on a false track than to assume that he can proceed without a firm understanding of the studies already completed. It is our hope that the material assembled in this bibliography and guide will be used as an important tool in the search for a deeper understanding of Canadian urban development in particular and urbanization in general and that it will contribute to a significant reduction in the fragmentation and compartmentalization of knowledge. Whether researchers approach their topic under the category of urban as setting, as process, or as site, they can benefit from the observation, insights, methods, and conclusions of those who preceded them.

Notes

These notes use the abbreviations contained in the *List of Abbreviations* found in the preliminary pages of this volume.

1. Bruce M. Stave, "A Conversation with H. J. Dyos: Urban History in Great Britain," *JUH* 5 (1979):478-79 and passim.
2. Gilbert A. Stelter, "Current Research in Canadian Urban History," *UHR* 9 (June 1980):110-28.
3. Alan F. J. Artibise and Gilbert A. Stelter, "The Past in the Present: Exploring the Relevance of Canada's Urban Past," in Artibise and Stelter, *The Usable Urban Past: Planning and Politics in the Modern Canadian City* (Toronto, 1979), pp. 1-3.
4. H. J. Dyos, ed., *The Study of Urban History* (London, 1968); Michael Frisch, "American Urban History as an Example of Recent Historiography," *History and Theory* 18 (1979):350-77; Theodore Hershberg, "The New Urban History: Toward an Interdisciplinary History of the City," *JUH* 5 (1978):3-40.
5. Frederick Armstrong, "Urban History in Canada," *UHR* 1-72 (February 1972):11-14; Gilbert A. Stelter, "A Sense of Time and Place: The Historian's Approach to Canada's Urban Past," in Stelter and Artibise, eds., *The Canadian City: Essays in Urban History* (Toronto, 1977), pp. 420-41; John C. Weaver, "Urban Canada: Recent Historical Writing," *QQ* 86 (1979):75-97.
6. James Lemon, "Study of the Urban Past: Approaches by Geographers," CHA, *HP* (1973):179-90; John Marshall, "Geography's Contribution to the Historical Study of Urban Canada," *UHR* 1-73 (May 1973):15-24.
7. Harold Kalman, "Recent Literature on the History of Canadian Architecture," *Journal of the Society of Architectural Historians* 31 (1972):312-23; Deryck Holdsworth, "Built Forms and Social Realities: A Review Essay of Recent Work on Canadian Heritage Structures," *UHR* 9 (October 1980):123-38.
8. Bruce M. Stave, *The Making of Urban History: Historiography through Oral History* (Beverly Hills, 1977).
9. Stave, "A Conversation with H. J. Dyos," and Stave, "A Conversation with Graeme Davison: Urban History in Australia," *JUH* 5 (1978):69-92.
10. Stave, "Urban History in Canada: A Conversation with Alan F. J. Artibise," *UHR* 8 (February 1980):110-43; Stave, "A Conversation with Gilbert A. Stelter: Urban History in Canada," *JUH* 6 (1980):177-210.
11. An extensive list can be found in the guide section of this volume.
12. Hershberg, "The New Urban History," and Eric Lampard, "The Dimensions of Urban History: A Footnote to the 'Urban Crisis,' " *PHR* 39 (1970):268.
13. James Simmons, *Canada as an Urban System: A Conceptual Framework*, Research Paper #62 (Toronto: CUCS, 1974); J. M. S. Careless, "Metropolis and Region: The Interplay between City and Region in Canadian History before 1914," *UHR* 3-78 (February 1979):99-118.
14. Harvey Lithwick and Gilles Paquet, "Urban Growth and Regional Contagion," in Lithwick and Paquet, eds., *Urban Studies: A Canadian Perspective* (Toronto, 1968), p. 37.
15. Careless, "Aspects of Urban Life in the West, 1870-1914," in Stelter and Artibise, *The Canadian City*, pp. 125-41; Artibise, "The Urban West: The Evolution of Prairie Towns and Cities to 1930," *Prairie For* 4 (1979):237-62; Careless, "Aspects of Metropolitanism in Maritime Canada," in Mason Wade, ed., *Regionalism in the Canadian Community, 1867-1967* (Toronto, 1969), pp. 117-29; Spelt, *Urban Development in South-Central Ontario* (1972).
16. L. D. McCann, "Urban Growth in a Staple Economy: The Emergence of Vancouver as a Regional Metropolis, 1886-1914," in L. J. Evenden, ed., *Vancouver: Western Metropolis* (Victoria, 1978), pp. 17-42; L. D. McCann, "Staples and the New Industrialism in the Growth of Post-Confederation Halifax," *Acadiensis* 8 (Spring 1979):47-79; and Phillips, "The Prairie Urban System, 1911-1961: Specialization and Change," in Artibise, ed., *Town and City: Aspects of Western Canadian Urban Development* (Regina, 1981), pp. 7-30. See also R. A. J.

McDonald, "Victoria, Vancouver, and the Economic Development of British Columbia, 1886-1914," in ibid., pp. 31-55.
17. Gilbert A. Stelter and Alan F. J. Artibise, eds., "Canadian Resource Towns," Special Issue, *Plan Canada* 18 (1978):7-71.
18. Stelter, "Community Development in Toronto's Commercial Empire: The Industrial Towns of the Nickel Belt, 1883-1931," *Laurentian Univ R* 6 (June 1974):3-53.
19. F. A. Dahms, "The Changing Functions of Villages and Hamlets in Wellington County, 1881-1971," *UHR* 8 (February 1980):3-19.
20. Norbert MacDonald, "Population Growth and Change in Seattle and Vancouver, 1880-1960," *PHR* 39 (1970):279-321; Artibise, "Patterns of Population Growth and Ethnic Relationships in Winnipeg, 1874-1974," *HS* 9 (1976): 297-335.
21. For an example of how these topics are handled at the international level, see Eric Lampard, "The Urbanizing World," in H. J. Dyos and Michael Wolff, *The Victorian City: Images and Realities* (London, 1973), pp. 3-58.
22. The evolutionary conception is outlined in some detail in John B. Sharples and Sam Bass Warner, Jr., "Urban History," *American Behavioural Scientist* 21 (1977):221-44. Several of the following paragraphs draw heavily on this excellent article.
23. See, for example, Artibise, "Continuity and Change: Elites and Prairie Urban Development, 1914-1950," in *The Usable Urban Past*, pp. 130-55; and the articles by Phillips and McDonald in *Town and City*. A forthcoming article in the *UHR* adopts the most sophisticated analysis of the evolutionary process to date. It is Paul Phillips and D. Hum, "Growth, Trade and Urban Development of Staple Regions." The necessity of combining both external and internal levels of explanation is made explicit by Leonard Gertler and Ronald Crowley in a section of their *Changing Canadian Cities* (Toronto, 1977) entitled "Growth Forces."
24. For suggestions about this process, see J. M. S. Careless, "Urban Development in Canada," *UHR* 1-74 (June 1974): 9-13; Stelter, "The Urban Frontier in Canadian History," *CI* 1 (1975):99-114.
25. For one discussion of this process in western Canada see Artibise, "Boosterism and the Development of Prairie Cities, 1871-1913," in *Town and City*, pp. 209-35.
26. This argument is made in J. G. Williamson and J. A. Swanson, "The Growth of Cities in the American Northeast, 1820-1870," *Explorations in Entrepreneurial History*, 2d series, 4 (1966), supplement.
27. Rutherford, ed., *Saving the Canadian City: The First Phase, 1880-1920* (Toronto, 1974); Van Nus, "The Fate of City Beautiful Thought in Canada, 1893-1930," in *The Canadian City*, pp. 162-85; Smith, "The Principle of Utility and the Origins of Planning Legislation in Alberta, 1912-1975," in *The Usable Urban Past*, pp. 196-225; and Gunton, "The Ideas and Policies of the Canadian Planning Profession, 1909-1931," in ibid., pp. 177-95.
28. Bloomfield, "Economy, Necessity, Political Reality: Town Planning Efforts in Kitchener-Waterloo, 1912-1925," *UHR* 9 (June 1980):3-48; Foran, "Land Development Patterns in Calgary, 1884-1945," in *The Usable Urban Past*, pp. 292-315.
29. L. D. McCann, "The Changing Structure of Resource Towns," *Plan Canada* 18 (1978):45-59; Oiva Saarinen, "The Influence of Thomas Adams and the British New Towns Movement in the Planning of Canadian Resource Communities," in *The Usable Urban Past*, pp. 268-92.
30. Bottomley, "Ideology, Planning, and Landscape: The Business Community, Urban Reform and the Establishment of Town Planning Vancouver, British Columbia, 1900-1940," Ph.D. thesis, British Columbia, 1977.
31. Dahr, "The Emergence of Land Use Planning in Ontario, with Special Emphasis on Planning in the City of Toronto," M.A. thesis, Waterloo, 1980.
32. Van Nus, "Towards the City Efficient: The Theory and Practice of Zoning, 1919-1939," in *The Usable Urban Past*, pp. 226-46.
33. Linteau, "Histoire de la ville de Maisonneuve, 1883-1918," Thèse de Ph.D., Montréal, 1975, and "Town Planning in Maisonneuve," *Can Coll* 13 (1978):82-85.
34. Linteau and Robert, "Land Ownership and Society in Montreal: An Hypothesis," in *The Canadian City*, pp. 17-36.
35. Doucet, "Building the Victorian City: The Process of Land Development in Hamilton, Ontario, 1847-1881," Ph.D. thesis, Toronto, 1977.

36. Weaver, "From Land Assembly to Social Maturity: The Suburban Life of Westdale (Hamilton), Ontario, 1911-1951," *HS* 11 (1978):411-40.
37. The best single account is John Saywell, *Housing Canadians: Essays on the History of Residential Construction in Canada* (Ottawa, 1975).
38. See, for example, Terry Copp, *The Anatomy of Poverty: The Condition of the Working Class in Montreal, 1897-1929* (Toronto, 1974).
39. K. A. H. Buckley, "Urban Building and Real Estate Fluctuations in Canada," *CJEPS* 18 (1952):41-66; James Pickett, "Residential Capital Formation in Canada, 1871-1921," *CJEPS* 29 (1963):40-58.
40. Two recent examples are Richard Binns, *Montreal's Electric Streetcars: An Illustrated History of the Tramway Era, 1872-1959* (Montreal, 1973); and F. F. Angus and R. J. Sandusky, *Loyalist City Streetcars: The Story of Street Railway Transit in Saint John, New Brunswick* (Toronto, 1979).
41. John Cooper, *Montreal, A Brief History* (Montreal, 1969), pp. 122-26.
42. H. J. Selwood, "Urban Development and the Streetcar: The Case of Winnipeg," UHR 3-77 (February 1978):34-41.
43. Doucet, "Mass Transit and the Failure of Private Ownership: The Case of Toronto," UHR 3-77 (February 1978):3-33.
44. Davis, "Mass Transit and Private Ownership: An Alternative Perspective on the Case of Toronto," *UHR* 3-78 (February 1979):60-98.
45. Phyllis Lambert, "Building in Montreal: A Break with Tradition," *Can Coll* 13 (1978):77-81; Harold Kalman and Douglas Richardson, "Building for Transportation in the Nineteenth Century," *Journal of Canadian Art History* 3 (1976):21-43.
46. Holdsworth, "House and Home in Vancouver: Images of West Coast Urbanism," in *The Canadian City*, pp. 186-211.
47. Holdsworth, "Built Forms and Social Realities."
48. Rutherford, "Tomorrow's Metropolis: The Urban Reform Movement in Canada, 1880-1920," in *The Canadian City*, pp. 368-92.
49. John Weaver, "Tomorrow's Metropolis Revisited: A Critical Assessment of Urban Reform in Canada, 1890-1920," in *The Canadian City*, pp. 393-418; James Anderson, "The Municipal Government Reform Movement in Western Canada, 1880-1920," in *The Usable Urban Past*, pp. 73-111.
50. J. E. Rea, "Political Parties and Civic Power: Winnipeg 1919-1975," in *The Usable Urban Past*, pp. 155-67. See also P. H. Wichern, "Winnipeg's Civic Political History and the Logic of Structural Urban Reform: A Review Essay," *UHR* 1-78 (June 1978):111-21.
51. Jones and McCalla, "Toronto Waterworks, 1840-1877: Continuity and Change in Nineteenth Century Toronto Politics," *CHR* 60 (1979):300-323.
52. Terry Copp, "Montreal's Municipal Government and the Crisis of the 1930s," in *The Usable Urban Past*, pp. 112-29.
53. John Taylor, "The Urban West: Public Welfare and a Theory of Urban Development," in A. R. McCormack and Ian MacPherson, eds., *Cities in the West* (Ottawa, 1975), pp. 286-313. See also Taylor, " 'Relief from Relief': The Cities Answer to Depression Dependency," *J Can St* 14 (Spring 1979):16-23.
54. Hershberg, "Toward a New Urban History," p. 12.
55. Ibid., p. 13.
56. Davey and Doucet, "The Social Geography of a Commercial City, c. 1853," Appendix 1 of Katz, *The People of Hamilton, Canada West* (Cambridge, 1975). Artibise's *Winnipeg: A Social History of Urban Growth, 1874-1914* (Montreal, 1975) also contains elements of urban as process.
57. Nicolson, "The Roman Catholic Church and the Irish in Victorian Toronto," Ph.D. thesis, Guelph, 1980.
58. Petroff, "Macedonians in Toronto: From Encampment to Settlement," *UHR* 2-78 (October 1978):58-74. This article forms part of a special issue of the *UHR* entitled "Immigrants in the City."
59. Betke, "The Original City of Edmonton: A Derivative Prairie Community," in Artibise, *Town and City*, pp. 309-45.

60. See, for example, Russell G. Hann, Gregory S. Kealey, Linda Kealey, Peter Warrian, *Primary Sources in Canadian Working Class History* (Kitchener, 1973), pp. 9-20; Gregory S. Kealey and Peter Warrian, eds., *Essays in Canadian Working Class History* (Toronto, 1976), pp. 7-12; and Bryan Palmer, "Working-Class Canada: Recent Historical Writing," *QQ* 86 (1979):594-617.

Directions for Users

1. This bibliography can be approached in a variety of ways. The table of contents is quite detailed, and for most users this will be the most appropriate way to locate material. The volume has been organized into almost two hundred categories and sub-categories. Under the various headings are listed the books, articles, and theses bearing on that particular topic.
2. The bibliography can also be approached through three separate indexes. The author index lists all the authors cited in the volume.
3. The subject index has a special note to users immediately preceding the index itself. The subject index is the most fruitful approach to material on what might be termed "social-cultural" topics, such as ethnicity, religion, education, and entertainment. We did not list these in the general section because most of the material on these topics was written in the context of a particular region or place.
4. The volume also contains a place index. This section is particularly useful for quickly locating material on places listed in the "other centres" categories noted in the table of contents.
5. In addition to the obvious uses, the subject and place indexes are necessary for locating books, articles, or theses which deal with more than one place. In the interests of space, we usually have not repeated such entries. For example, an article on St. John's and Victoria will be cited only in the St. John's section. But the place and subject indexes will list all the material on a particular place or subject.
6. As a convenience to users, reprintings or new editions have been indicated whenever possible.
7. The general section of the bibliography has a section devoted to "bibliographies and guides to sources." For bibliographies on specific themes or places, refer to the beginning of the relevant sections and/or to the indexes.
8. Edited volumes have usually been listed both as individual volumes and as separate articles. Thus, for example, *The Canadian City: Essays in Urban History* is listed in the general section and the articles contained in the volume are cited under appropriate headings elsewhere in the bibliography. In the latter case, the article citation refers by entry number to the volume citation. Users wishing full bibliographic information will thus have to refer to the original volume citation.
9. For several large urban centres with numerous citations—such as Montreal, Toronto, and Vancouver—we have divided the material into chronological sections.

10. The preliminary pages of this volume contain a list of abbreviations used throughout the bibliography. This list, however, does not include commonly used abbreviations such as J (Journal), R (Review), Can (Canadian), etc.
11. This volume contains material that we believe is accessible to the average student of the city. Unpublished manuscript material, government reports, maps and plans, photographs, etc. are discussed in the guide portion of this volume. Since research on almost any topic cannot be complete without the use of some of these primary materials, we see the guide as an essential part of the volume.

List of Abbreviations

AAAG	*Annals of the Association of American Geographers*
A ARCH	*American Archivist*
ACA	Association of Canadian Archivists
Ac Ec	*L'Actualité économique*
ACGE	*Acta Geographica*
ACTU	Architecture
Ag Hist	*Agricultural History*
AHR	*American Historical Review*
AJS	*American Journal of Sociology*
Alta Hist	*Alberta History*
Alta HR	*Alberta Historical Review*
Ann Am Ac Pol Soc Sc	*Annals of the American Academy of Political and Social Sciences*
APT Bull	*Association of Planning Technology Bulletin*
Arch Can	*Architecture Canada*
Arch J	*Architects' Journal*
Arch R	*Architectural Review*
ARCS	*American Review of Canadian Studies*
Atl Ad	*Atlantic Advocate*
BC Hist N	*B.C. Historical News*
BCHQ	*B.C. Historical Quarterly*
BC Lib Q	*B.C. Library Quarterly*
BC Per	*B.C. Perspectives*
BRH	*Bulletin de recherches historiques*
BSGQ	*Bulletin des societés de géographie de Québec et de Montréal*
CAB	*Canadian Architect and Builder*
Cah géogr Q	*Cahiers de géographie de Québec*
Cah int Soc	*Cahiers internationaux de Sociologie*
CAMJ	*Canadian Association of Mining Journal*
Can Arch	*Canadian Architect*
Can Bus	*Canadian Business*
Can Cart	*Canadian Cartographer*
Can Coll	*Canadian Collector*
Can For	*Canadian Forum*

Can Geogr	*Canadian Geographer/Le géographe canadien*
Can Lib J	*Canadian Library Journal*
Can Mun J	*Canadian Municipal Journal*
Can Pub Admin	*Canadian Public Administration/Administration publique du Canada*
Can R Soc Anth	*Canadian Review of Sociology and Anthropology/Revue canadienne de sociologie et d'anthropologie*
Can Wel	*Canadian Welfare*
CBC	Canadian Broadcasting Corporation
CCHA	*Canadian Chartered Accountant*
CCHA, *Trans*	Canadian Catholic Historical Association/Société canadienne d'historie de l'église catholique, *Transactions*
CCHS	Canadian Church Historical Society
CES	*Canadian Ethnic Studies/Etudes ethniques au Canada*
CF	*Canada français*
CFMM	Canadian Federation of Mayors and Municipalities
CGEJ	*Canadian Geographical Journal*
CHA	Canadian Historical Association
CHA, *AR*	Canadian Historical Association, *Annual Report*
CHA, *HP*	Canadian Historical Association, *Historical Papers*
CHR	*Canadian Historical Review*
CI	*Canadian Issues*
City Mag	*City Magazine*
CJE	*Canadian Journal of Economics*
CJEPS	*Canadian Journal of Economics and Political Science*
CJPS	*Canadian Journal of Political Science/Revue canadienne de science politique*
CL	*Cité libre*
CLA	Canadian Library Association
CMAJ	*Canadian Medical Association Journal*
CMHC	Central/Canada Mortgage and Housing Corporation
CnL	*Conservation of Life*
CNST	*Construction*
CPR	*Community Planning Review*
CPSA	Canadian Political Science Association
CRAS	*Canadian Review of American Studies*
CUCS	Centre for Urban and Community Studies, University of Toronto

Dal Rev	*Dalhousie Review*
DBS	Dominion Bureau of Statistics
Dom Ill Mon	*Dominion Illustrated Monthly*
D.S.W.	Doctor of Social Work
Econ Annal	*Economic Annalist*
Emp Di	*Empire Digest*
ENCR	*Engineering and Contract Record*
Geogr	*Geography*
GEOR	*Geographical Review*
GGJO	*Geographical Journal*
Hist Educ Q	*History of Education Quarterly*
Hist Meth N	*Historical Methods Newsletter*
HK	*Historic Kingston*
HS	*Histoire sociale/Social History*
HSSM, *Trans*	Historical and Scientific Society of Manitoba, *Transactions*
HSST	*History and Social Science Teacher*
ICEE	Institute of Civic Engineers
INCA	*Industrial Canada*
I.O.D.E.	Imperial Order Daughters of the Empire
JAIP	*Journal of the American Institute of Planners*
J Can St	*Journal of Canadian Studies/Revue d'études canadiennes*
J Fam Hist	*Journal of Family History*
JLPE	*Journal of Political Economy*
JOGG	*Journal of Geography*
JNB Mus	*Journal of the New Brunswick Museum*
JRAIC	*Journal, Royal Architectural Institute of Canada*
JSH	*Journal of Social History*
JUH	*Journal of Urban History*
Labour	*Labour/Le Travailleur*
LMHS, *Trans*	London and Middlesex Historical Society, *Transactions*
M. Arch.	Master of Architecture
M.B.A.	Master of Business Administration

Mat Hist Bull	*Material History Bulletin*
M.C.P.	Master of City Planning
MIT	Massachusetts Institute of Technology
M.P.E.	Master of Physical Education
M.R.P.	Master of Regional Planning
M&S	McClelland and Stewart
MSUA	Ministry of State for Urban Affairs
M.S.W.	Master of Social Work
Mun Rev Can	*Municipal Review of Canada*
Mun W	*Municipal World*
Nat Mun R	*National Municipal Review*
NBHS	New Brunswick Historical Society
NMM	National Museum of Man
NSHQ	*Nova Scotia Historical Quarterly*
NSHS	Nova Scotia Historical Society
NS Med Bull	*Nova Scotia Medical Bulletin*
OH	*Ontario History*
OHS, *PR*	Ontario Historical Society, *Papers and Records*
OISE	Ontario Institute for Studies in Education
Ont Lib R	*Ontario Library Review*
OUP	Oxford University Press
PA	*Public Affairs*
PAC	Public Archives of Canada
PANB	Provincial Archives of New Brunswick
PANS	Public Archives of Nova Scotia
PHEJ	*Public Health Journal*
PHR	*Pacific Historical Review*
PNQ	*Pacific Northwest Quarterly*
Prairie For	*Prairie Forum*
Progress Arch	*Progressive Architecture*
Pub Admin Rev	*Public Administration Review*
QQ	*Queen's Quarterly*
RCGG	*Revue canadienne de géographie*
RCU	*Revue canadienne d'urbanisme*
Rech soc	*Recherches sociographiques*
Rev inst soc	*Revue de l'institut de sociologie*
RHAF	*Revue d'histoire de l'Amérique française*

RSC, *Trans*	Royal Society of Canada/Société royale du Canada, *Transactions*
RTCN	*Revue trimestrielle canadienne*
SS	*Sociologie et sociétés*
TBHMS, *PR*	Thunder Bay Historical Museum Society, *Papers and Records*
To Pl CnL	*Town Planning and Conservation of Life*
TPICJ	*Town Planning Institute of Canada, Journal*
UBCP	University of British Columbia Press
UHGN	*Urban History Group Newsletter*
UHR	*Urban History Review/Revue d'histoire urbaine*
UHYb	*Urban History Yearbook*
UL	*Urban Life*
UMCA	*Union médical du Canada*
UPP	*Urbanism: Past and Present*
Urb For	*Urban Forum: Journal of the Urban Research Council of Canada*
UT Mon	*University of Toronto Monthly*
UTP	University of Toronto Press
UTQ	*University of Toronto Quarterly*
WB	*Wentworth Bygones*
W Bus Indus	*Western Business and Industry*
W Can J Ant	*Western Canadian Journal of Anthropology*
WCHSO, *Trans*	Women's Canadian Historical Society of Ottawa, *Transactions*
WHS, *AR*	Waterloo Historical Society, *Annual Report*
W Ont Hist N	*Western Ontario Historical Notes*

I

General

1. General

   a. *Bibliographies and Guides to Sources*

   1. **Anderson, B. L.** *Special Libraries and Information Centres in Canada: A Directory.* Ottawa: CLA, 1970.
   2. **Artibise, Alan F. J.** "Canadian Urban Studies." *Communique* 3 (April 1977):1-130.
   3. **Association of Canadian Archivists.** *Directory of Canadian Records and Manuscript Repositories.* Ottawa: ACA, 1977.
   4. **Bryfogle, R. C.** *Urban Problems: A Bibliography of Non-Print and Audio-Visual Material for a Secondary Geography Course.* Monticello, IL: Council of Planning Librarians, Exchange Bibliography No. 259, 1972.
   5. _____. *City in Print: An Urban Studies Bibliography.* Agincourt: GLC, 1975.
   6. **Canadian Council on Urban and Regional Research.** *Urban and Regional References, 1945-1969.* Ottawa, 1970 [Supplements annually to 1976.]
   7. **Dahl, Edward H., ed.** "Resources for the Study of Urban History in the Public Archives of Canada." Special Issue. *UHR* 2-72 (June 1972):1-13.
   8. **Finan, W. M.** *Urban Reference Series and Its Implementation at the Local Level.* Ottawa: Canadian Council on Urban and Regional Research, 1975.
   9. **Granatstein, J. L., and Steven, Paul, eds.** *Canada Since 1867: A Bibliographical Guide.* 1974. 2d ed. Toronto: Hakkert, 1977.
   10. **Hamilton, William B.** *The Macmillan Book of Canadian Place Names.* Toronto: Macmillan, 1978.
   11. **Haworth, Kent M.** "Local Archives: Responsibilities and Challenges for Archivists." *Archivaria* 3 (1976-77):28-39.
   12. **Hayward, Robert J.** "Sources for Urban Historical Research: Insurance Plans and Land Use Atlases." *UHR* 1-73 (May 1973):2-9.
   13. _____. "Chas. E. Goad and Fire Insurance Cartography." Association of Canadian Map Libraries, *Proceedings* 8 (1974):50-72.
   14. _____. *Fire Insurance Plans in the National Map Collection.* Ottawa: PAC, 1977.
   15. **Ketchum, J. D.** "Census Data and Urban Research." *CJEPS* 5 (1939):512-15.
   16. **Lambert, R., and Lavallée, Laval.** *Bibliography of Canadian Land Market Mechanisms and Land Information Systems.* Ottawa: MSUA, 1976.
   17. **Lauder, Kathleen, and Lavallée, Laval.** *A Canadian Bibliography of Urban and Regional Information System Activity.* Ottawa: MSUA, 1975.

18. **Lochhead, Douglas.** *Bibliography of Canadian Bibliographies.* 1960. 2d rev. ed. Toronto: UTP and Bibliographical Society of Canada, 1972.
19. **Marsh, Leonard.** *Communities in Canada: Selected Sources.* Toronto: M&S, 1970.
20. **May, Betty F.** *County Atlases of Canada: A Descriptive Catalogue.* Ottawa: PAC, 1970.
21. **MSUA.** *Directory of Canadian Urban Information Sources 1977.* Ottawa, 1977.
22. **Muise, D. A.** "The Dun and Bradstreet Collection: A Report." *UHR* 3-75 (February 1976):23-26.
23. **Ogden, R. Lynn.** "The Records of Business and the Urban Historian." *UHR* 3-72 (November 1972):2-5.
24. **Phelps, E.** *Catalogue of Fire Insurance Plans of the Dominion of Canada, 1885-1973.* London, Ont.: Phelps, 1976.
25. **Reynolds, Reg., and Russell, M. E.** "Fire Insurance Records: A Versatile Resource." *A Arch* 38 (1975):15-21.
26. **Stelter, Gilbert A.** *Canadian Urban History: A Selected Bibliography.* Sudbury: Laurentian UP, 1972.
27. **Thibault, Claude.** *Bibliographia Canadiana.* Toronto: Longmans, 1973.
28. **Wood, W. D.; Kelly, L. A.; and Reimer, P.** *Canadian Graduate Theses, 1919-1967: An Annotated Bibliography.* Kingston: Industrial Relations Centre, Queen's University, 1970.

b. General Works

29. **Artibise, Alan F. J., and Stelter, Gilbert A., eds.** *The Usable Urban Past: Planning and Politics in the Modern Canadian City.* Toronto: Macmillan, 1979.
30. **Axworthy, Lloyd, and Gillies, J. M., eds.** *The City: Canada's Prospects, Canada's Problems.* Toronto: Butterworths, 1973.
31. **Baxter, David.** "On the Contemporary City." *Alta Geogr* 5 (1968-69):4-11.
32. **Bellan, R. C.** *The Evolving City.* Toronto: Copp Clark, 1971.
33. **Blumenfeld, Hans.** *The Modern Metropolis: Its Origins, Growth, Characteristics and Planning.* Montreal: Harvest House, 1967.
34. **Bollens, J. C., and Schmandt, H. J.** *The Metropolis: Its People, Politics and Economic Life.* New York: Harper and Row, 1965.
35. **Borah, Woodrow; Hardoy, Jorge E.; and Stelter, Gilbert A., eds.** *Urbanization in the Americas: The Background in Comparative Perspective.* Ottawa: NMM, 1981.
36. **Bryfogle, R. C., and Krueger, Ralph R., eds.** *Urban Problems: A Canadian Reader.* 1971. 2d rev. ed. Toronto: Holt, Rinehart and Winston, 1975.
37. **Canada Commission of Conservation.** *Urban and Rural Development in Canada.* Report of Conference in Winnipeg, May, 1917. Ottawa: 1917.
38. **Careless, J. M. S.** "Urban Development in Canada." *UHR* 1-74 (June 1974):9-13.
39. _____. *The Rise of Cities in Canada before 1914.* CHA Booklet #32. Ottawa: CHA, 1978.
40. **Castells, Manuel.** *The Urban Question: A Marxist Approach.* London: Edward Arnold, 1977.
41. **Clark, S. D.** "Canadian Urban Development." *UHR* 1-74 (June 1974):14-19.
42. **Davis, K.** "The Origin and Growth of Urbanization in the Western World." *AJS* 60 (1955):429-37.
43. **Dickinson, R. E.** *City and Region: A Geographical Interpretation.* New York: Humanities Press, 1964.
44. **Dyos, H. J., and Wolff, M., eds.** *The Victorian City: Images and Realities.* 2 vols. London and Boston: Routledge and Kegan Paul, 1973.
45. **Forward, Charles N.** "A Canadian's Eye-View of Australian Cities." *CGEJ* 78 (1969):26-39.

46. **Gertler, Leonard O., and Crowley, Ronald W.** *Changing Canadian Cities: The Next Twenty-Five Years.* Toronto: M&S, 1977.
47. **Hammerström, Ingrid, and Hall, Thomas, eds.** *Growth and Transformation of the Modern City.* Stockholm: Swedish Council for Building Research, 1979.
48. **Harvey, David.** *Social Justice and the City.* London: Edward Arnold, 1973.
49. **Horsman, A. L.** "Popular Attitudes toward Urban Issues: Some Observations." M.A. thesis, British Columbia, 1974.
50. **Jackson, John N.** *The Canadian City: Space, Form, Quality.* Toronto: McGraw-Hill Ryerson, 1973.
51. **Jacobs, Jane.** *Canadian Cities and Sovereignty Association [:The 1979 Massey Lectures].* Toronto: CBC, 1979.
52. **Johnston, R. J.** "Regarding Urban Origins, Urbanization and Urban Patterns." *Geogr* 62 (January 1977):1-7.
53. **Kaplan, Harold.** *The Regional City: Politics and Planning in Metropolitan Areas.* Toronto: CBC, 1965.
54. **Kirkland, John S.** *An Overview of Small Communities in Canada.* Ottawa: CMHC, 1976.
55. **Lampard, Eric E.** "Historical Aspects of Urbanization." In #**137**, pp. 519-54.
56. **Leman, A. B., and Leman, I. A., eds.** *Great Lakes Megalopolis: From Civilization to Ecumenization.* Ottawa: MSUA, 1976.
57. **Lithwick, N. H.** "The City: Problems and Policies." In *Canadian Economic Problems and Policies,* edited by L. H. Officer and L. B. Smith, pp. 258-74. Toronto: McGraw-Hill, 1970.
58. _____. *Urban Canada: Problems and Prospects.* Ottawa: CMHC, 1970.
59. _____, **and Paquet, Gilles, eds.** *Urban Studies: A Canadian Perspective.* Toronto: Methuen, 1968.
60. **Lloyd, Antony John.** *Community Development in Canada.* Ottawa: Canadian Research Centre for Anthropology, University of Ottawa, 1965.
61. **McMullin, Stanley E., and Koroscil, Paul M., eds.** "The Canadian Urban Experience." *CI* 1 (1975):1-145.
62. **Mandel, Eli.** "The City in Canadian Poetry." In *Another Time,* by Eli Mandel. Erin, Ont.: Press Porcepic, 1977.
63. **Mooney, George S.** "Our Cities: A New Perspective for New Dimensions." *CPR* 7, no. 4 (1957):156-59.
64. **Mumford, Lewis.** *The City in History: Its Origins, Its Transformations, and Its Prospects.* New York: Harcourt Brace, 1961.
65. **Nader, G. A.** *Cities of Canada.* Vol. 1: *Theoretical, Historical and Planning Perspectives.* Toronto: Macmillan, 1975; Vol. 2: *Profiles of Fifteen Metropolitan Centres.* Toronto: Macmillan, 1976.
66. **Oberlander, H. Peter.** "The City: The Most Critical Instrument of Social Change." *CPR* 21, no. 2 (1971):16-17.
67. **Pearson, Norman.** "The Modern City and Society." *QQ* 67 (1960-61):578-85.
68. _____. "From Villages to Cities." In *The Canadians, 1867-1967,* edited by J. M. S. Careless and R. C. Brown, pp. 621-38. Toronto: Macmillan, 1967.
69. **Plunkett, Thomas J.** *Understanding Urban Development in Canada.* Toronto: Canadian Foundation for Economic Education, 1977.
70. **Powell, Alan, ed.** *The City: Attacking Modern Myths.* Toronto: M&S, 1972.
71. **Preston, Richard E., and Russwurm, Lorne H., eds.** *Essays on Canadian Urban Process and Form II.* Waterloo: University of Waterloo, Department of Geography Publication Series, No. 15, 1980.
72. **Rashleigh, E. T.** "Observations on Canadian Cities, 1960-1961." In *Readings in Canadian Geography,* edited by R. M. Irving, pp. 146-58. Toronto: Holt, Rinehart and Winston, 1968.

73. **Ray, David Michael.** *Canada: The Urban Challenge of Growth and Change.* Ottawa: MSUA, 1974.
74. _____, **and Murdie, Robert A.** "Canadian and American Urban Dimensions." In *City Classifications Handbook: Methods and Applications,* edited by Brian J. L. Berry, pp. 181-210. Englewood Cliffs, NJ: Prentice-Hall, 1971.
75. **Richardson, Boyce.** *The Future of Canadian Cities.* Toronto: New Press, 1972.
76. **Russwurm, Lorne H.; Preston, Richard E.; and Martin, Larry R. G., eds.** *Essays on Canadian Urban Process and Form.* Waterloo: University of Waterloo, Department of Geography Publication Series, No. 10, 1977.
77. **Saarinen, Eliel.** *The City: Its Growth, Its Decay, Its Future.* Cambridge, MA: MIT Press, 1943.
78. **Simmons, James W.** *Canada: Choices in a National Urban Strategy.* Research Paper #70. Toronto: CUCS, University of Toronto, 1975.
79. _____, **and Simmons, Robert.** *Urban Canada.* 2d ed. rev. Toronto: Copp Clark, 1974.
80. **Sjoberg, Gideon.** *The Pre-Industrial City—Past and Present.* New York: Free Press, 1960.
81. **Spreiregen, Paul D., ed.** *Metropolis and Beyond: Selected Essays by Hans Blumenfeld.* New York: Wiley, 1979.
82. **Stelter, Gilbert A.** "The Urban Frontier in Canadian History." *CI* 1 (1975):99-114.
83. _____, **ed.** "The Canadian City in the 19th Century." Special Issue. *UHR* 1-75 (June 1975):2-54.
84. _____, **and Artibise, Alan F. J.** "Cities in the Wilderness: Canadian Urban History before 1850." In #85, pp. 5-16.
85. _____, **and Artibise, Alan F. J., eds.** *The Canadian City: Essays in Urban History.* Toronto: M&S, 1977. [Reprinted by Macmillan of Canada, 1979].
86. **Stevens, J., ed.** *The Urban Experience.* Toronto: Macmillan, 1975.
87. **Tabb, William K., and Sawers, Larry, eds.** *Marxism and the Metropolis.* New York: OUP, 1978.
88. **Thernstrom, Stephan, and Sennett, Richard, eds.** *Nineteenth-Century Cities: Essays in the New Urban History.* New Haven: Yale UP, 1969.
89. **Tremblay, M. A., and Anderson, W. J., eds.** *Rural Canada in Transition: A Multidimensional Study of the Impact of Technology and Urbanization on Traditional Society.* Ottawa: Agricultural Economics Research Council of Canada, 1966.
90. **Vance, James E., Jr.** *This Scene of Man: The Role and Structure of the City in the Geography of Western Civilization.* New York: Harper and Row, 1977.
91. **Warner, Sam Bass, Jr.** *The Urban Wilderness: A History of the American City.* New York: Harper and Row, 1972.
92. _____, **and Fleisch, Sylvia.** "The Past of Today's Present: A Social History of America's Metropolises, 1960-1860." *JUH* 3 (1976):3-118.
93. **Wolforth, J., and Leigh, R.** *Urban Prospects.* Toronto: M&S, 1971.
94. **Yeates, Maurice.** *Main Street: Windsor to Quebec City.* Toronto: Macmillan, 1975.

c. *Historiography and Methodology*

95. **Adams, Thomas.** "Preparation of City and Town Maps." *Cn L* 3, no. 4 (1917):79-85.
96. **Aristarco, Guido.** "La ville, les possibilités du cinéma et les films." *SS* 8 (1976):91-116.
97. **Armstrong, Frederick H.** "Urban History in Canada." *UHGN* 28 (1969):1-10.
98. _____. "Urban History in Canada: Present State and Future Prospects." *UHR* 1-72 (February 1972):11-14.
99. **Artibise, Alan F. J., and Stelter, Gilbert A.** "The Past in the Present: Exploring the Relevance of Canada's Urban Past." In #29, pp. 1-4.

100. **Baldwin, M.** "Exhibition as a Medium for the Study and Teaching of History: Town Planning in Early Days in Canada." CHA, *AR* (1941):55-64.
101. **Bender, Thomas.** "Studying Nineteenth-Century Cities." *Hist Educ Q* 12 (1972):89-97.
102. **Berry, Brian J. L.** "Research Frontiers in Urban Geography." In #**137**, pp. 403-30.
103. **Binford, Henry C.** "Never Trust the Census Taker, even when he's Dead." *UHYb* (1975):22-28.
104. **Bowsfield, H.** "Writing Local History." *Alta HR* 17, no. 3 (1964):10-19.
105. **Brown, R. A., and Tyrrell, W. G.** *How to Use Local History.* Washington: National Council for Social Studies, 1961.
106. **Burke, Peter.** "Some Reflections on the Pre-Industrial City." *UHYb* (1975):13-21.
107. **Careless, J. M. S.** "Somewhat Narrow Horizons." CHA, *AR* (1968):1-10.
108. _____. "Nationalism, Pluralism and Canadian History." *Culture* 30 (March 1969):19-26.
109. _____. "Localism or Parochialism in Canadian History?" *BC Per* 2 (1972):4-14.
110. **Carry, J. H.** "Some Canadian Cities [Meaning and Origin of Names]." *CGEJ* 26, no. 6 (1943):297 [continued in subsequent issues].
111. **Carter, Harold.** *The Study of Urban Geography.* London: Edward Arnold, 1972.
112. _____. "The Map in Urban History." *UHYb* (1979):11-31.
113. **Carver, Humphrey.** "Urban Mapping: An Elementary Manual." *CPR* 1, no. 1 (1951):26-29.
114. **Castells, Manuel.** "Théorie et idéologie en société urbaine." *SS* 1 (1969):171-92.
115. **Cernushi-Salkoff, Serafin.** "L'historicité du concept de ville." *Cah int Soc* 50 (1971):83-94.
116. **Chinnery, G. A.** *Studying Urban History in Schools.* London: Historical Association, 1971.
117. **Conzen, M. R. G.** "The Use of Town Plans in the Study of Urban History." In #**123**, pp. 113-30.
118. **Cook, G. L.** "Some Uses of Local and Regional History as an Introduction to the Study of History." *BC Per* 2 (1972):15-24.
119. **Cronin, James E.** "The Problem with Urban History: Reflections on a Recent Meeting." *UPP* 9 (1979-80):40-43.
120. **Davey, P.** "Quantitative Methods in the Study of Local History." *HSST* 10, no. 2 (1974):9-16.
121. **Dempsey, Hugh A.** *How to Prepare a Local History.* Calgary: Glenbow Institute, 1979.
122. **Douch, R.** *Local History and the Teacher.* London: Routledge and Kegan Paul, 1967.
123. **Dyos, H. J., ed.** *The Study of Urban History.* London: Edward Arnold, 1968.
124. _____. *Urbanity and Suburbanity: An Inaugural Lecture.* Leicester: Leicester UP, 1973.
125. **Finberg, H. R. P.** *The Local Historian and His Theme.* Leicester: Leicester UP, 1952.
126. **Frisch, Michael.** "American Urban History as an Example of Recent Historiography." *History and Theory* 18 (1979):350-77.
127. **Gibbs, J. P., ed.** *Urban Research Methods.* Toronto: Van Nostrand, 1961.
128. **Glaab, Charles N.** "Historical Perspective on Urban Development Schemes." In #**164**, pp. 197-220.
129. **Goldfield, D. R.** "Living History: The Physical City as Artifact and Teaching Tool." *History Teacher* 8 (1975):535-56.
130. **Graff, Harvey J.** "Counting on the Past: Quantification in History." *Acadiensis* 6 (Autumn 1976):115-28.
131. **Hall, Peter.** "The Future of Cities and the Future of Urban Research." In *The Geographer and Society,* edited by W. R. Derrick Sewell and Harold D. Foster, pp. 210-33. Western Geographical Series, Vol. 1. Victoria: University of Victoria, 1970.
132. **Hamilton, William B.** "Structuring a Program in Local History." *HSST* 10, no. 2 (1974):3-8.

133. **Handlin, O., and Burchard, J., eds.** *The Historian and the City.* Cambridge, MA: Harvard UP, 1963.
134. **Harris, R. Colebrook.** "Historical Geography in Canada." *Can Geogr* 11 (1967):235-50.
135. **Harvey, D. C.** "The Importance of Local History in the Writing of General History." *CHR* 13 (1932):244-51.
136. **Hauser, P. M.** *Handbook for Social Research in Urban Areas.* Paris: UNESCO, 1969.
137. _____, **and Schnore, L. F., eds.** *The Study of Urbanization.* New York: Wiley, 1965.
138. **Hepburn, A. C.** "Teaching Urban History." *UHYb* (1976):35-36.
139. **Hershberg, Theodore.** "The New Urban History: Toward an Interdisciplinary History of the City." *JUH* 5 (1978):3-40.
140. **Johnson, J. H.** *Urban Geography: An Introductory Analysis.* Toronto: Pergamon, 1967.
141. **Knight, David B., and Clark, John.** "Some Reflections on a Conference on the Historical Urbanization of North America." *UHR* 1-73 (May 1973):10-14.
142. _____, **and Taylor, John H.** "Canada's Urban Past: A Report on the Canadian Urban History Conference." *UHR* 2-77 (October 1977):72-86.
143. **Lees, Lynn.** "The Study of Cities and the Study of Social Processes: Two Directions in Recent Urban History." *JSH* 7 (1974):330-37.
144. **Lemon, James T.** "Study of the Urban Past: Approaches by Geographers." CHA, *HP* (1973):179-90.
145. _____. "Can We Reform/Radicalize the Past?" In *The Settlement of Canada; Origins and Transfer: Proceedings of the 1975 British-Canadian Symposium on Historical Geography,* edited by Brian S. Osborne, pp. 183-201. Kingston: Queen's University, 1976.
146. **Long, Norton E.** "Political Science and the City." In #**164**, pp. 243-62.
147. **Lubove, R.** "The Urbanization Process: An Approach to Historical Research." *JAIP* 33, no. 1 (1967):33-58.
148. **Lutz, Burkart.** "Réflexions sur le problème sociologique de la ville." *SS* 4 (1972):139-53.
149. **McCann, L. D.** "The Local Historian and the Urban Past." Archival Association of Atlantic Canada, *Newsletter* 4, no. 2 (1976):21-23.
150. **Macfarlane, Alan.** *Reconstructing Historical Communities.* Cambridge: Cambridge UP, 1977.
151. **McLeod, Hugh.** "Religion in the City." *UHYb* (1978):7-22.
152. **Marshall, John U.** "Geography's Contribution to the Historical Study of Urban Canada." *UHR* 1-73 (May 1973):15-24.
153. **Martin, Yves.** "Les études urbaines." *Rech soc* 3 (1962):119-28.
154. **Mayer, Harold M.** "Urban Geography and City and Metropolitan Planning." In #**164**, pp. 221-38.
155. **Mercer, John.** "On Continentalism, Distinctiveness, and Comparative Urban Geography: Canadian and American Cities." *Can Geogr* 23 (1979):119-39.
156. **Michelson, William.** "Urban Sociology as an Aid to Urban Physical Development: Some Research Strategies." *Arch Can* 44 (1967):69-71.
157. **Murphy, R.** "Historical and Comparative Urban Studies." *JOGG* 65 (1966):212-19.
158. **Paquet, Gilles, and Wallot, Jean-Pierre.** "Pour une méso-histoire du XIXe siècle canadien." *RHAF* 33 (1979):387-426.
159. _____. "Canadian Cities as Social Technologies: An Exploratory Essay." In #**35**.
160. **Pentland, H. C.** "Recent Developments in Economic History: Some Implications for Local and Regional History." H.S.S.M. *Trans,* ser. 3, 24 (1967-68):7-15.
161. **Pressman, N. E. P.** "The Built Environment: A Planning Approach to the Study of Urban Settlement." *Contact: Bull Envir St* 6 (1974):6-13.
162. **Preston, Richard A.** "Is Local History Really History?" *Sask Hist* 10 (1957):97-103.

163. **Radford, John P.** "A Note on the Spatial Analysis of Sets of Highly Disaggregated Data." *Hist Meth N* 5 (1972):115-17.
164. **Schnore, L. F.**, ed. *Social Science and the City: A Survey of Urban Research*. New York: Praeger, 1968.
164A. _____. *The New Urban History: Quantitative Explorations by American Historians*. Princeton: Princeton UP, 1975.
165. **Sharples, John, and Warner, Sam Bass, Jr.** "Urban History." *American Behavioural Scientist* 21 (1977):221-44.
166. **Simmons, James W.** "Urban Geography in Canada." *Can Geogr* 11 (1967):341-56.
167. **Smith, Peter J.** "Geography and Urban Planning: Links and Departures." *Can Geogr* 19 (1975):267-78.
168. **Stave, Bruce M.** *The Making of Urban History: Historiography through Oral History*. Beverly Hills: Sage Publications, 1977.
169. _____. "A Conversation with Graeme Davison: Urban History in Australia." *JUH* 5 (1978):69-92.
170. _____. "A Conversation with H. J. Dyos: Urban History in Great Britain." *JUH* 5 (1979):469-500.
171. _____. "Urban History in Canada: A Conversation with Alan F. J. Artibise." *UHR* 8 (February 1980):110-43.
172. _____. "A Conversation with Gilbert A. Stelter: Urban History in Canada." *JUH* 6 (1980):177-210.
173. **Stelter, Gilbert A.** "The Use of Selected Quantifiable Sources in Canadian Urban History." *UHR* 1-72 (February 1972):15-18.
174. _____. "Current Research in Canadian Urban History." *UHR* 3-75 (February 1976):27-36.
175. _____. "Canada's Urban Past: Canadian Urban History Conference." *UHR* 1-77 (June 1977):3-32.
176. _____. "A Sense of Time and Place: The Historian's Approach to Canada's Urban Past." In #85, pp. 420-41.
177. _____. "Urban History in North America: Canada." *UHYb* (1977):24-29.
178. _____. "Urban History in Canada." *HSST* 14 (1979):185-94.
179. _____. "Current Research in Canadian Urban History." *UHR* 9 (June 1980):110-28.
180. _____, and **Artibise, Alan F. J.** "Urban History Comes of Age: A Review of Current Research." *City Mag* 3, no. 1 (1977):22-36.
181. **Symonds, H.**, ed. *The Teacher and the City*. Toronto: Methuen, 1971.
182. **Taylor, Donald.** "Inexpensive Base Maps for Small Communities." *CPR* 1, no. 3 (1951):103-5.
183. **Thernstrom, Stephan.** "Reflexions on the New Urban History." *Daedalus* 100 (1971):359-75.
184. **Thrupp, Sylvia L.** "Pedigree and Prospects of Local History." *BCHQ* 4 (1940):253-65.
185. **Trotier, Louis.** "Les études urbaines: Le point de vue géographique." *Rech soc* 3 (1962):129-30.
186. **Ward, David.** "Victorian Cities: How Modern?" *J Hist Geogr* 1 (1975):135-51.
187. **Warner, Sam Bass, Jr.** "If All the World Were Philadelphia: A Scaffolding for Urban History, 1774-1930." *AHR* 74 (1968):26-43.
188. _____. "A Research Strategy for Urban History." In #47, pp. 163-70.
189. **Weaver, John C.** "Living in and Building up the Canadian City: A Review of Studies on the Urban Past." *Plan Canada* 15 (1975):111-17.
190. _____. "Urban Canada: Recent Historical Writing." *QQ* 86 (1979):75-97.
191. **Winchester, I., and Davey, P.** "Record of the Past—A Way to Study Canadian History." *Orbit* 7, no. 1 (1976):3-7.

2. Growth and Economic Development

a. Economic Growth: General

192. **Bourne, L. S.; Siegel, J.; and Simmons, James W., eds.** *Urban Futures for Central Canada: Perspectives on Forecasting Urban Growth and Form.* Toronto: UTP, 1974.
193. **Brevis, I. N.** *Regional Economic Policies in Canada.* Toronto: Macmillan, 1969.
194. **Buck, W. P.; Middleton, Diana; and Walker, David.** "Encouraging Innovative Entrepreneurship: A Neglected Aspect of Development Policy." In *The Human Dimension in Industrial Development,* edited by David Walker, pp. 17-29. Waterloo: University of Waterloo, Dept. of Geography Publications Series, No. 16, 1980.
195. **Campeau, Charles-Edouard.** "Patterns of Metropolitan Expansion." In *Proceedings of the 7th Annual Conference of the Institute of Public Administration of Canada, Halifax, September 1955,* pp. 171-77. Toronto: UTP, 1956.
196. **Crowley, Ronald W., and Hartwick, J. M.** *Urban Economic Growth: The Canadian Case.* Ottawa: MSUA, 1973.
197. **Faris, R. E. L.** "Interrelated Problems of the Expanding Metropolis." *CJEPS* 5 (1939):341-47.
198. **Gillespie, W. I.** *The Urban Public Economy.* Ottawa: CMHC, 1971.
199. **Goheen, Peter G.** "Some Aspects of Canadian Urbanization from 1850 to 1921." In #35.
200. **Goldrick, Michael D.** "Present Issues in the Growth of Cities." *Can Pub Admin* 14 (1971):452-59.
201. **Hamilton, W.** "Urban Development and Economic Base for Canadian Cities, 1931-1961." M.A. thesis, Waterloo, 1970.
202. **Harrison, P.** "The Retailing Structure of Canadian Metropolitan Areas: A Comparison of Central Place Structures versus Socio-Economic Structure as Predictors of Inter-metropolitan Area Variations in Retailing Patterns." M.A. thesis, Victoria, 1971.
204. **Higgs, Robert; Williamson, J. G.; and Swanson, J. A.** "On City Growth: A Critique." *Explorations in Entrepreneurial History* 8 (1970-71):203-11.
205. **Hodge, Gerald.** *Comparisons of Structure and Growth of Urban Areas in Canada and the U.S.A.* Research Paper #9. Toronto: CUCS, University of Toronto, 1969.
206. **Jacobs, Jane.** *The Economy of Cities.* New York: Random House, 1969.
207. **Jacobs, Phillip.** "The Meaning of Qualitative Differences in Urban Growth Processes." M.A. thesis, McGill, 1968.
208. **Johnson, H.** *Urbanization and Economic Growth in Canada, 1851-1971.* Dept. of Economics, Research Report No. 7321. London: University of Western Ontario, 1973.
209. **Kerr, Donald P.** "Metropolitan Dominance in Canada." In *Canada: A Geographical Interpretation,* edited by J. Warkentin, pp. 531-35. Toronto: Methuen, 1968.
210. **Krebs, H. H.** "A Model of Urban Development for the Canadian Economy." M.A. thesis, Dalhousie, 1975.
211. **Lamarche, François.** "Les fondements économiques de la question urbaine." *SS* 4 (1972):15-42.
212. **Lampard, Eric E.** "The History of Cities in the Economically Advanced Areas." *Economic Development and Cultural Change* 3 (1955):81-136.
213. **Lithwick, N. H.** "An Economic Interpretation of the Urban Crisis." *J Can St* 7 (August 1972):36-49.
214. **Miron, J. R.** "Economic Bases in the Theory of City Growth." Ph.D. thesis, Toronto, 1974.
215. **Miyao, Takahiro.** "A Long-Run Analysis of Urban Growth over Space." *CJE* 10 (1977):678-86.

216. **Mooney, George S.** "Our Cities—Their Role in the National Economy." *Engineering J* 24 (1941):394-98.
217. _____, ed. *The Municipality's Role in the National Economy: A Selection of Papers Prepared for the Silver Jubilee of the Canadian Federation of Mayors and Municipalities.* Montreal: CFMM, 1962.
218. **Preston, Richard E.** "The Evolution of Urban Canada: The Post-1867 Period." In *Readings in Canadian Geography,* edited by Robert M. Irving, pp. 19-46. Toronto: Holt, Rinehart and Winston, 1978.
219. **Remy, Jean.** "Urbanisation de la ville et production d'un régime d'échanges." *SS* 4 (1972):101-20.
220. **Shindman, B.** "An Optimum Size for Cities." *Can Geogr* 1, no. 5 (1954):85-89.
221. **Slater, David W.** "The Political Economy of Urban Changes in Canada." *QQ* 67 (1961):586-604.
222. **Thompson, W. R.** *A Preface to Urban Economics.* Baltimore: Johns Hopkins Press, 1965.

b. Factors in Economic Growth

223. **Aitken, Hugh G.** "Defensive Expansionism: The State and Economic Growth in Canada." In *The State and Economic Growth,* edited by Hugh G. Aitken, pp. 79-114. New York: Social Science Research Council, 1959.
224. **Bertram, G. W.** "Economic Growth and Canadian Industry, 1870-1915: The Staple Model and the 'Take-Off' Hypothesis." *CJEPS* 29 (1963):162-84.
225. **Britton, John N. H., and Gilmour, James M.** *The Weakest Link: A Technological Perspective in Canadian Industrial Underdevelopment.* Ottawa: Science Council of Canada, 1978.
226. **Chambers, Edward J.** "Late Nineteenth Century Business Cycles in Canada." *CJEPS* 30 (1964):391-411.
227. _____, **and Bertram, G. W.** "Urbanization and Manufacturing in Central Canada, 1870-1890." In *Papers on Regional Statistical Methods,* edited by Sylvia Ostry and T. R. Rymes, pp. 225-28. Toronto: CPSA, 1966.
228. **Dales, J. H.** "Fuel, Power and Industrial Development in Central Canada." *Amer Econ Rev* 43 (1953):181-98.
229. **Easterbrook, W. T.** "The Entrepreneurial Function in Relation to Technological and Economic Change." In *Industrialization and Society,* edited by B. F. Hoselitz and W. E. Moore. Chicago: UNESCO, 1960.
230. **Fyfe, Stewart.** *Municipal Assistance to Industrial Location: A Canadian Study of Tax Concessions and Other Inducements.* Montreal: CFMM, 1960.
231. **Glenday, D.; Guindon, H.; and Turowetz, A., eds.** *Modernization and the Canadian State.* Toronto: Macmillan, 1978.
232. **Goheen, Peter G.** "Industrialization and the Growth of Cities in Nineteenth-Century America." *American Studies* 14 (1971):49-66.
233. **Gordon, David.** "Capitalist Development and the History of American Cities." In #87, pp. 25-63.
234. **Grassner, C.** "Specialization in Canadian Cities." M.A. thesis, Queen's, 1970.
235. **Hartland, Penelope.** "Factors in the Economic Growth of Canada." *J Econ Hist* 15 (1955):13-21.
236. **Hodgetts, J. E.** "The Public Corporation in Canada." In *Government Enterprise,* edited by W. G. Friedmann and J. F. Garver, pp. 201-26. New York: Columbia UP, 1970.
237. **Kellett, J. R.** "Municipal Socialism, Enterprise and Trading in the Victorian City." *UHYb* (1978):36-45.
238. **Langdon, I.** "The Political Economy of Capitalist Transformation: Central Canada from the 1840s to the 1870s." M.A. thesis, Carleton, 1972.

239. **Macmillan, David S.** "The 'New Men' in Action: Scottish Mercantile and Shipping Operations in the North American Colonies, 1760-1825." In *Canadian Business History: Selected Studies,* edited by David S. Macmillan, pp. 44-103. Toronto: M&S, 1972.
240. **Marshall, John U.** "City Size, Economic Diversity, and Functional Type: The Canadian Case." *Econ Geogr* 51 (January 1975):37-49.
241. **Masolf, L. D.** "Canadian Public Enterprise: A Character Study." *Am Pol Sci Rev* 50 (1956):405-21.
242. **Maxwell, J. W.** "The Functional Structure of Canadian Cities: A Classification of Cities." In *Readings in Canadian Geography,* edited by R. M. Irving, pp. 159-79. Toronto: Holt, Rinehart and Winston, 1968.
243. **Muller, Edward K.** "Regional Urbanization and the Selective Growth of Towns in North American Regions." *J Hist Geogr* 3 (1977):21-39.
244. **Norris, Darrell A.** "The Micro-Geography of Micro-Places: Late 19th Century Business Activity and Rural Society." In *The Settlement of Canada; Origins and Transfer: Proceedings of the 1975 British-Canadian Symposium on Historical Geography,* edited by Brian S. Osborne, pp. 139-61. Kingston: Queen's University, 1976.
245. **O'Carroll, Anthony Cecil.** "The Manufacturing Structure of Canadian Cities." M.A. thesis, British Columbia, 1970.
246. **O'Connor, K.** "Industrial Structure and Urban Growth of Canadian Cities, 1951-1961." Ph.D. thesis, McMaster, 1974.
247. **Parker, Keith A.** "The Staple Industries and Canadian Economic Development, 1841-1867." Ph.D. thesis, Maryland, 1966.
248. **Rice, R. E.** "Ship-Building in British America, 1787-1890." Ph.D. thesis, Liverpool, 1978.
249. **Smucker, Joseph.** *Industrialization in Canada.* Scarborough: Prentice-Hall, 1980.
250. **Vance, James E., Jr.** *The Merchant's World: The Geography of Wholesaling.* Englewood Cliffs, NJ: Prentice-Hall, 1970.
251. **Wrigley, E. A.** "Parasite or Stimulus: The Town in a Pre-industrial Economy." In *Towns in Societies: Essays in Economic History and Historical Sociology,* edited by Philip Abrams and E. A. Wrigley, pp. 295-309. Cambridge: Cambridge UP, 1978.

c. Urban Systems, Regionalism, and Metropolitanism

252. **Boisvert, Michel.** *The Correspondence between the Urban System and the Economic Base of Canada's Regions.* Ottawa: Economic Council of Canada, 1978.
253. **Bourne, L. S.** *Urban Systems: Strategies and Regulations: A Comparison of Policies in Britain, Sweden, Australia, and Canada.* Toronto: OUP, 1976.
254. _____, **and McKinnon, R. D.,** eds. *Urban Systems Development in Central Canada: Selected Papers.* Toronto: UTP, 1972.
255. **Careless, J. M. S.** "Frontierism, Metropolitanism, and Canadian History." *CHR* 35 (1954):1-21.
256. _____. "Metropolitan Reflections on 'Great Britain's Woodyard.' " *Acadiensis* 3, no. 1 (1973):103-9.
257. _____. "Metropolis and Region: The Interplay between City and Region in Canadian History before 1914." *UHR* 3-78 (February 1979):99-118.
258. **Colthart, A. J.** "The Metropolis-Hinterland Thesis and Regional Economic Development." M.A. thesis, Alberta, 1974.
259. **Conzen, Michael P.** "The Maturing Urban System in the United States, 1840-1910." *AAAG* 67 (1977):88-108.
260. **Cook, Ramsay.** "Frontier and Metropolis: The Canadian Experience." In *The Maple Leaf Forever: Essays on Nationalism and Politics in Canada,* by Ramsay Cook, pp. 148-57. Toronto: Macmillan, 1977.

261. **Dandel, M. F.** "Inter-urban Migration and the Modifications of the Urban System." M.A. thesis, Toronto, 1974.
262. **Hodge, Gerald.** "Urban Systems and Regional Policy." *Can Pub Admin* 9 (1966):181-93.
263. _____. "Comparisons of Urban Structure in Canada, the United States, and Great Britain." *Geogr Analysis* 3, no. 1 (1971):83-90.
264. **Kariel, H. G., and Welling, S. L.** "A Nodal Structure for a Set of Canadian Cities Using Graph Theory and Newspaper Deadlines." *Can Geogr* 21 (1977):148-63.
265. **Knight, David B., and Burrows, Susan.** "Centrality by Degrees: A 19th Century Canadian's Measurement for Central Location." *Can Cartographer* 12 (1975):109-20.
266. **Kuz, A. J.** "A Cross-Sectional and Longitudinal Analysis of Canadian Urban Systems: 1951, 1961, and 1951 to 1961." Ph.D. thesis, Pennsylvania State, 1972.
267. **Lower, A. R. M.** "Metropolis and Hinterland." *South Atlantic Q* 70 (1971):386-403.
268. **Lys-Cambridge, L.** "Regional Planning in the Metropolitan Shadow." M.A. thesis, Montreal, 1974.
269. **Marshall, John U.** *The Location of Service Towns: An Approach to the Analysis of Central Place Systems.* Toronto: Research Publication No. 3, Dept. of Geography, University of Toronto, 1969.
270. **Maxwell, J. W.** "The Functional Structure of Canadian Cities: A Classification of Cities." *Geogr Bull* 9, no. 4 (1967):61-87.
271. **Morse, Richard M.** "The Development of Urban Systems in the Americas in the Nineteenth Century." *J Interamerican Studies and World Affairs* 17 (1975):4-26.
272. **Pearson, Norman.** "The Regional City Exists." *CPR* 8, no. 4 (1958):112-15.
273. **Pred, Allan.** *City-Systems in Advanced Economies.* New York: Wiley, 1977.
274. **Rutherford, J. G.** "Interdependence of the Farm and City." Canadian Club of Winnipeg, *Speeches* (1915):57-60.
275. **Simmons, James W.** *Canada as an Urban System: A Conceptual Framework.* Research Paper #62. Toronto: CUCS, University of Toronto, 1974.
276. _____. *The Growth of the Canadian Urban System.* Research Paper #65. Toronto: CUCS, University of Toronto, 1974.
277. _____. *The Canadian Urban System: An Overview.* Research Paper #104. Toronto: CUCS, University of Toronto, 1979.
278. _____. *Mysteries of Urban Growth: A Cross-Sectional Analysis of the Canadian Urban System.* Research Paper #114. Toronto: CUCS, University of Toronto, 1979.
279. _____. "The Evolution of the Canadian Urban System." In #**29**, pp. 9-34.
280. **Thompson, Wilbur R.** "Urban Economic Growth and Development in a National System of Cities." In #**164**, pp. 431-90.
281. **Whitaker, J. R.** "Regional Contrasts in the Growth of Canadian Cities." *Scottish Geogr Mag* 53 (November 1937):373-79.

d. Transportation

282. **Blumenfeld, Hans.** "Transportation in the Modern Metropolis." *QQ* 67 (1961):640-53.
283. **Bryan, Nancy.** "Financing Urban Transportation." *Can Tax J* 17 (1969):142-47.
284. **Bush, Edward F.** "Thomas Coltrin Keefer." *OH* 66 (1974):211-22.
285. **Camu, Pierre.** "Transportation: The Basic Link Since 1534." RSC, *Trans*, 4th ser. 5 (1967):91-104.
286. **Carswell, R. E.** "Municipal Motor Vehicle User Taxes." *Can Tax J* 6 (1958):427-30.
287. **Due, John F.** *The Intercity Electric Railway Industry in Canada.* Toronto: UTP, 1966.
288. **Dutton, C. N.** "The Aorta of North American Commerce." *Can Mag* 1 (1893):255-60.

289. **Foster, Mark.** "City Planners and Urban Transportation: The American Response." *JUH* 5 (1979):365-96.
290. **Fraser, Graham.** "The Car as Architect." *City Mag* 2, no. 5 (1976):44-51.
291. **French, R. de L.** "Community Street Systems." In *Housing and Community Planning*. McGill University Monograph Series. Montreal, 1944.
292. **Graham, Gerald Sandford.** "The Origin of Free Ports in British North America." *CHR* 21 (1941):25-44.
293. **Grimble, L. G.** "Gaits: A Proposed Public Transit System." *CPR* 18, no. 3 (1968):4-9.
294. **Hilton, George W.** "Transport Technology and the Urban Pattern." *J Contemporary Hist* 4 (1969):123-36.
295. **Holt, Glen E.** "The Changing Perception of Urban Pathology: An Essay on the Development of Mass Transit in the U.S." In *Cities in American History*, edited by Kenneth Jackson and S. K. Schultz, pp. 324-43. New York: Knopf, 1972.
296. **Innis, H. A., ed.** *Essays in Transportation*. Toronto: UTP, 1941.
297. **Krim, Arthur J.** "The Innovation and Diffusion of the Street Railway in North America." M.A. thesis, Chicago, 1967.
298. **Lea, N. D., and Associates.** *Urban Transportation Developments in Eleven Canadian Metropolitan Areas*. Ottawa: Canadian Good Roads Association, 1966.
299. **Leo, Christopher.** *The Politics of Urban Development: Canadian Urban Expressway Disputes*. Monographs on Canadian Urban Government, vol. 3. Toronto: Institute of Public Administration in Canada, 1977.
300. **Mallach, Stanley.** "The Origins of the Decline of Mass Transportation in the United States, 1890-1930." *UPP* 8 (1979):1-17.
301. **Masters, D. C.** "T. C. Keefer and the Development of Transportation." CHA, *AR* (1940):36-44.
302. **Meen, Sharon P.** "Holy Day or Holiday? The Giddy Trolley and the Canadian Sunday." *UHR* 9 (June 1980):49-63.
303. **Nelles, H. V.** "Introduction." In *Philosophy of Railroads*, by T. C. Keefer, pp. ix-lxiii. Toronto: UTP, 1972.
304. **Purves, Donald F.** "The City and the Railway." *CPR* 14, no. 1 (1964):17-21.
305. **Ross, W. G.** "Development of Street Railways in Canada." *Can Mag* 18 (1902):276-78.
306. **Seurot, Paul.** "Transportation and the Development of Modern Cities." *TPICJ* 1, no. 7 (1921):9-13.
307. **Sewell, John.** "Public Transit in Canada: A Primer." *City Mag* 3, nos. 4 and 5 (1978):40-55.
308. **Slack, Brian.** *Harbour Redevelopment in Canada*. Ottawa: MSUA, 1974.
309. **Tangri, O. P.** *Transportation in Canada and the United States: A Bibliography of Selected References, 1945-1969*. 2 vols. Winnipeg: Centre for Transportation Studies, University of Manitoba, 1970.
310. **Wallace, Frederick W.** *Wooden Ships and Iron Men*. Toronto: Hodder and Stoughton, [c. 1925].
311. **Wilson, George H.** "The Application of Steam to St. Lawrence Valley Navigation, 1809-1840." M.A. thesis, McGill, 1961.
312. **Wilson, Norman D.** "Some Problems in Urban Transportation." In **#296**, pp. 85-117.

e. New and Company Towns

313. **Archer, H.** "A Classification and Definition of Single Enterprise Communities." M.A. thesis, Manitoba, 1969.
314. **Bradbury, John H.** "Toward an Alternate Theory of Resource-Based Town Development in Canada." *Econ Geogr* 55 (1979):147-66.

General   13

315. **Centre for Settlement Studies.** *Bibliography: Resource Frontier Communities.* 3 vols. Winnipeg: University of Manitoba, 1969 and 1970.
316. **Dietz, S. H.** *The Physical Development of Remote Resource Towns.* Ottawa: CMHC, 1968.
317. **Grimmer, A. K.** "The Development and Operation of a Company-Owned Resource Town." *Engineering J* 17 (1934):219-23.
318. **Hosken, Fran P.** "New Towns in U.S. and Europe." *Arch Can* 44 (1967):44-50.
319. **Institute of Local Government, Queen's University.** *Single Enterprise Communities in Canada.* Ottawa, CMHC, 1953.
320. **Kloppenborg, Anne.** "The New Frontier Towns." *Urban Reader* 6-7 (1979):25-30.
321. **Knight, Rolf.** *Work Camps and Company Towns in Canada and the U.S.: An Annotated Bibliography.* Vancouver: New Star, 1975.
322. **Langlois, Jean-Claude.** "L'aménagement des villes à industrie extractive du subarctique." Thèse de M.A., McGill, 1957.
323. _____. "Nos villes minières: Un échec?" *RCU* 7, no. 1 (1957):52-63.
324. **Larouche, Fernand.** "L'immigrant dans une ville minière: Une étude de l'interaction." *Rech soc* 14 (1973):203-28.
325. **Lauder, Kathleen S.** "Planning for Quality of Life in New Resource Towns." M.A. thesis, Waterloo, 1977.
326. **Lucas, Rex A.** *Minetown, Milltown, Railtown: Life in Canadian Communities of Single Industry.* Toronto: UTP, 1971.
327. **McCann, L. D.** "The Changing Internal Structure of Resource Towns." *Plan Canada* 18 (1978):46-59.
328. **McRae, Edward Davidson.** "New Communities for a New Era: The Instant Town." M.B.A. thesis, Simon Fraser, 1970.
329. **Mayell, J. F.** "Planned Non-Permanence or Transformable Community." B.Arch. thesis, British Columbia, 1972.
330. **Oberlander, H. Peter.** "Critique: Canada's New Towns." *Progres Arch* 9 (August 1956):113-19.
331. **Parker, Victor J.** *The Planned Non-Permanent Community: An Approach to Development of New Towns Based on Mining Activity.* Ottawa: Department of Northern Affairs and Natural Resources, 1963.
332. **Pearson, Norman.** "A Case for New Towns in Canada." In #36, pp. 180-87.
333. **Port, A. W.** "Decision Making in a One Industry Town." M.A. thesis, British Columbia, 1972.
334. **Porteous, J. Douglas.** "The Nature of the Company Town." *Trans British Geographers* 51 (1970):127-42.
335. _____. "The Company Town." In *Environment and Behaviour*, by J. Douglas Porteous, pp. 330-37. Reading, MA: Addison-Wesley, 1977.
336. **Pressman, N. E. P.** *Planning New Communities in Canada.* Ottawa: MSUA, 1975.
337. _____, ed. *New Communities in Canada: Exploring Planned Environments.* Waterloo: University of Waterloo, Faculty of Environmental Studies, 1976.
338. _____. and Lauder, Kathleen S. "Resource Towns as New Towns." *UHR* 1-78 (June 1978):78-95.
339. **Riffel, J. A.** *Quality of Life in Resource Towns.* Winnipeg: Centre for Settlement Studies, University of Manitoba, 1975.
340. **Roberge, Roger A.** "Resource Towns: The Pulp and Paper Communities." *CGEJ* 94, no. 1 (1977):28-35.
341. **Robinson, Ira M.** *New Industrial Towns on Canada's Resource Frontier.* Chicago: University of Chicago Press, 1962.
342. **Saarinen, Oiva.** "The Influence of Thomas Adams and the British New Town Movement in the Planning of Canadian Resource Communities." In #29, pp. 268-92.

343. **Shaw, W. G. S.** "Homes: The Neglected Element in Canadian Resource Town Planning." *Alta Geog* 7 (1971):43-49.
344. **Siemens, L. B.** "Single-Enterprise Communities on Canada's Resource Frontier." In #337, pp. 277-97.
345. **Stelter, Gilbert A., and Artibise, Alan F. J.** "Canadian Resource Towns in Historical Perspective." *Plan Canada* 18 (1978):7-16.
346. _____, eds. "Canadian Resource Towns." Special Issue. *Plan Canada* 18 (1978):7-71.
347. **Walker, Alexander.** "Company Towns." *TPICJ* 6, no. 3 (1927):97-101.
348. _____. "Planning of Company Towns in Canada." *Can Engineer* 53 (1927):147-50.
349. **Walker, H. W.** "Canadian 'New Towns.' " *CPR* 4 (1954):80-87.

3. Population

a. The Process of Urbanization

350. **Anderson, I. B.** "Components of Rural and Urban Population Change in Canada, 1921 to 1960." M.A. thesis, Saskatchewan, 1963.
351. **Barcelo, Michel.** "Urbanisme: Réalisations et obstacles." *Rech soc* 9 (1968):105-9.
352. **Bourne, L. S., and Simmons, James W.** *Canadian Settlement Trends: An Examination of the Spatial Pattern of Growth, 1971-1976.* Major Report Series #15. Toronto: CUCS, 1979.
353. **Casetti, Emilio.** "Urban Population Density Patterns: An Alternate Explanation." *Can Geogr* 11 (1967):96-100.
354. **Chevalier, Michel, et Choukrou, Jean-Marc.** "Un modèle de changement urbain au Canada." *SS* 4 (1972):83-100.
355. **Clark, S. D.** "The Role of Metropolitan Institutions in the Formation of a Canadian National Consciousness, with Special Reference to the United States." M.A. thesis, McGill, 1931.
356. **Clark, W. Harold.** "Buts à atteindre dans l'urbanisation du Canada." *RCU* 2, no. 4 (1952):99-101.
357. **Cudmore, S. A., and Caldwell, H. G.** "Rural and Urban Composition of the Canadian Population." In *Seventh Census of Canada, 1931.* Monographs, vol. 13, pp. 441-533.
358. **Drover, Glenn.** "Urban Density." *Can Wel* 32 (1956):236-39.
359. **Dusok, Watson.** "Urbanisme: Expression de son temps." *RCU* 2, no. 2 (1952):38-42.
360. **Freitag, Michel.** "De la ville-société à la ville-milieu: L'unité du procès social de constitution et de dissolution et l'objet urbain." *SS* 3 (1971):25-58.
361. **Gertler, Leonard O.** "Future Urban Growth." *Can Wel* 32 (1956):236-39.
362. **Kalbach, Warren E., and McVey, Wayne W.** *The Demographic Bases of Canadian Society.* Toronto: McGraw-Hill, 1971.
363. **Kasahara, Yoshiko.** "A Profile of Canada's Metropolitan Areas." *QQ* 70 (1963):303-13.
364. **Lampard, Eric E.** "Historical Contours of Contemporary Urban Society: A Comparative View." *J Contemporary Hist* 4 (1969):3-26.
365. _____. "The Urbanizing World." In *The Victorian City: Images and Realities,* Vol. I, edited by H. J. Dyos and Michael Wolff, pp. 3-58. London: Routledge and Kegan Paul, 1973.
366. **Lithwick, I.** "The Growth of Urban Population in Canada to 1976: An Economic Model." Ph.D. thesis, Western Ontario, 1974.
367. **Lithwick, N. H.** "The Process of Urbanization in Canada." In *Readings in Canadian Geography,* edited by R. M. Irving, pp. 130-45. Toronto: Holt, Rinehart and Winston, 1972.
368. **McCarthy, J. O.** "The Problem of the City." In Social Service Congress, *Reports of Addresses and Proceedings at Ottawa, 1914,* pp. 121-26. Toronto, 1914.
369. **Martin, Yves.** "Les agglomérations urbaines et les zones métropolitaines dans le recensement canadien." *Rech soc* 1 (1960):91-101.

370. **Mayer, Harold M.** "Metropolitan Shorelines of the Great Lakes." *Can Geogr* 8 (1964):197-202.
371. **Pearson, Norman.** "Conurbation Canada." *Can Geogr* 5, no. 4 (1961):10-17.
372. **Ricom-Singh, Françoise.** *Poles and Zones of Attraction.* 1971 Census Analytical Study. Ottawa: Statistics Canada, 1979.
373. **Rose, Albert.** "Forces Shaping Our Cities." *Can Wel* 35 (1959):163-68.
374. **Schnore, L. F., and Petersen, G. B.** "Urban and Metropolitan Development in the United States and Canada." *Ann Amer Acad Pol Soc Sc* 316 (March 1958):60-68.
375. **Slater, David W.** "Decentralization of Urban Peoples and Manufacturing in Canada." *CJEPS* 27 (1961):72-84.
376. **Stafford, J. D.** "Differential Urban Development in Canada, 1951-1961." Ph.D. thesis, Alberta, 1975.
377. **Stone, Leroy O.** *Urban Development in Canada.* Ottawa: DBS, 1967.
378. _____. "Recent Trends in Urbanization and Metropolitan Growth." *Canada Year Book* (1969):156-65.
379. **Yeomans, W. C.** "The Pressures of Urbanization." *CPR* 20, no. 4 (1970-71):4-9.

b. Social Characteristics of Population

380. **Balakrishnan, T. R.; Ebanks, G. E.; and Grindstaff, C. F.** *Patterns of Fertility in Canada.* 1971 Census Analytical Study. Ottawa: Statistics Canada, 1979.
381. **Brown, Graham.** "Marriage Data as Indicators of Urban Prosperity." *UHYb* (1978):68-73.
382. **Charles, E.** *The Changing Size of the Family in Canada.* Census Monograph no. 1, *Eighth Census of Canada, 1941.* Ottawa: King's Printer, 1948.
383. **Cimon, Jean.** "Le cancer urbain." *RCU* 7, no. 1 (1957):43-51.
384. **Clark, S. D.,** ed. *Urbanism and the Changing Canadian Society.* Toronto: UTP, 1961.
385. _____. "The Disadvantaged Rural Society: New Dimensions of Urban Poverty." In *Canadian Society in Historical Perspective,* by S. D. Clark, pp. 66-77. Toronto: McGraw-Hill Ryerson, 1976.
386. **Compeau, C.-E.** "Problèmes métropolitains." *RCU* 8, no. 2 (1958):52-58.
387. **Good, W. G.** "Canada's Rural Problem." Empire Club of Canada, *Speeches* (1915-16):299-310.
388. **Haggard, H. Rider.** "Back to the Land." Canadian Club of Ottawa, *Speeches* (1903-9):81-86.
389. **Henripin, Jacques.** *Trends and Factors of Fertility in Canada.* 1961 Census Monograph. Ottawa: Statistics Canada, 1972.
390. **Keyfitz, Nathan.** "The Impact of Technological Change on Demographic Patterns." In *Industrialization and Society,* edited by F. F. Hoselitz and W. E. Moore, pp. 218-36. Chicago: UNESCO, 1960.
391. **Lapierre-Adamcyk, Evelyne.** *Socio-economic Correlates of Fertility in Canadian Metropolitan Areas, 1961 and 1971.* 1971 Census Analytical Studies. Ottawa: Statistics Canada, 1979.
392. **Lovendan, P.** "Problèmes fondamentales de l'urbanisme." *Rev univ Laval* 4 (1950):950-59.
393. **MacLean, M. C.** "The Age Distribution of the Canadian People." In *Seventh Census of Canada, 1931.* Monographs, vol. 12, pp. 743-834.
394. **Macmillan, J. W.** "Problems of Population." Empire Club of Canada, *Speeches* (1911-12):73-85.
395. **Michelson, William.** *Man and His Urban Environment.* Don Mills: Addison-Wesley, 1970.
396. **Pelletier, A. J.; Thompson, F. D.; and Rochan, A.** "The Canadian Family." In *Seventh Census of Canada, 1931.* Monographs, vol. 12, pp. 3-214.

397. **Pessen, Edward.** "The Social Configuration of the Antebellum City: An Historical and Theoretical Inquiry." *JUH* 2 (1976):267-306.
398. **Strong-Boag, Veronica.** "The Response of Canadian Women to Industrialization, Urbanization and Immigration, 1876-1918." Ph.D. thesis, Toronto, 1971.
399. **Sutherland, Neil.** *Children in English-Canadian Society: Framing the Twentieth Century Consensus.* Toronto: UTP, 1976.
400. **Tracey, W. R.** "Fertility of the Population of Canada." In *Seventh Census of Canada, 1931.* Monographs, vol. 12, pp. 215-410.
401. **Wargon, Sylvia T.** *Canadian Households and Families.* 1971 Census Analytical Study. Ottawa: Statistics Canada, 1979.
402. **Winman, E.** "A Whirlwind of Disaster: Its Lessons [Growing Urban-Rural Disparity]." *Can Mag* 1 (1893):517-22.

c. Migration, Immigration, and Ethnicity

403. **Agocs, Carol.** "Ethnic Groups in the Ecology of North American Cities." *CES* 11, no. 2 (1979):1-18.
404. **Allyn, Nathaniel Constantine.** "European Immigration into Canada, 1946-1951." Ph.D. thesis, Stanford, 1953.
406. **Anderson, I. B.** "Components of Rural to Urban Population Change in Canada, 1921-1960." M.A. thesis, Saskatchewan, 1963.
407. **Anderson, Robert.** "Sweeping Migrants out of Town." *Can Wel* 33 (1957):209-10.
408. **Andracki, Stanislaw.** "The Immigration of Orientals into Canada with Special Reference to Chinese." Ph.D. thesis, McGill, 1958.
409. **Balakrishnan, T. R.** "Ethnic Residential Segregation in the Metropolitan Areas of Canada." *CJS* 1 (1976):481-98.
410. **Belkin, Simon.** *Through Narrow Gates: A Review of Jewish Immigration, Colonization and Immigrant Aid Work in Canada (1840-1940).* Montreal: Canadian Jewish Congress, 1967.
411. **Breton, Raymond, and Pinard, Maurice.** "Group Formation among Immigrants: Criteria and Processes." *CJEPS* 26 (1960):465-77.
412. **Brozowski, Roman.** "Revealed Preference in Intra-urban Migration." Ph.D. thesis, Western Ontario, 1977.
413. **Bryce, Peter H.** "The Public Health Aspects of European Immigration to Canada." In *Ontario, Provincial Board of Health, Twenty-Third Annual Report,* pp. 104-13. Toronto: Cameron, 1904.
414. _____. "Civic Responsibility and the Increase of Immigrants." Empire Club of Canada, *Speeches* (1906-7):186-97.
415. _____. "The Problem of Rural Depopulation: Its Meaning in Relation to Health and Its Possible Solution." *Can J Medicine and Surgery* 34 (1913):218-24.
416. _____. "Immigration and Its Effect upon the Public Health." *PHEJ* 4 (1913):641-47.
417. **Clark, S. D.** "Rural Migration and Patterns of Urban Growth." In *Canadian Society in Historical Perspective,* by S. D. Clark, pp. 78-90. Toronto: McGraw-Hill Ryerson, 1976.
418. **Driedger, Leo.** "A Perspective on Canadian Mennonite Urbanization." *Mennonite Life* 28 (1968):147-52.
419. _____. "Urbanization of Mennonites in Canada." In *Call to Faithfulness: Essays in Canadian Mennonite Studies,* edited by Henry Poettcker and Rudy Regehr, pp. 143-55. Altona, Man.: Friesen, 1972.
420. _____. "Canadian Mennonite Urbanism: Ethnic Villagers or Metropolitan Remnant?" *Mennonite Q Rev* 49 (1975):226-41.
421. _____. "Urbanization of Ukrainians in Canada: Consequences for Ethnic Identity." In *Changing Realities: Social Trends among Ukrainian Canadians,* edited by W. Roman Petryshyn, pp. 107-33. Edmonton: Canadian Institute of Ukrainian Studies, 1980.

422. **George, M. V.** *Internal Migration in Canada: Demographic Analyses.* 1961 Census Monograph. Ottawa: DBS, 1970.
423. **Harney, Robert F., and Troper, Harold, eds.** "Immigrants in the City." Special Issue. *CES* 9, no. 1 (1977):1-76.
424. **Hurd, W. Burton.** "Racial Origins and Nativity of the Canadian People." In *Seventh Census of Canada, 1931.* Monographs, vol. 13, pp. 537-828.
425. **Kalbach, Warren E.** *The Impact of Immigration on Canada's Population.* 1961 Census Monograph. Ottawa: DBS, 1970.
426. **Macdonald, Norman.** *Canada, 1763-1841; Immigration and Settlement: The Administration of the Imperial Land Regulations.* London: Longmans, Green, 1939.
427. _____. *Canada: Immigration and Colonization, 1841-1903.* Toronto: Macmillan, 1966.
428. **McDougall, D.** "Immigration into Canada, 1851-1921." *CJEPS* 27 (1961):461-75.
429. **Matwijiw, Peter.** "Ethnic Space in the Urban Region." M.A. thesis, Western Ontario, 1975.
430. **Philpott, Stuart Bowman.** "Trade Unionism and Acculturation: A Comparative Study of Urban Indians and Immigrant Italians." M.A. thesis, British Columbia, 1963.
431. **Richmond, Anthony H., and Kalbach, Warren E.** *Factors in the Adjustment of Immigrants and Their Descendants.* 1971 Census Analytical Study. Ottawa: Statistics Canada, 1980.
432. **Reid, F. L.** "The Supply of Immigrants to Canadian Cities, 1921-1961." M.A. thesis, Queen's, 1973.
433. **Ryder, N. B.** "The Interpretation of Origin Statistics." *CJEPS* 21 (1955):466-79.
434. **Shaver, J. M.** "Civic Problems Caused by the Immigrant." *PHEJ* 6 (1916):433-36.
435. **Shortt, Adam.** "The Social and Economic Significance of the Movement from the Country to the City." Canadian Club of Montreal, *Speeches* (1912-13):62-71.
436. **Simmons, James W.** *Migration and the Canadian Urban System: Part I, Spatial Patterns.* Research Paper #85. Toronto: CUCS, University of Toronto, 1977.
437. _____. *Migration and the Canadian Urban System: Comparing 1966-1971 and 1971-1976.* Research Paper #112. Toronto: CUCS, University of Toronto, 1979.
438. _____, **and Simmons, Robert.** "The Cultural Diversity of Canadian Cities." *CGEJ* 81, no. 4 (1970):124-29.
439. **Sinclair, A. M.** "Internal Migrations in Canada, 1871-1951." Ph.D. thesis, Harvard, 1966.
440. **Stone, Leroy O.** *Migration in Canada: Regional Aspects.* 1961 Census Monograph. Ottawa: DBS, 1969.
441. _____. *The Frequency of Geographic Mobility in the Population of Canada.* 1971 Census Analytical Study. Ottawa: Statistics Canada, 1978.
442. **Ward, David.** *Cities and Immigrants: A Geography of Change in Nineteenth Century America.* New York: OUP, 1971.
443. **Wilson, Robert.** "Migration Movements in Canada, 1868-1925." *CHR* 31 (1932):157-81.
444. **Younge, E. R.** "Population Movements and Assimilation of Alien Groups in Canada." *CJEPS* 10 (1944):371-80.

d. Native Population

445. **Breton, Raymond, and Akian, Gail G.** *Urban Institutions and People of Indian Ancestry: Suggestions for Research.* Ottawa: Institute for Research on Public Policy, 1978.
446. **Brody, Hugh.** *Indians on Skid Row: The Role of Alcohol and Community in the Adaptive Process of Indian Urban Migrants.* Ottawa: Department of Indian Affairs and Northern Development, 1971.
447. **Dosman, E. J.** *Indians: The Urban Dilemma.* Toronto: M&S, 1972.
448. **Evans, Marjorie.** "Fellowship Centres for Urban Canadian Indians." M.S.W. thesis, British Columbia, 1961.

449. **Gurstein, Michael.** *Urbanization and Indian People: An Analytical Literature Review.* Ottawa: Department of Indian and Northern Affairs, 1978.
450. **Kerri, James N.** "Indians in a Canadian City: Analyses of Social Adaptive Strategies." *Urban Anthr* 5 (1976): 143-56.
451. **McCaskill, Donald N.** "Migration, Adjustment and Integration of the Indian into the Urban Environment." M.A. thesis, Carleton, 1970.
452. **Manula, Francis A.** "Demographic Characteristics of Urban Indians." M.A. thesis, Calgary, 1973.
453. **Price, J., and McCaskill, Donald N.** "The Urban Integration of Canadian Native People." *CES* 4, No. 2 (1974):29-48.
454. **Ramsay, J. M.** "An Evaluation of Social Services for Urban Treaty Indians." M.A. thesis, Calgary, 1973.
455. **Ryan, Joan.** *Wall of Words: Betrayal of Urban Indians.* Toronto: Peter Martin, 1978.
456. **Smith, Doris Mae.** "Urban Native Adjustment Problems." M.A. thesis, Alberta, 1971.
457. **Trudeau, Joan.** "The Indian in the City." *Kerygma* 3 (1969):118-23.
458. **Zeitoun, L.** *Canadian Indians at the Crossroads: Some Aspects of Relocation and Urbanization in Canada.* Ottawa: Department of Manpower and Immigration, 1969.

e. Occupation and Class

459. **Acheson, T. W.** "The Social Origins of Canadian Industrialization: A Study in the Structure of Entrepreneurship." Ph.D. thesis, Toronto, 1971.
460. _____. "Changing Social Origins of the Canadian Industrial Elite, 1880-1910." In *Enterprise and National Development,* edited by Glenn Porter and Robert Cuff, pp. 51-79. Toronto: Hakkert, 1973.
461. **Ambrose, Peter J.** "Changes in the Employment Structure of Canadian Towns, Cities, Regions and Provinces between 1951 and 1961." M.A. thesis, McGill, 1965.
462. **Bowles, Roy T.** "Societal Economic Power in Canada: A Framework for Analysis." *J Can St* 14 (Spring 1979):106-13.
463. _____. *Social Impact Assessment in Several Canadian Communities.* Peterborough: Department of Sociology, Trent University, 1979.
464. **Crowley, Ronald W.** *Labour Force Growth and Specialization in Canadian Cities.* Ottawa: MSUA, 1971.
465. **D'Arcy, Kenneth Carl Ross.** "The Occupational Trends of the Male Labour Force in Canada and Canadian Urban Areas 1911-1961." M.A. thesis, Saskatchewan, 1968.
466. **Darroch, A. G., and Ornstein, M. D.** "Social Mobility in Nineteenth-Century Canada." *Hist Meth N* 8 (December 1974):49-50.
467. **Denton, Frank T., and George, Peter J.** "Socio-Economic Influences in School Attendance: A Study of a Canadian County in 1871." *Hist Educ Q* 14 (1974):223-34.
468. _____, **and Ostry, Sylvia.** *Historical Estimates of the Canadian Labour Force.* 1961 Census Monograph. Ottawa: DBS, 1967.
469. **Elliot, Brian.** "Le système urbain et la structure de l'inégalité." *SS* 4 (1972):121-38.
470. **Jones, F. S.** "Macro-economic Influences on Urban Employment Patterns: An Input-Output Analysis." Ph.D. thesis, McMaster, 1975.
471. **Kunin, R.** "Labour Force Participation Rates and Poverty in Canadian Metropolitan Areas." M.A. thesis, British Columbia, 1970
472. **Noble, G. W.** "Labour Relations in Canadian Municipalities." *Public Personnel Rev* 22 (1961):255-61.
473. **Ostry, Sylvia.** *The Occupational Composition of the Canadian Labour Force.* 1961 Census Monograph. Ottawa: DBS, 1967.

General 19

474. **Peet, Richard.** "Inequality and Poverty: A Marxist-Geographic Approach." *AAAG* 65 (1975):564-71.
475. **Pentland, H. C.** "The Development of a Capitalistic Labour Market in Canada." *CJEPS* 25 (1959):450-61.
476. _____. "Labour and the Development of Industrial Capitalism in Canada." Ph.D. thesis, Toronto, 1960.
477. **Podoluk, J. R.** *Incomes of Canadians.* 1961 Census Monograph. Ottawa: DBS, 1968.
478. **Simmons, James W.** "Short-Term Income Growth in the Canadian Urban System." *Can Geogr* 20 (1976):419-31.
479. **Stone, Leroy O.** *Occupational Composition of Canadian Migration.* 1971 Census Analytical Study. Ottawa: Statistics Canada, 1979.
480. **Thomas, John P.** "The Spatial Influence of Industries in Small Urban Centres on the Regional Labour Force," M.A. thesis, Western Ontario, 1970.

4. Urban Environment

a. Planning

481. **Adams, Thomas.** "Town Planning in Canada and the United States." *Town Plan R* 5, no. 2 (1914):155-59.
482. _____. "What Town Planning Really Means." *Can Mun J* 10 (1914):271-72.
483. _____. "Town Planning." Canadian Club of Hamilton, *Addresses* (1914-15):330-35.
484. _____. "The Scientific Planning of Roads in Towns and Cities." *ENCR* 29 (1915):358-63.
485. _____. "Town Planning, Housing and Public Health." In Canada, Commission of Conservation, *Report of the Seventh Annual Meeting, Held at Ottawa, January 1916,* pp. 117-36. Montreal: Federated Press, 1916.
486. _____. "The Town Planning Outlook in Canada." *Can Mun J* 12 (1916): 510-13.
487. _____. "Town Planning in Canada." *Garden Cities and Town Planning* 7 (1917):77-79.
488. _____. *Rural Planning and Development: A Study of Rural Conditions and Problems in Canada.* Ottawa: Commission of Conservation, 1917.
489. _____. "Influence of Town Planning on Social Life of the Community." *Can Mun J* 13 (July 1917):324-25.
490. _____. "Report on Housing, Town Planning and Municipal Government." In Canada, Commission of Conservation, *Report of the Tenth Annual Meeting, Held at Ottawa, February 1919,* pp. 95-105. Ottawa, 1919.
491. _____. "The Need for Scientific Investigation of Town Planning Problems." *Garden Cities and Town Planning* 10 (1920):191-99.
492. _____. "Town and Regional Planning in Relation to Industrial Growth in Canada." *TPICJ* 1, nos. 4-5 (1921):9-15.
493. _____. "The Value of the Agricultural Belt to Garden Cities." *Garden Cities and Town Planning* 11 (1921):143-45.
494. _____. "Relation of Zoning to City Planning." *Can Engineer* 40 (1921):127-28.
495. _____. "Planning a Metropolitan Region." *Mun Rev Can* 22, no. 4 (1926):118-20.
496. _____. *Outline of Town and City Planning: A Review of Past Efforts and Modern Aims.* New York: Russell Sage Foundation, 1935.
497. _____, and **Seymour, Horace L.** "Study in Problems of Urban Growth." *Can Engineer* 47 (1924):543-49.
498. _____, et al. *Recent Advances in Town Planning.* London: Churchill, 1932.
499. **Adshead, S. D.** "The Broader Aspects of Civic Improvement." *ENCR* 26 (1912):42-43.

500. **Anderson, Grant.** "Local Area Planning: The Dream and the Reality." *City Mag* 2, no. 7 (1977):35-43.
501. **Armstrong, Alan H.** "Thomas Adams and the Commission of Conservation." *Plan Canada* 1, no. 1 (1959):14-32.
502. **Armytage, W. H. G.** "A Planner Looks at Canada [James S. Buckingham in 1839]." *Dal Rev* 31 (1951):49-58.
503. **Artibise, Alan F. J., and Stelter, Gilbert A.** "Conservation Planning and Urban Planning: The Canadian Commission of Conservation in Historical Perspective." In *Planning for Conservation: An International Perspective,* edited by Roger Kain, pp. 17-36. London: Mansell, 1981.
504. **Ashworth, W.** *The Genesis of Modern British Town Planning.* London: Routledge and Kegan Paul, 1954.
505. **Baker, J.** "Private and Government Planning." In *Housing and Community Planning.* McGill University Monograph Series. Montreal, 1944.
506. **Beer, G. Frank.** "A Plea for City Planning Organization." In Canada, Commission of Conservation, *Report of the Fifth Annual Meeting, Held at Ottawa, January 1914,* pp. 108-16. Toronto: Bryant, 1914.
507. **Benevelo, L.** *The Origins of Modern Town Planning.* London: Routledge and Kegan Paul, 1967.
508. **Bland, John.** "Regional Planning." In *Housing and Community Planning.* McGill University Monograph Series. Montreal, 1944.
509. _____. "The Growth of Physical Planning." In *Housing and Community Planning.* McGill University Monograph Series. Montreal, 1944.
510. **Blumenfeld, Hans.** *Beyond the Metropolis.* Papers on Planning and Design, no. 12. Toronto: Dept. of Urban and Regional Planning, University of Toronto, 1977.
511. **Borah, Woodrow.** "European Cultural Influence in the Formation of the First Plan for Urban Centers." In *Urbanización y proceso social en América,* edited by R. P. Schaedel, pp. 34-54. Lima: Instituto de Estudios Peruanos, 1972.
512. **Buck, Frank E.** "Advantages of Town Planning." *TPICJ* 3, no. 2 (1924):8-11.
513. **Buckley, Alfred.** "The Garden City Idea." *TPICJ* 4, no. 3 (1925):4-8.
514. _____. "Garden Cities and the Social Renaissance." *TPICJ* 6, no. 3 (1927):89-97.
515. **Carver, Humphrey.** "Vision of the Great City." *CPR* 5, no. 2 (1955):45-49.
516. _____. "Planning in Canada." *Habitat* 3 (Autumn 1960):2-5.
517. _____. *Compassionate Landscape.* Toronto: UTP, 1975.
518. _____. "Building the Suburbs: A Planner's Reflections." *City Mag* 3, no. 7 (1978):40-45.
519. **Cassels, W. L.** "Curved Streets in Property Developments." *TPICJ* 2, no. 3 (1923):7-9.
520. **Cauchon, Noulan.** "Some Principles of Town Planning." *TPICJ* 1, no. 10 (1922):16-17.
521. _____. "Congestion: Its Effect upon Civic Life, Material and Social." *TPICJ* 2, no. 2 (1923):14-17.
522. _____. "Zoning—Its Financial Value." *TPICJ* 2, no. 3 (1923):11.
523. _____. "Memorandum on Zoning." *TPICJ* 2, no. 5 (1923):2-12.
524. _____. "Regional Settlement Planning as a National Policy." *TPICJ* 4, no. 2 (1925):8-12.
525. _____. "Arterial Highways and Hexagonal Planning." *TPICJ* 4, no. 3 (1923):7-9.
526. _____. "Town and Regional Planning." *TPICJ* 4, no. 6 (1925):14-17.
527. _____. "Memorandum and Diagrams re Hexagonal Planning Traffic Intercepter and Orbit." *TPICJ* 5, no. 1 (1926):11-16.
528. _____. "Health Properties of Hexagonal Planning." *TPICJ* 5, no. 6 (1926):23-27.
529. _____. "Town Planning." *JRAIC* 3 (1926):165-70.
530. _____. "Zoning and Town Planning Legislation." *TPICJ* 6, no. 5 (1927):177-81.
531. _____. "The Legislative Aspects of Town Planning in Canada." *TPICJ* 7, no. 1 (1928):4-10.

532. **Cherry, G. E.** *The Evolution of British Town Planning.* London: Leonard and Hill, 1974.
533. **Clark, Ron.** "The Crisis in Canadian City Planning." *City Mag* 1, no. 8 (1976):17-25.
534. **Cooper, I., and Hulchanski, J. D.** *Canadian Town Planning, 1900-1930: A Historical Bibliography.* Vol. 1. *Planning.* Bibliographic Report #7. Toronto: CUCS, University of Toronto, 1978.
535. **Cornish, F. J.** "The Municipal Council in the Planning Process." *CPR* 9, no. 2 (1959):42-43.
536. **Craig, J. D.** "The Modern Attitude to Town Building." *TPICJ* 7, no. 5 (1928):127-29.
537. **Crerar, A. D.** "The Loss of Farmland in the Metropolitan Regions of Canada." In *Regional and Resource Planning in Canada,* edited by Ralph R. Krueger, pp. 106-14. Toronto: Holt, Rinehart and Winston, 1963.
538. **Dalzell, A. G.** "A Contrast in City Planning: Showing the Economic Advantages of Modern Town Planning." *To Pl Cn L* 7, no. 1 (1921):7-11.
539. _____. "The Commercial Value of Civic Beauty." *TPICJ* 7, no. 3 (1928):58-63.
540. _____. "The Attitude of the Engineer towards Town Planning." *TPICJ* 8, no. 2 (1929):43-46.
541. _____. "The Need for Regional Planning." *TPICJ* 8, no. 3 (1929):64-67.
542. _____. "Town Planning in Canada: Misconceptions and Misunderstandings." *TPICJ* 9, no. 2 (1930):26-28.
543. _____. "National Planning and Public Welfare." *TPICJ* 9, no. 6 (1930):113-15.
544. **Dawson, Carl A.** "City Planning and Our North American Social Heritage." In *Housing and Community Planning.* McGill University Monograph Series. Montreal, 1944.
545. **Deacon, P. A.** "Community Planning in Canada." *Can For* 31 (November 1951):175-76.
546. **Dickinson, R. E.** *City Planning and Regionalism.* London: Kegan Paul, 1947.
547. **Evan-Parry, B.** "Zoning for Health." *TPICJ* 4, no. 3 (1925):18-23.
548. **Ewing, James.** "The Engineer and the Town Plan." *TPICJ* 4, no. 4 (1925):8-11.
549. **Faludi, E. G., and Adamson, Anthony.** "Plans for Eight Communities: Regina, Hamilton, Windsor, Peterborough, Stratford, Kenora, Terrace Bay, and Etobicoke." *JRAIC* 23, no. 11 (1946):276-93.
550. **Ferguson, G. H.** "Decentralization of Industry and Metropolitan Control." *TPICJ* 1, no. 3 (1921):13-14.
551. **Fleming, A. Grant.** "Planning for Health." *TPICJ* 5, no. 4 (1926):8-13.
552. **Ford, George B.** "Progress in Planning, 1925." *TPICJ* 4, no. 3 (1925):29-34.
553. **Fulton, D.** *Design for Small Communities.* Toronto: Macmillan, 1975.
554. **Gardiner, J.** "Town Planning from a Sanitary Standpoint." *PHEJ* 3 (1912):322-24.
555. **Gerecke, Kent.** "The Practice of Urban Planning in Canada." M.A. thesis, British Columbia, 1971.
556. _____. "Toward a New Model of Urban Planning." Ph.D. thesis, British Columbia, 1974.
557. _____. "The History of Canadian City Planning." *City Mag* 2, nos. 3 and 4 (1976):12-23.
558. **Gertler, Leonard O.** "Economic Problems of Urban Development: Causes and Costs of Urban Blight in Canada." *CPR* 1, no. 1 (1951):30-36.
559. _____. "Why Control the Growth of Cities?" *CPR* 5, no. 4 (1955):151-55.
560. _____. "Regional Planning and Development." In *Resources for Tomorrow: Conference Background Papers 1.* Ottawa, 1961.
561. _____. *Regional Planning in Canada: A Planner's Testament.* Montreal: Harvest House, 1972.
562. _____. *Urban Issues.* Toronto: Van Nostrand Reinhold, 1975.
563. _____, ed. *Planning the Canadian Environment.* Montreal: Harvest House, 1968.
564. _____; **Lord, Ian; and Stewart, Audrey.** "Canadian Planning: The Regional Perspective." *Plan Canada* 15 (1975):72-86.

565. **Gunton, Thomas I.** "The Ideas and Policies of the Canadian Planning Profession, 1909-1931." In #**29**, pp. 117-95.
566. **Haldeman, B. A.** "The Municipal Zone System." *Can Engineer* 23 (1912):457-59.
567. **Hall, Peter, and Clawson, Marion.** *Planning and Urban Growth: An Anglo-American Comparison.* Baltimore: Johns Hopkins UP, 1973.
568. **Hardoy, Jorge E.** "European Urban Forms in the Fifteenth to Seventeenth Centuries and Their Utilization in Latin America." In *Urbanization in the Americas from Its Beginnings to the Present,* edited by R. P. Schaedel, Jorge E. Hardoy, and N. S. Krinzer, pp. 215-48. The Hague: Mouton, 1978.
569. **Hartman, Edward T.** "Planning Boards and Their Work." *TPICJ* 7, no. 3 (1928):66-69.
570. **Hasan, Nino.** *The Emergence and Development of Zoning Controls in North American Municipalities: A Critical Analysis.* Papers on Planning and Design, no. 13. Toronto: Dept. of Urban and Regional Planning, University of Toronto, 1977.
571. **Hewett, G. T.** "Canada and the United States as a Field for the Garden City Movement." *Proceedings of the Sixth National Conference on City Planning.* Boston (1914):180-89.
572. **Hugo-Brunt, Michael.** *The History of City Planning: A Survey.* Montreal: Harvest House, 1972.
573. **Hulchanski, J. D.** *Citizen Participation in Planning: A Comprehensive Bibliography.* Papers on Planning and Design, no. 2. Toronto: Dept. of Urban and Regional Planning, University of Toronto, 1974.
574. ———. *Thomas Adams: A Biographical and Bibliographical Guide.* Papers on Planning and Design, no. 15. Toronto: Dept. of Urban and Regional Planning, University of Toronto, 1978.
575. ———. *Canadian Town Planning and Housing, 1930-1940: A Historical Bibliography.* Bibliographic Series #10. Toronto: CUCS, 1978.
576. ———. *Canadian Town Planning and Housing, 1940-1950: A Historical Bibliography.* Bibliographic Series #12. Toronto: CUCS, 1979.
577. **Jacobs, Jane.** *The Death and Life of Great American Cities.* New York: Random House, 1961.
578. **Jones, Murray V.** "Urban Focus and Regional Planning." *Can Pub Admin* 9 (1966):177-80.
579. **Kitchen, John M.** "What It Means to Zone." *TPICJ* 5, no. 4 (1926):3-8.
580. **Knowles, M.** "Development of Zoning in Town Planning." *Can Engineer* 45 (1923):308-10.
581. **Krueger, Ralph R.** "Community Planning and Local Government." *CPR* 18, no. 4 (1968):16-22.
582. **Lampard, Eric E.** "City Making and Mending in the United States: On Capitalizing a Social Environment." In #**35**.
583. **Le May, T. D.** "The Skyscraper Problem in Town Planning." *Can Engineer* 58 (1930):190-91.
584. **Marsh, Leonard.** "Government Planning in Canada." In *Housing and Community Planning.* McGill University Monograph Series. Montreal, 1944.
585. **Mawson, Thomas H.** "The Larger Problems of Town Planning." *ENCR* 29 (1915):390-92.
586. **Mayo, H. B.** "Joint Planning for Metropolitan Regions." *CPR* 6, no. 3 (1956):125-29.
587. **Meyerson, M., and Banfield, E. C.** *Politics, Planning and the Public Interest.* Toronto: Macmillan, 1955.
588. **Millward, H. A.** "The Convergence of Urban Plan Features: A Comparative Examination of Trends in Canada and England." Ph.D. thesis, Western Ontario, 1975.
589. **Milner, James B.** "Town and Regional Planning in Transition." *Can Pub Admin* 3 (1960):59-75.
590. **Mitchell, C. H.** "Town Planning and Civic Improvement." *Can Engineer* 23 (1912):911-15.
591. "Modern City Planning." *TPICJ* 1, no. 11 (1922):11-15.

592. **Nicolls, F. W.** "Community Planning/Urbanisme: 1940-1945." *CPR* 14, no. 2 (1964):2-4.
593. **Nobbs, Percy E.** *Report on Town Planning Legislation in the Provinces of Canada.* Montreal: Department of City Planning, 1946.
594. **Oberlander, H. Peter.** "Community Planning and Housing: An Aspect of Canadian Federalism." Ph.D. thesis, Harvard, 1956.
595. _____. "Community Planning and Housing: Stepchildren of Canadian Federalism." *QQ* 67 (1960-61):663-72.
596. _____. "Urban Planning and Federalism." *Proceedings of the 1964 Annual Conference of the American Institute of Planners.* Newark, NJ, 1964.
597. _____, ed. *Canada: An Urban Agenda.* Ottawa: Community Planning Press, 1976.
598. **Parent, Honoré.** "City Planning and the Law." In *Housing and Community Planning.* McGill University Monograph Series. Montreal, 1944.
599. **Parks, William T., and Robinson, Ira M.** *Urban and Regional Planning in a Federal State: The Canadian Experience.* Stroudsburg, PA: Dowden, Hutchinson and Ross, 1979.
600. **Pearson, Norman.** *Recreational Land-Use Planning.* Guelph: University of Guelph, Centre for Resource Development, Publication No. 63, 1972.
601. **Pressman, N. E. P.** "Urbanism—Toward a More Humanized Environment." *Plan Canada* 11, no. 1 (1970):13-22.
602. _____. "Hans Blumenfeld: Humanist and Urban Planner." *Plan Canada* 16, no. 1 (1976):25-36.
603. **Renfrew, Stewart.** "Commission of Conservation." *Douglas Library Notes* 19, no. 3-4 (1971):17-26.
604. **Reps, J. W.** *The Making of Urban America: A History of City Planning in the United States.* Princeton: Princeton UP, 1965.
605. **Rettig, George.** "Civic Improvement and Beautification." Canadian Club of Toronto, *Proceedings* (1911-12):123-26.
606. **Rowat, Donald Cameron.** "Planning and Metropolitan Government." *Can Pub Admin* 1, no. 1 (1958):14-21.
607. **Roweis, S. T.** *Urban Planning in Early and Late Capitalist Societies.* Papers on Planning and Design, no. 7. Toronto: Dept. of Urban and Regional Planning, University of Toronto, 1975.
608. **Rowland, K.** *The Shape of Towns.* London: Ginn, 1966.
609. **Sanford, Barbara.** *A Socio-Historical Approach to the Planning of Urban Residential Environments.* Papers on Planning and Design, no. 23. Toronto: Dept. of Urban and Regional Planning, University of Toronto, 1979.
610. **Scott, A. J., and Roweis, S. T.** *Urban Planning in Theory and Practice: A Reappraisal.* Papers on Planning and Design, no. 14. Toronto: University of Toronto, Dept. of Urban and Regional Planning, 1977.
611. **Scott, M.** *American Planning Since 1890.* Berkeley and Los Angeles: University of California Press, 1970.
612. **Shockey, William J.** "Industrial Development and Community Planning." *CPR* 9, no. 3 (1959):93-95.
613. **Shortt, Adam.** "Historical Aspects of Town Planning." *TPICJ* 1, nos. 4-5 (1921):15-16.
614. _____. "One Method of Financing Town Planning." *TPICJ* 1, no. 10 (1922):17-18.
615. **Slater, David W.** "Planning in Smaller Communities." *CPR* 11, no. 3 (1961):6-17.
616. **Smith, A. G., and Seymour, Horace L.** "High Buildings in Relation to Zoning." *TPICJ* 7, no. 1 (1928):18-22.
617. **Smith, C. Ray, and Witty, David R.** "Conservation, Resources, and Environment: An Exposition and Critical Evaluation of the Commission of Conservation, Canada." *Plan Canada* 11, no. 1 (1970):55-71; and 11, no. 3 (1972):199-216.
618. **Smith, Peter J.** "John Arthur Roebuck: A Canadian Influence on the Development of Planning Thought in the Early Nineteenth Century." *Plan Canada* 19 (1979): 200-210.

24   Canada's Urban Past

619. **Spragge, Godfrey L.** "Canadian Planners' Goals: Deep Roots and Fuzzy Thinking." *Can Pub Admin* 18 (1975):216-34.
620. **Sutcliffe, A. R.** *The History of Modern Town Planning: A Bibliographic Guide.* Birmingham: Centre for Urban and Regional Studies, University of Birmingham, 1977.
621. **Tanimura, H.** "Urban Development Models as Planning Tools." M.C.P. thesis, Manitoba, 1966.
622. **Tardif, J. P. E.** "An Ecological Interpretation of City Planning." M.C.P. thesis, Manitoba, 1969.
623. **Unwin, R.** "A Town Planning Scheme: Its Effect on Housing and Architecture." *ENCR* 28 (1914):923-28.
624. **Van Nus, Walter.** "The Plan-Makers and the City: Architects, Engineers, Surveyors, and Urban Planning in Canada, 1890-1939." Ph.D. thesis, Toronto, 1975.
625. ———. "Sources for the History of Urban Planning in Canada, 1890-1939." *UHR* 1-76 (June 1976):6-9.
626. ———. "The Fate of City Beautiful Thought in Canada, 1893-1930." In **#85**, pp. 162-85.
627. ———. "Towards the City Efficient: The Theory and Practice of Zoning, 1919-1939." In **#29**, pp. 226-46.
628. **Vivian, Henry.** "Garden Suburbs and Town Planning." Canadian Club of Toronto, *Proceedings* (1910-11):35-40.
629. **Wainwright, W. H.** "The Municipal Engineer and Town Planning." *Can Engineer* 21 (1911):168-70.
630. **Wark, L.** "Public Policy Alternatives in the Rural-Urban Fringe." M.A. thesis, Toronto, 1974.
631. **White, James.** "The Housing and Town Planning Work of the Commission of Conservation." *TPICJ* 1, no. 2 (1921):2-4.
632. **Whitnall, G. Gordon.** "Zoning." *TPICJ* 6, no. 4 (1927):135-39.
633. **Wynne-Roberts, R. O.** "Some Observations on the First Draft of the Town Planning Act." *ENCR* 28 (1914):831-34.
634. **Young, Stewart.** "The Necessity for Proper Direction and Advice by Provincial Authorities in Town Planning." *TPICJ* 6, no. 4 (1927):152-55.

b. Land and Development

635. **Adams, Thomas.** *Town Planning and Land Development.* Ottawa: Commission of Conservation, 1918.
636. **Ashton, Patrick.** "The Political Economy of Suburban Development." In **#87**, pp. 64-89.
637. **Aubin, Henry.** *City for Sale: International Finance and Canadian Development.* Toronto: Lorimer, 1977.
638. **Bartholomew, Harland.** *Land Uses in American Cities.* Cambridge, MA: Harvard UP, 1955.
639. **Blumenfeld, Hans.** *On Prices of Residential Lots and Houses: A Critical Evaluation of the Data and Conclusions of the 'Greenspan Report.'* Papers on Planning and Design, no. 25. Toronto: Dept. of Urban and Regional Planning, University of Toronto, 1980.
640. **Bourne, L. S.** "Urban Development under Stagnating Growth." *Urb For* 4, no. 4 (1979):10-15.
641. **Bryant, R. W. G.** *Land: Private Property/Public Control.* Montreal: Harvest House, 1972.
642. **Caron, J. P.; Chung, Joseph; and Jouandet-Bernadat, R.** "Zonage et valeurs foncières." *Rech soc* 16 (1975):181-206.
643. **Crerar, A. D.** "Land for Our Future—The High Cost of Sprawl." *CPR* 9, no. 2 (1959):44-48.
644. **Cutler, Maurice.** "How Foreign Owners Shape Our Cities." *CGEJ* 90 (June 1975):34-48.

645. **Dalzell, A. G.** "Development of Urban Communities." *Can Engineer* 56 (1929):267-72.
646. **Dyos, H. J.** *Victorian Suburb: A Study in the Growth of Camberwell.* 1961. 2d ed. Leicester: Leicester UP, 1973.
647. **Firey, Walter.** *Land Use in Central Boston.* Cambridge: Harvard UP, 1947.
648. **Gutstein, Donald.** "Genstar: Portrait of a Conglomerate Developer." *City Mag* 2, no. 1 (1976):23-31.
649. **Hoyt, Homer.** *One Hundred Years of Land Values in Chicago.* Chicago: University of Chicago Press, 1933.
650. **Lambert, R., and Lavallée, Laval.** *Bibliography on Canadian Land Market Mechanisms and Land Information Systems.* Ottawa: MSUA, 1976.
651. **Levin, Earl A.** "Land Planning and Land Costs." *CPR* 9, no. 2 (1959):54-64.
652. **Lorimer, James.** *The Developers.* Toronto: Lorimer, 1978.
653. **MacRossie, W.** "Land Policy." In *Housing and Community Planning.* McGill University Monograph Series. Montreal, 1944.
654. **Nobbs, Percy E.** "The Subdivision of Residential Suburban Property." *TPICJ* 5, no. 2 (1926):10-16.
655. **Pearson, Norman.** *The Effect of Urbanization on Agricultural Land.* Guelph: University of Guelph, Centre for Resource Development, Publication No. 65, 1972.
656. **Roweis, S. T., and Scott, A. J.** *The Urban Land Question.* Papers on Planning and Design, no. 10. Toronto: Dept. of Urban and Regional Planning, University of Toronto, 1976.
657. **Simmons, James W., and Huebert, Victor H.** "The Location of Land for Public Use in Urban Areas." *Can Geogr* 14 (1970):45-56.
658. **Spurr, P.** "Five Land Banks [Kingston, Peterborough, Hamilton, Saskatoon, Red Deer]." *City Mag* 2, no. 1 (1976):10-21.
659. _____. *Land and Urban Development: A Preliminary Study.* Toronto: Lorimer, 1976.
660. **Vance, James E., Jr.** "Land Assignment in the Pre-Capitalist, and Post-Capitalist City." *Econ Geogr* 47 (1979):101-20.
661. **Warner, Sam Bass, Jr.** *Streetcar Suburbs: The Process of Growth in Boston, 1870-1900.* Cambridge: Harvard UP, 1962.

c. Building and Architecture

662. **Adamson, Anthony.** "Form and the 20th Century Canadian City." *QQ* 69 (1962):49-68.
663. "Architectural Control—The Experimental Stage." *TPICJ* 8, no. 5 (1929):99-100.
664. **Astles, A. R.** "The Evolution and Role of Historic and Architectural Preservation within the North American City." M.A. thesis, Simon Fraser, 1972.
665. **Bacon, E. N.** *Design of Cities: An Account of the Development of Urban Form, from Ancient Athens to Modern Brasilia.* New York: Penguin, 1976.
666. **Buggey, Susan.** "Researching Canadian Buildings: Some Historical Sources." *HS* 20 (1977):409-26.
667. **Capling, A. J.** "Ornamental Aspects of Cities." M.A. thesis, McGill, 1967.
668. **Collier, R. W.** *Contemporary Cathedrals: Large Scale Developments in Canadian Cities.* Montreal: Harvest House, 1975.
669. *Criteria for Evaluating Buildings or Structures of Historic Significance.* Toronto: Ontario Heritage Administration, 1976.
670. **Dalzell, A. G.** "Should Shack-Towns Be Encouraged?" *TPICJ* 5, no. 2 (1926):23-29.
671. **Denhez, Marc.** "Conserving Neighbourhoods and Landmarks: The Canadian Problems." *Urb For* 2, no. 1 (1975):27-34.
672. **Erickson, Arthur.** "Architecture, Urban Development and Industrialization." *Can Arch* 20 (January 1975):35-38.

673. _____. *The Architecture of Arthur Erickson*. Montreal: Tundra Books, 1975.
674. **Falkner, Ann.** "The Canadian Inventory of Historic Buildings." *CGEJ* 86 (February 1973):44-53.
675. _____. *Without Our Past? A Handbook for the Preservation of Canada's Architectural Heritage*. Toronto: UTP, 1977.
676. **Fitch, James M.** *American Building: The Historical Forces That Shaped It*. 1947. 2d ed. New York: Schocken Books, 1966.
677. **Fox, M. F.** "Bird's Eye Views of Canadian Cities: A Review." *UHR* 1-77 (June 1977):38-45.
678. **Galt, George.** "Planning Better to Save Heritage Buildings." *CGEJ* 99 (October-November 1979):56-61.
679. **Gowans, Alan.** *Building Canada: An Architectural History of Canadian Life*. Toronto: OUP, 1966.
680. _____. "The Canadian National Style." In *The Shield of Achilles. Aspects of Canada in the Victorian Age*, edited by W. L. Morton, pp. 208-19. Toronto:M&S, 1968.
681. _____. "Towards a Meaningfully Built Environment." *CI* 1, no. 1 (1975):55-84.
682. **Gutstein, Donald.** "Arthur Erickson: The Corporate Artist-Architect." *City Mag* 1, no. 1 (1974):6-15.
683. **Hildebrand, Grant.** *Designing for Industry: The Architecture of Albert Kahn*. Cambridge, MA: MIT Press, 1974.
684. **Hubbard, Robert Hamilton.** "Canadian Gothic." *Arch Rev* 116 (1954):102-8.
685. **Jackson, J. T.** "The House as a Visual Indicator of Social Status Change, 1861-1915." M.A. thesis, Western Ontario, 1973.
686. **Jamieson, Walter.** "Architectural Conservation Training in Canada." *UPP* 8 (1979):46-49.
687. **Kalman, Harold.** "Recent Literature on the History of Canadian Architecture." *Journal of the Society of Architectural Historians* 31 (1972):312-23.
688. _____, and **Richardson, Douglas.** "Building for Transportation in the Nineteenth Century." *J Can Art Hist* 3 (1976):21-43.
689. **Koltun, Lilly.** *City Blocks, City Spaces: Historical Photographs of Canada's Urban Growth, c. 1850-1900*. Ottawa: National Photography Collection, PAC, 1980.
690. **Krishnamurti, U. K.** "Evolution of Capital Cities." M.Arch. thesis, McGill, 1968.
691. **Kuwabara, B., and Sampson, B.** "Diamond and Myers: The Form of Reform." *City Mag* 1, nos. 5 and 6 (1975):29-47.
692. **Lambert, Phyllis.** "The Record of Buildings as Evidence." In *Court House: A Photographic Document*, edited by Richard Pare, pp. 10-13. New York: Horizon Press, 1978.
693. **Lane, Barbara M.** "Changing Attitudes to Monumentality: An Interpretation of European Architecture and Urban Form, 1880-1914." In #**47**, pp. 101-14.
694. **Langton, W. A.** "High Building." *CAB* 16 (1903):63-64.
695. **Lasserre, F.** "Modern Architecture, the New Aesthetics and Concrete." *JRAIC* 15 (1938):145-47.
696. **McCann, L. D., and Frey, M. W.** "The Two-Storey House Type as Urban Architecture." *Alta Geogr*, no. 9 (1973):24-37.
697. **Marani, F. H.** "Sky Scrapers." *TPICJ* 2, no. 3 (1923):12.
698. **Milner, James B.** "The Centenary-Opportunity for City Building?" *CPR* 13, no. 4 (1963):13-16.
699. **Moorhouse, Walter.** "Building Height Limitations in Downtown Districts." *JRAIC* 1 (1924):57-59, 133-35.
700. **Nobbs, Percy E.** "Planning for Sunlight." *TPICJ* 1, no. 9 (1922):6-12.
701. _____. *Architecture in Canada*. London: Royal Institute of British Architects, 1924.
702. _____. "On the Control of Architecture." *TPICJ* 7, no. 5 (1928):120-22.

703. **O'Shaughnessy, Katherine.** "Heritage Conservation." *Mun W* 89 (October 1979):255-57, 274-75.
704. **Richardson, Douglas.** "Canadian Architecture in the Victorian Era: The Spirit of the Place." *Can Coll* 10 (1975):20-29.
705. **Ritchie, Thomas.** *Canada Builds, 1867-1967.* Toronto: UTP, 1967.
706. _____. "The Architecture of William Thomas." *Arch Can* 44 (May 1967):41-45.
707. **Scully, Vincent.** *American Architecture and Urbanism.* New York: Praeger, 1969.
708. **Shadbolt, Douglas.** "Postwar Architecture in Canada." *Can For* 63 (April 1978):7-9.
709. **Sheppard, E. S.** "Diffusion through the Urban System: The Construction of Shopping Centres in Canada." M.A. thesis, Toronto, 1974.
710. **Sise, Hazen.** "The Townscape Revealed." *CGEJ* 73 (1966):128-37.
711. **Smith, John F.** *A Critical Bibliography of Building Conservation: Historic Towns, Buildings, Their Furnishings and Fittings.* London: Mansell, 1978.
712. **Spreiregen, Paul D.** *Urban Design: The Architecture of Towns and Cities.* New York: McGraw-Hill, 1965.
713. **Stoughton, Arthur Alexander.** "The Contributions of Architecture and Its Control." *TPICJ* 8, no. 3 (1929):49-51.

d. Housing

714. **Adams, Thomas.** "Housing and Town Planning in Canada." *Town Plan R* 6, no. 1 (1915):20-26.
715. _____. "Housing and Town Planning in Canada." In Canada, Commission of Conservation, *Report of the Sixth Annual Meeting, Held at Ottawa, January 1915*, pp. 158-79. Toronto: Bryant, 1915.
716. _____. "Housing Conditions in Canada." *Cn L* 3, no. 1 (1916):10-11.
717. _____. "Cost of Land for Building Purposes: Effect on Housing in England and Canada." *Cn L* 3, no. 2 (1917):29-32.
718. _____. "Government Housing during War." *Cn L* 4, no. 2 (1918):25-33.
719. _____. "The Housing Problem and Production." *Cn L* 4, no. 3 (1918):49-57.
720. _____. "The Housing Problem." Canadian Club of Montreal, *Addresses* (1918-19):178-87.
721. _____. "Housing and Social Reconstruction." *Landscape Arch* 9 (1919):41-62.
722. _____. "Canada's Drive for Better Housing." *Nat Mun Rev* 8 (1919):354-59.
723. _____. "The Housing Situation in Canada." *Housing Betterment* 10, no. 1 (1921):40-42.
724. _____. "Bad Housing Conditions: Private and Public Responsibility in Canada." *Cn L* 7 (March 1921):12-15.
725. **Beer, G. Frank.** "Working Men's Houses and Model Dwellings in Canada." *Garden Cities and Town Planning* 4 (1914):104-9.
726. **Bourne, L. S., and Biernacki, C. M.** *Urban Housing Markets, Housing Supply and the Spatial Structure of Residential Change: A Working Bibliography.* Toronto: CUCS, University of Toronto, 1977.
727. **Bridle, Augustus.** "The Homes of Workingmen." *Can Mag* 22 (1903-4):33-40.
728. **Bryce, Peter H.** "The Land Problem in Relation to Housing." *PHEJ* 6 (1915):608-13.
729. **Buckley, K. A. H.** "Urban Building and Real Estate Fluctuations in Canada." *CJEPS* 18 (1952):41-66.
730. **CMHC.** *Housing and Urban Growth in Canada: A Brief to the Royal Commission on Canada's Economic Prospects.* Ottawa: CMHC, 1956.
731. **Chamberlain, S. B., and Crowley, D. F.** *Decision-Making and Change in Urban Residential Space: Selected and Annotated References.* Toronto: CUCS, University of Toronto, 1969.

732. **Clatworthy, S. J.** "A Location Model of Multiple Unit Rental Housing Development." M.A. thesis, Queen's, 1974.
733. **Cooper, I., and Hulchanski, J. D.** *Canadian Town Planning, 1900-1930: A Historical Bibliography.* Vol. 2. *Housing.* Bibliographic Report #8. Toronto: CUCS, University of Toronto, 1978.
734. **Dalzell, A. G.** *Housing in Canada: I. Housing in Relation to Land Development.* Toronto: Social Science Council of Canada, 1927.
735. _____. "The Housing of the Industrial Classes in Canada." *TPICJ* 7, no. 5 (1928):123-26.
736. _____. "Housing Industrial Classes in Canada." *Can Engineer* 55 (1928):350-51.
737. _____. *Housing in Canada: II. The Housing of the Working Classes.* Toronto: Social Science Council of Canada, 1928.
738. _____. "Current Trends in House Building." *TPICJ* 9, no. 2 (1930):26-32.
739. **Davies, Gordon W.** "A Model of the Urban Residential Land and Housing Markets." *CJE* 10 (1977):393-410.
740. **Dennis, Michael, and Fish, Susan.** *Programs in Search of a Policy: Low Income Housing in Canada.* Toronto: Hakkert, 1972.
741. **Dill, John, and Macri, Pamela.** *Current References Relating to Housing and Land Issues in Canada.* Monticello, IL: Council of Planning Librarians, Exchange Bibliography no. 842, 1975.
742. **Feldman, Lionel D.** "The Provision of Public Housing in Canada." M.A. thesis, Carleton, 1962.
743. **Firestone, O. J.** "Measurement of Housing Needs, Supply and Post-War Requirements." In *Housing and Community Planning.* McGill University Monograph Series. Montreal, 1944.
744. **Fukushima, M.** "An Analysis of the Transition between Community and Privacy in Urban Housing." M.Arch. thesis, McGill, 1975.
745. **Germain, Denis.** "La situation du logement au Canada depuis 1921." *AcEc* 36 (1960):44-71.
746. _____. "Certaines caractéristiques du logement au Canada." *AcEc* 36 (1960):467-86.
747. **Gilles, J. M.** "Canadian Housing Legislation: A Case Study of Housing Problems and Policies." Ph.D. thesis, Indiana, 1952.
748. **Godbout, Jacques.** "Ménages à faible revenu, développement urbain et politiques gouvernementales de l'habitation." *SS* 4 (1972):43-54.
749. **Goldberg, J.** "Changing Perspectives in Canadian Federal Housing Policy, 1960-1970." M.A. thesis, McGill, 1974.
750. **Greenway, H. F.** "Housing in Canada." In *Seventh Census of Canada, 1931.* Monographs, vol. 12, pp. 411-578.
751. **Gregg, Marjorie Wyeth.** "The Housing Problem in a City Block." M.A. thesis, Toronto, 1916.
752. **Hague, Ernest W. J.** "The Housing Problem." *PHEJ* 5 (1914):371-78.
753. **Hastings, Charles J.** "The Significance of Sanitary Housing." *INCA* 12 (1912):1284-86.
754. _____. "Suggestions for the Housing Problem." *INCA* 13 (1912):66-67.
755. **Havel, J.-E.** *Habitat et logement.* Paris: Press Universitaires de France,1968.
756. **Hellyer, Paul, et al.** *Report of the Federal Government Task Force on Housing and Urban Development.* Ottawa: Queen's Printer, 1969.
757. **Hellyer Task Force Report.** "A Program for Urban Canada." *CPR* 19, no. 1 (1969):4-8.
758. **Hodgetts, Charles A.** "Town Planning and Housing in Canada." *ENCR* 25 (1911):52-53.
759. _____. "Unsanitary Housing." In Canada, Commission of Conservation, *Report of the Second Annual Meeting, Held at Quebec, January 1911,* pp. 50-84. Montreal: Lovell, 1911.
760. _____. "Housing and Town Planning." In Canada, Commission of Conservation, *Report of the Third Annual Meeting, Held at Ottawa, January 1912,* pp. 130-46. Montreal: Lovell, 1912.

761. _____. "Town Planning and Housing." *PHEJ* 3 (1912):61-63.
762. _____. "Housing and Health." *Can Mun J* 16 (1920):86-87.
763. **James, F. C.** "The Economic Background of Housing and Community Planning in Post-War Canada." In *Housing and Community Planning*. McGill University Monograph Series. Montreal, 1944.
764. **Kellough, W. R., and Beaton, Wallace.** "Anatomy of the Housing Shortage." *CPR* 19, no. 1 (1969):18-26.
765. **Larson, Peter.** "Quelques aspects sur l'histoire de la politique du logement de l'état canadien." Thèse de Ph.D., Grenoble, 1976.
766. **McCullough, J. W. S.** "Housing and Health." In Canadian Conference on Social Work, *Proceedings of the First Annual Meeting at Montreal, April 1928*, pp. 185-91. Toronto, 1928.
767. **Macmillan, James A., and Nickel, Edith.** "An Economic Appraisal of Urban Housing Assistance: Rental Supplements versus Public Housing." *Can Pub Admin* 17 (1974):443-60.
768. **Morrison, Philip S.** *Mortgage Lending in Canadian Cities*. Research Paper #111. Toronto: CUCS, University of Toronto, 1979.
769. **Murray, J. A., ed.** *Housing in North America and the Public Interest: Proceedings of the Twentieth Annual University of Windsor Seminar on Canadian-American Relations*. Windsor: Institute of Canadian-American Studies, University of Windsor, 1979.
770. **Nevitt, Adela Adam, ed.** *The Economic Problems of Housing: Proceedings of a Conference Held by the International Economic Association*. Toronto: Macmillan, 1967.
771. **Phillips, D. A.** "Urban Housing Quality: The Importance of Attitudes in the Decision to Rehabilitate." M.A. thesis, British Columbia, 1976.
772. **Pickett, James.** "Residential Capital Formation in Canada, 1871-1921." *CJEPS* 29 (1963):40-58.
773. **Prince, Samuel.** "Co-operative Housing." *JRAIC* 20 (1943):156-58.
774. **Richardson, Nigel H.** "Let's Stop Building Tomorrow's Slums." *CPR* 9, no. 2 (1959):32-41.
775. **Robinson, B. B.** "Some Aspects of Canadian Housing." M.A. thesis, Duke, 1948.
776. **Saywell, John T.** *Housing Canadians: Essays on the History of Residential Construction in Canada*. Discussion Paper No. 24. Ottawa: Economic Council of Canada, 1975.
777. **Simpson, L.** "Housing of the Industrial Workers." *Cn L* 2, no. 1 (1915):17-20.
778. **Sizler, V. J.** *Housing Rehabilitation and Neighbourhood Change: Britain, Canada, and the U.S.A.: An Annotated Bibliography*. Toronto: CUCS, University of Toronto, 1975.
779. **Steele, Marion.** "Dwelling Starts in Canada, 1921-1940." Ph.D. thesis, Toronto, 1972.
780. _____. *The Demand for Housing in Canada*. 1971 Census Analytical Study. Ottawa: Statistics Canada, 1979.
781. **Stewart, Bryce.** "The Housing of Our Immigrant Workers." CPSA, *Papers and Proceedings* 1 (1913):98-111.
782. **Stone, Michael E.** "Housing, Mortgage Lending, and the Contradictions of Capitalism." In #87, pp. 179-208.
783. **Vinton, Warren J.** "The Planning of Public Housing." In *Housing and Community Planning*. McGill University Monograph Series. Montreal, 1944.
784. **Vivian, Henry.** "Town Planning and Housing." Canadian Club of Winnipeg, *Addresses* (1909-10):39-42.
785. _____. "Workingmen's Homes and the Garden City Movement in England." Canadian Club of Vancouver, *Addresses* (1909-10):97-105.
786. **Wiesman, Brahm,** "The Control of Residential Density." M.A. thesis, McGill, 1950.
787. **Wilson, A. D.** "Canadian Housing Legislation." *Can Pub Admin* 2 (1959):214-28.
788. **Willson, K.** *Housing Rehabilitation in Canada: A Review of Policy Goals and Program Design*. Major Report Series #16. Toronto: CUCS, University of Toronto, 1980.

e. Form and Internal Structure

789. **Adams, John S.** "Residential Structure of Midwestern Cities." *AAAG* 60 (1970):37-62.
790. **Adams, Thomas.** "Parks and Playgrounds in Cities." *Can Mun J* 16 (1920):345-48.
791. **Baird, Bonnie.** "How Urban Forests Improve City Life." *CGEJ* 94, no. 3 (1977):60-65.
792. **Bonnett, P. A.** "Nature in the Urban Landscape: A Review and Bibliography of Urban Ecology." M.A. thesis, Alberta, 1971.
793. **Booth, P. J.** "An Alternative Approach for Evaluation and Planning of Urban Public Recreational Facilities." M.A. thesis, Western Ontario, 1975.
794. **Borgfjord, M. R.** "Central Area Planning for Small Urban Centres." M.C.P. thesis, Manitoba, 1973.
795. **Bourne, L. S.** *Perspectives on the Inner City: A Review of Its Character, Decline and Revival.* Research Paper #94. Toronto: CUCS, University of Toronto, 1978.
796. _____, ed. *Internal Structure of the City: Readings on Space and Environment.* Toronto: OUP, 1971.
797. _____, and Simmons, James W., eds. *The Form of Cities in Central Canada: Selected Papers.* Toronto: UTP, 1971.
798. _____, and Barker, G. M. "Ecological Patterns of Small Urban Centres in Canada." *Econ Geogr* 47 (1971):258-65.
799. **Bowden, Martyn J.** "Downtown through Time: Delimitation, Expansion and Internal Growth." *Econ Geogr* 47 (1971):121-35.
800. _____. "Growth of the Central Districts in Large Cities." In **#164A**, pp. 83-88.
801. **Brown, Philip.** *The Canadian Inner City, 1971-1976: A Statistical Handbook.* Ottawa: CMHC, 1979.
802. **Calnan, D. M.** "Businessmen, Forestry and the Gospel of Efficiency: The Canadian Conservation Commission, 1909-1921." M.A. thesis, Western Ontario, 1976.
803. **Carver, Humphrey.** *Cities in the Suburbs.* Toronto: UTP, 1962.
804. **Clark, S. D.** *The Suburban Society.* Toronto: UTP, 1966.
805. **Condit, Carl W.** "The Evolution of Urban Form." *Technology and Culture* 11 (1970):428-33.
806. **Conzen, Michael P.** "Analytical Approaches to the Urban Landscape." In *Dimensions of Human Geography: Essays on Some Familiar and Neglected Themes,* edited by Karl Butzer, pp. 128-65. Chicago: University of Chicago, Dept. of Geography Research Paper No. 186, 1978.
807. _____. "The Morphology of Nineteenth-Century Cities in the United States." In **#35**.
808. **Dennis, R. I.** "Community Structure in Victorian Cities." In *The Settlement of Canada: Origins and Transfer: Proceedings of the 1975 British-Canadian Symposium on Historical Geography,* edited by Brian S. Osborne, pp. 105-38. Kingston: Queen's University, 1976.
809. **Detwyler, T. R.** *Urbanization and Environment: The Physical Geography of the City.* Belmont, CA: Duxbury Press, 1972.
810. **Federal Publications Service.** *Urbanisme et environnement/Urbanism and Environment.* Ottawa: Federal Publications Service, 1974.
811. **Forward, Charles N.** "A Comparison of Waterfront Land Use in Four Canadian Ports: St. John's, Saint John, Halifax and Victoria." *Econ Geogr* 45 (1969):155-69.
812. **Greer-Wooten, Bryn.** "Spatial Structure of the Urban Field." Ph.D. thesis, McGill, 1968.
813. **Hutton, Charles L. A.** "Use of Floor Space in the Functional Differentiation of Small Towns." *Geogr Bull* 9, no. 3 (1967):272-83.
814. **Johnston, R. J.** "On Spatial Patterns in the Residential Structure of Cities." *Can Geogr* 14 (1970):361-66.
815. **Kennedy, W. J. V.** "The Planned Industrial District: Its Significance for Urban Development in Canada." M.A. thesis, British Columbia, 1964.

816. **Leaning, John D.** "The Canadian Shopping Centre." M.A. thesis, McGill, 1957.
817. **Leigh, R.** "Analysis of the Factors Affecting the Location of Industries within Cities." *Can Geogr* 13 (1969):28-33.
818. **Li, Si-Ming.** "Factor Substitution, Technological Change and Location of Plants in an Urban Area." *Alta Geogr* 12 (1976):36-42.
819. **McLemore, R.; Aass, C.; and Keilhoffer, P.** *The Changing Canadian Inner City.* Ottawa: MSUA, 1975.
820. **Rosenfeld, R. C.** "Urban Sprawl and the Solution of Growth Planning: Legal Problems with Its Implementation in Canada and the United States of America." LL.M. thesis, Manitoba, 1976.
821. **Sawers, Larry,** "Urban Form and the Mode of Production." *Review of Radical Political Economics* 7 (1975):52-68.
822. **Schneider, Kenneth R.** "The Destruction of Urban Space." *CPR* 21, no. 1 (1971):12-16, 31-36.
823. **Seeley, J. R.; Sim, R. A.; and Loosley, E. W.** *Crestwood Heights: A Study of the Culture of Suburban Life.* Toronto: UTP, 1956.
824. **Sewell, John.** "The Suburbs." Special Issue. *City Mag* 2, no. 6 (1977):19-55.
825. **Sutton, S.B., ed.** *Civilizing American Cities: A Selection of Frederick Law Olmstead's Writings on City Landscape.* Cambridge, MA: MIT Press, 1979.
826. **Todd, Fred G.** "Character in Design of Parks." *TPICJ* 1, no. 7 (1921):16-17.
827. **Vance, James E., Jr.** "Focus on Downtown." *CPR* 16, no. 2 (1966): 9-15.
828. **Villeneuve, Paul Y.; Polèse, Mario; and Carlos, Serge.** "De la frontière à la métropole: La géographie sociale du Canada urbain." *Can Geogr* 20 (1976):72-110.
829. **Virak, Victor.** "The Structure and the Form of Central Areas of Particular Canadian Cities." M.A. thesis, McGill, 1963.
830. **Walford, Dorice C.** "Tendencies in the Evolution of the Centres of Canadian Cities." M.A. thesis, McGill, 1958.
831. **Warner, Sam Bass, Jr.** "The Public Invasion of Private Space and the Private Engrossment of Public Space." In #47, pp. 171-77.
832. **Whitehead, J. W. R.** "Fringe Belts: A Neglected Aspect of Urban Geography." *Trans British Geographers* 41 (1967):223-33.

f. Urban Renewal

833. **Adams, Thomas.** "Improvement of Slum Areas." *To Pl Cn L* 6, no. 2 (1920):36-39.
834. **Armstrong, Alan H.** "Federal Aids to Urban Repair and Replacement." *CPR* 4, no. 2 (1954):49-63.
835. **Beauregard, Robert A., and Halcomb, Briavel.** "Dominant Enterprises and Acquiescent Communities: The Private Sector and Urban Revitalization." *UPP* 8 (1979):18-31.
836. **Bourne, L. S.** "Trends in Urban Redevelopment: The Implications for Urban Form." *Appraisal J* 37 (1970):24-36.
837. **Bunge, John Christian.** "Urban Renewal in Canada: An Assessment of Current Practice." M.Sc. thesis, British Columbia, 1967.
838. **Carlson, David.** *Revitalizing North American Neighbourhoods: A Comparison of Canadian and U.S. Programs for Neighbourhood Preservation and Housing Rehabilitation.* Washington, DC: HUD, 1979.
839. **Carney, B.** "Residential Redevelopment: A Study of the Decision-Making Process." M.Sc. thesis, Toronto, 1970.
840. **Clark, Douglas.** "Urban Renewal and Municipal Taxation." *Can Tax J* 10 (1962):387-94; 11 (1963):76-82.

841. **Croll, David A.** "The Objectives of Redevelopment in Canadian Cities." *CPR* 6, no. 4 (1956):144-46.
842. **Cross, K. J.** "Urban Redevelopment in Canada." Ph.D. thesis, Cornell, 1958.
843. **Gertler, Leonard O.** "Economic Problems of Urban Redevelopment." M.A. thesis, Toronto, 1950.
844. **Gnandt, F. R.** "An Evaluation of Relocation in Urban Renewal." M.A. thesis, Alberta, 1976.
845. **Hartman, Chester, and Hessler, R.** "The Illusion and Reality of Urban Renewal." In #87, pp. 153-78.
846. **Lighthall, William D.** "Rehousing in Canada." *PHEJ* 3 (1912):446-49.
847. **Lowden, James David.** "Urban Renewal in Canada: Post Mortem." M.A. thesis, British Columbia, 1970.
848. **Mariyana, Soy.** "Urban Renewal, Planning and Design." M.A. Thesis, McGill, 1957.
849. **Owen, Davis S.** "Planning Downtown Redevelopment: What Kind of Organization Is Needed?" *CPR* 9, no. 4 (1959):124-25.
850. **Poon, C. L.** "Urban Railway Relocation: An Economic Evaluation." Ph.D. thesis, Western Ontario, 1976.
851. **Robert, Lionel.** "La rénovation urbaine et la stratégie fiscale des municipalités." *SS* 4 (1972):55-82.
852. **Rose, Albert.** *Citizen Participation in Urban Renewal.* Major Report Series #1. Toronto: CUCS, University of Toronto, 1974.
853. **Searles, John R., Jr.** "Urban Renewal: Eight Problems." *CPR* 9, no. 4 (1959):126-29.
854. **Silzer, V. J.** *Housing Rehabilitation and Neighbourhood Change: Britain, Canada, and the U.S.A.—An Annotated Bibliography.* Bibliographic Series #5. Toronto: CUCS, University of Toronto, 1975.
855. **Slater, David W.** "Economic Remedies for City Ills." *CPR* 11, no. 3 (1961):18-22.
856. **Somerville, M. M.** "The Human Element in Urban Renewal." *CPR* 18, no. 4 (1968):5-8.

5. Municipal Government

a. General Studies

857. **Anderson, George.** "A Comparative Study of Local Government Development in Canada, 1620-1870." M.A. thesis, Saskatchewan (Regina), 1975.
858. **Angers, Bernard.** "Certaines considérations relatives à la question municipale." *Can Pub Admin* 20 (1977):380-88.
859. **Basevi, Vincent.** "The Evolution of Municipal Government." *Can Mag* 39 (1912):367-72.
860. **Beecroft, Eric.** "Government for Metropolitan Regions." *CPR* 8, no. 3 (1958):102-5.
861. **Black, A., and Powell, M.** *Municipal Government and Finance: An Annotated Bibliography.* Ottawa: Policy and Planning Division, CMHC, 1971.
862. **Bourinot, J. G.** *Local Government in Canada: An Historical Study.* Baltimore: Johns Hopkins University, 1887. [Reprinted 1973 by Johnson Reprint Corp., New York.]
863. **Brittain, Horace L.** "Must Municipalities Muddle Along?" *Empire Club of Canada, Speeches* 31 (1933-34):118-28.
864. _____. *Local Government in Canada.* Toronto: Ryerson, 1951.
865. **Burns, R. M.** "Government in an Urban Society." *Can Pub Admin* 14 (1971):415-25.
866. **Callard, K.** "The Present System of Local Government in Canada." *CJEPS* 17 (1951):204-17.

General 33

867. **Civic Improvement League for Canada.** *Report of the Preliminary Conference Held under the Auspices of the Commission of Conservation at Ottawa.* Ottawa: Commission of Conservation, 1915.
868. **Cooper, J. A.** "The Municipal Survey." CPSA, *Papers and Proceedings* 1 (1913):124-31.
869. **Crawford, Kenneth Grant.** *Canadian Municipal Government.* Toronto: UTP, 1954.
870. **Feldman, Lionel D., and Goldrick, Michael D. eds.** *Politics and Government of Urban Canada: Selected Readings.* 1969. 3d ed. rev. Toronto: Methuen, 1976.
871. **Hall, G. E.** "Municipal Government's 100th Anniversary." *Mun W* 59 (December 1949):369-74.
872. **Harris, G. M.** *Comparative Local Government.* London: Hutchinson's, 1949.
873. **Higgins, D. J. H.** *Urban Canada: Its Government and Politics.* Toronto: Macmillan, 1977.
874. ———. "Municipal Politics and Government: Development of the Field in Canadian Political Science." *Can Pub Admin* 22 (1979):380-401.
875. **Hunt, T. A.** "Recent Canadian Municipal Progress." *Can Mun J* 9 (1013):352-54.
876. **Keith-Lucas, B.** "Metropolitan Local Government in Canada." *Pub Admin* 39 (1961):251-62.
877. **Levac, Anne Carswell.** *Urban Population Growth and Municipal Organization.* Local Government Reference Paper, No. 1. Kingston: Institute of Local Government, 1973.
878. **McVittie, J. I.** *Municipal Amalgamation and Annexation: Procedures in Canadian Provinces.* Halifax: Institute of Public Affairs, Dalhousie University, 1959.
879. **Maxwell, J. A.** "Reports on Local Government: A Review Article." *CJEPS* 17 (1951):377-82.
880. **Morse, C.** "Municipal Institutions in England and Canada." *Can Law J* 41 (1905):505-21.
881. **Municipal Publishing Company.** *Municipal Canada.* 1924. Rev. ed. Montreal: The company, 1926.
882. **Munro, W. B.** "Problems of City Government." *Dal Rev* 1 (1921):139-50.
883. **Plunkett, Thomas J.** *Municipal Organization in Canada.* Montreal: CFMM, 1955.
884. ———. "Metropolitan Government in Canada." *UT Law J* 14, no. 1 (1961):29-51.
885. ———. *Urban Canada and Its Government: A Study of Municipal Organization.* Toronto: Macmillan, 1968.
886. **Rowat, Donald Cameron.** *The Canadian Municipal System: Essays on the Improvement of Local Government.* Toronto: M&S, 1969.
887. ———. *Your Local Government: A Sketch of the Municipal System in Canada.* 1955. 2d ed. Toronto: Macmillan, 1975.
888. ———, ed. *The Government of Federal Capitals.* Toronto: UTP, 1973.
889. **Tindal, C. R., and Tindal, S. Nobes.** *Local Government in Canada: An Introduction.* Toronto: McGraw-Hill Ryerson, 1979.
890. **Viau, Jacques.** "Current Developments in Canada Local Government Law." *Can Tax J* 9 (1966):451-68.
891. **Whalen, Hugh J.** "Democracy and Local Government." *Can Pub Admin* 3 (1960):1-13.
892. ———. "Ideology, Democracy, and the Foundations of Local Self-Government." *CJEPS* 26 (1960):377-95.
893. **Wickett, S. Morley.** "City Government in Canada." *Can Mag* 18, no. 1 (1901):53-65.
894. ———. "Bibliography of Canadian Municipal Government." In #**895**, pp. 121-30, 193, 365.
895. ———, ed. *Municipal Government in Canada.* Toronto: University of Toronto Studies, History and Economics, 1907.
896. **Wickwar, W. H.** *The Political Theory of Local Government.* Columbia, SC: University of South Carolina Press, 1970.

b. Politics and Political Parties

897. **Anderson, James D.** "Nonpartisan Civic Politics in Canada and the United States." M.A. thesis, Alberta, 1971.
898. _____. "Nonpartisan Urban Politics in Canadian Cities." In #**925,** pp. 5-21.
899. **Axworthy, Lloyd.** "The Politics of Urban Innovation." In *Living in the Seventies,* edited by A. M. Linden, pp. 44-52. Toronto: Peter Martin, 1970.
900. **Bettison, David G.** *The Politics of Canadian Urban Development.* Edmonton: University of Alberta Press, 1975.
901. **Dant, Noel.** "People, Planning, Politics, Publicity and the Press." *CPR* 12, no. 2 (1962):3-12.
902. **Draper, J. A.,** ed. *Citizen Participation: Canada, A Book of Readings.* Toronto: New Press, 1971.
903. **Duncan, Lewis.** "The Political Basis of Municipal Democracy." *CJEPS* 8 (1942):427-32.
904. **Fowler, E. P., and Goldrick, Michael D.** "Patterns of Partisan and Nonpartisan Balloting." In #**925,** pp. 45-59.
905. **Fraser, Derek.** "Politics and the Victorian City." *UHYb* (1979):32-45.
906. **Gibbon, K. M., and Rowat, Donald Cameron,** eds. *Political Corruption in Canada: Cases, Causes, and Cures.* Toronto: M&S, 1976.
907. **Granatstein, J. L.** "The New City Politics." In #**925,** pp. 60-61.
908. **Hahn, H.** "Ethos and Social Class: Referenda in Canadian Cities." *Polity* 2 (1970):294-315.
909. **Hays, Samuel P.** "The Changing Political Structure of the City in Industrial America." *JUH* 1 (1974):6-38.
910. **Joyce, J. G.** "Municipal Political Parties in Canada." M.A. thesis, Western Ontario, 1969.
911. _____, **and Hossé, Hans A.** *Civic Parties in Canada.* Ottawa: CFMM, 1970.
912. **Keating, Donald R.** "Looking Back at Community Organizing." *City Mag* 3, no. 6 (1978):36-43.
913. **Lightbody, James W.** "The Rise of Party Politics in Canadian Local Elections." *J Can St* 6, no. 1 (1971):39-44.
914. _____. "Political Integration of Urban Minority Groups." Ph.D. thesis, Queen's, 1977.
915. **Lighthall, William D.** "The Elimination of Political Parties in Canadian Cities." *Nat Mun Rev* 6 (1917):207-9. Reprinted in #**925,** pp. 30-32.
916. **Lithwick, N. H.** "Towards a New Urban Politics." *CPR* 22, no. 3 (1972):3-8.
917. **Long, J. A., and Slemko, B.** "The Recruitment of Local Decision-Makers in Five Canadian Cities." *CJPS* 7 (1974):550-59.
918. **Lorimer, James.** "Expertise versus Participation: Who Will Govern Canada's Cities in the Seventies?" In *Living in the Seventies,* edited by A. M. Linden, pp. 37-43. Toronto: Peter Martin, 1970.
919. _____. *The Real World of City Politics.* Toronto: James Lewis and Samuel, 1970.
920. _____. *A Citizen's Guide to City Politics.* Toronto: James Lewis and Samuel, 1972.
921. _____, **and Ross, Evelyn,** eds. *The City Book: The Planning and Politics of Canada's Cities.* Toronto: Lorimer, 1976.
922. _____. *The Second City Book: Studies of Urban and Suburban Canada.* Toronto: Lorimer, 1977.
923. **MacLennan, Ian.** "Towards Urban Freedom." *CPR* 20, no. 4 (1970):16-21.
924. **Masson, Jack K.** *The Demise of 'Alphabet Parties': The Rise of Responsible Party Politics in Cities.* Occasional Paper No. 4. Edmonton: University of Alberta, Dept. of Political Science, 1976.
925. _____, **and Anderson, James D.,** eds. *Emerging Party Politics in Urban Canada.* Toronto: M&S, 1972.

926. **Mollenknopf, John H.** "The Postwar Politics of Urban Development." In **#87**, pp. 117-52.
927. **Punnett, R. M.** "Party Politics and Canadian Municipal Government." *J Can St* 4 (1969):46-53.
928. **Stinson, Arthur, Ed.** *Citizen Action: An Annotated Bibliography of Case Studies.* Ottawa: Community Planning Association of Canada, 1975.
929. **Weaver, John C.** *Shaping the Canadian City: Essays on Urban Politics and Policy, 1890-1920.* Monographs on Canadian Urban Government, vol. 1. Toronto: Institute of Public Administration of Canada, 1977.
930. **Wellman, B.** *Community-Network-Communications: An Annotated Bibliography.* 2d rev. ed. Toronto: CUCS, University of Toronto, 1974.

c. Structure, Administration and Reform

931. **Aitchison, J. H.** "The Municipal Corporations Act of 1849." *CHR* 30 (1949):107-22.
932. **Ames, Herbert Brown.** "The 'Machine' in Honest Hands." *Can Mag* 3 (1894):101-9.
933. _____. "Some Problems of Municipal Government." Canadian Club of Toronto, *Proceedings* (1903-4):89-93.
934. **Andras, Robert.** "Formation of the Federal Ministry of Urban Affairs." *CPR* 21, no. 1 (1971):4-11.
935. "Aspects of Municipal Administration: A Symposium." *Can Pub Admin* 11 (1968):18-96.
936. **Beecroft, Eric.** "The Government of Metropolitan Regions." *CPR* 8, no. 3 (1958):102-6.
937. _____. "Agenda for Regional Government." *Can Pub Admin* 5 (1962):219-28.
938. _____, ed. *Changes Confronting Small Cities and Towns: A Selection of Papers.* Montreal: CFMM, 1964.
939. **Blumenfeld, Hans.** "The Role of the Federal Government in Urban Affairs." *J Liberal Thought* 11, no. 2 (1966):35-44.
940. **Bolduc, Roch.** "Incidences du rôle accru de l'état sur la démocratie locale." *Can Pub Admin* 23 (1980):60-75.
941. **Bourassa, Guy.** "L'administration municipale." *Rech soc* 9, no. 1-2 (1968):45-55.
942. **Cameron, K. D., ed.** "National Urban Policy." Special Issue. *Plan Canada* 12, no. 1 (1972):4-128.
943. **CFMM.** *Report of the Special Committee on Dominion-Provincial-Municipal Relations.* Montreal: CFFM, 1948.
944. _____. *The Federation and the Federal Government.* Montreal: CFMM, 1960.
945. **Chipperfield, G. H.** "The City Manager and Chief Administrative Officer." Institute of Public Administration of Canada, *Proceedings* 16 (1964):123-32.
946. **Crawford, Kenneth Grant.** "Urban Growth and Boundary Readjustments." *Can Pub Admin* 3 (1960):51-58.
947. **Curtis, Clifford A., and Chatters, Carl H.** "The Changing Form of Municipal Government." *Can Tax J* 6 (1958):339-45.
948. **Davies, P. G.** "Administration in the Regional City." *CPR* 8, no. 4 (1958):116-18.
950. **Faucher, Albert.** "Le fonds d'emprunt municipal dans le Haut-Canada, 1852-1867." *Rech soc* 1 (1960):7-32.
951. **French, J. R.** "City Manager Plan in Canada." Institute of Public Administration of Canada, *Proceedings* 6 (1954):63-73.
952. **Fyfe, Stewart.** "Governing Urban Communities." *QQ* 67 (1960-61):605-16.
953. **Gaetz, H. H.** "Municipal Legislation." In **#925**, pp. 26-29.
954. **Hickey, Paul.** "The Changing Structure of Municipal Government in Canada." *CCHA* 89 (1966):182-86.

955. **Higgins, D. J. H.** "Community and Local Government: Boundary Determination." Ph.D. thesis, Carleton, 1973.
956. **Hocken, H. C.** "The Increasing Complexity of Municipal Government." *Can Mun J* 9 (1913):397-98.
957. _____. "The New Spirit in Municipal Government." Canadian Club of Ottawa, *Addresses* (1914-15):85-97.
958. **Humes, Samuel.** *The Structure of Local Governments throughout the World*. The Hague: Nijhoff, 1961.
959. **Kunka, Gloria Mae.** "Urban Problems and Inter-Governmental Relations." M.A. thesis, Carleton, 1969.
960. **Lighthall, William D.** "The People as Municipalities." Canadian Club of Toronto, *Proceedings* (1904-5):31-38.
961. **Lithwick, N. H.** "Urban Policy-Making: Shortcomings in Political Technology." *Can Pub Admin* 15 (1972):571-84.
962. **McCarthy, Michael P.** "On Bosses, Reformers and Urban Growth: Some Suggestions for a Political Typology of American Cities." *JUH* 4 (1977):29-38.
963. **Macfarland, H. B. F.** "Union of Canadian Municipalities and the Twentieth Century City." *PHEJ* 2 (1911):540-41.
964. **McIver, John M.** "A Survey of the City Manager Plan in Canada." *Can Pub Admin* 3 (1960):216-32.
965. **Mooney, George S.** "The Canadian Federation of Mayors and Municipalities: Its Role and Function." *Can Pub Admin* 3 (1960):82-92.
966. **Morton, W. L.** "The Extension of the Franchise in Canada: A Study in Democratic Nationalism." CHA, *AR* (1943):72-81.
967. **Nelles, H. V., and Armstrong, Christopher.** "The Great Fight for Clean Government." *UHR* 2-76 (October 1976):50-66.
968. **Peterson, B. H.** "Recruitment and Selection for Public Administration in a Municipal Perspective." *Can Pub Admin* 7 (1964):215-26.
969. **Plunkett, Thomas J.** "Structural Reform of Local Government in Canada." *Pub Admin Rev* 33, no. 1 (1973):40-51.
970. _____, **and Betts, George Michael.** *The Management of Canadian Urban Government: A Basic Text for a Course in Urban Management*. Kingston: Institute of Local Government, Queen's University, 1978.
971. **Robson, William A.** "Metropolitan Government: Problems and Solutions." *Can Pub Admin* 9 (1966):45-54.
972. **Rogers, I. M.** *The Law of Canadian Municipal Corporations*. Toronto: Carswell, 1959.
973. **Rose, Albert.** *Problems of Canadian City Growth: An Essay on Metropolitan Administration and Planning*. Ottawa: Community Planning Association of Canada, 1950.
974. _____. "The Challenge of Metropolitan Growth." *CPR* 4, no. 4 (1954):97-103.
975. **Rowat, Donald C.** "Do We Need the Manager Plan?" *Can Pub Admin* 3 (1960):42-50.
976. _____. "The Role of Canada's Urban Municipalities in Governmental Decision-Making." *Studies in Comparative Local Government* 8, no. 1 (1974):43-49.
977. _____. "The Problem of Federal-Urban Relations in Canada." *Q Can St* 3 (1975):214-24.
978. **Rutherford, Paul F. W.** "Tomorrow's Metropolis: The Urban Reform Movement in Canada, 1880-1920." In #**85**, pp. 368-92.
979. _____, ed. *Saving the Canadian City: The First Phase, 1890-1920: An Anthology of Articles on Urban Reform*. Social History of Canada, vol. 22. Toronto: UTP, 1974.
980. **Scanlon, T. J.** "Board of Control: Its Merits and Defects." *Can Pub Admin* 3 (1960):331-36.
981. **Suski, Julian G.** "The Structure of Municipal Government in Canada and in Europe." *Can Pub Admin* 8 (1965):307-24.

982. **Thayer, Frederick C.** "Regional Administration: The Failure of Traditional Theory in the United States and Canada." *Can Pub Admin* 15 (1972):449-64.
983. **Tindal, C. R.** *Structural Changes in Local Government: Government for Urban Regions.* Monographs on Canadian Urban Government, vol. 2. Toronto: Institute of Public Administration of Canada, 1977.
984. **Underhill, Frank.** "Commission Government in Cities." *The Arbor* (University of Toronto) 1-2 (1910-11):284-94.
985. **Weaver, John C.** "Elitism and the Corporate Ideal: Businessmen and Boosters in Canadian Civic Reform, 1890-1920." In *Cities in the West,* edited by A. R. McCormack and I. MacPherson, pp. 48-73. Ottawa: NMM, 1975.
986. _____. "Tomorrow's Metropolis Revisited: A Critical Assessment of Urban Reform in Canada, 1890-1920." In **#85**, pp. 393-418.
987. _____, ed. "Approaches to the History of Urban Reform." Special Issue. *UHR* 2-76 (October 1976):3-66.
988. **Wickett, S. Morley.** "The Problems of City Government." Empire Club of Canada, *Speeches* 5 (1907-8):107-15.
989. _____. "City Government by Commission." Canadian Club of Hamilton, *Addresses* (1912-13):17-31.
990. **Woodruff, C. R.** "The Newer Civic Life." Canadian Club of Toronto, *Proceedings* (1907-8):45-50.
991. **Wrenshall, C. M.** *Municipal Administration and Accounting.* Toronto: Pitman, 1937.
992. **Young, Dennis A.** "Canadian Local Government Development: Some Aspects of the Commissioner and City Manager Forms of Administration." *Can Pub Admin* 9 (1966):55-68.

d. Finance and Taxation

993. **Andres, James M.** "Canadian Municipal Debt Structure and Borrowing, 1946-1959." M.A. thesis, Ottawa, 1961.
994. **Barber, Clarence E.** "Prospective Developments in Municipal Finance." *Can Tax J* 4, no. 4 (1956):284-89.
995. **Beedle, A.** "Municipal Accounting in Canada and Its Relevance to Reality." *Can Pub Admin* 9 (1966):69-85.
996. **Bélanger, Gérard.** "Questions de base à toute réforme du financement municipal." *Can Pub Admin* 20 (1977):370-79.
997. **Berry, David B.** "Provincial and Municipal Expenditures." *Can Tax J* 16, no. 5 (1968):395-97.
998. **Bird, R. M.** "The Taxation of Land Values in Canada and Australasia." M.A. thesis, Columbia, 1960.
999. **Bowland, James G.** "Planning a Municipal Capital Budget." *Can Pub Admin* 6 (1963):463-69.
1000. **Brazer, Harvey E.** "The Value of Industrial Property as a Subject of Taxation." *Can Pub Admin* 4 (1961):137-47.
1001. **Burnett, A. A.** "Financing Municipal Government in Canada." Ph.D. thesis, McGill, 1960.
1002. **CFMM.** *Municipal and Intergovernmental Finance, 1930-1951.* Montreal: CFMM, 1953.
1003. _____. *The Politics of Government Finance.* Montreal: CFMM, 1969.
1004. **Carswell, R. E.** "Municipal Finances." *Can Tax J* 6, no. 1 (1958):49-51.
1005. **Chanette, François.** "Le financement des gouvernements municipaux par l'emprunt obligatoire." *Can Banker* 71, no. 3 (1964):71-77.
1006. **Chappell, C. H.** "Municipal Problems Associated with Certain Types of Industrial Taxation." *Can Pub Admin* 4 (1961):148-53.

1007. **Clark, R. M.** "Some Aspects of the Development of Personal Income Tax in the Provinces and Municipalities of Canada to 1930." Ph.D. thesis, Harvard, 1946.
1008. _____. "Municipal Business Tax." *Can Tax J* 8, no. 5 (1960):339-42.
1009. **Clayton, F. A.** "Distribution of Urban Residential Property Tax Burdens and Expenditure Benefits in Canada." Ph.D. thesis, Queen's, 1966.
1010. **Crawford, Kenneth Grant.** "Some Problems of Assessment." *Can Pub Admin* 7 (1964):324-32.
1011. **Curtis, Clifford A., and Chatters, Carl H.** "Municipal Finance and Provincial-Federal Relations." *CJEPS* 17 (1951):297-306.
1012. _____. "Canadian Municipal Finance." *Can Tax J* 1 (1953):532-39.
1013. **Digman, R. G.** "Some Facts and Conclusions Respecting Canadian Municipal Bonds." M.A. thesis, Toronto, 1912.
1014. **Douglas, J. M.** "Canadian Municipal Securities." M.A. thesis, McMaster, 1936.
1015. **Emerson, Bruce E.** "Municipal Tort Liability in the Common Law Provinces." *UBC Law Rev* 1 (1960):147-76.
1016. **Finnis, F. H.** "Local Tax Concessions in Canadian Municipalities." *Can Tax J* 9, no. 1 (1961):61-65.
1017. _____. "Local Assessment and Taxation of Industry." *Can Tax J* 10, no. 1 (1962):63-64.
1018. _____. "Site Valuation and Local Government. *Can Tax J* 11, no. 2 (1963):118-26.
1019. _____. "Measuring the Local Tax Base." *Can Tax J* 12, no. 1 (1964):43-49.
1020. _____. "Slums and Property Taxation." *Can Tax J* 16, no. 2 (1968):154-58.
1021. **Froom, A. M.** "Canadian Municipal Debts and Methods of Their Repayment." M.A. thesis, McMaster, 1916.
1022. **Goldenberg, H. Carl.** *Municipal Finance in Canada: A Study Prepared for the Royal Commission on Dominion-Provincial Relations*. Ottawa: King's Printer, 1939.
1023. _____. "Municipal Finance and Taxation—Problems and Prospects." *Can Tax J* 4, no. 3 (1956):158-65.
1024. **Graham, John F.** "The Application of the Fiscal Equity Principle to Provincial-Municipal Relations." *Can Pub Admin* 3 (1960):24-30.
1025. **Haig, R. M.** *The Exemption of Improvements from Taxation in Canada and the United States: A Report Prepared for the Committee on Taxation of the City of New York*. New York: City of New York, 1915.
1026. **Hardy, Eric.** "Provincial-Municipal Relations: With Emphasis on the Financial Relationships between Provinces and Local Government." *Can Pub Admin* 3 (1960):14-24.
1027. _____. "The Serious Problems of Municipal Finance." *Can Pub Admin* 4 (1961):154-63.
1028. **Higgins, B. H.** "Financial Planning at the Community Level." In *Housing and Community Planning*. McGill University Monograph Series. Montreal, 1944.
1029. **Jack, L. B.** "Control of Local Government Finance in Three Federal Countries: Canada, the United States, and Australia." Ph.D. thesis, McGill, 1943.
1030. **Johnson, I. C.** "Provincial and Municipal Debt in Canada, 1946-1966." M.A. thesis, Western Ontario, 1971.
1031. **Johnson, J.A.** "Provincial-Municipal Intergovernment Fiscal Relations." *Can Pub Admin* 12 (1969):166-80.
1032. **McInnes, J. R.** "Municipal Revenue—Possible New or Additional Sources." *Can Tax J* 5, no. 4 (1957):299-303.
1033. **Manning, H. E.** *Assessment and Rating: Municipal Taxation in Canada*. Toronto: Cartwright, 1951.
1034. **Marshall, A. H.** *Financial Administration in Local Government*. Toronto: Nelson, 1960.
1035. **Meekison, John Peter.** "Major Aspects of Federal-Municipal Financial Relations." M.A. thesis, Western Ontario, 1962.

1036. **Michas, N. A.** "Variations in the Level of Provincial-Municipal Expenditures in Canada [1951-1961]: An Econometric Analysis." *Public Finance* 24 (1969):597-617.
1037. **Migue, J. L.** "Histoire des finances municipales canadiennes, 1866-1939." Thèse de M.A., Montréal, 1956.
1038. **Newcomer, Mabel, and Hutchinson, Ruth Gillette.** "Taxation of Land Values in Canada." *JLPE* 40 (1932):366-78.
1039. **O'Connell, Martin P.** "Municipal Borrowing: Problems and Prospects." *Can Pub Admin* 6 (1963):64-83.
1040. **Oliver, J.** "Municipal Revenue Other Than Government Grants." *Can Pub Admin* 6 (1963):57-63.
1041. **Owens, H. T.** *Land Value Taxation in Canadian Local Government.* Quebec: Henry George Foundation of Canada, 1953.
1042. **Perry, J. Harvey.** *Taxes, Tariffs and Subsidies: A History of Canadian Fiscal Development.* 2 vols. Toronto: UTP, 1955.
1043. _____. "Municipal Finance Needs and Federal Fiscal Policy." *Can Tax J* 7 (1959):308-17.
1044. **Pierce, Dixwell L.** "City Sales Taxes." *Can Tax J* 1 (1953):564-75.
1045. **Plunkett, Thomas J.** *The Financial Structure and the Decision-Making Process of Canadian Municipal Government.* Ottawa: CMHC, 1972.
1046. **Powell, C. W.** "Provincial-Municipal Financing." *Can Pub Admin* 6 (1963):84-91.
1047. **Raney, E. F.** "Municipal Taxation in Canada: A Reconstruction." Ph.D. thesis, Toronto, 1912.
1048. **Robeye, Lactance.** "Urbanisme et finance." *RCU* 9, no. 3 (1959):88-89.
1049. **Santos, B. R.** "Property Taxation and Housing Market Analysis." Ph.D. thesis, Manitoba, 1974.
1050. **Silver, Sheldon.** "The Feasibility of a Municipal Income Tax in Canada." *Can Tax J* 16 (1968):398-406.
1051. **Slater, David W.** "Urban Growth and Municipal Finance." *Can Banker* 70, no. 2 (1963):5-17.
1052. **Stoughton, Arthur Alexander.** "The Town Planning Comptroller and His Work." *TPICJ* 1, no. 6 (1921):8-10.
1053. **Thomas, J. W. N.** "Municipal Debt Financing in Canada." M.A. thesis, Queen's, 1964.
1054. **Vineberg, S.** *Provincial and Local Taxation in Canada.* London: King, 1912.
1055. **Wagdin, G. A.** "Statistical Approaches in Municipal Finance." *Mun Fin* 39, no. 1 (1966):30-37.
1056. **Yorath, C. J.** "Municipal Finance and Administration." *Cn L* 3, no. 3 (1917):64-67; no. 4 (1917):75-78.

e. Services

1057. **Atherton, William Henry.** "Child Welfare and the City." *PHEJ* 2 (1911):461-66.
1058. **Baker, H. R.** "The Impact of Central Government Services on the Small Community." *Can Pub Admin* 3 (1960):97-106.
1059. **Bates, Gordon.** "The Value of Social Hygiene to a Community." *PHEJ* 16 (1925):401-9.
1060. **Brown, C. A. B., and Hughes, J. E.** "Municipal Playgrounds." Canadian Club of Toronto, *Proceedings* (1909-10):69-74.
1061. **Carswell, R. E.** "Cities Help the Unemployed." *Can Tax J* 6 (1958):128-33.
1062. **Chatters, Carl H., and Curtis, Clifford A.** "War-Time Problems of Local Governments." *CJEPS* 9 (1943):394-407.

1063. **Cooper, I., and Hulchanski, J. D.** *Canadian Town Planning, 1900-1930: A Historical Bibliography.* Vol. 3. *Public Health.* Bibliographic Report #9. Toronto: CUCS, University of Toronto, 1978.
1064. **Cousineau, A.** "Planning Public Services." In *Housing and Community Planning.* McGill University Monograph Series. Montreal, 1944.
1065. **Feldman, Lionel D.** "Administration of Justice—A Municipal Burden?" *Can Tax J* 10 (1952):203-9.
1066. **Fingard, Judith.** "The Winter's Tale: The Seasonal Contours of Pre-Industrial Poverty in British North America, 1815-1860." CHA, *HP* (1974):65-94.
1067. **Hareven, Tamara.** "An Ambiguous Alliance: Some Aspects of American Influences on Canadian Social Welfare." *HS* 3 (1969):2-98.
1068. **Hastings, C. H.** "Guarding a City's Health." Canadian Club of Toronto, *Proceedings* (1916-17):120-28.
1069. **Hibbard, F. W.** "The Control of Public Utilities." Empire Club of Canada, *Speeches* 8 (1910-11):209-17.
1070. **Jones, Howard.** "Metropolis, Community and Family." *Can Wel* 35 (1959):220-26.
1071. **Kitchen, Harry M.** "Some Organizational Implications of Providing an Urban Service: The Case of Water." *Can Pub Admin* 18 (1975):297-308.
1072. **Krueger, Ralph R.** "Community Planning and Local Government." *CPR* 18, no. 4 (1968):16-21.
1073. **Laberge, J. E.** "Town Planning and Civic Authorities." *PHEJ* 3 (1912):126-29.
1074. **Lamb, A. S.** "Planning for Health and Recreation." In *Housing and Community Planning.* McGill University Monograph Series. Montreal, 1944.
1075. **Leigh, Amy.** "Municipalities and Public Welfare." *Can Wel* 40 (1964):16-22.
1076. **Lighthall, William D.** "War-Time Experiences of Canadian Cities." *Nat Mun Rev* 7, no. 1 (1918):19-23.
1077. **McCarthy, J. O.** "Some Social Problems of Civic Government." Canadian Club of Hamilton, *Addresses* (1912-13):77-84.
1078. **MacKinnon, Fred R.** "Local Government and Welfare." *Can Pub Admin* 3 (1960):31-41.
1079. **Markusen, Ann R.** "Class and Urban Social Expenditure: A Marxist Theory of Metropolitan Government." In *#87*, pp. 90-111.
1080. **Morgan, John S., and Leigh, Amy.** "The Contribution of the Municipality to the Administration of Public Welfare." *Can Pub Admin* 7 (1964):137-57.
1081. **Murray, T. A.** "The Purification of Public Water Supplies." *PHEJ* 2 (1911):114-19.
1082. _____. "The Evolution of Sewage Disposal Methods in Canada." *ENCR* 28 (1914):580-86.
1083. **Outhet, R. A.** "Municipal Powers in Dealing with Town Planning Schemes." *PHEJ* 3 (1912):483-85.
1084. **Riendeau, Roger.** "A Clash of Interests: Dependency and the Municipal Problem in the Great Depression." *J Can St* 14 (Spring 1979):50-58.
1085. **Riis, Jack.** "The Value of Playgrounds to the Community." Canadian Club of Toronto, *Proceedings* (1912-13):271-79.
1086. **Seunath, M. A.** "Community Development in Urban Areas." M.S.W. thesis, Calgary, 1971.
1087. **Small, F. L.** *The Influent and the Effluent: The History of Urban Water Supply and Sanitation.* Saskatoon: Modern Press, 1974.
1088. **Smith, W. Richmond.** "Britain's Experience of Public Ownership." Empire Club of Canada, *Speeches* 3 (1905-6):184-203.
1089. **Squire, S. L.** "Good Roads as a Municipal Problem." *ENCR* 31 (1917):850-51.
1090. **Taylor, John H.** "Urban Social Organization and Urban Discontent: The 1930s." In *Western*

Perspectives 1, edited by David Jay Bercuson, pp. 33-44. Toronto: Holt, Rinehart and Winston, 1974.

1091. _____. " 'Relief from Relief': The Cities Answer to Depression Dependency." *J Can St* 14 (Spring 1979):16-23.

1092. _____, **ed.** "Fire, Disease, and Water in the Nineteenth Century City." Special Issue. *UHR* 8 (June 1979):7-116.

1093. Tufts, L. R. "Community Social Services: A Study of the Range, Nature and Incidence of Human Problems Which Require Service in a Low-Income Urban Community." M.S.W. thesis, Dalhousie, 1973.

1094. Webster, Donald H. *Urban Planning and Municipal Public Policy.* New York: Harper, 1958.

1095. White, John. "Public Ownership of Public Utilities." Empire Club of Canada, *Speeches* (1905-6):143-54.

1096. Willows, Maurice. "Efficiency in Caring for the Poor, the Sick and the Delinquent, as a Factor in the Healthy Development of a City." Canadian Club of Winnipeg, *Addresses* (1913):12-15.

1097. Woodsworth, James Shaver. *My Neighbour: A Study of City Conditions, A Plea for Social Service.* 1911. Reprint, with an introduction by Richard Allen. Social History of Canada, vol. 3. Toronto: UTP, 1972.

II

Maritimes

1. General

1098. **Acheson, T. W.** "The Maritimes and Empire Canada." In *Canada and the Burden of Unity*, edited by David J. Bercuson, pp. 87-114. Toronto: Macmillan, 1977.
1099. _____. "The National Policy and the Industrialization of the Maritimes, 1880-1910." In #**85**, pp. 93-124.
1100. **Allison, D.** "Notes on 'A General Return of the Several Townships in the Province of Nova Scotia for the First Day of January, 1767.'" NSHS *Collections* 7 (1889-91):44-71.
1101. **Archibald, B.** "The Development of Underdevelopment in the Maritimes." M.A. thesis, Dalhousie, 1971.
1102. **Arnell, J. C.** "The Ports of the Maritimes and Their Trade and Commerce in 1880." *CGEJ* 78, no. 1 (1969):12-17.
1103. **Atlantic Development Board.** *Urban Centres in the Atlantic Provinces*. Ottawa: Queen's Printer, 1967.
1104. "Atlantic Provinces: Urban Growth for a Non-Urban Area." *Progres Arch* 53 (September 1972):108-11.
1105. **Bailey, Alfred G.** "Creative Moments in the Culture of the Maritime Provinces." *Dal Rev* 29 (1949):231-51.
1106. **Baker, John F.** "The Underdevelopment of Atlantic Canada, 1867-1920: A Study of the Development of Capitalism." M.A. thesis, McMaster, 1977.
1107. **Bird, J. Brian.** "Settlement Patterns in Maritime Canada, 1687-1786." *GEOR* 45 (1955):385-404.
1108. **Brenton, G. W.** "Migration and Development in the Maritimes." M.A. thesis, Queen's, 1974.
1109. **Brookes, Alan A.** "Out-Migration from the Maritime Provinces, 1860-1900: Some Preliminary Considerations." *Acadiensis* 5 (Spring 1976):26-55.
1110. **Brown, Wallace.** "William Cobbett in the Maritimes." *Dal Rev* 56 (1976):448-61.
1111. **Brym, Robert J., and Sacouman, R. James,** eds. *Underdevelopment and Social Movements in Atlantic Canada*. Toronto: New Hogtown Press, 1979.
1112. **Butler, Peter M.** "Earnings and Transfers: Income Sources in Atlantic Canada and Their Relationship to Work Settings." *CRSA* 16 (1979):32-46.
1113. **Cameron, John R.** *Provincial-Municipal Relations in the Maritime Provinces*. Fredericton: Maritime Union Study, 1970.
1114. **Careless, J. M. S.** "Aspects of Metropolitanism in Atlantic Canada." In *Regionalism in the Canadian Community, 1867-1967*, edited by Mason Wade, pp. 117-29. Toronto: UTP, 1969.

1115. **Clark, S. D.** "The Rural Village Society of the Maritimes." In *The Developing Canadian Community,* edited by S. D. Clark, pp. 41-62. Toronto: UTP, 1962.
1116. **Coke, J.** "Trends in Rural Population in Canada with Particular Reference to the Maritimes." *Econ Anal 21* (August 1951):85-91.
1117. **Davis, J. M.** "Considerations in the Investigation, Analysis and Planning of the Central Areas of Maritime Cities." In *Issues in Regional/Urban Development of Atlantic Canada,* edited by Neil B. Ridler, pp. 129-36. Saint John: University of New Brunswick, 1978.
1118. **Fingard, Judith.** "The Decline of the Sailor as a Ship Labourer in 19th-Century Timber Ports." *Labour* 3 (1978):63-108.
1119. _____. "The Relief of the Unemployed: The Poor in Saint John, Halifax, and Saint John's, 1815-1860." In #**85**, pp. 341-67.
1120. **Fischer, Lewis R., and Sager, Eric W., eds.** *The Enterprising Canadians: Entrepreneurs and Economic Development in Eastern Canada, 1820-1914.* St. John's: Memorial University, 1979.
1121. **Fisher, Gerald.** "Atlantic Canada." *Communique* 3 (January 1977):1-69.
1122. **Forward, Charles N.** "Cities: Function, Form, and Future." In *The Atlantic Provinces,* edited by Alan Macpherson, pp. 137-76. Toronto: UTP, 1972.
1123. **Frederickson, Mary.** *Local Studies.* Halifax: Atlantic Institute of Education, 1976.
1124. **Frost, James D.** "Principles of Interest: The Bank of Nova Scotia and the Industrialization of the Maritimes, 1880-1910." M.A. thesis, Queen's, 1979.
1125. **Grant, John N.** "Post-1812 Negro Immigration and Settlement in the Maritimes." M.A. thesis, New Brunswick, 1970.
1126. **Hamilton, William B.** *Local History in Atlantic Canada.* Toronto: Macmillan, 1974.
1127. **Hemmean, Douglas.** "A Maritime Small Town in the Nineties." *Dal Rev* 13 (1933):209-16.
1128. **Hugo-Brunt, Michael.** "The Origin of Colonial Settlements in the Maritimes." In #**563**, pp. 42-83.
1129. _____. "Portsmouth: Prototype of Canadian Maritime Settlement." *Plan Canada* 1 (1960):144-70; 2 (1961):58-74.
1130. **MacLellan, O.** *Towns of the Maritimes.* Moncton: Moncton *Daily Times,* 1947.
1131. **Mannion, John J.** *Irish Settlements in Eastern Canada.* Toronto: UTP, 1974.
1132. **Matthews, Keith.** "The Shipping Industry of Atlantic Canada: Themes and Problems." In *Ships and Shipbuilding in the North Atlantic Region,* edited by Keith Matthews and Gerald Panting, pp. 1-18. St. John's: Memorial University, 1978.
1133. **Morley, William F. E.** *Canadian Local Histories: A Bibliography.* Vol. 1, *The Atlantic Provinces.* Toronto: UTP, 1967.
1134. **Murray, W. C.** "Local Government in the Maritime Provinces." In #**895**, pp. 221-68.
1135. **Nablo, R. W.** "Social Structure Related to Business and Finance in a Seaport City." M.A. thesis, New Brunswick, 1960.
1136. *Our Dominion: Historical and Other Sketches of the Mercantile and Manufacturing Interests of Fredericton, Marysville, Woodstock, Moncton, New Brunswick, Yarmouth, N.S., etc.* Toronto: Historical Publishing Co., 1889.
1137. **Peterson, Roger.** "Transportation and Development in Atlantic Canada." In *Issues in Regional/Urban Development of Atlantic Canada,* edited by Neil B. Ridler, pp. 59-65. Saint John: University of New Brunswick, 1978.
1138. **Saunders, Stanley Alexander.** *The Economic History of the Maritime Provinces.* Ottawa: Royal Commission on Dominion-Provincial Relations, 1939.
1139. **Whalen, Hugh J.** "Recent Municipal Fiscal Trends in the Atlantic Provinces." *Can Pub Admin* 2 (1959):154-71.
1140. **Winks, Robin W.** "Negroes in the Maritimes: An Introductory Survey." *Dal Rev* 48 (1968-69):453-71.

III

Nova Scotia

1. General

1141. **Antoft, Kell,** ed. *A Guide to Local Government in Nova Scotia.* Halifax: Institute of Public Affairs, Dalhousie University, 1977.
1142. **Barovick, B. M.** "Economic Conditions and Foreign Real Estate and Industrial Investments in Nova Scotia." M.A. thesis, Rhode Island, 1974.
1143. **Beck, M. J.** *The Government of Nova Scotia.* Toronto: UTP, 1957.
1144. _____. *The Evolution of Municipal Government in Nova Scotia, 1749-1973.* Halifax: Royal Commission on Education, Public Services and Provincial-Municipal Relations, 1974.
1145. **Belcher, Jonathan.** "Description and State of New Settlements in Nova Scotia in 1761." In *Report of the Public Archives of Canada for 1904,* pp. 287-300. Ottawa: King's Printer, 1905.
1146. **Bell, F. H.** "Municipal Taxation in Nova Scotia." *Dal Rev* 1 (1921):264-80.
1147. **Birkett, Patricia.** "The Social Influences of the Churches in Nova Scotia, 1829-1867." Ph.D. thesis, Dalhousie, 1969.
1148. **Blakeley, Phyllis R.** "Music in Nova Scotia 1605-1867: Part I." *Dal Rev* 31 (1951):94-101; "Part II," pp. 223-30.
1149. **Campbell, D. F.** "A Comparative Study of the Reading Ability of Rural and Urban School Children in Nova Scotia." M.A. thesis, Catholic University of America, 1951.
1150. **Chard, Donald F.** "Joseph Howe and the Struggle for Railways in Nova Scotia, 1830-1858." *NSHQ* 8 (1978): 289-97.
1151. **Clark, Andrew H.** *Acadia: The Geography of Early Nova Scotia to 1760.* Madison: University of Wisconsin Press, 1968.
1152. **Dua, A. S.** "An Econometric Analysis of Per Capita Municipal Expenditures in Nova Scotia, 1968 and 1971." M.A. Thesis, Catholic University of America, 1951.
1153. **Evans, Reginald Dickey.** "Stage Coaches in Nova Scotia, 1815 to 1867." NSHS *Collections* 24 (1938):107-34.
1154. _____. "Transportation and Communication in Nova Scotia, 1815 to 1850." M.A. thesis, Dalhousie, 1936.
1155. **Fay, S. F. J.** "Municipal Finance in Nova Scotia and Prince Edward Island, 1945-1955." M.A. thesis, New Brunswick, 1959.
1156. **Fergusson, Charles Bruce.** *Local Government in Nova Scotia.* Halifax: Institute of Public Affairs, Dalhousie University, 1961.
1157. _____. "Local Government in Nova Scotia." PANS *Bulletin* 17 (1961):1-18.
1158. _____. *Place Names and Places in Nova Scotia.* Halifax: PANS, 1967.

1159. **Fingard, Judith.** "The Church of England in Nova Scotia, 1783-1816." M.Phil. thesis, London, 1967.
1160. **Forsey, Eugene A.** *Economic and Social Aspects of the Nova Scotia Coal Industry.* Toronto: Macmillan, 1926.
1161. **Gentilcore, R. Louis.** "The Agricultural Background of Settlement in Eastern Nova Scotia." *AAAG* 46 (1956):378-404.
1162. **Graham, John F.** "Provincial-Municipal Fiscal Relations and Economic Development in a Low Income Province: Nova Scotia." Ph.D. thesis, Columbia, 1959.
1163. _____. "New Municipal Services Program in Nova Scotia: An Evaluation." *Can Tax J* 15 (1967):493-505.
1164. **Guy, R. M.** "Industrial Development and Urbanization of Pictou County, Nova Scotia to 1900." M.A. thesis, Acadia, 1962.
1165. **Hansford, G. R.** "The Shipbuilding Industry of Nova Scotia during the Nineteenth Century." M.A. thesis, Acadia, 1953.
1166. **Harvey, D. C.** "The Struggle for the New England Form of Township Government in Nova Scotia." CHA, *AR* (1933):15-22.
1167. _____. "The Intellectual Awakening of Nova Scotia." *Dal Rev* 13 (1933):1-22.
1168. _____. "Early Public Libraries in Nova Scotia." *Dal Rev* 14 (1935):429-43.
1169. **Henry, Frances.** *Forgotten Canadians: The Blacks of Nova Scotia.* Toronto: Longmans, 1973.
1170. **Hollingsworth, S.** *An Account of the Present State of Nova Scotia.* Edinburgh: Creech, 1786.
1171. **Hunter, James Jamison, Jr.** "The Organization and Administration of the Public School System in the Province of Nova Scotia." Ph.D. thesis, Syracuse, 1943.
1172. **Johnson, Peter Graham.** "The Union of Nova Scotia Municipalities as a Pressure Group." M.A. thesis, Dalhousie, 1967.
1173. **Johnston, Andrew J. B.** "The Protestant Spirit of Colonial Nova Scotia: An Inquiry into Mid-Nineteenth Century Anti-Catholicism." M.A. thesis, Dalhousie, 1978.
1174. **Kerr, W. B.** "The Merchants of Nova Scotia and the American Revolution." *CHR* 13 (1932):20-36.
1175. **Lomas, A. A.** "The Industrial Development of Nova Scotia, 1830-1854." M.A. thesis, Dalhousie, 1950.
1176. **Long, R. S.** *Nova Scotia Municipal and Regional Planning in the Seventies: Report/Evaluation of the Town Planning Act Review.* Halifax: N.S. Dept. of Municipal Affairs and CMHC, 1972.
1177. **MacKinnon, Ian F.** *Settlements and Churches in Nova Scotia, 1749-1776.* Halifax: Allen, 1930.
1178. **Macmillan, Arvo Arnold.** "The Systems Approach in the Analysis of the Official Town Plan, Zoning By-law, and Subdivision Regulations: A Case Study of the Town Planning Act of Nova Scotia." M.A. thesis, British Columbia, 1968.
1179. **Magill, D. W.** "Migration and Occupational Mobility from a Nova Scotia Coal Mining Town." M.A. thesis, McGill, 1966.
1180. **Martell, J. S.** *Immigration to and Emigration from Nova Scotia, 1815-1838.* Halifax: PANS, 1942.
1181. **Morse, Robert.** "Report on Nova Scotia, 1784." *Report of the Public Archives of Canada for 1884,* pp. xvii-lix. Ottawa: Maclean, Roger, 1885.
1182. **Morse, Susan Longley.** "Immigration to Nova Scotia, 1839-1851." M.A. thesis, Dalhousie, 1946.
1183. **Pross, A. Paul.** *Planning and Development: The Case of Two Nova Scotia Communities.* Halifax: Institute of Public Affairs, Dalhousie University, 1976.

1184. **Robertson, Harold H.** "The Commercial Relationship between Nova Scotia and the British West Indies, 1788-1822." M.A. thesis, Dalhousie, 1975.
1185. **Roper, J. I.** "Public Utility Regulation in Nova Scotia." *Dal Rev* 17 (1937):67-79.
1186. **Ross, Winifred M.** "Child Rescue: The Nova Scotia Society for the Prevention of Cruelty, 1880-1920." M.A. thesis, Dalhousie, 1975.
1187. **Rowat, Donald Cameron.** *The Reorganization of Provincial-Municipal Relations in Nova Scotia: A Report Prepared for the Government of Nova Scotia by the Nova Scotia Municipal Bureau.* Halifax: Institute of Public Affairs, Dalhousie University, 1949.
1188. ———. "Reorganization of Provincial-Municipal Relations in Nova Scotia." *PA* 13 (1950):39-47.
1189. **Sarty, L. I.** "Electric Power Development in Nova Scotia." M.A. thesis, Acadia, 1937.
1190. **Saxton, P.** "Nova Scotia, 1760-1775: The Paragon of Localism." M.A. thesis, St. Mary's, 1974.
1191. **Sexton, F. H.** "Education for Industry in Nova Scotia." *Dal Rev* 1 (1921):66-74.
1192. **Smith, William.** "The Early Post Office in Nova Scotia, 1755-1867." NSHS *Collections* 19 (1918):53-73.
1193. **Speller, R. G.** "Some Aspects of Provincial-Municipal Fiscal Relations in Nova Scotia." M.A. thesis, Dalhousie, 1949.
1194. **Tennyson, Brian.** *Cape Breton: A Bibliography.* Halifax: N.S. Dept. of Education, 1978.
1195. **Thorpe, Wendy L.** "The Local Government Records of Nova Scotia in the Public Archives of Nova Scotia." *Archival Association of Atlantic Canada, Newsletter* 4 (April 1976):3-6.
1196. **Tratt, Gertrude.** *A Survey and Listing of Nova Scotia Newspapers, 1752-1957.* Halifax: Dalhousie, 1979.
1197. **Vaison, Robert.** *Studying Nova Scotia: Its History and Present State, Its Politics and Economy: A Bibliography and Guide.* Halifax: Mount Saint Vincent University, 1974.
1198. ———. *Nova Scotia, Past and Present: A Bibliography.* Halifax: N.S. Dept. of Education, 1976.
1199. **Wallace, Arthur W.** *An Album of Drawings of Early Buildings in Nova Scotia.* Halifax: Heritage Trust of Nova Scotia, 1976.
1200. **Webb, Ross Allan.** "The Mechanization of Transport in Nova Scotia, 1825-1967." Ph.D. thesis, Pittsburgh, 1956.
1201. **Wilson, E. C.** "The Impact of a Century of Irish Immigration in Nova Scotia, 1750-1850." Ph.D. thesis, Ottawa, 1961.
1202. **Wood, K., and Verge, H.** *A Study of the Problems of Certain Cape Breton Communities.* Halifax: Institute of Public Affairs, Dalhousie University, 1966.
1203. "Wretched Housing Conditions in Nova Scotia Mining Areas." *TPICJ* 5 (1926):20-22.

2. Amherst

1204. **Bird, Will R.** *Amherst, Nova Scotia: Diamond Jubilee, 1889-1949.* Amherst: News-Sentinel Press Ltd., 1949.
1205. **Lamy, R.** "The Development and Decline of Amherst as an Industrial Centre." B.A. essay, Mount Allison, 1930.
1206. **Reilly, J. Nolan.** "Notes on the Amherst General Strike and the One Big Union." *Bulletin of the Committee on Canadian Labour History* 3 (1977):5-8.
1207. **Steele, David A.** *A History of the Amherst Baptist Church, to Which Is Appended Historical Notes on the Town of Amherst.* Amherst: Black, 1895.

3. Annapolis Royal

1208. **Blackmer, Hugh A.** "Agricultural Transportation in a Regional System: The Annapolis Valley, Nova Scotia." Ph.D. thesis, Stanford, 1976.

1209. Calnek, William A., ed. *History of the County of Annapolis, Including Old Port Royal and Acadia; with Memoirs of Its Representatives in the Provincial Parliament, and Biographical and Genealogical Sketches of Its Early English Settlers and Their Families.* Toronto: Briggs, 1897.

1210. Johnson, John. *Annapolis Royal and Area from 1605: Guide to Historical Projects and Events.* Annapolis Royal: Annapolis Royal Historical Association, 1977.

1211. Macvicar, William M. *A Short History of Annapolis Royal, the Port Royal of the French, from Its Settlement in 1604 to . . . 1854.* Toronto: Copp Clark, 1897.

1212. Miller, J. D. and Associates Ltd. *Town of Annapolis Royal: A Feasibility Study on Heritage Conservation and Development Opportunities.* Halifax, 1978.

1213. Perkins, Charlotte I. *The Romance of Old Annapolis Royal . . . .* 1934. Rev. Ed. Annapolis Royal: Historical Association of Annapolis Royal, 1952.

1214. Runciman, J. Herbert. *The Historic Garrison at Annapolis Royal. Some of Its Early History, as Told by One of Its Defenders.* Annapolis Royal: Banks, 1886.

4. Antigonish

1215. *Antigonish, Town and Country.* Antigonish: Town Council and Board of Trade, 1916.

1216. MacGillivray, C. J. *Timothy Hierlihy and His Times: The Story of the Founder of Antigonish, N.S.* Antigonish: Casket Print, 1936.

1217. Maclean, Raymond A., ed. *History of Antigonish.* 2 vols. Antigonish: Formac, 1976.

1218. Whidden, David G. *Genealogical Record of the Antigonish Whiddens, and a Brief Historical Outline of the Province of Nova Scotia and of the County and Town of Antigonish.* Wolfville: Davidson, 1930.

1219. _____. *The History of the Town of Antigonish.* Wolfville: The Casket, 1934.

5. Halifax-Dartmouth

a. General

1220. Aikins, T. *History of Halifax City.* 1895. Reprint. Belleville: Mika, 1973.

1221. *Allen's Souvenir Guide to Halifax.* Halifax: Allen, 1887.

1222. Archibald, Stephen. "Civic Ornaments: Ironwork in Halifax Parks." *Mat Hist Bull* 5 (Spring 1978):1-11.

1223. Bassett, John M. *Samuel Cunard.* Toronto: Fitzhenry and Whiteside, 1975.

1224. Bell, F. H. *Taxation in Halifax.* Halifax: Halifax Printing Co., 1897.

1225. Best, J. Linden. "Box, Pit, and Gallery: The Theatre Royal at Spring Gardens." *Dal Rev* 53 (1973):520-28.

1226. Bilson, Geoffrey. "Two Cholera Ships in Halifax." *Dal Rev* 53 (1973):449-60.

1227. Blakeley, Phyllis R. "Incidents in Victorian Halifax." CHA, *AR* (1949):40-45.

1228. _____. "The Theatre and Music in Halifax." *Dal Rev* 29 (1949):8-20.

1229. Borrett, William C. *More Tales Told under the Old Town Clock.* Halifax: Imperial Publishing Co., 1943.

1230. _____. *Historic Halifax.* Toronto: Ryerson, 1949.

1231. Brown, W. M. "Recollections of Old Halifax." NSHS *Collections* 13 (1908):75-102.

1232. Buggey, Susan. "Halifax Waterfront Buildings: An Historical Report." *Canadian Historic Sites: Occasional Papers in Archaeology and History* 9 (1975):117-68.

1233. Burns, Terrence. "An Historical Study of the Catholic Schools of the City of Halifax, 1850-1900." M.A. thesis, St. Mary's, 1962.

1234. Butler, George Frederic. "The Early Organization and Influence of Halifax Merchants." NSHS *Collections* 25 (1942):1-16.

1235. **Carre, W. H.** *Art Work on Halifax.* Halifax: Carre, 1899.
1236. **Collins, Louis W.** *In Halifax Town: On Going for a Walk in Halifax, Nova Scotia.* Halifax: Halcraft Printing, 1975.
1237. **Copeland, Pat.** "Restoration, Revelation and Some Regret [Halifax Citadel]." *Commercial News* (March 1978):2-6.
1238. **Daley, Timothy T.** "Social Planning in Halifax-Dartmouth: Fact or Fiction?" *Dal Law J* 2 (1976):658-81.
1239. **Dalhousie College, Centenary Committee of.** *One Hundred Years of Dalhousie, 1818-1918.* Halifax: Centenary Committee, 1919.
1240. **De Bard, August A.** "Council-Manager Government in Halifax." *Can Pub Admin* 3 (1960):76-81.
1241. **Denhez, Marc.** "An Evaluation and Protection System for Heritage Resources in Halifax." *Urb For* 3 (1977):30-32.
1242. **Desrossiers, Lise.** "The Problems of Putting Old Buildings to Work." *Halifax* 1 (1978):34-39.
1243. **Doyle, Frank W.** "Halifax and War." *Can Banker* 53 (1946):131-40.
1244. **Duffus, A. F.** *The West House, Brunswick Street, Halifax.* Halifax: Heritage Trust of Nova Scotia, 1973.
1245. **Eaton, Arthur W. H.** *Chapters in the History of Halifax, Nova Scotia.* New York: National American Society, 1915-21.
1246. **Fergusson, Charles Bruce.** "The Rise of the Theatre in Halifax." *Dal Rev* 29 (1950):419-27.
1247. _____. "The Halifax Post Office." *Dal Rev* 38 (1958):39-46.
1248. _____. "The Establishment of the United States of America in Halifax." *NSHQ* 3 (1973):57-73.
1249. _____. "Halifax Has a Winner: Historic Properties." *CGEJ* 97 (1978):34-39.
1250. **Flemming, H. A.** "Halifax Currency." NSHS *Collections* 20 (1921):111-37.
1251. **Fogarty, Donald William.** "A History of the Halifax School for the Blind." M.A. thesis, St. Mary's, 1960.
1252. **Gillis, Allison Ronald.** "Structural Assimilation among Jews in Halifax." M.A. thesis, Dalhousie, 1970.
1253. _____, and **Whitehead, Paul C.** "The Halifax Jews: A Community within a Community." In *Immigrant Groups,* edited by Jean Leonard Elliott, pp. 84-94. Scarborough: Prentice-Hall, 1971.
1254. **Gordon, James D.** *Halifax: 'Its Sins and Sorrows.'* Reprint. Halifax: Friends of the Old Town Clock, 1973.
1255. **Greenough, John Joseph.** "The Colonel and the Cows: Frolics and Citadel Hill." *Conservation Can* 3 (1978):10-12.
1256. **Halifax, City of.** *The Advantages of Halifax as a Manufacturing Centre.* Halifax: Imperial Publishing Co., 1904.
1257. _____. *Halifax, Nova Scotia: The Great Harbour.* Halifax: John Quinpool, 1941.
1258. *The Halifax Guide Book.* Halifax: Morton, 1878.
1259. **Hallam, W. T.** *When You Are in Halifax: Sketches of Life in the First English Settlement in Canada.* Toronto: Church Book Room, 1937.
1260. **Harnett, Ken O.** *Encounter on Urban Environment: Historian's Report.* Halifax: Voluntary Economic Planning Board, 1970.
1261. **Harrington, A. R.** "Encounter at Halifax." *CPR* 20, no. 2 (1970):26-27.
1262. **Harris, John E.** *Taxation in Halifax City: A Review.* Halifax: Institute of Public Affairs, Dalhousie University, 1966.
1263. **Harris, R. V.** "In and about Halifax." *Acadiensis* 8 (1908):12-31.

1264. _____. *The Church of St. Paul in Halifax, Nova Scotia, 1749-1949.* Toronto: Ryerson, 1949.
1265. **Harvey, D. C.** "The Dalhousie Idea." *Dal Rev* 17 (1937):131-43.
1266. _____. "The Early Struggles of Dalhousie." *Dal Rev* 17 (1937):311-26.
1267. _____. "From College to University." *Dal Rev* 17 (1938):411-31.
1268. _____. *An Introduction to the History of Dalhousie University.* Halifax: McCurdy Printing Co., 1938.
1269. _____. "A View of Halifax, 1749-1949." RSC, *Trans,* 3d ser. 43 (1949):71-87.
1270. _____. "Halifax—1749-1949." *CGEJ* 38 (1949):6-37.
1271. **Heritage Trust of Nova Scotia.** *Founded upon a Rock: Historical Buildings of Halifax and Vicinity Standing in 1967.* Halifax, 1967.
1272. **Hill, George William.** "History of St. Paul's Church, Halifax, Nova Scotia." NSHS *Collections* 1 (1878):35-58; 2 (1879-80): 63-99.
1273. _____. "Nomenclature of the Streets of Halifax." NSHS *Collections* 15 (1911):1-22.
1274. **Howard, W. H.** *Glimpses in and out of Halifax.* Halifax, 1896.
1275. **Jensen, L. B.** *Vanishing Halifax.* Halifax: Petheric Press, 1968.
1276. **Johnson, Arthur L.** "The Boston-Halifax Steamship Lines." *American Neptune* 37 (1977):231-38.
1277. **Johnston, Andrew J. B.** *Defending Halifax: Ordnance, 1825-1906.* Manuscript Report Series. Ottawa: Historic Sites, Parks Canada, 1977.
1278. **Johnston, H. W.** "Halifax Water Works." *NS Institute of Science* 12 (1906-7):22-89.
1279. **Jones, Murray V., and Associates Limited.** *Report on Regional Development: District of Halifax, Dartmouth and Halifax County.* 2 vols. Toronto, 1969.
1280. **King, Edwin D., and Quigley, J. Gordon.** *150 Years of the First Baptist Church, Halifax, N.S., 1927-1977.* Halifax: Mitchell Printing, 1978.
1281. **Lambert, Barbara.** "On the Waterfront: The Story of Halifax's Oldest Buildings." *Heritage Canada* 3 (1977):20-24.
1282. **Lane, Richard B.** *The Halifax Citadel.* Manuscript Report Series. Ottawa: Historic Sites, Parks Canada, 1965.
1283. **Lawson, M. J.** *History of the Townships of Dartmouth, Preston and Lawrencetown, Halifax County, N.S.* Belleville: Mika, 1972.
1284. **Linkletter, Z. A.** "Administration of the Municipality and the County of Halifax." M.A. thesis, Dalhousie, 1945.
1285. **Logan, J. W.** "A History of the Halifax Grammar School, High School, and Academy, 1789-1894." NSHS *Collections* 23 (1936):117-35.
1286. **MacDonald, Nancy K.** "The Wanderers' Amateur Athletic Club of Halifax 1882-1925: Its Contribution to Amateur Sport." M.P.E. thesis, Dalhousie, 1974.
1287. **McFarlane, M.** "The Civic Culture of Negroes in Halifax." M.A. thesis, Dalhousie, 1969.
1288. **McGee, Timothy J.** "Music in Halifax, 1749-1799." *Dal Rev* 49 (1969):377-87.
1289. **McKay, Ian.** "The Working Class of Metropolitan Halifax, 1850-1889." B.A. Hons. essay, Dalhousie, 1975.
1290. _____. "Capital and Labour in the Halifax Baking and Confectionery Industry during the Last Half of the Nineteenth Century." *Labour* 3 (1978):63-108.
1291. **McLennan, C. Prescott.** "Church Memories of Halifax." *Dal Rev* 22 (1942):170-84.
1292. _____. "Press Memories of Halifax." *Dal Rev* 23 (1944):425-32.
1293. **MacLennan, H.** "Halifax." *Habitat* 10, nos. 3-6 (1967):14-17.
1294. **MacMechan, Archibald.** "Halifax in Books." *Acadiensis* 6 (1906):103-23, 201-17.
1295. _____. "Storied Halifax." *Can Mag* 35 (1910):291-99.
1296. _____. "Changing Halifax." *Can Mag* 41 (1913):327-36.

1297. _____. "The Rise of Samuel Cunard." *Dal Rev* 9 (1929):202-10.
1298. _____. "Halifax in Trade." *CGEJ* 3 (1931):151-74.
1299. **Major, Marjorie.** "The Great Pontack Inn." *NSHQ* 3 (1973):171-90.
1300. **Martin, John Patrick.** *The Story of Dartmouth.* Dartmouth, 1957.
1301. **Merkel, Andrew.** "Then and Now (1849-1949)." *Dal Rev* 29 (1949): 65-72.
1302. **Metzler, N.** *Illustrated Halifax: Its Civil, Military and Naval History.* Montreal: McConniff, 1891.
1303. **Mitchell, J. R.** "Port of Halifax—Warden of the North." *Atl Ad* 47 (January 1957):23-30.
1304. **Mitchell, V. W.** "Halifax Police Department." *RCMP Q* 30, no. 4 (1965):3-8.
1305. **Moore, Marian F.** "A Case for Preservation [The Old Ordnance Yard in Halifax]." *Atl Ad* 55, no. 5 (1965):61-66.
1306. **Mullane, G.** "Old Inns and Coffee Houses of Halifax, N.S." NSHS *Collections* 22 (1933):1-24.
1307. **Murray, R.** "Historic Landmarks of Halifax." *Westminster* 5 (1904):299-305.
1308. **Murray, W. C.** "History of St. Matthew's Church, Halifax." NSHS *Collections* 16 (1912):137-40.
1309. **Norton, J. T.** "The Port of Halifax: Its Role in the Economic Development of Nova Scotia." B.A. essay, Carleton, 1974.
1310. **Nova Scotia Association of Architects.** *Exploring Halifax.* Toronto: Greey de Pencier, 1976.
1311. *Our Dominion: Mercantile and Manufacturing Interests, Historical and Commercial Sketches of Halifax and Environs.* Toronto: The Historical Publishing Co., 1887.
1312. **Payne, A. M.** "The Life of Samuel Cunard." NSHS *Collections* 19 (1918):75-91.
1313. **Payzant, Joan, and Payzant, Lewis.** *Like a Weaver's Shuttle [:The Halifax-Dartmouth Ferries Since 1752].* Halifax: Nimbus Publishing, 1979.
1314. **Perry, Margaret L.** "The Founding of St. Matthew's [United Church, Halifax]." *Atl Ad* 65 (November 1974):29-30.
1315. **Phillips-Cleland, Jennifer.** *An Evaluation and Protection System for Heritage Resources in Halifax.* Halifax: City of Halifax Planning Dept., 1976.
1316. **Piers, H.** *The Evolution of the Halifax Fortress, 1749-1928.* Halifax: PANS, 1947.
1317. **Punch, Terrence M.** "Beamish of Kilvarra and Halifax." *NSHQ* 9 (1979):269-81.
1318. **Raddall, J. H.** *Halifax: Warden of the North.* Toronto: M&S, 1974.
1319. **Regan, J. W.** *Sketches and Traditions of the Northwest Arm.* Halifax: McAlpine, 1908.
1320. **Rhude, F.** "Halifax Grows Young Gracefully." *INCA* 68 (April 1968):27-32.
1321. **Rogers, George W.** *A Sense of Place: Granville Street, Halifax, Nova Scotia.* Halifax: Heritage Trust of Nova Scotia, 1970.
1322. **Rosinski, Maud.** "Halifax's Brunswick Street." *Heritage Canada* (1976):26-27.
1323. **Saunders, E. A.** *Halifax: A Gateway of Canada, Facts and Figures for Exporters and Importers.* Halifax: McNab, 1925.
1324. **Seth, James.** "Halifax Revisited." *Dal Rev* 1 (1922):333-39.
1325. **Shaw, Patrick Vincent.** "A History of the Halifax School for the Deaf." M.A. thesis, St. Mary's, 1960.
1326. **Shaw, R. E.** "History of the Disciples of Christ in Halifax, Nova Scotia." NSHS *Collections* 34 (1963):121-40.
1327. **Stacey, C. P.** "Halifax as an International Strategic Factor, 1749-1949." CHA, *AR* (1949):46-56.
1328. **Sutherland, David Alexander.** "Halifax, 1815-1914: Colony to Colony." *UHR* 1-75 (June 1975):7-11.
1329. **Thomas, C. E.** "St. Paul's Church, Halifax, Revisited." NSHS *Collections* 33 (1961):21-55.

1330. **Thompson, A. Audley.** "The Tradition and Progress of Halifax." *Mun Rev Can* 30 (August 1934):37-40.
1331. **Tremaine, M.** "Social Life in Halifax." *Dom Ill Mon* 1 (1892):473-81.
1332. **Tupper, E. S.** "The Attractions of Halifax." *Can Mag* 13 (1899):347-54.
1333. **Vannin, E.** "Gentlemen of the Town." *Atl Ad* 56, no. 5 (1966):26-34.
1334. **Vernon, Charles W.** *The Story of Christ Church, Dartmouth: A Hundred Years and More in the Life of a Nova Scotian Parish.* Halifax: Weeks, 1917.
1335. **Watkins, Lyndon.** "Halifax Historic Properties: Recycling the Past to Enhance the Future." *Habitat* 18 (1976):2-9.
1336. **Watson, J. Wreford.** "Relict Geography in an Urban Community: Halifax, Nova Scotia." In *Geographical Essays in Memory of Alan G. Ogilvie*, edited by R. Miller and J. W. Watson, pp. 110-43. London: Nelson, 1959.
1337. **Wentzells Ltd.** *The Years Between: Halifax, 1820-1923.* Halifax: Wentzells, 1923.
1338. **White, G. A.** *Halifax and Its Business.* Halifax: Nova Scotia Printing Co., 1876.
1339. **Whitman, J.** "Halifax." *Can Mon* 2 (1879):421-28.
1340. **Wood, J. T.** "Halifax: The Open Door of Canada." *Can Mag* 12 (1899):521-27.

b. Pre-1870

1341. **Andres, Gwenyth.** "The Establishment of Institutional Care in Halifax in the Mid-Nineteenth Century." B.A. Hons. essay, Dalhousie, 1974.
1342. **Bains, Yashdip Singh.** "The Articulate Audience and the Fortunes of the Theatre in Halifax in 1816-1819." *Dal Rev* 57 (1977-78):726-36.
1343. ———. "The Spectator's Eye: Impressions of Halifax Theatre in the Early Nineteenth Century." *Dal Rev* 59 (1979):40-50.
1344. **Blakeley, Phyllis R.** "Halifax at the Time of Confederation." *Dal Rev* 27 (1948):391-409.
1345. **Burant, James K. P.** "Pre-Confederation Photography in Halifax, Nova Scotia." *J Can Art Hist* (1977):25-44.
1346. ———. "The Development of Visual Arts in Halifax, N.S., 1815-1867." M.A. thesis, Carleton, 1979.
1347. **Burns, J. E.** "The Development of Roman Catholic Church Government in Halifax from 1760-1853." NSHS *Collections* 23 (1936):89-115.
1348. **Dickie, Robert.** "The Halifax Grammar School—1850." M.A. thesis, St. Mary's, 1960.
1349. **Douglas, W. A. B.** "Halifax as an Element of Sea Power, 1749-1766." M.A. thesis, Dalhousie, 1962.
1350. **Eaton, Arthur W. H.** "Halifax in 1793." *Report of the Public Archives of Canada for 1946,* pp. xxiv-xxvii. Ottawa: King's Printer, 1947.
1351. **Elliott, Shirley B.** "Impressions of Halifax, 1854." *J Educ* 6th Series, 1 (Fall 1974):35-36.
1352. ———. "Nova Scotia's Economic Profile, 1774." *J Educ* 6th Series, 2 (Winter 1974-75):35-37.
1353. **Ells, Margaret.** "Dartmouth Whalers." *Dal Rev* 15 (1935):85-95.
1354. **Evans, Roger Albert.** "The Army and Navy at Halifax in Peace Time, 1783-1793." M.A. thesis, Dalhousie, 1970.
1355. **Fergusson, Charles Bruce.** "Eighteenth Century Halifax." CHA, *AR* (1949):32-39.
1356. ———. "Isaac Hildrith (c. 1741-1807): Architect of Government House, Halifax." *Dal Rev* 50 (1970-71):510-16.
1357. **Fingard, Judith.** "Attitudes towards the Education of the Poor in Colonial Halifax." *Acadiensis* 2, no. 2 (1973):15-42.
1358. **Fischer, Lewis R.** "The Halifax Merchants in the Era of the American Revolution, 1749-1775." Ph.D. thesis, York, 1978.

1359. Fraser, D. G. "The Origin and Function of the Court of Vice-Admiralty in Halifax, 1749-1759." NSHS *Collections* 33 (1961):57-80.
1360. Gouett, Paul M. "The Halifax Orphan House, 1752-1787." *NSHQ* 6 (1976):281-91.
1361. Grant, Marguerite H. L. "Historical Sketches of Hospitals and Alms Houses in Halifax, Nova Scotia, 1749 to 1859." *NS Med Bull* 27 (1938):229-38, 294-304, 491-512.
1362. Greenough, John Joseph. *The Halifax Citadel, 1825-1860: A Narrative and Structural History.* Canadian Historic Sites Series, 17. Ottawa: Parks Canada, 1977.
1363. Hart, G. E. "The Halifax Poor Man's Friend Society, 1820-1827: An Early Social Experiment." *CHR* 34 (1953):109-23.
1364. Hill, George William. *Domestic Life in Early Halifax.* Halifax: NS Museums, 1972.
1365. Howell, David F. "A History of Horseracing in Halifax, Nova Scotia, 1749-1867." M.P.E. thesis, Dalhousie, 1972.
1366. Jewitt, A. R. "Early Halifax Theatres." *Dal Rev* 5 (1926):444-59.
1367. Johnson, C. H. "Halifax under the Eye of the *Guardian,* 1838-1841." NSHS *Collections* 30 (1954):207-29.
1368. Keane, Patrick. "A Study in Early Problems and Policies in Adult Education: The Halifax Mechanics' Institute." *HS* 16 (1975):225-74.
1369. "Letter from Governor Cornwallis Relating to the First Steps in the Founding of Halifax." *Report of the Public Archives of Canada for 1939,* pp. 47-49. Ottawa: King's Printer, 1940.
1370. Lynch, P. "Early Reminiscences of Halifax." NSHS *Collections* 16 (1912):171-204.
1371. MacDonald, James S. "Hon. Edward Cornwallis: Founder of Halifax." NSHS *Collections* 12 (1905):1-17.
1372. MacNutt, W. S. "Why Halifax Was Founded." *Dal Rev* 12 (1933):524-32.
1373. Martell, J. S. "Halifax during and after the War of 1812." *Dal Rev* 23 (1943):289-304.
1374. Maybee, Janet A. "Theatre in Halifax, 1850-1880." M.A. thesis, Dalhousie, 1965.
1375. Oland, Sidney C. M. "Materials for a History of the Theatre in Early Halifax." M.A. thesis, Dalhousie, 1966.
1376. "Papers Relating to the First Settlement of Halifax, 1749-1756." In *Selections from the Public Documents of Nova Scotia,* edited by Thomas B. Akins, pp. 495-706. Halifax: Annand, 1869.
1377. Punch, Terrence M. "The Halifax Connections, 1748-1848: A Century of Oligarchy in Nova Scotia." M.A. thesis, St. Mary's, 1972.
1378. _____. "Assessment Roles of Halifax County, 1792-93." NSHS *Genealogical Newsletter* 15 (April 1976):14-23.
1379. _____. "Halifax Town: The Census of 1838." *NSHQ* 6 (1976):233-58.
1380. _____. "Irish Deserters at Halifax, Nova Scotia, during the Napoleonic Wars." *Irish Ancestor* 8, no. 1 (1976):33-35.
1381. _____. "The Wests of Halifax and Lunenburg." *NSHQ* 6 (1976):69-86.
1382. _____. "The Irish in Halifax, 1836-1871: A Study in Ethnic Assimilation." M.A. thesis, Dalhousie, 1977.
1383. _____, and Marble, Allan E. "The Family of John Howe, Halifax Loyalist and King's Printer." *NSHQ* 6 (1976):317-27.
1384. Rogers, Joseph. *Rogers' Photographic Advertising Album.* Halifax, 1871. Reprinted as *A Century Ago: Halifax, 1871.* Halifax: Heritage Trust of Nova Scotia, 1971.
1385. Sainte-Mesmin, Benique-Charles. "Halifax in 1793." *Report of the Public Archives of Canada for 1946,* pp. xxiv-xxviii. Ottawa: King's Printer, 1947.
1386. Spindel, Donna J. "Anchors of Empire: Savannah, Halifax, and the Atlantic Frontier." *ARCS* 6, no. 2 (1976):88-103.
1387. Stewart, Herbert Leslie. *The Irish in Nova Scotia: Annals of the Charitable Irish Society of Halifax (1786-1836).* Kentville: Kentville Publishing Co., [c. 1949].

1388. **Sutherland, David Alexander.** "The Merchants of Halifax, 1815-1850: A Commercial Class in Pursuit of Metropolitan Status." Ph.D. thesis, Toronto, 1975.
1389. ———. "Halifax Merchants and the Pursuit of Development, 1783-1850." *CHR* 59 (1978):1-17.
1390. **Wright, A. Jeffrey.** "The Halifax Riot of April 1863." *NSHQ* 4 (1974):277-99.

c. Post-1870

1391. **Adams, Thomas.** "The Planning of New Halifax." *ENCR* 32 (1918): 680-83.
1392. **Armstrong, Christopher, and Nelles, H. V.** "Getting Your Way in Nova Scotia. 'Tweaking' Halifax, 1909-1917." *Acadiensis* 5 (Spring 1976):105-31.
1393. **Baillie, Murray.** *Municipal Government in Metropolitan Halifax: A Bibliography.* 1971. 2d ed. Halifax: Saint Mary's University, 1977.
1394. **Bernard, A.; Léveillé, J.; and Lord, G.** *Profile: Halifax-Dartmouth. The Political and Administrative Structures of the Metropolitan Region of Halifax-Dartmouth.* Ottawa: MSUA, 1974.
1395. **Best, J. Linden.** "The Post-Confederation Theatres of Halifax." M.A. thesis, New Brunswick, 1972.
1396. **Bird, Michel J.** *The Town That Died: The True Story of the Greatest Man-Made Explosion before Hiroshima.* New York: Putnam, 1963.
1397. **Blakeley, Phyllis R.** *Glimpses of Halifax, 1867-1900.* Halifax: PANS, 1949.
1398. ———. "Halifax Coal Shortage—1871." *Atl Ad* 64 (January 1974):46-47, 50-52, 63.
1399. **Bronson, H. L.** "Some Notes on the Halifax Explosion." *RSC, Trans,* 12 (1918):31-36.
1400. **Butler, A. N.** *Halifax Relief Commission, 1918-1976.* Ottawa: Dept. of Finance, 1976.
1401. **Clairmont, D. H., and Magill, D. W.** *Africville: The Life and Death of a Canadian Black Community.* Toronto: M&S, 1974.
1402. **Conrad, W. Hugh.** "Sudden Explosion of Dartmouth City, A Rival to Halifax." *Atl Ad* 58 (January 1968):18-22, 24.
1403. **Forward, Charles N.** "Parallelism of Halifax and Victoria." *CGEJ* 90, no. 3 (1975):34-43.
1404. **Frost, James D.** "The Business and Political Careers of John F. Stairs of Halifax, 1879-1891." B.A. Hons. essay, Dalhousie, 1976.
1405. **Frowd, W. A.** "The Maritime Munitions Disaster in Halifax." *Chambers'* 99 (January 1922):55-59.
1406. **Healey, Denis.** "The University of Halifax, 1875-1881." *Dal Rev* 53 (1973):39-56.
1407. **Henson, Guy.** "A Regional City [Halifax-Dartmouth] Plans Its Future." *CPR* 11, no. 1 (1961):13-27.
1408. **Higgins, D. J. H., and Christiansen-Ruffman, Linda.** "Halifax-Dartmouth: The Politics of Public Waterfront Development." *City Mag* 3, no. 1 (1977):37-51.
1409. **Himmelman, Melody.** " 'For Whom the Bell Tolls': A Quantitative Sketch of Marriage Patterns, Halifax, 1871-81." B.A. Hons. essay, Dalhousie, 1979.
1410. **Horwood, Joan.** *The Great Halifax Explosion, Dec. 6, 1917.* St. John's: Avalon, 1976.
1411. **Johnston, Keith L.** "The Halifax Drink Trade, 1879-1895." B.A. Hons. essay, Dalhousie, 1977.
1412. **Jozsa, J. M.** "A Method for the Analysis of Economic Polarization: Two Case Studies—Halifax-Dartmouth, Nova Scotia, and Quebec City, Quebec." M.A. thesis, McMaster, 1975.
1413. **Little, C. H.** "Halifax: Container Port." *CGEJ* 86 (1973):126-33.
1414. **McCann, L. D.** "Staples and the New Industrialism in the Growth of Post-Confederation Halifax." *Acadiensis* 8 (Spring 1979):47-79.

1415. **MacKinnon, C. I.** "The Imperial Fortresses in Canada: Halifax and Esquimalt, 1871-1906." Ph.D. thesis, Toronto, 1965.
1416. **Metson, Graham,** ed. *The Halifax Explosion, December 6, 1917, Including the complete text of The Halifax Disaster by Archibald MacMechan.* Toronto: McGraw-Hill Ryerson, 1978.
1417. **Morrison, K. Margaret.** "The Social Evil in Halifax in the late Nineteenth Century." B.A. Hons. essay, Dalhousie, 1979.
1418. "Planning the Greater Halifax." *Cn L* 4 (1918):82-88.
1419. **Powell, Ken.** "Fighting Back in Halifax." *Arch J* 170 (1979):547-50.
1420. **Prince, Samuel Henry.** "Catastrophe and Social Change: A Sociological Study of the Halifax Disaster." Ph.D. thesis, Columbia, 1920.
1421. **Richardson, Evelyn M.** "The Halifax Explosion, 1917." *NSHQ* 7 (1977):305-30.
1422. **Ross, G. A.** "The Halifax Disaster and Rehousing." *Construction* 12 (1919):293-307.
1423. **Rowat, Donald Cameron.** "Halifax: A Case for a Metropolitan Authority." *CPR* 1 (1951):131-41.
1424. **Sinclair, A.** *The Economic Base of the Halifax Metropolitan Region.* Halifax: Institute of Public Affairs, Dalhousie University, 1961.
1425. **Stephens, Gary P.** "A History of Male Basketball in Halifax, 1894-1930." M.P.E. thesis, Dalhousie, 1977.
1426. **Stephenson, Gordon.** *A Redevelopment Study of Halifax, Nova Scotia.* Halifax: City of Halifax, 1957.
1427. **Sutherland, David Alexander.** "The Personnel and Policies of the Halifax Board of Trade, 1890-1914." In #1120, pp. 203-30.
1428. **Thompson, Fred.** "A Rebel Voice: Fred Thompson Remembers Halifax, 1919-1920." *This Magazine* 12 (1978):7-11.
1429. **Van Steen, Marcus.** "New Halifax Faces Old Problems." *CGEJ* 51 (1955):118-27.
1430. **Varson, R., and Aucoin, P. C.** "Municipal Politics in Canada: Class and Voting in the 1968 Halifax Mayoralty Election." *Univ Windsor Rev* 5, no. 2 (1970):68-78.
1431. **Waite, Catherine Ann.** "The Longshoremen of Halifax, 1900-1930: Their Living and Working Conditions." M.A. thesis, Dalhousie, 1978.
1432. **Weaver, John C.** "Reconstruction of the Richmond District in Halifax: A Canadian Episode in Public Housing and Town Planning, 1918-1921." *Plan Canada* 16 (1976):36-47.

6. Louisbourg

1433. **Almon, Albert.** *Louisburg: The Dream City of America.* Glace Bay: The Author, 1934.
1434. ———. *Rochefort Point: A Silent City in Louisbourg.* Glace Bay: Macdonald, 1940.
1435. **Arsenault, Bona.** *Louisbourg, 1713-1758.* Québec: Conseil de la vie française en Amérique, 1971.
1436. **Bower, Peter John.** "Louisbourg: The Chimera, 1745-48." M.A. thesis, Dalhousie, 1975.
1437. **Chard, Donald F.** "The External Relations of Louisbourg, Isle Royale, 1713-1760." Ph.D. thesis, Ottawa, 1976.
1438. **Clark, Andrew H.** "New England's Role in the Underdevelopment of Cape Breton during the French Regime, 1713-58." *Cape Breton's Magazine* 21 (1978):29-35.
1439. **Crowley, Terence Allan.** "Government and Interests: French Colonial Administration at Louisbourg, 1713-1758." Ph.D. thesis, Duke, 1976.
1440. **Dickason, Olive Patricia.** "Louisbourg and the Indians: A Study in Imperial Race Relations, 1713-1760." *History and Archaeology,* no. 6. Ottawa: National Historic Parks and Sites Branch, Dept. of Indian Affairs and Northern Development, 1976.
1441. **Downey, Fairfax Davis.** *Louisbourg: Key to a Continent.* Englewood Cliffs, NJ: Prentice-Hall, 1965.

1442. **Edwards, Joseph Plimsoll.** "Louisbourg: An Historical Sketch." NSHS *Collections* 9 (1893-95):137-96.
1443. **Fortier, John.** *Fortress of Louisbourg.* Toronto: OUP, 1979.
1444. **Fortier, Margaret.** "The Development of the Fortifications at Louisbourg." *Canada, An Historical Magazine* 1 (June 1974):16-31.
1445. **Gesner, Claribel.** "Louisbourg: A Town out of Time." *Atl Ad* 60 (1970):37-45.
1446. **Greer, Allan.** "Mutiny at Louisbourg, December 1744." *HS* 10 (1977):305-36.
1447. **Gwyn, Julian.** "War and Economic Change: Louisbourg and the New England Economy in the 1740s." *Univ Ottawa Q* 47 (1977):114-31.
1448. **Harris, Donald.** "La fortresse et la porte de Louisbourg." *Dossiers de l'archéologie* 27 (1978):88-95.
1449. **Hitsman, J. Mackay, and Bond, Courtney Claude Joseph.** "Louisbourg: A Foredoomed Fortress." *Can Army J* 10 (1956):178-87.
1450. **Howard, Richard.** *Louisbourg.* Toronto: Clarke Irwin, 1968.
1451. "Journal and Census of Ile Royale prepared by le Sieur de la Roque in 1752." *Report of the Public Archives of Canada for 1905,* 2, Appendix A, pp. 1-172. Ottawa: King's Printer, 1906.
1452. **Krause, E. R.** "Private Buildings in Louisburg, 1713-1758." *Canada, An Historical Magazine* 1 (June 1974):47-59.
1453. **McLennan, John S.** *Louisbourg from Its Foundation to Its Fall, 1713-1758.* London: Macmillan, 1918.
1454. **Moore, Christopher.** "The Maritime Economy of Isle Royale." *Canada, An Historical Magazine* 1 (June 1974):32-46.
1455. _____. "The Merchant Community of Louisbourg, Ile Royale, 1714-1758." M.A. thesis, Ottawa, 1977.
1456. _____. "The Other Louisbourg: Trade and Merchant Enterprise in Ile Royale, 1713-58." *HS* 12 (1979):79-96.
1457. **Morgan, Robert J., and MacLean, T. D.** "Social Structure and Life in Louisbourg." *Canada, An Historical Magazine* (June 1974):60-77.
1458. **Pothier, Bernard.** "Acadien Immigration to Ile Royale after the Treaty of Utrecht (1713 to 1758)." M.A. thesis, Ottawa, 1967.
1459. **Proulx, Gilles.** "Histoire du costume militaire à Louisbourg, 1713-1758." Thèse de M.A., Montréal, 1970.
1460. **Rawlyk, George A.** "The Fall of Louisbourg, 1745, Comic Opera Affair?" *QQ* 74 (1967):92-103.
1461. _____. *Yankees at Louisbourg.* Orono: University of Maine Press, 1967.
1462. **Rogers, Grace McLeod.** *Louisbourg.* Toronto: Ryerson, 1928.
1463. **Thibault, Henri-Paul.** "L'organisation matérielle d'un ensemble de propriétés urbaines: Louisbourg, 1713-1758." Thèse de M.A., Montréal, 1970.
1464. _____. "L'orientation des recherches historiques à Louisbourg." *RHAF* 24 (1970):408-12.
1465. **Wood, William C. H.** *The Great Fortress: A Chronicle of Louisbourg, 1720-1760.* Toronto: Glasgow, Brock, 1915.
1466. **Young, J. C.** "Louisburg, Nova Scotia in Historical Fact and Fiction." M.A. thesis, Maine, 1968.

7. Pictou

1467. **Cameron, James Malcolm.** "The Pictou Bank." *NSHQ* 6 (1976):118-30.
1468. **Dunlop, Allan C.** "Pharmacist and Entrepreneur: Pictou's J. D. B. Fraser." *NSHQ* 4 (March 1974):1-21.

1469. **Guy, R. M.** "Industrial Development and Urbanization of Pictou Co., N.S. to 1900." M.A. thesis, Acadia, 1962.
1470. **MacDonald, Bruce F.** "Intellectual Forces in Pictou, 1803-1843." M.A. thesis, New Brunswick, 1977.
1471. **Pictou Heritage Society.** *Wood and Stone: Pictou, Nova Scotia*. With drawings by L. B. Jensen. Halifax: Petheric Press, 1972.
1472. **Sherwood, Roland H.** "The Founding of Pictou." *NSHQ* 1 (1971):325-34.
1473. _____. *Pictou Pioneers: A Story of the First Hundred Years in the History of Pictou Town*. Windsor, N.S.: Lancelot Press, 1973.
1474. _____. "The Laws of Pictou." *NSHQ* 7 (1977):101-9.
1475. **Sitwell, O. F. G.** "Land Use and Settlement Pattern in Pictou County, Nova Scotia." Ph.D. thesis, Toronto, 1968.

8. Shelburne

1476. **Edwards, Joseph Plimsoll.** "The Shelburne That Was and Is Not." *Dal Rev* 2 (1922):179-97.
1477. _____. "Vicissitudes of a Loyalist City." *Dal Rev* 2 (1922):313-28.
1478. **McLeod, R. R.** "Historical Sketch of the Town of Shelburne, Nova Scotia." *Acadiensis* 8 (1908):35-52.
1479. **Raymond, W. O.** "The Founding of Shelburne: Benjamin Marston at Halifax, Shelburne and Miramichi." NBHS *Collections* 3 (1907):204-97.
1480. **Smith, T. Watson.** "The Loyalists at Shelburne." NSHS *Collections* 6 (1887-88):53-89.

9. Springhill

1481. **Brown, Roger David.** *Blood on the Coal: The Story of the Springhill Mining Disasters*. Windsor: Lancelot Press, 1976.
1482. **Campbell, Bertha J.** "Early History of St. Andrew's-Wesley United Church of Canada, Springhill, Nova Scotia." *NSHQ* 6 (1976):173-92.
1483. _____. "Early History of Presbyterians of Springhill, Nova Scotia." *NSHQ* 7 (1977):1-30.
1484. **Heffernan, Jean D.** "Recollections of a Nova Scotia Town, Springhill: Travelling Shows of the 1890s." *Bluenose Magazine* 3 (1978):30-32.
1485. **Morrow, Robert A. H.** *Story of the Springhill Disaster: Comprising a Full and Authentic Account of the Great Coal Mining Explosion . . . February 21, 1891, Including a History of Springhill and Its Collieries*. Saint John: Morrow, 1891.

10. Sydney and Cape Breton

1486. **Beck, C. W.** "The Geography of the Iron and Steel Industry of Sydney, Nova Scotia." M.A. thesis, Kent State, 1950.
1487. **Boothroyd, P. D.** "Urban Functional Organization in the Cape Breton Industrial Area." M.A. thesis, Toronto, 1963.
1488. **Cameron, James Malcolm.** *Industrial History of the New Glasgow District*. New Glasgow: Hector Pub. Co., 1960.
1489. "Conditions in Sydney in 1789." *Report of the Public Archives of Canada for 1944*, pp. xxxvii-xxxviii. Ottawa: King's Printer, 1945.
1490. **Frank, David.** "Coal Masters and Coal Miners: The 1922 Strike and the Roots of Class Conflict in the Cape Breton Coal Industry." M.A. thesis, Dalhousie, 1974.

1491. _____. "Class Conflict in the Coal Industry: Cape Breton, 1922." In *Essays in Canadian Working Class History,* edited by Gregory S. Kealey and Peter Warrian, pp. 161-84. Toronto: M&S, 1976.
1492. _____. "The Cape Breton Coal Industry and the Rise and Fall of the British Empire Steel Corporation." *Acadiensis* 7, no. 1 (1977):3-34.
1493. Gray, F. W. "The Future of the Sydney Coalfield." *Dal Rev* 21 (1941):178-83.
1494. Gray, Helen M. *Sydney, A Gateway to Canada.* Sydney: Louisbourg Chapter, I.O.D.E., 1941.
1495. Harvey, R. *Sydney: An Urban Study.* Toronto: Clarke, Irwin, 1970.
1496. Jackson, E. E. *Windows on the Past: North Sydney, N.S.* Windsor: Lancelot Press, 1974.
1497. McDermid, G. E. "The Religious and Ecclesiastical Background of the Scottish Emigrants to Cape Breton, Nova Scotia." Ph.D. thesis, Aberdeen, 1969.
1498. MacEwan, Paul. *Miners and Steelworkers: Labour in Cape Breton.* Toronto: Hakkert, 1976.
1499. Macgillivray, Donald W. "Industrial Unrest in Cape Breton, 1919-1925." M.A. thesis, New Brunswick, 1971.
1500. _____. "Henry Melville Whitney Comes to Cape Breton: The Sign of a Gilded Age Entrepreneur." *Acadiensis* 9 (Autumn 1979):44-70.
1501. MacKinnon, J. G. *Old Sydney: Sketches of the Town and Its People in Days Gone By.* Reprint. Belleville: Mika, 1973.
1502. Magill, D. W. "Migration and Occupational Mobility from a Nova Scotia Coal Mining Town." M.A. thesis, McGill, 1964.
1503. Martell, J. S. "Early Coal Mining in Nova Scotia." *Dal Rev* 25 (1945):156-72.
1504. Morgan, Robert J. "Cape Breton, 1784-1820: The Failure of an Associate Colony." Ph.D. thesis, Ottawa, 1968.
1505. Murray, John. *The History of the Presbyterian Church in Cape Breton.* Truro: News Publishing Co., 1921.
1506. Nova Scotia Steel and Coal Co. Ltd. *Souvenir, 1908.* New Glasgow: The Company, 1908.
1507. Schwartzman, David. "Mergers in the Nova Scotia Coal Fields: A History of the Dominion Coal Company, 1893-1940." Ph.D. thesis, California (Berkeley), 1953.
1508. Sunderland, Terry. *Still Standing [Historic Buildings of Cape Breton].* Sydney: College of Cape Breton Press, 1979.
1509. Tennyson, Brian D. "Cape Breton in 1867." *NSHQ* 6 (1976):193-206.
1510. _____, ed. *Essays in Cape Breton History.* Windsor, N.S.: Lancelot Press, 1973.
1511. Wood, K., and Verge, H. *A Study of the Problems of Certain Cape Breton Communities.* Halifax: Institute of Public Affairs, Dalhousie University, 1966.

11. Windsor

1512. Copeland, Mary. "A View of Windsor, Nova Scotia." *Can Coll* 14 (1979):40-43.
1513. Jones, George P. *Windsor: Its History, Points of Interest, and Representative Business Men.* Windsor: Anslow, 1893.
1514. Pope, William. *Portrait of Windsor.* Windsor: Lancelot Press, 1974.
1515. Shand, G. V. "The Industries of Windsor, Nova Scotia, 1850-1900." NSHS *Collections* 34 (1963):141-68.
1516. _____. "Windsor: A Centre of Shipbuilding." NSHS *Collections* 37 (1970):39-66.
1517. Windsor Board of Trade. *Windsor, Nova Scotia; Dedicated to History, Literature and Commerce.* Windsor: Tribune Publishing Co., [c. 1900].
1518. *Windsor, Nova Scotia.* Windsor: Board of Trade, 1923.

12. Yarmouth

1519. **Aitken, R. M.** "Localism and National Identity in Yarmouth, Nova Scotia, 1830-1870." M.A. thesis, Trent, 1975.
1520. **Alexander, David.** "The Port of Yarmouth, Nova Scotia, 1840-1889." In *Ships and Shipbuilding in the North Atlantic Region,* edited by Keith Matthews and Gerald Panting, pp. 77-103. St. John's: Memorial University, 1978.
1521. _____, **and Panting, Gerald.** "The Mercantile Fleet and Its Owners: Yarmouth, Nova Scotia, 1840-1889." *Acadiensis* 7, no. 2 (1978):3-28.
1522. **Brown, George Stanley.** *Yarmouth, Nova Scotia: A Sequel to Campbell's History . . . .* Boston: Rand Avery, 1888.
1523. **Kenney, J. E.** *The Port of Yarmouth and Its Development: A Brief Historical Sketch from the Early Days to the Present.* Yarmouth: Herald Print, 1931.
1524. **Lawson, J. Murray.** *Yarmouth, Past and Present: A Book of Reminiscences.* Yarmouth: Yarmouth Herald Office, 1902.
1525. **Marshall, M. V.** "Yarmouth and Argyle, 1814-1851." *NSHQ* 3 (1973):281-302.
1526. **Panting, Gerald.** "Cradle of Enterprise: Yarmouth, Nova Scotia, 1840-1889." In #**1120**, pp. 253-72.
1527. **Reilly, Sharon.** *Selected Buildings in Yarmouth, Nova Scotia.* Manuscript Report Series. Ottawa: Historic Sites, Parks Canada, 1977.
1528. **Ricker, Helen S.** "Glenwood, Yarmouth County, 1895-1909." *NSHQ* 7 (1977):257-65.

13. Other Centres

1529. **Barss, Peter.** *Images of Lunenburg County.* Toronto: M&S, 1978.
1530. **Boucher, Neil.** "The Development of an Acadian Village: Surette's Island, 1857-1970." M.A. thesis, Acadia, 1973.
1531. **Brown, D. M.** "Simon Perkins of Liverpool, Nova Scotia, 1766-1797." M.A. thesis, Queen's, 1978.
1532. **Coward, Elizabeth Ruggles.** *Bridgetown, Nova Scotia: Its History to 1900.* Kentville: Kentville Publishing Co., 1955.
1533. **Desbrisay, Mather Byles.** *History of the County of Lunenburg.* 1895. Reprint. Belleville: Mika, 1972.
1534. **Deveau, J. Alphonse.** *Along the Shores of Saint Mary's Bay: The Story of a Unique Community.* 2 vols. Church Point, N.S.: Imprimerie de l'université Sainte-Anne, 1977.
1535. **Fillmore, Charles L.** *The Streets of Truro: Location and Origins of Names.* Truro: Colchester Historical Society, 1976.
1536. **Grant, John N.** "The Development of Sherbrooke Village to 1880." *NSHQ* 2 (1972):41-54.
1537. **Greenwood, J. L.** *The History of Freeport.* Yarmouth: Davis, 1934.
1538. **Hartling, Philip L.** *Where the Broad Atlantic Surges Roll: A History of Beaver Harbour, Port Dufferin, Quoddy, Harrigan Cove, Moose Head, Moser River, Necum Teuch, and Ecum Secum.* Antigonish: Formac, 1979.
1539. **Lacey, Laurie, ed.** *Lunenburg County Folklore and Oral History: Project '77.* Ottawa: NMM, Mercury Series, 1979.
1540. **Pross, A. Paul.** "The Role of Provincial Government in Development Planning: The Case of Two Nova Scotia Communities [Port Hawkesbury and Bridgewater]." *Urb For* 1, no. 3 (1975):6-12; 1, no. 4 (1975-76):17-24.
1541. **Robinson, Cyril.** "Glace Bay." *CGEJ* 69 (1964):88-95.
1542. **Smith, James F.** *A History of Pugwash.* Oxford, N.S.: North Cumberland Historical Society, 1978.

1543. Stephens, D. E. "Boom Town of Iron and Steel [Londonderry, Nova Scotia]." NSHS *Collections* 4 (1974):23-30.
1544. *Town of Truro Centennial, 1875-1975, Marking 100 Years as an Incorporated Community.* Truro: Centennial Committee, 1975.
1545. Wallace, Mrs. Ernest. "The History of the Municipality of East Hants." *NSHQ* 8 (1978):51-79.
1546. Watt, John. "Migration Patterns and Worker Attitudes in an Industrial Growth Centre: The Strait of Canso, Nova Scotia." In *The Human Dimension in Industrial Development,* edited by David Walker, pp. 31-53. Waterloo: University of Waterloo, Dept. of Geography Publication Series, No. 16, 1980.
1547. White, William J. "Left-Wing Politics and Community: A Study of Glace Bay, 1930-1940." M.A. thesis, Dalhousie, 1978.

IV

New Brunswick

1. General

1548. **Adams, J. Gordon.** *Urban Centres in New Brunswick.* Ottawa: Geographical Branch, 1968.
1549. **Allen, Edwin G.** *Municipal Organization in New Brunswick.* Fredericton: NB Dept. of Municipal Affairs, 1967.
1550. **_____, and Fyfe, Stewart.** "Municipal Reform in New Brunswick." In *A Look to the North: Canadian Regional Experience,* pp. 71-82. Washington: Advisory Commission on Intergovernmental Relations, 1974.
1551. **Anderson, Nels, and Chanteloup, R. E.** "Leadership Roles of Cities." In *The Problem of Leadership in Urban Communities,* edited by the Division of Social Science, University of New Brunswick, pp. 5-43. Saint John: Graphic Services, 1977.
1552. **Andrews, A.** "Social Crisis and Labour Mobility: A Study of Economic and Social Change in a New Brunswick Railway Community." M.A. thesis, New Brunswick, 1967.
1553. **Argaez, G.** "The Economic Impact of the Shipbuilding and Shipping Industries on Nineteenth-Century New Brunswick." RSC, *Trans,* 4th ser. 15 (1977):315-23.
1554. **Brookes, Alan A.** "Doing the Best I Can: The Taking of the 1861 New Brunswick Census." *HS* 9 (May 1976):70-91.
1555. **Condon, Ann K. Gordon.** "The Settlement of New Brunswick by the American Loyalists [1783]." Ph.D. thesis, Harvard, 1964.
1556. **Cyr, Georges.** "La réforme du système de gouvernement municipal au Nouveau-Brunswick." Thèse de M.A., Ottawa, 1970.
1557. **Fellows, Robert F.** *Early New Brunswick Photographs. Vol. I: Cities, Towns, and Villages.* Fredericton, 1978.
1558. **Felt, Paula C., and Felt, Lawrence F.** "Capital Industrial Development in Nineteenth Century New Brunswick: Some Preliminary Comments." In #**1120**, pp. 55-70.
1559. **Ganong, W. F.** "A Monograph of the Origins of Settlements in the Province of New Brunswick." RSC, *Trans,* 2d ser. 10 (1904):3-185.
1560. **Greenhous, Brereton.** "Paupers and Poorhouses: The Development of Poor Relief in Early New Brunswick." *HS* 1 (1968):103-28.
1561. **Guérette, G.** "Urbanism in a Regional Context with Special Reference to Northwestern New Brunswick." M.C.P. thesis, Manitoba, 1970.
1562. **Krueger, Ralph R.** "The Provincial-Municipal Government Revolution in New Brunswick." *Can Pub Admin* 13 (1970):51-99.
1563. **McClelland, Peter D.** "The New Brunswick Economy in the Nineteenth Century." Ph.D. thesis, Harvard, 1966.

1564. **McKee, D. L.** "Municipal Finance in New Brunswick and Newfoundland, 1951-1956." M.A. thesis, New Brunswick, 1959.
1565. **New Brunswick.** Royal Commission on Finance and Municipal Taxation. *Report* [The Bryne Report]. Fredericton: Dept. of Municipal Affairs, 1964.
1566. **Plunkett, Thomas J.** "The Report of the Royal Commission on Finance and Municipal Taxation in New Brunswick: A Review and Commentary." *Can Pub Admin* 8 (1965):12-23.
1567. **Ridler, Neil.** "Fiscal Constraints on Municipal Leadership with Special Reference to New Brunswick." In *The Problem of Leadership in Urban Communities,* edited by the Division of Social Science, University of New Brunswick, pp. 80-102. Saint John: Graphic Services, 1977.
1568. **Ruff, Norman J.** "Administrative Reform and Development: A Study of Administrative Adaptation to Provincial Developmental Goals and the Reorganization of Provincial and Local Government in New Brunswick, 1963-1967." Ph.D. thesis, McGill, 1973.
1569. **Sealy, Nanciellen D.** "Ethnicity and Ethnic Group Persistence in an Acadian Village in Maritime Canada." Ph.D. thesis, Southern Illinois, 1975.
1570. **Temperley, Howard.** "Frontierism, Capital and the American Loyalist in Canada." *J Amer St* 13 (1979):5-27.
1571. **Wassingham, D. G.** "An Economic and Financial Assessment of the Report of the Royal Commission on Finance and Municipal Taxation in New Brunswick." M.A. thesis, New Brunswick, 1969.
1572. **Webster, J. Clarence.** *An Historical Guide to New Brunswick.* Fredericton: Bureau of Information and Tourist Travel, 1938.
1573. **Whalen, Hugh J.** *The Development of Local Government in New Brunswick.* Fredericton: Queen's Printer, 1963.
1574. **Wynn, Graeme.** "Industrialism, Entrepreneurship, and Opportunity in the New Brunswick Timber Trade." In #**1120**, pp. 5-22.
1575. _____. "The Assault on the New Brunswick Forest, 1780-1850." Ph.D. thesis, Toronto, 1974.

2. Fredericton

1576. **Baird, Francis.** *Fredericton's 100 Years: Then and Now.* Fredericton: Wilson, 1948.
1577. **Bell, Geoffrey.** "When Fredericton Had Its Own Bank." *Atl Ad* 66 (May 1976):26-27.
1578. _____, **and Eisenhauer, Harry.** "The Birth, Maturation, and Demise of the Bank of Fredericton (1836-39)." *Canadian Paper Money J* 11 (July 1975):81-83, 96, 102.
1579. **Belliveau, Hector.** "Alphée Belliveau, 40 ans de vie française à Fredericton, 1880-1920: Un témoignage." La société historique acadienne, *Les cahiers* 7 (1976):27-33.
1580. **Cumming, Marion.** "Etchings of Fredericton." *Heritage Canada* 1 (Summer 1975):14-19.
1581. **DeWitt, R. L.** "The Lutheran Church in Fredericton." M.A. thesis, New Brunswick, 1965.
1582. **Fellows, Robert F.,** ed. *The Fredericton Census of 1871.* Fredericton: PANB, 1974.
1583. **Foote, Raymond Leslie.** "The Fredericton Jewish Community: A Study in Class, Status, and Religion." M.A. thesis, New Brunswick, 1967.
1584. **Fredericton Central Area Concept Plan.** *History of Fredericton: A Review of the Historical Development of the Downtown and Inner City.* Fredericton: City of Fredericton Planning Department, 1979.
1585. "Fredericton, New Brunswick." *Anglo-American Mag* 4 (1854):242-44.
1586. **Gorham, Raymond P.** "Fredericton, Capital of New Brunswick." *CGEJ* 10 (1935):247-55.
1587. **Hill, Isabel Louise.** *Fredericton, New Brunswick, British North America.* Fredericton: York-Sunbury Historical Society, 1968.

1588. **Jansson, D. W.** "Fredericton: Beauty and Change." *Atl Ad* 53, no. 6 (1963):38-42.
1589. **Keirstead, W. C.** "The University of New Brunswick: Past and Present." *Dal Rev* 22 (1942):344-54.
1590. **Pacey, Mary,** ed. *Walking Tours of Fredericton: The Colonial Capital.* Fredericton: Fredericton Heritage Trust, 1977.
1591. **Peck, Mary.** *A Study of the Legislative Building, Fredericton, New Brunswick.* Fredericton: Historical Resources Administration, 1977.
1592. **Phillips, F.** *Fredericton: The Early Years (An Exhibition of Photographs from the Provincial Archives of New Brunswick).* Fredericton: PANB, 1974.
1593. **Phillips, Fred H.** "Fredericton—Centennial City." *CGEJ* 36 (1948):80-93.
1594. *The Story of Fredericton: Fredericton's 100 Years: Then and Now.* Fredericton: The Mayor and the Council of the City of Fredericton, 1948.
1595. **Thompson, Marjorie.** "Mrs. Ewing in Fredericton [1867-69]." *Atl Ad* 55, no. 6 (1965):38-42.
1596. **Werthman, W. C.** "Old Houses of Fredericton." *Atl Ad* 55, no. 6 (1965):61-64.
1597. **Wright, Esther Clark.** "Fredericton." *Habitat* 10, nos. 3-6 (1967):22-26.
1598. **Younkin, Rebecca J.** "Three Periods of Growth in a Maritime Centre: A Social History of Fredericton, N.B., 1783-1851." M.A. thesis, Guelph, 1979.

3. Moncton

1599. **Anderson, Amos McIntyre.** "Educational Administration in the City of Moncton." M.A. thesis, New Brunswick, 1936.
1600. **Belliveau, John E.** "Few Homes Like This . . . Moncton's Williams House in Mint Condition." *Atl Ad* 65, no. 1 (1974):28-30.
1601. **Gallant, Susan.** "Moncton Historical Analysis." *Arts Atlantic* 1 (1978):32-35.
1602. *The Hub of the Maritimes.* Moncton: W. J. Edington and Premier Sales and Advertising Service, 1934.
1603. **Johns, Anthony.** "Moncton Rises Again." *Atl Ad* 55, no. 1 (1964): 22-26.
1604. **Le Blanc, E.** "Moncton." *Habitat* 10, nos. 3-6 (1967):18-21.
1605. **Lemon, Donald P.** "Public Relief Policy in Moncton: The Depression Years, 1929-1939." M.A. thesis, New Brunswick, 1977.
1606. **McKee-Allain, Isabelle.** "Les migrants francophones à Moncton, Nouveau-Brunswick, et leur participation dans le milieu." Thèse de M.A., Université Laval, 1975.
1607. **Machum, L. A.** *A History of Moncton, Town and City, 1855-1965.* Moncton: City of Moncton, 1965.
1608. **Medjuck, Sheva.** "Wooden Ships and Iron People: The Lives of the People of Moncton, New Brunswick, 1851-1871." Ph.D. thesis, York, 1978.
1609. _____. "Family and Household Composition in the Nineteenth Century: The Case of Moncton, New Brunswick, 1851-1871." *CJS* 4 (1979):275-86.
1610. **Michaud, Marguerite.** "La musée de la cathédrale de Moncton." *RHAF* 8 (1954):236-42.
1611. **Pincombe, Charles Alexander.** "The History of Moncton Township, 1700-1875." M.A. thesis, New Brunswick, 1969.
1612. **Richard, Camille.** "Le milieu social francophone de Moncton." *Rev univ Moncton* 2 (1969):31-35.
1613. **Robinson, Arthur S.** "The Bend [The Early History of Moncton]." *NBHS Collections* 18 (1963):229-36.
1614. **Steeves, Helen I.** *The Story of Moncton's First Store and Storekeeper: Life around "The Bend" a Century Ago.* Saint John: McMillan, 1924.

4. Sackville

1615. **Dixon, Louise.** "Early History of Sackville." NBHS *Collections* 18 (1963):219-28.
1616. **Milner, William C.** *History of Sackville, New Brunswick.* Sackville: Tribune Printing Co., 1934.
1617. **Moffat, Charles W.** *Introducing Sackville, New Brunswick, Canada: The Official Book on the Most Central Town in the Maritime Provinces, Compiled with the Official Endorsation of the Sackville Town Council and the Sackville Board of Trade.* Sackville: Board of Trade, 1946.

5. St. Andrews

1618. **Cockburn, M. N.** "The Town of Saint Andrews. Some of Its Early History." *Acadiensis* 7 (1907):203-49.
1619. **Jack, David Russell.** "St. Andrews-by-the-Sea." *Acadiensis* 3 (1903):157-62.
1620. **Mowat, Grace Helen.** *The Diverting History of a Loyalist Town: A Portrait of St. Andrews, New Brunswick.* 2d ed. Fredericton: Brunswick Press, 1953.
1621. **Nason, R.** "The Economic Development of St. Andrews, New Brunswick, 1783-1795." M.A. thesis, New Brunswick, 1979.
1622. **Thornley, Betty.** *St. Andrews-by-the-Sea.* Montreal: Canadian Pacific Railway, 1917.

6. Saint John

1623. **Acheson, T. W.** "The Great Merchant and Economic Development in Saint John, 1820-1850." *Acadiensis* 8 (Spring 1979):3-28.
1624. **Angus, Fred F., and Sandusky, Robert J.** *Loyalist City Streetcars: The Story of Street Railway Transit in Saint John, New Brunswick.* Toronto: Railfare/Fitzhenry and Whiteside, 1979.
1625. **Babcock, Robert H.** "Economic Development in Portland, Maine and Saint John, New Brunswick during the Age of Iron and Steam, 1850-1914." *ARCS* 9, no. 1 (1979):3-37.
1626. **Belding, A. M.** "Saint John as a Winter Port." *Can Mag* 12 (1898-99):398-99.
1627. **Bilson, Geoffrey.** "The Cholera Epidemic in Saint John, N.B., 1854." *Acadiensis* 4, no. 1 (1974):85-99.
1628. **Boyaner, Eli.** "The Settlement and Development of the Jewish Community of Saint John." NBHS *Collections* 5, no. 15 (1959):79-86
1629. **Braddock, John.** "Inside and Out: Changes in St. John." *Atl Ad* 55 (March 1965):14-17.
1630. **Burley, David V.** "An Archaeological Reconnaissance of Saint John, New Brunswick." *Man in the Northeast* 20 (1976):33-40.
1631. **Campbell, Roderick Calvin.** "Simonds, Hazen and White: A Study of a New Brunswick Firm in the Commercial World of the Eighteenth Century." M.A. thesis, New Brunswick, 1970.
1632. **Conwell, Russell H.** *History of the Great Fire in Saint John, June 20 and 21, 1877.* Saint John: Jones and Morrison, 1877.
1633. **Costello, Evelyn Paula.** "A Report on the Saint John Mechanics' Institute, 1838-1890." M.A. thesis, New Brunswick, 1974.
1634. **Cushing, J. E.; Casey, Teresa; and Robertson, Monica.** *A Chronicle of Irish Emigration to Saint John, New Brunswick, 1847.* Saint John: NB Museum, 1979.
1635. **Duggan, G. H.** "Superstructure of the St. John Arch." *ICEE* 206 (1917-18):255-68.
1636. **Durrant, D. A.** "A Development Model for North Saint John, N.B." M.A. thesis, Western Ontario, 1968.

1637. **Ellis, F.** "St. John, Past and Present." *Acadiensis* 4 (1904):320-30.
1638. **Fleming, P. W.** "The Development of Secondary Education in St. John, New Brunswick, Canada, from 1805." M.A. thesis, Leeds, 1977.
1639. **Forward, Charles N.** "A Comparison of Waterfront Land Use in Four Canadian Ports: St. John's, Saint John, Halifax and Victoria." *Econ Geogr* 45 (1969):155-69.
1640. **Garnett, N. G.** "The Loyalist City—Saint John, New Brunswick." *Maritime Advocate and Busy East* 45 (November 1954):19.
1641. **Gilbert, Beth.** "A Study of Mandatory Retirement in Saint John." In *The Aged in Society,* edited by D. Stewart, pp. 17-24. Saint John: University of New Brunswick at Saint John, 1979.
1642. **Goshen, D.** "The Metamorphosis of Saint John." *Atl Ad* 50, no. 7 (1960):16-26.
1643. **Hamilton, John R.** *Saint John, and the Province of New Brunswick. A Handbook for Travellers, Tourists, and Business Men.* Saint John: Hamilton, 1884.
1644. **Hannay, J.** *Saint John and Its Business: A History of Saint John.* Saint John: Chubb, 1875.
1645. **Harper, J. Russell.** "The Theatre in Saint John, 1789-1817." *Dal Rev* 34 (1954):260-69.
1646. **Hay, Elizabeth.** "Saint John." *Emp Di* 5, no. 11 (1948):51-56.
1647. **Haynes, E. Russell.** "The Proposed Development of Courtnay Bay, Saint John, New Brunswick, 1912-1923." M.A. thesis, New Brunswick, 1969.
1648. **Hughes, Gary.** "The Harbour, 1889-1976: The Port of Saint John Loses Its Colour." *J NB Mus* 1 (1977):16-26.
1649. **Isaacs, I. J.** *The Metropolis of New Brunswick: Its Facilities and Interests.* Saint John: Barnes, 1908.
1650. **Jack, David Russell.** *Centennial Prize Essay on the History of the City and County of St. John . . . 1783-1883.* Saint John: McMillan, 1883.
1651. _____. "Historic Landmarks of Saint John." *Westminster* 4 (1904):381-86.
1652. _____. *History of St. Andrew's Church, St. John, N.B.* Saint John, 1913.
1653. **Keith, Gerald.** "Saint John in 1853." NBHS *Collections* 5, no. 14 (1955):62-66.
1654. **Lawrence, Joseph W.** "The Medical Men of St. John." NBHS *Collections* 1 (1894-97):273-305.
1655. **Livingston, Gordon.** *Livingston's Hand Book and Visitor's Guide to Saint John with an Account of Fredericton and the St. John River.* Saint John: Chubb, 1869.
1656. **Lovatt, Bill.** "Saint John: Canada's Oldest Incorporated City." *Atl Ad* 54, no. 7 (1964):22-31.
1657. **Lower, A. R. M.** "Loyalist Cities: Saint John, New Brunswick and Kingston, Ontario." *QQ* 72 (1966):657-64.
1658. **McGahan, Elizabeth M. W.** "The Port of Saint John, New Brunswick, 1867-1911: Exploration of an Ecological Complex." *UHR* 3-76 (February 1977):3-13.
1659. _____. "The Port in the City: Saint John, New Brunswick (1867-1911) and the Process of Integration." Ph.D. thesis, New Brunswick, 1979.
1660. **MacKay, Michael.** "Saint John in Federal Politics, 1885-1887." M.A. thesis, New Brunswick, 1973.
1661. **MacKinnon, John Stephen.** "The Development of Local Government in the City of Saint John, 1785-1795." M.A. thesis, New Brunswick, 1968.
1662. **MacLeod, G. W.** "The Port of Saint John, Container Transportation Synthesis." M.Eng., New Brunswick, 1975.
1663. **MacQuarrie, M. R.** *Saint John, New Brunswick: A City in Transition.* Saint John: City of Saint John, 1970.
1664. **Matheson, Marion H.** "The Hinterlands of Saint John." *Geogr Bull* 7 (1955):65-102.
1665. **Merrett, J. Campbell.** *A Plan for Saint John.* Saint John: Barnes-Hopkins, 1946.
1666. _____. "Saint John, N.B." *JRAIC* 23 (1946):296-98.

1667. **Millidge, J. W.** "Some Reminiscences of the City of Saint John, Province of New Brunswick." NBHS *Collections* 12 (1928):340-49.
1668. **Milner, William C.** *Saint John in the Forties.* Saint John: Daily Telegraph, 1923.
1669. **Nesbit, W. C.** "The Development of the Saint John School System to 1871." M.Ed. thesis, New Brunswick, 1970.
1670. **Northrup, D. A.** "Saint John, N.B., 1871-1891: The Changing Residential Structure of a Slow-Growth City." M.A. thesis, York, 1979.
1671. *Our Dominion. Mercantile and Manufacturing Interests, Historical and Commercial Sketches of St. John and Environs.* Toronto: Historical Pub. Co., 1887.
1672. **Oxley, J. M.** "The Liverpool of Canada." *National Monthly of Canada* (1904):238-56.
1673. **Payne, Marilyn.** "The Saint John Woodcarvers." *J NB Mus* 3 (1979):38-43.
1674. **Potrin, G.** *City of Saint John Urban Renewal Study.* Toronto: Garden City Press, 1957.
1675. **Pratley, P. L.** "Design and Erection of St. John Bridge." *ICEE* 206 (1917-18):269-91.
1676. **Price, S. R.** "Amalgamation of Municipal Governments: Metropolitan Saint John." *NB Municipal Monthly* 25, no. 9 (1969):6-11.
1677. **Rayburn, J. A.** "Some Factors Affecting the Movement of Foreign Traffic through Saint John." *Geogr Bull* 7, no. 1 (1965):17-25.
1678. **Rayburn, W. O.** "Incidents in the History of St. John, New Brunswick." NBHS *Collections* 12 (1928):313-19.
1679. **Rees, R.** "Changing Saint John: The Old and the New." *CGEJ* 90, no. 5 (1975):12-17.
1680. **Rice, James Richard.** "A History of Organized Labour in Saint John, New Brunswick, 1813-1890." M.A. thesis, New Brunswick, 1968.
1681. _____. "The Wrights of Saint John: A Study of Shipbuilding and Shipowning in the Maritimes, 1839-1855." In *Canadian Business History: Selected Studies,* edited by D. S. Macmillan, pp. 317-37. Toronto: M&S, 1972.
1682. **Roberts, David.** "Social Structure in a Commercial City: Saint John, 1871." *UHR* 2-74 (October 1974):15-18.
1683. **Roberts, Theodore Goodridge.** "The Old Grey Port of Saint John." *CGEJ* 5 (1932):215-26.
1684. **Robinson, Charlotte M.** "The Pioneers of King Street." NBHS *Collections* 5, no. 14 (1955):29-45.
1685. **Saint John Board of Trade.** *The Book of Saint John. Issued by the Citizens and Business Firms of the City.* Saint John: Saint John Telegraph Pub. Co., 1903.
1686. "St. John, New Brunswick." *Anglo-American Mag* 3 (1853):566-70.
1687. **Saint John, N.B., Common Council.** *Saint John, New Brunswick, Canada; Canada's Winter Shipping Port.* Saint John, 1914.
1688. **Saint John, N.B.** *Canada's First City, Saint John. The Charter of 1785 and Common Council Proceedings under Mayor G. G. Ludlow, 1785-1795. With Foreword by Mayor Eric L. Teed.* Saint John: Lingley Printing Co., 1962.
1689. **Scovil Brothers.** *Saint John. An Historical Sketch, 1783-1909.* Saint John: Globe Printers, 1909(?).
1690. **Smith, Brian F.** "Federal Politics in Saint John, 1900-1904." M.A. thesis, New Brunswick, 1971.
1691. **Smith, Mary Elizabeth.** "Theatre in Saint John: The First Thirty Years." *Dal Rev* 59 (1979):28-39.
1692. **Stevens, Thalia O.** "The St. John River Commission, 1909-1916." M.A. thesis, Maine, 1969.
1693. **Stewart, George.** *The Story of the Great Fire in St. John, N.B., June 20th, 1877.* Toronto, 1877.
1694. **Trueman, Stuart.** "Exploring Saint John and Its Great River." *CGEJ* 88 (February 1974):10-19.

1695. **Wallace, Carl M.** "Saint John, New Brunswick, 1800-1900." *UHR* 1-75 (June 1975):12-21.
1696. _____. "Saint John Boosters and the Railroads in Mid-Nineteenth Century." *Acadiensis* 6, no. 1 (1976):71-91.
1697. **Wallace, F. W.** *The Romance of a Great Port.* Saint John: Barnes, 1935.
1698. **Ward, Clarence.** "The First Common Council." *Acadiensis* 3 (1903):267-80.
1699. **Weaver, Emily P.** "Saint John: The City of Loyalists." *Can Mag* 35 (1910):449-57.
1700. **Webster, Jackie.** "Saint John's Market, A Century of Faithful Service." *New Brunswick* 1 (September 1976):1-4.
1701. **Weis, Eduardo.** "Saint John Iron Works Ltd., Saint John, New Brunswick, Canada." *Maritimes Shipping Herald and Marine Engineering Journal* 1 (February-March 1975):12-13, 19-22.
1702. **Whalen, James M.** "The Nineteenth-Century Almshouse System in Saint John County." *HS* 7 (1971):5-28.
1703. **Willett, J.** "Epitomized History of Saint John, New Brunswick: Street Names and for Whom Called." NBHS *Collections* 11 (1927):143-205.
1704. **Williams, J. S.** "The Federal Election of 1911 in the Constituency of Saint John City, N.B." M.A. thesis, New Brunswick, 1974.
1705. **Wood-Holt, B.** *Early Marriage Records of New Brunswick, Saint John City and County, from the Conquest to 1839.* Saint John, 1978.
1706. **Wright, Esther Clark.** *Saint John Ships and Their Builders.* Wolfville, 1976.

7. Other Centres

1707. **Acheson, T. W.** "A Study in the Historical Demography of a Loyalist County." *HS* 1 (1968):53-65.
1708. _____. "Denominationalism in a Loyalist Country: A Social History of Charlotte, 1783-1840." M.A. thesis, New Brunswick, 1969.
1709. **Andrews, A.** "Social Crisis and Labour Mobility: A Study of Economic and Social Change in a New Brunswick Railway Community." M.A. thesis, New Brunswick, 1967.
1710. *Bathurst, the Convention Centre of the North Shore.* Bathurst: Golden Jubilee Organization, 1962.
1711. **Bell, Fannie C.** *A History of Old Shediac, New Brunswick.* Moncton: National Print Ltd., 1937.
1712. **Caragianis, Eva M.** "The Development of Urban Form through Planning Administration with Specific Reference to Oromocto, New Brunswick." M.Arch. thesis, McGill, 1958.
1713. **Carson, G. S.** "Hampton—Past and Present." NBHS *Collections* 18 (1963):195-203.
1714. **Delottinville, Peter.** "The St. Croix Cotton Manufacturing Co. and Its Influence on the St. Croix Community, 1880-1892." M.A. thesis, Dalhousie, 1979.
1715. **Finley, A. Gregg.** "The Morans of St. Martins, N.B., 1850-1880: Toward an Understanding of Family Participation in Maritime Enterprise." In #1120, pp. 35-54.
1716. _____. "The Social Organization of a Shipbuilding Community: St. Martin's, New Brunswick, 1815-1900." M.A. thesis, New Brunswick, 1978.
1717. **Fraser, James A.** *'By Favourable Winds'; A History of Chatham, New Brunswick.* Chatham: Town of Chatham, 1975.
1718. **Glendenning, B. G. S.** "The Birchill Lumbering Firm: A Study in New Brunswick Entrepreneurship, 1850 to 1900." M.A. thesis, Concordia, 1978.
1719. **Knowlton, Isaac C.** *Annals of Calais, Maine and St. Stephen, New Brunswick; Including the Village of Milltown, Me., and the Present Town of Milltown, N.B.* Calais: Sears, 1875.
1720. **Lagace, Anita.** *How Grand Falls Grew.* Saint John: McMillan, 1945.

1721. **MacAllister, Edith.** *Newcastle on the Miramichi: A Brief History.* Newcastle, 1974.
1722. **MacGowan, D. F.** "Clifton, New Brunswick: The Rise and Fall of a Shipbuilding Community." M.A. thesis, New Brunswick, 1955.
1723. **Murray, Jack.** "Spotlight on Woodstock: New Brunswick's Oldest Incorporated Town." *Current Events* 11 (January-February 1963):4-9.
1724. **Naegele, Kaspar D.** "Picture of a Maritime Mill Town (Marysville, N.B.)." *PA* 11 (1947):11-15.
1725. **Rogers, Jerry.** "McAdam, un village à la croisée des chemins." *Le Nouveau-Brunswick* 2 (1977):10-13.
1726. **Sealy, Nanciellen.** "Ethnicity and Ethnic Group Persistence in an Acadian Village in Maritime Canada." Ph.D. thesis, Southern Illinois, 1975.
1727. _____. "Consequences of Development Strategies in an Acadian Maritime Village." In Canadian Ethnology Society, *Papers from the Fourth Annual Congress,* edited by Richard J. Preston, pp. 71-83. Ottawa: National Museums of Canada, 1978.
1728. **Spray, W. A.** "Early Northumberland County: A Study in Local Government." M.A. thesis, New Brunswick, 1963.
1729. **Swartzen, Gordon W.** "The Impact of a Military Installation on a Local Economy: A Case Study of Camp Gagetown and the Town of Oromocto." M.A. thesis, Ottawa, 1965.
1730. **Thompson, Ethel A.** *The Tides of Discipline: A Personal History of Three Traditional Fishing Communities: Chance Harbour, Dipper Harbour and Maces Bay, Situated on the South Shore of New Brunswick.* St. Stephen: Print 'N Press, 1978.
1731. **Tribble, S. P.** "Pulptown, Canada: A Study of Migration to a Planned New Brunswick Community." M.A. thesis, New Brunswick, 1973.
1732. **Watson, R. G.** "Local Government in a New Brunswick County, 1784-1850." M.A. thesis, New Brunswick, 1969.
1733. **Webster, John C.** *A History of Shediac, New Brunswick.* Shediac: Privately Printed, 1928.
1734. **Williams, M. E.** "Early History of Education in the District of Bathurst." M.A. thesis, Ottawa, 1951.

V

Prince Edward Island

1. General

1735. **Baglole, Harry.** "Land and Politics in Prince Edward Island to 1860." M.A. thesis, Memorial, 1969.
1736. _____, ed. *Exploring Island History: A Guide to the Historical Resources of Prince Edward Island.* Belfast, P.E.I.: Ragweed Press, 1977.
1737. **Bolger, Francis W. P., ed.** *Canada's Smallest Province: A History of P.E.I.* Charlottetown: PEI Centennial Commission, 1973.
1738. **Clark, Andrew H.** *Three Centuries and the Island.* Toronto: UTP, 1959.
1739. **Fay, S. F. J.** "Municipal Finance in Nova Scotia and Prince Edward Island, 1945-1955." M.A. thesis, New Brunswick, 1959.
1740. **Fischer, Lewis R.** "The Port of Prince Edward Island, 1840-1889: A Preliminary Analysis." In *Ships and Shipbuilding in the North Atlantic Region,* edited by Keith Matthews and Gerald Panting, pp. 41-70. St. John's: Memorial, 1978.
1741. _____. "The Shipping Industry of Nineteenth Century Prince Edward Island: A Brief History." *The Island Magazine* 4 (1978):15-21.
1742. **Greenhill, Basil, and Giffard, Ann.** *Westcountrymen in Prince Edward's Isle.* Toronto: UTP, 1967.
1743. **Hodge, Gerald.** *Rural and Urban Development Capability in Prince Edward Island.* Toronto: Acres Research and Planning, 1967.
1744. _____. "Urban Structure and Regional Development." Regional Science Association, *Papers* 21 (1968):101-23.
1745. **Holman, H. T.** "Local Government Records of Prince Edward Island in the Public Archives of Prince Edward Island." Archival Association of Atlantic Canada, *Newsletter* 4 (April 1976):9-11.
1746. **MacKinnon, Frank.** *The Government of Prince Edward Island.* Toronto: UTP, 1951.
1747. **MacKinnon, Wayne Emerson.** "The Politics of Planning: A Case Study of the P.E.I. Development Plan." M.A. thesis, Dalhousie, 1975.
1748. **Meacham, J. H.** *Illustrated Historical Atlas of P.E.I.* 1880. Reprint. Belleville: Mika, 1973.
1749. **Paris, Jacques, and Hodge, Gerald.** *The System of Central Places in P.E.I.* Toronto: Acres Research and Planning, 1967.
1750. **Tuck, Robert C.** "Georgetown: The Town That Time Forgot." *The Island Magazine* 4 (1978):22-28.

2. Charlottetown

1751. **Becker, J. Richard.** "The Bank of Charlottetown—Fact or Fraud?" *Canadian Paper Money J* 10 (1974):107-14.
1752. **Bremner, Benjamin.** *Memories of Long Ago: Being a Series of Sketches Pertaining to Charlottetown in the Past.* Charlottetown: Irwin Print Co., 1930.
1753. *The Central Christian Church, Its Origins and Growth.* Charlottetown: Central Christian Church, 1975.
1754. *The Charlottetown Centennial.* Charlottetown: Charlottetown Centennial Committee, 1955.
1755. **Cullen, Mary K.** "The Late Nineteenth Century Development of the Queen Square Gardens, Charlottetown, P.E.I." *APT Bulletin* 9 (1977): 1-20.
1756. **Harvey, D. C.** "Charlottetown." *CGEJ* 4 (1932):201-19.
1757. **Lafferty, Louis W.** *The Structure of Opportunity: An Analysis of Business and Industry in the Economy of King's County and Charlottetown, P.E.I.* Montague, P.E.I.: P.E.I. New Start, 1969.
1758. **MacKenzie, Ruth Heartz.** *West Street Revisited.* Charlottetown, 1977.
1759. **MacKinnon, Frank.** "Charlottetown's Centennial." *CGEJ* 51 (1955):238-43.
1760. ———. "Charlottetown." *Habitat* 10, nos. 3-6 (1967):10-13.
1761. **McLeod, Ada.** "Travels in Prince Edward Island in 1820." *Dal Rev* 3 (1923):31-41.
1762. **Mellish, John T.** *Outlines of the History of Methodism in Charlottetown, P.E.I.* Charlottetown, 1888.
1763. **Mullaly, Emmet J.** "A Sketch of the Life and Times of the Right Reverend Angus Bernard MacEachern, the First Bishop of the Diocese of Charlottetown." CHA, *AR* (1945-46):71-106.
1764. **Prince Edward Island. Dept. of Industry and Commerce. Industrial Intelligence Unit.** *A Community Profile of Charlottetown.* Charlottetown, 1973.
1765. **Sinnot, J. Cyril.** *A History of the Charlottetown Clinic.* Charlottetown, 1975.
1766. **Smith, Rebecca L.** "Charlottetown Amateur Theatre to 1824." *Dal Rev* 59 (1979):5-27.
1767. **Turner, Jonni.** "Charlottetown: A Redevelopment." *Arts Atlantic* 1 (1978):20-23.

VI

Newfoundland

1. General

1768. **Adams, J. Gordon.** *Urban Centres in Newfoundland.* Report of the Planning Division of the Atlantic Development Board. Ottawa: Dept. of Energy, Mines and Resources, 1967.
1769. _____. "Newfoundland Population Movements, with Particular Reference to the Post-War Period." Ph.D. thesis, McGill, 1971.
1770. **Alexander, David.** "Development and Dependence in Newfoundland 1880-1970." *Acadiensis* 4, no. 1 (1974):3-31.
1771. _____. "The Political Economy of Fishing in Newfoundland." *J Can St* 11, no. 1 (1976):32-40.
1772. **Allston, J. T.** "The Growth and Planning of Communities in Newfoundland." In #1820, v. 6, pp. 605-13.
1773. **Bonnycastle, Richard.** *Newfoundland in 1842.* London: Colburn, 1842.
1774. **Callum, C.** "Rural Communities in Decline: The Newfoundland Experience." *Ekistics* 41 (1976):99-101.
1775. **Chiarmonte, Louis J.** *Craftsmen-Client Contracts: Interpersonal Relations in a Newfoundland Fishing Community.* Newfoundland Social and Economic Studies, no. 10. St. John's: Memorial, 1970.
1776. **Cohen, Anthony P.** *The Management of Myths, The Politics of Legitimation in a Newfoundland Community.* Newfoundland Social and Economic Studies, no. 14. St. John's: Memorial, 1975.
1777. **Copes, Parzival.** *The Resettlement of Fishing Communities in Newfoundland.* Ottawa: Canadian Council on Rural Development, 1972.
1778. **Courtney, D. S.** "The Newfoundland Household Resettlement Programs: A Case Study in Spatial Reorganization and Centre Strategy." M.A. thesis, Memorial, 1973.
1779. **Crosbie, John C.** "Local Government in Newfoundland." *CJEPS* 22 (1956):332-46.
1780. **Delaney, R. E.** "Scots Kinship, Migration and Early Settlement in Southwestern Newfoundland." M.A. thesis, Memorial, 1970.
1781. **Fay, C. R.** *Life and Labour in Newfoundland.* Toronto: UTP, 1956.
1782. **Firestone, Melvin M.** "Socialization and Interaction in a Newfoundland Outport." *UL* 7 (April 1978):91-110.
1783. **Forward, Charles N.** "The Shipping Trade of the Island of Newfoundland." *GGJO* 11 (1958):5-35.
1784. **Fox, Arthur.** *The Newfoundland Constabulary.* St. John's: Robinson-Blackmore, 1971.
1785. **Hamdani, D.** "The Role of Public Finance in the Development of Newfoundland." M.A. thesis, Memorial, 1967.

1786. **Handcock, W. G.** "Migration from S.W. England to Newfoundland during the Late 18th and Early 19th Centuries." Ph.D. thesis, Birmingham, 1972.
1787. **Handelman, Donald.** "Bureaucratic Interpretation: The Perception of Child Abuse in Urban Newfoundland." In *Bureaucracy and World View: Studies in the Logic of Official Interpretation,* by D. Handelman and Elliot Leyton, pp. 15-70. Newfoundland Social and Economic Studies, No. 22. St. John's: Memorial, 1978.
1788. **Hatton, Joseph, and Harney, Moses.** *Newfoundland: Its History, Its Present Condition, and Its Prospects in the Future.* Boston: Doyle and Whittle, 1883.
1789. **Hawco, J. R.** "Change, Dependency and the Catholic Church in Five Newfoundland Communities." M.A. thesis, Alberta, 1979.
1790. **Head, Clifford Grant.** *Eighteenth Century Newfoundland: A Geographer's Perspective.* Toronto: M&S, 1976.
1791. **Hefferton, S. J.** "Planning for Small Towns in Newfoundland." *CPR* 8, no. 1 (1958):11-15.
1792. **Hickman, George Albert.** "The History of Education in Newfoundland." M.A. thesis, Acadia, 1941.
1793. **Hugo-Brunt, Michael.** "Two Worlds Meet: A Survey of Newfoundland Settlement. Part 1: The Great Fishery and Early Settlement." *Plan Canada* 5, no. 1 (1964):22-36; "Part 2: Development in the 19th and 20th Centuries." 5, no. 2 (1964):59-83.
1794. **Hutchison, Thomas.** *Hutchison's Newfoundland Directory, for 1864-65.* St. John's: McConnan, 1864.
1795. **Iverson, Noel, and Matthews, Ralph.** *Communities in Decline: An Examination of Household Resettlement in Newfoundland.* St. John's: Institute of Social and Economic Research, Memorial, 1968.
1796. **Kerr, Kenneth J.** "A Social Analysis of the Members of the Newfoundland House of Assembly, Executive Council, and Legislative Council for 1855-1914." M.A. thesis, Memorial, 1973.
1797. **Lamarre, Nicole.** "Kinship and Inheritance Patterns in a French Newfoundland Village." In *Communities and Culture in French Canada,* edited by G. L. Gold and M.-A. Tremblay, pp. 142-53. Toronto: Holt, Rinehart and Winston, 1973.
1798. "Local Government Records in Newfoundland." Archival Association of Atlantic Canada, *Newsletter* 4 (April 1976):7-8.
1799. **McCutcheon, Henry R.** "The Changing Structure of the Tertiary Economy of Newfoundland." *Urb For* 1, no. 2 (1975):16-20.
1800. **McKee, D. L.** "Municipal Finance in New Brunswick and Newfoundland, 1951-1956." M.A. thesis, New Brunswick, 1959.
1801. **Mannion, John J.** "Settlers and Traders in Western Newfoundland." In *The Peopling of Newfoundland: Essays in Historical Geography,* edited by John J. Mannion, pp. 234-75. Newfoundland Social and Economic Papers, No. 8. St. John's: Memorial, 1977.
1802. **Matthews, Keith.** "The Irish in Newfoundland." In *Lectures on the History of Newfoundland, 1500-1830,* by Keith Matthews, pp. 219-28. St. John's: Memorial, 1973.
1803. _____. *Checklist of Research Studies Pertaining to the History of Newfoundland in the Archives of the Maritime History Group.* St. John's: Memorial, 1974.
1804. _____. "Historical Fence Building: A Critique of the Historiography of Newfoundland." *Nfld Q* 74 (Spring 1978):21-30.
1805. **Matthews, Ralph.** "Communities in Transition: An Examination of Government Initiated Community Migration in Rural Newfoundland." M.A. thesis, Minnesota, 1970.
1806. _____. *'There's No Better Place Than Here': Social Change in Three Newfoundland Communities.* Toronto: Peter Martin Associates, 1976.
1807. **Mayo, H. B.** "Municipal Government in Newfoundland." *PA* 4 (March 1941):136-39.
1808. **Mosdell, H. M.** "Ten Towns of Newfoundland." In #1820, v. 6, pp. 421-32.

1809. Mott, H. Y. *Newfoundland Men: A Collection of Biographical Sketches.* Concord, NH: Cragg, 1894.

1810. Munske, R. R. "Development of the Urban System in Newfoundland." M.A. thesis, George Washington, 1974.

1811. O'Dea, A. C. *A Newfoundland Bibliography: 1611-1960.* St. John's: Memorial, 1960.

1812. O'Flaherty, Patrick. "Looking Backwards: The Milieu of the Old Newfoundland Outports." *J Can St* 10 (February 1975):3-9.

1813. O'Neill, Paul, and O'Dea, Shane, eds. *Ten Historic Towns: Heritage Architecture of Newfoundland.* St. John's: Valhalla-Newfoundland Historic Trust, 1979.

1814. Philbrook, T. V. *Fisherman, Logger, Merchant, Miner: Social Change and Industrialism in Three Newfoundland Communities.* Newfoundland Social and Economic Studies, No. 1. St. John's: Memorial, 1966.

1815. Powell, C. W. "Problems Arising from Lack of Organized Municipalities in Newfoundland." Institute of Public Administration of Canada, *Proceedings* (1947):168-82.

1816. Prowse, D. W. "Local Government in Newfoundland." In #**895**, pp. 269-78.

1817. Rowe, F. W. *The Development of Education in Newfoundland.* Toronto: Ryerson, 1964.

1818. Sim, Victor W. "A Comparison of the Site and Function of Four Towns in Northeast Newfoundland." M.A. thesis, Clark, 1957.

1819. Stolnik, Michael, L., ed. *Viewpoints on Communities in Crisis.* Newfoundland Social and Economic Papers, No. 1. St. John's: Memorial, 1968.

1820. Smallwood, Joseph R., ed. *The Book of Newfoundland.* 6 Vols. St. John's: Newfoundland Book Publishers, 1937-1967.

1821. Smith, Margaret. "Newfoundland, 1815-1840: A Study of a Merchantocracy." M.A. thesis, Memorial, 1968.

1822. Stavely, Michael. "Population Dynamics in Newfoundland: The Regional Patterns." In *The Peopling of Newfoundland: Essays in Historical Geography,* edited by John J. Mannion, pp. 49-76. Newfoundland Social and Economic Papers, No. 8. St. John's: Memorial, 1977.

1823. Summers, F. "A Geographical Analysis of Population Trends in Newfoundland." Ph.D. thesis, McGill, 1957.

1824. Tocque, Philip. *Newfoundland: As It Was, and As It Is.* London: Sampson, Low, Marston, Searle and Rivington, 1878.

1825. Wadel, Cato. *Marginal Adaptations and Modernization in Newfoundland, A Study of Strategies and Implications in the Resettlement and Redevelopment of Outport Fishing Communities.* Newfoundland Social and Economic Studies, No. 7. St. John's: Memorial, 1969.

1826. Whiteley, W. H. "Newfoundland, Quebec and the Labrador Merchants, 1783-1809." *Nfld Q* 73 (1977):18-26.

1827. Wicks, René. "Newfoundland Social Life: 1750-1856." *Nfld Q* 70 (Fall 1974):17-23.

1828. Wonders, William C. "Parasite Communities of Newfoundland." *CPR* 2, no. 1 (1953):27-29.

2. Corner Brook

1829. Beattie, Kim. "Newfoundland's Surprise City." *Civic Admin* 2, no. 9 (1950):31-32, 65.

1830. Callahan, W. R. "Cornerbrook; Newfoundland's Second City Bids for First Place." *Atl Ad* 53, no. 10 (1963):42-44, 49-50.

1831. Fay, C. R. "Grand Falls and Corner Brook." In #**1781,** pp. 191-211.

1832. Plunkett, Thomas J. "Local Government in Greater Corner Brook, Newfoundland." M.A. thesis, McGill, 1955.

1833. Wonders, William C. "The Corner Brook Area, Newfoundland." *Geogr Bull* 5 (1954):29-58.

1834. Young, Ewart. *Corner Brook, Newfoundland, 1923-1948: 25 Years of Progress.* Corner Brook: Western Publishing Co., 1948.

3. St. John's

1835. **Allston, J. T.** "Town and Country Planning Comes to Newfoundland." In #1820, v. 4, pp. 414-16.
1836. **Amy, W. Lacey.** "St. John's: The Impossible Possible." *Can Mag* 48 (February 1912):373-78.
1837. **Baker, Melvin.** *St. John's Bibliography, 1870-1914.* St. John's: Memorial University, 1974.
1838. _____. "The Politics of Municipal Reform in St. John's, Newfoundland, 1888-1892." *UHR* 2-76 (October 1976):12-29.
1839. **Ball, Jean.** "St. John's: Sketchy Impressions." *Heritage Canada* 2 (Winter 1975-76):9-16.
1840. **Bellows, G.** "The Foundation of Memorial University College." *Nfld Q* 71 (Summer 1975):5-9.
1841. **Byrnes, John Maclay.** *The Paths to Yesterday: Memories of Old St. John's, Newfoundland.* Boston: Meador, 1931.
1842. **Cahulk, A.** "The St. John's Chamber of Commerce." M.A. thesis, Memorial, 1967.
1843. **Copes, Parzival.** *St. John's and Newfoundland: An Economic Survey.* St. John's: Board of Trade, 1961.
1844. **Crosbie, John C.** "The Boom in Municipal Development." In #1820, v. 4, pp. 405-13.
1845. **Cryderman, B.** "Comparison of Two Urban Citizen Action Groups, St. John's, Newfoundland." M.A. thesis, Memorial, 1976.
1846. **Devine, P. K.** *Ye Olde St. John's, 1750-1936.* St. John's: Newfoundland Directories, 1936.
1847. **Duder, R., ed.** *The Kirk, 1842-1942.* St. John's: Robinson, 1942.
1848. **Fay, C. R.** "The St. John's Chamber of Commerce." In #1781, pp. 146-62.
1849. _____. "Ordeal by Fire." In #1781, pp. 163-90.
1850. **Foran, Edward B.** "St. John's City: Historic Capital of Newfoundland." In #1820, v. 2, pp. 1-25.
1851. _____. "The New Old St. John's." In #1820, v. 4, pp. 89-95.
1852. **Forward, Charles N.** "The Distribution of Commercial Establishments in St. John's, Newfoundland." *Can Geogr* 2 (1957):30-48.
1853. _____. "Recent Changes in the Form and Function of the Port of St. John's, Newfoundland." *Can Geogr* 11 (1967):101-16.
1854. **Fraser, A.** "The Recapture of St. John's." *Atl Ad* 56, no. 8 (1966):42-47.
1855. **Grattan, Patricia.** "St. John's Heritage." *Arts Atlantic* 1 (1978):29-31.
1856. **Harney, Moses, and O'Meara, Henry.** *The Great Fire in St. John's, Newfoundland.* Boston: Relief Committee, 1892.
1857. **Harrington, Michael Francis.** "St. John's, Newfoundland." *CGEJ* 81 (1970):74-85.
1858. _____. "St. John's: On Signal Hill." *Heritage Canada* 2 (Winter 1976):17-18.
1859. **Higgins, Brian E.** "The Port of St. John's." In #1820, v. 4, pp. 85-88.
1860. **Horwood, H.** "St. John's." *Habitat* 10, nos. 3-6 (1967):4-9.
1861. **Joy, John.** "The Growth and Development of Trades and Manufacturing in St. John's, 1870-1914." M.A. thesis, Memorial, 1977.
1862. **Kennedy, R.** "The Development of a Community Resource Directory for the St. John's Area." M.Ed. thesis, Memorial, 1977.
1863. **Kent, W. J.** "The Great Fire of '92." In #1820, v. 5, pp. 102-7.
1864. **Lang, V.** "Land Use Problems and Priorities in the Fringes of St. John's, Newfoundland." *Urb For* 11, no. 2 (1976):12-15.
1865. **Le Messurier, Henry W.** *The Church of St. Thomas and Its Rectors, 1836-1928.* St. John's: The Church of St. Thomas, 1928.

1866. _____. "The Dramatic History of St. John's." In #1820, v. 5, pp. 72-85.
1867. **Lewis, D. E.** "Saint John's, Newfoundland." *Dal Rev* 25 (1945): 331-38.
1868. **McGrath, P. T.** "Capitals of Greater Britain: St. John's, Newfoundland." *Pall Mall Mag* 18 (1899):4-15.
1869. **Matthews, Keith.** "The Rise of St. John's." In *Lectures on the History of Newfoundland, 1500-1830,* by Keith Matthews, pp. 243-48. St. John's: Memorial, 1973.
1870. _____. "The Class of '32: St. John's Reformers on the Eve of Representative Government." *Acadiensis* 6, no. 2 (1977):80-94.
1871. **Moyles, Robert Gordon.** "Fire, Frost, and Famine: St. John's in 1817." *Nfld Q* 67, no. 3 (1970):9-10.
1872. _____. "St. John's: A Century of Struggle." In *'Complaints Is Many and Various but the Odd Divil Likes It': Nineteenth Century Views of Newfoundland,* by R. G. Moyles, pp. 1-30. Toronto: Peter Martin, 1975.
1873. **Murphy, Michael P.** *The Story of the Colonial Building.* St. John's: Newfoundland and Labrador Provincial Archives, 1972.
1874. _____. *Pathways through Yesterday.* St. John's: Town Crier Pub. Co., 1976.
1875. **Newfoundland Historic Trust.** *A Gift of Heritage: Historic Architecture of St. John's.* St. John's: Valhalla Press, 1975.
1876. **Nichols, John W.** *A Century of Methodism in St. John's, 1815-1915.* St. John's: Dicks, 1915.
1877. **O'Dea, Shane.** *The Domestic Architecture of Old St. John's.* Pamphlet No. 2. St. John's: Newfoundland Historical Society, 1974.
1878. _____. *The Architectural Heritage of St. John's: An Evaluation Inventory.* St. John's: Newfoundland Historic Trust, 1976.
1879. **O'Neill, Paul.** *Everyman's Complete St. John's Guide.* St. John's: Valhalla Press, 1975.
1880. _____. *The Oldest City: The Story of St. John's, Newfoundland.* Vol. 1. Erin, Ont.: Press Porcepic, 1975.
1881. _____. *A Seaport Legacy: The Story of St. John's, Newfoundland.* Vol. 2. Erin, Ont.: Press Porcepic, 1976.
1882. **Pearson, R. E.** *Atlas of St. John's, Newfoundland.* St. John's: Memorial University, Dept. of Geography, 1969.
1883. **Perlin, A. B.** "St. John's: Newfoundland's Ancient Capital Takes on New Dimensions." *Atl Ad* 50, no. 10 (1960):37-50.
1884. **Pitt, David G.** *Windows of Agates.* St. John's: Gower Street United Church, 1966.
1885. **Rockwood, Jim.** "Historic St. John's." *Atl Ad* 62, no. 7 (1972):36-39.
1886. **Rowe, C. Francis.** *A Record of the 275th Anniversary of the Cathedral Parish of Saint John the Baptist, St. John's, Newfoundland, 1699-1974.* St. John's: The Parish, 1975.
1887. **Sager, Eric W.** "The Merchants of Water Street and Capital Investment in Newfoundland's Traditional Economy." In #1120, pp. 75-96.
1888. _____. "The Port of St. John's, Newfoundland, 1840-1889: A Preliminary Analysis." In *Ships and Shipbuilding in the North Atlantic Region,* edited by Keith Matthews and Gerald Panting, pp. 19-40. St. John's: Memorial, 1978.
1889. **St. David's Church, St. John's, Nfld.** *Early History of the Congregational Church in Newfoundland.* St. John's, 1975.
1890. **Shrimpton, Mark.** "An Examination of the Relationships between Social Areas and Social Interaction: A Case Study of St. John's, Newfoundland." M.A. thesis, Memorial, 1976.
1891. _____, **and Fuchs, Richard.** "Neighbourhood Changes and Vandalism in Central St. John's." *Aspects* 10 (1979):22-25.
1892. _____, **and Sharpe, Christopher A.** "An Inner City in Decline: St. John's, Newfoundland." *UHR* 9 (June 1980):90-109.

1893. **Story, George M.** *George Street United Church, 1873-1973.* St. John's: George Street United Church, 1973.
1894. _____. "Judge Prowse: Historian and Publicist." *Aspects* 4, no. 3 (1972):15-25.
1895. **Wadden, Brian.** "The St. John's Street Railway Co." *Nfld Q* 64, no. 1 (1965):3-5, 27-30; 64, no. 2 (1965):10-13, 27-28.
1896. **Whiteway, Louise.** "Christmas in St. John's—One Hundred Years Ago." *Atl Ad* 61 (December 1970):26-27.
1897. _____. "The Athenaeum Movement: St. John's Athenaeum (1861-1898)." *Dal Rev* 50 (1970-71):534-49.
1898. **Winton, A. C.** "Newfoundland and Its Capital." *Dom Ill Mon* 1 (1892):657-66.
1899. **Withers, J. W.** "Dirty, Diseased and Dangerous—And Always Exciting: St. John's in 1897." In #1820, v. 5, pp. 54-71.
1900. **Young, Ewart.** *St. John's, Newfoundland: Capital of Canada's Newest Province.* Montreal: Guardian Associates, 1949.

4. Other Centres

1901. **Blackmore, Laura.** "Paper Town: Grand Falls." *Atlantic Guardian* 3, no. 8 (1947):9-21.
1902. **Brown, Howard C.** "The Impact of Modernization on the Traditional Economy and Society of Inner Placentia Bay." M.A. thesis, Memorial, 1975.
1903. _____. "A Study of the Curling Area, 1860-1920." *Nfld Q* 71 (March 1975):17-25; 71 (Summer 1975):17-24.
1904. **Carson, Terry M.** "Political Culture and Community Development in the Harbour Breton Area." M.A. thesis, Memorial, 1971.
1905. **De Witt, Robert L.** *Public Policy and Community Protest: The Fogo Case.* Newfoundland Social and Economic Studies, No. 8. St. John's: Memorial, 1969.
1906. **Firestone, Melvin M.** *Brothers and Rivals: Patrilocality in Savage Cove.* Newfoundland Social and Economic Studies, No. 5. St. John's: Memorial, 1967.
1906A. _____. "Socialization and Interaction in a Newfoundland Outport." *UL* 7 (1978):91-110.
1907. **Mills, David E.** "The Development of Folk Architecture in Trinity Bay." In *The Peopling of Newfoundland: Essays in Historical Geography,* edited by John J. Mannion, pp. 77-101. Newfoundland Social and Economic Papers, No. 8. St. John's: Memorial, 1977.
1908. **Neary, Peter F.** " 'Traditional' and 'Modern' Elements in the Social and Economic History of Bell Island and Conception Bay." CHA, *HP* (1973):105-36.
1909. **Philbrook, T. V.** "Industrialization in a Small Community: A Study of Three Newfoundland Communities [Cod Cove, Ore Blight, and Fiber]." Ph.D. thesis, Minnesota, 1964.
1910. **Proulx, Jean-Pierre.** "Placentia: 1713-1811." *History and Archaeology* 26 (1979):115-90.
1911. **Roberts, Peter Job.** "Harbour Grace Elections, 1832-1883." M.A. thesis, New Brunswick, 1969.
1912. **Russell, Edgar A.** "Bay Roberts." *Atlantic Guardian* 5, no. 4 (1948):16-22.
1913. **Smith, Phillip.** *Brinco: The Story of Churchill Falls.* Toronto: M&S, 1975.
1914. **Thornton, Patricia A.** "The Demographic and Mercantile Bases of Initial Permanent Settlement in the Strait of Belle Isle." In *The Peopling of Newfoundland,* edited by John J. Mannion, pp. 152-83. Newfoundland Social and Economic Papers, No. 8. St. John's: Memorial, 1977.
1915. **Tucker, Walter B.** "Grand Falls: Our Most Prosperous Town." In #1820, v. 6, pp. 295-99.
1916. **Young, Ewart.** *Grand Falls, Botwood, Bishop's Falls, Badger, Millertown, Terra Nova, Newfoundland: Paper and Pulpwood Towns of the Interior.* Montreal: Guardian Associates, 1951.

VII

Quebec

1. General

1917. **Adams, Thomas.** "Town and Country Planning in Quebec." *To Pl Cn L* 6, no. 4 (1920):77-79.
1918. **Alcorn, Richard S., and Igartua, José E.** "Du rang à la ville: Le processus d'urbanisation au Québec et en Ontario." *RHAF* 29 (1975):417-20.
1919. **Angers, Majella.** *Liste de publications reliées aux 63 principales agglomerations du Québec.* Québec: Ministère des affaires municipales, 1975.
1920. *Architecture et urbanisme au Québec.* Montréal: Presses de l'université de Montréal, 1971.
1921. **Ballahan, Maurice Bernard.** "A Regional Study of the Richelieu Valley: The Urban Centres." M.A. thesis, McGill, 1952.
1922. **Barber, G. M., and Britton, John N. H.** *Occupational Structure and Population Growth in the Ontario-Quebec Urban System, 1941-1966.* Research Paper #49. Toronto: CUCS, 1971.
1923. **Beaulieu, André; Bonenfant, Jean-Charles; and Hamelin, Jean.** *Répertoire des publications gouvernementales du Québec de 1867 à 1964.* Québec: Imprimeur de la reine, 1968.
1924. **Beaulieu, André, and Hamelin, Jean.** *Les journaux du Québec de 1764 à 1964.* Québec: Presses de l'université de Laval, 1966.
1925. _____. *La presse québécoise.* Québec: Presses de l'université Laval, 1973.
1926. **Beaulieu, André, and Morley, William F. E.** *Canadian Local Histories: A Bibliography.* Vol. 2. *La Province de Québec.* Toronto: UTP, 1971.
1927. **Bédard, Robert-J.** *La bataille des annexions.* Montréal: Jour, 1965.
1928. **Bélanger, Marcel.** "De la région naturelle à la région urbaine: Problèmes d'habitat." In #1954, pp. 45-63.
1929. **Bergevin, G.-M.** "De l'organisation de la vie culturelle dans une petite ville." *Education des adultes* 9 (1961):51-58.
1930. **Bertrand, Jean-Pierre.** *Chronologie de mise en marché des matériaux et produits de la construction au XIXe et XXe siecle.* Montréal: CRIU, 1978.
1931. *Bibliographie du Québec métropolitain.* Québec: Conseil des oeuvres de Québec, 1971.
1932. **Bonnier, L.** "La caisse populaire et la communauté québecoise." *Rev Desjardins* 30 (1964):74-76.
1933. **Bouchard, Gaétan.** *La coopérative d'habitation du Québec métropolitain.* Québec: Gouvernement du Québec, 1967.
1935. **Bouchette, Joseph.** *A Topographical Description of the Province of Lower Canada, with Remarks upon Upper Canada, and on the Relative Connexion of Both Provinces with the United States of America.* 1815. St. Lambert: Canada East Reprints, 1973.

1936. **Boudreault, M.** "Géographie et urbanisme: Les leçons des politiques urbanisatiques en vigeur sur la rive sud du Saint-Laurent." Thèse de M.A., Ottawa, 1970.
1937. **Bourassa, Guy.** "Le système municipal québécois." In *Le système politique du Canada,* edited by L. Sabourin, pp. 337-50. Ottawa: Editions de l'université d'Ottawa, 1968.
1938. **Bourdon, Jean.** *Plans of the First French Settlements on the St. Lawrence, 1635-1642.* Montreal: McGill University Library, 1958.
1939. **Bourne, L. S., and Baker, Alan Maurice.** *Urban Development in Ontario and Quebec: Outline and Overview.* Research Paper #1. Toronto: CUCS, 1968.
1940. **Bourne, L. S., and Mather, C. A.** *Comparative Explorations of City-Size Distributions: The Ontario-Quebec Urban System.* Research Paper #27. Toronto: CUCS, 1970.
1941. **Brien, G.** "Structure routière et structure urbaine: Un exemple d'approche méthodologique: Le cas de la 5ᵉ région économique Québécoise." Thèse de M.A., Sherbrooke, 1973.
1942. **Brochu, M.** *Le défi du Nouveau-Québec.* Montréal: Jour, 1962.
1943. **Brouillette, Benoît.** "Les régions géographiques et économiques de la province de Québec." In *Mélanges géographiques canadiens offerts à Raoul Blanchard,* edited by L.-E. Hamelin, pp. 65-84. Québec: Presses de l'université Laval, 1959.
1944. **Brousseau, Margo.** "Les zones d'influence des principales villes du Québec: Etude de quelques charactéristiques." Thèse de M.A., Laval, 1967.
1945. **Bussières, Roger.** *Le régime municipal de la province de Québec.* Québec: Ministère des affaires municipales, 1964.
1946. **Campeau, Charles-Edouard.** "Problèmes métropolitains." *RCU* 8, no. 2 (1958):52-58.
1947. **Camu, Pierre.** "L'axe économique de Saint-Laurent, entre Kingston et Québec." Thèse de Ph.D., Montréal, 1952.
1948. _____. "Villes-moyennes du Québec: Problème urgent d'urbanisme." *RCU* 7, no. 1 (1957):10-13.
1949. _____. "Le paysage urbain du Québec." *Geogr Bull* 10 (1957):23-25.
1950. _____. "Les ports de la province de Québec." *Cah géogr Q* 3 (1959): 393-401.
1951. **Careless, William.** "The Architecture of French Canada." *JRAIC* 2 (1925):141-45.
1952. **Castelli, Mireille D.** "L'habitation urbaine en Nouvelle-France." *Cah de droit* 16 (1975):403-30.
1953. **Charette, François.** "Le financement des gouvernements municipaux par l'emprunt obligataire." *Can Bank* 71, no. 3 (1963):71-77.
1954. **Charney, Melvin, and Bélanger, Marcel.** *Architecture et urbanisme au Québec.* Montréal: Presses de l'université de Montréal, 1971.
1955. **Charpentier, Alfred.** "La grève du textile dans le Québec en 1937." *Relat indus* 20, no. 1 (1965):86-128.
1956. **Château, J.-P.** "Croissance et structure des secteurs manufacturiers au Québec et en Ontario, 1949-63." *Ac Ec* 44 (1968):492-527.
1957. **Cimon, Jean.** "L'explosion urbaine au Canada français." *Relations* 236 (1960):205-7.
1958. **Clark, S. D.** "The Position of the French-Speaking Population in the Northern Industrial Community." In *Canadian Society in Historical Perspective,* by S. D. Clark, pp. 91-114. Toronto: McGraw-Hill Ryerson, 1976.
1959. **Coupal, Michel.** "Le financement des municipalités." Thèse de M.A., Montréal, 1965.
1960. **Davies, J. B.** "An Analysis of City Size Distribution in Ontario and Quebec." M.A. thesis, Toronto, 1970.
1961. **Dechêne, Louise, and Robert, Jean-Claude.** "Le choléra de 1832 dans le Bas-Canada: Mesure des inégalités devant la mort." In *The Great Mortalities: Methodological Studies of Demographic Crises in the Past/Les Grandes Mortalités: Etude méthodologique des crises démographiques du passé,* edited by Hubert Charbonneau and André Larose, pp. 229-56. Liège: Ondina, 1979.
1962. **Demers, Armand.** "Esquisse sur l'urbanisme régional au 'Royaume du Saguenay.' " *RCU* 7, no. 1 (1957):64-68.

1963. **Denis, Paul Yves.** "La présence urbaine au Québec et dans l'Ontario: Aspects et tendances de son évolution mis en relief par quelques critères de comparaison." *RCGG* 17 (1963):3-8.
1964. **Deschamps, Clement E.** *Municipalités et paroisses dans la province de Québec.* Quebec: Brousseau, 1896.
1965. **Desjardins, Bertrand; Beauchamp, Pierre; and Légaré, Jacques.** "Automatic Family Reconstruction: The French-Canadian Seventeenth Century Experience." *J Fam Hist* 2 (1977):56-76.
1966. **Desjardins, Micheline.** *Québec. Initiation à la géographie urbaine.* Montréal: Holt, Rinehart et Winston, 1970.
1967. **Desrochers, Gilles.** "Les avantages économiques à attendre des fusions municipales." *Ac Ec* 40 (1965):816-23.
1968. **Dorion, C.-N.** "Evolution de la législation générale et spéciale concernant les corporations municipales de la province de Québec après la Confederation." Dans *Mémoire présenté à la Commission Tremblay par l'union des municipalités de la province de Québec,* pp. 316-484. Québec, 1954.
1969. **Doucet, Jean-Louis.** *Composition et pouvoirs des commissions d'urbanisme.* Québec: Ministère des affaires municipales, 1962.
1970. **Drapeau, Julien.** "Histoire du régime municipal au Québec (première partie)." *RCU* 18, no. 4 (1968):12-15; "Deuxième partie," 19, no. 1 (1969):27-29; "Troisième partie," 19, no. 2 (1969):24-27.
1971. **Dubuc, Alfred.** "Problems in the Study of the Stratification of Canadian Society from 1760-1840." CHA, *AR* (1965):12-29.
1972. **Dugas, R.** "La polarisation spatiale: Le cas de capitales régionales au Québec." Thèse de M.A., Laval, 1975.
1973. **Duncan, M.** "The French Canadian Population: Its Distribution and Development." M.A. thesis, Aberdeen, 1944.
1974. **Durand, Guy.** "Le tissu urbain québécois, 1941-1961: Evolution des structures urbaines de l'industrie et des occupations." *Rech soc* 18 (1977):133-57.
1975. **Durocher, René, and Linteau, Paul-André.** *Histoire du Québec: Bibliographie selective (1867-1970).* Montréal: Boréal Express, 1974.
1976. **Durrand, Gilles.** "Histoire urbaine: Sources." *Archives* 2 (1973): 23-34.
1977. **Falardeau, Jean-Charles.** "The Seventeenth Century Parish in French Canada." In *French Canadian Society,* edited by Marcel Rioux and Yves Martin, pp. 19-32. Vol. 1. Toronto: M&S, 1964.
1978. **Faucher, Albert.** "L'émigration des Canadiens français au XIXe siècle." *Rech soc* 5 (1964):277-317.
1979. _____. *Québec en Amérique au XIXe siècle.* Montréal: Fides, 1973.
1980. _____, and Lamontagne, Maurice. "History of Industrial Development." In *Essais sur le Québec contemporain,* edited by Jean-Charles Falardeau, pp. 23-37. Québec: Presses de l'université Laval, 1953.
1981. **Fauteux, Joseph-Noël.** *Essai sur l'industrie au Canada sous le régime français.* Quebec: Proulx, 1927.
1982. **Fizet, Edouard.** "Vers un organisme provincial d'urbanisme." *RCU* 1, no. 3 (1951):83-87.
1982A.**Fortin, Gérald.** "Le Québec: Une ville à inventer." *Rech soc* 9, nos. 1-2 (1968):11-21.
1983. _____. *La fin d'un règne.* Montréal: Hurtubise HMH, 1971.
1984. _____. "La sociologie urbaine au Québec: Un bilan." *SS* 4 (1972):7-13.
1985. **Fournier, Laval.** "Une typologie des centres urbains du Québec." Thèse de M.A., Ottawa, 1976.
1986. **Fraser, Graham.** "The Urban Politics of the P.Q." *City Mag* 3, no. 6 (1978):21-31.
1987. **Gagnon, Antoine.** "Organisation municipale." *CV* 7 (1964):51-59.

1988. **Gagnon, R.** *Les cantons de l'est.* Montréal: Holt, Rinehart et Winston, 1970.
1989. **Galarneau, Claude.** *La France devant l'opinion canadienne, 1760-1815.* Québec: Presses de l'université Laval, 1970.
1990. **Gariépy, Wilfrid.** *La paroisse urbaine.* Montréal: Institut social populaire, 1953.
1991. **Garigue, Philippe.** "French Canadian Kinship and Urban Life." In *French-Canadian Society,* edited by Marcel Rioux and Yves Martin, pp. 358-71. Vol. 1. Toronto: M&S, 1964.
1992. _____. "Une enquête sur l'industrialisation de la Province de Québec." *Ac Ec* 33 (1957):419-36.
1993. **Germain, Annick.** "Histoire urbaine et histoire de l'urbanisation au Québec: Brève revue des travaux réalisés au cours de la décennie." *UHR* 3-78 (février 1979):3-22.
1994. **Gervais, Gaetan.** "L'expansion du réseau ferroviaire québecois, 1875-1895." Thèse de Ph.D., Ottawa, 1978.
1995. **Godin, J.** "Mécanismes de participation et démocratie locale: Quatre municipalités de la vallée du Richelieu." Thèse de M.A., Québec à Montréal, 1972.
1996. **Golant, S., and Bourne, L. S.** *Growth Characteristics of the Ontario-Quebec Urban System.* Research Paper #4. Toronto: CUCS, 1968.
1997. **Goldberg, S. A.** "The French Canadians and the Industrialization of Quebec." M.A. thesis, McGill, 1940.
1998. **Golding, P.** "British Settlement and Imperial Interests in Lower Canada, 1820-1841." Ph.D. thesis, London, 1978.
1999. **Gosselin, Emile.** "Principes généraux de l'administration municipale: Sa nature, ses fonctions, son territoire." *Mémoire présenté à la Commission royale d'enquête sur les problèmes constitutionnels par l'Union des municipalités de la province de Québec.* Etudes speciales, I. Québec, 1954.
2000. **Gouvernement du Québec.** *Répertoire des municipalités/Municipal Guide.* Québec: Ministère de l'industrie et du commerce, 1964.
2001. **Gowans, Alan.** "The Earliest Church Architecture of New France from the Foundation to 1665." *JRAIC* 26 (1949):291-98.
2002. _____. "The Baroque Revival in Quebec." *J Soc Arch Hist* 14 (1955):8-14.
2003. **Grant, George M.** *French Canadian Life and Character; with Historical and Descriptive Sketches of the Scenery and Life in Quebec, Montreal, Ottawa and Surrounding Country.* Chicago: Belford, 1889.
2004. **Greening, W. E.** *History of the Eastern Townships.* Montreal: Harvest House, 1977.
2005. **Greenwood, Frank M.** "The Development of a Garrison Mentality among the English in Lower Canada, 1793-1811." Ph.D. thesis, British Columbia, 1971.
2006. **Groupe de travail sur l'urbanisation.** "Rappel historique de l'évolution urbaine au Québec." In *L'urbanisation au Québec,* pp. 23-29. Quebec: Editeur officiel du Québec, 1976.
2007. **Hamel, P., and Rouleau, P.** *Orientations et tendances de la politique urbanistique au Québec.* Montréal: CRIU, 1972.
2008. **Hamelin, Louis-Edmond.** "Un puissant exemple d'émigration rurale à l'échelon paroissial." *Géogr canad* 5 (1955):53-61.
2009. **Harvey, Fernand.** "Nouvelles perspectives sur l'histoire sociale du Québec." *RHAF* 24 (1971):567-81.
2010. _____. "Technologie et organisation du travail à la fin au XIXe: Le cas du Québec." *Rech soc* 18 (1977):397-414.
2011. _____. *Révolution industrielle et travailleurs. Une enquête sur les rapports entre le capital et le travail au Québec à la fin du 19e siècle.* Montréal: Boréal Express, 1978.
2012. **Hébert, Serge.** "L'histoire de l'industrie textile des cantons de l'est." Thèse de M.A., Sherbrooke, 1976.

2013. **Henripin, Jacques, and Martin, Yves.** *La population du Québec et de ses régions, 1961-1981.* Québec: Presses de l'université Laval, 1964.
2014. **Hilton, D. K.** "The Iron Mining Communities of Quebec-Labrador: A Study of a Resource Frontier." M.A. thesis, McGill, 1968.
2015. **Hughes, Everett C.** "Industry and the Rural System in Quebec." *CJEPS* 4 (1938):341-49.
2016. ———. "The Problem of Planning in Quebec." In *Housing and Community Planning*, pp. 156-65. McGill University Monograph Series. Montreal, 1944.
2017. **Jones, Murray V.** "Local Government Boundaries in Québec." M.A. thesis, McGill, 1951.
2018. **Keyfitz, Nathan.** "L'exode rural dans la province de Québec, 1951-1961." *Rech soc* 3, no. 3 (1962):303-16.
2019. **King, Leslie J.** "Discriminatory Analysis of Urban Growth Patterns in Ontario and Quebec, 1951-1961." *AAAG* 57 (1967):566-78.
2020. **Laberge, L.** "L'immigration et l'industrialisation du Canada français." *Culture* 18 (1957):14-20.
2021. ———. "Le Québec et les migrations interrégionales au Canada." *Culture* 18 (1957):155-72.
2022. **Lamonde, Yvan.** *Guide d'histoire du Québec.* Montréal: Boréal Express, 1976.
2023. **Lamontagne, Maurice, and Falardeau, Jean-Charles.** "The Life Cycle of French Canadian Urban Families." *CJEPS* 13 (1947):233-47.
2024. **Lanctôt, Gustave.** "Le régime municipal en Nouvelle-France." *Culture* 9 (1948):255-83.
2025. **Laneuville, André.** "Le financement de la rénovation urbaine." Thèse de M.A., Montréal, 1964.
2026. **Langlois, Georges.** *Histoire de la population canadienne-française.* Montréal: Lévesque, 1935.
2027. **Lapointe, Gérard.** "Le pouvoir municipal: Une recherche sociologique." *Rech soc* 2 (1961):401-36.
2028. **Laporte, Pierre.** "L'urbanisme dans la province de Québec en 1963." *RCU* 13, no. 4 (1963):24-25.
2029. **Laurin, J.-E.** *Histoire économique de Montréal et des cités et villes du Québec.* Ottawa: Laurin, 1942.
2030. **Lavedan, Pierre.** "Problèmes de l'urbanisme" *Rev univ Laval* 4B (1950):950-59.
2031. **Lavigne, Jacques.** "Mesure des migrations internes au Canada sous le régime français." Thèse de M.A., Montréal, 1974.
2032. **Lavoie, Yolande.** *L'émigration des Canadiens aux Etats-Unis avant 1930. Mesure du phénomène.* Montréal: Presses de l'université de Montréal, 1972.
2033. **Légaré, Anne.** *Les classes sociales au Québec.* Montréal: Presses de l'université du Québec, 1977.
2034. **Lessard, Marc-André.** "Bibliographie des villes du Québec." *Rech soc* 9 (1968):143-209.
2035. ———, **and Montminy, Jean-Paul, eds.** *L'urbanisation de la société canadienne-française.* Québec: Presses de l'université Laval, 1967.
2036. **Lessard, Michel, and Marquis, H.** "La maison québécoise, une maison qui se souvient." *Forces* 17 (1971):4-22.
2036A.**Letarte, Jacques.** *Atlas d'histoire économique et sociale du Québec, 1851-1901.* Montréal: Fides, 1971.
2037. **Lieff, P. J.** "The Urbanization of the French Canadian Parish." M.A. thesis, McGill, 1940.
2038. **Linteau, Paul-André.** "L'histoire urbaine au Québec: Bilan et tendances." *UHR* 1-72 (février 1972):7-10.
2039. ———. "Quelques réflexions autour de la bourgeoisie québécoise 1850-1914." *RHAF* 30 (1976):55-66.

2040. _____; Durocher, René; and Robert, Jean-Claude. *Histoire du Québec contemporain de la Confédération à la crise.* Montréal: Boréal Express, 1979.

2041. **Little, Jack.** "French Canadian Colonization of the Eastern Townships, 1850-1893." Ph.D. thesis, Ottawa, 1976.

2042. **McCullough, J. W. S.** "Early History of Public Health in Upper and Lower Canada." *Can J Medicine and Surgery* 51 (1922):60-84.

2043. **Mangala, M.** "Urbanisation et innovations en transport: L'exemple du Québec méridional." Thèse de M.A., Ottawa, 1973.

2044. **Manseau, H.** "La petite ville et le gros village du Québec." Thèse de M.A., Montréal, 1974.

2045. **Marier, Georges.** "Développements urbains dans Québec." *RCU* 4 (1954):41-44.

2046. **Marsan, Jean-Claude.** "Architecture in Quebec." *Can Coll* 13 (1978):72-76.

2047. **Martin, J.-M.** "La croissance urbaine dans le Québec." *RCU* 7, no. 1 (1957):6-9.

2048. **Martin, J.-P.** "Villes et régions du Québec au XIXe siècle: Approche géographique." Thèse 3e cycle, Louis Pasteur (Strasbourg), 1975.

2049. **Martin, Yves.** "Les agglomérations urbaines et les zones métropolitaines dans le recensement canadien." *Rech soc* 1 (1960):91-101.

2050. _____. "Les études urbaines." In *Situation de la recherche sur le Canada français,* edited by F. Dumont and Yves Martin, pp. 119-32. Québec: Presses de l'université Laval, 1962.

2051. _____. "Urban Studies in French Canada." In *French-Canadian Society,* edited by Marcel Rioux and Yves Martin, pp. 245-56. Vol. 1. Toronto: M & S, 1964.

2053. **Masters, D. C.** "The English Communities in Winnipeg and in the Eastern Townships of Quebec." In *Regionalism in the Canadian Community, 1867-1967,* edited by Mason Wade, pp. 130-59. Toronto: UTP, 1969.

2054. **Mayrand, Pierre.** "Relations spatiotemporelles de l'architecture et de l'urbanisme en Nouvelle-France." Conseil des monuments et sites du Québec, *Bulletin* 6 (1978):22-27.

2055. **Ménard, G.** "Décentralisation de la population urbaine et de l'industrie dans le Québec." Thèse, HEC (Montréal), 1950.

2056. **Messier, Camille, and Marois, Michèle R.** *L'intégration urbaine des migrants de l'est du Québec. Les Gaspésiens de la ville.* 2 vols. Montréal: Conseil de développement social du Montréal métropolitain, 1971.

2057. **Michaud, Laurent.** "Le déséquilibre urbain québecois." *Ac Ec* 44 (1968):128-40.

2058. **Miquelon, Dale.** *Dugard of Rouen: French Trade to Canada and the West Indies, 1729-1770.* Montreal: McGill-Queen's UP, 1978.

2059. **Moogk, Peter N.** "A Social History of Skilled Labour in New France." Ph.D. thesis, Toronto, 1968.

2060. _____. *Building a House in New France, An Account of the Perplexities of Client and Craftsmen in Early Canada.* Toronto: M&S, 1977.

2061. _____. "Manual Education and Economic Life in New France." *Studies in Voltaire and the Eighteenth Century* 167 (1977):125-68.

2062. **Morin, Denis.** "Allométrie du systèi.ie urbain du Québec (1941-1971)." *Cah géogr Q* 46 (1975):17-37.

2063. **Morin, R.** "L'analyse de localisation spatiale de trois centres commerciaux regionaux du Québec métropolitain." Thèse de M.A., Sherbrooke, 1975.

2064. **Morrison, N. M.** "Industry and Municipal Politics in Quebec." M.A. thesis, McGill, 1940.

2065. **Niellon, Françoise.** "Les sites fortifiés de Nouvelle-France." *Dossiers de l'archéologie* 27 (1978):81-86.

2066. **Norbert, Roland.** "Crédit municipal dans la province de Québec." Thèse de M.A., Montréal, 1936.

2067. **Olivier, M.** "Les logements ouvriers." *RTCN* 7 (1921):485-94.

2068. **Ouellet, Fernand.** *Histoire économique et sociale du Québec, 1760-1850. Structure et conjoncture.* Montréal: Fides, 1966. Revised and translated as *Economic and Social History of Quebec, 1760-1850.* Toronto: Macmillan, 1980.

2069. _____. "Dualité économique et changement technologique au Québec (1760-1790)." *HS* 18 (1976):256-96.

2070. _____. *Le Bas-Canada, 1791-1840: Changements structuraux et crise.* Ottawa: Editions de l'université d'Ottawa, 1976. Revised and translated as *Lower Canada, 1791-1840: Social Change and Nationalism.* Toronto: M&S, 1979.

2071. _____. "Officiers de milice et structure sociale au Québec (1660-1815)." *HS* 12 (1979):37-65.

2072. **Ouellet, J.** "Les caractéristiques de l'habitation urbaine au Québec en 1961." Thèse de D.E.S., Montréal, 1971.

2073. **Paquet, Gilles, and Wallot, Jean-Pierre.** "International Circumstances of Lower Canada, 1786-1810: Prolegomenon." *CHR* 53 (1972):371-401.

2074. **Parent, Gilles.** "Deux efforts de colonisation française dans les cantons de l'est, 1848 et 1851." Thèse de M.A., Sherbrooke, 1978.

2075. **Parenteau, Roland.** "L'administration municipale au Québec: les finances." *CCHA* 86 (1965):449-52.

2076. _____. "La législation fédérale sur l'habitation et ses résultats." *Ac Ec* 32 (1956):210-30.

2077. **Parizeau, Gérard.** *La société canadienne-française au XIXe siècle: Essais sur le milieu.* Montréal: Fides, 1975.

2078. **Parker, W. H.** "The Towns of Lower Canada in the 1830s." In *Urbanization and Its Problems,* edited by R. P. Beckinsale and J. N. Houston, pp. 391-425. Oxford: Basil Blackwell, 1970.

2079. **Péloquin, Bonaventure.** "Québec et l'urbanisme." *BRH* 63, no. 2 (1957):57-67.

2080. **Piché, Odessa.** *Municipalités, paroisses, cantons, etc., de la province de Québec de 1896 à 1924.* Québec: Ministère de la colonisation et des pêcheries, 1924.

2081. **Pierre-Deschenes, Claudine.** "La tuberculose au Québec au début au XXe siècle: Problème social et réponse réformiste." Thèse de M.A., Québec à Montréal, 1980.

2082. **Polèse, Mario, and Turpin, Pierre.** "L'évolution de la hierarchie tertiaire de villes: Le cas de la région du sud-est de Montréal, 1931-1966." *Ac Ec* 48 (1972):398-413.

2083. **Porter, John R.** "L'architecture québécoise dans l'oeuvre de Joseph Légaré." Conseil des monuments et sites du Québec, *Bulletin* 6 (1978):19-21.

2084. **Prézeau, Pierre.** "La prise de décision dans les problèmes métropolitains." Thèse de M.A., Laval, 1964.

2085. **Québec, Ministère des affaires municipales, Direction générale de la planification.** "La communauté urbaine: Une formule d'organisation et de gestion des agglomérations." *Annuaire du Québec* (1971): 1-40.

2086. **Raynault, André.** *Croissance et structure économique de la Province de Québec.* Québec: Ministère de l'industrie et du commerce, 1961.

2087. **Reynolds, Lloyd George.** *The British Immigrant: His Social and Economic Adjustment in Canada.* Toronto: OUP, 1935.

2088. **Rioux, Marcel.** "Kinship Recognition and Urbanization in French Canada." In *French-Canadian Society,* edited by Marcel Rioux and Yves Martin, pp. 372-85. Vol. 1. Toronto: M & S, 1964.

2089. **Robert, Georges.** "Plaidoyer pour un urbanisme québécois." *RCU* 12, no. 1 (1962):11-13.

2090. _____. "Recherche du concept d'aménagement d'un centre civique de ville moyenne au Québec." *RCU* 13, no. 3 (1962):26-33.

2091. **Robins, R.** "Liens inter-industriels et connexions inter-urbaines dans trois agglomérations importantes du Québec." Thèse de M.A., McGill, 1974.

2092. **Robitaille, André.** "Evolution de l'habitat au Canada français." *Architecture-Bâtiment-Construction* 21 (1966):32-38.

2093. **Rouillard, Jacques.** "L'action politique ouvrier au début du 20ᵉ siècle." In *Le mouvement ouvrière au Québec*, edited by Fernand Harvey, pp. 185-213. Montréal: Boréal Express, 1980.
2094. **Routaboule, D.** "Villes moyennes du Québec." *UL* 4 (1966):281-316.
2095. **Roy, Jean-Louis.** "Livres et société bas-canadienne, croissance et expansion de la librairie Fabre (1816-1855)." *HS* 5 (1972):117-43.
2096. _____. *Edouard-Raymond Fabre. Libraire et patriote canadien (1799-1854).* Montréal: HMH, 1974.
2097. **Roy, Jean-Marie.** "Québec, esquisse de géographie urbaine." *Can Geogr* 2 (1952):83-98.
2098. **Roy, Raymond; Landry, Yves; and Charbonneau, Hubert.** "Quelques comportements des Canadiens au XVIIᵉ siècle d'après les registres paroissiaux." *RHAF* 31 (1977):49-74.
2099. **Rudin, Ronald.** "The Development of Four Quebec Towns, 1840-1914: A Study of Urban and Economic Growth in Quebec." Ph.D. thesis, York, 1977.
2100. **Ryan, William F.** *The Clergy and Economic Growth in Quebec, 1896-1914.* Quebec: Presses de l'université Laval, 1966.
2101. **Sales, Arnaud.** *La bourgeoisie industrielle au Québec.* Montréal: Presses de l'université de Montréal, 1979.
2102. **Séguin, Normand.** *La conquête du sol au 19ᵉ siècle.* Montréal: Boréal Express, 1977.
2103. **Simard, Sylvain.** "L'image du Canada en France, 1850-1914." Thèse de Ph.D., Bordeaux III, 1975.
2104. **Smith, Charles D.** "The Role of Land Alienation, Colonization and the British American Land Company on Quebec's Development, 1800-1850." M.A. thesis, McGill, 1974.
2105. **Smith, F. N.** "The Establishment of Religious Communities in the Eastern Townships of Lower Canada, 1799 to 1851." M.A. thesis, McGill, 1976.
2106. **Southam, Peter.** "Evolution du gouvernement municipal au Québec de 1920 à 1939." Thèse de M.A., Laval, 1969.
2107. **Stamp, Robert M.** "Urbanization and Education in Ontario and Quebec, 1867-1914." *McGill J Educ* 3 (1968):127-35.
2108. **Taylor, Griffith.** "Town Patterns on the Gulf of Saint Lawrence." *CGEJ* 30 (1945):254-75.
2109. **Thouez, Jean-Pierre.** "Caractéristiques physio-chimiques de l'eau potable et la mortalité ischémique du coeur: Application aux municipalités des cantons de l'est (Québec)." *Can Geogr* 23 (1979):208-21.
2110. *Transformations municipales 1931-1961.* Québec: Ministère de l'industrie et du commerce, 1961.
2111. **Traquair, Ramsay.** "The Old Architecture of the Province of Quebec." *JRAIC* 2 (1925):25-30.
2112. _____. *The Old Architecture of Quebec: A Study of the Buildings Erected in New France from the Earliest Explorers to the Middle of the Nineteenth Century.* Toronto: Macmillan, 1947.
2113. **Tremblay, M.** *Inventaire descriptif des villes constituées au Québec de 1941 à 1971.* Québec: Université de Laval, 1974.
2114. **Trotier, Louis.** "Some Functional Characteristics of the Main Service Centres of the Province of Québec." In *Mélanges géographiques canadiens offerts à Raoul Blanchard,* edited by L.-E. Hamelin, pp. 243-59. Québec: Presses universitaires Laval, 1959.
2115. _____. "Transformations récentes de l'agglomération québécoise: Fonctions, population et organisation de l'espace." *Cah géogr Q* 13 (1962-63):7-26.
2116. _____. "Caractères de l'organisation urbaine de la province de Québec." *RCGG* 18 (1964):279-85.
2117. _____. "La genèse du réseau urbain du Québec." *Rech soc* 9 (1968):23-32.
2118. **Trudeau, Michelle.** "Classification of Centres in the Montreal Environs and Eastern Township Regions." M.A. thesis, McGill, 1966.

2119. **Trudel, Jacques.** "Notre environnement urbain." *Parti-pris* 2, no. 4 (1964):21-32.
2120. **Trudel, Marcel.** *Atlas historique du Canada français.* Québec: Presses de l'université Laval, 1961.
2121. _____. *La population du Canada en 1663.* Montréal: Fides, 1973.
2122. _____. *Le terrier du Saint-Laurent en 1663.* Ottawa: Editions de l'université d'Ottawa, 1973.
2123. **Turner, Philip J.** "The Development of Architecture in the Province of Quebec since Confederation." *CNST* 20 (June 1927):189-95.
2124. **Union des municipalités de la province de Québec.** *Mémoire soumis à la Commission royale d'enquête sur la fiscalité.* Montreal, 1964.
2125. **Vallières, M.** "Les industries manufacturières du Québec, 1900-1959: Essai de normalisation des données statistiques en dix-sept groupes industriels et étude sommaire de la croissance de ces groupes." Thèse de M.A., Laval, 1973.
2126. **Viau, Pierre.** *Les municipalités du Québec.* Montréal: Editions de la Place, 1969.
2127. **Weir, R. Stanley.** "Municipal Institutions in the Province of Quebec." In **#895,** pp. 165-92.
2128. **Woodhead, K. H.** "L'administration municipale au Québec: Problèmes de gestion." *CCHA* 86 (1965):370-76.

2. Arvida

2129. **Bélanger, Léonidas.** "La ville de l'Aluminium. Quelques données de base pour son histoire." *Saguenayensia* 13 (1971):62-67.
2130. **Eberts, E. H.** "Arvida and Kitimat: The Story of Two Industrial Community Development Properties." *Canadian Labour* 3 (1958):10-13.
2131. **Merrill, C. R.** "Model City Built by Aluminum Industry, Arvida, Québec." *ENCR* 58, no. 7 (1945):60-65.
2132. **Routhier, François.** *Jonquière-Kénogami-Arvida.* Québec: Centre de recherches en sociologie religieuse, 1965.

3. Asbestos

2133. **David, Hélène.** "La grève et le bon Dieu: La grève de l'amiante au Québec." *SS* 1 (1969):249-76.
2134. **Ethier, Jean-Marie.** "Le coût de la vie à Asbestos, en 1945." Thèse de M.A., Laval, 1946.
2135. **Isbister, Alexander Fraser.** "Another Look at the Asbestos Workers' Strike of 1949." M.A. thesis, Bishops, 1965.
2136. **McKenzie, Grace M.** "The Asbestos Strike, The Press and Public Opinion." M.A. thesis, Toronto, 1951.
2137. **Pépin, Fernand.** "La grève de l'amiante à Asbestos." Thèse de M.A., Montréal, 1952.
2138. **Ross, W. Gilles.** "Encroachment of the Jeffrey Mine on the Town of Asbestos, Quebec." *GEOR* 57 (1967):523-37.
2139. **Shay, Margaret E.** "The Asbestos Strike: A Case Study in the Breakdown in Industrial Communication." Ph.D. thesis, Fordham, 1951.
2140. **Trudeau, Pierre Elliott, ed.** *La grève de l'amiante.* Montréal: Jour, 1970. Translated as *The Asbestos Strike.* Toronto: James Lewis and Samuel, 1974.

4. Chicoutimi and the Saguenay Region

2141. **Angers, Lorenzo.** "Chicoutimi, poste de traite, 1720-1740." *Saguenayensia* 12, no. 1 (1970):2-8.

2142. _____. *Chicoutimi, poste de traite, 1676-1856*. Montréal: Leméac, 1971.
2143. **Bélanger, René.** *Les Escoumins*. Chicoutimi: Société historique du Saguenay, 1946.
2144. **Bouchard, Gérard.** "L'histoire démographique et le problème des migrations: L'exemple de Laterrière." *HS* 15 (1975):21-33.
2145. _____. "L'histoire de la population et l'étude de la mobilité sociale au Saguenay, XIXe-XXe siècles." *Rech soc* 17 (1976):353-72.
2146. _____. "Family Structures and Geographic Mobility at Laterrière, 1851-1935." *J Fam Hist* 2 (1977):350-69.
2147. _____. "Introduction à l'étude de la société saguenayenne aux XIXe et XXe siècles." *RHAF* 31 (1977):3-27.
2148. _____, and **Séguin, Normand.** "Pour une histoire de l'occupation du sol et de la propriété foncière au Saguenay." *Protée* 3, no. 3 (1971):33-39.
2149. _____, and **Bergeron, Michel.** "L'arpenteur J.-B. Duberger et les premiers recensements de la population saguenayenne au XIXe siècle." *Archives* 8, no. 3 (1976):11-20.
2150. **Bouchard, Louis-Marie.** "La conurbation du Haut-Saguenay, quelques aspects spatiaux." *Protée* 1 (1971):9-25.
2151. _____. "Les structures spatiales et l'interdépendance des villes dans la conurbation du Saguenay." *Cah géogr Q* 16 (1972):77-97.
2152. _____. *Les villes du Saguenay: Etude géographique*. Montréal: Leméac, 1973.
2153. **Brouillette, Benoît.** "L'habitat et la population au Saguenay." *Ac Ec* 22 (1947):646-71.
2154. **Cauchon, Noulan.** "Town Planning Project Act, Chicoutimi." *Can Engineer* 54 (1928):421-32.
2155. "Chicoutimi." *Commerce* 55, no. 10 (1953):24-39.
2156. **Delisle, A.** "Chicoutimi industriel." Thèse de M.A., Laval, 1951.
2157. **Drolet, Jean-Claude.** "Les problèmes pastoraux du diocèse de Chicoutimi d'après les décrets de Mgr. Racine." *Saguenayensia* 12 (1970):94-96.
2158. _____. "Un affrontement libéral-ultramontain au diocèse de Chicoutimi en 1888." *Saguenayensia* 13 (1971):74-76.
2159. _____. "Le chapitre de Chicoutimi." *Saguenayensia* 14 (1972):2-5.
2160. _____. "Un parlement-modèle au Séminaire de Chicoutimi en 1912-1913." *Saguenayensia* 14 (1972):74-83.
2161. _____. "Un collège-séminaire à Chicoutimi en 1873." *Saguenayensia* 14 (1972):118-34.
2162. **Fortin, Jacinthe.** "La guignolée à Chicoutimi autour des années '30." *Saguenayensia* 13 (1971):161-63.
2163. **Harvey, Jacquelin.** "Le port de Chicoutimi." *Rev géogr Mtl* 22 (1968):149-57.
2164. **Higgs, R. W.** "Chicoutimi—L'aire métropolitaine oubliée." *RCU* 16, no. 1 (1966):15-19.
2165. **Ouellet, M.-F.** "Evolution des fonctions urbaines de Chicoutimi." *Can Geogr* 1 (1951):25-30.
2166. "Regional Plan for the Saguenay District and the Hinterland of Quebec." *TPICJ* 7, no. 2 (1928):31-233.
2167. **Rheault, C.** "Etude comparative des monts urbains dans les villes de Chicoutimi, Jonquière, Kénagami et Chicoutimi-Nord." Thèse de L ès L., Laval, 1972.
2168. **Rouillard, O. E.** "Chicoutimi et Lac St. Jean." *BSGQ* 2 (1911):157-84.
2169. **Rouleau, Jean-Paul.** *Chicoutimi: Contexte socio-religieux et adaptation pastorale*. Québec: Université de Laval, 1968.
2170. **Simard, André.** *Les evêques et les prêtres séculiers du diocèse de Chicoutimi (1878-1968): Notices biographiques*. Chicoutimi: Chancellerie de l'évêché, 1969.
2171. **Tremblay, Victor.** "Les fondateurs de Chicoutimi." *Saguenayensia* 12 (1970):51-52.
2172. _____. "La fondation de Chicoutimi." *Saguenayensia* 13 (1971):59-61.

5. Drummondville

2173. **Biron, Robert.** "Drummondville, centre industriel et commercial des cantons de l'est." Thèse, HEC (Montréal), 1947.
2174. *The City of Drummondville, Quebec, Canada: An Economic Appreciation of Its Industrial, Commercial, Social, and Cultural Aspects.* Montreal: Dominion Management Associates, 1951.
2175. **Fournier, Jocelyn.** "Napoléon Garceau (1868-1945): Un Drummondvillais méconnu de l'histoire." Thèse de M.A., Sherbrooke, 1978.
2176. **Gauvin, D.** "Evolution de la structure industrielle de Drummondville." Thèse de L. ès L., Laval, 1973.
2177. **Hughes, Everett C.** *French Canada in Transition.* Chicago: University of Chicago Press, 1943. Translated as *Rencontre de deux mondes: La crise d'industrialisation du Canada français.* 1944. Reprint. Montréal: Boréal Express, 1972.
2178. **Pésant, Y.** "Expérience de rénovation urbaine dans le secteur Saint-Joseph à Drummondville." Thèse de L. ès L., Laval, 1973.
2179. **Poirier, R.** "Evolution de l'habitat urbain de Drummondville." Essai de B.A., Sherbrooke, 1974.
2180. **Rajotte, E. C.** *Drummondville: 150 ans de vie quotidienne au coeur du Québec.* Drummondville: Cantons, 1972.

6. Granby

2181. **Begin, Benoît-J., and Robert, Georges.** "Résumé du Rapport d'accompagnement du plan directeur d'urbanisme de la ville de Granby." *ACTU* 15 (1960):288-93.
2182. **Brodeur, Serge.** "L'avenir économique de Granby." Thèse, HEC (Montréal), 1963.
2183. **Fontaine, Gabriel.** "Granby, ville industrielle." *Ac Ec* 24 (1948):112-32.
2184. **Lavallée, Jean.** "Granby, étude de géographie urbaine." Thèse de M.A., Montréal, 1968.

7. Hull

2185. **Andrew, Caroline; Blais, André; and Des Rosiers, Rachel.** "Le logement public à Hull." *CJPS* 8 (1975):403-30.
2186. **Aubin, V.-P., and Bérubé, A.-E.** *Hull industriel.* Hull, 1908.
2187. **Bilodeau, B.** "Structure spatiale du commerce de détail dans le quartier Montcalm à Hull." Thèse de L. ès L., Laval, 1972.
2188. **Bordeleau, S., and Guimont, A.** "Luttes urbaines à Hull." Thèse de M.A., Laval, 1976.
2189. **Boult, Jean-Claude.** "Bibliographie de l'histoire de Hull: Inventaire préliminaire." *Asticou* 9 (1972):31-42.
2190. **Boutet, Edgar.** *85 ans de théâtre à Hull.* Hull: Société historique de l'ouest du Québec, 1969.
2191. **Brault, Lucien.** *Hull, 1800-1950.* Hull: Editions de l'université d'Ottawa, 1950.
2192. _____. *Un siècle d'administration scolaire: La commission des écoles catholiques de Hull, 1866-1966.* Hull: Commission des écoles catholique de Hull, 1966.
2193. **Brown, Roger James.** "The City of Hull." B.A. essay, Toronto, 1952.
2194. **Carrière, Gaston.** *Le Père Louis-Etienne Reboul, organisateur de la vie religieuse de Hull et apôtre des chantiers.* Ottawa: Editions de l'université d'Ottawa, 1959.
2195. _____. "L'établissement de l'église à Hull et dans la région." *Rev univ Ottawa* 39 (1969):586-626.
2196. **Cinq-Mars, Eugène.** *Hull, son origine, ses progrès, son avenir.* Hull: Bérubé, 1908.

2197. **Côté, Denise.** "La participation des citoyens aux organismes communautaires de Hull: Une étude de l'assemblée générale de l'Ile de Hull." Thèse de M.A., Ottawa, 1975.
2198. **Craigie, Cynthia Helen.** "The Influence of the Timber Trade and Philemon Wright on the Social and Economic Development of Hull Township, 1800-1856." M.A. thesis, Carleton, 1969.
2199. **Desjardins, M. A.** "La rénovation urbaine à Hull." *CV* 7 (1964):34-39.
2200. **Elliot, Bruce S.** " 'The Famous Township of Hull': Image and Aspirations of a Pioneer Quebec Community." *HS* 24 (1979):339-67.
2201. **Guértin, Pierre-S.** "Rénovation urbaine d'un quartier résidentiel désaffecté de la cité de Hull." *Architecture-Bâtiment-Construction* 18 (1963):38-42.
2202. **Kayser, Edmond.** "Industry in Hull: Its Origins and Development, 1800-1961." M.A. thesis, Ottawa, 1967.
2203. **Labelle, Rhéal.** "Monographie industrielle de la compagnie E. B. Eddy, Hull." Thèse de M.A., Laval, 1953.
2204. **Laflamme, H.** "Monographie de la ville de Hull." Thèse de M.A., Montréal, 1964.
2205. **Lapointe, Michelle.** "Le syndicat catholique des allumettières de Hull, 1919-1924." *RHAF* 32 (1979):603-28.
2206. **Lelièvre, A. B.** "Settlement of Hull." WCHSO, *Trans* 3 (1910):5-12.
2207. **Lendray-Zwicki, Joseph B.** "Shopping Centre Growth and the Decline of the Central Business District in an Urban System: A Case Study of the Ottawa-Hull Census Metropolitan Area." M.A. thesis, Ottawa, 1978.
2208. **Materazzi, F.** "Urban Growth and Land Use in Hull." M.A. thesis, McGill, 1979.
2209. **May, Edward G., and Millen, Walter H.** *The History of the Parish of Hull, Quebec, 1823-1923.* Ottawa: Dodson Merrill, 1923.
2210. **Rheault, Michel.** "Structure routière et structure urbaine: Un exemple d'approche typologique: Le cas de la région fonctionnelle d'Ottawa-Hull." Thèse de M.A., Ottawa, 1973.
2211. **Rossignol, Léo F.** "Aux origines de Hull." *Rev univ Ottawa* 10 (1940):408-17.
2212. ———. "Débuts de Hull, 1792-1842." Thèse de M.A., Ottawa, 1940.
2213. ———. "Histoire documentaire de Hull, 1792-1900." Thèse de Ph.D., Ottawa, 1941.
2214. ———; **Lapointe, Pierre-Louis; and Carrière, Gaston.** *Hull, 1800-1975: Histoire illustrée.* Hull: Comité de la Grande fête de Hull, 1975.
2215. **Rugg, Robert D.** "The Use and Non-Use of Urban Parks: Accessibility and Social Characteristics in Relation to Public Outdoor Recreation in Selected Neighbourhoods of Ottawa-Hull." Ph.D. thesis, Ottawa, 1974.
2216. **Saint-Amour, Jean-Pierre.** *L'Outaouais québécois—Guide de recherche et bibliographie sélective.* Hull: Centre d'études universitaires dans l'ouest québécois, Université du Québec, 1978.

8. Joliette

2217. **Beauregard, Ludger.** "Joliette, pépinière de petites industries." *Technique* 28, no. 2 (1953):95-102.
2218. **Corbeil, Wilfrid.** "Le musée d'art de Joliette." *Vie des Arts* 28 (1971):40-43.
2219. **Fontaine, L.** "Joliette, centre industriel." Thèse, HEC (Montréal), 1944.
2220. **Hamelin, Louis-Edmond.** "Aspects de la géographie sociale de la cité de Joliette." Thèse de M.A., Laval, 1948.
2221. **Maheux, Louis-Philippe.** "Etude économique de Joliette." Thèse, HEC (Montréal), 1948.
2222. **Malo, Roch.** "La ville de Joliette, les facteurs de développement économique." Thèse de licence, Montréal, 1962.
2223. **Marsolais, Jean-Marc.** "La région de Joliette." Thèse de licence, Laval, 1948.

2224. **Martel, Pierre-G.** "Joliette: Dix ans d'évolution psychiatrique." *Laval Médical* 42 (1971):1-3.
2225. **Robert, Jean-Claude.** "L'activité économique de Barthelemy Joliette et la fondation du village d'Industrie (Joliette), 1822-1850." Thèse de M.A., Montréal, 1971.
2226. _____. "Un seigneur entrepreneur: Barthelemy Joliette et la fondation du village d'Industrie (Joliette), 1822-1850." *RHAF* 26 (1972):375-95.
2227. **Simard, Réal.** "Les centrales diocésaines de Joliette." Thèse de M.A., Montréal, 1955.

9. Montreal and Environs

a. General

2228. **Andrew, Caroline.** "Synthèse bibliographique: Espace et politique: le cas de Montréal." *CJPS* 12 (1979):369-83.
2229. **Atherton, William Henry.** *Montreal (1534-1914)*. 3 vols. Montreal: Clarke, 1914.
2230. _____. *History of the Harbour Front of Montreal*. Montreal: City Improvement League, 1935.
2231. **Aubin, Henry.** *Les vrais propriétaires de Montréal*. Montréal: Etincelle, 1977. Translated as *City for Sale*. Toronto: Lorimer, 1978.
2232. **Auclair, Elie-J.** *Saint-Jean Baptiste de Montréal, monographie paroissiale, 1874-1924*. Québec, 1924.
2232A. _____. *Histoire de Châteauguay, 1735-1935*. Montréal: Beauchemin, 1935.
2233. _____. "Les origines de Châteauguay." RSC, *Trans*, 29 (1935):57-66.
2234. _____. *Saint-Henri des Tanneries de Montréal*. Montréal, 1942.
2235. **Baillargeon, Georges.** *La survivance du régime seigneurial à Montréal: Un régime qui ne veut pas mourir*. Montréal: Cercle du livre de France, 1968.
2236. **Baillargeon, H.-P.** *Le Carmel de Montréal: Ses racines, sa spiritualité, sa vie*. Montréal: Fides, 1977.
2237. **Barbeau, Victor.** *Ville, ô ma ville*. Montréal: Société des ecrivains canadiens, 1941.
2238. _____, éd. *Regards sur Montréal*. Montréal: Cahier de l'académie canadienne-française, 1966.
2239. **Beaudin, François.** "Guide des archives judiciaires de Montréal." *Archives* 70, no. 2 (1970):43-56.
2240. **Beaulieu, Claude.** "The Preservation of Old Montreal." *Can Coll* 9, no. 3 (1974):20-28.
2241. **Beauregard, Ludger.** "Montréal, métropole industrielle de Québec." *Technique* 28, no. 7 (1953):461-69.
2242. _____. "La plaine du Richelieu, banlieue agricole de Montréal." *RCGG* 13 (1959):19-37.
2243. _____, ed. *Montréal. Guide d'excursions—Field Guide*. 22e Congrès international de géographie. Montréal: Presses de l'université de Montréal, 1972.
2244. **Bélanger, Marcel, and Trotier, Louis.** *L'urbanisation de la région de Montréal: Essai de bibliographie analytique*. Québec: Université de Laval, Dept. de géographie, 1975.
2245. **Bellman, David.** *Mont-Royal Montréal/Mount Royal Montreal*. Montréal: McCord Museum, 1977.
2246. **Bensley, Edward Horton.** *The Montreal General Hospital since 1821*. Montreal, 1971.
2247. **Bernier, Jeanne.** *Trois siècles de charité à l'Hôtel-Dieu de Montréal*. Montréal: Therien, 1949.
2248. **Bertrand, Camille.** *Histoire de Montréal, 1760-1940*. 2 vols. Montréal: Beauchemin, 1935-1942.
2249. **Blanchard, Raoul.** *L'ouest du Canada français. Tome premier: Montréal et sa région*. Montréal: Beauchemin, 1953.

2250. **Bland, John.** "Domestic Architecture in Montreal." *Culture* 9 (1948):399-407.
2251. _____. "Effect of Nineteenth Century Manners on Montreal." *JRAIC* 33 (1956):414-17.
2252. **Borthwick, John Douglas.** *History of the Montreal Prison.* Montreal: Périard, 1886.
2253. _____. *History and Biographical Gazetteer of Montreal to the Year 1892.* Montreal: Lovell, 1892.
2254. _____. *History of Montreal including the Streets of Montreal.* Montreal: Gallagher, 1897.
2255. **Bourassa, Guy.** "The Political Elite of Montreal: From Aristocracy to Democracy." In #870, pp. 124-34.
2256. **Bourdon, Joseph-Pierre.** *Montréal-Matin: Son histoire, ses histoires.* Montréal: La Presse, 1978.
2257. **Bourguignon, J. C.** "Montréal, ville portuaire, 1535-1867." *RCU* 13 (1963):18-25.
2258. **Brouillard, Pierre.** "Bref aperçu des archives du port de Montréal." *Archives* 8 (1976):10-15.
2259. **Brouillette, Benoît.** "Le port de Montréal." *Ac Ec* 11 (1935):113-45.
2260. _____. "Le développement industriel du port de Montréal." *Ac Ec* 14 (1938):201-21.
2261. _____. "Le port de Vancouver (comparé au port de Montréal)." *Ac Ec* 29 (1953):448-80.
2262. _____. "Le port de Montréal, hier et aujourd'hui." *Rev géogr Mtl* 21 (1967):195-233.
2263. **Bruchési, Jean.** *De Ville-Marie à Montréal.* Montréal: L'Arbre, 1942.
2264. **Burrill, M. F.** "Studies in the Industrial Geography of Montreal." Ph.D. thesis, Clark, 1930.
2265. **Campeau, Charles-Edouard.** *Les espaces libres à Montréal.* Montréal: Beauchemin, 1926.
2266. _____. "La canalisation du Saint-Laurent et la région de Montréal." *Relations* 173 (1955):120-22; 175 (1955):187-88; 176 (1955):205-6.
2267. **Camu, Pierre.** "Types de maisons dans la région suburbaine de Montréal." *Can Geogr* no. 9 (1957):21-29.
2268. **Carter, David G.** "Le musée des beaux-arts de Montréal." *Vie des Arts* 63 (1971):20-27.
2269. *Catalogue de la bibliothèque administrative des archives municipales et inventaire chronologique des cartes et des plans de Montréal, 1534-1918.* Montréal, 1918.
2270. **Chambers, Ernest J.** *The Book of Montreal: A Souvenir of Canada's Commercial Metropolis.* Montreal: Book of Montreal Co., 1903.
2271. **Chevrette, F.; Marx, H.; and Tremblay, A.** *Les problèmes constitutionels posés par le restructuration scolaire de l'Ile de Montréal.* Québec: Editeur officiel du Québec, 1972.
2272. **Choko, Marc Henri.** *Cent ans de crises du logement à Montréal: Bibliographie chronologique.* Montréal: CRIU, 1978.
2273. **Choquette, R.** *Montréal.* Montréal: Leméac, 1965.
2274. **Collard, Edgar A.** *Montreal Yesterdays.* Don Mills: Longmans, 1962.
2275. _____. *Call Back Yesterdays.* Don Mills: Longmans, 1965.
2276. _____. *The Story of Dominion Square, Place du Canada.* Don Mills: Longmans, 1971.
2277. _____. *A Very Human Story: A Brief History of the Royal Trust Company, Its First 75 Years.* Montreal: Royal Trust Co., 1975.
2278. _____. *Montreal: The Days That Are No More.* Toronto: Doubleday, 1976.
2279. **Collard, K. B.** "Montreal and Toronto." In *Great Cities of the World,* edited by W. A. Robson, pp. 353-82. New York: Macmillan, 1957.
2280. **Conklin, E. N.** "Women's Voluntary Associations in French Montreal: A Study of Changing Institutions and Attitudes." Ph.D. thesis, Illinois (Urbana), 1972.
2281. **Cooper, J. J.** "Hotels in Montreal." *JRAIC* 33 (1956):420-23.
2282. **Cooper, John Irwin.** *Montreal: The Story of Three Hundred Years.* Montreal: Lamirande, 1942.
2283. _____. *The Blessed Communion: The Origins and History of the Diocese of Montreal, 1760-1960.* Montreal: Archives Committee of the Diocese of Montreal, 1960.

2284. _____. *Montreal: A Brief History*. Montreal: McGill-Queen's UP, 1967.
2285. **Crone, Kennedy.** "La Ville de Montréal." *CGEJ* 3 (1931):3-45.
2286. **Cross, Harold C.** *100 Years of Service: The Story of the Montreal Y.M.C.A.* Montreal: Southam Press, 1951.
2287. **Culliton, John, ed.** *Leacock's Montreal*. Toronto: M&S, 1963.
2288. **Dale, Allan.** "Châteauguay." *CGEJ* 11 (1935):33-41.
2289. **Davidson, N. M.** "Montreal's Dominance of the Canadian Men's Fine Clothing Industry." M.A. thesis, Western Ontario, 1969.
2290. **Davis, Richard E.** "The Montreal Young Men's Christian Association as a Religious and Social Organization." M.A. thesis, McGill, 1927.
2291. **Dawson, C. A.** "The City as an Organism." *TPICJ* 5, no. 4 (1926):17-20.
2292. **DeGrandmont, Eloi, and Martin-Tard, Louis.** *Montréal-Guide*. Montréal: Jour, 1967.
2293. **Delfosse, Georges.** *Vieux Montréal historique*. Montréal: Delfosse, 1932.
2294. **Denis, Paul-Yves.** "L'évolution des quartiers/The Development of the Various Districts." In #2243, pp. 78-89.
2295. **Denison, Merrill.** *Canada's First Bank: A History of the Bank of Montreal*. Toronto: M&S, 1966.
2296. **Desjardins, Edouard.** "Un duel résultant d'une polémique autour de l'Hôtel-Dieu et du Montreal General Hospital." *UMCA* 100 (1971):530-35.
2297. _____. "Le centenaire de la Société Médicale de Montréal." *UMCA* 100 (1971):1188-94.
2298. **De Volpi, C. P., and Winkworth, P. S.** *Montreal: A Pictorial Record, 1535-1885*. 2 vols. Montreal: Dev-Sco, 1963.
2299. **Déziel, Julien.** *Essai d'histoire de Verdun*. Verdun: Comité du Centenaire, 1976.
2300. **D'Iberville-Moreau, Luc.** *Lost Montreal*. Toronto: OUP, 1975.
2301. _____. "Le château Dufresne et la conservation du jeune patrimoine." *Vie des arts* 87 (1977):12-15.
2302. **Dolmat, Waclaw B.** "Histoire des paroisses polonaises à Montréal." Thèse de M.A., Montréal, 1952.
2303. **Douglas, Muriel H.** "A History of the Society for the Protection of Women and Children in Montreal, 1882-1966." M.S.W. thesis, McGill, 1967.
2304. **Doyon Charles.** "The Guarantee Trust Company: A Study in Bonding." M.A. thesis, McGill, 1980.
2305. **Edwards, M. J.** "Fiction and Montreal, 1769-1885." Ph.D. thesis, Toronto, 1969.
2306. **Feindel, Susan T., et al.** *Mansions of the Golden Square Mile*. Montreal: Concordia University, 1976.
2307. **Ferland-Angers, Albertine.** "La citadelle de Montréal (1658-1820)." *RHAF* 3 (1950):492-517.
2308. **Gérin-Lajoie, Henri.** "Les archives municipales de la ville de Montréal." *UHR* 2-74 (octobre 1974):2-4.
2309. **Germano, J.** "Histoire de la charité à Montréal." *Rev canad* 32 (1896):423-38.
2310. **Gibbard, Harold A.** "The Means and Modes of Living of European Immigrants in Montreal." M.A. thesis, McGill, 1934.
2311. **Gibbon, J. M.** *Our Old Montreal*. Toronto: M&S, 1947.
2312. **Gibbs, Phillip F.** "The Physical Characteristics of Suburban Development with Special Reference to the Lakeshore Communities of Montreal." M.Arch. thesis, McGill, 1971.
2313. **Goshorn, Warner S.** "Landscape Architecture in Montreal." *CPR* 6, no. 1 (1956):39-43.
2314. **Gosling, S. M.** *The Development of the Port of Montreal*. Reading: University of Reading, 1932.
2315. **Gourdeau-Côté, Suzanne, and Smith, André.** "L'université McGill a 150 ans." *Forces* 15 (1971):19-25.

2316. **Graham, F. T.** *Histrionic Montreal.* 1902. Reprint. New York: Arno Press, 1976.
2317. **Gray, Clayton.** *The Montreal Story.* Montreal: Whitecombe and Gilmour, 1949. Translated as *Le vieux Montréal.* Montréal: Jour, 1964.
2318. **Groulx, Lionel.** *Ville-Marie, 1642-1942.* Montréal: L'Oeuvre des tracts, 1942.
2319. **Groupe de recherche en art populaire (GRAP).** *Rapport:Travaux et Conferences, 1975-1979.* Montréal: Dépt. de l'histoire de l'art, université du Québec à Montréal, juin, 1979.
2320. **Groupe de recherche sur la société Montréalaise au XIXe siècle (GRSM).** *Montréal au XIXe siècle: Répertoire des rues.* Québec: Ministère des affaires culturelles, 1976.
2321. **Gubbay, Aline, and Hooff, Sally.** *Montreal's Little Mountain: A Portrait of Westmount/La petite montagne: Un portrait de Westmount.* Montréal: Trillium, 1979.
2322. **Guitard, Michèle.** "Pour une histoire de l'Institut Canadien de Montréal." *RHAF* 27 (1973):403-7.
2323. **Halliday, H. A.** "Terrebonne: From Seigneury to Suburb." *CGEJ* 84 (1972):131-39.
2324. **Hamelin, Jean, and Provencher, Jean.** "La vie de relations sur le Saint-Laurent entre Québec et Montréal au milieu du XVIIIe siècle." *Cah géogr Q* 11 (1967):243-52.
2325. **Hardy, Eric.** "Montreal and Toronto." In *Great Cities of the World,* edited by W. A. Robson and D. E. Regan, pp. 985-1038. London: Allen & Unwin, 1972.
2326. **Hébert, Gérard.** "Grève de la construction à Montréal." *Relations* 337 (1969):106-10.
2327. **Hendrie, Lillian M.** *Early Days in Montreal and Rambles in the Neighbourhood.* Montreal: Mercury Press, 1932.
2328. **Heroux, J.-P.** *Troisième centenaire de Montréal.* Montréal: Commission de IIIe centenaire de Montréal par Therrien et Frères, 1942.
2329. **Hinshelwood, N. M.** *Montreal and Vicinity; Being a History of the Old Town, A Pictorial Record of the Modern City.* . . . Montreal: Desbarats, 1903.
2330. **Hollier, R.** *Montréal, ma grand'ville.* Montréal: Déom, 1963.
2331. **Hopkins, Henry Whitmer, ed.** *Atlas of the City and Island of Montreal, Including the Counties of Jacques Cartier and Hochelaga.* Montreal: Provincial Surveying and Pub. Co., 1879.
2332. **Innis, F. C., and Lundgren, J.** "Montreal: The National and International City." *Geogr Mag* 43 (1970):36-47.
2332A. **Janisset, M.-F.** "Les quartiers de Ville Saint Laurent, au sud de Côte-Vertu." Thèse de M.A., Montreal, 1963.
2333. **Jenkins, Kathleen.** *Montreal: Island City of the St. Lawrence.* Garden City, NY: Doubleday, 1966.
2334. **Johnson, John S.** "History and Organization of the Montreal Stock Exchange." M.A. thesis, McGill, 1934.
2335. **Jupp, G. A.** "The Role and Functions of the Tavern in Montreal." M.A. thesis, Calgary, 1969.
2336. **Keating, C., and Keating, D.** *Guide to Montreal.* Toronto: McGraw-Hill, 1967.
2337. **King, M. J.** *Montreal and Quebec: A Pictorial and Historical Guide.* Toronto: Dent, 1955.
2338. **Knoff, L. L., and Lavigueur, H.** *Montréal: L'age d'or/The Golden Years.* Toronto: M&S, 1965.
2339. **Knott, Leonard L.** *City in a Wilderness.* Montreal: Editorial Associates, 1938.
2340. **Knowles, Valerie.** "Early Guardians of Montreal's Waterfront [The Montreal River Police]." *RCMP Q* 30, no. 2 (1964):3-8.
2341. **Lacoste, Norbert.** "La recherche sur la pratique religieuse dans la zone metropolitaine de Montréal." *Rech soc* 3 (1962):361-66.
2342. _____. "Bibliographie sommaire des études sur Montréal." *Rech soc* 6 (1965):277-81.
2343. **Lahaise, Robert.** *L'Hôtel-Dieu du Vieux-Montréal, 1642-1861.* Montréal: Hurtubise HMH, 1973.
2344. _____. *Les édifices conventuels du Vieux-Montréal: Aspects ethnohistoriques.* Montreal: Hurtubise HMH, 1980.

2345. **Lajeunesse, J. M.** *History of Public Transportation in Montreal.* Montreal: Apollon, 1973.
2346. **Lambert, Phyllis.** "The State of the Historic District of Old Montreal." In *Proceedings of New Life for Old Buildings—British Columbia and Yukon Heritage Conference,* pp. 132-39. Vancouver: Community Arts Council, 1977.
2347. _____. "A Selection of Documentary Prints of Montreal, with Notes on Urban Growth." In #2245, pp. 511-29.
2348. _____. "Photographic Documentation and Buildings: Relationships Past and Present." *Archivaria* 5 (1977-78):60-77.
2349. **Lamonde, Yvan.** "L'enseignement de la philosophie au collège de Montréal, 1790-1876." *Culture* 31 (1970):109-23, 213-24, 312-26.
2350. _____. *Les bibliothèques de collectivités à Montréal (17e-19e siècles).* Montréal: Bibliothèque nationale du Québec, 1979.
2351. **Lamothe, J.-C.** *Histoire de la corporation de la cité de Montréal depuis son origine jusqu'à nos jours.* Montréal: Laviolette et Massé, 1903.
2352. **Lanctôt, Gustave.** "L'histoire française de Ville Marie." *Rev univ Ottawa* 12 (1942):279-301.
2353. **Langlois, Jean-Claude.** "Problems of Urban Growth in Greater Montreal." *Can Geogr* 5, no. 3 (1961):1-11.
2354. _____. "Le centre de Montréal et son évolution." *Habitat* 7, no. 1 (1964):14-19.
2355. **Laurin, J.-E.** *Histoire économique de Montréal et des cités et villes du Québec.* Ottawa: Laurin, 1942.
2356. **Leacock, Stephen.** *Montreal, Seaport and City.* Toronto: M&S, 1948.
2357. **Leblanc, André E.** "The Labour Movement Seen through the Pages of Montreal's *Le Monde Ouvrier/The Labour World* (1916-1926)—An Analysis of Thought and a Detailed Index." M.A. thesis, Montreal, 1971.
2358. **Leblond de Brumath, A.** *Histoire populaire de Montréal depuis ses origines jusqu'à nos jours.* Montréal: Granger, 1890.
2359. **Leduc, Pierre.** *Promenade dans le Vieux Montréal.* Montréal: Office municipal du tourisme, 1969.
2360. **Lefebvre, Fernand.** "L'histoire du guet à Montréal." *RHAF* 6 (1952):263-73.
2361. **Lewis, D. S.** *Royal Victoria Hospital, 1887-1947.* Montreal: McGill UP, 1969.
2362. **Lighthall, William D.** *Sights and Shrines of Montreal.* Montreal: Grafton, 1892.
2363. **Linteau, Paul-André, and Thivierge, J.** *Montréal au 19e siècle: Bibliographie.* Montréal: GRSM, 1972.
2364. **Loiselle, Roland.** "Evolution du développement de la banlieue montréalaise." Thèse de M.A., Montréal, 1965.
2365. **Longstreet, T. Morris.** *Quebec, Montreal and Ottawa.* New York: Century Co., 1933.
2366. **MacDermot, Hugh E.** *A History of the Montreal General Hospital.* Montreal: General Hospital, 1950.
2367. **McIver, John Mackay.** "The Administration of Montreal: Past, Present, and Future." M.A. thesis, Carleton, 1961.
2368. **MacKay, Robert W. S.** *The Stranger's Guide to the Island and City of Montreal, Containing a Brief Description of All That Is Remarkable in Either.* Montreal: Lowell and Gibson, 1848.
2369. **McLean, Eric, and Wilson, R.D.** *Le passé vivant de Montréal—The Living Past of Montreal.* Montreal: McGill UP, 1964.
2370. **McLean, F. H.** "Municipal Government of Montreal." *Ann Am Ac Pol Sci* 18 (1901):359-63.
2371. **MacLennan, H.** "City of Two Souls: The Fascinating Story of Montreal." *Holiday* 10 (1951):48-55.
2372. _____. *McGill: The Story of a University.* London: Allen & Unwin, 1960.

2373. **MacMillan, Cyrus.** *McGill and Its Story, 1821-1921.* Toronto: OUP, 1921.
2374. **Marsan, Jean-Claude.** *Montréal en évolution: Historique du développement de l'architecture et de l'environnement montréalais.* Montréal: Fides, 1974.
2375. **Mason Philip.** "Man Conquers Mountain [A History of Montreal's Mountain Park Railway]." *Can Rail* 209 (1969):108-12.
2376. **Massicote, E.-Z.** *La cité de Sainte-Cunégonde.* Montréal: Houle, 1893.
2377. **Mather, Edith.** *Montreal Architecture.* Montreal: Tundra, 1977.
2378. _____, **and Chicoine, René.** *Les rues de Montréal. Façades et fantaisie/Touches of Fantasy on Montreal Streets.* Montreal: Tundra, 1977.
2379. **Maurault, Olivier.** "La basilique de Montréal." *RTCN* 5 (1919): 253-66.
2380. _____. "L'église Notre-Dame de Montréal." *RTCN* 6 (1920):396-98.
2381. _____. "Montréal: Capitale." *RTCN* 13 (1927):20-36.
2382. _____. *La paroisse: Histoire de l'église Notre-Dame de Montréal.* Montréal: Carrière, 1929.
2383. _____. "Les vitraux d'histoire de Notre-Dame de Montréal." *Rev univ Ottawa* 3 (1933):461-91.
2384. _____. "L'Université de Montreal." *Cah des dix* 17 (1952): 11-54.
2385. **Medam, Alain.** *Montréal interdite.* Paris: Presses universitaires de la France, 1978.
2385A.**Mercier, Bernard-E.** "De paroisse rurale à paroisse urbaine: Notre-Dame-des-Anges de Cartierville (1910-1956). Essai géographique et démographique." *RCGG* 20, nos. 3-4 (1958):79-115.
2386. **Miller, Emile.** "Inventaire chronologique des cartes et des plans de Montréal, 1611-1915, avec annotations." *Rapport annuel du département des archives municipales pour l'année 1915.* Appendix 3, pp. 39-80. Montréal: Perrault, 1916.
2387. **Miller, Evelyn.** "The History of the Montreal Jewish Public Library and Archives." *Can Arch* 2 (1970):49-55.
2388. **Montpetit, Raymond.** "La construction des théâtres à Montréal aux XIXe siècle: Critique de l'historiographie." In #2319, pp. 48-66.
2389. _____, **and Dufresne, Sylvie.** "Formes et fonctions du loisir public à Montreal au XIXe siècle." In #2319, pp. 1-47.
2390. **Montreal Society of Architecture.** *Exploring Montreal: Its Buildings, People and Places.* Toronto: Greey de Pencier, 1974. Translated as *Decouvrir Montreal.* Montreal: Jour, 1975.
2391. **Montreal Urban Community Transit Commission.** *Urban Transit in Montreal: The Last Hundred Years, 1861-1961.* Montreal: The Commission, 1970. Reprinted by Yagon Book Services, 1978.
2392. **Morin, Victor.** *Le vieux Montréal. Fondation. Developpement. Visite.* Montréal: Editions des dix, 1942.
2393. _____. "Aux sources de l'histoire de Montréal." *RSC, Trans,* 36 (1942):83-94.
2394. _____. *La légende dorée de Montréal.* Montréal: Editions des dix, 1949.
2395. **Nish, Cameron.** *Inventaire sommaire des archives de la société historique de Montréal.* Montréal: Sir George Williams University, 1968.
2396. **Percival, W. P.** *The Lure of Montreal.* 1945. Rev. ed. Toronto: Ryerson, 1964.
2397. **Perrault, Claude.** "Les marchés Saint-Anne—Le parlement et la Place Youville, 1833-1901." *RHAF* 23 (1969):393-403.
2398. **Puxley, Evelyn.** *Poverty in Montreal.* Montreal: Dawson College Press, 1971.
2399. **Racine, Jean-Bernard.** "La genèse d'une métropole/The Genesis of a Metropolis." In #2243, pp. 107-15.
2400. **Régnier, Michel.** *Montréal, Paris d'Amérique.* Montréal: Jour, 1961.
2401. **Reynolds, Lloyd George.** "The Occupational Adjustment of the British Immigrant in Montreal." M.A. thesis, McGill, 1933.

2402. **Rich, Edwin Ernest.** *Montreal and the Fur Trade.* Montreal: McGill UP, 1966.
2403. **Ricour, Françoise.** "Outremont, monographie urbaine." Thèse de M.A., Montréal, 1962.
2404. _____. "Les quartiers d'Outremont." *Rev géogr Mtl* 18, no. 1 (1964):65-85.
2405. _____. "Suburbanisation et structures urbaines à l'Ile Jésus." Thèse de Ph.D., Montréal, 1969.
2406. **Roberts, Leslie.** "Westmount." *Habitat* 10, no. 306 (1967):56-59.
2407. _____. *Montreal: From Mission Colony to World City.* Toronto: Macmillan, 1969.
2408. **Robillard, Claude.** "Montréal la magnifique." *RCU* 8, no. 2 (1958):59-62.
2409. **Rocher, Guy.** "Industrialisation et culture urbaine. Note préliminaire à l'étude de la région métropolitaine de Montréal." *Contributions à l'étude des sciences de l'homme* 1 (1952):165-70.
2410. **Rosenberg, Louis.** *A Study of the Changes in the Geographic Distribution of the Jewish Population in Metropolitan Montreal, 1851-1951.* Canadian Jewish Population Studies, 4. Montreal: Canadian Jewish Congress, 1955.
2411. **Ruddick, S.** "Study of a Nineteenth Century Working Class Neighbourhood in Montreal's Inner City." M.A. thesis, McGill, 1979.
2412. **Rumilly, Robert.** *Histoire de l'Ecole des hautes études commerciales de Montréal, 1907-1967.* Montréal: Beauchemin, 1967.
2413. _____. *Histoire de Saint-Laurent.* Montréal: Beauchemin, 1970.
2414. _____. *Histoire de Montréal.* 5 vols. Montréal: Fides, 1970-74.
2415. _____. *Histoire de Longueuil.* Longueuil: Société d'histoire de Longueuil, 1974.
2416. _____. *Histoire d'Outremont, 1875-1975.* Montréal: Leméac, 1975.
2416A. _____. *Histoire de la Société Saint-Jean-Baptiste de Montréal. Des patriotes au fleurdelisé, 1834-1948.* Montreal: Aurore, 1975.
2417. **Sancton, Andrew B.** "Governing Montreal: The Impact of French-English Differences on Metropolitan Politics." Ph.D. thesis, Oxford, 1979.
2418. **Sandham, Alfred.** *Ville Marie, or, Sketches of Montreal, Past and Present.* Montreal: Bishop, 1870.
2419. **Sheehy-Casey, M. T.** "The Development of the Port of Montreal." *Can Engineer* 47, no. 18 (1924):513-18.
2420. **Shepherd, Francis J.** *Origin and History of the Montreal General Hospital.* Montreal: General Hospital, 1925.
2421. **Schoenaver, Norbert.** "The Influence of Urban Growth upon Surrounding Villages with Special Reference to Montreal and Villages in the Richelieu Valley." M.A. thesis, McGill, 1959.
2422. **Sinclair, M. H.** "The Industrial Geography of the Beauharnois Canal Area." M.A. thesis, McGill, 1954.
2423. **Sirois, A.** *Montréal dans le roman canadien.* Montréal: Didier, 1969.
2424. **Société Canadienne de Science Economique.** *Montreal . . . problèmes de croissance et éléments d'une stratégie de développement.* Montréal: HEC, 1975.
2425. **Société historique de Montréal.** *Les origines de Montréal.* IIe livraison. Montréal: Ménard, 1917.
2425A. _____. *Montréal. Artisans, histoire, patrimoine.* Montréal: Fides, 1979.
2426. **Solomon, David N.** "The Young Men's Hebrew Association of Montreal." M.A. thesis, McGill, 1942.
2427. **Stanislas, Frère.** *Historique de Ville-La Salle, Le vieux Lachine.* La Salle, 1950.
2428. **Sweeney, Robert.** *A Guide to the History and Records of Selected Montreal Businesses before 1947/Guide pour l'étude d'entreprises montréalaises et de leur archives avant 1947.* Montreal: Montreal Business History Project, 1979.
2429. **Tanghe, Raymond.** *Montréal.* Montréal: Lévêque, 1936.

2430. **Tata, S. B.** *Montreal.* Toronto: M&S, 1963.
2431. **Terrill, Frederick W.** *A Chronology of Montreal and of Canada, From A.D. 1752 to A.D. 1893. . . .* Montreal: Lovell, 1893.
2432. **Toker, Franklin.** *The Church of Notre-Dame in Montreal: An Architectural History.* Montreal: McGill-Queen's UP, 1970.
2433. **Tombs, L. C.** *The Port of Montreal.* McGill Economic Studies, #6. Toronto: Macmillan, 1926.
2434. **Tranquair, Ramsay.** "The Building of McGill University." *JRAIC* 2 (1925):45-63.
2435. **Trépanier, Leon.** *Les rues du Vieux Montréal, au fil du temps.* Montréal: Fides, 1968.
2436. **Trudeau, Michelle.** "A Classification of Centres in the Montreal Environs and Eastern Townships Region." M.A. thesis, McGill, 1966.
2437. **Wilson, E. L.** "The Montreal Parks and Playgrounds Association Inc. A Historical Study of the Association from the Year of Its Founding in 1896 to 1949." M.A. thesis, McGill, 1953.
2438. **Wilson, Laurence M.** *This Was Montreal.* Montreal: Château de Ramezay, 1960.

b. The French Regime to 1760

2439. **Adair, Edward Robert.** "The Evolution of Montreal under the French Regime." CHA, *AR* (1942):20-41.
2440. **Beaudoin, Marie-Louise.** *Les premières et les Filles du Roi à Ville-Marie.* Montréal: Soeurs de la Congrégation de Notre-Dame, 1971.
2441. **Bertrand, Camille.** *Histoire de Montréal, 1535-1760.* Montréal: Beauchemin, 1935.
2442. **Charbonneau, Hubert.** "A propos de démographie urbaine en Nouvelle-France." *RHAF* 30 (1976):263-69.
2443. **Choplin, Robert.** "Un mouvement français d'expansion coloniale au XVIIe siècle: La fondation de Montréal." Thèse de M.A., Montréal, 1951.
2444. **Décarie-Audet, Louise.** "Les textiles à Montréal de 1740 à 1760 à travers une collection d'actes notaires." Thèse de M.A., Laval, 1977.
2445. **Dechêne, Louise.** "L'évolution du régime seigneurial au Canada. Le cas de Montréal aux XVIIe et XVIIIe siècles." *Rech soc* 12 (1971):143-84.
2446. _____. *Habitants et marchands de Montréal au XVIIe siècle.* Paris: Plon, 1974.
2447. _____. "La croissance de Montréal au XVIIIe siècle." *RHAF* 27 (1973):163-79. Translated as "The Growth of Montreal in the 18th Century." In *Canadian History before Confederation,* edited by J. M. Bumsted, pp. 154-67. Georgetown: Irwin-Dorsey, 1979.
2448. **Desjardins, Edouard.** "La médecine à forfait aux débuts de Ville-Marie." *UMCA* 98 (1969):239-42.
2449. _____. "L'hôpital général des frères Charon à Ville-Marie." *UMCA* 98 (1969):2108-12.
2450. **Dollier de Casson, François.** *Histoire de Montréal, 1640-1672.* Montréal: Sénécal, 1871. Translated as *A History of Montreal, 1640-1672.* New York: Dutton, 1928.
2451. **Dupuis, Aurore.** "Les contrats de bancs d'Eglise à Montréal au XVIIIe siècle (1692-1760)." Thèse de M.A., Sherbrooke, 1978.
2452. **Faillon, Etienne Michel.** *Vie de Mme. d'Youville, fondatrice des soeurs de la charité de Ville-Marie, dans l'Ile de Montréal, en Canada.* St.-Jovite: Ed. Magnificat, 1971.
2453. **Genest, Nicole.** "Habitation et aménagement intérieur à Montréal au milieu du XVIIIe siècle." Thèse de M.A., Laval, 1977.
2454. **Gosselin, Auguste.** "Le 'Traité de Fortifications' of Chaussegros de Léry." *BRH* 7 (1901):157-58.
2455. **Hébert, N. T.** "Les incendies à Montréal sous le régime français." *Assurances* 37 (1970):301-4.

2456. **Lachance, André.** "Le Bureau des Pauvres de Montréal, 1698-1699: Contribution à l'étude de la société montréalaise de la fin du XVIIe siècle." *HS* 4 (1969):99-112.

2457. **Lanctôt, Gustave.** "L'histoire française de Ville Marie." *Rev univ Ottawa* 12 (1942):279-301.

2458. _____. "Images et figures de Montréal sous la France, 1642-1763." RSC, *Trans,* 3d ser. 37 (1943):53-78.

2459. _____. "Montréal avant Maisonneuve." *Rev univ Laval* (1956-57):576-84.

2460. _____. *Montréal sous Maisonneuve, 1642-1665.* Montréal: Beauchemin, 1966. Translated as *Montreal under Maisonneuve.* Toronto: Clarke Irwin, 1969.

2461. **Marchal, Léon.** *Les origines de Montréal: Ville-Marie, 1642-65.* Montréal: Beauchemin, 1942.

2462. **Massicotte, E.-Z.** "Les colons de Montréal de 1642 à 1667." RSC, *Trans,* 3d ser. 7 (1913):3-65.

2463. _____. "Les premières concessions de terre à Montréal, sous de Maisonneuve, 1648-1665." RSC, *Trans,* 3d ser. 8 (1914):215-29.

2464. _____. "Inventaire des cartes et plans de l'île et de la ville de Montréal." *BRH* 20, no. 2 (1914):33-41; 20, no. 3 (1914):65-73.

2465. _____. "L'incendie du vieux Montréal en 1721." *Can Antiquarian and Numismatic J* 12 (1915):51-92.

2466. _____. *Montréal sous le régime français: Repertoire des arrêts, édits, mandements, ordonnances et règlements, conservés dans les archives du Palais de Justice de Montréal, 1640-1760.* Montréal: Ducharme, 1919.

2467. _____. "Auberges et cabarets d'autrefois: Notes sur l'industrie de l'hôtellerie à Montréal sous le régime français." RSC, *Trans,* 3d ser. 21 (1927):97-112.

2468. _____. "Maçons, entrepreneurs, architectes." *BRH* 35 (1929):132-42.

2469. _____. "Memento historique de Montréal, 1636-1760." RSC, *Trans,* 3d ser. 27 (1933):111-31.

2470. _____. "Quelques rues et faubourgs du vieux Montréal." *Cah des dix* 1 (1936):105-56.

2471. _____. "Evocation du vieux Montréal." *Cah des dix* 3 (1938):131-64.

2472. _____. "Montréal se transforme." *Cah des dix* 5 (1940):177-215.

2473. _____. "Quelques maisons du vieux Montréal." *Cah des dix* 10 (1945):231-62.

2474. _____. "Les incendies à Montréal sous le régime français." *Assurances* 37 (1970):301-4.

2475. **Maurault, Olivier.** "Montréal et Louisiane." *RHAF* 2 (1949):513-21.

2476. _____."La seigneurie de Montréal." *Cah des dix* 22 (1957):69-82.

2477. **Moogk, Peter N.** "The Ancestor of Quebec's Craft Union: The Montreal Shoemaker's Protest of 1729." Histoire des travailleurs québécois, *Bulletin* 5 (1978):34-39.

2478. **Perreault, J.-A. Claude.** "The Montreal Seigneurie, 1636-1760." M.A. thesis, McGill, 1971.

2479. **Raymond, Raoul.** "Hôpital Général de Montréal, Registre de l'entrée des pauvres (1691-1741)." *Mémoires de la Société Généalogique Canadienne-Française* 20 (1969):238-42.

2480. **Sigouin, Alice.** "Louis-Hector Callières, gouverneur de Montréal, 1684-1699." Thèse de M.A., Ottawa, 1970.

2481. **Trudel, Marcel.** "Les débuts d'une société: Montréal, 1642-1663." *RHAF* 23 (1969):185-207.

2482. _____. *Montréal: La formation d'une société (1642-1663).* Montréal: Fides, 1976.

2483. **Vermette, Luce.** "Les feux domestiques à Montréal, de 1740 à 1760." Thèse de M.A., Laval, 1977.

c. 1760-1850

2484. **Adam, Richard.** "La crise à Montréal en 1849." Thèse de M.A., Montréal, 1968.

2485. **Audet, Francis J.** *Les députés de Montréal, 1792-1867.* Montréal: Editions des dix, 1943.

2486. **Audet, P. H.** "Apprenticeship in Early Nineteenth Century Montreal." M.A. thesis, Concordia, 1976.
2487. **Bazin, Jules.** "Un peintre américain à Montréal en 1820." *Vie des Arts* 66 (1972):19-23.
2488. **Beaudin, François.** "L'influence de La Mennais sur Mgr. Lartigue, premier évêque de Montréal." *RHAF* 24 (1971):225-38.
2489. **Bell, J. Jones.** "Burning of the Parliament Buildings: Montreal, 1849." *Can Mag* 20 (1903):501-6.
2490. **Bensley, Edward Horton.** "The Beginning of Teaching at McGill University." *McGill J Educ* 6 (1971):23-24.
2491. **Bernard, Jean-Paul; Linteau, Paul-André; and Robert, Jean-Claude.** "La structure professionnelle de Montréal en 1825." *RHAF* 30 (1976):383-416.
2492. **Blanchette-Lessard, Lucie, and Daigneault-Saint-Denis, Nicole.** "Groupes sociaux patriotes et les rébellions de 1837-38." Thèse de M.A., Québec à Montréal, 1975.
2493. **Bosworth, N.** *Hochelaga Depicta: The Early History and Present State of the City and Island of Montreal.* 1839. Reprint. Toronto: Coles, 1974.
2494. **Charland, Thomas M.** "The Lake Champlain Army and the Fall of Montreal." *Vermont Hist* 28 (1960):293-301.
2495. **Chausse, Gilles.** "Un évêque nationaliste Mgr. Jean-Jacques Lartigue, premier évêque de Montréal." CCHA, *Rapport* (1968):9-20.
2496. **Conroy, Mary P.** "History of Theatre in Montreal prior to Confederation." M.A. thesis, McGill, 1936.
2497. **Cooper, John Irwin.** "The Origins and Early History of the Montreal City and District Saving Banks." CCHA, *Rapport* (1945-46):15-25.
2498. _____. "Irish Immigration and the Canadian Church before the Middle of the Nineteenth Century." CCHS, *Journal* 2 (May 1955):1-20.
2499. **Corley, N. T.** "The Montreal Ship Canal, 1805-1865." M.A. thesis, McGill, 1961.
2500. **DeLorimier, Michel.** "Chevalier DeLorimier, notaire et patriote Montréalais de 1837-38." Thèse de M.A., Québec à Montréal, 1975.
2501. **Dewey, Alex. G.** "The First Fifteen Years of British Administration in Montreal, 1760 to 1775." M.A. thesis, McGill, 1913.
2502. _____. "Beginnings of British Commerce at Montreal." *Can Mag* 43 (1914):3-14.
2503. **Dubuc, Alfred.** "Montréal et les débuts de la navigation à vapeur sur le Saint-Laurent." *Rev histoire économique et sociale* 45 (1967):105-18.
2504. _____. "Thomas Molson, entrepreneur canadien, 1791-1863." Thèse de doctorat d'Etat, Lettres, Paris, 1969.
2505. **Farrell, David R.** "Anchors of Empire: Detroit, Montreal, and the Continental Interior, 1760-1775." *ARCS* 7, no. 1 (1977):33-54.
2506. **Forêtier, Pierre.** "Notes and Reminiscences of an Inhabitant of Montreal during the Occupation of that City by the Bostonians from 1775 to 1776." *Report of the Public Archives of Canada for 1945*, pp. xxiii-xxvi. Ottawa: King's Printer, 1946.
2507. **Foster, Josephine.** "The Montreal Riot of 1849." *CHR* 32 (1951):61-65.
2508. **Galarneau, France.** "L'élection partielle du quartier-ouest de Montréal en 1832: Analyse politico-sociale." *RHAF* 32 (1979):565-84.
2509. **Giguère, Georges-Emile.** "Les biens de Saint-Sulpice et 'The Attorney General Stuart's Opinion Respecting the Seminary of Montréal' (10 décembre 1828)." *RHAF* 24 (1970):45-78.
2510. **Guimond, Lionel.** "La *Gazette* de Montréal de 1785 à 1790." Thèse de M.A., Montréal, 1957.
2511. **Hare, John E.** "Le théâtre de société à Montréal, 1789-1791." *Bulletin du Centre de recherche en civilisation canadienne-française* 16 (1978):22-26.
2512. **Harvey, Janice.** "Upper-Class Reaction to Poverty in Mid-Nineteenth Century Montreal: A Protestant Example." M.A. thesis, McGill, 1978.

2513. **Igartua, José E.** "A Change in Climate: The Conquest and the Marchands of Montreal." CHA, *HP* (1974):115-35.
2514. _____. "The Merchants and Negociants of Montreal, 1750-75: A Study in Socio-Economic History." Ph.D. thesis, Michigan State, 1974.
2515. _____. "The Merchants of Montreal at the Conquest: Socio-Economic Profile." *HS* 16 (1976):275-93.
2516. _____. "Le comportement démographique des marchands de Montréal vers 1760." *RHAF* 33 (1979):427-45.
2517. **Keep, G. R. C.** *The Irish Migration to Montreal, 1847-1867.* Montreal: McGill UP, 1948.
2518. _____. "The Irish Adjustment in Montreal." *CHR* 31 (1950):39-46.
2519. _____. "D'Arcy McGee and Montreal." *Culture* 12 (1951):16-28.
2520. **Klassen, Henry C.** "L. H. Holton: Montreal Business Man and Politician, 1817-1867." Ph.D. thesis, Toronto, 1970.
2521. **Knowles, David C.** "The American Presbyterian Church of Montreal 1822-65." M.A. thesis, McGill, 1957.
2522. **Lapointe-Roy, Huguette.** "Paupérisme et assistance sociale à Montréal, 1832-1865." Thèse de M.A., McGill, 1972.
2523. **Lefebvre, André.** *La Montréal Gazette et le nationalisme canadien, 1835-1842.* Montréal: Guerin, 1970.
2524. **Lefebvre, Fernand.** "La vie à la prison du Montréal au XIXe siècle." *RHAF* 7 (1954):524-37.
2525. **Linteau, Paul-André, and Robert, Jean-Claude.** "Propriété foncière et société à Montréal: Une hypothèse." *RHAF* 28 (1974):17-39. Translated as "Land Ownership and Society in Montreal: An Hypothesis." In #**85,** pp. 17-36.
2526. _____. "Un recensement et son recenseur: Le cas de Montréal en 1825." *Archives* 8 (1976):29-36.
2527. **MacDermaid, M. A.** "Bishop Lartigue and the First Rebellion in the Montreal Area." M.A. thesis, Carleton, 1968.
2528. **MacDermot, Hugh E.** "The Early Admission Books of the Montreal General Hospital." *CMAJ* 36 (1937):524-29.
2529. **MacDonald, Mary L.** "The Literary Life of English and French Montreal from 1817 to 1830 as Seen through the Periodicals of the Time." M.A. thesis, Carleton, 1977.
2530. **McDougall, Elizabeth A.** "The American Element in the Early Presbyterian Church in Montreal, 1786-1822." M.A. thesis, McGill, 1965.
2531. **MacLeod, Paul G.** "Montreal and Reciprocity, 1846-1854." M.A. thesis, Rochester, 1967.
2532. **Marion, S.** "Le voltairianisme de la *Gazette* littéraire de Montréal." *Rev univ Ottawa* 9 (1939):393-408; 10 (1940):7-28.
2533. _____. "La *Gazette* de Montréal de 1778, berceau de la critique littéraire au Canada français." *Rev univ Ottawa* 10 (1940):330-53.
2534. **Massicotte, E.-Z.** "Hôtelleries, clubs et cafés à Montréal de 1760 à 1850." RSC, *Trans,* 3d ser. 22 (1928):37-62.
2536. **Monet, Jacques.** "La crise Metcalfe and the Montreal Election, 1843-1844." *CHR* 44 (1963):1-19.
2537. **Ouellet, Fernand.** "Papineau et la rivalité Québec-Montréal, 1820-1840." *RHAF* 13 (1959):311-27.
2538. _____. "Structures des occupations et ethnicité dans les villes de Québec et de Montréal, 1819-1844." In *Eléments d'histoire sociale du Bas Canada,* pp. 177-205. Montréal: Hurtubise HMH, 1972.
2539. **Paquet, Gilles, and Wallot, Jean-Pierre.** "Les inventaires après décès à Montréal au tournant du XIXe siècle: Préliminaires à une analyse." *RHAF* 30 (1976):163-221.

2540. **Pendergast, R. A.** "The Economics of the Montreal Traders." *W Can J Ant* 3, no. 1 (1971):34-42.
2541. **Pouliot, Léon.** "La difficile érection du diocèse de Montréal (1836)." *RHAF* 16 (1963):506-35.
2542. **Query, Jacques.** "Montréal sous l'occupation américaine." Thèse de M.A., Montréal, 1977.
2543. **Rabottin, Maurice.** "Langue et société. Le français de Montréal en 1840." Thèse 3e cycle, Nice, 1972.
2544. **Rioux, Jean Roch.** "Les débuts de l'Institut canadien et du journal *L'Avenir*, 1844-1849." Thèse de Ph.D., Laval, 1964.
2545. **Robert, Jean-Claude.** "Les notables de Montréal au XIXe siècle." *HS* 15 (1975):54-76.
2546. _____. "Montréal, 1821-1871: Aspects de l'urbanisation." Thèse 3e cycle, Ecole des Hautes Etudes en Sciences Sociales (Paris), 1977.
2547. **Rousseau, Louis.** *La prédication à Montréal de 1800 à 1830: Approche religiologique.* Montréal: Fides, 1976.
2548. **Ste. Croix, Lorne J.** "The First Incorporation of the City of Montreal, 1826-1836." M.A. thesis, McGill, 1972.
2549. **Senior, Elinor.** "The British Garrison in Montreal in the 1840s." *J Society for Army Historical Research* 52 (Summer 1974):111-27.
2550. _____. "An Imperial Garrison in Its Colonial Setting: British Regulars in Montreal, 1832-54." Ph.D. thesis, McGill, 1976.
2551. _____. "The Influence of the British Garrison on the Development of the Montreal Police, 1832-1853." *Military Affairs* 43, no. 2 (1979):63-68.
2552. **Tousignant, Pierre.** "La *Gazette* de Montréal de 1791 à 1796." Thèse de M.A., Montréal, 1960.
2553. **Tremblay, Robert.** "La formation matérielle de la classe ouvrière à Montréal entre 1790 et 1830." *RHAF* 33 (1979):39-50.
2554. **Tremblay, Yves.** "Etude de la société de Montréal au début du régime anglais." Thèse de M.A., Ottawa, 1968.
2555. **Tulchinsky, Gerald J. J.** "The Construction of the First Lachine Canal, 1815-1826." M.A. thesis, McGill, 1960.
2556. _____. "The Montreal Business Community, 1837-1853." In *Canadian Business History: Selected Studies, 1497-1971*, edited by D. S. Macmillan, pp. 125-43. Toronto: M&S, 1972.
2557. _____. *The River Barons: Montreal Businessmen and the Growth of Industry and Transportation, 1837-1853.* Toronto: UTP, 1977.
2558. **Viger, Jacques.** *Rapports sur les chemins, rues, ruelles, et ponts de la cité et paroisse de Montréal, avril et mai, 1840.* Montréal: Lovell, 1841.
2559. **Vincelli, B. M.** "The Symbolic Function of the Bank of Montreal Building on the Place D'Armes, 1846: An Image of the English Mercantile Aristocracy." M.A. thesis, Victoria, 1979.

d. 1850-1920

2560. **Adams, Thomas.** "Town Planning and the Housing Problem, with Especial Reference to the City of Montreal." Canadian Club of Montreal, *Addresses* (1914-15):121-30.
2561. **Ames, Herbert Brown.** *The City below the Hill: A Sociological Study of a Portion of the City of Montreal, Canada.* 1897. Reprint, with an introduction by Paul F. W. Rutherford. Social History of Canada, vol. 6. Toronto: UTP, 1972.
2562. **Ballantyne, C. C.** "The Port of Montreal." Canadian Club of Toronto, *Proceedings* (1912-13):106-15.

2563. **Bernier, Jacques.** "La condition ouvrière à Montréal à la fin du 19e siècle, 1874-1896." Thèse de M.A., Laval, 1971.
2564. _____. "La condition des travailleurs, 1851-1896." In *Les travailleurs québécois, 1851-1896*, edited by Jean Hamelin, pp. 31-60. Montréal: Presses de l'université du Québec, 1973.
2565. **Binns, Richard M.** *Montreal's Electric Streetcars: An Illustrated History of the Tramway Era: 1892-1959*. Montreal: Railfare Enterprises, 1973.
2566. **Bisson, Margaret M.** "Le théâtre français à Montréal, 1878-1931." Thèse de M.A., McGill, 1931.
2567. **Bradbury, Bettina.** "The Family Economy and Work in an Industrializing City: Montreal in the 1870s." CHA, *HP* (1979):71-96.
2568. **Brault, Lucien.** "Le premier tramway au Canada." *BRH* 45 (1939):80.
2569. **Brouillard, Pierre.** "Le développement du port de Montréal, 1850-1896." Thèse de M.A., Québec à Montréal, 1977.
2570. **Bruchési, L. P. N.** "Les petites soeurs des pauvres à Montréal." *CF* 1 (1888):183-92.
2571. **Burgess, Joanne.** "L'industrie de la chaussure à Montréal, 1840 à 1870: De l'artisanat à la fabrique." Thèse de M.A., Québec à Montréal, 1977.
2572. _____. "L'industrie de la chaussure à Montréal, 1840-1870: Le passage de l'artisanat à la fabrique." *RHAF* 31 (1977):187-210.
2573. **Carman, A. R.** "H. B. Ames." *Can Mag* 23 (1904):308-11.
2574. **Charpentier, Alfred.** "Le mouvement politique ouvrier de Montréal, 1883-1929." *Relat indus* 10 (1956):74-95.
2575. **Cooper, John Irwin.** "The Social Structure of Montreal in the 1850s." CHA, *AR* (1956):63-73.
2576. **Copp, Terry.** "The Condition of the Working Class in Montreal, 1897-1920." CHA, *HP* (1972):157-80.
2577. _____. *The Anatomy of Poverty: The Condition of the Working Class in Montreal, 1897-1929*. Toronto: M&S, 1974. Translated as *Classe ouvrière et pauvreté. Les conditions de vie des travailleurs montréalais 1897-1929*. Montréal: Boréal Express, 1978.
2578. **Cousineau, A.** "L'habitation à Montreal." *RTCN* 6 (1920):85-94.
2579. **Cowie, F. W.** "The Great National Port of Canada: Features of the Important Extension Works in Progress in Montreal Harbour." *Can Engineer* 22 (1911):178-83.
2580. _____. "Transportation Problems in Canada and Montreal Harbour." *ICEE* 198 (1914):104-207; 199 (1915):337-46.
2581. **Craik, W. A.** "The Linking of Montreal and Toronto." *Can Mag* 28 (1906):40-44.
2582. **Cross, Dorothy Suzanne.** "The Irish in Montreal, 1867-1896." M.A. thesis, McGill, 1969.
2583. _____. "The Neglected Majority: The Changing Role of Women in the 19th Century Montreal." In #85, pp. 255-81.
2584. _____, and **Dudley, J. G.** "Comparative Study of Street Directories and Census Returns for 1871." *UHR* 3-72 (November 1972):12-16.
2585. **De Bonville, Jean.** *Jean-Baptiste Gagnepetit. Les travailleurs montréalais à la fin du XIXe siècle*. Montreal: Aurore, 1975.
2586. **Dufresne, Sylvie.** "Le carnaval d'hiver à Montréal, 1883-1889." Thèse de M.A., Québec à Montréal, 1980.
2587. **Dumas-Rousseau, Michèle.** "L'université de Montréal de 1852 à 1865: Tentatives de fondation." Thèse de M.A., Montréal, 1967.
2589. **Dupont-Hébert Roger.** "Le développement industriel de Montréal depuis l'Union à 1900." Thèse, HEC (Montréal), 1940.
2590. **Fahos, J. G.; Milde, G. T.; and Weinmayr, M. V.** *Frederick Law Olmsted, Sr.: Founder of Landscape Architecture in America*. Amherst: University of Massachusetts Press, 1968.

2591. *La fin d'une époque/The End of an Era: Montréal, 1880-1914.* Montreal: McCord Museum, 1977.

2592. Gagnon, Eugene. "Notes on the Early History and Evolution of the Department of Health of Montreal." *PHEJ* 39 (1938):216-21.

2593. Gauvin, Michel. "The Municipal Reform Movement in Montreal, 1886-1914." M.A. thesis, Ottawa, 1972.

2594. _____. "The Reformer and the Machine: Montreal Civic Politics from Raymond Prefontaine to Méderic Martin." *J Can St* 13, no. 2 (1978):27-41.

2594A. Goad, C.-E. *Atlas of the City of Montreal, From Special Survey and Official Plans, Showing All Buildings and Names of Owners.* 2 vols. Montreal, 1881-1890.

2594B. _____. *Atlas of the City of Montreal and Vicinity in Four Volumes, From Official Plans and Special Surveys, Showing Cadastral Numbers, Buildings, and Lots.* 4 vols. Montreal, 1912-1914.

2595. Guay, Michèle. "La Saint-Jean-Baptiste à Montréal au XIXe siècle et au début au XXe siècle." Thèse de M.A., Ottawa, 1972.

2596. Hanna, David B. "The New Town of Montreal." M.A. thesis, Toronto, 1977.

2597. _____, **and Remiggi, Frank W.** *Montreal Neighbourhoods: The Dynamics and Diversity of Montreal Neighbourhoods in Expansion at the End of the 19th Century.* Montreal: Canadian Association of Geographers, 1980.

2598. Harper, J. Russell, and Triggs, Stanley. *Portrait of a Period: A Collection of Notman Photographs, 1856-1915.* Montreal: McGill UP, 1967.

2599. Harvey, Janice. "Upper-Class Reaction to Poverty in Mid-Nineteenth Century Montreal: A Protestant Example." M.A. thesis, McGill, 1978.

2600. Hatton, Warwick, and Hatton, Beth. *A Feast of Ginger Bread from our Victorian Past/Pâtisserie maison de notre charmant passé.* Montreal: Tundra, 1976.

2601. Heap, Margaret. "La grève des charretiers à Montréal, 1864." *RHAF* 31 (1977):371-95.

2602. _____, **and Galarneau, F.** *Montréal au XIXe siècle: Répertoire des rues.* Québec: Ministère des affaires culturelles, 1976.

2603. Horovitz, William B. "An Index of Retail Prices in Montreal 1843-67." M.A. thesis, McGill, 1967.

2604. Janin, G. "The Water Supply Problem of Montreal." *Can Engineer* 18 (1910):25-28.

2605. Johnston, John A. "The Presbyterian College, Montreal, 1865-1915." M.A. thesis, McGill, 1951.

2606. Lajeunesse, Marcel. "Associations littéraires et bibliothèques à Montréal au XIXe siècle et au début du XXe siècle: L'apport sulpicien." Thèse de Ph.D., Ottawa, 1977.

2607. Lambert, Phyllis. "The Architectural Heritage of Montreal: A Sense of Community." *Artscanada* 202/203 (1975-76):22-27.

2608. _____, **and Lemire, Robert.** *Inventaire des bâtiments du vieux Montréal du quartier Saint Antoine et de la ville de Maisonneuve construits entre 1880 et 1915.* Québec: Ministère des affaires culturelles, 1977.

2609. _____. "Building in Montreal: A Break with Tradition." *Can Coll* 13 (1978):77-81.

2609A. Lavallée, André. *Québec contre Montréal. La querelle universitaire, 1876-1891.* Montréal: Presses de l'université de Montréal, 1974.

2610. Lavigne, Marie, and Stoddart, Jennifer. "Ouvrières et travailleuses Montréalaises, 1900-1940." In *Les femmes dans la société québécoise,* edited by M. Lavigne and Y. Pinard, pp. 125-44. Montréal: Boréal Express, 1977.

2611. Lavigne, Marie; Pinard, Yolande; and Stoddart, Jennifer. "La Fédération nationale Saint-Jean-Baptiste et les revendications feministes au debut du 20e siècle." *RHAF* 29 (1975):353-73.

2612. Leduc, Pierre. "Les origines et le développement de l'art association de Montréal (1860-1912)." Thèse de M.A., Montréal, 1963.

2613. **Legge, Charles.** *A Glance at the Victoria Bridge and the Men Who Built It.* Montréal: Lovell, 1860.
2614. **Lighthall, William D.** "Westmount: A Municipal Illustration." In **#895**, pp. 25-34.
2615. **Linteau, Paul-André.** "Le développement du port de Montréal au début du 20ᵉ siècle." CHA, *HP* (1972):181-206.
2616. _____. "La Société Montréalaise au 19ᵉ siècle: Bilan des travaux." *UHR* 3-73 (février 1974):17-19.
2617. _____. "Les travailleurs montréalais au 19ᵉ siècle." *Bulletin du regroupement de chercheurs en histoire des travailleurs québécois* 1, no. 2 (1974):13-15.
2618. _____. "Montréal, 1850-1914." *UHR* 1-75 (juin 1975):31-35.
2619. _____. "Histoire de la ville de Maisonneuve, 1883-1918." Thèse de Ph.D., Montréal, 1975.
2620. _____. "Town Planning in Maisonneuve." *Can Coll* 13 (1978):82-85.
2621. **McConniff, J.** *Illustrated Montreal, the Metropolis of Canada.* Montreal: Desbarats, 1890.
2622. **MacLean, John S.** "Montreal: A Great Commercial City." *Can Mag* 33 (1909):3-10.
2623. **Martell, Eve.** "L'industrie à Montréal en 1871." Thèse de M.A., Québec à Montréal, 1976.
2624. **Martineau, Paul G.** "The Civic Administration of Montreal." In **#895**, pp. 201-22.
2625. **Masters, D. C.** "Toronto vs. Montreal: The Struggle for Financial Hegemony." *CHR* 22 (1941):133-46.
2626. **Maurault, Olivier.** "La congrégation irlandaise de Montréal." *RTCN* 8 (1922):267-90.
2627. **Metcalfe, Alan.** "Organized Sport and Social Stratification in Montreal: 1840-1901." In *Canadian Sport: Sociological Perspectives,* edited by R. S. Gruneau and J. G. Albinson, pp. 77-101. Don Mills: Addison-Wesley, 1976.
2628. _____. "The Evolution of Organized Physical Recreation in Montreal, 1840-1895." *HS* 21 (1978):144-66.
2629. **Morin, L.-E.** *Histoire des travaux de la commission du havre dans le port de Montréal.* Montréal: Moniteur du commerce, 1894.
2630. **Muddiman, B.** "The Spell of Montreal." *Can Mag* 27 (1915):92-95.
2631. "Municipal Reform in Montreal." *Can Mag* 12 (1899):457-60.
2632. **Murray, A. L.** "Frederick Law Olmsted and the Design of Mount Royal Park." *J Soc Arch Hist* 36 (1967):163-71.
2633. **Nantel, Guillaume-Alphonse.** *La métropole de demain. Avenir de Montréal.* Montréal: Mesnard, 1910.
2634. **Nichol, Helen R.** "Investigation of Labour Conditions of Children and Young Persons in Montreal." M.A. thesis, McGill, 1921.
2635. **Olmsted, Frederick Law.** *Mount Royal, Montreal.* New York: Putnam, 1881.
2636. **Perin, Robert.** "Bourget and the Dream of a Free Church in Quebec, 1862-1878." Ph.D. thesis, Ottawa, 1975.
2637. **Pinard, Yolande.** "La féminisme à Montréal au commencement du XXᵉ siècle, 1893-1920." Thèse de M.A., Québec à Montréal, 1976.
2637A. _____. "Les debuts du mouvement des femmes." In *Les femmes dans la société québécoise,* edited by M. Lavigne and Y. Pinard, pp. 61-87. Montréal: Boréal Express, 1977.
2638. **Pollack, Gladys.** "The Sun Life Insurance Company of Montreal, 1872-1900." M.A. thesis, McGill, 1980.
2639. **Price, Enid M.** *The Changes in the Industrial Occupations of Women in the Environment of Montreal during the War Period, 1914-1918.* Montreal: McGill, 1919.
2640. **Ramirez, Bruno, and Del Balso, Michael.** *The Italians of Montreal: From Sojourning to Settlement, 1900-1921.* Montreal: Courant, 1980.

2641. **Robbins, M. C.** "Mount Royal, Montreal." *Garden and Forest* 6 (1892):23-24.
2642. **Ronish, Donna A.** "The Montreal Ladies' Educational Association, 1871-1885." *McGill J Educ* 6 (1971):78-83.
2643. _____. "The Development of Higher Education for Women at McGill University from 1857 to 1899 with Special Reference to the Role of Sir John William Dawson." M.A. thesis, McGill, 1972.
2644. **Russell, Daniel J.** "H. B. Ames and Municipal Reform." M.A. thesis, McGill, 1972.
2645. **Saint-Cyr, J.-F.** "Le contrat des tramways de Montréal." *RTCN* 7 (1921):207-32.
2646. **Sandham, Alfred.** *Montreal and Its Fortifications*. Montreal: Rose, 1874.
2647. **Sibley, C.** "Canada's Great National Port." *Can Mag* 60 (1922):128-34.
2648. **Slemon, P.** "Montreal's Musical Life under the Union, with an Emphasis on the Terminal Years, 1841 and 1867." M.A. thesis, McGill, 1976.
2649. **Soucy-Roy, C.** "Le quartier Ste-Marie, 1850-1900." Thèse de M.A., Québec à Montréal, 1977.
2650. **Stephens, G. W.** "The Administration of Montreal." Canadian Club of Montreal, *Addresses* (1913-14):205-9.
2651. **Sylvain, Robert.** "Le 9 juin 1853 à Montréal." *RHAF* 14 (1960):173-216.
2652. **Tetrault, Martin.** "L'état de santé des Montréalais, 1880-1914." Thèse de M.A., Montréal, 1979.
2653. **Walsh, Henry Cecil.** "Montreal Homes." *Can Mag* 12 (1898):51-56.
2654. **Weir, R. Stanley.** "Some Notes on the Charters of Montreal and Related Statutes." In **#895**, pp. 279-300.
2655. **Williams, David M.** *Montreal, 1850-1870: City Life in Canada One Hundred Years Ago*. Scarborough: Gage, 1971.
2656. **Young, Brian J.** "The Defeat of George Etienne Cartier in Montreal-East in 1872." *CHR* 51 (1971):386-407.
2657. _____. "Railway Politics in Montreal, 1867-1878." CHA, *HP* (1972):89-108.
2658. _____. *Promoters and Politicians: The North-Shore Railways in the History of Quebec, 1854-1885*. Toronto: UTP, 1978.

e. 1920-Present

2659. **Aikin, Dorothy.** "The Role of the Montreal Council of Social Agencies in the Establishment of Public Assistance." M.A. thesis, Chicago, 1950.
2660. **Arès, Richard.** "Comportement linguistique des groupes ethniques à Montréal." *Relations* 336 (1969):77-79.
2661. _____. "Langues parlées par les neo-Québécois à Montréal." *Relations* 337 (1969):102-05.
2662. **Audet, Lucille.** *Chinatown*. Montreal: Mission Chinoise, 1950.
2663. **Auyang, Antonia C.** "Evolution of Commercial Land Use in Cities with Special Reference to Montreal." M.A. thesis, McGill, 1965.
2664. **Barcelo, Michel.** "Montreal Planned and Unplanned." *Arch Design* 37 (1967):307-10.
2665. **Bayley, C. M.** "The Social Structure of the Italian and Ukrainian Communities in Montreal, 1935-1937." M.A. thesis, McGill, 1939.
2666. **Beaudry, G.** "Le regroupement municipal [à Laval]: Une solution pour réaliser une politique d'urbanisme." Thèse de M.A., Montréal, 1968.
2667. **Beaulieu, Claude.** "Le contrôle architectural à Montréal." *RCU* 7, no. 1 (1957):40-42.
2668. **Beauregard, Ludger.** "Géographie manufacturière de Montréal." In *Mélanges géographiques canadiens offerts à Raoul Blanchard*, pp. 275-94. Québec: Presses Universitaires Laval, 1959.

2669. **Belanger, Claude.** "Analyse de quelques thèmes dans le Quartier latin, 1919-1945." Thèse de M.A., Ottawa, 1970.

2670. **Belanger, Marcel.** "Le complexe périmétropolitan Montréalais: Une analyse de l'évolution des populations totales." *Rev géogr Mtl* 26 (1972):241-49.

2671. **Bélanger, Noël.** "L'idéologie du Montréal *Daily Star*, 1929-1933." Thèse de M.A., Laval, 1971.

2672. **Bélanger, R.** *Les vieux logements de Montréal.* Montréal: Commission metropolitaine, 1937.

2673. **Benjamin, J.** *La communauté urbaine de Montréal: Une reforme ratée.* Montréal: L'Aurore, 1975.

2674. **Berku, Dida.** "Saving Montreal." *City Mag* 1, no. 4 (1975):38-46.

2675. **Berman, Alf.** "The Construction Industry in Montreal with Special Reference to Seasonal Unemployment." M.A. thesis, McGill, 1931.

2676. **Bernard, A.; Léveillé, J.; and Lord, G.** *Profile: Montreal. The Political and Administrative Structures of the Metropolitan Region of Montreal.* Ottawa: MSUA, 1974.

2677. **Blanchard, Raoul.** *Montréal, esquisse de géographie urbaine.* Grenoble: Allier, 1947.

2678. _____. "Montréal, esquisse de géographie." *Rev géogr alpine* 35 (1947):133-328.

2679. _____. "Montréal, esquisse de géographie urbaine." *RCGG* 1-2 (1950):31-46.

2680. **Blishen, Bernard R.** "A Sociological Study of Three Philanthropic Financial Campaigns in Montreal." M.A. thesis, McGill, 1950.

2681. **Blouin, A.** "Montréal au XXe siècle." *JRAIC* 33 (1956):420-23.

2682. **Boissevain, Jeremy.** "Les Italians de Montréal: L'adaptation dans une société pluraliste." *Documents de la Commission royale d'enquête sur le bilinguisme et le biculturalisme*, no. 7. Ottawa: Information Canada, 1971. Translated as *The Italians of Montreal: Social Adjustments in a Plural Society.* New York: Arno, 1971.

2683. **Bouchard, Diana.** "Spatial Patterns of Selected Retail Activities, Montreal 1950-70." M.A. thesis, McGill, 1972.

2684. **Bougie, M.** "Quelques aspects économiques du transport en commun à Montréal." Thèse, HEC (Montréal), 1958.

2685. **Boulkind, Mabel.** "Vocational Training Facilities for Women in Montreal." M.A. thesis, McGill, 1938.

2686. **Bourassa, Guy.** "Remarques sur le comportement électoral des Montréalais." *CL* 14 (janvier 1963):18-21.

2687. _____. "La connaissance politique de Montréal: Bilan et perspectives." *Rech soc* 6, no. 2 (1965):163-80.

2688. _____. "Les groupes de pression à Montréal. Les citoyens et la legislation." *Cah ICEA* 2 (1966):61-78.

2689. _____. "La structure du pouvoir à Montréal: Le domaine de l'éducation. *Rech soc* 8, no. 2 (1967):125-50.

2690. _____. "Les relations ethniques dans la vie politique montréalaise." *Documents de la Commission royale d'enquête sur le bilinguisme et le biculturalisme*, no. 10. Ottawa: Information Canada, 1971.

2691. **Bourguignon, J. C.** "Montréal et son port." *RCU* 11, no. 2 (1961): 21-28.

2692. **Brazeau, Joseph.** "The French-Canadian Doctor in Montreal." M.A. thesis, McGill, 1951.

2693. _____. "La question linguistique à Montréal." *Rev inst soc* 1 (1968):31-52.

2694. **Brédimas-Assimopoulos, Nadia.** "Intégration civique sans acculturation. Les Grecs à Montréal." *SS* 7 (1975):129-42.

2695. **Bridger, M. K.** "The Relationship between Landscape and Residential Growth Patterns: The Example of Western Montreal Island." M.A. thesis, McGill, 1964.

2696. _____, and Greer-Wooten, Bryn. "Landscape Components and Residential Urban Growth in Western Montreal Island." *Rev géogr Mtl* 19 (1965):75-90.
2697. **Brouillette, Benoit.** "La géographie de Montréal." *L'Enseignement primaire* 3e série, 1 (1942):804-13.
2698. **Brown, Wilfrid Harold.** "The Slovakian Community in Montreal." M.A. thesis, McGill, 1927.
2699. **Burdett, Gillian M.** "The High School for Girls, Montreal." M.A. thesis, McGill, 1963.
2700. **Cameron, Jean.** *A Study of Housing Conditions of Old People in Montreal.* Ottawa: CMHC, 1957.
2701. **Campeau, Charles-Edouard.** "Montreal's Master Plan for Improved Traffic." *Engineering J* 34 (1951):768-75.
2702. _____. "Problèmes d'urbanisme dans la métropole." *L'Ingénieur* 167 (1956):7-13.
2703. _____. "Town Planning from the Air, As Applied to the City of Montreal." *CASU* 8, no. 3 (1956):157-63.
2704. _____. "Planning Problems in Montreal." *CPR* 7, no. 1 (1957):31-39.
2705. **Camu, Pierre.** 'Effets du projet de canalisation du Saint-Laurent sur le port de Montréal." *Ac Ec* 28 (1953):619-37.
2706. _____. "Le port de Montréal à la veille de l'ouverture de la nouvelle voie navigable du Saint-Laurent." *Can Geogr* 5 (octobre 1958-mai 1959):85-95.
2707. **Caron, Roland.** "Les ports concurrents de Montréal sur le fleuve Saint-Laurent." Thèse, HEC (Montréal), 1944.
2708. **Chan, David W.** "Design Considerations in Urban Low-Income Housing Redevelopment with Special Reference to Montreal." M.Arch. thesis, McGill, 1970.
2709. **Charbonneau, Hubert, and Legaré, Jacques.** "L'extrême mobilité urbaine au Canada: L'exemple de Montréal entre 1956 et 1961." *Rev géogr Mtl* 21 (1967):235-65.
2710. **Charbonneau, Hubert; Henripin, Jacques; and Legaré, Jacques.** "L'avenir démographique des francophones au Québec et à Montréal en l'absence de politiques adéquates." *Rev géogr Mtl* 24 (1970):199-202.
2711. **Charney, Melvin.** "The Old Montreal No One Wants to Preserve." *Montrealer* 38 (1964):20-23.
2712. **Chichekian, Gars.** "Armenian Immigrants in Canada and Their Distribution in Montreal." *Cah géogr Q* 21 (1977):62-82.
2713. **Choko, Marc Henri.** *Crises du logement à Montréal.* Montréal: Albert Saint-Martin, 1980.
2714. **Cobb, Henri.** "Some Notes on the Design of Place Ville Marie." *JRAIC* 40 (1963):54-60.
2715. **Coleman, Romalis.** "The Reaction of Montreal Jews toward French Nationalism and Separatism." M.A. thesis, McGill, 1967.
2716. **Copp, Terry.** "The Montreal Working Class in Prosperity and Depression." *CI* 1 (1975):85-98.
2717. _____. "Montreal's Municipal Government and the Crisis of the 1930s." In #29, pp. 112-29.
2718. **Côté, Alphonse.** "Une agglomération polono-ukrainienne de Montréal." Thèse de M.A., Montréal, 1948.
2719. **Coulon, Jacques.** "Old Montreal Renewal: A Love Affair." *CGEJ* 84 (1972):24-31.
2720. **Cousineau, Aimé.** "City Planning Activities in Montreal." *JRAIC* 20, no. 4 (1943):51-53.
2721. **Dagenais, Pierre.** "Montréal, métropole canadienne." *Le français dans le monde* 23 (1964):7-12.
2722. _____. "La métropole du Canada: Montréal ou Toronto?" *Rev géogr Mtl* 23 (1969):27-38.
2723. **Daly, Margaret.** "Montreal Poor Challenge Mayor Drapeau's Regime." In #925, pp. 76-82.
2724. **Davidson, J. R.** "The Westward Migration of Montreal's English Speaking People." M.A. thesis, Brigham Young, 1974.

2725. **Davidson, Mary.** "The Social Adjustment of British Immigrant Families in Verdun and Pointe-Saint-Charles." M.A. thesis, McGill, 1933.
2726. **Davidson, N. M.** "Montreal's Dominance of the Canadian Men's Fine Clothing Industry." M.A. thesis, Western Ontario, 1969.
2727. **De Guise, J.-G.** "Monographie historique du conseil central des syndicats nationaux de Montréal, 1920 à 1955." Thèse de M.A., Montréal, 1962.
2728. **De Jong, Nicolas J.** "Spatial Aspects of Real Estate Transactions: An Exploratory Study of the Island of Montreal, 1947-1967." M.A. thesis, McGill, 1971.
2729. **Delâge, Jean.** "Analyse du commerce de détail à Montréal en 1939." *Ac Ec* 17 (1941):54-77.
2730. **Dell'Aniello, Paul.** "Montréal, métropole financière." *Ac Ec* 43 (1967):112-16.
2731. **De Lorme, Pierre.** "La politique urbaine: Fondements théoriques et application pratique: Analyse du projet de l'autoroute est-ouest à Montréal." Thèse de M.A., Ottawa, 1976.
2732. **Denis, Paul Yves.** "Conditions géographiques et postulats démographiques d'une rénovation urbaine à Montréal." *Rev géogr Mtl* 21 (1967):149-64.
2733. ———. "Montréal: Bilan décennal d'une morphologie en transition." *Rev géogr Mtl* 25 (1971):281-91.
2734. **Dernsi, Louis-Antoine.** "Housing in the Suburban Region of Montreal, 1951-1961." M.A. thesis, McGill, 1964.
2735. **Desbarats, Guy.** "Montréal—laboratoire urbain." *Habitat* 10 (janvier-février 1967):26-32.
2736. **Deschamp, Jean.** "L'habitation à Montréal." *Ac Ec* 23 (1947):446-72.
2737. **Desjardins, Edouard.** "L'enseignement medical à Montréal au milieu du XXe siècle." *UMCA* 100 (1971):305-9.
2738. **Divay, Gérard, and Hurtubise, Luc.** *Les promoteurs d'habitation dans la région de Montréal.* Montréal: Institut national de la recherche, 1972.
2739. **Dubois, A.** "La communauté urbaine de Montréal, les forces en présence." Thèse de M.A., Montréal, 1974.
2740. **Dubreuil, G., and Rioux, Marcel.** "Une étude de communauté à la péripherie de la banlieue montréalaise." *Rech soc* 4 (1963):107-11.
2741. **Ducharme, O.** "Monographie économique du quartier Saint-Henri (Montréal)." Thèse de M.A., Montréal, 1941.
2742. **Dupire, Jean.** "Le service d'éducation du syndicat national des fonctionnaires municipaux de Montréal." *Relat indus* 12 (1957):231-37.
2742A. **Dupoint, Claude.** "Camillien Houde, politicien de carrière." Thèse de M.A., Ottawa, 1972.
2743. **Ewing, James.** "The Montreal Situation with Reference to Town Planning." *TPICJ* 1, no. 7 (1921):4-9.
2744. ———. "Suggested Mountain Roadway for Mount Royal Park, Montreal." *TPICJ* 1, no. 8 (1922):6-7.
2745. ———. "Plain Words for Montreal." *TPICJ* 4, no. 4 (1925):12-15.
2746. ———. "Corrective Planning Methods." *TPICJ* 5, no. 2 (1926):17-20.
2747. **Feberdy, L. I.** "Intergovernmental Functions in Respect to Regional Planning [in the Montreal Region]." M.A. thesis, McGill, 1969.
2748. **Ferland, Yvan.** *Croissance de la population et besoins en logement dans la zone métropolitaine de Montréal.* Montréal: Conseil des oeuvres de Montréal, 1967.
2749. **Fernandez, Ronald.** "Ethnicity as a Symbol System: A Theoretical Discussion Exemplified by Case Studies of Spaniards in Montreal." M.A. thesis, McGill, 1972.
2750. ———. "A Logic of Ethnicity: A Study of the Significance and Classification of Ethnic Identity among Montreal Portuguese." Ph.D. thesis, McGill, 1978.
2751. **Fiset, Edouard.** "Introduction of an Urban Concept in the Planning of the Exposition." *JRAIC* 42 (1965):55-62.

2752. **Fisher, David.** "Montreal Regional Industrial Pattern as Compared with That of Toronto." M.A. thesis, McGill, 1940.
2753. **Fleming, C. E. B., and Krohn, R. G.** "Neighbourhood Economy and the Urban Housing Problem: Landlords and Tenants in a Working Class Montreal Locality." *W Can J Ant* 3, no. 2 (1972):45-64.
2754. **Foggin, Peter M.** "Changes in the Intra-Urban Land-Value Surface: The Impact of Transportation, Land-Use and Socio-Economic Factors in Central Montreal." Ph.D. thesis, McGill, 1970.
2755. _____. "Les formes de l'utilisation du sol à Montréal/Urban Land Use Patterns: The Montreal Case." In #**2243**, pp. 32-45.
2756. _____, **and Polèse, Mario.** *The Social Geography of Montreal in 1971.* Research Paper #88. Toronto: CUCS, 1977.
2757. **Fortin, Berthe.** "Le problème du logement à Montréal." Thèse de M.A., Montréal, 1946.
2758. **Fortin, I.** "Considération sur un projet d'organisation et sur les fonctions d'une commission d'urbanisme de l'Ile de Montréal." *RTCN* 10 (1924):254-69.
2759. **Fournier, Pierre.** "A Political Analysis of School Reorganization in Montreal." M.A. thesis, McGill, 1971.
2760. **Frei, John W.** "Client Power in Montreal." *Can Wel* 44 (1968):8-11.
2761. **Gabeline, D.; Lanken, D.; and Pape, G.** *Montreal at the Crossroads.* Montreal: Harvest House, 1975.
2762. **Gagnon, Gilbert.** "La fonction commerciale du port de Montréal depuis 1946." Thèse, HEC (Montréal), 1963.
2763. **Gagnon-Lacasse, Francine.** "Evolution des institutions politiques de la ville de Montréal (1921-1965)." Thèse de M.A. Montréal, 1967.
2764. **Gariépy, Gérard.** "Le plan directeur des espaces libres pour Montréal." *RCU* 6, no. 1 (1956):35-38.
2765. **Gauthier, Paul.** "Montréal et ses quartiers." *BRH* 67 (1961):115-35.
2766. **Gellert, Judith.** "The Social Adjustment of Hungarian Refugees in Montreal." M.S.W. thesis, McGill, 1964.
2767. **Germain, Claude.** "Evolution démographique et polarisation de la région de Montréal." *Ac Ec* 38 (1962):245-76.
2768. _____. "Mouvements migratoires et croissance démographique de Montréal." *Ac Ec* 38 (1962):411-24.
2769. _____. "Le rapport du conseil du travail de Montréal sur la pauvreté." *Ac Ec* 42 (1966):141-46.
2770. **Germain, Denis.** "Le besoin de logement à Montréal." *Ac Ec* 36 (1961):681-700.
2771. _____. "Le problème du logement à Montréal." *Ac Ec* 38 (1962):71-80.
2772. _____. "Montréal, métropole industrielle." *Ac Ec* 43 (1967):117-27.
2773. **Gibbard, Harold A.** "The Means and Modes of Living of European Immigrants in Montreal." M.A. thesis, McGill, 1934.
2774. **Gilmour, Gillian M.** "Some Aspects of Residential Mobility in Urban Social Space [Montreal, 1951-61]." M.A. thesis, McGill, 1969.
2775. **Granbois, A.** "Montreal." *Habitat* 10, no. 3-6 (1967):52-55.
2776. **Graser, Otto.** "A Survey of Industrial Estates with Special Reference to Montreal." M.Arch. thesis, McGill, 1964.
2777. **Gratton, Valmore.** "Industrial Montreal." *Mun Rev Can* 46 (1950):22-23.
2778. _____. *Transportation in the Montreal Region.* Montréal: Service de la circulation de la cité de Montréal, 1958.
2779. **Greer-Wootten, Bryn.** "Changing Social Areas and the Intra-Urban Migration Process." *Rev géogr Mtl* 26 (1972):271-92.

2780. _____, and Marshall, John V. "Le système urbain/The Urban System." In #2243, pp. 157-69.
2781. **Grenon, Hector.** *Camillien Houde.* Montreal: Stanké, 1979.
2782. **Groulx, Adelard.** "La mortalité maternelle et la mortalité infantile à Montréal." *UMCA* 72 (1943):1415-17.
2783. **Guérin, Marc-Aimé.** "L'aménagement du sol dans la banlieue rurale de Montréal." *RCGG* 6 (1952):19-27.
2784. **Gutwirth, J.** "The Structure of a Hassidic Community in Montreal." *Jewish J Soc* 14, no. 1 (1972):43-62.
2785. **Handelman, Donald.** "West Indian Associations in Montreal." M.A. thesis, McGill, 1964.
2787. **Harney, Robert F.** "Montreal's King of Italian Labour: A Case Study of Padronism." *Labour* 4 (1979):57-84.
2788. **Harvey, Pierre.** "L'industrie manufacturière dans la zone métropolitaine de Montréal." *Ac Ec* 31 (1955):136-45.
2789. **Hébert, Jean-Paul.** "Le commerce de détail à Montréal et à Toronto." Thèse, HEC (Montréal), 1952.
2790. **Henripin, Jacques.** "Les facteurs sociaux de la mortalité infantile à Montréal." *Union médicale du Canada* 89 (1960):3-11; 91 (1962):65-71.
2791. _____. "L'inégalité sociale devant la mort: La mortalité et la mortalité infantile à Montréal." *Rech soc* 2, no. 1 (1961):3-34.
2792. **Hoffman, Andrew.** "City Squares and Open Spaces with Special Reference to Montreal." M.A. thesis, McGill, 1962.
2793. **Hughes, Everett C., and McDonald, Margaret L.** "French and English in the Economic Structure of Montreal." *CJEPS* 7 (1941):493-505.
2794. **Isenberg, Seymour.** "Industrial Location in the City of St. Laurent." M.A. thesis, McGill, 1967.
2795. **Israël, Wilfrid Emerson.** "The Montreal Negro Community." M.A. thesis, McGill, 1928.
2796. **Jamieson, S. M.** "French and English in the Institutional Structure of Montreal: A Study of the Social and Economic Division of Labour." M.A. thesis, McGill, 1938.
2797. **Johnson, Rodrigue.** "Les attitudes professionnelles des instituteurs de Montréal." Thèse de 3e cycle, Paris, 1967.
2798. **Jones, C. F.** "The Grain Trade of Montreal." *Econ Geogr* 1 (1925):53-72.
2799. **Kardos, R.** "Political Power and Urban Redevelopment: A Case Study of Montreal." M.A. thesis, McGill, 1969.
2800. **Kentridge, Leon R.** "A Survey of New Towns about Metropolitan Areas with Special Reference to Montreal." M.Arch. thesis, McGill, 1961.
2801. **Khor, Ean.** "Evolution of Patterns of Land Subdivision with Special Reference to Montreal." M.A. thesis, McGill, 1964.
2802. **Kovitz, M.** "Landlord Subsidization by Tenants in East End Montreal." M.A. thesis, McGill, 1975.
2803. **Laberge, L.** "Aspects de geographie sociale de la population polonaise de Montreal." Thèse L. ès L., Laval, 1972.
2804. **Lacoste, Norbert.** *Les caractéristiques sociales de la population du grand Montréal.* Montréal: Faculté des sciences sociales, Université de Montréal, 1958.
2805. _____. "Les traits nouveaux de la population du grand Montréal." *Rech soc* 6 (1965):265-72.
2806. _____. "La morphologie religieuse de Montréal." *Rev inst soc* 1 (1968):67-72.
2807. **Laforest, M.** "Le port de Montréal, 1914-1940." Thèse, HEC (Montréal), 1942.
2808. **Lampson, Réal.** "Le scrutin du 28 juillet 1930 dans la région de Montréal." Thèse de M.A., Laval, 1972.

2809. **Langlois, Claude.** "The State of Local Government in Greater Montreal." *Can Geogr* 8 (1964):160-62.
2810. **Langral, Georges.** "Région de Montréal." *Commerce* 61, no. 8 (1959):29-71; 61, no. 9 (1959):21-60; 61, no. 10 (1959):35-55.
2811. **Lapierre, Richard.** "Aspects géographiques du tourisme à Montréal." *Cah géogr Q* 6 (1959):295-303.
2812. **Laplante, Jean de.** "La communauté montréalaise." *Contributions à l'étude des sciences de l'Homme* 1 (1952):57-107.
2813. **Larivière, Claude.** *Crise économique et contrôle social: Le cas de Montréal, 1929-1937.* Montréal: Saint-Martin, 1977.
2814. **Larouche, Pierre.** "Modèle de développement residentiel de la région de Montréal." Thèse de M.A., Yale, 1964.
2815. **Lash, H. N.** "Montreal, Rural-Urban Land Use, Sampling Methods of Study." M.A. thesis, McGill, 1949.
2816. **Lasry, J.-C., and Bloomfield-Schachter, E.** "Jewish Intermarriage in Montreal, 1962-1972." *Jewish Soc Stud* 37 (1975):267-78.
2817. **Laurence, L.** "Finances municipales comparées de Montréal, Toronto, et Vancouver." Thèse de M.A., Montréal, 1957.
2818. **Lavallée, Jean.** *Laval—ville nouvelle.* Montreal: Holt, Rinehart and Winston, 1969.
2819. **Lavigne, Marie, and Stoddart, Jennifer.** "Analyse du travail féminin à Montréal entre les deux guerres." Thèse de M.A., Québec à Montréal, 1974.
2820. ———. "Les travailleuses montréalaises entre les deux guerres." *Labour* 2 (1977):170-84.
2821. **Lefebvre, Guy.** "Les revenus et dépenses de la province de Québec. La contribution et la part imputable à la région de Montréal." Thèse, HEC (Montréal), 1963.
2822. **Lefrançois, Pierre-C.** "Montréal, métropole commerciale." *Ac Ec* 43 (1967):106-11.
2823. **Legault, Guy-R.** "Le métro de Montréal." *Arch Can* 43 (1966):44-48.
2824. **Léonard, Jean-François.** "L'évolution du rôle du service d'urbanisme de la ville de Montréal dans l'orientation de la politique, d'aménagement de la ville de Montréal, 1941-1971." Thèse de M.A., Québec à Montréal, 1974.
2825. ———, **and McGraw, Donald.** "Le contrôle du redéveloppement urbain par les groupes populaires à Montréal: Du carcan intellectuel aux alternatives politiques." *Urb For* 2, no. 1 (1976):5-12.
2826. **Lepine, Y.** "Intégration d'une communauté rurale de la banlieue maraîchère de Montréal à la société urbaine post-industrielle." Thèse de M.A., Laval, 1972.
2827. **Leroy, Vély.** "Le règlement de zonage concernant le flanc sud du Mont-Royal." *Ac Ec* 38 (1963):569-85.
2828. **Lesage, J.** "Le syndicalisme chez les fonctionnaires municipaux de la ville de Montréal." Thèse de M.A., Montréal, 1957.
2829. **Léveillée, Jacques.** "Développement urbain et politiques gouvernementales urbaines dans l'agglomération montréalaise, 1945-1975." Thèse de Ph.D., Montréal, 1976.
2830. ———. "Contextes socio-économiques, configuration des classes sociales et enjeux structurels de l'agglomération montréalaise, 1945-1976." *Urb For* 3, no. 1 (1977):26-36.
2831. ———. "Les stratégies urbaines fédérales et québécoises en rapport avec les enjeux structurels montréalais." *Urb For* 3, no. 2 (1977):26-35.
2832. ———. "Réactions des gouvernements supérieurs aux enjeux structurels montréalais." *Urb For* 3, no. 4 (1977):20-29.
2833. **Levesque, Robert, and Migner, Robert-Maurice.** *Camillien et les années vingt. Suivi de Camillien au Goulag. Cartographie du Houdisme.* Montréal: Brûlés, 1978.
2834. **Levinson, Harvey.** "Montreal's Response to the Spanish Civil War." M.A. thesis, Concordia, 1976.
2835. **Lewis, A. C.** "Survey and Replanning of Montreal." *JRAIC* 21 (1944):146-51.

2836. **Li, Ying H.** "Street Patterns in Residential Areas with Special Reference to Montreal." M.Arch. thesis, McGill, 1965.
2837. **Lieberson, S.** "Bilingualism in Montreal: A Demographic Analysis." *AJS* 71 (1965):10-23.
2838. **Limoges, Thérèse.** *La prostitution à Montréal.* Montréal: L'Homme, 1967.
2839. **Lord, G.; Tremblay, A.; and Trépanier, M.-O.** *Les communautés urbaines de Montréal et de Québec.: Premier bilan.* Montréal: Presses de l'université de Montréal, 1975.
2840. **Louder, Frederick.** "Montreal's Downtown Moves East." *City Mag* 1, no. 7 (1975):32-39.
2841. **McDougall, W.** "An Inquiry into Residential Development in Pointe-Claire, Quebec over the Last Forty Years." *HSST* 10, no. 2 (1974):35-43.
2842. **McGraw, Donald.** "Les causes de la modification de la pratique politique et ideologigue des groupes populaires en milieu urbain à Montréal, entre 1963 et 1968." Thèse de M.A., Québec à Montréal, 1979.
2843. **Mailhiot, Bernard.** "La psychologie des relations inter-ethniques à Montréal." *Contributions à l'étude des sciences de l'homme* 3 (1956):7-24.
2844. _____. "Les relations entre les groupes ethniques à Montréal: Zones de conflit et zones d'échange." *Education des adultes* 7 (1961):1-17.
2845. **Mallory, James R.** "Montreal: Problem Metropolis." *CPR* 5, no. 1 (1955):4-9.
2846. **Manchur, S. W.** "The Economic and Social Adjustment of Slavic Immigrants in Canada with Special Reference to the Ukrainian in Montreal." M.A. thesis, McGill, 1935.
2847. **Mandelle, Roméo.** "La préservation du passé à Montréal." *Habitat* 5, no. 4 (1962):24-28.
2848. **Martin, Dan.** "Caractéristiques du logement dans la région métropolitaine de Montréal." Thèse, HEC (Montréal), 1956.
2849. _____, **and Prus, V.** "Rockland Shopping Center, Town of Mount-Royal." *Can Arch* 5 (1960):64-75.
2850. **Martin, Fernand.** *Montreal: An Economic Perspective.* Montreal: C. D. Howe Research Institute, 1979.
2851. **Martin, Gérald.** "Etude des facteurs qui ont déterminé la localisation de l'industrie à Montréal et dans les banlieues." *RTCN* 20 (1934):297-334.
2852. **Martin, Jacques.** "Les chevaliers du travail et le syndicalisme international à Montréal." Thèse de M.A., Montréal, 1965.
2853. **Massue, Huet.** *Financial and Economic Situation of Montreal Compared with That of Toronto.* Montreal: Shawinigan Water and Power, 1940.
2854. **Melancon, J.-M.** "Montréal-Nord et ses problèmes de développement." Thèse, HEC (Montréal), 1963.
2855. **Ménard, Denis.** "Le marché des produits du pétrole des raffineries de Montréal." Thèse, HEC (Montréal), 1963.
2856. **Mercer, John.** "City Manager Communities in the Montreal Metropolitan Area." *Can Geogr* 18 (1974):352-66.
2857. **Metton, Alain.** "L'électricité à Montréal." *Rev géogr Mtl* 25 (1971):221-33.
2858. **Meyer, John.** "Will the Seaway Doom Montreal?" *Can Bus* 28 (1955):32-38.
2859. **Migner, Robert-Maurice.** "Camillien Houde et le houdisme." Thèse de M.A., Montréal, 1971.
2860. _____. "Le bossisme politique à Montréal: Camillien Houde remplace Méderic Martin (1923-1929)." *UHR* 1-74 (juin 1974):2-8.
2861. **Minville, Esdras, ed.** *Montréal économique: Etude préparée à l'occasion du troisième centenaire de la ville.* Montréal: Fides, 1943.
2862. **Mollmann, Albert Von.** *Das Deutschtum in Montreal.* Jena: Fischer, 1937.
2863. **Montréal, Qué., Service d'urbanisme.** *Urbanisation. Etude de l'expansion urbaine dans la région de Montréal.* Bulletin technique no. 5. Montréal, 1968.
2864. **Murricane, K.** "Inter-urban Industrial Linkages in Montreal's Hinterland." M.A. thesis, McGill, 1975.

2865. **Musée d'art contemporain, Montréal.** *Borduas et les automatistes, Montréal, 1942-1955.* Montréal: Editeur officiel du Québec, 1971.
2866. **Ng, Che L.** "The Development of Complex Commercial Projects in Central Areas with Special Reference to Montreal." M.Arch. thesis, McGill, 1965.
2867. **Nobbs, Percy E.** "City Owned Land and the Housing Problem in Montreal." In *Housing and Community Planning*, pp. 196-203. McGill University Monograph Series. Montreal, 1944.
2868. **O'Brien, Michael.** "The Development and History of the Federation of English-Speaking Catholic Teachers, Incorporated, of Montreal." M.A. thesis, McGill, 1973.
2869. **Ossenberg, R. J.** "The Social Integration and Adjustment of Post-War Immigrants in Montreal and Toronto." *Can R Soc Anth* 1 (1964): 202-15.
2870. **Paint, H. M.** "The St. Lawrence Seaway—Part Three: The Port of Montreal." *Can Bank* 64 (1957):21-37.
2871. **Paré, A.** "L'annexion des municipalités modifiera-t-elle le fardeau des contribuables de Montréal?" Thèse, HEC (Montréal), 1962.
2872. **Parenteau, Roland.** "La question des tramways à Montréal." *Ac Ec* 26 (1951):779-94.
2873. **Parisella, John E.** "Pressure Group Politics: A Case Study of the St. Leonard School Crisis." M.A. thesis, McGill, 1971.
2874. **Parrisset, Marie-Françoise.** "Saint-Laurent, secteur sud." Thèse de M.A., Montréal, 1963.
2875. **Patenaude, J.-Z. Leon.** *Le vrai visage de Jean Drapeau.* Montréal: Jour, 1962.
2876. **Paumier, Cyril.** "New Town at Montreal's Front Door." *Landscape Arch* 57 (1966):67.
2877. **Pelletier, Jean, and Beauregard, Ludger.** "Le centre-ville de Montréal." *Geogr Bull* 9, no. 4 (1967):89-124.
2878. **Perks, W. T.** "Planning in the Province of Quebec: The Montreal Metropolitan Region." *Town Plan R* 36 (1965):29-48.
2879. **Perreault, Louis.** "L'habitation et l'évolution de l'urbanisme à Montréal de la période de crise à la création de la société d'habitation du Québec, 1935-1968." Thèse de M.A., Laval, 1979.
2880. **Pick, Alfred John.** *The Administration of Paris and Montreal: A Comparative Study.* Montreal: Witness, 1940.
2881. **Picker, A.** "L'évolution des professions primaires, secondaires et tertiaires à Montréal et à Toronto, de 1931 à 1961: Concept et realité." Thèse, HEC (Montréal), 1966.
2882. "The Planning of Montreal." *TPICJ* 5, no. 6 (1926):21-23.
2883. **Potter, H. H.** "The Occupational Adjustments of Montreal Negroes, 1941-1948." M.A. thesis, McGill, 1949.
2884. **Prezeau, Pierre.** "Politique et annexions." *Parti-pris* 2, no. 4 (1964):33-45.
2885. **Prost, Robert.** "Connaissance et action: Ou les deux faces opposées d'une reforme gouvernementale [Montréal]." *CJPS* 10 (1977):43-63.
2886. **Racine, Jean-Bernard.** "Exurbanisation et metamorphisme péri-urbain. Introduction à l'étude de la croissance du grand Montréal." *Rev géogr Mtl* 21 (1967): 313-41.
2887. **Racine, Louis.** "Etude comparative des industries manufacturières de Montréal et de Toronto, avant et après la guerre." Thèse, HEC (Montréal), 1951.
2888. **Raina, S. K.** "Development of High-rise Habitation in Central Urban Areas with Special Reference to Montreal." M.Arch. thesis, McGill, 1974.
2889. *Rapport de la Commission d'étude des problèmes intermunicipaux dans l'Ile de Montréal (Rapport Blier).* Québec: Imprimerie de la reine, 1964.
2890. *Rapport de la Commission d'étude du système administratif de Montréal.* 2 vols. Québec: Gouvernement du Québec, 1960-1961.
2891. **Rawin, S.** "Social Mobility in the Home-Building Industry in Montreal 1951-61." M.A. thesis, McGill, 1962.
2891A. **Raynault, Adhémar.** *Témoin d'une époque.* Montréal: Jour, 1970.

2892. **Renaud, Charles.** *L'imprévisible Monsieur Houde.* Montréal: Les Editions de l'Homme, 1964.
2893. **Rennie, D. L. C.** "The Ethnic Division of Labour in Montreal, 1931-1951." M.A. thesis, McGill, 1953.
2894. *A Report on Housing and Slum Clearance for Montreal.* Montreal: Joint Committee of the Montreal Board of Trade and the Civic Improvement League, 1935.
2895. **Ribordy, F.-X.** "Conflit de culture et criminalité des Italians à Montréal." Thèse de Ph.D., Montréal, 1970.
2896. **Richard, Mireille.** "L'oeuvre des réfugiés hongrois et l'adaptation à Montréal d'un groupe de réfugiés hongrois." Thèse de M.A., Montréal, 1961.
2897. **Richardson, Nigel A.** "A Study of the Relationship between Ecological and Non-ecological Factors in the Development of Natural Areas of Montreal." M.A. thesis, McGill, 1954.
2898. **Robert, Percy A.** "Dufferin District: An Area in Transition." M.A. thesis, McGill, 1928.
2899. **Robertson, Barbara.** "Occupational Traits in Clerical Work: A Study of Employed and Unemployed Women in Montreal." M.A. thesis, McGill, 1935.
2900. **Romalis, Coleman.** "The Reaction of Montreal Jews toward French Nationalism and Separatism." M.A. thesis, McGill, 1967.
2901. **Roquebrune, R. de.** *Le Quartier Saint-Louis.* Montréal: Fides, 1966.
2902. **Rosenberg, Louis.** *Population Characteristics of the Jewish Community of Montreal.* Canadian Jewish Population Studies, 5. Montreal: Canadian Jewish Congress, 1955.
2903. ———. *Population Characteristics of the Jewish Community of Montreal.* Canadian Jewish Population Studies, 6. Montreal: Canadian Jewish Congress, 1956.
2904. **Ross, Aileen.** "The French and English Social Elites of Montreal." M.A. thesis, McGill, 1941.
2905. **Ross, Herman Russell.** "Juvenile Delinquency in Montreal." M.A. thesis, McGill, 1932.
2906. **Rowan, Jan C.** "The Story of Place Ville Marie." *Progres Arch* 41 (1960):123-35.
2907. **Saint-Maurice, D.** "Etude du réseau de transport en commun de l'Ile de Montréal." Thèse de Ph.D., Laval, 1973.
2908. **Sancton, Andrew B.** "The Impact of Language Differences on Metropolitan Reform in Montreal." *Can Pub Admin* 22 (1979):227-50.
2909. **Santiago, A. M.** "Residential Rehabilitation: With Special Reference to Montreal." M.Arch. thesis, McGill, 1975.
2910. **Savoie, Gerald.** "La criminalité à Montréal." Thèse de M.A., Montréal, 1961.
2911. **Schoenauer, Norbert.** "The Influence of Urban Growth upon Surrounding Villages with Special Reference to Montreal and the Richelieu Valley." M.A. thesis, McGill, 1959.
2912. **Seidel, Judith.** "The Development and Social Adjustment of the Jewish Community in Montreal." M.A. thesis, McGill, 1940.
2913. **Shaffir, William.** "The Montreal Chassidic Community; Community Boundaries and the Maintenance of Ethnic Identities." M.A. thesis, McGill, 1970.
2914. **Shank, Wesley I.** "The Clustering of Skyscrapers with Special Reference to Montreal." M.Arch. thesis, McGill 1965.
2915. **Sharma, Brajesh.** "Industrial Land Use in Urban Areas with Special Reference to Montreal." M.A. thesis, McGill, 1971.
2916. **Shepard, W. C.** "The Genesis of the Montreal Council of Social Agencies." M.S.W. thesis, McGill, 1957.
2917. **Shooner, Pierre.** "Les taxes sur l'industrie manufacturière à Montréal et à Toronto." Thèse de M.A., Montréal, 1961.
2918. **Shortt, George E.** *Metropolitan Government and Regional Planning Problem and Practice and Application to Montreal.* Montreal: Montreal Board of Trade, 1956.
2919. ———. "Metropolitan Government and Regional Planning in the Montreal Area." *CPR* 7, no. 1 (1957):22-30.
2920. **Sise, Hazan.** "The Future of Mount-Royal." *CPR* 13, no. 3 (1963):34-43.

2921. La situation des immigrants à Montréal: Etude sur l'adaptation occupationnelle, les conditions residentielles et les relations sociales. Montréal: Conseil des oeuvres de Montréal, 1959.
2922. **Slack, Brian.** "The Impact of the St. Lawrence Seaway on the Port of Montreal." M.A. thesis, McGill, 1963.
2923. **Sprougate, G. P.** "Housing and Public Accommodations for the Montreal Negro." *Expression* 1, no. 2 (1965):13-23.
2924. **Steed, Guy P. F.** "Standardization, Scale, Incubation and Inertia: Montreal and Toronto Clothing Industries." *Can Geogr* 20 (1976):298-309.
2925. **Tanghe, Raymond,** *Géographie humaine de Montréal.* Montréal: Librairie d'action canadienne française, 1928.
2926. _____. "Analyse du budget de la ville de Montréal." *Ac Ec* 12 (1936):254-68.
2927. _____. "L'administration de Montréal." *CF* 23, no. 2 (1935):123-34.
2928. _____. "La population de Montréal." *Ac Ec* 18, no. 2 (1942):163-80.
2929. **Thibodeau, J.-C.** *Implantation manufacturière de la région de Montréal, 1962-1967.* Montréal: Presses de l'université du Québec, 1972.
2930. **Tremblay, A.** "Le cauchemar de Drapeau sera son nouveau défi." In #*925,* pp. 68-75.
2931. **Trépanier, Léon.** "Les attributs de la mairie de Montréal." *Cah des dix* 31 (1966):203-12.
2932. **Turcot, Jean.** "Le rôle des filiales américaines dans le développement industriel de Montréal." Thèse de M.A., Montréal, 1940.
2933. **Turcotte, Georges E.** "Dossier sur le pouvoir municipal à Montréal." *Maintenant* 103 (février 1971):48-61.
2934. **Upton, Phyllis G.** "A Study of the Expressed Employment Needs of Montreal, Implications for Business Education Curriculum." M.A. thesis, McGill, 1966.
2935. **Vaucrosson, Noel V.** "Housing Design within the Urban Social Redevelopment Project Area of Montreal." M.Arch. thesis, McGill, 1967.
2936. **Veltman, Calvin J.; Boulet, J.-A.; and Castonguay, Charles.** "The Economic Context of Bilingualism and Language Transfer in the Montreal Metropolitan Area." *CJE* 12 (1979):468-79.
2937. **Versailles, Yvan.** "Le développement industriel de l'est de Montréal." Thèse de M.A., Montréal, 1938.
2938. **Wassef, Nadia.** "The Egyptians in Montreal: A New Colour in the Canadian Ethnic Mosaic." M.A. thesis, McGill, 1978.
2939. **Wellbourne, Arthur J.** "A Study of Educational Practices in the Schools in the Island of Montreal." M.A. thesis, McGill, 1946.
2940. **Wesley, George J.** "Montreal, Que.—Planning and Policies." *CPR* 20, no. 3 (1970):22-23.
2941. **Wright, Frederick.** "Montreal Borough Commission." *Am Pol Sci Rev* 22 (1928):381-83.
2942. _____, ed. *The Borough System of Government for Greater Montreal.* Montreal: Municipal Service Bureau, 1947.
2943. **Wusaty, N.** "Ukrainians in Montreal: The First Seventy-Five Years." B.A. essay, McGill, 1974.
2944. **Zakuta, Leo.** "The Natural Areas of the Montreal Metropolitan Community." M.A. thesis, McGill, 1948.

10. Quebec City

a. General

2945. **Acland, J. H.** "Quebec City." *Canadian Archives* 8 (1963):60-65.
2946. **Anderson, Ross Cardwell.** "The Architecture of Quebec City." *Can Arch* 11, no. 5 (1966):63-70.

2947. **Angus, A. D.** *Old Quebec.* Montreal: Carrier, 1955.
2948. **Association des guides historiques de Québec.** *Hier et aujourd'hui—Québec—Past and Present.* Québec, n.d.
2949. **Azard-Malaurie, Marie Madeleine.** "De l'architecture monumentale classique à Québec." *Vie des Arts* 49 (1967-68):42-49.
2950. **Barbeau, C. M.** *I Have Seen Quebec.* Toronto: Macmillan, 1957. Translated as *J'ai vu Québec.* Québec: Garneau, 1957.
2951. _____. "Notre ancienne architecture." *Rev Q indus* 5, no. 2 (1940):4-9.
2952. **Beaudin, François.** "Archives de la ville de Québec. Repertoire numérique des registres antérieurs à 1840." *Archives* 71, no. 2 (1971):21-32.
2953. **Blanchard, Raoul.** *Le Québec par l'image.* Montréal: Beauchemin, 1949.
2954. **Bland, J.** "Comment conserver, et restaurer la ville de Québec." *RCU* 13, no. 3 (1963):6-17.
2955. **Boutwell, W. D.** "Quebec: Capital of French Canada." *Nat Geog Mag* 57 (1930):507-522.
2956. **Brown, Clément.** *Québec, croissance d'une ville.* Québec: Presses universitaires Laval, 1952.
2957. **Bruchési, Jean.** "Québec, ville forte." *Cah des dix* 22 (1957):53-67.
2958. **Carle, Claude, and Perreault, Guy.** *Images du vieux Québec.* Québec: Pélican, 1967.
2959. **Carrel, Frank.** *The Québec Tercentenary Commemorative History.* Quebec: *Daily Telegraph,* 1908.
2960. _____. *Guide to the City of Quebec.* Quebec, 1924.
2961. **Casgrain, Henri Raymond.** *Histoire de l'Hôtel-Dieu de Québec.* Montréal: Beauchemin, 1888.
2962. **Chandonnet, Jean.** "Le problème de la syndicalisation dans le commerce de détail de Québec." Thèse de M.A., Laval, 1956.
2963. **Chouinard, H. J. J. B.** *Fêtes du troisième centenaire de la fondation de Québec par Champlain, 1608-1908.* Québec: Laflamme et Proulx, 1908.
2964. **Cimon, Jean.** "Autopsie du vieux Québec." *RCU* 8, no. 3 (1958):93-95.
2965. _____. "Intéressant projet de rénovation urbaine à Québec." *CV* 5 (1962):34-38.
2966. *La cité de Québec, son passé est glorieux et son avenir est brillant.* Québec: Poitras, 1955.
2967. **Cloutier, Raoul.** *The Lure of Quebec: An Illustrated Descriptive Guide to the Historical and Picturesque Landmarks and Plans of Interest in Quebec and Environs.* Toronto: Musson, 1923.
2968. **Comité de rénovation et de mise en valeur du Vieux Québec.** *Concept général de réaménagement du Vieux Québec.* Québec: Société historique de Québec, 1970.
2969. **Commission urbaine de Québec.** *A pied dans le vieux Québec/Walking Tour of Old Quebec.* Québec, 1972.
2970. **Davies, Blodwen.** *The Storied Streets of Quebec.* Toronto: Ryerson, 1931.
2971. **De la Roche, Mazo.** *Quebec: Historic Seaport.* Garden City, NY: Doubleday, 1944.
2972. **Desjardins, Micheline.** *Québec: Initiation à la géographie urbaine.* Montreal: Holt, Rinehart and Winston, 1970.
2973. **De Volpi, C. P.** *Quebec: A Pictorial Record, 1608-1875.* Toronto: Longman, 1971.
2974. **Dompierre, J.** "Rôle de l'aménagement des berges de la rivière Saint-Charles dans la cadre du renouveau urbain de la ville de Québec." Thèse de Ph.D., Laval, 1973.
2975. **Doughty, Arthur George.** *Quebec of Yesteryear.* Toronto: Nelson, 1932.
2976. _____. *The Fortress of Quebec, 1608-1903.* Quebec: Dussault et Proulx, 1904.
2977. _____, **and Dionne, N. E.** *Quebec under Two Flags: A Brief History of the City.* Quebec: *Quebec News,* 1903.
2978. **Doyle-Frenière, Murielle.** "Les archives de la ville de Québec." *UHR* 1-77 (juin 1977):33-37.

2979. **Duval, André.** *Québec romantique.* Montréal: Boréal Express, 1978.
2980. _____. *La capitale.* Montréal: Boréal Express, 1979.
2981. **Duval, Monique.** *Québec depuis 1608.* Québec: Ministère des affaires culturelles, 1973.
2982. **Falardeau, Jean-Charles.** *Etude générale de la ville de Québec.* Québec, 1949.
2983. **Fiset, Edouard, and Bédard, Roland.** "Le Québec historique." *RCU* 7 (1957):69-75.
2984. **Gaumond, Michel.** *Place Royale: Its Houses and Their Occupants.* Québec: Ministère des affaires culturelles, 1971.
2985. **Goldthorpe, Harry.** *Quebec Streets.* Bradford: Sunbeam Press, 1962.
2986. **Gouin, Paul.** "Conservation des sites historiques." *RCU* 13, no. 4 (1963):17-23.
2987. **Hitsman, J. Mackay.** *Safeguarding Canada, 1763-1871.* Toronto: UTP, 1968.
2988. **Hubert, J.** *La ville de Québec.* Québec: Les Archives de la ville de Québec, 1971.
2989. **Jean, Luce.** "Les bibliothèques paroissiales de la ville de Québec." Thèse de M.A., Laval, 1949.
2990. **Jobin, Albert.** *La petite histoire de Québec.* Québec: Institut Saint-Jean-Bosco, 1948.
2991. **King, M. J.** *Montreal and Quebec: A Pictorial and Historical Guide.* Toronto: Dent, 1955.
2992. **Lemoine, James M.** *Histoire des fortifications et des rues de Québec.* Québec: Le canadien, 1875.
2993. _____. *Quebec Past and Present: A History of Quebec.* Quebec: Côté, 1876.
2994. _____. *Quebec: Its Gates and Environs.* Quebec: *Morning Chronicle,* 1880.
2995. _____. *Picturesque Quebec: A Sequel to Quebec Past and Present.* Montreal: Dawson, 1882.
2996. _____. *Historical Notes on Quebec and Its Environs.* Quebec: Darveau, 1888.
2997. _____. *The Port of Quebec: Its Annals, 1535-1900.* Quebec: Chronicle Printing Co., 1901.
2998. **Letendre, A.** "Analyse financière de la communauté urbaine de Québec." Thèse de M.Sc., Laval, 1971.
2999. **Longstreet, T. Morris.** *Quebec, Montreal, and Ottawa.* New York: Century Co., 1933.
3000. **McArthur, Duncan.** "Quebec, 1629-1929." *QQ* 36 (1929):506-16.
3001. **MacPherson, Charlotte H. G.** *Reminiscences of Old Quebec.* Montreal: Lovell, 1890.
3002. **Marquis, Georges-Emile.** *Les monuments commémoratifs de Québec.* Québec: Garneau, 1958.
3003. **Masters, D. C.** "Mountain Family Circle: A Study in Canadian Urban Culture." RSC, *Trans,* 3d ser. 52 (1958):15-28.
3004. **Moon, Robert.** "Restoring 17th Century Lower Town Quebec." *CGEJ* 91, no. 3 (1975):38-45.
3005. **Nicholson, Bryon.** *In Old Quebec and Other Sketches.* Quebec: Commercial Printing, 1908.
3006. **Noppen, Luc.** *Les églises du Québec, 1600-1850.* Montréal: Fides, 1977.
3007. _____, **and Porter, John R.** *Les églises de Charlesbourg et l'architecture religieuse du Québec.* Québec: Editeur officiel du Québec, 1971.
3008. **Noppen, Luc; Paulette, Claude; and Tremblay, Michel.** *Québec: Trois siècles d'architecture.* Québec: Libre Expression, 1979.
3009. **Oliver, Thomas J.** *Guide to the City of Quebec and Environs.* Quebec: Demers, 1883.
3010. _____. *Haliwell's New Guide to the City of Quebec and Environs with Map of the City.* Quebec: Haliwell, 1888.
3011. **Ouellet, Fernand.** *Histoire de la Chambre de Commerce de Québec.* Québec: Centre de recherche de la faculté de commerce de l'université Laval, 1959.
3012. *Une page d'histoire de Québec, magnifique essor industriel.* Montréal: Société historique nationale, in collaboration with the Industrial Historical Society, 1955.
3013. **Picard, François.** *La batterie royale, de la fin du XVIIe siècle à la fin du XXe siècle.* Québec: Ministère des affaires culturelles, 1978.

3014. **Pitcher, Rosemary.** *Chateau Frontenac.* Montreal: McGraw-Hill Ryerson, 1971.
3015. **Pouliot, Adrien.** "Le troisième centenaire de la congrégation de la Haute-Ville de Québec." CCHA, *Rapport* (1956-57):103-21.
3016. **Provost, Honorius.** "Historique de Séminaire de Québec." *Rev univ Laval* 17 (1963):591-99.
3017. _____. "Les séminaires des Missions-Etrangères de Paris et de Québec." CCHA, *Rapport* (1971):1-16.
3018. **Richardson, A. J. H.** "The Old City of Quebec and Our Heritage in Architecture." CHA, *AR* (1963):31-41.
3019. _____. "Guide to the Architecturally and Historically Most Significant Buildings in the Old City of Quebec." APT *Bull* 2 (1970):1-144.
3020. **Roy, Pierre-Georges.** *Les rues de la cité de Lévis.* Lévis, 1931.
3021. _____. *Les rues de Québec.* Lévis, 1932.
3022. _____. *A travers l'histoire de l'Hôtel-Dieu de Québec.* Lévis, 1939.
3023. _____. *La traverse entre Québec et Lévis.* Lévis, 1942.
3024. **Sirois, F. B., and La Flamme, A.** *Guide de la cartothèque.* Québec: Archives de la ville de Québec, 1975.
3025. **Société historique du Québec.** *Inventaire du vieux Québec.* Québec: Université Laval, 1956.
3026. **Steppler, Glenn A.** *Quebec: The Gibraltar of North America.* Manuscript Report Series. Ottawa: Historic Sites, Parks Canada, 1976.
3027. **Stokes, C. W.** "Quebec, the Ancient Capital of Quebec." *Can Mag* 52 (1918):569-78.
3028. **Thibault, Henri-Paul.** *Bibliographie de la ville de Québec (1534-1972) et inventaire des sources concernant les fortifications (1759-1871).* Ottawa: Parcs Canada, 1973.
3029. **Tourangeau, Rémi.** "Le théâtre au Québec, condamné et réhabilité par les clercs." *Cah de Cap-Rouge* 6 (1978):41-50.
3030. **Trudelle, Joseph.** *Les jubilés et les églises et chapelles de la ville et de la banlieue de Québec, 1608-1901.* 2 vols. Québec: Le Soleil, 1901-4.
3031. **Vincent, Rodolfe.** *Québec, ville historique.* Montréal: Centre de psychologie et de pédagogie, 1966.
3032. **Weaver, Emily P.** *Old Quebec: The City of Champlain.* Toronto: Briggs, 1907.
3033. **Wilson, S., and Anderson, B.** "The Walled City of Quebec." *Habitat* 10, nos. 3-6 (1967):34-41.
3034. **Wood, William.** "Historic Seaport of Quebec: From Immemoriality to the Present Day." *CHR* 26 (1945):392-400.

b. The French Regime to 1760

3035. **Audet, Louis-Philippe.** "Les annonces d'école dans la Gazette de Québec." *Rev univ Laval* 6A (1951):111-15.
3036. _____. "Programme et professeurs du Collège de Québec (1635-1763)." *Cah des dix* 34 (1969):13-18.
3037. **Baillargeon, Noël.** "Le séminaire de Québec sous l'épiscopat de Mgr. de Laval (1663-1688)." Thèse de Ph.D., Laval, 1970.
3038. _____. *Le Séminaire de Québec 1685 à 1760.* Québec: Presses de l'université Laval, 1977.
3039. **Beaudet, L.** *Recensement de la ville de Québec pour 1716.* Québec: Côté, 1887.
3040. **Beaudry, René.** "Les plans en relief de Québec, Montréal et Louisbourg." *RHAF* 16 (1962):213-18.
3041. **Bechard, Auguste.** "Fortifications du Canada sous le régime français." In *L'Ancien Québec,* pp. 55-76. Québec: Belleau, 1890.

3042. **Bosher, John F.** "Le ravitaillement de Québec en 1758: Quelques documents." *HS* 9 (1972):79-85.
3043. **Chabot, Marie-Emmanuel.** "Constitution et règlements des premières Ursulines de Québec (1647-1681)." *Rev univ Laval* 19A (1964):105-20.
3044. **Chouinard, François-Xavier.** *La ville de Québec, histoire municipale.* Vol. 1. *Régime français.* Québec: Société historique de Québec, 1963.
3045. **D'Allaire, Micheline.** "Les prétentions des religieuses de l'Hôpital-Général de Québec sur le Palais Episcopal de Québec." *RHAF* 23 (1969):53-67.
3046. _____. "Origine sociale des religieuses de l'Hôpital-Général de Québec (1692-1764)." *RHAF* 23 (1970):559-81.
3047. _____. *L'Hôpital-Général de Québec, 1692-1764.* Montréal: Fides, 1971.
3048. **Delvaux, Paul-Henri.** "Fondation établissement et fonctionnement de l'Hôtel-Dieu de Québec, premier hôpital du Canada (1638-1693)." Thèse de M.A., Montréal, 1972.
3049. **Desloges, Yvon.** "Gaspard Chaussegros de Lery et les fortifications de Québec, 1745-1754: Théorie et réalisation." In *Le Parc de l'artillerie et les fortifications de Québec-études historiques,* edited by Louis Richer, pp. 57-76. Ottawa: Parcs Canada, 1976.
3050. **Doughty, Arthur George.** *The Cradle of New France: A Story of the City Founded by Champlain.* Montreal: Cambridge Corp., 1908.
3051. **Gauthier, Raymonde.** "L'architecture civile et conventuelle à Québec (1680-1726)." Thèse de M.A., Laval, 1976.
3052. _____. "Une carte de Jean Bourdon de 1640." *J Can Art Hist* 3 (1976): 99-100.
3053. **Genest, Nicole, and Kirjan, C.** "Fondation de Québec par Champlain." *Dossiers de l'archéologie* 27 (1978):72-80.
3054. **Hamelin, Jean, and Provencher, Jean.** "La vie de relations sur le Saint-Laurent entre Québec et Montréal au milieu du XVIIIe siècle." *Cah géogr Q* 11 (1967):243-52.
3055. **Hardy, Jean-Pierre, and Ruddell, David Thierry.** *Les apprentis artisans à Québec, 1660-1815.* Montréal: Presses de l'université du Québec, 1977.
3056. **Hébert, Jean-Claude.** *Le siège de Québec en 1759, par trois témoins.* Québec: Editeur officiel du Québec, 1972.
3057. **Lachance, André.** "La criminalité à Québec sous le régime français: Etude statistique." *RHAF* 20 (1966):409-14.
3058. **Laframboise, Yves.** *L'architecture traditionnelle au Québec: Glossaire illustré de la maison aux 17e et 18e siècles.* Montréal: L'Homme, 1975.
3059. **La France, Marc.** *Etude sur l'évolution physique de la ville de Québec, 1608-1763.* Ottawa: Ministère des affaires indiennes, Service des lieux historiques nationaux, 1972.
3060. _____. "Evolution physique et politiques urbaines: Québec sous le régime français." *UHR* 3-75 (février 1976):3-22.
3062. **Lapalme, Loretta.** "The Hôtel-Dieu of Quebec—The First Hospital North of Rio Grande under Its First Two Superiors." *CCHA, Study Sessions* 41 (1974):53-64.
3063. **Le Blant, Robert.** "Les prémices de la fondation de Québec 1607-1608." *RHAF* 20 (1966):44-55.
3064. **Létourneau, Hubert, and Labrèque, Lucille.** "Inventaire de pièces détachées de la prévôté de Québec (1668-1759)." *Rapport des archives nationales du Québec* 49 (1971):51-413.
3065. **Mathieu, Jacques.** "La vie à Québec au milieu du XVIIe siècle—Etude des sources." *RHAF* 23 (1969):404-24.
3066. _____. "Un négociant de Québec à l'époque de la conquête, Jacques Perrault, l'aîné." *Rapport des archives nationales du Québec* 48 (1970):27-81.
3067. _____. *La construction navale royale à Québec, 1739-1759.* Québec: Société historique de Québec, 1971.
3068. **Miquelon, Dale.** "Havy and Lefebvre of Quebec: A Case Study of Metropolitan Participation in Canadian Trade, 1730-60." *CHR* 56 (1975):1-24.

3069. **Noppen, Luc.** *Québec au XVIIIe siècle: Douze dessins gravés de Richard Short.* Québec: Pélican, 1978.
3070. **Olivier-Lacamp, Gael, and Légaré, Jacques.** "Quelques caractéristiques des ménages de la ville de Québec entre 1666 et 1716." *HS* 23 (1979):66-78.
3071. **Paradis, Wilfrid H.** "L'érection du diocèse de Québec et l'opposition de l'archévêque de Rouen, 1662-1674." *RHAF* 9 (1956):465-501.
3072. **Parker, Gilbert, and Bryan, Claude G.** *Old Quebec: The Fortress of New France.* Toronto: Copp Clark, 1903.
3073. **Reid, Allana Gertrude.** "The Development and Importance of the Town of Quebec, 1608-1760." Ph.D. thesis, McGill, 1950.
3074. ———. "General Trade between Quebec and France during the French Régime." *CHR* 34 (1953):18-32.
3075. **Rousseau, François.** L'hospitalisation en Nouvelle-France, l'Hôtel-Dieu de Québec, 1689-1698." Thèse de M.A., Laval, 1975.
3076. ———. "Hôpital et société en Nouvelle-France: L'Hôtel-Dieu de Québec à la fin du XVIIe siècle." *RHAF* 31 (1977):29-48.
3077. **Roy, Pierre-Georges.** *La ville de Québec sous le régime français.* 2 vols. Québec: Archives du gouvernement de la province de Québec, 1930.
3078. **Samson, Denis.** "Histoire des fortifications de Québec sous le régime français." Thèse de M.A., Laval, 1971.
3079. **Stacey, C. P.** *Quebec, 1759: The Siege and the Battle.* Toronto: Macmillan, 1959.
3080. **Sulte, Benjamin.** "Québec de 1620 à 1632." *BRH* (1899):292-304, 324-40.
3081. **Trudel, Marcel.** "Le séminaire de Québec sous le régime militaire, 1759-1764." *Rev univ Laval* 8 (1953-54):312-32, 399-420, 505-29, 599-613.
3082. ———. "Québec, il y a 370 ans ou plus." *Forces* 43 (1978):30-39.
3083. **Vachon, A.** "La restauration de la Tour de Babel ou 'La vie a Québec au milieu du XVIIe siècle.' " *RHAF* 24 (1970):167-250.

c. 1760-1850

3084. **Allaire, Emilia-B.** "La vie des gens à la Place royale." In *Rapport de la semaine d'histoire tenue à Québec, 1976, sous le thème: Québec 1800-1835,* edited by G.-H. Dagneau, pp. 218-25. Québec: Editeur officiel du Québec, 1977.
3085. **Audet, Francis J.** "Les habitants de la ville de Québec en 1769-1770." *BRH* 27 (1921):81-88.
3086. **Bernier, Jacques.** "La construction domiciliaire à Québec, 1810-1820." *RHAF* 31 (1978):547-61.
3087. ———. *Les intérieurs domestiques des menuisiers et charpentiers de la région de Québec, 1810-1819.* Ottawa: NMM, 1978.
3088. **Brunet, Michel, and Harper, J. Russell.** *Québec 1800—W. H. Bartlett.* Montréal: L'Homme, 1968.
3089. **Cameron, Christina, and Trudel, Jean.** *The Drawings of James Cockburn: A Visit through Quebec's Past.* Toronto: Gage, 1977.
3090. **Cestre, Gilbert.** "Québec: Evolution des limites municipales depuis 1831-1832." *Cah géogr Q* 20 (1976):561-67.
3091. **Chabot, Marie-Emmanuel.** "Les Ursulines de Québec en 1850." *CCHA, Rapport* (1969):75-94.
3092. **Dahl, Edward H.; Espesset, H.; La France, Marc; and Ruddell, David Thierry.** *La ville de Québec, 1800-1850: Un inventaire de cartes et de plans.* Ottawa: NMM, History Division, 1975.

3093. **Desloges, Yvon.** "Québec et ses fortifications, de 1800 à 1835." In *Rapport de la semaine d'histoire tenue à Québec sous le thème: Québec 1800-1835,* edited by G.-H. Dagneau, pp. 109-12. Québec: Editeur officiel au Québec, 1977.
3094. **Drolet, Antonio.** "La bibliothèque du séminaire de Québec et son catalogue de 1782." *CF* 28 (1940):266-81.
3095. _____. *La ville de Québec: Histoire municipale.* Vol. 2. *Régime anglais jusqu'à l'incorporation, 1759-1833.* Québec: Société historique de Québec, 1965.
3096. _____. *La ville de Québec: Histoire municipale.* Vol. 3. *De l'incorporation à la confédération (1833-1867).* Québec: Société historique de Québec, 1967.
3097. **Faucher, Albert.** "The Decline of Shipbuilding at Quebec in the Nineteenth Century." *CJEPS* 23 (1957):195-215.
3099. **Gagne, Jean-A.** "Aspect juridique et municipal de la vie à Québec entre 1800 et 1835." In *Rapport de la semaine d'histoire tenue à Québec sous le thème: Québec 1800-1835,* edited by G.-H. Dagneau, pp. 93-102. Québec: Editeur officiel du Québec, 1977.
3100. **Gagnon, F. E. A.** "Notes sur le Château St. Louis incendié en 1834, et le Château Haldimand ou vieux Château, Québec." Literary and Historical Society of Quebec, *Trans* (1887-89):171-76.
3101. **Hardy, Jean-Pierre, and Ruddell, David Thierry.** "Le monde du travail au Québec au XVIIIe et au XIXe siècles: Historiographie et état de la question." *RHAF* 25 (1972):499-539.
3102. **Hardy, René.** "Note sur certaines manifestations du réveil religieux de 1840 dans la paroisse Notre-Dame de Québec." *CCHA, Rapport* (1968):81-98.
3103. **Hare, John E.** "La population de la ville de Québec, 1795-1805." *HS* 13 (1974):23-47.
3104. _____. "Le comportement de la paysannerie rurale et urbaine de la région de Québec pendant l'occupation américaine, 1775-76." *Rev univ Ottawa* 47 (1977):145-50.
3105. **Hawkins, Alfred.** *Hawkins Picture of Quebec; with Historical Recollections.* Quebec: Neilson and Cowan, 1834.
3106. **Jarrell, R. A.** "The Rise and Decline of Science at Quebec, 1824-1844." *HS* 19 (1977):77-91.
3107. **Jordan, John A.** *The Grosse-Isle Tragedy and the Monument to the Irish Fever Victims, 1847.* Quebec: Telegraph Printing Co., 1909.
3108. **Lacelle, Claudette.** "La garnison Britannique dans la ville de Québec vue par les journaux de 1764 à 1840." In *Le Parc de L'Artillerie et les fortifications de Québec—Etudes historiques,* edited by Louis Richer, pp. 37-55. Ottawa: Parcs Canada, 1976.
3109. **La France, Marc, and Ruddell, David Thierry.** "Eléments de l'urbanisation de la ville de Québec, 1790-1840." *UHR* 1-75 (juin 1975):22-30.
3110. **Langelier, F.** *Lettres sur les affaires municipales de la cité de Québec.* Québec: Imprimerie de l'Evénement, 1868.
3111. **Maheux, Arthur.** "Le séminaire de Québec en 1848." *Rev univ Laval* 6B (1952):701-9, 795-801.
3112. **Noppen, Luc.** "Le renouveau architectural proposé par Thomas Baillairgé au Québec, de 1820 à 1850." Thèse 3e cycle, Toulouse-le-Mirail, 1976.
3113. _____. *La maison Maizerets, le Château Bellevue: Deux exemples de la diffusion de l'architecture du séminaire de Quebec aux XVIIIe et XIXe siècles.* Québec: Ministre des affaires culturelles, 1978.
3114. **O'Gallagher, Marianna.** "A History of the Irish in Quebec City from 1830-1860." M.A. thesis, Ottawa, 1976.
3115. _____. "Care of the Orphaned and the Aged by the Irish Community of Quebec City, 1847 and the Years Following." *CCHA, Study Sessions* 43 (1976):39-56.
3116. **Ouellet, Fernand.** "Papineau et la rivalité Québec-Montréal, 1820-1840." *RHAF* 13 (1959):311-27.

3117. _____. "Structures des occupations et ethnicité dans les villes de Québec et de Montréal, 1819-1844." In *Eléments d'histoire sociale du Bas-Canada*, pp. 177-205. Montréal: Hurtubise HMH, 1972.

3118. **Paillé, Michel-P.** "Accroissement et structure de la population à Québec au début du XIXe siècle (à propos d'un article de John Hare)." *HS* 9 (1976):187-97.

3119. **Parker, W. H.** "Quebec City in the 1830s." In *Mélanges géographiques canadiens offerts à Raoul Blanchard,* edited by L.-H. Hamelin, pp. 261-73. Québec: Presses de l'université Laval, 1959.

3120. **Plouffe, M.** "Quelques particularités sociales et politiques de la charte du système administratif et du personnel politique de la cité de Québec, 1833-1867." Thèse de M.A., Laval, 1971.

3121. **Provost, Abbé, ed.** *Recensement de la ville de Québec en 1818 par le curé Joseph Signay.* Cahiers d'histoire, 29. Québec: Société historique de Québec, 1976.

3122. **Roberts, David.** "George Allsopp: Quebec Merchant, 1773-1805." M.A. thesis, Queen's, 1974.

3123. **Roche, J. F.** "Quebec under Siege, 1775-1776: The 'Memorandums' of Jacob Danford." *CHR* 50 (1969):68-85.

3124. **Roy, Camille.** *L'Université Laval et les fêtes du cinquantienaire.* Québec: Dussault, 1903.

3125. **Stewart, C. M.** "Quebec City in the 1770s." *History Today* 23 (1973):116-21.

d. 1850-1920

3126. **Buies, Arthur.** *Québec en 1900.* Québec: Brousseau, 1893.

3127. **The Commercial Magazine Co. Ltd.** *The Town of Levis and Environs, P.Q., Canada.* Montreal: Commercial Magazine Co., 1912.

3128. **Cooper, John Irwin.** "The Quebec Ship Labourers Benevolent Society." *CHR* 30 (1949):336-43.

3129. **De Celles, A. D.** "Laval University." *Can Mag* 8 (1896):207-13.

3130. **Gale, George.** *Quebec 'twixt Old and New.* Quebec: Telegraph Printing Co., 1915.

3131. **Gamache, J. Charles.** *Histoire de Saint-Roch de Québec et de ses institutions, 1829-1929.* Québec: Charrier et Dugal, 1929.

3132. **Hardy, René.** "L'activité sociale du curé de Notre-Dame de Québec: Aperçu de l'influence du clergé au milieu du XIXe siècle." *HS* 6 (1970):5-32.

3133. **Larocque, Paul.** "La condition socio-économique des travailleurs de la ville de Québec (1896-1914)." Thèse de M.A., Laval, 1971.

3134. **MacDougall, Alex.** "The Presbyterian Church in the Presbytery of Quebec, 1875-1925." M.A. thesis, McGill, 1960.

3135. **MacTavish, Newton.** "Our Three Hundredth Birthday." *Can Mag* 31 (1908):387-401.

3136. **Maheux, Arthur.** "Un marchand de Québec: William Price." *Rev univ Laval* 9B (1955):717-22.

3137. **Marquis, Georges-Emile.** *Les fortifications de Québec, un centenaire: 1823-1923.* Québec: Telegraph Printing Co., 1923.

3138. **Mathieu, Jacques.** "L'idéologie des annales de la Société Saint-Jean Baptiste de Québec, 1880-1902." *Rech soc* 10 (1969):438-48.

3139. _____. "La condition ouvrière dans l'industrie du cuir à Québec de 1900 à 1930, d'après les procès-verbaux d'un syndicat." Thèse de M.A., Laval, 1970.

3140. **Murphy, Achille.** "Les projets d'embellissements de la Ville de Québec proposés par Lord Dufferin en 1875." *J Can Art Hist* 1 (1974):18-29.

3141. **Nicholson, Byron.** "Attractions of Quebec." *Can Mag* 16 (1901):554-59.

3142. **Rivet, Monique.** "Les Irlandais à Québec (1870-1968)." Thèse de M.A., Laval, 1969.

3143. **Routhier, Adolphe Basile.** *Quebec et Lévis à l'aurore du XXe siècle.* Montréal: Publications Samuel de Champlain, 1900.
3144. **Roy, Camille.** *Les fêtes du troisième centenaire de Québec, 1608-1908.* Québec: Comité du Livre Souvenir des fêtes jubilaires, 1911.
3145. **Roy, P.-G.** *La Chambre de Commerce de Lévis: 1872-1947.* Lévis: Quotidien, 1947.
3146. **Savard, Pierre.** "Les canadiens français vus par les consuls de France à Québec et à Montréal de 1859 à 1900." *RHAF* 21 (1967):217-29.
3147. _____. *Le consulat général de France à Québec et à Montréal de 1859 à 1914.* Québec: Cahiers de l'Institut d'Histoire, no. 15, 1970.
3148. _____. *La ville de Québec au miroir de la littérature, 1860-1900.* Québec: Société historique de Québec, 1971.
3149. **Smith, Pemberton.** "The Passing of the Sailing Ship at Quebec." CHA, *AR* (1923):65-71.
3150. **Waterston, Elizabeth.** "Howells and the City of Quebec." *CRAS* 9 (1978):155-67.
3151. **Wood, William C. H.** "Petition of the City of Quebec to Queen Victoria in 1857, Edited by Col. W. Wood." *CHR* 2 (1921):363-68.

e. 1920-Present

3152. **Bailly, A. S., and Polèse, Mario.** "Processus urbains et modèles spatiaux: Ecologie factorielle comparée Edmonton-Québec." *Can géogr* 21 (1977):59-80.
3153. **Beaudet, Colett.** "Banlieue réelle et ville de Québec." Thèse de M.A., Laval, 1947.
3154. **Bédard, Roland.** "The Greater Quebec of Tomorrow: A Master Plan for Quebec City." M.R.P. thesis, Cornell, 1947.
3155. **Bernard, A.; Léveillé, J.; and Lord, G.** *Profile: Quebec. The Political and Administrative Structures of the Metropolitan Region of Quebec.* Ottawa: MSUA, 1975.
3156. **Bernier, Paul-Etienne.** "Le fait juif à Québec." Thèse de M.A., Laval, 1941.
3157. **Brann, Esther.** "A Quebec Sketch Book." *CGEJ* 1 (1930):105-30.
3158. **Butcher, Wilfred F.** "The 'English' of Quebec City." *Can For* 33 (1953):148-51.
3159. **Camu, Pierre.** *Etude du port de Québec.* Etudes géographiques, #17. Ottawa: Ministère des mines et relevés techniques, 1959.
3160. **Charbonneau, Gaétan.** "Etude sur les revenus des familles dans la ville de Québec en 1939 et en 1945." Thèse de M.A., Laval, 1947.
3161. **Corrivault, Claude; Gagné, Raymond; and Caron, J.-C.** "Le Québec metropolitain." *Commerce* 1 (1959):15-46.
3162. **Côté, Michelle.** "Sillery, Banlieue residentielle de Québec." Thèse de M.A., Laval, 1962.
3163. **Denault, Hayda.** "Les services sociaux à Quebec." Thèse de M.A., Laval, 1945.
3164. **Desmeules, Jean.** "Etude géographique et sociale de la population de Sainte-Foy en 1958." Thèse de M.A., Laval, 1959.
3165. **Diamant, Claude.** "La région économique de Québec." *Québec industriel* 21 (1966):41-80.
3166. **Duffy, Lise, and Carrier, André.** "Etude du personnel politique de la ville de Québec, 1920-1965." Thèse de M.A., Montréal, 1966.
3167. **Escojido, André.** "La mentalité du chef d'entreprise dans la région socio-économique de Québec." Thèse de M.A., Laval, 1960.
3168. **Falardeau, Jean-Charles.** "Evolution et métabolisme contemporain de la ville de Québec." *Culture* 5 (1944):121-31.
3169. _____. "A Survey of Quebec City Families." *PHEJ* 38 (1947):515-27.
3170. _____. "Délimitation d'une banlieue de grande ville (Québec)." *RCU* 1 (1951):16-22.
3171. **Fry, Henry.** "Ship Building at Quebec." *Can Mag* 5 (1895):3-8.

3172. **Gagnon, Gabriel.** "La population et le territoire de la ville de Québec." Thèse de M.A., Laval, 1960.
3173. _____. "Les zones sociales de l'agglomération de Québec." *Rech soc* 1 (1960):255-68.
3174. **Godbout, Jacques.** "La formation de la communauté urbaine de Québec et le rôle de l'état dans la restructuration des pouvoirs locaux." *Rech soc* 12 (1971):185-205.
3175. **Grenier, Fernand.** "La région de Québec." *Can géogr Q* 7 (1963):37-57.
3176. _____, **and Dorion, Henri.** "Québec, région économique." *Commerce* 63 (1961):35-74, 245-56.
3178. **Hulbert, F.** "Le rayonnement et l'impact économique du carnaval de Québec." *Cah géogr Q* 15 (1971):77-104.
3179. **Jozsa, J. M.** "A Method for the Analysis of Economic Polarization: Two Case Studies; Halifax-Dartmouth, Nova Scotia, and Quebec City, Quebec." M.A. thesis, McMaster, 1975.
3180. **Lamontagne, G.** "Contribution à l'étude de la rue Saint-Jean: Analyse de deux aspects fondamentaux de sa fonction commerciale." Thèse de M.A., Laval, 1965.
3181. **Lapointe, Gérard.** *La côte de Beauport. De la dispersion rurale à la banlieue residentielle.* Québec: Centre de recherches en sociologie religieuse, Université Laval, 1964.
3182. **Leclerc, Gilberte.** "La population et l'économie du quartier Saint-Roch: Etudes d'interrelations." Thèse de M.A., Laval, 1967.
3183. **Lemieux, Vincent.** "La Cité de Lévis: Essai de sociologie municipale." Thèse de M.A., Laval, 1957.
3184. _____. "L'organisation municipale à Lévis: Etude de sociologie politique." *Rech soc* 2 (1961):437-72.
3185. **Lord, G.; Tremblay, A.; and Trépanier, M.-O.** *Les communautés urbaines de Montréal et de Québec: Premier bilan.* Montréal: Presses de l'Université de Montréal, 1975.
3186. **Marier, Claude.** "Déclin de la Chambre de Commerce de Québec, 1924-1945." Thèse de M.A., Laval, 1949.
3187. **Morin, R.** "L'analyse de localisation spatiale de trois centres commerciaux régionaux du Québec métropolitain." Thèse de M.A., Sherbrooke, 1975.
3188. **Neil, Edmund.** "Monographie de Sainte-Foy." Thèse de M.A., Laval, 1952.
3189. **Papillon, Marthe.** "Etude des familles de la ville de Québec." Thèse de M.A., Laval, 1946.
3190. **Paré, Simone.** "Social Participation in Beauport, Quebec." Ph.D. thesis, Columbia, 1960.
3191. **Pineault, Gilles, and Pineault, Laval.** "Evolution territoriale de la cité de Québec." Thèse de M.A., Laval, 1965.
3192. **Poisson, Yves, ed.** *Programme d'expansion économique pour la région métropolitaine de Québec.* 4 vols. Québec: Bureau de l'industrie et du commerce du Québec métropolitain, 1967.
3193. **Rajotte, F.** "The Quebec City Recreational Hinterland." Ph.D. thesis, McGill, 1973.
3194. *Rapport de la commission d'étude du système administratif de la cité de Québec (Rapport Sylvestre).* Québec: Imprimeur de la reine, 1964.
3195. **Richard, Camille.** *Etude de la population de Sainte-Foy.* Québec: Commission scolaire de Sainte-Foy, 1964.
3196. **Roy, Gilles.** "Le Rond-Point de Lévis." *Cah géogr Q* 5 (1958):97-105.
3197. **Roy, Jean-Marie.** "Québec: Esquisse de géographie urbaine." *Can Geogr* no. 2 (1952):83-98.
3198. **Saint-Cyr, Michel.** "L'administration du personnel et sa condition dans les entreprises de la ville de Québec." Thèse de M.A., Laval, 1955.
3199. **Saint-Laurent, Jacques.** *La situation de la main-d'oeuvre dans la région métropolitaine de Québec.* Québec: Université Laval, 1962.
3200. **St. Pierre, Jocelyn.** "Le quartier Saint-Roch de Québec, l'environment socio-économique des travailleurs, 1941-1971." Thèse de M.A., Laval, 1971.

3201. "Town Planning Commission for Quebec City." *TPICJ* 7, no. 2 (1928):29-33.
3202. **Tremblay, Louis-Marie.** "Le marché du travail dans la région de Québec." Thèse de M.A., Laval, 1957.
3203. **Velloni, Pietro.** "Les immigrants italiens à Québec." Thèse de M.A., Laval, 1961.

11. Rimouski

3204. **Benoist, Emile.** *Rimouski et les pays d'en bas.* Montréal: Devoir, 1945.
3205. **Bernier, Réal.** "Rimouski, métropole du Bas Saint-Laurent." Thèse, HEC (Montréal), 1941.
3205A. **Caron, Marie Ange.** *Mosaïque rimouskoise: Une histoire de Rimouski.* Rimouski, 1979.
3206. **Dextraze, Pierre.** *Rimouski, métropole régionale.* Rimouski: CEGEP de Rimouski, 1977.
3207. **Dubé, Yves, and Martin, Yves.** "Rimouski: Population et économie." *Rech soc* 1 (1960):269-308.
3208. **Dumas, Monique.** *L'église de Rimouski dans un contexte de développement régional, 1963-1972.* Montréal: Fides, 1978.
3209. **Frenette, J.-V.** "Rimouski: Etude de géographie urbaine." Thèse de M.A., Montréal, 1956.
3210. **Guerette, Réal, and Guimond, Paul-Henri.** *Rimouski, évolution démographique.* Rimouski: Collège de Rimouski, 1976.
3211. **Légaré, Jean-Paul.** "Rimouski planifie son expansion." *CV* 4, no. 8 (1961):18-23.
3211A. **Lechasseur, Antonio.** "Propriété foncière et clergé: Rimouski, 1881-1911." Thèse de M.A., Québec à Montréal, 1980.
3212. **Matte, Gilbert.** "Rimouski, part d'été et d'hiver." Thèse, HEC (Montréal), 1932.
3213. **Saint-Pierre, Ruth, and Nadeau, Mireille.** *Rimouski, ville de services.* Rimouski: CEGEP de Rimouski, 1977.
3214. **Thibault, Suzel.** "La ville de Rimouski et la coopération." Thèse de M.A., Montréal, 1946.

12. Rouyn-Noranda

3215. **Gourd, Benoît-Beaudry.** *Bibliographie de l'Abitibi-Témiscamingue.* Rouyn: Université du Québec, 1973.
3215A. ———. "Les travailleurs miniers et l'implementation du syndicalisme dans les mines de l'Abitibi-Témiscamingue 1925-1950." *De l'Abitibi-Témiscaming* 4 (1977):45-111.
3216. **Hogg, A. M.** "Municipal Developments at Noranda, Quebec." *Can Engineer* 54 (1928):136-37.
3217. **Larouche, Fernand.** "L'immigrant dans une ville minière: Une étude de l'interaction." *Rech soc* 14 (1973):204-28.
3218. **Roberts, Leslie.** *Noranda.* Toronto: Clarke, Trevor, 1956.
3219. **Rowe, R. C.** "Historical Sketch of Noranda Mines." *CAMJ* 55 (1934):144-48.
3220. ———. "Town Planning and Social Relationships (Noranda)." *CAMJ* 55 (1934):205-7.
3221. **Vincent, Roger.** "Etude du roulement de la main-d'oeuvre à la Canadian International Paper Co. (Division Noranda) pour l'année 1947-48." Thèse de M.A., Montréal, 1953.

13. Saint-Jean D'Iberville

3222. **Brousseau, Jean-D.** *Saint-Jean de Québec. Origine et développement.* Saint-Jean: Le Richelieu, 1938.

3223. **Laghaout, M.** "St.-Jean-D'Iberville, centre régional et ville satellite (essai de géographie active)." Thèse de M.A., Montréal, 1970.
3224. **Lanctôt, Gustave.** *Brève histoire de St.-Jean-du-Richelieu.* Montréal, 1947.
3225. "Saint-Jean d'Iberville," *Commerce* 56 (1954):31-35.

14. St. Jérôme

3226. **Auclair, Elie-J.** *Saint-Jérôme de Terrebonne.* Saint-Jérôme: Labelle, 1934.
3227. **Drouin-Lapointe, Denise.** "Les travailleurs de la compagnie Rolland et quelques aspects de la vie économique et du travail (Saint-Jérôme)." Thèse de M.A., Laval, 1962.
3228. **Dumont, Fernand, and Fortin, Gerald.** "Un sondage de pratique religieuse en milieu urbain." *Rech soc* 1 (1960):500-502.
3229. **Dumont, Y., and Martin, Yves.** *L'analyse des structures sociales régionales: Etude sociologique de la région de St.-Jerome.* Montreal: Presses de l'université Laval, 1963.
3230. **Fortin, Marc.** "Saint-Jérome: Reine des Laurentides." *Commerce* 56, no. 3 (1954):50-54.

15. Saint-Hyacinthe

3231. **Aubry, Pierre.** "Développement urbain de St.-Hyacinthe et ses implications financières." Thèse de M.A., Montréal, 1965.
3232. **Beaudry, Françoise.** "La petite industrie à St.-Hyacinthe et St. Jean, étude de comparabilité." Thèse de M.A., Montréal, 1966.
3233. **Beauregard, Ludger.** "Saint-Hyacinthe, bastion de notre industrie textile." *Technique* 27 (1952):395-403.
3234. **Belhumeur, David.** "Le service d'électricité de la cité de Saint-Hyacinthe." Thèse, HEC (Montréal), 1945.
3235. **Boucher, Réal.** "L'endettement de l'évêché de St.-Hyacinthe au XIXe siècle: Le rôle décisif de Charles La Rocque dans l'extinction de cette dette." *RHAF* 33 (1980):557-74.
3236. **Choquette, C.-P.** *Histoire de la ville de Saint-Hyacinthe.* Saint-Hyacinthe: Richer, 1930.
3237. **Commercial Magazine Co. Ltd.** *Saint-Hyacinthe, P.Q., Canada.* Montreal: Commercial Magazine, 1912.
3238. **Francoeur, Jean.** "Saint-Hyacinthe, esquisse de géographie urbaine." Thèse de M.A., Montréal, 1953.
3239. **Jacobs, Philip.** "The Meaning of Qualitative Difference in Urban Growth Processes (St.-Hyacinthe and Trois-Rivières)." M.A. thesis, McGill, 1968.
3240. **Lapointe, Laurent.** "La formation de la Banque de Saint-Hyacinthe et le développement économique regional." Thèse de M.A., Montréal, 1976.
3241. **Ostiguy, Jean.** "Monographie de Saint-Hyacinthe." Thèse, HEC (Montréal), 1940.
3242. **Phaneuf, Georges-Etienne.** *La diocèse de Saint-Hyacinthe: Etude sociologique du milieu et des institutions.* Cahiers de l'Institut social populaire, no. 3. Montréal, 1957.
3243. **Rudin, Ronald.** "Regional Complexity and Political Behaviour in a Quebec County, 1867-1886 [:A Case Study of Saint-Hyacinthe]." *HS* 17 (1976):92-110.

16. Schefferville

3244. **Derbyshire, Edward.** "Amenities and the Notion of Permanence in Schefferville, Quebec." *ACGE* 16, no. 4 (1957-58):1-16.
3245. _____. "Notes on the Social Structure of a Canadian Pioneer Town [Schefferville, Quebec]." *Soc Rev* 8 (1960):63-75.

3246. **Garigue, Philippe.** "Une enquête sur l'industrialisation de la province de Québec: Schefferville." *Ac Ec* 33 (1957):419-36.
3247. **Humphrys, Graham.** "Schefferville, Quebec: A New Pioneering Town." *GEOR* 48 (1958):151-66.
3248. "The Operations of the Iron Ore Company of Canada Limited (Schefferville and Sept-Iles)." *CAMJ* 76 (1955):39-47.

17. Shawinigan

3249. **Bachand, Benoît.** "Monographie économique de Shawinigan Falls et Grand'Mère." Thèse, HEC (Montréal), 1938.
3250. **Beauregard, Ludger.** "Shawinigan, coeur industriel de la Mauricie." *Technique* 27 (1952):233-43.
3251. **Bégin, Benoît-J., and Robert, Georges.** "Shawinigan-Sud: Un municipalité de banlieue qui a son plan directeur mais qui n'a pas le statut légal pour l'appliquer." *Architecture* 15 (1960):121-25.
3252. **Boisvert, Jean-Jacques.** "Shawinigan: Etude de géographie urbaine." Thèse de M.A., Laval, 1951.
3252A. **Briere, J.; Decarie, D.; and Desjardins, R.** "Shawinigan-Sud: Organisation de l'espace et glissement de terrain." Essai de B.A., Québec à Montréal, 1973.
3253. **Brouillette, Normand.** "Les facteurs du déclin industriel de Shawinigan." *Cah géogr Q* 17 (1973):123-34.
3254. **Chambers, F. T. D.** "Shawinigan: The City in the Forest." *Westminster* 6 (1909):153-60.
3255. **Doucet, R.** "Monographie économique de la cité de Shawinigan Falls." Thèse de M.A., Laval, 1949.
3256. **Dupré, P.** "Shawinigan Falls industriel." Thèse de M.A., Laval, 1950.
3257. **Filteau, Gérard.** *L'épopoée de Shawinigan.* Shawinigan Falls: Guertin et Gignac, 1944.
3258. *Industrial Shawinigan.* Shawinigan: Shawinigan *Standard,* 1937.
3259. **Lavergne, Gérald.** "Monographie industrielle de la ville de Shawinigan." Thèse, HEC (Montréal), 1949.

18. Sherbrooke

3260. **Blaise, P.** "Monographie de Sherbrooke." Thèse de M.A., Laval, 1941.
3261. **Brunelle-Lavoie, L.** "Le mouvement ouvrier à Sherbrooke jusqu'à 1919." Thèse de M.A., Sherbrooke, 1977.
3262. **Buckley, Alfred.** "Garden Suburb at Sherbrooke, Quebec." *To Pl Cn L* 6, no. 1 (1920):10-11.
3263. **Cazalis, Pierre.** "Sherbrooke: Sa place dans la vie de relations des cantons de l'est." *Cah géogr Q* 16 (1964):165-98.
3264. **Choquette, Fernand.** "Commerce et industrie à Sherbrooke." Thèse, HEC (Montréal), 1942.
3265. **Damphousse, R.** "La francisation progressive de Sherbrooke—Etude de répartition des deux ethnies principales dans la ville de Sherbrooke." Thèse de Ph.D., Sherbrooke, 1971.
3266. **Demers, Louis-Philippe.** *Sherbrooke . . . Découvertes—Légendes—Documents.* Sherbrooke, 1969.
3267. **Finestone, Harold.** "Trends in the Population Structure in the Sherbrooke Sub-Region." M.A. thesis, McGill, 1944.
3268. **Gosselin, E.** "Les catholiques du diocèse de Sherbrooke (localisation, population et dette)." Thèse de Ph.D., Sherbrooke, 1971.

3269. **Goulet, Elie.** "Lueurs du côté de Sherbrooke." *Rev univ Laval* 6B (1952):406-11.
3270. **Gravel, Albert.** *Pages d'histoire régionale.* Sherbrooke, 1960.
3271. **Greening, W. E.** "Sherbrooke: The Queen of the Eastern Townships." *CGEJ* 69 (1964):12-19.
3272. **Kesteman, Jean-Pierre.** "Les travailleurs à la construction du chemin de fer dans la région de Sherbrooke (1851-1853)." *RHAF* 31 (1978):525-46.
3273. **Martel, J.** "Les troubles de 1837-38 dans la région de Sherbrooke." *Rev univ Sherbrooke* 5 (1964):39-58.
3274. **Michaud, C.** "Le comportement résidentiel des ménages en milieu suburbain: Le cas de Sherbrooke." Thèse de M.A., Sherbrooke, 1976.
3275. **Nadeau, Jacques.** "La ville de Sherbrooke." Thèse, HEC (Montréal), 1940.
3276. **O'Neil, Pierre.** "Essai de sociologie des comportements politiques municipaux dans la ville de Sherbrooke." Thèse de M.A., Laval, 1958.
3277. **Rudin, Ronald.** "Land Ownership and Urban Growth: The Experience of Two Quebec Towns, 1840-1914 [Sherbrooke and Sorel]." *UHR* 8 (October 1979):23-46.
3278. **Saint-Onge, C.** "Le commerce d'alimentation de détail à Sherbrooke." Thèse de M.A., Sherbrooke, 1974.
3279. **Thouez, Jean-Pierre.** "L'utilisation des cartes historiques dans l'analyse de l'évolution des sols en milieu urbain: Le cas de Sherbrooke, 1863-1951." *UHR* 3-78 (février 1979):50-60.

19. Sorel

3280. **Beaudry, Yvon.** *Sorel, 1642-1942.* Sorel: Ed. du IIIe centenaire, 1943.
3281. **Beauregard, Ludger.** "Sorel, pôle industriel du Québec." *Technique* 27 (1952):108-20.
3282. **Bruneau, A.-A.** "Sorel." *RTCN* 12 (1926):390-402.
3283. **Champagne, F.** "Evolution économique de Sorel." Thèse, HEC (Montréal), 1949.
3284. *The City and Port of Sorel.* Sorel: Chamber of Commerce, 1930.
3285. **Couillard-Després, Abbé A.** *Histoire de Sorel de ses origines à nos jours.* Montréal: Imprimerie des Sourds-Muets, 1926.
3286. **Daneau, Jean-Jacques.** "Sorel: Essai de monographie urbaine." Thèse de M.A., Montréal, 1961.
3287. **De Lorimier, François C.** "Les grèves de Sorel (1937)." Thèse de M.A., Montréal, 1952.
3288. **Enos, Kathleen.** "The Economic Evolution of the Seigneurie of Sorel." M.A. thesis, Ottawa, 1968.
3289. *The Industrial City of Sorel in Eastern Canada.* Sorel: Marine Industries, Sorel Industries, and Sorel Steel Foundries, 1945.
3290. **Legendre, D.** "Sorel-Tracy—Une agglomération—Deux paysages." Thèse de M.A., Montréal, 1972.
3291. **St.-Germain, G.** "Les problèmes du développement industriel de la région de Sorel." Thèse, HEC (Montréal), 1963.
3292. **Salvail, Narcisse.** "Monographie économique de la ville de Sorel." Thèse, HEC (Montréal), 1945.
3293. *Sorel, 1642-1942.* Sorel: Editions du IIIe centenaire, 1942.
3294. **Weston, D. R.** "Sorel, Past and Present." *CGEJ* 51 (1955):84-89.

20. Témiskaming (Kipawa)

3295. **Adams, Thomas.** "Pulp and Paper Company Plan of Model Townsite at Kipawa, P.Q." *ENCR* 33 (1919):288-90.

3296. **Asselin, Maurice, and Gourd, Benoît-Beaudry,** eds. *L'Abitibi et Témiskaming: Hier et aujourd'hui.* Rouyn: Bibliothèque Nationale du Québec, 1975.
3297. **Commission of Conservation.** "The Town of Kipawa." *Report of the Tenth Annual Meeting.* Appendix VII, pp. 110-12. Ottawa: Commission of Conservation, 1919.
3298. **Grimmer, A. K.** "The Development and Operation of a Company-Owned Industrial Town (Temiscaming)." *Engineering J* 17 (1934):219-23.
3299. **Perreault, G.** "Analyse socio-économique d'une région: Le cas de l'Abitibi-Témiscamingue." Thèse de M.A., Sherbrooke, 1975.
3300. "Planning and Building New Towns in Canada: Kipawa." *Cn L* 5 (1919):10-16.
3301. **Saarinen, Oiva.** "The Influence of Thomas Adams and the British New Towns Movement in the Planning of Canadian Resource Communities [Iroquois Falls, Ontario, and Témiscaming, Quebec]." In #29, pp. 268-92.

21. Thetford Mines

3302. **Adams, Cléophas.** *Thetford Mines. Historique et Biographie.* Thetford Mines: Le Mégantic, 1929.
3303. **Cloutier, Pierre.** "Les villes de l'amiante, Thetford Mines et Black Lake." Thèse de M.A., Laval, 1966.
3304. **Hallé, Robert.** "Monographie économique de Thetford-Mines." Thèse de M.A., Laval, 1947.
3305. **Paulin, Jean-Claude, and Fecteau, Nelson.** *La cité de l'or blanc. Thetford Mines, 1876-1976.* Thetford Mines, 1975.
3306. **Tanguay, C.** "Thetford Mines, centre-ville—Variables problématiques d'intégration d'une structure spatiale archaique à un potential normal de développement commercial." Thèse de L. ès L., Laval, 1972.

22. Trois-Rivières

3307. **Audet, Francis J.** *Les députés des Trois-Rivières (1808-1838).* Trois-Rivières: Bien-Public, 1934.
3308. **Balcer, Georges.** *The City of Three Rivers as a Seaport and Her Network of Railroads.* Trois-Rivières: Journal des Trois-Rivières, 1880.
3309. **Barthe, J.-B.-M.** *Trois-Rivières, Album illustré, Histoire, géographie, industrie.* Trois-Rivières, 1903.
3310. **Beauregard, Ludger.** "Trois-Rivières, reine de l'industrie papetière." *Technique* 27 (1952):531-42.
3311. **Bégin, Benoît J., and Robert, Georges.** "Plan directeur de la cité de Trois-Rivières." *Architecture* 16 (1961):38-50.
3312. **Bergeron, Cécile.** "Le Collège Séraphique des Trois-Rivières: 1952-1968." Thèse de M.A., Sherbrooke, 1971.
3313. **Blanchard, Raoul.** *La Mauricie.* Trois-Rivières: Bien-Public, 1950.
3314. **Bonenfant, Jean-Charles.** "Le journal des Trois-Rivières et la naissance de la Confédération." *Cah des dix* 35 (1970):39-54.
3315. **Camu, Pierre.** "Le port et l'arrière-pays de Trois-Rivières." *Geogr Bull* 1 (1951):30-56.
3316. **Charbonneau, C.** "Trois-Rivières industriel." Thèse de M.A., Laval, 1947.
3317. **Cloutier, St.-Georges.** "Three Rivers." *Ac Ec* 15 (1939):147-67.
3318. **Cotret, René de.** "Monographie industrielle de la ville de Trois-Rivières." Thèse, HEC (Montréal), 1949.
3319. **Coulon, Jacques.** "Trois-Rivières doit s'agrandir." *CV* 3 (1960):26-27.

3320. **Douville, Raymond.** *Visages du vieux Trois-Rivières.* Trois-Rivières: Bien-Public, 1955.

3321. **Foulché-Delbosc, Isabel.** "Women of Three Rivers, 1651-1663." In *The Neglected Majority: Essays in Canadian Women's History,* edited by Susan Mann Trofimenkoff and Alison Prentice, pp. 14-26. Toronto: M&S, 1977.

3322. **Gauthier, Raymonde.** *Trois Rivières, disparue ou presque.* Québec: Fides, 1978.

3323. *The Great Port of Three Rivers.* Trois-Rivières: Three Rivers Harbour Board, 1932.

3324. **Greening, W. E.** "Trois-Rivières—Historic Gateway to the ː Maurice." *CGEJ* 59 (1959):204-11.

3325. **Jacobs, Philip.** "The Meaning of Qualitative Differences in Urban Growth Processes [St.-Hyacinthe and Trois-Rivières]." M.A. thesis, McGill, 1968.

3326. **Lamothe, J.** "L'avenir industriel des Trois-Rivières." Thèse, HEC (Montréal), 1951.

3327. **Langston, W. J.** "Record of Trois-Rivières: Industrial Growth." *INCA* 29 (1928):44-47.

3328. **Legge, Arthur E. E.** *The Anglican Church in Three Rivers (1768-1956).* Trois-Rivières, 1956.

3329. **Lessard, Claude.** "Répertoire des greffes de notaires qui se trouvent aux archives du palais de justice de Trois-Rivières." *Archives* 70 (1970):59-73.

3330. **Magnan, A., and Panneton, G.** *Le diocèse de Trois-Rivières.* Trois-Rivières: Bien-Public, 1962.

3331. **Nadon, Pierre.** "Les forges de Saint-Maurice." *Dossiers de l'archéologie* 27 (1978):96-101.

3332. **Richard, Louis.** *Histoire du Collège des Trois-Rivières: Première periode de 1860 à 1874.* Trois-Rivières: Ayotte, 1885.

3333. **Sulte, Benjamin.** *Histoire de la ville des Trois-Rivières et de ses environs.* Montréal: Senecal, 1870.

3334. **Tessier, Albert.** *Les Trois-Rivières—Quatre siècles d'histoire, 1535-1935.* Trois-Rivières: Le Nouvelliste, 1934.

3335. ———. "Trois-Rivières." *Habitat* 10, no. 3-6 (1967):42-45.

3336. **Theriault, Yvan.** *Trois-Rivières: Ville de reflet.* Trois-Rivières: Bien-Public, 1954.

3337. ———. *Etude du centre commercial des Trois-Rivières en fonction du projet de mail en 1962.* Trois-Rivières, 1962.

3338. **Trudel, Marcel.** "Le gouvernement des Trois-Rivières sous le régime militaire, 1760-1764." *RHAF* 5 (1951):69-98.

3339. ———. *Le Régime militaire dans le Gouvernement des Trois-Rivières, 1760-1764.* Trois-Rivières: Bien-Public, 1952.

3340. **Uren, P. E.** "The Historical Geography of the Saint-Maurice Valley, with Special Reference to Urban Occupancy." M.A. thesis, McGill, 1949.

3341. **Voisine, Nive.** "Un diocèse divisé contre lui-même. Trois-Rivières (1852-1885)." *Rev univ Ottawa* 47 (1977):226-36.

23. Other Centres

3342. **Bélanger, B.** "Ste-Marie: Ville industrielle." Thèse de L. ès L., Laval, 1965.

3343. **Bélanger, Joseph.** "Les services publics municipalisés à Rivière-du-Loup." Thèse de M.A., Laval, 1951.

3344. **Bellemare, J.-E.** *Histoire de Nicolet, 1669-1924.* Athabasca: Imprimerie d'Athabaska, 1924.

3345. **Bergeron, Arthur.** *Pierreville, 1853-1953: Un siècle de vie paroissiale et l'aurore du suivant.* Pierreville: Comité du centenaire, 1960.

3346. **Bergevin, J. C.** "Intégration d'un village à la péripherie urbaine de Québec (St-Jean-de-Boischatel)." Thèse de L. ès L., Laval, 1971.

3347. **Biays, P.** 'Une ville d'Abitibi: Senneterre." *Cah géogr Q* 3 (1957):63-74.
3348. **Bolduc, Roger.** *Saint-Georges d'hier et d'aujourd'hui.* Saint-Georges de Beauce: Beauce Publications, 1969.
3349. **Bourget, M.** "Monographie de la cité du Cap-de-la-Madeleine." Thèse de M.A., Laval, 1951.
3350. **Brouillette, Benoît.** "Montmagny, ville et paroisse." *BSGQ* 2 (1943):65-88.
3351. **Chagnon, Claude.** "Sainte-Agathe-des-Monts, centre touristique." *Cah géogr Q* 13 (1969):121-30.
3352. _____. "Sainte-Agathe-des-Monts." *RCU* 20, no. 3 (1970):24-28.
3353. **Chamard, L.** "Evolution de la ville de la Pocatière de 1927 à 1970." Thèse de L. ès L., Laval, 1971.
3354. **Clunie, David.** "Two New Northern Communities (Fermont, Quebec, and Leaf Rapids, Manitoba)." In #337, pp. 309-15.
3355. **Coté, Y.** "L'évolution et la régression d'un ville minière: Duparquet." Thèse de L. ès L., Laval, 1972.
3356. **Dandenault, Roch.** *Histoire de Coaticook, 1818-1976.* Sherbrooke: Editions Sherbrooke, 1976.
3357. **Déom, André.** "La grève de Lachute." Thèse de M.A., Montréal, 1951.
3358. **Frenette, Marcel.** "Monographie économique de Lachute." Thèse, HEC (Montréal), 1950.
3359. **Gagnon, Antoine.** *Monographie de Matane.* Rimouski: Imprimerie Générale, 1945.
3360. _____. *Histoire de Matane, 1677-1977: Tricentaire de la seigneurie.* Rimouski: Société d'histoire de Matane, 1977.
3361. **Garry, Robert.** "Chibougamau, ville minière." *RCGG* 9, no. 1 (1955):47-52.
3362. **Guérette, Fernand.** "Monographie économique de la municipalité de Causapscal." *Ac Ec* 20 (1945):340-64.
3363. **Hamelin, Louis-Edmond.** *Le cadre naturel de Sainte-Marie-de-Beauce.* Québec: Institut de géographie de l'université Laval, 1953.
3364. _____; **Martin, Yves; Robitaille, René; and Cimon, Jean.** "Sainte-Marie de Beauce: Etudes d'urbanisme." *RCU* 5, no. 3 (1955):91-105.
3365. **Hiess, A.** "St. Jean, Quebec 1871: A Socio-Economic Profile." M.A. thesis, Concordia, 1976.
3366. **Hilton, Kenneth D.** "The Iron Mining Communities of Quebec-Labrador: A Study of a Resolute Frontier." M.A. thesis, McGill, 1968.
3368. **Kremenliev, Gregor.** "The Company and the Town: A History of the Pulp and Paper Town of Chandler, Quebec, 1912-1971." M.A. thesis, Concordia, 1976.
3369. **Larouche, Léonidas.** *Le second registre de Tadoussac, 1668-1700.* Montréal: Presses de l'université du Québec, 1972.
3370. **Laverdière, Camille.** "La région de Sept-Iles, côte nord du Saint-Laurent: Etude morphologique." Thèse de M.A., Université de Montréal, 1954.
3371. **Lazure, L.** "Le port de Valleyfield: Son implantation, sa situation, ses fonctions." Thèse de L. ès L., Laval, 1972.
3372. **Léger, Albert-Ange.** "Salaberry-de-Valleyfield, esquisse de géographie urbaine." Thèse de M.A., Montréal, 1961.
3373. **Legget, Robert F.** "Development of a Pulpwood Shipping Harbour, Forestville, Quebec." *Engineering J* 36 (1953):1287-94.
3374. **Lemieux, Marc.** "Lauzon: Etude de géographie urbaine." Thèse de M.A., Laval, 1967.
3375. **Marchand, Jean-René.** *Une ville du Nord, Sainte-Thècle: Cent ans d'histoire, 1874-1974.* Trois-Rivières: Bien-Public, 1974.
3376. **Matte, E.** "Monographie de la ville de La Tuque." Thèse de M.A., Laval, 1946.

3378. **Michaud, Laurent.** "Le phénomène urbain du comté de Chambly." Thèse de M.A., Université de Montréal, 1962.
3379. **Michie, George.** "Sept-Iles: Canada's Newest Seaport." M.A. thesis, McGill, 1956.
3380. **Morisseau, H.** "Un collège classique à Saint-Denis-sur-Richelieu dès 1805." *Rev univ Ottawa* 18 (1948):356-66.
3381. **Norbert, Prosper.** "Monographie économique du Cap-de-la-Madeleine." Thèse, HEC (Montréal), 1951.
3382. **Pacreau, C.** *Tadoussac.* Montmagny: Marquis, 1947.
3383. **Pépin, Pierre-Yves.** "Parent, ville en régression." *RCGG* 10 (1956):236-39.
3384. **Provost, Honorius.** *Sainte-Marie de la Nouvelle-Beauce. Histoire civile.* Québec: Nouvelle-Beauce, 1970.
3385. **Robitaille, André.** "Sainte-Marie de Beauce: Le plan directeur." *RCU* 5, no. 4 (1955):134-42.
3386. **Ross, W. Gillies.** *Three Eastern Townships Mining Villages since 1863: Albert Mines, Capelton, and Eustis, Quebec.* Lennoxville: Bishop's University, 1974.
3387. **Routhier, François.** *Jonquière-Kenogami-Arvida.* Québec: Centre de recherches en sociologie religieuse, 1965.
3388. **Rowe, K. C.** "A Paper Mill and a Town in the Making (Baie-Comeau)." *Pulp and Paper Magazine of Canada* 37 (1936):623-42.
3389. **Schoenauer, Norbert.** "Fermont: A New Version of the Company Town." In #337, pp. 316-20.
3390. **Séguin, Normand.** "Héberville au Lac Saint-Jean, 1830-1900: Un exemple québécois de colonisation au XIXe siècle." CHA, *HP* (1973):251-68.
3391. "Sept-Iles." *Saguenayensia* 12 (1970):149-53.
3392. **Smith, Willard Vandine.** "The Evolution of a Fall Line Settlement: Buckingham, Quebec." M.A. thesis, Ottawa, 1967.
3393. **Tessier, J.-G.** "Implications du regroupement des fermes dans le secteur de Saint-Hermas, région aeroportuaire de Mirabel." Thèse de M.A., Laval, 1974.

VIII

Ontario

1. General

3394. **Adams, Thomas.** "Planning of Cities in Ontario." *To Pl Cn L* 6, no. 1 (1920):1-8.
3395. **Adler, G. M.** *Land Planning by Administrative Regulation. The Policies of the Ontario Municipal Board.* Toronto: UTP, 1971.
3396. **Aitchison, J. H.** "The Municipal Corporations Act of 1849." *CHR* 30 (1950):107-22.
3397. _____. "The Development of Local Government in Upper Canada, 1783-1850." Ph.D. thesis, Toronto, 1953.
3398. **Aitken, Barbara B.** *Local Histories of Ontario Municipalities, 1951-1977: A Bibliography.* Toronto: Ontario Library Association, 1978.
3399. **Anderson, C. E., and Co.** *Province of Ontario Gazetteer and Directory.* Toronto: Anderson, 1869.
3400. **Armstrong, Frederick H., and Hultin, Neil C.** "The *Anglo-American Magazine* Looks at Urban Upper Canada on the Eve of the Railway Era." In *Profiles of a Province,* edited by Edith G. Firth, pp. 43-58. Toronto: Ontario Historical Society, 1967.
3401. **Armstrong, G. H.** *The Origin and Meaning of Place Names in Canada.* Toronto: Macmillan, 1930.
3401A. **Bain, Ian.** "The Role of J. J. Kelso in the Launching of the Child Welfare Movement in Ontario." M.S.W. Thesis, Toronto, 1954.
3402. **Balciumas, T.** "Views of the Small Ontario Town in Selected Canadian Fiction, 1894-1912." M.A. thesis, Toronto, 1968.
3403. **Ball, N. R.** "The Technology of Settlement and Land Clearing in Upper Canada prior to 1840." Ph.D. thesis, Toronto, 1979.
3404. **Bannister, J. A.** "The Romance of Forgotten Towns." *W Ont Hist N* 21, no. 2 (1965):46-76.
3405. **Barber, G. M., and Britton, John N. H.** *Occupational Structure and Population Growth in the Ontario-Quebec Urban System, 1941-1966.* Research Paper #49. Toronto: CUCS, 1971.
3406. **Barron, F. L.** "The Genesis of Temperance in Ontario, 1828-1850." Ph.D. thesis, Guelph, 1976.
3407. **Bates, Hilary, and Sherman, Robert.** *Index to the Publications of the Ontario Historical Association, 1899-1972.* Toronto: Ontario Historical Society, 1974.
3408. **Beattie, R. N.** "The Impact of Hydro on Ontario." In *Profiles of a Province,* edited by Edith G. Firth, pp. 166-72. Toronto: Ontario Historical Society, 1967.
3409. **Bédard, Robert-J.** "The Economic Impact of the St. Lawrence Seaway on the Canadian Great Lake Ports." M.A. thesis, Ottawa, 1971.

3410. **Beer, G. Frank.** "Better Housing in Canada: The Ontario Plan." *Imperial Health Conference* (1914):123-32.
3411. **Biggar, C. R. W.** "Some Notes on the Growth of Municipal Institutions in Canada: Ontario, 1788-1849." *Can Law J* 33 (1897):7-18.
3412. **Bishop, Olga B.; Irwin, B.I.; and Miller, C.G.** *Bibliography of Ontario History, 1867-1976.* 2 vols. Toronto: UTP, 1980.
3413. **Bland, Warren R.** "The Changing Locational Pattern of Manufacturing in Southern Ontario from 1881 to 1932." Ph.D. thesis, Indiana, 1970.
3414. _____. "The Location of Manufacturing in Southern Ontario in 1881." *Ont Geogr* 8 (1974):9-39.
3415. _____. "The Changing Location of Metal-Fabricating and Clothing Industries in Southern Ontario: 1881-1932." *Ont Geogr* 9 (1975):34-57.
3416. **Bleasdale, Ruth E.** "Irish Labourers on the Cornwall, Welland, and Williamsburg Canals." M.A. thesis, Western Ontario, 1976.
3417. **Bockus, Elton C.** "The Common School of Upper Canada, 1786-1843." M.A. thesis, McGill, 1967.
3418. **Bogue, Margaret B., and Palmer, Virginia A.** *Around the Shores of Lake Superior: A Guide to Historic Sites.* Madison: University of Wisconsin Press, 1979.
3419. **Bourne, L. S., and Baker, Alan Maurice.** *Urban Development in Ontario and Quebec: Outline and Overview.* Research Paper #1. Toronto: CUCS, 1968.
3420. **Boyle, Terry, and Stokes, Peter J.** *Under This Roof: Family Homes of Southern Ontario.* Toronto: Doubleday, 1980.
3421. **Bradshaw, T.** "Maintenance of Public Credit and Its Relation to the Present Financial Position of Many Ontario Municipalities." CCHA, *Study Sessions* 26 (1935):119-33.
3422. **Brandon, K. F.** "Public Health in Upper Canada." *PHEJ* 25 (1934):461-65.
3423. **Brown, Ron.** *Ghost Towns of Ontario.* Langley: Stagecoach, 1977.
3424. **Brozowski, Roman.** "Population Changes in Ontario Towns and Villages, 1941-1966." M.A. thesis, Windsor, 1971.
3425. **Burnell, A. E. K.** "Recent Planning Developments in Ontario." *TPICJ* 7, no. 5 (1928):120-27.
3426. _____. "Community Planning in Ontario." *PA* 10 (1947):260-63.
3427. **Burnett, Jean Robertson.** "Ethnic Groups in Upper Canada." M.A. thesis, Toronto, 1943.
3428. **Byrnes, T. C.** "The Automotive Industry in Ontario." M.A. thesis, Toronto, 1951.
3429. **Campbell, Maurice A., and Nixon, Peter G.** *Four Cities: Studies in Regional Planning [Windsor, Sarnia, London, Waterloo-South Wellington].* Toronto: M&S, 1971.
3430. **Camu, Pierre.** "L'axe économique de Saint Laurent, entre Kingston et Québec [City]." Thèse de Ph.D., Montréal, 1952.
3431. **Careless, J. M. S.** "Some Aspects of Urbanization in Nineteenth-Century Ontario." In *Aspects of Nineteenth-Century Ontario,* edited by F. H. Armstrong, H. A. Stevenson, and J. D. Wilson, pp. 65-79. Toronto: UTP, 1974.
3432. **Carol, H.** "Development Regions in Southern Ontario Based on City-Centred Regions." *Ont Geogr* 4 (1969):13-29.
3433. **Cartwright, D. G.** "Institutions on the Frontier: French-Canadian Settlement in Eastern Ontario in the Nineteenth Century." *Can Geogr* 21 (1977):1-21.
3434. **Cassidy, H. M.** *Unemployment and Relief in Ontario, 1929-1932: A Survey and Report.* Toronto: Dent, 1932.
3435. **Chadwick, Edward Marion.** *Ontario Families.* 2 vols. Toronto: Ralph, Smith and Co., 1895-98.
3436. **Chimbos, Peter D.** "A Comparison of the Social Adaptation of Dutch, Greek and Slovak Immigrants in a Canadian Community." *International Migration Rev* 6 (1972):230-44.

3437. **Christie, R.** "The Development of the Furniture Industry in the Southwestern Ontario Furniture Manufacturing Region." M.A. thesis, Western Ontario, 1964.
3438. **Clarke, John.** "A Geographical Analysis of Colonial Settlements in the Western District of Upper Canada, 1788-1850." Ph.D. thesis, Western Ontario, 1970.
3439. _____; **Taylor, H. W.; and Wightman, W. R.** "Areal Patterns of Population Change in Southern Ontario, 1831-1891: Core, Frontier and Intervening Space." *Ont Geogr* 12 (1978):27-48.
3440. **Copp, Terry.** "The Experience of Unionism in Four Ontario Towns." Committee on Canadian Labour History, *Bulletin* 6 (1978):4-11.
3441. **Crawford, Kenneth Grant.** "Municipal Government in Ontario." Ph.D. thesis, Toronto, 1930.
3442. _____. "The Independence of Municipal Councils in Ontario." *CJEPS* 6 (1940):543-45.
3443. **Crawford, Patricia, et al.** *Architecture in Ontario: A Select Bibliography on Architectural Conservation and the History of Architecture with Special Reference to the Province of Ontario.* Kingston: Frontenac Historic Foundation, 1976.
3444. **Culham, David John.** "Urban Ownership of Rural Land on the Niagara Escarpment, Ontario. Implications for Resource Management." M.A. thesis, Western Ontario, 1967.
3445. **Cullingworth, J. B.** *Ontario Planning: Notes on the Conroy Report on the Ontario Planning Act.* Papers on Planning and Design, no. 19. Toronto: University of Toronto, Dept. of Urban and Regional Planning, 1978.
3446. **Curtis, Clifford A.** "Municipal Government in Ontario." *CJEPS* 8 (1942):416-26.
3447. **Dahms, Frederick A.** "Declining Villages?" In *Proceedings of the Second Annual Agricultural History of Ontario Seminar,* edited by T. A. Crowley, pp. 50-65. Guelph: University of Guelph, 1977.
3448. _____, **and Forbes, James A.** "A Comparison of Three Central Place Systems: Guelph, Barrie, and Owen Sound." *Can Geogr* 20 (1976):439-44.
3449. **Davies, J. B.** "An Analysis of City Size Distribution in the Cities of Ontario and Quebec." M.A. thesis, Toronto, 1970.
3450. **Davy, B. W.** "Temporal Changes in Centrality of Small Urban Places." M.A. thesis, McMaster, 1970.
3451. **Deacon, Nadine A. H.** "Geographical Factors and Land Use in Toronto." *CGEJ* 29 (1944):80-99.
3452. **Dean, W. G., ed.** *Economic Atlas of Ontario.* Toronto: UTP, 1969.
3453. **Demko, D.** "Cognition of Southern Ontario Cities in a Potential Migration Context." *Econ Geogr* 1, no. 1 (1974):20-34.
3454. **Denis, Paul-Yves.** "La présence urbaine au Québec et dans l'Ontario: Aspects et tendances de son évolution mis en relief par quelques critères de comparaison." *RCGG* 17 (1963):3-8.
3456. **De Volpi, C. P.** *The Niagara Peninsula, 1697-1880: A Pictorial Record.* Montreal: Dev-Sco, 1966.
3457. **Dewar, Kenneth.** "State Ownership in Canada: The Origins of Ontario Hydro." Ph.D. thesis, Toronto, 1975.
3458. **Dolbey, I. J.** "Inter-Municipal Special Purpose Bodies in the Province of Ontario." M.A. thesis, Queen's, 1966.
3459. **Dupré, J. Stephen.** *Intergovernmental Finance in Ontario: A Provincial-Local Perspective.* Toronto: Queen's Printer, 1968.
3460. **English, John.** "New and Old History in Ontario." *Acadiensis* 3, no. 2 (1974):110-16.
3461. **Evans, J. A. S.** "The Classical Tradition in Ontario Architecture." *CGEJ* 44 (1962):66-69.
3462. **Faucher, Albert.** "Le fonds d'emprunt municipal dans le Haut-Canada, 1852-1867." *Rech soc* 1 (1960):7-32.
3463. **Feldman, Lionel D.** "Legislative Control of Municipalities in Ontario." *Can Pub Admin* 4 (1961):294-301.

3464. **Ferris, T. T. M.** "Growth and Financing of Municipal Government in Ontario, 1850-1900." Ph.D. thesis, Western Ontario, 1964.
3465. _____. "Local Government Reform in Upper Canada." *Can Pub Admin* 12 (1969):387-410.
3466. **Field, N. C., and Kerr, Donald P.** *Geographical Aspects of Industrial Growth in the Metropolitan Toronto Region.* Toronto: Ontario Dept. of Treasury and Economics, 1968.
3467. **Finnis, F. H.** "Municipal Affairs (Ontario Committee on Taxation)." *Can Tax J* 15 (1967):527-42.
3468. _____. "Ontario Tax Reform: Municipal Taxation and Structural Reform." *Can Tax J* 17 (1969)132-35.
3469. **Foucault, E. A.** "A Planning Policy for Single-Enterprise Communities in Northeastern Ontario." M.A. thesis, Western Ontario, 1977.
3470. **Fowke, V. C.** "The Myth of the Self-Sufficient Canadian Pioneer." RSC, *Trans,* 3d series, 61 (1962):23-37.
3471. **Fraser, Mary,** ed. *Conserving Ontario's Main Streets: Proceedings of the Conference at Trent University, Peterborough, August 1978.* Toronto: Ontario Heritage Foundation, 1979.
3472. **Gaffield, Chad M.** "Cultural Challenge in Eastern Ontario: Land, Family and Education in the 19th Century." Ph.D. thesis, Toronto, 1978.
3473. **Galvin, Martin J.** "Catholic-Protestant Relations in Ontario, 1864-1875." M.A. thesis, Toronto, 1962.
3474. **Gentilcore, R. Louis.** "Lines on the Land: Crown Surveys and Settlement in Upper Canada." *OH* 61 (1969):57-73.
3475. _____, ed. *Ontario: Studies in Canadian Geography.* Toronto: UTP, 1972.
3476. _____, **and Wood, J. David.** "A Military Colony in a Wilderness: The Upper Canada Frontier." In #3639, pp. 32-50.
3477. **Gidney, R. E.** "Education and Society in Upper Canada, 1791-1850." M. Phil. thesis, London, 1970.
3478. **Gilmour, James M.** *Spatial Evolution of Manufacturing: Southern Ontario, 1851-1891.* Toronto: UTP, 1972.
3479. **Glazebrook, G. P. de T.** *Life in Ontario: A Social History.* Toronto: UTP, 1968.
3480. _____. "The Origins of Local Government." In *Aspects of Nineteenth-Century Ontario,* edited by F. H. Armstrong, H. A. Stevenson, and J. D. Wilson, pp. 36-47. Toronto: UTP, 1974.
3481. **Golant, S., and Bourne, L. S.** *Growth Characteristics of the Ontario-Quebec Urban System.* Research Paper #4. Toronto: CUCS, 1968.
3482. **Gourlay, Robert F.** *Statistical Account of Upper Canada.* 1822. Reprint. New York: Johnson Reprint Corp., 1966.
3483. **Greenhill, Ralph; MacPherson, Ken; and Richardson, Douglas.** *Ontario Towns.* Ottawa: Oberon, 1974.
3484. **Hall, Carl A. S.** "Electrical Utilities in Ontario and under Private Ownership, 1890-1914." Ph.D. thesis, Toronto, 1968.
3484A. **Hall, C. J.** "The Image of the Small Ontario Town in Fiction, 1900-1918: A Case Study in Humanistic Geography." M.A. thesis, Queen's, 1979.
3485. **Hann, Russell.** *Farmers Confront Industrialism: Some Historical Perspectives of Ontario Agrarian Movements.* 3d ed. rev. Toronto: New Hogtown Press, 1975.
3486. **Harrington, Lyn.** "Gingerbread Architecture in Ontario." *CGEJ* 85 (1972):196-99.
3487. **Heidenreich, C. E.** "A Study of Functions and Forms in Business Districts of Some Small Urban Centres in Southern Ontario." M.A. thesis, Toronto, 1964.
3488. **Heron, Craig, and Palmer, Bryan D.** "Through the Prism of the Strike: Industrial Conflict in Southern Ontario, 1901-1914." *CHR* 58 (1977):423-58.
3489. **Herrington, W. S.** "The Evolution of Municipal Government in Upper Canada." RSC, *Trans,* 3d ser. 25 (1931):1-19.

3490. **Hickey, Paul.** "Financial Control of Ontario Municipalities." CCHA, *Study Sessions* 70 (1957):313-18.
3491. _____. "Ontario's Responsibility for Municipal Finance Administration." *Mun Fin* 36 (1963):34-39.
3492. _____. *Decision-Making Processes in Ontario's Local Governments*. Toronto: Queen's Printer, 1973.
3493. **Hills, C. A.; Love, D. V.; and Lacote, D. S.** *Developing a Better Environment: Ecological Land-Use Planning in Ontario*. Toronto: Ontario Economic Council, 1970.
3494. **Hodgins, J. G.** *Documentary History of Education in Upper Canada, from the Passing of the Constitutional Act of 1791 to 1876*. 28 vols. Toronto: Warwick and Rutter, 1894-1910.
3495. **Holman, Lois C.** "The Ontario Municipal Board." M.A. thesis, Western Ontario, 1956.
3496. **Houston, Susan E.** "Politics, Schools, and Social Change in Upper Canada." *CHR* 53 (1972):249-71.
3497. _____. "The Impetus to Reform: Urban Crime, Poverty and Ignorance in Ontario, 1850-1875." Ph.D. thesis, Toronto, 1974.
3498. **Institute of Local Government, Queen's University.** *The Municipal Council and Councillor in Ontario*. Kingston: Queen's University, 1966.
3499. **Isbister, John.** "Agriculture, Balanced Growth, and Social Change in Central Canada since 1850: An Interpretation." *Economic Development and Cultural Change* 5 (1977):673-97.
3500. **Jackson, John D.** "French-English Relations in an Ontario Community." In *Immigrant Groups*, edited by Jean Leonard Elliott, pp. 160-74. Toronto: Prentice-Hall, 1971.
3501. **Jackson, W. A. D.** "A Geographical Study of Early Settlement in Southern Ontario." M.A. thesis, Toronto, 1949.
3502. **Keddie, Vincent.** "A Study of Manual Workers' Attitudes towards Social Class in Four Ontario Communities." Ph.D. thesis, McMaster, 1974.
3503. **Keith, J. Clark.** "Regional Planning in Western Ontario: Planning the Suburban Zone." *TPICJ* 3, no. 3 (1924):3-6.
3504. _____. "Regional Planning." *TPICJ* 7, no. 5 (1928):137-40.
3505. **Kerr, Donald P., and Spelt, Jacob.** "Some Aspects of Industrial Location in Southern Ontario." *Can Geogr* 15 (1960):12-25.
3506. **King, Leslie J.** "Discriminatory Analysis of Urban Growth Patterns in Ontario and Quebec, 1951-1961." *AAAG* 57 (1967):566-78.
3507. **Kirk, D. W.** "Southwestern Ontario: The Areal Pattern of Urban Settlements in 1850." Ph.D. thesis, Northwestern, 1949.
3508. **Knight, David B., and Burrows, Susan.** "Centrality by Degrees: A 19th-Century Canadian's Measurement for Central Location." *Can Cart* 12 (1975):109-20.
3509. **Koop, R. H.** "Urban and Rural Migration Flows in Southern Ontario, 1951-1961." M.Sc. thesis, Guelph, 1967.
3510. **Kreuger, Ralph R.** "Urbanization of the Niagara Fruit Belt." *Can Geogr* 32 (1978):179-94.
3511. **Landon, Fred.** "The Evolution of Local Government in Ontario." *OH* 42 (1950):1-5.
3512. _____. *Western Ontario and the American Frontier*. Toronto: M&S, 1967.
3513. **Langman, R. C.** *Patterns of Settlement in Southern Ontario: Three Studies*. Toronto: M&S, 1971.
3514. **Langmuir, J. W.** "Asylums, Prisons and Public Charities of Ontario, and Their System of Management." *Can Mon* 5 (1880):239-47.
3516. **Lee, Chun-Fen.** "The Middle Grand River Valley of Ontario: A Study in Regional Geography." Ph.D. thesis, Toronto, 1943.
3517. **Lee, Judith M.** "Inventive Activity and Its Relation to Industrial Development in Southern Ontario, 1881-1911." M.A. thesis, Western Ontario, 1972.
3518. **Lévesque, J. R.** "Municipal Finance in Ontario, 1946-1964." M.A. thesis, Ottawa, 1967.

3519. **Lithwick, N. H.** "An Economic Interpretation of the Urban Crisis." *J Can St* 7, no. 3 (1972):36-49.

3520. **McArthur, N. M.** "River to Seaway—Study of Probable Effects of the St. Lawrence Seaway upon the Economy at Cornwall, Morrisburg, Iroquois, Cardinal, Prescott and Brockville." Ph.D. thesis, Michigan, 1955.

3521. **McCabe, R. W.** *Shopping Centre Proposals: Some Implications of a Decision by the Ontario Municipal Board.* Papers on Planning and Designs, no. 8. Toronto: University of Toronto, Dept. of Urban and Regional Planning, 1975.

3521A. **McCallum, John.** *Unequal Beginnings: Agriculture and Economic Development in Quebec and Ontario.* Toronto: UTP, 1980.

3522. **McCammon, Andrew.** "British Colonialism, Governor Simcoe, and Local Government in Upper Canada." M.A. thesis, Guelph, 1980.

3523. **McCullough, J. W. S.** "Early History of Public Health in Upper and Lower Canada." *Can J Medicine and Surgery* 51 (1922):60-84.

3524. **McCurry, R. K.** "Provincial Control of Local Government Bodies: An Ontario Study." M.A. thesis, Toronto, 1963.

3525. **McDougall, Harry.** "The Fortresses of Lake Ontario." *CGEJ* 77 (1968):115-64.

3526. **Macdougall, J. B.** *Building the North.* Toronto: M&S, 1919.

3527. **McGaughey, Charles Eustace.** "The Development of Municipal Institutions in Ontario, 1785-1888." M.A. thesis, Queen's, 1939.

3528. **McIlwraith, Thomas.** "The Adequacy of Rural Roads in the Era before Railways: An Illustration from Upper Canada." *Can Geogr* 14 (1970):344-60.

3529. **MacIver, I.** "Urban Water Supply Alternatives: Perception and Choice in the Grand Basin, Ontario." Ph.D. thesis, Chicago, 1969.

3530. **McKay, K. W.** "Municipal Organization in Ontario." In #**895**, pp. 89-120.

3531. **McKenna, Bruce.** "The Ontario Municipal Board: Citizens as Losers." *City Mag* 1, no. 7 (1975):40-46.

3532. **McLeod, Judy.** "Decision Making in Ontario New Communities." M.A. thesis, Waterloo, 1975.

3533. **MacLeod, Malcolm.** "Fortress Ontario or Forlorn Hope? Simcoe and the Defence of Upper Canada." *CHR* 53 (1972):149-78.

3534. **MacRae, Marion, and Adamson, Anthony.** *The Ancestral Roof: Domestic Architecture of Upper Canada.* Toronto: UTP, 1963.

3535. _____. *Hallowed Walls: Church Architecture in Upper Canada.* Toronto: Clarke Irwin, 1975.

3536. **Mactaggart, H. I., and Sundquist, K. E.** *Publications of the Government of Ontario, 1956-1971.* Toronto: Government Services, 1975.

3537. **Marple, David.** "The Utility of Quantitative Sources in the Study of Transportation and the Growth of the Ontario and Quebec Urban Hierarchy, 1861-1901." *UHR* 2-73 (October 1973):2-7.

3538. **Marshall, John U.** "The Urban Network." In #**3475**, pp. 64-82.

3539. _____, **and Smith, W. Randy.** "The Dynamics of Growth in a Regional Urban System: Southern Ontario, 1851-1971." *Can Geogr* 22 (1978):22-40.

3540. **Mavor, James.** "Municipal Ownership of Public Utilities." *Publications of the Michigan Political Science Association* 4 (1904):1-10. Reprinted in #**979**, pp. 45-52.

3541. **Mika, Nick, and Mika, Helma.** *Places in Ontario: Their Name Origins and History. Part 1: A to E.* Belleville: Mika, 1977.

3542. **Milanson, Harold.** *Urban and Economic Development in Northern Ontario.* Ottawa: Queen's Printer, 1962.

3543. **Miller, Orlo.** *A Century of Western Ontario.* Toronto: Ryerson, 1949.

Ontario   137

3544. **Mills, John M.** *Traction on the Grand: The Story of Electric Railways along Ontario's Grand River Valley.* Toronto: Railfare, 1977.
3545. **Morley, William F. E.** *Canadian Local Histories: A Bibliography.* Vol. 3. *Ontario and the Canadian North.* Toronto: UTP, 1978.
3546. **Morrison, T. R.** "The Child and Urban Social Reform in Late Nineteenth Century Ontario." Ph.D. thesis, Toronto, 1971.
3547. **Muir, Doris J.; Woodcock, Judith-Anne; and Irvine, Lorraine.** *Good Beginnings: An Annotated Bibliography of Selected Primary Sources [for the Study of Kirkland Lake, North Bay, Sudbury, Tri-Town, Cobalt, Haileybury, and New Liskeard].* Sudbury: Laurentian University, 1975.
3548. **Munro, Don.** "The Care of the Dependent Poor in Ontario, 1891-1921: A Study of the Impact of Social Change on the Organization of Welfare Services in Ontario." M.S.W. thesis, Toronto, 1966.
3549. **Murphy, Larry.** *Thomas Keefer.* Toronto: Fitzhenry and Whiteside, 1976.
3550. **Mutambirwa, Christopher C.** "Modelling Differentials in Urban Growth with Applications to the Ontario Urban Growth System." Ph.D. thesis, Western Ontario, 1973.
3551. **Nicholson, N. L.** "The Religious Factors in the Location of Ontario Universities." *Ont Geogr* 7 (1972):37-49.
3552. **Nitkin, D. A.** "Negro Colonization as a Response to Racism: An Historical Geography of the Southwestern Ontario Experience." M.A. thesis, York, 1974.
3553. **Norcliffe, G. B., and Kotseff, L. E.** "Local Industrial Complexes in Ontario." *AAAG* 70 (1980):68-79.
3554. **O'Brien, Allan.** "Father Knows Best: A Look at the Provincial-Municipal Relationship in Ontario." In *Government and Politics of Ontario,* edited by Donald C. MacDonald, pp. 154-71. Toronto: Macmillan, 1975.
3555. **Ondaatje, Kim, and Mackenzie, Lois.** *Old Ontario Houses.* Agincourt: Gage, 1977.
3556. **Ontario. Department of Health.** "The Development of Public Health in Ontario." *PHEJ* 26 (1935):110-23.
3557. **Ontario. Department of Municipal Affairs.** "Local Histories of Municipalities." *Lib Bull* 8 (24 June 1970).
3558. **Ontario. Department of Trade and Development, and the Ontario Development Corporation.** *Industrial Directory of Municipal Data.* Toronto, 1960-69.
3559. **Ontario. Department of Treasury and Economics, and the Department of Municipal Affairs.** *A Strategy for Southwestern Ontario Development.* Toronto, 1970.
3560. **Ontario. Department of Treasury and Economics, Regional Development Branch.** *Design for Development: Northeastern Ontario Region, Phase 1: Analysis.* Toronto: 1971.
3561. **Overton, David.** "An Examination of Models of Port Development: Lake Erie North Shore, 1784-1870." M.A. thesis, Western Ontario, 1970.
3562. **Parr, G. J.** "The Welcome and the Wake: Attitudes in Canada West toward the Irish Famine Migration." *OH* 56 (1974):101-13.
3563. **Payne, Hilary.** "The Restructuring of Ontario Local Government." M.A. thesis, Windsor, 1975.
3564. **Pearson, Norman.** "Regional Government and Development." In *Government and Politics of Ontario,* edited by Donald C. MacDonald, pp. 172-93. Toronto: Macmillan, 1975.
3565. **Percival, Ray N.** "New Towns for Ontario, Short Story of the Origin and Design Techniques." *Town and Country Planning* 25 (February 1957):80-83.
3566. **Petersen, J.** "Technology and Social Change in the Mining Communities of Northern Ontario." Ph.D. thesis, Toronto, 1977.
3567. **Phillips, R. A. J.** *Up the Streets of Ontario.* Ottawa: Heritage Canada, 1976.
3568. **Philp, John.** "The Economic and Social Effects of the British Garrisons in the Development of Western Upper Canada." *OH* 41 (1949):37-48.

3569. **Piva, Michael J.** "Workers and Tories: The Collapse of the Conservative Party in Urban Ontario, 1908-1919." *UHR* 3-76 (February 1977):23-39.
3570. **Preston, Richard E.** "The Recent Evolution of Ontario Central Place Systems in the Light of Christaller's Concept of Centrality." *Can Geogr* 23 (1979):201-21.
3571. **Price, Mary J.** "The Professionalization of Medicine in Ontario during the Nineteenth Century." M.A. thesis, McMaster, 1977.
3572. **Price, Trevor,** ed. *Regional Government in Ontario.* Toronto: Science Research Associates, 1971.
3573. **Proctor, F. B.** *The Law of Municipal Corporations in Ontario.* Toronto: Burroughs, 1931.
3574. "Proposed Town Planning Legislation for Ontario." *TPICJ* 1, no. 12 (1922):10-17.
3575. **Punter, L. B.** "Shopping Centre Development in Small Cities and Towns in Ontario." M.A. thesis, York, 1975.
3576. **Ramsay, Dean P.** "The Development of Child Welfare Legislation in Ontario." M.S.W. thesis, Toronto, 1949.
3577. **Ray, David Michael.** "Settlement and Rural Out Migration in Easternmost Ontario, 1783-1956." M.A. thesis, Ottawa, 1961.
3578. _____. *Market Potential and Economic Shadow: A Quantitative Analysis of Industrial Location in Southern Ontario.* Chicago: University of Chicago, Dept. of Geography, Research Paper no. 101, 1965.
3579. **Reed, M.** *Site Plan Control in Ontario.* Papers on Planning and Design, no. 20. Toronto: University of Toronto, Dept. of Urban and Regional Planning, 1978.
3580. **Rempel, John.** "The History and Development of Early Forms of Building Construction in Ontario." *OH* 52 (1960):235-44; 53 (1961):1-35.
3581. _____. *Building with Wood and Other Aspects of Nineteenth-Century Building in Ontario.* Toronto: UTP, 1977.
3582. **Reynolds, Roy.** *A Guide to Educational Materials in Municipal Records, Records of Committees and Commissions and Other Miscellaneous Papers in the Ontario Archives.* Toronto: OISE, 1976.
3583. **Richards, J. H.** "Land Use and Settlement Patterns on the Fringe of the Shield in Southern Ontario." Ph.D. thesis, Toronto, 1954.
3584. **Richards, T.** "Toward an Optimal Organization for Municipal Water Supply in South West Ontario." M.A. thesis, Western Ontario, 1966.
3585. **Richardson, Douglas,** ed. *Architecture in Ontario: A Select Bibliography on Architectural Conservation and the History of Architecture.* Toronto: Ontario Ministry of Culture and Recreation, 1976.
3586. **Richmond, D. R.** *Government Reform in Ontario.* Toronto: Ontario Economic Council, 1969.
3587. **Ross, R. K.** *Local Government in Ontario.* Toronto: Canada Law Book Company, 1962.
3588. **Routley, H. T.** "The Development of Townsites in New Ontario." *Can Engineer* 42 (1922):270-72.
3589. **Russwurm, Lorne H.** "Expanding Urbanization in the London to Hamilton Area of Western Ontario, 1941-1961." Ph.D. thesis, Illinois, 1964.
3590. _____. *Development of an Urban Corridor: Toronto to Stratford Area, 1941-1961.* Toronto: Ontario Dept. of Treasury and Economics, 1970.
3591. **Saarinen, Oiva,** ed. *Proceedings of the Conference on Regional Development in Northeastern Ontario.* Sudbury: Laurentian University, 1976.
3592. **Scollie, F. Brent.** "Every Scrap of Paper: Access to Ontario's Municipal Records." *Can Lib J* 31, no. 1 (1974):8-16.
3593. **Seaborn, Edwin.** *The March of Medicine in Western Ontario.* Toronto: Ryerson, 1944.
3594. **Seifried, Neil R. M.** "A Study of Changes in Manufacturing in Mid-Western Ontario, 1951-1964." Ph.D. thesis, Washington, 1969.

3595. **Semple, Neil.** "The Impact of Urbanization on the Methodist Church in Central Canada, 1854-1884." Ph.D. thesis, Toronto, 1979.
3596. **Seymour, Horace L.** "New Town Planning Powers in Ontario." *TPICJ* 1, nos. 4-5 (1921):22-23.
3597. **Shortt, Adam.** "The Beginnings of Municipal Government in Ontario." *Transactions of the Canadian Institute* 7 (1901-2):409-24.
3598. _____. "Municipal Government in Ontario: An Historical Sketch." In **#895**, pp. 59-88.
3599. **Simcoe, Elizabeth.** *The Diary of Mrs. John Graves Simcoe.* 1911. Reprint. Toronto: Coles, 1973.
3600. **Sissons, C. B.** "A Housing Policy for Ontario." *Can Mag* 53 (1919):241-48.
3601. **Sitwell, O. F. G.** "The Great Lake Ports of Ontario." M.A. thesis, Toronto, 1959.
3602. **Smart, J. D.** "The Patrons of Industry in Ontario in the 1890s." M.A. thesis, Carleton, 1969.
3603. **Smith, W. Randy.** "Rail Network Development and Changes in Ontario's Urban System 1850-1890." M.A. thesis, York, 1975.
3604. **Spelt, Jacob.** *Urban Development in South Central Ontario.* Toronto: M&S, 1972.
3605. **Spragge, G. W.** "The Districts of Upper Canada." *OH* 39 (1947):91-100.
3606. **Stacey, Robert.** " 'Salvage for Us These Fragments': C. W. Jefferys and Ontario's Historic Architecture." *OH* 70 (1978):147-70.
3607. **Stamp, Robert M.** "Urbanization and Education in Ontario and Quebec, 1867-1914." *McGill J Educ* 3 (1968):127-35.
3608. **Stankovic, D.** "Spatial and Temporal Patterns in Short Term Employment Change within the Southern Ontario Urban System." M.A. thesis, McMaster, 1975.
3609. **Stelter, Gilbert A.** "Urban Planning and Development in Upper Canada before 1850." In **#35**.
3610. _____, **and Rowan, John.** *Community Development in Northeastern Ontario: A Selected Bibliography.* Sudbury: Laurentian University, 1972.
3611. **Stevenson, H. A., and Armstrong, Frederick H.** *Approaches to Teaching Local History, Using Upper Canadian and Ontario Examples.* Toronto: OUP, 1969.
3612. **Stevenson, M. A.** *Case Studies of Ontario's Business Improvement Area Program: Toronto, Oshawa, Acton and Willard.* Papers on Planning and Design, no. 21. Toronto: University of Toronto, Dept. of Urban and Regional Planning, 1979.
3613. **Stoddart, P. J.** "The Development of the Southern Ontario Steam Railway Network Competitive Conditions: 1830-1914." M.A. thesis, Guelph, 1976.
3614. **Taylor, Griffith.** "The Seven Ages of Towns." *Econ Geogr* 21 (1945):157-60.
3615. _____. "Towns and Townships in Southern Ontario." *Econ Geogr* 21 (1945):88-96.
3616. **Taylor, I. C.** "Components of Population Change, Ontario, 1850-1940." M.A. thesis, Toronto, 1967.
3617. **Thoman, R. S.** *Design for Development in Ontario: The Initiation of a Regional Development Process.* Toronto: Allister, 1971.
3618. **Thomas, John P.** "The Spatial Influence of Industries in Small Urban Centres on the Regional Work Force." M.A. thesis, Western Ontario, 1970.
3619. **Tyrrell, T. A. C.** "Ontario Planning and Urban Growth." *CPR* 7, no. 3 (1957):114-23.
3620. **Waldron, Gordon.** "The Depopulation and Impoverishment of Rural Ontario." Canadian Club of Toronto, *Speeches* (1910-11):63-70.
3621. **Walker, David F.** "The Role of Coal as a Location Factor in the Development of Manufacturing Industry in Southern Ontario, 1871-1921." M.A. thesis, Toronto, 1967.
3622. _____. "The Energy Sources of Manufacturing Industry in Southern Ontario, 1871-1921." *Ont Geogr* 6 (1971):56-66.
3623. _____. "Transportation of Coal into Southern Ontario, 1871-1921." *OH* 53 (1971):15-30.

140   Canada's Urban Past

3624. _____. "Energy and Industrial Location in Southern Ontario, 1871-1921." In **#3625**, pp. 41-68.
3625. _____, **and Bater, James H.**, eds. *Industrial Development in Southern Ontario: Selected Essays*. Waterloo: University of Waterloo, Dept. of Geography, 1974.
3626. Wall, Geoffrey, ed. *Recreational Land Use in Southern Ontario*. Waterloo: University of Waterloo, Dept. of Geography, 1979.
3627. Warrian, Peter. " 'Sons of Toil': The Impact of Industrialization on Craft Workers in Late 19th Century Ontario." In **#3625**, pp. 69-99.
3628. Watson, Joyce N. "Tracing the History of a House: Some Notes for the Amateur Historian." *Ont Lib Rev* 60 (1976):34-38.
3629. Watson, John Wreford. "Rural Depopulation in Southern Ontario." *AAAG* 37 (1947):145-54.
3630. Weaver, Emily P. *The Story of the Counties of Ontario*. Toronto: Bell and Cockburn, 1913.
3631. Weekes, F. E. "Provincial-Municipal Relations in Social Service Administration in Ontario." M.A. thesis, Toronto, 1945.
3632. Westhues, Kenneth. *Village in Crisis*. Toronto: Holt, Rinehart and Winston, 1974.
3633. Whebell, C. F. J. "The Geographical Basis of Local Government in Southern Ontario." Ph.D. thesis, London, 1961.
3634. _____. "Corridors: A Theory of Urban Systems." *AAAG* 59 (1969):1-26.
3635. _____. "Robert Baldwin and Decentralization, 1841-49." In *Aspects of Nineteenth Century Ontario*, edited by F. H. Armstrong, H. A. Stevenson, and J. D. Wilson, pp. 48-64. Toronto: UTP, 1974.
3636. _____. "Two Polygonal Settlement Schemes from Upper Canada." *Ont Geogr* 12 (1978):85-92.
3637. Wolfe, R. I. "Recreational Land Use in Ontario." Ph.D. thesis, Toronto, 1956.
3638. Wood, C. E. "Fiscal Problems of the Province of Ontario, 1929-1959." M.A. thesis, Queen's, 1960.
3639. Wood, J. David, ed. *Perspectives on Landscape and Settlement in Nineteenth Century Ontario*. Toronto: M&S, 1975.
3640. Wynn, Graeme. "Notes on Society and Environment in Old Ontario." *J Social Hist* 13 (1979):49-65.

2. Belleville

3641. Boyce, Gerald E. *Belleville: Birth of a City*. Belleville: Ellis, 1977.
3642. Mika, Nick, and Mika, Helma. *Mosaic of Belleville: An Illustrated History of a City*. Belleville: Mika, 1966.
3643. _____. *Belleville: Friendly City*. Belleville: Mika, 1973.
3644. _____. *Belleville: The Good Old Days*. Belleville: Mika, 1975.
3645. Mikel, W. C. *City of Belleville History*. Picton: Picton *Gazette*, 1943.

3. Brantford

3646. Brown, Robert F. *A Guide to Historical Brantford and Brant County*. Brantford, 1952.
3647. Clark, Robert, et al. *A Glimpse of the Past: A Centennial History of Brantford and Brant Country*. Brantford: Brant Historical Society, 1967.
3648. Johnston, Charles M. *Brant County: A History, 1784-1945*. Toronto: OUP, 1967.
3649. Reville, Frederick D. *History of the County of Brant*. 2 vols. Brantford: Hurley, 1920.
3650. Russell, Paul G. *Brantford: Sketches of a Town*. Brantford: Glenhyrst Arts Council, 1967.

4. Brockville

3651. **Chisamore, Dale, et al.** *Brockville: A Social History, 1890-1930.* Brockville: Waterway Press, 1975.
3651A. **Cole, W. H.** "Local History of the Town of Brockville." OHS, *PR* 12 (1914):33-41.
3652. **Donnison, D. V.** *Welfare Services in a Canadian Community: A Study of Brockville, Ontario.* Toronto: UTP, 1958.
3653. **Richards, Elva M.** "The Joneses of Brockville and the Family Compact." *OH* 60 (1968):169-84.

5. Cambridge (formerly Galt, Hespeler and Preston)

3654. **Brewster, Winfield.** *The Street of Business: Queen Street, Hespeler, Ontario.* Hespeler: T&T Press, 1954.
3655. **Dunford, J. R.** "Political Opinion in South Waterloo, 1857-1873." M.A. thesis, Toronto, 1955.
3656. **Kerr, James E.** "Early Days in Galt." WHS, *AR* 60 (1972):26-35.
3657. **Klotz, Otto.** "Sketch of the History of the Village of Preston [written in 1886]." WHS, *AR* 60 (1972):16-25.
3658. **Panabaker, D. N.** "The Town of Hespeler." WHS, *AR* 60 (1972):36-49.
3659. **Peck, T.** "Galt Sixty Years Ago." WHS, *AR* 13 (1925):144-53.
3660. **Perry, Robert L.** *Galt, U.S.A.: The American Presence in a Canadian City.* Toronto: Maclean & Hunter, 1971.
3661. **Stevenson, John A.** "The Founder of Galt." *QQ* 54 (1947):336-42.

6. Cobalt

3662. **Baldwin, Douglas.** "The Life of the Silver Miner in Northern Ontario." *Labour* 2 (1977):79-107.
3663. _____. "The Development of an Unplanned Community: Cobalt, 1903-1914." *Plan Canada* 18 (1978):17-29.
3664. _____. "Primary Source Materials for the History of Northern Ontario Mining Towns: The Case of Cobalt." *UHR* 3-77 (February 1978):80-85.
3665. _____. "Imitation vs. Innovation: Cobalt as an Urban Frontier Town." *Laurentian Univ Rev* 11 (1979):23-42.
3666. _____, and **Dunn, John A.** *Cobalt: A Pictorial History of the Development of Silver Mining.* Cobalt: Highway Bookshop, 1976.
3667. **Brown, L. Carson.** "Cobalt Blooms Again." *CGEJ* 47 (1953):24-35.
3668. _____. " 'Cobalt': The Town with the Silver Lining." *CGEJ* 67 (1963):2-13.
3669. **Cole, A. A.** "Cobalt: Bonanza Silver District of Ontario." *Engineering Mining J* 118 (1924):325-30.
3670. **Gard, Anson.** *The Real Cobalt: The Story of a Great Silver Mining Camp.* Toronto: Ryerson, 1908.
3671. **Grant, H. T.** "A Mining Camp in Retrospect." *Blackwood's* 221 (1927):832-43.
3672. **Hogan, Brian F.** *Cobalt: Year of the Strike, 1919.* Cobalt: Highway Bookshop, 1978.
3673. **Jarvis, W. H. P.** *Trails and Tales in Cobalt.* Toronto: William Briggs, 1908.
3674. **Loudon, J. D.** "Cobalt." *UT Mon* 6 (1905-6):10-14.
3675. **Robson, Frederic.** "Cobalt: A Mistaken Idol." *Can Mag* 31 (1908):99-105.
3676. **Tretheway, W. G.** "Early Days in Cobalt." *CAMJ* 30 (1909):20-22.

7. Cobourg

3677. **Baskerville, Peter.** "The Entrepreneur and the Metropolitan Impulse: James Gray Bethune and Cobourg, 1825-1836." In **#3686**, pp. 56-70.

3678. **Calnan, D. M.** "Postponed Progress: Cobourg Common Schools, 1850-1871." In **#3686**, pp. 182-202.

3679. **Carter-Edwards, Dennis.** "Cobourg: A Nineteenth Century Response to the 'Worthy Poor.' " In **#3686**, pp. 167-81.

3680. **Ennals, Peter M.** "Cobourg and Port Hope: The Struggle for the Control of 'the Back Country.' " In **#3639**, pp. 183-96.

3681. **Guillet, Edwin C.** "The Town of Cobourg, 1798-1945." *CGEJ* 30 (1945):288-98.

3682. _____. "The Cobourg Conspiracy." In **#3686**, pp. 108-31.

3683. **Muntz, M.** "William Weller: Stage Coach Magnate." In **#3686**, pp. 71-84.

3684. **Petryshyn, J.** "James Cockburn: Cobourg Politician." In **#3686**, pp. 132-44.

3685. _____. "Nineteenth Century Cobourg: A Historical Profile." In **#3686**, pp. 11-27.

3686. _____, ed. *Victorian Cobourg: A Nineteenth Century Profile.* Belleville: Mika, 1976.

3687. **Pickford, Frank A.** *Two Centuries of Change. The United Counties of Northumberland and Durham, 1767-1967.* Cobourg: Centennial Book Committee, 1967.

3688. **Scatterly, P.** "The Cobourg-Peterborough Railway: Destiny Denied." In **#3686**, pp. 85-107.

3689. **Stokes, John.** "The Preservation of Victoria Hall." In **#3686**, pp. 28-55.

8. Elliot Lake

3690. **Brown, L. Carson.** "Elliot Lake: The World's Uranium Capital." *CGEJ* 75 (1967):120-33.

3691. **Code, Douglas.** "Elliot Lake: A Geographic-Planning Perspective of a Single-Enterprise Community." B.A. essay, Laurentian, 1974.

3692. **Downey, Terrence J.** "The Political Economy of Uranium: Elliot Lake, 1948-1970." M.A. thesis, Western Ontario, 1972.

3693. **Hall, Oswald.** "The Social Consequences of Uranium Mining." *UTQ* 26 (1957):226-43.

3694. _____. "The New Planned Community." *Can Wel* 36 (1960):9-14.

3695. **Jones, R. W.** "Elliot Lake: A Unique Case of Community Organization." *International Review of Community Development* 2 (1958):105-13.

3696. **Lundgren, R.** "Town Determined to Live." *Habitat* 11 (1968):21-23.

3697. **Naegele, Kaspar D.** "New Town of Elliot Lake." *Ontario Planning* 3 (March 1956):1-7.

3698. **Pearson, Norman.** "Elliot Lake: 'The Best-Planned Mining Town.' " *Can Arch* 3 (1958):54-61.

3699. _____. "Elliot Lake: Experiment in Conformity." *Town and Country Planning* 27 (1959):199-203.

3700. **Percival, Ray N.** "Elliot Lake: Another View." *Town and Country Planning* 28 (1960):61-65.

9. Goderich

3701. **Clark, Louisa.** *Louisa Clark's Annual, 1841: Life and Literature in British North America by a Lady Writer Residing in the Town of Goderich, Canada West,* edited by Beverly Cline. Erin: Press Porcepic, 1976.

3702. **Johnston, Hugh.** "Stratford and Goderich in the Days of the Canada Company." *OH* 63 (1971):71-85.

3703. **Lauriston, V.** "A Century of Goderich." *CGEJ* 5 (1932):83-96.
3704. **Lewis, Paul.** "The Goderich Mechanic's Institute, 1852-1870." *W Ont Hist N* 26 (1972):19-24.
3705. **Lizars, Robina.** *In the Days of the Canada Company: The Story of the Settlement of the Huron Tract and a View of the Social Life of the Period, 1825-1850.* 1896. Rev. ed. Toronto: Coles, 1972.
3706. **Scott, James.** *The Settlement of Huron County.* Toronto: Ryerson, 1966.
3707. **Wallace, Dorothy,** ed. *Memories of Goderich: The Prettiest Town in Canada.* Goderich, 1977.

10. Guelph

3708. **Bawtinheimer, R.** "The Young George Drew and His Guelph Background, 1894-1925." M.A. thesis, Guelph, 1976.
3709. **Bell, W. J.** *Municipal Ownership and Civic Government.* Guelph: Board of Trade, 1909.
3710. **Bradshaw, Brian.** "Patterns of Residence, Occupations, and Preferred Work-Places among Italians in Guelph, Ontario, 1920-1960." M.A. thesis, Guelph, 1980.
3711. **Byerly, A. E.** *The Beginning of Things in Wellington and Waterloo Counties with Particular Reference to Guelph, Galt and Kitchener.* Guelph: Guelph Publishing Co., 1935.
3712. **Cameron, James Malcolm.** "Guelph and the Canada Company, 1827-1851: An Approach to Resource Development." M.Sc. thesis, Guelph, 1966.
3713. _____. "The Canada Company and Land Settlement as Resource Development in the Guelph Block." In #3639, pp. 141-58.
3714. _____, and **Cameron, J.** *The Early Days in Guelph: Guelph and the Canada Company.* Guelph, 1967.
3715. **Chambers, Debra.** "The People of a Commercial Town in Canada West: Guelph in 1861." M.A. thesis, Guelph, 1980.
3716. **Coleman, Thelma.** *The Canada Company.* Stratford: Perth County Historical Board, 1978.
3717. **Connon, John P.** *The Early History of Elora, Ontario, and Vicinity.* Rev. ed. Introduction by Gerald Noonan. Waterloo: Wilfrid Laurier UP, 1974.
3718. **Corke, Charles.** "Early Photography and Photographers in Guelph and Area." *Historic Guelph, the Royal City* 17 (1978):55-67.
3719. **Couling, Gordon.** *Where Guelph Began: A Walking Tour of the Original Market Square Area.* Guelph: Guelph Arts Council, 1979.
3720. **Coulman, Donald E.** *Guelph, Take a Look at Us.* Cheltenham: Boston Mills Press, 1977.
3721. **Cutts, A. B.** "The Old Scottish Architecture of Ontario." *CGEJ* 39 (1949):202-17.
3722. **Dahms, Frederick A.** "Citizen Participation and Inter-Agency Cooperation: Some Planning Procedures in Guelph." *CPR* 25, no. 2 (1975):3-6.
3723. _____. "Some Quantitative Approaches to the Study of Central Places in the Guelph Area, 1851-1970." *UHR* 2-75 (October 1975):9-30.
3724. _____. "How Ontario's Guelph District Developed." *CGEJ* 94, no. 1 (1977):48-55.
3725. _____. *Historical Background, Population Change and Agriculture: Wellington County, 1840-1976.* Vol. 1. *A Statistical and Cartographic Survey.* Guelph: University of Guelph, Centre for Resource Development, 1978.
3726. _____. "The Changing Functions of Villages and Hamlets in Wellington County, 1881-1971." *UHR* 8 (February 1980):3-19.
3727. _____, and **Forbes, James A.** "Central Places in the Golden Triangle: The Guelph System 1970." In *The Waterloo County Area: Selected Geographical Essays,* edited by A. G. McLellan, pp. 113-27. Waterloo: University of Waterloo, 1971.
3728. **Drummond, Albert W.** *Guelph, the Royal City.* Guelph, 1924.
3729. **Duncan, Dorothy.** "The Bell Organ Company." *Can Coll* 13 (1978):40-41.

3730. **Duncan, Kenneth J.** "Aspects of Scottish Settlement in Wellington County." Colloquium on Scottish Studies, *Proceedings* 3 (1970):15-20. Guelph: University of Guelph, 1970.
3731. **Forbes, James A.** "The Guelph Central Place System." M.A. thesis, Guelph, 1975.
3732. **Gordon, Ian A.** *John Galt: The Life of a Writer.* Toronto: UTP, 1972.
3733. *Guelph Centennial, 1827-1927.* Guelph: Guelph *Mercury,* 1927.
3734. **Hacking, J. H.** *Directory of the Town of Guelph, 1873, with a Brief Sketch of the Rise and Progress of the Town.* Guelph, 1873.
3735. **Hinds, Ann.** *Pioneer Inns and Taverns of Guelph.* Cheltenham: Boston Mills Press, 1977.
3736. *Illustrated Historical Atlas of Wellington County, Ontario.* 1906. Reprint. Belleville: Mika, 1972.
3737. **Johnson, Leo A.** *History of Guelph, 1827-1927.* Guelph: Guelph Historical Society, 1977.
3738. **Johnson, Nora.** "Guelph and Goderich: Tadmores in Upper Canada." *JRAIC* 35 (1958):386-90.
3739. **Karr, Clarence.** *The Canada Land Company: The Early Years.* Toronto: Ontario Historical Society, 1974.
3740. **Kennedy, David.** *Incidents of Pioneer Days at Guelph and the County of Bruce.* 1903. Rev. ed. Toronto: Bruce County Historical Society, 1973.
3741. **Lee, Robert C.** "The Canada Company, 1826-1853: A Study in Direction." M.A. thesis, Guelph, 1967.
3742. **Marett, Clara M.** "The Ontario Agricultural College (1874-1974): Some Developments in Scientific Agriculture." M.A. thesis, Guelph, 1975.
3743. **Marston, Katharine A., and Zuk, Nancy.** *A Historical Tour of Elora.* Elora: Elora *Express,* 1972.
3744. **Miller, R. J.** "The Stone Buildings of Guelph—A Geographical Study." B.A. essay, Guelph, 1970.
3745. **Mills, Richard E.** "Elora." WHS, *AR* 23 (1938):164-68.
3746. **Nasby, Judith M.** "A Painter of Guelph—David Johnston Kennedy." *Historic Guelph, the Royal City* 17 (1978):36-49.
3747. **Parnall, M. B.** "The Senior Public Schools and the Neighbourhood Schools of Guelph." M.Ed. thesis, Toronto, 1958.
3748. **Reid, W. Stanford.** *A Century and a Half of Witness: The Story of St. Andrew's Presbyterian Church, Guelph, Ontario, 1828-1978.* Mississauga: Mayers and Smart, 1980.
3749. **Ross. Alexander M.** *The College on the Hill: A History of the Ontario Agricultural College, 1874-1974.* Guelph: OAC Alumni Association, 1974.
3750. **Russwurm, Lorne H.** "Urban Fringe and Urban Shadow in the Waterloo-Southeast Wellington County Area Land Space Matrix." In *The Waterloo County Area: Selected Geographical Essays,* edited by A. G. McLellan, pp. 97-111. Waterloo: University of Waterloo, 1971.
3751. **Shutt, Greta.** *The High Schools of Guelph.* Toronto: UTP, 1961.
3752. **Strothard, J.** "John Galt and the Canada Company." M.Litt. thesis, Edinburgh, 1979.
3753. **Templin, Hugh.** *Fergus: The Story of a Little Town.* Fergus: Fergus *News-Record,* 1933.
3754. **Thompson, Robert.** *A Brief Sketch of the Early History of Guelph.* 1877. Rev. ed. Guelph: Civic Museum, 1977.
3755. **Vaughan, Edgar.** "The Guayrians at Guelph in Upper Canada." *Historic Guelph, the Royal City* 18 (1979):7-112.
3756. **Waterston, Elizabeth.** "John Galt, the Founder of Guelph." *Historic Guelph, the Royal City* 17 (1978):4-15.
3757. **Wellington County, Centennial Committee.** *Centennial, 1854-1954, the County of Wellington.* Fergus: Beattie, 1954.
3758. **Wolfe, J. S., and Burghardt, Andrew F.** "The Neighbourhood Effect in a Local Election." *Can Geogr* 22 (1978):298-305.
3759. **Wood, Frank.** "Guelph: Its Founding and Its Growth." *CGEJ* 68 (1964):122-31.

11. Hamilton

a. General

3760. **Abrams, Percy.** "A Study of the Jewish Immigrants in Hamilton and Their Relationship with the Jewish Community Centre." M.S.W. thesis, Toronto, 1955.
3761. **Asling, S. E.** "Historical St. Paul's." *Wentworth Historical Society* 3 (1902):19-29.
3762. **Bailey, Thomas M., and Carter, C. M.** *Hamilton, Famous and Fascinating: Two Centuries of a Colorful City.* Hamilton: Griffen, 1972.
3763. **Bennett, M. B.** *A History of Your Local Hydro Commission.* Hamilton: Hydro Electric Commission, 1967.
3764. **Brown, I. D., and Brink, A. W.** *The Dundas Heritage.* Dundas: Dundas Heritage Association, 1971.
3765. **Burkholder, Mabel.** *The Story of Hamilton.* Hamilton: Davis-Lisson, 1938.
3766. **Campbell, M. F.** "70 Years with Hamilton's Street Railway." *WB* 2 (1960):16-22.
3767. _____. *A Mountain and a City: The Story of Hamilton.* Toronto: M&S, 1966.
3768. _____. "Hamilton." *Habitat* 10, nos. 3-6 (1967):82-87.
3769. **Campbell, M. J.** *The Hamilton General Hospital, School of Nursing, 1890-1955.* Toronto: Ryerson, 1956.
3770. **Canada Life Assurance Company.** *Hamilton, the Birmingham of Canada.* Hamilton, 1892.
3771. **Carter, J. Smyth.** *The Story of Dundas from 1784 to 1904.* 1905. Rev. ed. Belleville: Mika, 1973.
3772. **Craig, Martha, ed.** *The Garden of Canada: Burlington, Oakville and District.* 1902. Rev. ed. Burlington: Burlington Historical Society, 1973.
3773. **Croil, James.** *Dundas; or a Sketch of Canadian History.* 1861. Rev. ed. Belleville: Mika, 1972.
3774. **Davidson, W. A., ed.** *Picturesque Dundas.* 1896. Rev. ed. Dundas: Dundas Historical Society Museum, 1972.
3775. **Emery, Claire, and Ford, Barbara.** *From Pathway to Skyway: A History of Burlington.* Burlington: Confederation Centennial Committee of Burlington, 1967.
3776. **Ennals, Peter M.** "Land and Society in Hamilton Township, Upper Canada, 1797-1861." Ph.D. thesis, Toronto, 1978.
3777. **Evans, L. C.** *Hamilton: The Story of a City.* Toronto: Ryerson, 1970.
3778. **Forrester, J.** *Making Steel in Hamilton.* Toronto: Ginn, 1967.
3779. _____; **Birchall, G.; Gray, D. M.** *Longhouse to Blast Furnace: Growth of an Industrial Community.* Toronto: Fitzhenry and Whiteside, 1973.
3780. **Freeman, Bill, and Hewitt, Marsha.** *Their Town: The Mafia, the Media and the Party Machine.* Toronto: James Lorimer, 1979. Major excerpts published by *City Mag,* Special Issue 4 (1980).
3781. **Furry, C. G.** *History of the Hamilton Waterworks System.* Hamilton: Corporation of the City of Hamilton, 1959.
3782. **Griffin, J. A.** "A Backward Look." *Wentworth Historical Society* 8 (1919):62-68.
3783. **Grimsby Historical Society.** *Grimsby, 1816-1876.* 1959. Rev. ed. Grimsby, 1967.
3785. **James, William, and James, E. M.** *'A Sufficient Quantity of Pure and Wholesome Water': The Story of Hamilton's Old Pumphouse.* London: Phelps, 1978.
3786. **Johnston, Charles M.** *The Head of the Lake: A History of Wentworth County.* Hamilton: Wentworth County Council, 1967.
3787. **Kilbourn, William.** *The Elements Combined: A History of the Steel Company of Canada.* Toronto: Clarke, Irwin, 1960.

146 Canada's Urban Past

3788. **Kurman, Louis A.** "The Hamilton Jewish Community." *WB* 8 (1969):8-12.
3789. **Logan, R.** "The Geography of Intermunicipal Relations: A Case Study in the Grimsby Area, Ontario." Ph.D. thesis, McMaster, 1973.
3790. **Middleton, Diana J., and Walker, David F.** "Entrepreneurship and the Establishment of Hamilton as a Major Industrial Center." In *The Human Dimension in Industrial Development*, edited by David Walker, pp. 1-14. Waterloo: University of Waterloo, Dept. of Geography Publication Series, No.16, 1980.
3791. **Mills, John M.** *Cataract Traction: The Railway of Hamilton.* Toronto: Upper Canada Railway Society, 1971.
3792. **Roberts, David Wayne, ed.** *The Hamilton Working Class, 1820-1977: A Bibliography.* Hamilton: McMaster University, Labour Studies Programme, 1978.
3793. **Russell, David.** "A Financial History of Hamilton." B.A. thesis, McMaster, 1936.
3794. **Shumski, Gary.** "The Primary Iron and Steel Industry in Hamilton." B.A. essay, Brock, 1969.
3795. **Torrance, Gordon V.** "The History of Law Enforcement in Hamilton from 1833 to 1967." *WB* 7 (1967):67-78.
3796. **Walker, Howard V.** *All Roads Lead to Dundas: A Tour.* Toronto: Architectural Conservancy of Ontario, 1977.
3797. **Wallace, Arthur W.** "Historic Architecture in Hamilton." *JRAIC* 40, no. 4 (1963):47-50.
3798. **Ward, H. B.** "Hamilton, Ontario, as a Manufacturing Center." Ph.D. thesis, Chicago, 1934.
3799. **Watson, John Wreford.** "Hamilton and Its Environs." *CGEJ* 30 (1945):240-52.
3800. **Weaver, John C.** "From Land Assembly to Social Maturity: The Suburban Life of Westdale (Hamilton), Ontario, 1911-1951." *HS* 11 (1978):411-40.
3801. **Westland, S. I.** "The Land Transport Geography of Hamilton." M.A. thesis, McMaster, 1950.
3802. **Winchester, I.** *The Canadian Social History Project: Report Number 5:1973-74.* Toronto: OISE, 1974.
3803. **Wingfield, Alexander H., ed.** *Hamilton Centennial, 1846-1946: One Hundred Years of Progress.* Hamilton: Hamilton Centennial Committee, 1946.
3804. **Wood, Harold A.** *The Site of Hamilton and Its Influence on the Development of the City.* Bulletin no. 7. Montreal: Education Committee, Canadian Association of Geographers, 1961.
3805. **Woodhouse, T. Roy.** *The History of the Town of Dundas.* 3 vols. Dundas: Dundas Historical Society, 1965-68.

b. Pre-1921

3806. **Armstrong, Frederick H.** "The Hamilton Election of 1841: A Contemporary Analysis." *W Ont Hist N* 22, no. 2 (1965):1-5.
3806A. **Bird, T. R.** "Cultural Conflict and Crime among Irish Immigrants in Hamilton, Ontario in 1891." M.A. thesis, Queen's, 1977.
3807. **Blaine, W. E.** *Ride through the Garden of Canada. A Short History of the Hamilton, Grimsby and Beamsville Electric Railway Company, 1894-1931.* Grimsby, 1967.
3808. **Charlton, B. E.** "Notes on Incidents in the Early History of Hamilton and Vicinity." Hamilton Association, *J and Proc* (1891):13-22.
3809. **Davey, Ian E.** "School Reform and School Attendance: The Hamilton Central School, 1853-1861." M.A. thesis, Toronto, 1972.
3810. _____. "Educational Reform and the Working Class: School Attendance in Hamilton, 1851-1891." Ph.D. thesis, University of Toronto, 1975.
3811. _____, **and Doucet, Michael J.** "The Social Geography of a Commercial City, c. 1853." In #3827, pp. 319-42.

3812. **Denton, Frank T., and George, Peter J.** "An Exploratory Statistical Analysis of Some Socioeconomic Characteristics of Families in Hamilton, Ontario, 1871." *HS* 5 (1970):16-44.

3813. _____. "Socio-economic Characteristics of Families in Wentworth County, 1871: Some Further Results." *HS* 7 (1974):103-10.

3814. **Doucet, Michael J.** "Working Class Housing in a Small Nineteenth Century Canadian City: Hamilton, Ontario, 1852-1881." In *Essays in Canadian Working Class History,* edited by Gregory S. Kealey and Peter Warrian, pp. 83-105. Toronto: M&S, 1976.

3815. _____. "Building the Victorian City: The Process of Land Development in Hamilton, Ontario, 1847-1881." Ph.D. thesis, University of Toronto, 1977.

3816. _____. "The Role of the *Spectator* in Shaping Attitudes towards Land in Hamilton, Ontario, 1847-1881." *HS* 11 (1979):431-43.

3817. **Graff, Harvey J.** "Towards a Meaning of Literacy: Literacy and Social Structure in Ham ton, Ontario." *Hist Educ Q* 12 (1972):411-31.

3818. *Hamilton, the Birmingham of Canada.* Hamilton: Times Printing, 1892.

3819. **Katz, Michael B.** *The "Hamilton Project": An Interim Report.* Toronto: OISE, 1969.

3820. _____. "Social Structure in Hamilton, Ontario." In *#88,* pp. 209-44.

3821. _____. *The "Hamilton Project": An Interim Report, no. 2.* Toronto: OISE, 1970.

3822. _____. *The Canadian Social History Project: Interim Report no. 3.* Toronto: OISE, 1971.

3823. _____. *The Canadian Social History Project: Interim Report no. 4.* Toronto: OISE, 1972.

3824. _____. "The People of a Canadian City, 1851-1852." In *#85,* pp. 227-54.

3825. _____. "Who Went to School, [in Hamilton, Ontario, 1851-1861]." *Hist Educ Q* 12 (1972):432-54.

3826. _____. "The Entrepreneurial Class in a Canadian City: The Mid-Nineteenth Century." *JSH* 8 (1975):1-29.

3827. _____. *The People of Hamilton, Canada West: Family and Class in a Mid-Nineteenth-Century City.* Cambridge, MA: Harvard UP, 1975.

3828. _____, and **Davey, Ian E.** "School Attendance and Early Industrialization in a Canadian City: A Multivariate Analysis." *Hist Educ Q* 18 (1978):271-94.

3829. **Lister, Herbert.** *Hamilton, Canada: Its History, Commerce, Industry and Resources.* Hamilton: City Council, 1913.

3830. **Lucas, Richard.** "The Conflict over Public Power in Hamilton, Ontario, 1906-1914." *OH* 68 (1976):236-46.

3831. **McCalla, Douglas.** "The Decline of Hamilton as a Wholesale Centre." *OH* 65 (1973):247-54.

3832. _____. "The Canadian Grain Trade in the 1840s: The Buchanans' Case." CHA, *HP* (1974):95-114.

3833. _____. *The Upper Canada Trade, 1834-72: A Study of the Buchanans' Business.* Toronto: UTP, 1979.

3834. **McKay, Alexander G.** *Victorian Architecture in Hamilton.* Hamilton: Architectural Conservancy of Ontario, 1967.

3835. **MacRae, Marion.** *MacNab of Dundurn.* Toronto: Clarke, Irwin, 1971.

3836. **Medjuck, Sheva.** "The Importance of Boarding for the Structure of the Household in the Nineteenth Century: Moncton, New Brunswick and Hamilton, Canada West." *HS* 13 (1980):207-14.

3837. **Middleton, Diana J., and Walker, David F.** "Manufacturers and Industrial Development Policy in Hamilton, 1890-1910." *UHR* 8 (February 1980):20-46.

3838. **Palmer, Bryan D.** *A Culture in Conflict: Skilled Workers and Industrial Capitalism in Hamilton, Ontario, 1860-1914.* Montreal: McGill-Queen's UP, 1979.

3839. **Roberts, James.** "The Housing Situation, Hamilton." *Can Mun J* 8 (1912):255-56.

3840. **Roberts, Richard D.** "The Changing Patterns in Distribution and Composition of Manufacturing Activity in Hamilton between 1861 and 1921." M.A. thesis, McMaster, 1964.
3841. **Siemiatycki, Myer.** "Munitions and Labour Militancy: The 1916 Hamilton Machinists' Strike." *Labour* 3 (1978):131-51.
3842. **Smith, Carl.** "The Political Career of Allan Napier MacNab (1825-1836)." M.A. thesis, Guelph, 1971.
3843. **Smith, J. H.** *Historical Sketch of the County of Wentworth and the Head of the Lake.* 1897. Reprint. Hamilton: Wentworth Historical Society, 1922.
3844. _____. "Historical Landmarks of Hamilton." *Westminster* 5 (1904):399-405.
3845. _____. "City of Hamilton." *Wentworth Historical Society* 6 (1915):64-73.
3846. **Spector, David.** "The Knights of Labour in Hamilton and Toronto, 1882-1887." M.A. thesis, Trent, 1976.
3847. **Storey, Robert H.** "Industrialization in Canada: The Emergence of the Hamilton Working Class, 1850-1870." M.A. thesis, Dalhousie, 1975.
3848. **Swanborough, R.** "The Early History of the Hamilton Fire Department, 1816-1905." *WB* 8 (1969):23-33.
3849. **Synge, Jane.** "Immigrant Communities—British and Continental European—in Early Twentieth Century Hamilton." *Oral History* 4 (1976):38-51.
3850. **Vickers, Elizabeth Smith.** "The Victorian Buildings of Hamilton." *WB* 7 (1967):46-56.
3851. **Warnick, Paul C.** "The History of Rail Transportation in the Hamilton Area, 1845-1865." M.A. thesis, McMaster, 1954.
3852. **Wells, E. P.** "McMaster University." *Can Mag* 3 (1894):309-16.
3853. **Wells, W. D.** "The Hamilton Region, 1800-1882. The Interrelationships between Transportation and Industrial Development." M.A. thesis, Waterloo, 1973.
3854. **Woodhouse, T. Roy.** "The Beginnings of the History of Hamilton." *WB* 5 (1964):23-27.

c. Post-1921

3855. **Adams, Robert M.** "The Development of the United Steelworkers of America, 1936-1951." M.A. thesis, Queen's, 1957.
3856. **Bailey, D. H. R.** "Electoral Cleavages in Metropolitan Hamilton: An Ecological Analysis of the Federal and Provincial Elections, 1962-1972." M.A. thesis, McMaster, 1973.
3857. **Bernard, A.; Léveillé, J.; and Lord, G.** *Profile: Hamilton-Wentworth. The Political and Administrative Structures of the Metropolitan Region of Hamilton-Wentworth.* Ottawa: MSUA, 1975.
3858. **Bradino, D.** "The Italians in Hamilton, 1921 to 1945." M.A. thesis, Western Ontario, 1977.
3859. **Brock, R. W.** "Hamilton as an Industrial Centre Occupies Commanding Position in Ontario." *INCA* 30 (March 1930):52-58.
3860. **Chandler, David B.** "The Residential Location of Occupational and Ethnic Groups in Hamilton." M.A. thesis, McMaster, 1965.
3861. **Dear, Michael, and Burghardt, Andrew F.** "How Hamilton and Its Suburbs Are Coping with Pressures for Growth." *CGEJ* 93, no. 2 (1976):22-31.
3862. **Eastham, Francis.** "The Relationship between the N.D.P. and the Principal Labour Unions in Hamilton." M.A. thesis, McMaster, 1973.
3863. **Falkenhagen, J. D.** "A Study of Single Unemployed Men in Hamilton." M.S.W. thesis, Toronto, 1965.
3864. **Faludi, E. G.** *A Master Plan for the Development of the City of Hamilton.* Hamilton: City Planning Committee, 1947.
3865. **Fenton, Charles Stephen.** "Assimilation Processes among Immigrants: A Study of German and Italian Immigrants to Hamilton." M.A. thesis, McMaster, 1968.

3866. **Foster, Matthew James.** "Ethnic Settlement in the Barton Street Region of Hamilton, 1921-1961." M.A. thesis, McMaster, 1965.
3867. **Freeman, Bill.** "Hamilton's Civic Square: The First Eleven Years." *City Mag* 1, no. 8 (1976):26-41.
3868. **Friar, J.** "Hamilton's Central Business District." M.A. thesis, McMaster, 1963.
3869. **Haak, L. A.** "Housing Survey in Hamilton." *Social Welfare* 19 (March 1937):4-6.
3870. **Jacek, Henry.** "Central Government Planning *versus* Conflicting Local Elites: Regional Government in Hamilton-Wentworth." In *Government and Politics of Ontario*, edited by Donald C. MacDonald, pp. 48-64. Toronto: Macmillan, 1975.
3871. ———; **McDonough, John; Skimizu, Ronald; and Smith, Patrick.** "Social Articulation and Aggregation in Political Party Organizations in a Large Canadian City." *CJPS* 8 (1975):274-98.
3872. **Jones, F. E.** "The Social Origins of High School Teachers in a Canadian City." *CJEPS* 29 (1963):529-35.
3873. **McMenemy, John M.** "Lion in a Den of Daniels: A Study of Sam Lawrence, Labour in Politics." M.A. thesis, McMaster, 1965.
3874. **Martin, Ann.** "Up-Along: Newfoundland Families in Hamilton." M.A. thesis, McMaster, 1974.
3875. **Mercer, John.** "Some Aspects of the Spatial Pattern of Multiple Occupancy Residential Structures in Hamilton." M.A. thesis, McMaster, 1966.
3876. **Moore, Dan.** "The 1946 Steel Strike in Hamilton." M.A. thesis, Carleton, 1979.
3877. **Pearson, Norman.** "Hamilton: Setting for Disaster." *CPR* 8, no. 3 (1958):90-92.
3878. **Proulx, D.** *Pardon My Lunch Bucket: A Look at the New Hamilton.* Hamilton: City of Hamilton, 1971.
3879. **Reeds, L. G.** "The Changing Face of Hamilton and District." *CPR* 8 (1958):85-89.
3880. **Riddett, R. H.** "Differential Business Mortality in an Urban Renewal Scheme as an Indicator of Current Changes in Retail Activity." *Ont Geogr* 6 (1971):9-16.
3881. **Stone, Ken.** *Steel Strike, Hamilton 1946.* Toronto: Canadian Party of Labour, 1976.
3882. **Thompson, A. W.** "Assimilation of West Indians in London and Hamilton, Ontario." M.A. thesis, Western Ontario, 1970.
3883. **Thrall, Grant Ian.** "Spatial Inequalities in Tax Assessment: A Case Study of Hamilton, Ontario." *Econ Geogr* 55 (1979):123-34.
3884. **Vincent, Patrick.** "The Assimilation Process, with Special Reference to Italian Children in the Hamilton School System." M.A. thesis, McMaster, 1968.

12. Kapuskasing

3886. **Butcher, P. J.** "The Establishment of a Pulp and Paper Industry at Kapuskasing by the Spruce Falls Companies." M.A. thesis, Western Ontario, 1978.
3887. **Hall, Alfred V.** "Considerations in the Lay-Out of the Town of Kapuskasing." *TPICJ* 1, no. 10 (1922):5-12.
3888. **Kirkconnell, Watson.** "Kapuskasing—An Historical Sketch." *QQ* 27 (1921):264-78.
3889. **Saarinen, Oiva.** *Provincial Land Use Planning Initiatives in the Town of Kapuskasing.* Sudbury: Laurentian University, Dept. of Geography, 1980.

13. Kingston

a. General

3890. **Anderson, Allan J.** *The Anglican Churches of Kingston.* Kingston: Diocese of Ontario, 1963.

3891. **Angus, Margaret.** *Kingston General Hospital: A Social and Institutional History.* Montreal: McGill-Queen's UP, 1973.
3892. _____. "John A. Lived Here." *Canada: An Historical Magazine* 2 (1974):8-21.
3893. **Baines, James.** *Historical Record of Princess Street United Church, Kingston, Ontario.* Kingston: Foster and North, 1947.
3894. **Bell, J. Jones.** "Queen's University and Its Founders." *Can Mag* 7 (1896):19-27.
3895. **Calvin, Delano D.** *Queen's University at Kingston.* Kingston: Queen's University Trustees, 1941.
3896. **Campbell, Mary I.** *One Hundred Years of Service: Orphans' Home and Widows' Friend Society, 1857-1957.* Kingston, 1957.
3897. **Carlyle, R.** "Royal Military College." *Can Mag* 35 (1910):121-28.
3898. **Creighton, Donald Grant.** "Sir John Macdonald and Kingston." CHA, *AR* (1950):72-80.
3899. **Davis, Bruce P., and Davis, Carol L.** *The Davis Family and the Leather Industry, 1834-1934.* Toronto: Ryerson, 1934.
3900. **Defoe, Deborah.** "Kingston: A Selected Bibliography." *HK* 21 (1973):78-101.
3901. _____. "Kingston: A Select Bibliography: Addendum, 1977." Kingston: Kingston Public Library, 1977.
3902. **Dolan, George R.** "The Past and Present Fortifications at Kingston." OHS, *PR* 12 (1914):72-80.
3903. **Doyle, James, and Doyle, Trudy.** *Kingston: Portrait of a City.* Gananoque: Doyle, 1972.
3904. **Draper, William G.** *History of the City of Kingston.* Kingston: Creighton, 1862.
3905. **Dyde, D. F.** "History of Kingston and District: A Selected List." *Ont Lib Rev* 34 (1950):226-28.
3906. **Edmison, J. Alexander.** "Kingston Penitentiary a Century Ago." *Can Wel* 25 (1949):29-32.
3907. _____. "The History of Kingston Penitentiary." *HK* 3 (1954):26-35. Reprinted in #3924.
3908. **Electa, Mary.** "The History of the Community of the Sisters of Providence of St. Vincent de Paul, Kingston." *HK* 7 (1958):28-42. Reprinted in #3924.
3909. **Ellis, W. S.** "Some Events in the History of Kingston." OHS, *PR* 8 (1907):78-89.
3910. **Flynn, Louis J.** *At School in Kingston, 1850-1973.* Kingston: Roman Catholic Separate School Board, 1973.
3911. _____. "The History of Saint Mary's Cathedral of the Immaculate Conception, Kingston, Ontario, 1843-1973." CCHA, *Study Sessions* (1973):35-40.
3912. _____. *Built on a Rock: The Story of the Roman Catholic Church in Kingston, 1826-1876.* Kingston: Archdiocese of Kingston, 1976.
3913. _____. *Historic Kingston: An Historic Tour of the City of Kingston.* Kingston: Kingston Historical Society, n.d.
3914. **Geiger, Dorothy.** "A History of the Kingston Waterfront and Water Lots." *HK* 19 (1971):3-16.
3915. **Gérin, Léon.** "Cataraqui, Fort Frontenac, Kingston: Trois stades de notre évolution sociale." RSC, *Trans,* 3d ser. 5 (1933):193-214.
3916. **Grant, W. L.** "Historic Landmarks of Kingston." *Westminster* 4 (1904):239-43.
3917. **Gundy, H. Pearson.** "Libraries in Kingston." *Ont Lib Rev* 33 (1949):7-11.
3918. _____. "Publishing and Bookselling in Kingston since 1810." *HK* 10 (1961):22-36. Reprinted in #3924.
3919. _____. *Queen's University at Kingston.* Kingston: Queen's Alumni, 1967.
3920. **Johnson, Arthur L.** "The Transportation Revolution on Lake Ontario, 1817-1867: Kingston and Ogdensburg." *OH* 68 (1975):199-209.
3921. **Johnson, J. K.** "John A. Macdonald and the Kingston Business Community." In #3961, pp. 141-55.

3922. **Kent, D. M.** *Bibliography of Books Relating to the History of Kingston.* Toronto: University of Toronto Library School, 1933.
3923. **King, Margaret M.** *The Old Limestone City.* Kingston: Jackson Press, 1910.
3924. **Kingston Historical Society.** *Historic Kingston: Transactions of the Kingston Historical Society.* Vols. 1-10. Belleville: Mika, 1974.
3925. **Kingston Social Planning Council.** *Health, Welfare and Recreation Needs in Kingston and District.* Kingston, 1967.
3926. *Kingston 300—A Social Snapshot.* Kingston: Kingston 300 Editorial Committee, 1973.
3927. **Kirkconnell, Watson.** "Fort Henry, 1812-1914." *QQ* 28 (1920):78-88.
3928. **Lapp, Donald A.** "The Schools of Kingston: Their First One Hundred and Fifty Years." M.A. thesis, Queen's, 1937.
3929. **Levine, G. J.** "Residential Mobility in Kingston 1800-1861." M.A. thesis, Queen's, 1975.
3930. **Lovell, Walter S.** "The History of the Present Fortifications at Kingston." OHS, *PR* 30 (1936):155-77.
3931. _____. *Pioneering with Youth: History of the Young Men's Christian Association of Kingston, Canada, 1855-1935.* Kingston: Hanson and Edgar, 1936.
3932. **Lower, A. R. M.** "Some Reflections on Kingston's Architecture." *HK* 6 (1957):3-12. Reprinted in #3924.
3933. _____. "Loyalist Cities: Saint John, New Brunswick and Kingston, Ontario." *QQ* 72 (1966):657-64.
3934. _____. "The Character of Kingston." In #3961, pp. 17-36.
3935. **Luciuk, Lubomyr Y.** "Ukrainians in the Making: Their Kingston Story." M.A. thesis, Queen's, 1979.
3936. **MacDermaid, Anne.** "The City of Kingston Archives." *UHR* 1-78 (June 1978):3-8.
3937. **Macdonnell, G. M., and Dyde, S. W.** "Queen's and Her Future." *QQ* 17 (1910):218-36.
3938. **McHoull, W. Donald.** "The Founding and Early History of Queen's University." M.A. thesis, Queen's, 1935.
3939. **Machar, Agnes M.** "An Old Canadian Town." *Can Mon* 4 (July 1873):1-18.
3940. _____. "Some Epochs of the Story of Old Kingston." OHS, *PR* 8 (1907):102-23.
3941. _____. *The Story of Old Kingston.* Toronto: Musson, 1908.
3942. **Mackie, John.** *The Orangemen of Kingston.* Kingston, 1889.
3943. **Mika, Nick.** *Mosaic of Kingston.* Belleville: Mika, 1969.
3944. _____. *Kingston City Hall.* Belleville: Mika, 1974.
3945. **Neatby, Hilda.** "Queen's University: Town and Gown to 1877." In #3961, pp. 331-41.
3946. "An Old Canadian Town." *Can Mon* 4 (1873):1-18.
3947. **Osborne, Brian S.** "Kingston in the Nineteenth Century: A Study in Urban Decline." In #3639, pp. 159-82.
3948. **Pense, Fred.** "Kingston's Newspapers." *HK* 4 (1955):33-36. Reprinted in #3924.
3949. **Perley, M. E.** "Kingston and Harbour." WCHSO, *Trans* (1909):39-45.
3950. **Preston, Richard A.** "The History of the Port of Kingston." *OH* 46 (1954):201-12; 47 (1954):13-22; 47 (1955):23-38.
3951. _____. "R.M.C. and Kingston: The Effect of Imperial and Military Influences on a Canadian Community." *OH* 60 (1968):105-23.
3952. _____. *Canada's R.M.C.: A History of the Royal Military College.* Toronto: UTP, 1969.
3953. _____. "The British Influence of RMC." In #3961, pp. 119-37.
3954. **Price, Brian J.** "The Archives of the Archdiocese of Kingston." CCHA, *Study Sessions* (1973):21-26.
3955. **Reynolds, T.** "Interpreting the Demand Surface of a Single Transport Mode: Taxicab Movements in Kingston." M.A. thesis, Queen's, 1975.

3956. **Spurr, John W.** "Garrison and Community, 1815-1870." In **#3961,** pp. 103-18.
3957. **Stanley, George F. G.** "Historic Kingston and Its Defences." *OH* 46 (1954):21-35.
3958. _____, **and Preston, Richard A.** *A Short History of Kingston as a Military and Naval Centre.* Kingston: RMC, 1950.
3959. **Stewart, J. Douglas, and Wilson, Ian E.** *Heritage Kingston.* Kingston: Agnes Etherington Art Centre of Queen's University, 1973.
3960. **Taylor, C. J.** "The Kingston, Ontario Penitentiary and Moral Architecture." *HS* 24 (1979):385-408.
3961. **Tulchinsky, Gerald J. J., ed.** *To Preserve and Defend: Essays on Kingston in the Nineteenth Century.* Montreal: McGill-Queen's UP, 1976.
3962. **Tunbridge, T. E.** "Separation of Residence from Workplace: A Kingston Example." *UHR* 3-78 (February 1979):23-32.
3963. **Walkem, Richard T.** "The Old Fortifications on Points Frederik and Henry, Kingston." *QQ* 5 (1897):53-61.
3964. **Wallace, Robert C.** *Queen's University: A Centenary Volume, 1841-1941.* Toronto: Ryerson, 1941.
3965. _____. *Some Great Men of Queen's.* Toronto: Ryerson, 1971.
3966. **Watson, J.** "Thirty Years in the History of Queen's University." *QQ* 10 (1902):188-96.
3967. **Way, Ronald L.** "Kingston and the British Army." *HK* 1 (1952):28-39. Reprinted in **#3924.**
3968. **Webster, T. Stewart.** "John A. Macdonald and Kingston." M.A. thesis, Queen's, 1944.
3969. **Whalley, George.** "Growth of an Orchestra: The Kingston Symphony Orchestra." *Can Composer* 37 (February 1919):12-15.
3970. **Yeigh, Frank.** "Kingston, Past and Present." *CGEJ* 1 (1930):576-86.
3971. **Young, Anna G.** *Great Lakes' Saga: The Influence of One Family [Gildersleeves of Kingston] on the Development of Canadian Shipping on the Great Lakes, 1816-1931.* Owen Sound: Richardson, 1965.

b. Pre-1850

3972. **Angus, Margaret.** "Some Old Kingston Homes and the Families Who Lived in Them." *HK* 4 (1955):3-13. Reprinted in **#3924.**
3973. _____. "The Macaulay Family of Kingston." *HK* 5 (1956):3-12. Reprinted in **#3924.**
3974. _____. *The Old Stones of Kingston: Its Buildings before 1867.* Toronto: UTP, 1966.
3975. _____. "Health, Emigration and Welfare in Kingston, 1820-1840." In *Oliver Mowat's Ontario,* edited by D. Swainson, pp. 120-35. Toronto: Macmillan, 1972.
3971. **Arber, Ross D.** "The Impact of Military and Naval Factors upon Kingston, 1673-1819: A Study of Site-Situation Relationships." B.A. essay, Queen's, 1964.
3977. **Betts, George Michael.** "Municipal Government and Politics, 1800-1850." In **#3961,** pp. 223-44.
3978. **Bindon, Katryn M.** "Kingston: A Social History, 1785-1830." Ph.D. thesis, Queen's, 1979.
3979. **Cross, H. F.** "The Struggle for Self-Government as Waged at Kingston, 1839-1844." B.A. essay, Queen's, 1922.
3980. **Cumberland, R. W.** "The United Empire Loyalist Settlements between Kingston and Adolphustown." *QQ* 31 (1923):395-419.
3981. **Dendy, J.** "The Fortifications of Kingston, 1790-1850: Documents, Plans and Commentary." B.A. essay, RMC, 1960.
3982. **Gibson, Thomas.** *A Short Account of the Early History of the Kingston General Hospital.* Kingston: Hanson and Edgar, 1935.

3983. **Gundy, H. Pearson.** "Hugh C. Thomson: Editor, Publisher, and Politician, 1791-1834." In **#3961**, pp. 203-22.
3984. **Hagarty, W. G.** "Fort Frontenac." *HK* 2 (1953):14-25. Reprinted in **#3924**.
3985. **Hodgetts, J. E.** "The Civil Service When Kingston Was the Capital of Canada." *HK* 5 (1956):13-24. Reprinted in **#3924**.
3986. **Horsey, E. E.** *Kingston a Century Ago*. Kingston: Kingston Historical Society, 1938.
3987. **Houston, Samuel.** "Early History of Presbyterianism in Kingston and Vicinity." *QQ* 2 (1894):93-102.
3988. **Lamontagne, Léopold.** "Kingston's French Heritage." *OH* 45 (1953):109-21.
3989. _____, ed. *Royal Fort Frontenac*. Toronto: Champlain Society, Ontario Series, vol. 2, 1958.
3990. **Levine, G. J.** "Residential Mobility in Kingston 1800-1861: An Experiment in Record Linkage." M.A. thesis, Queen's, 1975.
3991. **McDowall, Duncan L.** "Kingston, 1841-54: A Study of Economic Change in a Mid-Nineteenth Century Community." M.A. thesis, Queen's, 1973.
3992. **McMorine, J. K.** "Early Anglicanism in Kingston, 1793-1844." *QQ* 4 (1896):1-13.
3993. _____. "Early History of the Anglican Church in Kingston." OHS, *PR* (1907):90-101.
3994. **Magill, Max.** "The Failure of the Commercial Bank." In **#3961**, pp. 169-81.
3995. **Malcolmson, Patricia E.** "The Poor in Kingston, 1815-1850." In **#3961**, pp. 281-97.
3996. **Osborne, Brian S.** "The Settlement of Kingston's Hinterland." In **#3961**, pp. 63-79.
3997. **Palmer, Bryan D.** "Kingston Mechanics and the Rise of the Penitentiary, 1833-1836." *HS* 13 (1980):7-32.
3998. **Pierce, D. J., and Pritchett, J. P.** "The Choice of Kingston as the Capital of Canada, 1839-1841." CHA, *AR* (1929):57-63.
3999. **Preston, Richard A.,** ed. *Kingston before the War of 1812: A Collection of Documents*. Toronto: Champlain Society, Ontario Series, vol. 3, 1959.
4000. **Roy, Antoine,** "Le Fort Frontenac sous le régime français." CHA, *AR* (1950):51-57.
4001. **Roy, J. A.** *Kingston: The King's Town*. Toronto: M&S, 1952.
4002. **Schurman, D. M.** "Bishop Strachan and the Archdeaconry of Kingston." *HK* 8 (1959):24-33. Reprinted in **#3924**.
4003. _____. "John Travers Lewis and the Establishment of the Anglican Diocese." In **#3961**, pp. 299-310.
4004. **Short, A.** "Life in Kingston the Year after Waterloo." *QQ* 8 (1901):180-90.
4005. **Smith, F. P.** "Early Schools in Kingston." *HK* 5 (1956):25-29. Reprinted in **#3924**.
4006. **Stanley, George F. G.** "Kingston as Early Tourists Saw It." *HK* 1 (1952):15-27. Reprinted in **#3924**.
4007. _____. "Kingston and the Choice of Canada's Capital." *HK* 24 (1976):18-37.
4008. _____. "Kingston and the Defense of British North America." In **#3961**, pp. 83-101.
4009. **Stewart, J. Douglas.** "Architecture for a Boom Town: The Primitive and the Neo-Baroque in George Brown's Kingston Buildings." In **#3961**, pp. 37-61.
4010. **Thompson, F. F.** "A Chapter of Early Methodism in the Kingston Area." *HK* 6 (1957):32-45. Reprinted in **#3924**.
4011. **Walkem, Richard T.** "Notes on Fort Frontenac and the Old Fortifications of Kingston." *QQ* 4 (1897):276-300.
4012. **Wise, S. F.** "Tory Factionalism: Kingston Elections and Upper Canada Politics, 1820-1836." *OH* 57 (1965):205-25.
4013. _____. "John Macaulay: Tory for All Seasons." In **#3961**, pp. 185-202.
4014. **Young, Maurice M.** "The Development of Municipal Government in the Bay of Quinte Area." *HK* 8 (1959):40-49. Reprinted in **#3924**.

c. 1850-1921

4015. Barnett, Robert F. J. "A Study of Price Movements and the Cost of Living in Kingston, Ontario, for the Years 1865 to 1900." M.A. thesis, Queen's, 1963.
4016. Flynn, Louis J. "The Early Years of the Kingston Historical Society, 1893-1906." *HK* 11 (March 1963):35-46.
4017. Green, Alan G. "Immigrants in the City: Kingston as Revealed in the Census Manuscripts of 1871." In **#3961,** pp. 311-30.
4018. Kemp, F. A. "The Kingston Locomotive Works, 1850-1969." *Can Rail* 240 (1972):16-23.
4019. Livermore, J. D. "The Orange Order and the Election of 1861 in Kingston." In **#3961,** pp. 245-59.
4020. MacDermaid, Anne. "Kingston in the Eighteen-Nineties: A Study of Urban-Rural Interaction and Change." *HK* 20 (1972):35-45.
4021. McDowall, Duncan L. "Kingston, 1846-1854: A Study of Economic Change in a Mid-Nineteenth Century Canadian Community." M.A. thesis, Queen's, 1973.
4022. McInnis, Marvin. *Kingston in the Canadian Economy of the Late Nineteenth Century.* Kingston: Queen's University, Institute for Economic Research, Discussion Paper No. 132, 1974.
4023. Neatby, Hilda. *Queen's University: I. 1841-1917: And Not to Yield.* Montreal: McGill-Queen's UP, 1978.
4024. Richardson, George. "The Canadian Locomotive Company." In **#3961,** pp. 157-67.
4025. Swainson, Donald, "Kingstonians in the Second Parliament: Portrait of an Elite Group." In **#3961,** pp. 261-77.

d. Post-1921

4026. Hallsworth, A. G. "The Housing Decision Process and Social Areas: A Study of Kingston, Ontario." M.A. thesis, Queen's, 1971.
4027. Kirkland, John S. "Housing Filtration in Kingston, 1953-1968." M.A. thesis, Queen's, 1970.
4028. Obright, D. C. "The Residential Location Decision: A Study of Four Operationally Defined Residential Areas within Ten Miles of Downtown Kingston." M.A. thesis, Queen's, 1973.
4029. Skepple, Adolphus D. "Potential Influence of Public Interest on Perceived Areas of Change within the Urban Environment with special Reference to the Kingston Waterfront." M.A. thesis, Queen's, 1971.
4030. Webster, G. "The Application of Location-Allocation Models to the Design of a Public Facility System: A Case Study of the Kingston Public School System." M.A. thesis, Queen's, 1973.

14. Kirkland Lake

4031. Barnes, Michael. *Gold Camp Pioneer: Roza Brown of Kirkland Lake.* Cobalt: Highway Bookshop, 1973.
4032. _____. *The Town That Stands on Gold.* Cobalt: Highway Bookshop, 1978.
4033. Brown, L. C. "Kirkland Lake: 50 Golden Years." *CGEJ* 76 (1969):2-15.
4034. Dike, M. L. "The Changing Economic Structure of Kirkland Lake." M.A. thesis, Western Ontario, 1969.
4035. MacDowell, Laurel. "Remember Kirkland Lake: The History and Effects of the Kirkland Lake Gold Miners' Strike, 1941-42." Ph.D. thesis, Toronto, 1979.
4036. McMillan, J. G. "Early Mining Days in the Kirkland-Larder Lakes District." *CAMJ* 65 (1944):296-99.

4037. **Pain, S. A.** *Three Miles of Gold: The Story of Kirkland Lake.* Toronto: Ryerson, 1960.
4038. **Pollock, John W.** "The Cultural History of Kirkland Lake District, Northeastern Ontario." M.A. thesis, McMaster, 1976.
4039. **Todd, E. W.** *Kirkland Lake Gold Area.* Toronto: King's Printer, 1928.

15. Kitchener-Waterloo

4040. **Baird, K. A.** "Kitchener-Waterloo, Ontario." *CGEJ* 76 (1969):90-99.
4041. **Bloomfield, Elizabeth.** "Economy, Necessity, Political Reality: Town Planning Efforts in Kitchener-Waterloo, 1912-1925." *UHR* 9 (June 1980):3-48.
4042. **Breithaupt, W. H.** "Some Features of Town Planning, with Application to the City of Kitchener." *TPICJ* 1, no. 6 (1921):5-8.
4043. **Brown, H. W.** "Kitchener and Waterloo Collegiate and Vocational School: Its History." WHS, *AR* 25 (1927):268-84.
4044. **Canadian Chamber of Commerce.** *Kitchener-Waterloo Survey: A Fact finding Survey for Post-War Planning.* Montreal: Canadian Chamber of Commerce, 1944.
4045. **Chapman, J. S.** "Commercial Structure of Kitchener and Waterloo." B.A. essay, Waterloo, 1975.
4046. **Collishaw, W., and Preston, B., eds.** *Recollections of 125 years.* Kitchener: Allprint, 1979.
4047. **Copp, Terry, ed.** *Industrial Unionism in Kitchener, 1937-1947.* Elora: Cumnock Press, 1976.
4048. **Cumming, Ross, ed.** *Illustrated Atlas of the County of Waterloo, 1881; County of Waterloo Directory, 1877-1878; Illustrated Atlas of the County of Wellington, 1877.* Owen Sound: Richardson, Bond and Wright, 1972.
4049. **Diamond, Mrs. Clarence.** "The History of New Hamburg." WHS, *AR* 64 (1976):39-47.
4050. **Dickson, F. W. R.** "Bridgeport." WHS, *AR* 53 (1966):12-18.
4051. **Donohoe, E. F., ed.** *Kitchener Centennial, 1854-1954.* Kitchener, 1954.
4052. **Dudycha, D. J.** "A Simulation Model of Suburban Residential Development: Kitchener-Waterloo." M.A. thesis, Waterloo, 1972.
4053. **Dunham, Mabel.** "Waterloo County. House of Industry and Refuge." WHS, *AR* 42 (1948):19-29.
4054. **Durst, H.** "Urban Growth in Waterloo Township." B.A. essay, Waterloo, 1963.
4056. **Eby, Ezra.** *A Biographical History of Early Settlers and Their Descendants in Waterloo Township.* 1895. Rev. ed. Kitchener: Aljon, 1971.
4057. **Ferguson, M.** "The Pre-development Land Market and the Initiation of the Rural-Urban Land Conversion Process: A Case Study in the Former Township of Waterloo." M.A. thesis, Waterloo, 1975.
4058. **Haldane, Elizabeth.** "The Historical Geography of Waterloo Township, 1800-1855." M.A. thesis, McMaster, 1963.
4059. **Heick, Welf H.** "The Lutherans of Waterloo County, Ontario, 1810-1859: A Historical Study." M.A. thesis, Queen's, 1959.
4060. ———. "Becoming an Indigenous Church. The Lutheran Church in Waterloo County, Ontario." *OH* 56 (1964):249-60.
4061. **Heintz, Gladys J.** "German Immigration into Upper Canada and Ontario from 1783 to the Present Day." M.A. thesis, Queen's, 1938.
4062. **Huck, Marilyn Glynn.** "Early Settlement in Waterloo County (Upper Canada)." M.A. thesis, Toronto, 1960.
4063. **Kaufman, Alvin.** "Town Planning in Kitchener after Three Years Trial." *TPICJ* 7, no. 5 (1928):134-37.

4064. **Kitchener Urban Renewal Committee.** *Downtown Kitchener, Ontario.* Toronto: Smith, 1964.
4065. **Klinck, George.** "The Early Days of Elmira." WHS, *AR* 15 (1927):285-96.
4066. **Krueger, Ralph R.** "The Kitchener Market Fight: Another View." *Urb For* 2, no. 2 (1976):40-47.
4067. **Kurokawa, Minako.** "Mennonite Children in Waterloo County." In *Immigrant Groups,* edited by Jean Leonard Elliott, pp. 33-46. Scarborough: Prentice-Hall, 1971.
4068. **Lee, Chun-Fen.** "Twin Cities of Waterloo and Kitchener." *Econ Geogr* 22 (1946):142-47.
4069. **Leibbrandt, Gottlieb.** *Jubilaums Ausgabe: Nachrichten/Centennial Issue: Concordia Club, 1873-1973.* Kitchener: Concordia Club, 1973.
4070. _____. *Little Paradise: Aus Geschichte und Leben der Deutschkanadier in der County Waterloo, Ontario, 1800-1975.* Kitchener: Allprint Co., 1977.
4071. **Lim, J. L.** "The Pattern of Apartment Development and Planning Controls: Kitchener (1960-1974)." M.A. thesis, Waterloo, 1975.
4072. **McKegney, Patricia.** "Berlin, Ontario—1914/1919." M.Phil. thesis, Waterloo, 1979.
4073. **McLellan, A. G.,** ed. *The Waterloo County Area: Selected Geographical Essays.* Waterloo: University of Waterloo, Dept. of Geography, 1971.
4074. **Mage, Julius, and Murdie, Robert A.** "The Mennonites of Waterloo County." *CGEJ* 80 (1970):10-17.
4075. **Manly, C. M.** "Conestogo." *Can Mag* 31 (1908):25-32.
4076. **Moyer, William.** *This Unique Heritage: The Story of Waterloo County.* Kitchener: Radio Station CHYM, 1971.
4077. _____, **and Crook, Robert.** *Kitchener: Yesterday Revisited.* Kitchener: Kitchener Chamber of Commerce, 1979.
4078. **Norcliffe, G. B.** "Territorial Influences in Urban Political Space: A Study of Perception in Kitchener-Waterloo." *Can Geogr* 18 (1974):311-29.
4079. **Pando, Robert Ian.** "A Description and Analysis of Urban Land Use Expansion in Waterloo's Urban Fringe." M.A. thesis, Waterloo, 1969.
4080. **Pasternak, Jack.** *The Kitchener Market Fight.* Toronto: Samuel Stevens, Hakkert, 1975.
4081. **Reed, H. R., Jr.** "The Journey to Work for Manufacturing Workers: A Case Study in Kitchener, Ontario." M.A. thesis, Waterloo, 1969.
4082. **Reive, T. G.** "The Industrial Background of Waterloo County to 1914." B.A. essay, Waterloo Lutheran, 1970.
4083. **Russwurm, Lorne H.** "The Rural-Urban Fringe, with Comparative Reference to London, Kitchener-Waterloo, and Sarnia." M.A. thesis, Western Ontario, 1961.
4084. **Scott, James.** *Of Mud and Dreams: University of Waterloo, 1957-1967.* Toronto: Ryerson, 1967.
4085. **Seymour, Horace L.** "Planning of Kitchener and Waterloo, Ontario." *Can Engineer* 47 (1924):125-30.
4086. _____. "Report of Town Planning Survey of Waterloo, Ontario." *TPICJ* 3, no. 1 (1924):3-8.
4087. _____. "A Plan for the City of Kitchener." *TPICJ* 4, no. 1 (1925):2-4.
4088. **Sherk, A. B.** "The Pennsylvania Germans of Waterloo County, Ontario." *OH* 7 (1906):98-109.
4089. **Smith, A. R. G.** "Early History of Haysville and Vicinity." WHS, *AR* 4 (1916):10-12.
4090. **Soeder, R. R.; Russwurm, Lorne H.; and Russwurm, L. M.** "Changing Retail Functions in the Central Business Districts of Kitchener and Waterloo." In #**4073**, pp. 129-46.
4091. **Spricenieks, Alfred.** "Historical Geography of Industrial Development of Kitchener, Waterloo and Bridgeport, 1801-1956." B.A. essay, Waterloo, 1961.
4092. **Stroh, Jacob.** "Reminiscences of Berlin." WHS, *AR* 66 (1978):71-123.

4093. **Tiessen, Paul,** ed. *Berlin, Canada, a Self-Portrait.* 1912. Rev. ed. St. Jacobs: Sand Hill Books, 1979.
4094. **Uliana, J. A.** "An Analysis of Land Use Stability and Succession in the Zone of Transition: The Case of Kitchener, Ontario." M.A. thesis, Waterloo, 1974.
4095. **Uttley, W. V.** "Joseph Schneider: Founder of the City." WHS, *AR* 17 (1929):111-19.
4096. ———. *A History of Kitchener, Ontario.* 1937. 2d ed. Waterloo: Wilfrid Laurier UP, 1975.
4097. **Vey, W. E.** "The German Immigrants of Waterloo County, 1840-1900." M.A. thesis, Western Ontario, 1977.
4098. **Wells, Clayton W.** "A Historical Sketch of the Town of Waterloo, Ontario." WHS, *AR* 16 (1928):22-67.

16. London

a. General

4099. **Armstrong, Frederick H., and Brock, Daniel J.** *Reflections on London's Past.* London: City of London, 1975.
4100. **Armstrong, Frederick H., and Phelps, Edward C.** "Urban Preservation and the Municipal Advisory Committee in London, Ontario." *UHR* 2-77 (October 1977):10-19.
4101. **Bice, C.** "London." *Habitat* 10, nos. 3-6 (1967):88-93.
4102. **Bremner, A.** *City of London, Ontario, Canada: The Pioneer Period and the London of Today.* 1897. Rev. ed. London: London Public Library Board, 1967.
4103. **Chambers, Jack; Curnoe, W. Glen; and Boyle, John.** *The Heart of London.* Toronto: NC Press, 1976.
4104. **Clarke, B. Frank.** "Case Studies of the Elite of London." M.A. thesis, Western Ontario, 1978.
4105. **Curnoe, W. Glen.** *Around London, 1900-1950: A Picture History.* London, 1973.
4106. **Farrell, John K. A.** "Michael Francis Fallon, Bishop of London, Ontario, Canada (1909-1931): The Man and His Controversies." CCHA, *Study Sessions* 35 (1968):73-90.
4107. **Ferris, T. T. M.** "History of the London and Port Stanley Railway, 1852-1946." M.A. thesis, Western Ontario, 1946.
4108. **Fraser, Alexander,** ed. *Minutes of the Quarter Sessions for the London District, 1800-1809, 1813-1818.* Toronto: Ontario Archives Report, 1933.
4109. **Garvey, John.** *Social, Business and Economic Development of London and the Talbot Settlement.* London: London *Echo*, 1949.
4110. **Geraghty, E.** *Telephone History, London, Ontario, 1880-1972.* Montreal: Telephone Historical Collection, 1972.
4111. **Graham, J. E.** "Residential and Migration Patterns of Italians in London, Ontario, 1891-1971." B.A. essay, Western Ontario, 1972.
4112. **Gwynne-Timothy, John.** *Western's First Century.* London: University of Western Ontario, 1978.
4113. **Halwa, T. L.** "An Application of the Griffin and Preston Transition Zone Concept to London, Ontario." M.A. thesis, Western Ontario, 1974.
4114. **Hamil, Fred C.** "Colonel Talbot and the Early History of London." *OH* 43 (1951):159-76.
4115. **Ibbotson, Leonard.** "Brief History of Town Planning in London, Ontario, Canada." *TPICJ* 7, no. 5 (1928):145-54.
4116. **James, N. C.** "The Western University." LMHS, *Trans* 5 (1914):41-47.
4117. **Janelle, Donald.** "Scale Components in the Descriptive Analysis of Urban Land Use Change: London, Ontario, 1850-1960." *Ont Geogr* 7 (1972):66-76.

4118. **London Ontario Chamber of Commerce.** *Seventy-Seven Years of Service in Community Building, London, Canada, 1857-1934.* London, 1935.
4119. **Lutman, John H.** "Conducting Urban Heritage Surveys: A Case Study of London Ontario." *UHR* 1-77 (June 1977):46-54.
4120. _____. *The Historic Heart of London.* London: City of London, 1977.
4121. _____. *The South and West of London: An Historical and Architectural Guide.* London: City of London, 1979.
4122. **McArthur, N. M.** "The Middle Towns of the London Area." M.A. thesis, Western Ontario, 1950.
4123. **Miller, Orlo.** "London, Ontario, Pioneer Welfare Planner." *Can Wel* 36 (1960):249-56.
4124. _____. "The Fat Years and the Lean Years: London in Boom and Depression." *OH* 53 (1961):73-80.
4125. _____. *Gargoyles and Gentlemen: A History of St. Paul's Cathedral, London, Ontario, 1834-1964.* Toronto: Ryerson, 1966.
4126. _____. *A Century of Western Ontario: The Story of London, 'The Free Press,' and Western Ontario, 1849-1949.* 1949. Rev. ed. Westport, CT: Greenwood Press, 1972.
4127. **Onn, Gerald.** "The History of the London Street Railway Company (1873-1951)." M.A. thesis, Western Ontario, 1958.
4128. **Oxley, J. M.** "London: The Forest City." *National Monthly of Canada* 4 (1904):73-86.
4129. **Palmer, Bryan D.** " 'Give Us the Road and We Will Run It'; The Social and Cultural Matrix of an Emerging Labour Movement." In *Essays in Canadian Working Class History,* edited by Gregory S. Kealey and Peter Warrian, pp. 106-24, Toronto: M&S, 1976.
4130. **Priddis, H.** "Naming of London Streets." LMHS, *Trans* 2 (1909):7-30.
4131. **Scott, B. S.** "Oil Refining in London." *W Ont Hist N* 6 (September-December 1948):38-45.
4132. **Talman, J. J.** "Rise of the University of Western Ontario." *W Ont Hist N* 5 (June 1947):26-31.
4133. _____. *Huron College, 1863-1963.* London: Huron College, 1963.
4134. **Taube, E.** "The Growth of London, Ontario." *CGEJ* 33 (1946):102-16.

b. Pre-1921

4135. **Armstrong, Frederick H.** "George Jervis Goodhue: Pioneer Merchant of London, Upper Canada." *OH* 63 (1971):217-32.
4136. _____, and **Brock, Daniel J.** "The Rise of London: A Study of Urban Evolution in Nineteenth-Century Southwestern Ontario." In *Aspects of Nineteenth-Century Ontario,* edited by Frederick H. Armstrong, H. A. Stevenson, and J. D. Wilson, pp. 80-100. Toronto: UTP, 1974.
4137. **Baehre, R. K. F.** "The Lunatic Asylum of London, Ontario, in the 19th Century." M.Phil. thesis, Waterloo, 1977.
4138. **Brock, Daniel J.** "Richard Talbot, the Tipperary Irish and the Formative Years of London Township: 1818-1826." M.A. thesis, Western Ontario, 1969.
4139. **Brunger, Alan G.** "A Spatial Analysis of Individual Settlements in Southern London District, Upper Canada, 1800-1836." Ph.D. thesis, Western Ontario, 1974.
4140. **Burley, Kevin.** "Occupational Structure and Ethnicity in London, Ontario, 1871." *HS* 11 (1978):390-410.
4141. **Campbell, C. T.** "Founding of London." LMHS, *Trans* 1 (1908):12-28.
4142. _____. "Beginning of London." OHS, *PR* 9 (1910):61-74.
4143. _____. "The Settlement of London." LMHS, *Trans* 4 (1911):9-51.
4144. _____. "The Village of London." LMHS, *Trans* 9 (1918):5-25.

4145. _____. *Pioneer Days in London.* London: *Advertiser,* 1921.
4146. **Cruikshank, E. A.** "The Early Years of the London District." OHS, *PR* 24 (1927):145-280.
4147. **Cuddy, S.** "Strathroy, 1832-1925." LMHS, *Trans* 12 (1927):35-48.
4148. **Davis, Ruth Helen.** "The Beginnings and Development of the University of Western Ontario, 1878-1924." M.A. thesis, Western Ontario, 1925.
4149. **Davis, W. L.** "A History of the Early Labour Movements in London, Ontario." M.A. thesis, Western Ontario, 1930.
4150. **Dillon, Willard Francis.** "The Irish in London, Ontario, 1826-1861." M.A. thesis, Western Ontario, 1963.
4151. **Echenberg, H. D.** "Urbanization, Integration and Organized Sport in Nineteenth Century Ontario: London, 1850-1900." M.A. thesis, Western Ontario, 1979.
4152. **Edwards, C. B.** "London Public Schools, 1848-1871." LMHS, *Trans* 5 (1914):14-29.
4153. **Farrell, John K. A.** "The History of the Roman Catholic Church in London, Ontario, 1826-1931." M.A. thesis, Western Ontario, 1949.
4154. **Fuller, Paul G.** "Aspects of London's Cultural Development from the Turn of the Century to World War One." M.A. thesis, Western Ontario, 1966.
4155. **Gardner, W. H.** *London, Ontario: A Presentation of Her Resources, Achievements, and Possibilities.* London: Advertising Job Printing, 1914.
4156. _____. *London and Its Men of Affairs.* London: Advertising Job Printing, 1915.
4157. **Hamil, Fred C.** *Lake Erie Baron (Thomas Talbot).* Toronto: Macmillan, 1955.
4158. **Henderson, J. L.** "A Study of the British Garrison in London, Canada West, 1838-1869." M.A. thesis, Windsor, 1967.
4159. **Hines, F. R.** "Concert Life in London, Ontario, 1870-1880." M.Mus. thesis, Western Ontario, 1977.
4160. **Hopkinson, M. W.** "The London Region and the French-Canadian Question, 1864-1890." M.A. thesis, Western Ontario, 1969.
4161. **Jackson, J.** "The House as a Visual Indicator of Social Status Change: The Example of London, Ontario, 1861-1915." M.A. thesis, Western Ontario, 1973.
4162. _____. "Houses as Urban Artifacts: A Case Study of London, Ontario, 1845-1915." *Ont Geogr* 12 (1978):49-68.
4163. **Judd, William W., ed.** *Minutes of the London Mechanics' Institute (1841-1895).* London: London Public Library and Art Museum, 1976.
4164. **Kirk, J. Michael.** "Some Aspects of the Military History of London, Ontario: 1850-1900." M.A. thesis, Guelph, 1972.
4165. **Landon, Fred.** "Fugitive Slaves in London before 1860." LMHS, *Trans* 10 (1919):25-38.
4166. _____. "Some Early Newspapers and Newspaper Men of London." LMHS, *Trans* 12 (1927):26-34.
4167. _____. "London and Its Vicinity, 1837-38." *OH* 24 (1927):410-38.
4168. **Miller, Orlo.** "The History of the Newspaper Press in London, 1830-1875." OHS, *PR* 32 (1937):114-39.
4169. **Nelles, Douglas H.** "Topographical Survey of London, Ontario and the Use of Aerial Maps." *TPICJ* 1, nos. 4-5 (1921):24-25.
4170. **Ross, Ian C.** "London East, 1854-1885: The Evolution, Incorporation and Annexation of a Satellite Municipality." M.A. thesis, Western Ontario, 1977.
4171. **Scott, B. S.** "The Economic and Industrial History of the City of London, Canada, from the Building of the First Railway, 1855, to the Present, 1930." M.A. thesis, Western Ontario, 1930.
4172. **Spicer, Elizabeth, ed.** *Descriptions of London and Environs, 1799-1854.* London: London Public Library and Art Museum, 1975.

4173. **Tamblyn, W. F.** "A University in the Making (Western University, London, Ontario)." *Can Mag* 55 (1920):417-25.
4174. **Woolcock, H. R.** "Attitudes to Health and Disease in London, Canada, 1826-1854." M.A. thesis, Western Ontario, 1977.
4175. **Yealland, F. T.** "The London of Canada." *United Empire* 4 (1913):655-59.

c. Post-1921

4176. **Andress, D. D.** "The Impact of Apartment Building and Townhouse Development on School Planning, London, Ontario." M.A. thesis, Western Ontario, 1967.
4177. **Assaly, L.C.W.** "Chain and Independent Grocery Store Prices in London, Ontario." *Q Rev Commerce* 7 (Summer 1940):287-98.
4178. **Binns, M. A.** "Cultural Pluralism in Canada: An Exploratory Study of the Italians and the Ukrainians in London, Ontario." M.A. thesis, Western Ontario, 1971.
4179. **Carr, N.** "A Profile of Political Activists in London, Ontario." M.A. thesis, Western Ontario, 1970.
4180. **Crawford, Kenneth Grant.** "The Finances and the Financial Administration of the City of London." M.A. thesis, Western Ontario, 1926.
4181. **Doney, H. J.** "The Neighbourhood Concept in Urban Planning: A Sample Analysis in London, Ontario." M.A. thesis, Western Ontario, 1973.
4182. **Drewery, Ellen M.** "Community Action in London." *CPR* 18, no. 2 (1968):22-25.
4183. **Elliot, Una.** "Comparative Roles of the People of Italian and Netherlandish Origin in the Creation of a Homogeneous Population in the City of London." M.A. thesis, Western Ontario, 1964.
4184. **Fesenmaier, Daniel R.; Goodchild, Michael F.; and Morrison, Sandra.** "The Spatial Structure of the Rural-Urban Fringe: A Multivariate Approach." *Can Geogr* 23 (1979):255-65.
4185. **Flaman, Richard.** "A Path Analysis of Residential Land Use Determinants in London, Ontario." *Ont Geogr* 9 (1975):19-33.
4186. **Flanders, D.** "Case Studies in the Problem of Urban Church Residency, 1914-1975, with Particular Reference to London, Ontario, and the Parkdale District of Toronto." M.A. thesis, Western Ontario, 1976.
4187. **Fleming, Jane I.** "The Effect of Committee of Adjustment Decisions on Urban Development: A Case Study of London, Ontario, 1965-69." M.A. thesis, Western Ontario, 1970.
4188. **Fraser, F. W.** "Local Political Party Officeholders in the City of London, Ontario." M.A. thesis, Western Ontario, 1974.
4189. **Haydu, G.** "The Urban System of the London, Ontario, Region: A Central Place Analysis." M.A. thesis, York, 1973.
4190. **Hessel, R. H.** "The Labour Movement in London. Some Personal Recollections." *W Ont Hist N* 21 (March 1965):49-50.
4191. **Heubert, V. H.** "Public Land-Use in London, Ontario." M.A. thesis, Western Ontario, 1967.
4192. **Krueger, Ralph R.** "Urban Blight with Specific Reference to London, Ontario." M.A. thesis, Western Ontario, 1955.
4193. **Mennill, David C.** "Residence and Employment Locations in London, Ontario." M.A. thesis, Western Ontario, 1966.
4194. _____. "Simulation of New Residential Growth in London, Ontario." *Ont Geogr* 1 (1967):5-11.
4195. **Millward, H. A.** "Simulation of Urban Spatial Growth, with Reference to London, Canada, and West Nottinghamshire, England." M.A. thesis, Western Ontario, 1972.

4196. **Muncaster, Russell W.** "A Model for Mixed Urban-Place Hierarchies: An Application to the London, Ontario Urban-Place System." Ph.D. thesis, Clark, 1972.
4197. _____. "The Empirical Structure of Urban Systems: The London, Ontario, Example." *Can Geogr* 22 (1978):306-18.
4198. **Newall, P. D.** "Changing Conceptions of the Efficient Use of Space: A Case Study of Railways with Specific Reference to the C.P.R. Right-of-Way in London, Ontario." M.A. thesis, Western Ontario, 1977.
4199. **Nixon, G. P., and Campbell, Maurice A.** *Four Cities [Windsor, Sarnia, London, Waterloo]: Studies in Urban and Regional Planning.* Toronto: M&S, 1971.
4200. **Owens, G. B.** "Evaluating a Highway Locational Model: The London 402 Controversy." M.A. thesis, Western Ontario, 1975.
4201. **Pincombe, P. G.** "An Analysis of the Recreational Activities of Urban Adults—Case Study: London, Ontario." M.A. thesis, Western Ontario, 1970.
4202. **Russwurm, Lorne H.** "Expanding Urbanization in the London to Hamilton Area of Western Ontario, 1941-1961." Ph.D. thesis, Illinois, 1964.
4203. _____. "Country Residential Development and the Regional City Farm in Canada." *Ont Geogr* 10 (1976):79-96.
4204. **Saleh, M.** "Spatial Patterns of the Hotel Industry of London, Ontario." M.A. thesis, Western Ontario, 1972.
4205. **Saunders, J. M.** "Population Changes in Ontario, 1951-1956, with Special Reference to the London Region." M.A. thesis, Western Ontario, 1959.
4206. **Sherman, Max.** "Effects of Rezoning on Adjacent Property Values: From Case Studies in London, Ontario." M.A. thesis, Western Ontario, 1973.
4207. **Sullivan, G. V.** "Urban Recreation: An Overview. A Case Study of London, Ontario." M.A. thesis, Western Ontario, 1969.
4208. **Tanner, T.** "London's Loyalties. The 1935 Federal Election in London, Ontario." *W Ont Hist N* 21 (Autumn 1965):30-45.
4209. **Thompson, A. W.** "Assimilation of West Indians in London and Hamilton, Ontario." M.A. thesis, Western Ontario, 1970.
4210. **Thompson, W. A.** "Consumer Purchasing outside the City of London." *Q Rev Commerce* 3 (Winter 1935):15-23.
4211. **Troughton, Michael.** "Comparative Profiles of Land Holding Types in the Rural-Urban Fringe of London." *Ont Geogr* 10 (1976):27-53.
4212. **Ward, H. F.** "The London-St. Thomas-Port Stanley Axis of Development." M.Sc. thesis, Western Ontario, 1950.
4213. **Waters, J. W.** "Geographical Study of Villages in the London Area." M.Sc. thesis, Western Ontario, 1950.
4214. **Waters, N. M.** "Methodology for Servicing the Geography of Urban Fire: An Exploration with Special Reference to London, Ontario." Ph.D. thesis, Western Ontario, 1977.
4215. **Wilson, Charles.** "Industrial Trends of the London Area." M.A. thesis, Western Ontario, 1960.
4216. **Yeung, Y. M.** "The Commercial Structure of London, Ontario." M.A. thesis, Western Ontario, 1966.

17. North Bay

4217. **Campbell, H. A.** *Life and Adventures of a Pioneer.* North Bay: Northland, 1970.
4218. **Gard, Anson.** *North Bay: The Gateway to Silverland.* Toronto: Emerson, 1909.
4219. **Kennedy, W. K. P.** *North Bay: Past, Present, Prospective.* Toronto: Best, 1961.
4220. **North Bay Board of Trade.** *The Nipissing District, Province of Ontario, Canada.* North Bay: Board of Trade, 1897.

4221. Parker, L. J. "North Bay." *Habitat* 10, nos. 3-6 (1967):94-97.
4222. "Town Plan for North Bay." *TPICJ* 7, no. 2 (1928):35-38.

18. Orillia

4223. *The First Hundred Years, the Orillia Presbyterian Church, 1851-1951.* Orillia: Packet and Times, 1951.
4224. Gaffield, Chad M., and Levine, David. "Dependency and Adolescence on the Canadian Frontier: Orillia, Ontario in the Nineteenth Century." *Hist Educ Q* 18 (1978):35-47.
4225. Leacock, Stephen. *Sunshine Sketches of a Little Town.* 1912. Reprint. Toronto: M&S, 1970.
4226. Nichols, C. M., and Hyde, F. D., eds. *Review Number, Magazine of Industry.* Barrie: Barrie Gazette, 1911.
4227. Noble, E. J. "Entrepreneurship and Nineteenth Century Urban Growth: A Case Study of Orillia, Ontario, 1867-1898." *UHR* 9 (June 1980):64-89.
4228. Orillia Historical Society. *Orillia Portraits.* Vol. 1. Orillia: Stubly, 1966.

19. Oshawa

4229. Harkness, John Graham. *Stormont, Dundas and Glengarry, A History 1784-1945.* Oshawa: Mundy-Goodfellow, 1946.
4230. Hood, M. M. *Oshawa: A History of "Canada's Motor City."* Oshawa: McLaughlin Public Library Board, 1968.
4231. Kaiser, T. E. *Historic Sketches of Oshawa.* Oshawa: Reformer Printing and Publishing, 1921.
4232. McDonald, Donald. "A City Plan for Oshawa, Ontario." M.R.P. thesis, Cornell, 1948.
4233. Pendergast, James A. "Labour and Politics in Oshawa and District, 1928-1943." M.A. thesis, Queen's, 1973.

20. Ottawa

a. General

4234. Adams, Thomas. "The Future of Ottawa." *Cn L* 6 (1920):32-35, 45-47.
4235. Armond, Y. "L'Ottawa vue par les français." *Rev univ Ottawa* 8 (1938):381-408.
4236. Audet, F. J. *Historique des journaux d'Ottawa.* Ottawa: Bureau, 1896.
4237. Bond, Courtney Claude Joseph. "Tracks into Ottawa: The Construction of Railways into Canada's Capital." *OH* 57 (1965):123-34.
4238. _____. *The Ottawa Country: A Historical Guide to the National Capital Region.* Ottawa: National Capital Commission, 1968.
4239. _____. *City on the Ottawa.* 1965. 2d rev. ed. Ottawa: Queen's Printer, 1971.
4240. _____, **and Hughson, J. W.** *Hurling down the Pine: The Story of the Wright, Gilmour and Hughson Families, Timber and Lumber Manufacturers in the Hull and Ottawa Region, 1800-1920.* Old Chelsea: Historical Society of the Gatineau, 1964.
4241. Bourns, Brian. "Ottawa Regional Planning: Winners Take $300,000,000." *City Mag*, Preview Edition (Summer 1974):23-28.
4242. Bradley, W. H. "The Diocese of Ottawa." *Can Churchman* 79 (February 1952):38-39.
4243. Brault, Lucien. *Ottawa: Capitale du Canada, de son origine à nos jours.* Ottawa: Editions de l'université d'Ottawa, 1942.

4244. _____. *Ottawa, Old and New.* Ottawa: Ottawa Historical Information Institute, 1946.
4245. _____. "Bibliographie d'Ottawa." *Rev univ Ottawa* 24 (1954):345-75.
4246. _____. *Une siècle d'administration scholaire: La commission des écoles catholiques de Hull, 1866-1966.* Hull: La commission des écoles catholiques de Hull, 1966.
4247. **Carr-Harris, B.** "Historic Landmarks of Ottawa." *Westminster* 5 (1904):8-13.
4248. **Carrière, Gaston.** "Bibliographie des professeurs oblats des facultés ecclesiastiques de l'université d'Ottawa." *Rev univ Ottawa* 32 (1962):81-104.
4249. **Cummings, H. R., and MacSkimming, W. T.** *The City of Ottawa Public Schools: A Brief History.* Ottawa: Ottawa Board of Education, 1971.
4250. **Davies, Blodwen.** *The Charm of Ottawa.* Toronto: M&S, 1932.
4251. _____. *Ottawa, Portrait of a Capital.* Toronto: McGraw-Hill, 1954.
4252. **De Volpi, C. P.** *Ottawa, 1807-1882: A Pictorial Record.* Montreal: Dev-Sco, 1964.
4253. **Duhamel, R.** "Ville, ô ma ville." *Rev univ Ottawa* 12 (1942):184-88.
4254. **Eggleston, Wilfrid.** *The Queen's Choice: The Story of Canada's Capital.* Ottawa: Queen's Printer, 1961.
4255. **Finn, T. D.,** ed. *Centenary of Ottawa, 1854-1954: "The Capital Chosen by a Queen."* Ottawa: City of Ottawa, 1954.
4256. **Gillis, Robert Peter.** "Ottawa and Hull, 1870-1930: A Description and Analysis of Their Industrial Structure." In #**4306**, pp. 13-20.
4257. **Gravel, L.** "Les espaces récreatifs de la Région de la Capitale Nationale (leur intégration dans le processus d'urbanisation)." Thèse de M.A., Montréal, 1974.
4258. **Greening, W. E.** *The Ottawa.* Toronto: M&S, 1961.
4259. _____. "The Lumber Industry in the Ottawa Valley and the American Market in the 19th Century." *OH* 62 (1970):134-36.
4260. **Guillet, Edwin C.** "Ottawa of Yesterday." *CGEJ* 34 (1947):40-48.
4261. **Haig, R. B.** *Ottawa: City of Big Ears.* Ottawa: Haig and Haig, 1970.
4262. **Heritage Ottawa.** *Walking in New Edinburgh, Ottawa.* Ottawa, 1974.
4263. _____, *Walking in Sandy Hill, Ottawa.* Ottawa, 1974.
4264. **Hill, Hamnett P.** *History of Christ Church Cathedral, Ottawa, 1832-1932.* Ottawa: Runge, 1932.
4265. **Horsey, A.** "Gleanings from Ottawa Scrap-Books." *OHS, PR* 13 (1915):36-41.
4266. **Hubbard, Robert Hamilton.** "Architecture in Ottawa." *JRAIC* 32 (1955):410-28.
4267. _____, *Rideau Hall.* Ottawa: Queen's Printer, 1967.
4268. _____. *Cathedral in the Capital: A Short History of Christ Church Cathedral.* Ottawa: Cathedral Centennial Committee, 1972.
4269. _____. *An Illustrated History of Government House, Ottawa, from Victorian Times to the Present Day.* Montreal: McGill-Queen's UP, 1977. Translated as *Histoire illustrée de la Résidence du Gouverneur général à Ottawa.* Montreal: McGill-Queen's UP, 1979.
4270. **Hunter, E. L.** "History of Ottawa and District: A Selected List." *Ont Lib Rev* 33 (1949):342-44.
4271. **Jefferson, R., and Johnson, L. L.** *Faith of Our Fathers: The Story of the Diocese of Ottawa.* Ottawa: Anglican Book Society, 1957.
4272. **Kalman, Harold, and Mackie, Joan.** *The Architecture of W. E. Noffke.* Ottawa: Heritage Ottawa, 1976.
4273. **Leaning, John D.** *The Revitalization of Older Residential Districts* [Glebe district of Ottawa]. Ottawa: MSUA, 1974.
4274. **Legget, Robert F.** *Ottawa Waterway: Gateway to a Continent.* 1962. Rev. ed. Toronto: UTP, 1975.
4275. **Legros, Hector.** *Le diocèse d'Ottawa, 1847-1948.* Ottawa: *Le Droit,* 1949.
4276. **Lett, W. P.** "Bytown to Ottawa, 1827-1873." *WCHSO, Trans* 8 (1922):23-24.

4277. **Longstreet, T. Morris.** *Quebec, Montreal and Ottawa.* New York: Century, 1933.
4278. **Lower, A. R. M.** "The Lumberjack's River." *QQ* 60 (1953):24-40.
4279. **Lucas, G. C.** "Presbyterians in Carleton County to 1867." M.A. thesis, Carleton, 1973.
4280. **McPhail, J. G.** *St. Andrew's Church, Ottawa: The First Hundred Years, 1828-1928.* Ottawa: Merrill, 1932.
4281. **Mahatty, R. V.** "Ottawa Journalism, 1860-1950." *OH* 42 (1950):205-11.
4282. **Mallory, Enid.** "Ottawa Lumber Era." *CGEJ* 48 (1954):60-73.
4283. **May, J.** "Bush Life in the Ottawa Valley." OHS, *PR* 12 (1914):152-63.
4284. **Minton, Eric.** "Ottawa's First Suburb." *Habitat* 9, no. 5 (1968):18-20.
4285. ———. *Ottawa: Reflections of the Past.* Toronto: Nelson, Foster, and Scott, 1974.
4286. **Muddiman, B.** "Ottawa." *Westminster* 22 (1913):129-36.
4287. **Nagy, T. L.** *Ottawa in Maps: A Brief Cartographical History of Ottawa, 1825-1973.* Ottawa: PAC, 1974.
4288. **National Capital Commission.** *A Bibliography of History and Heritage of the National Capital Region.* 1976. Rev. ed. Ottawa: National Capital Commission, 1978.
4289. **Purdy, M. J.** "An Inquiry into the Functions of a Ribbon Road: A Case Study of Bank Street, Ottawa, Ontario, 1891-1972." M.A. thesis, Carleton, 1974.
4290. **Rivers, P. E.** "The Learning Group as a Perceptual Filter: A Study of Residential Preferences in Ottawa." M.A. thesis, Carleton, 1974.
4291. **Roger, Charles.** *Ottawa Past and Present.* Ottawa: *Times,* 1871.
4292. **Ross, A. H. D.** *Ottawa Past and Present.* Toronto: Musson, 1927.
4293. **Ross, P. D.** *Retrospect of a Newspaper Person.* Toronto: OUP, 1931.
4294. **Rossignol, Martin.** "Monographie de la ville d'Ottawa." Thèse de M.A., Montréal, 1948.
4295. **Russell, Hilary.** " 'All that Glitters': A Memorial to Ottawa's Capital Theatre and Its Predecessors." *Canadian Historic Sites: Occasional Papers in Archaeology and History* 13 (1975):5-105.
4296. **Sabourin, Joanne M.** "The Ottawa Centre Area: The Application of Principal Components Analysis to the Study of an Urban Landscape." M.A. thesis, Ottawa, 1975.
4297. ———. "The Evolution of the Ottawa Central Area." In #**4306**, pp. 53-64.
4298. **Scott, Mary McKay.** "Some Historic Buildings in Ottawa." WCHSO, *Trans* 10 (1928):81-92.
4299. **Small, H. Beaumont.** *The Resources of the Ottawa District.* Ottawa: *Times,* 1872.
4300. **Taylor, John H.** "Ottawa: City as Conglomerate." *UHR* 1-75 (June 1975):36-37.
4301. ———. "Fire, Disease and Water in Ottawa: An Introduction." *UHR* 8 (June 1979):7-37.
4302. **Thorburn, C. H.** "Ottawa, 1867-1927." WCHSO, *Trans* 10 (1928):5-29.
4303. **Tremblay, Louis.** "L'Académie De-La-Salle d'Ottawa au XXe siècle: Problèmes d'accréditation et clientèle scolaire." Thèse de M.A., Ottawa, 1969.
4304. **Walker, H. J. N.** *Carleton Saga.* Ottawa: Runge, 1968.
4305. **Welch, Edwin.** "The City of Ottawa Archives." *UHR* 1-76 (June 1976):10-13.
4306. **Wesche, Rolf, and Kugler-Gagnon, Marianne, eds.** *Ottawa-Hull, Spatial Perspectives and Planning/Perspectives spatiales et aménagement.* Ottawa: University of Ottawa, Dept. of Geography and Regional Planning, 1978.
4307. **Whitton, Charlotte.** "Ottawa." *Habitat* 10, nos. 3-6 (1967):60-73.
4308. **You, A.** "L'Ottawa vue par les français." *Rev univ Ottawa* 8 (1938):381-408.
4309. **Young, A. H.** "Ottawa a Hundred Years Ago." OHS, *PR* 28 (1932):35-40.

b. Pre-1850

4310. **Audet, Francis J.** "Les députés de la vallée de l'Ottawa, 1792-1867." *CHR* 16 (1935):5-23.

4311. **Blue, Charles S.** "John By: Founder of a Capital." *Can Mag* 38 (1912):573-79.
4312. **Bond, Courtney Claude Joseph.** "Alexander James Christie, Bytown Pioneer." *OH* 56 (1964):16-36.
4313. **Borobé, P.-H.** "Mgr. Joseph-Thomas Duhamel, premier archevêque d'Ottawa." *Rev univ Ottawa* 17 (1947):181-207.
4314. **Campbell, W. W.** "The Old Bytown Canal." *Can Mag* 42 (1914):459-63.
4315. **Carrière, Gaston.** "Les Oblats dans la vallée de l'Outaouais (1841-1861)." CCHA, *Rapport* 22 (1954-55):25-57.
4316. _____. "Le Collège de Bytown." *Rev univ Ottawa* 26 (1956):56-78, 224-45, 317-49.
4317. **Cross, Michael S.** "The Lumber Community of Upper Canada, 1815-1867." *OH* 52 (1960):213-33.
4318. _____. "The Age of Gentility: The Creation of an Aristocracy in the Ottawa Valley." CHA, *HP* (1967):105-17.
4319. _____. "Dark Druidical Groves: The Lumber Community and the Commercial Frontier in British North America to 1854." Ph.D. thesis, Toronto, 1968.
4320. _____. "Stony Monday, 1849: The Rebellion Losses Riots in Bytown." *OH* 63 (1971):177-90.
4321. _____. "The Shiners' War: Social Violence in the Ottawa Valley in the 1830s." *CHR* 54 (1973):1-26.
4322. **Hill, Hammett P.** "The *Bytown Gazette:* A Pioneer Newspaper." OHS, *Trans* 8 (1922):38-51.
4323. **Lett, W. P.** *Recollections of Bytown and Its Old Inhabitants*. Ottawa: Citizen Printing and Publishing Co., 1874.
4324. **National Capital Commission.** *Lower Town, Ottawa, 1826-1854*. Ottawa: National Capital Commission, 1979.
4325. **Pigeon, L. B.** "Notes on Some of the Prominent Citizens of the Early Days of Bytown." WCHSO, *Trans* 8 (1922):20-22.
4326. **Scott, R. W.** *Recollections of Bytown: Some Incidents in the History of Ottawa*. Ottawa: Mortimer, 1931.
4327. **Stewart, McLeod.** *First Half Century of Ottawa*. Ottawa: Esdale, c. 1910.
4328. **Welch, Edwin, ed.** *Bytown Council Minutes, 1847-1848*. Ottawa: City of Ottawa Archives, 1978.
4329. **Wilson, Andrew.** *A History of Old Bytown, Now the City of Ottawa*. Ottawa: *News*, 1876.

c. 1850-1921

4330. **Bennett, Edward H.** "Some Aspects of City Planning, with General Reference to a Plan for Ottawa and Hull." Canadian Club of Ottawa, *Addresses* (1914-15):7-29.
4331. **Bond, Courtney Claude Joseph.** "The Canadian Government Comes to Ottawa, 1865-1866." *OH* 55 (1963):23-34.
4332. **Bridle, Augustus.** "Ottawa the Unusual." *Can Mag* 36 (1911):211-17.
4333. **Carrière, Gaston.** "En marge d'un centenaire: La charte de l'université d'Ottawa (15 août 1866)." *Rev univ Ottawa* 36 (1966):383-407.
4334. **Charteris, J. F.** "Seeing Ottawa and the Duke." *Can Mon* 18 (1915):76-91, 123-24.
4335. **Cole, Frederick.** *The Struggle for the Capital of Canada*. Ottawa, 1938.
4336. **Cook, Frederick.** "City Government in Ottawa." In #**895**, pp. 323-38.
4337. **Cross, L. Doreen.** "Locating Selected Occupations: Ottawa, 1870." *UHR* 2-74 (October 1974):5-14.
4338. **Edgar, James D.** *Canada and Its Capital, with Sketches of Political and Social Life at Ottawa*. Toronto: Morang, 1898.

4339. **Fear, Jon.** " 'The Lumber Piles Must Go': Ottawa's Lumber Interests and the Great Fire of 1900." *UHR* 8 (June 1979):38-66.

4340. **Gard, Anson.** *The Hub and the Spokes, or, the Capital and Its Environs.* Ottawa: Emerson, 1904.

4341. _____. *Ottawa: The Beautiful Capital.* Ottawa: Emerson, 1907.

4342. **Gibson, James A.** "Sir Edmund Head's Memorandum on the Choice of Ottawa as the Seat of Government of Canada." *CHR* 16 (1935):411-17.

4343. _____. "How Ottawa Became the Capital of Canada." *OH* 46 (1954):213-22.

4344. **Gillis, Robert Peter.** "The Ottawa Lumber Barons and the Conservation Movement, 1880-1914." *J Can St* 9, no. 1 (1974):14-30.

4345. _____. "Big Business and the Origins of the Conservative Reform Movement in Ottawa, 1890-1912." *J Can St* 15, no. 1 (1980):93-109.

4346. **Grant, George M.** *French Canadian Life and Character; with Historical and Descriptive Sketches of the Scenery and Life in Quebec, Montreal, Ottawa and Surrounding Country.* Chicago: Beeford, 1889.

4347. **Groulx, Lionel.** "Le choix de la capitale du Canada." *RHAF* 5 (1951-52):522-30.

4348. **Hammond, M. O.** "Ashes of History: Events Recalled by the Parliamentary Buildings Fire at Ottawa." *Can Mag* 46 (1916):474-83.

4349. **Hill, Hammett P.** *Robert Randall and the Le Breton Flats: An Account of the Early Legal and Political Controversies Respecting a Large Portion of the Present City of Ottawa.* Ottawa: Hope, 1919.

4350. **Holt, H. S.** *Report of the Federal Plan Commission on a General Plan for the Cities of Ottawa and Hull, 1915.* Ottawa: Federal Plan Commission, 1916.

4351. **Knight, David B.** "Boosterism and Locational Analysis." *UHR* 3-73 (February 1974):10-16.

4352. _____. *A Capital for Canada: Conflict and Compromise in the Nineteenth Century.* Chicago: University of Chicago, Dept. of Geography, Research Paper no. 182, 1977.

4353. _____. "The Persistance of an Idea amid Divergent Regional Forces: How Ottawa Became Capital." In #**4306**, pp. 3-12.

4354. _____, ed. *Choosing Canada's Capital: Jealousy and Friction in the 19th Century.* Toronto: M&S, 1977.

4355. **Lloyd, Sheila.** "The Ottawa Typhoid Epidemics of 1911 and 1912: A Case Study of Disease as a Catalyst for Urban Reform." *UHR* 8 (June 1979):66-89.

4356. **McCready, J. E. B.** "Ottawa, a Retrospect." *Can Mag* 29 (1907):16-19.

4357. **Randal, F. H.** "Rideau Hall, Past and Present." *Can Mag* 12 (1898):149-56.

4358. **Scott, M. O.** "The Washington of the North [Ottawa]." *Can Mag* 30 (1908):321-26.

4359. **Scott, R. W.** *The Choice of the Capital.* Ottawa: Mortimer, 1907.

4360. **Trotman, James.** "Ottawa in 1878: Land Use Patterns in a Canadian City." M.A. thesis, Carleton, 1977.

4361. **Warfe, Chris.** "The Search for Pure Water in Ottawa, 1910-1915." *UHR* 8 (June 1979):90-112.

d. Post-1921

4362. **Amery, A. D.** "Geographic and Occupational Wage Differentials in Quebec and Ottawa." M.A. thesis, McGill, 1961.

4363. **Annan, Ernest.** "Downtown Ottawa-Hull." *Can Arch* 21, no. 8 (1976):21-39.

4364. **Balharrie, Watson.** "The Intended Appearance of the National Capital." *CPR* 2, no. 2 (1952):43-47.

4365. **Banks, W. J.** "Ottawa—Canada's Changing Capital." *Empire Review* 482 (1941):109-41.

4366. **Bernard, A.; Léveillé, J.; and Lord, G.** *Profile: Ottawa-Hull. The Political and Administrative Structures of the Metropolitan Region of Ottawa.* Ottawa: MSUA, 1974.
4367. **Bezanson, T.** "An Analysis of the Decision-Making Process in the Development of Land Use Policy in the Ottawa Region." M.A. thesis, Carleton, 1978.
4368. **Blair, Gladys, and Blackburn, Clyde.** *The National Capital Region's Towns and Villages.* Ottawa: National Capital Commission, 1976.
4369. **Blumenfeld, Hans.** "National Capital Plan: Glories and Miseries of a Master Plan." *Arch Can* 44, no. 4 (1967):32-35.
4370. "Canada's Capital Today—Through the Camera's Eye." *CGEJ* 94, no. 2 (1977):10-31.
4371. **Cauchon, Noulan.** "Town Planning and the Proposal for a Federal District of Ottawa and Hull." *TPICJ* 1, nos. 4-5 (1921):25-27.
4372. _____. "Plan for Ottawa South." *TPICJ* 2, no. 2 (1923):7-9.
4373. _____. "Draft of Zoning By-Law for Ottawa." *TPICJ* 3, no. 4 (1924):2-24.
4374. _____ "The Federal District Commission for Ottawa." *TPICJ* 6, no. 3 (1927):109-12.
4375. "Cauchon's Plans for Ottawa." *TPICJ* 4, no. 4 (1925):8-11.
4376. **Coleman, A.** *The Planning Challenge of the Ottawa Area.* Ottawa: Queen's Printer, 1969.
4377. **Courtney, J. L.** "Residential Development and Differentiation in Ottawa: A Spatial Overview." M.A. thesis, Waterloo, 1969.
4378. **Department of Planning and Works.** *Urban Renewal.* Ottawa: City of Ottawa, 1967.
4379. "A Federal District for Ottawa." *TPICJ* 1, no. 9 (1922):3-6.
4380. **Fox, M. F.** "The Analysis of Office Distributional Patterns in Central Ottawa, 1940-1970." M.A. thesis, Carleton, 1973.
4381. **Fullerton, Douglas H.** *The Capital of Canada: How Should It Be Governed? A Special Study on the National Capital.* 2 vols. Ottawa: Information Canada, 1974.
4382. **Gréber, Jacques.** "L'aménagement de la capitale nationale." *Rev univ Ottawa* 20 (1950):265-71.
4383. _____. "Plan d'aménagement de la capitale nationale du Canada." *UL* 55 (1950):23-69.
4384. _____. *Plan for the National Capital: General Report.* Ottawa: King's Printer, 1950.
4385. **Hay, Alan K.** "The National Capital Plan." *CGEJ* 63 (1961):202-17.
4386. **Hossé, Hans A.** "Ottawa's Greenbelt and Its Anticpated Effects." *Can Geogr* 4, no. 17 (1960):35-40.
4387. _____. "The Greenbelt and Ottawa's 'Urban Containment.' " In #4306, pp. 93-100.
4388. **Ketchum, C. J.** *Federal District Capital.* Ottawa: Runge, 1939.
4389. **Kinniburgh, James.** *Ottawa the Capital.* London: Stockwell, 1938.
4390. **Kitchen, John M.** "Preparing Zoning Bylaws for the City of Ottawa." *TPICJ* 3, no. 3 (1924):22-24.
4391. **Lamarche, Rodolphe, and Bosquet, Jean-Claude.** "Ottawa-Hull dans le système métropolitaine canadien." In #4306, pp. 21-32.
4392. **Lamarche, Rudolphe, and Perron, Linda.** "Ottawa-Hull: Social Structure and Spatial Differentiation." In #4306, pp. 73-80.
4393. **Leary, R. M.** "Capital on the Ottawa." *Town Plan Rev* 41 (1970):3-14.
4394. **Le Cavalier, Patricia F.** "The Perception of Neighbourhood Strain: A Community Case Study [Ottawa Urban Renewal]." M.A. thesis, Ottawa, 1975.
4395. **Lendray-Zwicki, Joseph B.** "Shopping Centre Growth and the Decline of the Central Business District in an Urban System: A Case Study of the Ottawa-Hull Census Metropolitan Area." M.A. thesis, Ottawa, 1978.
4396. **McRae, K. D.,** ed. *The Federal Capital: Government Institutions.* Ottawa: Queen's Printer, 1969.
4397. **Maheux, Arthur, and Fontaine, H.** "Le congrès de l'Alliance canadienne à Ottawa, 1960." *Rev univ Laval* 15B (1961):526-30.

4398. **Murch, B., and Palko, S.** *Language and Income, Ottawa-Hull, 1961-71.* Ottawa: Carleton University, Dept. of Geography, 1975.
4399. **Mutswairo, Solomon M.** "Geographic Analysis of Land Use Patterns in Ottawa." M.A. thesis, Ottawa, 1964.
4400. **Nga, Nguyen Thuy.** "Planificateurs et résidents: Une perspective différente de l'environnement physique: Rénovation urbaine dans le secteur est de la basse ville d'Ottawa." Thèse de Ph.D., Ottawa, 1972.
4401. **Nwala, V. E.** "The Spatial Dynamics of the Journey to Work from a Low and a High Income Residential Neighbourhood: A Case Study of Lower Town East and Rockcliffe Park Village." M.A. thesis, Ottawa, 1963.
4402. **O'Leary, M. Grattan.** "Ottawa: More Than a City." *CGEJ* 2 (1931):183-99.
4403. "Ottawa: The National Capital Plan." *Can Arch* 5, no. 5 (1960):52-70.
4404. "The Ottawa Planning Situation." *TPICJ* 7, no. 4 (1928):98-102.
4405. "Ottawa's Town Planning Tribulations." *TPICJ* 5, no. 6 (1926):29-32.
4406. **Ottawa Welfare Council.** *Survey of Ottawa's Child and Family Services.* Ottawa, 1953.
4407. "Ottawa Zoning By-Law." *TPICJ* 5, no. 1 (1926):16-23.
4408. **Ploegaerts, Léon.** "L'impact des plans d'aménagement dans l'organisation spatiale du milieu urbain: Le cas d'Ottawa, capitale canadienne." In #**4306**, pp. 149-57.
4409. **Putnam, J. H.** *City Government, Ottawa.* Ottawa: Hope, 1919.
4410. *Report of the Federal Plan Commission on a General Plan for the Cities of Ottawa and Hull.* Ottawa: Federal Plan Commission, 1915.
4411. **Rheault, Michel.** "Structure routière et structure urbaine: Un exemple d'approche typologique: Le cas de la région fonctionnelle d'Ottawa-Hull." Thèse de M.A., Ottawa, 1973.
4412. **Rowat, Donald Cameron.** *The Proposal of a Federal Territory for Canada's Capital.* Toronto: Advisory Committee on Confederation, 1966.
4413. _____. "The Problem of Governing Federal Capitals." *CJPS* 1 (1968):345-56.
4414. _____. "Ottawa." In *The Government of Federal Capitals,* edited by Donald Cameron Rowat, pp. 315-40. Toronto: UTP, 1973.
4415. _____, ed. *Urban Politics in Ottawa-Carleton: Research Essays.* Ottawa: Carleton University, Dept. of Political Science, 1974.
4416. **Rubin, K.** *Sandy Hill—A Case Study of Neighbourhood Participation in City Planning.* Ottawa: City of Ottawa Planning Branch, 1972.
4417. **Rugg, Robert D.** "The Use and Non-Use of Urban Parks: Accessibility and Social Characteristics in ·Relation to Public Outdoor Recreation in Selected Neighbourhoods of Ottawa-Hull." Ph.D. thesis, Ottawa, 1974.
4418. _____. "The Municipal Park System of Ottawa." In #**4306**, pp. 81-92.
4419. **Sabourin, Bernard.** "A Case Study of Municipal Finance: The Corporation of the City of Ottawa, 1939-1954." M.A. thesis, Ottawa, 1957.
4420. **Sabourin, Joanne M.** "The Ottawa Central Area: The Application of Principle Components Analysis in the Study of an Urban Landscape." M.A. thesis, Ottawa, 1975.
4421. **Schouten, Jaap.** "Public Land Policy and Metropolitan Development: The Case of Canada's Capital." *Contact: J Urban and Environmental Affairs* 9, no. 3 (1977):2-15.
4422. **Shimwell, Joseph.** "The Physical Composition and Dynamic of Centre City with Special Reference to Ottawa." M.Arch. thesis, McGill, 1970.
4423. **Smith, J. F. C.** "Design for a National Capital." *Maclean's* 51 (1 July 1938):8-9.
4424. **Tate, Alan.** "The Sparks Street Experiment. Part 1." *CPR* 10, no. 3 (1960):2-5.
4425. _____. "The Sparks Street Experiment. Part 2." *CPR* 11, no. 1 (1961):9-12.
4426. **Tennant, R. D.** "The Ottawa Electric Railway." *Can Rail* 216 (1969):310-30.
4427. **Thrift, Eric W.** "Open Space—Parks—A Capital Region Programme." *CPR* 15, no. 4 (1965):2-13.

4428. _____. "Building Canada's Capital: The National Capital Commission." *CGEJ* 72 (1966):166-79.
4429. **Tochon, Nelson.** "Le concept d'aménagement de la communauté régionale de l'Outaouais." In #**4306,** pp. 127-34.
4430. **Tomovcik, Vladimir.** "The Gréber Plan for Ottawa." M.A. thesis, Waterloo, 1977.
4431. **Wood, Edward I.** "Landscape Architecture in the National Capital." *CPR* 6, no. 1 (1956):13-24.
4432. **Wright, John M.** "The Regional Municipality of Ottawa-Carleton: Planning Objectives, Concepts, and Principal Policies." In #**4306,** pp. 117-26.

21. Parry Sound

4433. **Brunton, S., ed.** *Notes and Sketches on the History of Parry Sound.* Parry Sound: Historical Society, 1969.
4434. **McKean, F. K.** *The Beattys of Parry Sound.* Parry Sound: North Star Publishing, 1963.
4435. _____. "Early Parry Sound and the Beatty Family." *OH* 56 (1964): 167-84.

22. Peterborough

4436. **Bliss, Michael.** " 'Better and Purer': The Peterborough Methodist Mafia and the Renaissance of Toronto." *York Pioneer* (Fall 1979):14-24.
4437. **Boeckh, John L.** "The Role of Locational Relationships in the Utilization of In-Patient Mental Care Facilities in the Peterborough Region." B.A. Hons. essay, Trent, 1978.
4438. **Boland, Edgar J.** *From the Pioneers to the Seventies: A History of the Diocese of Peterborough, 1882-1975.* Peterborough: Maxwell Review, 1976.
4439. **Bolton, Robert J.** *History of the Central Public School, Peterborough, 1860-1960.* Peterborough, 1960.
4440. **Borg, R., ed.** *Peterborough, Land of Shining Waters: An Anthology.* Peterborough: City and County of Peterborough, 1966.
4441. **Brunger, Alan G.** "Early Settlement in Contrasting Areas of Peterborough County." In #**3639,** pp. 117-40.
4442. **Brydon, Dianne.** "The Impact of the Lumbering Industry on the Spatial Distributions of Occupations in Peterborough, 1852-1881." B.A. Hons. essay, Trent, 1978.
4443. **Cole, A.O.C., ed.** *Illustrated Historical Atlas of Peterborough County, 1825-1875.* Peterborough: Peterborough Historical Foundation, 1975.
4444. **Coleman, J.** *The Settlement and Growth of the Otonabee Sector.* Peterborough: Trent-Severn Waterway Interpretive Program, 1978.
4445. **Corbett, Gail, ed.** *Portraits: Peterborough Area Women, Past and Present.* Woodview: Portraits Group, 1975.
4446. **Craw, G. Wilson.** *The Peterborough Story: Our Mayors, 1850-1951.* Peterborough: *Examiner,* 1967.
4447. **Crozier, M. J., ed.** *Little Lake Survey: An Examination of the Physical Environment of Little Lake, Peterborough,* Peterborough: Trent University, 1972.
4448. **Dobbin, Francis H.** *The Peterborough Fire Brigade.* Peterborough, 1925.
4449. _____. *Our Old Home Town.* Toronto: Dent, 1943.
4450. **Donnellan, Brian, et al.** *A Political and Cultural History of Peterborough, 1832-1918.* Peterborough: Trent University, 1975.
4451. **Doyle, Kevin.** "Assimilation, Integration and Social Mobility of the Irish in Mid-Victorian Canada: The Case of Peterborough, 1850-1870." Ph.D. thesis, Dalhousie, 1980.

4452. Edimson, J. Alexander, and Pammett, H. T. *Through the Years in Douro.* Peterborough: Newson, 1967.

4453. Fairlie, Anne, et al. *A Practical Study of Land Ownership in Peterborough and Victoria Counties: Trends, 1955-1975.* Peterborough: Trent University, 1975.

4454. Ferguson, Guy. "The Peter Robinson Emigration of 1876 and Some Factors Influencing the Location of Emigrants." B.A. Hons. essay, Trent, 1972.

4455. Guillet, Edwin C., ed. *The Valley of the Trent.* Toronto: Champlain Society, 1957.

4456. Jones, Elwood. *St. John's, Peterborough: The Sesquicentennial History of an Anglican Parish.* Peterborough: Maxwell Review, 1976.

4457. Kidd, Martha Ann. *Peterborough's Architectural Heritage.* Peterborough: Peterborough Architectural Conservation Advisory Committee, 1978.

4458. La Branche, Bill. *Peterborough Scrap-Books: A Pictorial History of the City of Peterborough, 1825-1975.* Peterborough: Maxwell Review, 1975.

4459. Londerville, John J. D. "The Schools of Peterborough: Their First Hundred Years." M.A. thesis, Queen's, 1942.

4460. Morris, Janet. "A Study of the Downtown Area of Peterborough." B.A. Hons. essay, Trent, 1971.

4461. Morrison, G. E. "Spatial and Temporal Population Density Patterns in Middle-Sized Cities: Peterborough, 1951-1971." B.A. Hons. essay, Trent, 1975.

4462. Mulvaney, C. Pelham. *History of the County of Peterborough, Ontario.* Toronto: Robinson, 1884.

4463. O'Neil, Lynne E., ed. *Studies in the Historical Geography of the Peterborough Area.* Peterborough: Trent University Geographical Society, 1977.

4464. Pammett, H. T. "The Emigration from Ireland to Upper Canada under Peter Robinson in 1825." M.A. thesis, Queen's, 1934.

4465. ———. "The Irish Emigrant Settler in the Pioneer Kawarthas." *Families* 17 (1978):154-74.

4466. Poole, Thomas W. *A Sketch of the Early Settlement and Subsequent Progress of the Town of Peterborough and of Each Township in the County of Peterborough.* 1867. Reprint, with additions, 1941. Reprint. Peterborough: Peterborough Printing Co., 1967.

4467. Smith, Douglas Frederick. "Peterborough's C.B.D.: Structure and Change, 1950-1972." B.A. essay, York, 1972.

4468. Sneddon, R. "The Central Business District of Peterborough, Ontario: Retail Function and Structure." M.A. thesis, Chicago, 1962.

4469. Sullivan, Genevieve. "Peterborough Centennial, 1950: A Century of Progress." *Ont Lib Rev* 35 (1951):43-46.

4470. ———. "History of Peterborough and District: A Selected List." *Ont Lib Rev* 35 (1951):146-48.

4471. Taylor-Vaisey, Robert D., ed. *Peterborough Region.* Vol. 1 of *Ontario's Heritage: A Guide to Archival Resources.* Cheltenham: Boston Mills, 1978.

4472. Wagner, Michael J. "Gentry Perception and Land Utilization in the Peterborough-Kawartha Lakes Region, 1818-1851." M.A. thesis, Toronto, 1968.

4473. Wood, J. W. "Citizen Input for Planning: A Case Study of Peterborough's Waterfront." M.A. thesis, Western Ontario, 1973.

23. Sarnia

4474. Brown, Robert Stewart. "Joseph Warner Murphy and the Mechanics of Political Survival, 1945-1963." M.A. thesis, Western Ontario, 1979.

4475. Elford, Jean. "Sarnia, Canada's Chemical Valley." *CGEJ* 55 (1957):170-85.

4476. Lauriston, V. *Lambton County's Hundred Years, 1849-1949.* Sarnia: Haines Frontier Printing, 1949.

4477. **Maclean, J.** "The Town That Rocked the Oil Cradle (Petrolia)." *Imperial Oil Rev* 39 (June 1955):6-10.
4478. **Phelps, Edward C.** "John Henry Fairbanks of Petrolia, 1831-1914. A Canadian Entrepreneur." M.A. thesis, Western Ontario, 1965.
4479. _____. *A Bibliography of Lambton County and the City of Sarnia, Ontario.* London: University of Western Ontario Library Bulletin, 1970.
4480. _____. *Petrolia, 1874-1974.* Petrolia: Petrolia Print and Litho, 1974.
4481. **Smith, George, and Smith, Leslie K.** *A History of Sarnia to 1900.* Bright's Grove, 1973.
4482. **Smith, Leslie K., and Smith, George.** "Reminiscence of the First Sarnia Survey." *OH* 59 (1967):79-88.
4483. **Whipp, C., and Phelps, Edward C., comps.** *Petrolia, 1866-1966.* Petrolia: Petrolia *Advertiser-Topic*, 1966.

24. Sault Ste. Marie

4484. **Beeson, Louis, ed.** "Sault Ste. Marie in the 1850s." *Michigan Hist* 30 (1955):281-311.
4485. **Collins, A. B.** *Stories of the Past: 300 Years of Soo History.* Sault Ste. Marie: Sault *Star*, 1967.
4486. **Colloton, F. W.** *Historic Sault Ste. Marie.* Sault Ste. Marie: Central Algoma Teacher's Institute, 1951.
4487. _____. "The Story of Algoma, 1830-1939." CCHS, *Journal* 11 (April 1954):18-27.
4488. **Faludi, E. G.** *Rebuilding a City. The Urban Renewal of Greater Sault Ste. Marie, 1960-1980.* Sault Ste. Marie: City of Sault Ste. Marie, 1961.
4489. **Hamilton, Raphael N.** "Jesuit Mission at Sault Ste-Marie (1632-1706)." *Michigan Hist* 52 (1968):122-32.
4490. **Heath, Francis M, et al.** *50 Years of Labour in Algoma: Essays on Aspects of Algoma's Working Class History.* Sault Ste. Marie: Algoma University College, 1978.
4491. **Konarek, J.** "Algoma Central and Hudson Bay Railway. Its Beginnings." *OH* 62 (1970):73-81.
4492. **Lach, E.** "The History of the Pre-1920 Italian Settlement at Sault Ste. Marie, Ontario." M.A. thesis, Western Ontario, 1979.
4493. **McDowall, Duncan L.** "Steel at the Sault: Sir James Dunn and Algoma Steel, 1906-1956." Ph.D. thesis, Carleton, 1978.
4494. **MacPhail, Cathy.** *A Bibliography of Works on the Two Soos and Their Surroundings.* Sault Ste. Marie: Sault Area International Library Association, 1972.
4495. **Mills, James C.** "The Gateway of the Inland Sea [Sault Ste. Marie]." *Can Mag* 38 (1911):27-35.
4496. **Prior, L. C.** "Sault Ste. Marie and the Algoma Steel Corporation." M.A. thesis, Toronto, 1956.
4497. **Punch, Katherine.** "Sault Ste. Marie." *CGEJ* 63 (1966):198-207.
4498. **Sullivan, Alan.** *The Rapids.* 1922. Reprint, with an introduction by Michael Bliss. Social History of Canada, vol. 8. Toronto: UTP, 1972.
4499. **Van Emery, M.** Francis Hector Clerque and the Rise of Sault Ste. Marie as an Industrial Centre." *OH* 56 (1964):191-202.
4500. **Whitaker, J. R.** "Sault Ste. Marie, Michigan and Ontario: A Comparative Study in Urban Geography." Geographical Society of Philadelphia, *Bulletin* 32 (1934):88-107.

25. St. Catharines and the Niagara Region

4501. **Adams, Thomas.** "Regional Planning of the Niagara District." *ENCR* 33 (1919):563-66.

4502. Armstrong, G. M. *The First Eighty Years of the Women's Literary Club of St. Catharines, 1892-1972.* St. Catharines: Women's Literary Club of St. Catharines, 1976.
4503. Augustine, H. A. "The Industrial Geography of the Welland, Ontario Area." M.A. thesis, Indiana, 1967.
4504. Canniff, W. D. "Settlement and Original Survey of Niagara Townships." *Proceedings Can Institute* 1 (1890):96-101.
4505. Carnochan, Janet. "Queenstown in Early Years." *Niagara Historical Society* 25 (1913):19-31.
4506. _____. *History of Niagara.* 1912. Rev. ed. Belleville: Mika, 1973.
4507. _____. *Niagara 100 Years Ago: The Ancient Capital and Its Vicinity.* Welland: Lundy's Lane Historical Society, 1892.
4508. Coombs, Albert Ernest. *City of St. Catharines: Historical Facts.* St. Catharines: St. Catharines *Standard*, 1947.
4509. Creasey, B. J. "Niagara Revisited." *United Empire* 22 (1931):179-83.
4510. Creed, Catherine. "Some Notes on Municipal Proceedings in the Niagara District, 1849-1870." OHS, *PR* 29 (1933):160-70.
4511. Cruikshank, E. A. *Story of Butler's Rangers and the Settlement of Niagara.* 1893. Rev. ed. Niagara Falls: Lundy's Lane Historical Society, 1975.
4512. _____. "Ten Years of the Colonization of Niagara, 1780-1790." *Niagara Historical Society* 17 (1908):1-50.
4513. De Volpi, C. P. *The Niagara Peninsula, 1697-1880: A Pictorial Record.* Montreal: Dev-Sco, 1966.
4514. Fessenden, E. J. "Niagara on the Canadian Shore." *Wentworth Historical Society* 2 (1899):38-48.
4515. Fisher, Val. *St. Catharines—Canada's Garden City.* Toronto: Canadian Business Research Bureau, 1933.
4516. Fleming, David. *History of the Town of Niagara-on-the-Lake (1791-1970).* Manuscript Report Series. Ottawa: Historic Sites, Parks Canada, 1971.
4517. Greenhill, Ralph, and Mahoney, T. D. *Niagara.* Toronto: UTP, 1969.
4517A. Greenwald, Michelle; Levitt, Alan; Peebles, Elaine. *The Welland Canal: Historical Resource Analysis and Preservation Alternatives.* Toronto: Ministry of Culture and Recreation, 1979.
4518. Heit, M. "The Relationship between Distance from a Point of Location Attractiveness and Private Recreational Land Use: The Model Industry of Niagara Falls, Ontario." M.A. thesis, New York (Buffalo), 1974.
4519. Jackson, John N. *Welland and the Welland Canal, the Canal By-Pass Project.* Belleville: Mika, 1975.
4520. _____. *St. Catharines Ontario: Its Early Years.* Belleville: Mika, 1976.
4521. _____, **and Burtniak, John.** *Railways in the Niagara Peninsula: Their Development, Progress and Community Significance.* Belleville: Mika, 1978.
4522. Jackson, John N., and White, Carole. *The Industrial Structure of the Niagara Peninsula.* St. Catharines: Brock University, Dept. of Geography, 1971.
4523. Jones, V. C., ed. *St. Catharines Centennial History.* St. Catharines: Advance Print, 1967.
4524. Kirby, W. *Annals of Niagara.* 1896. Reprint. London: Phelps, 1972.
4525. Kiwanis Club, Stamford, Ont. *Niagara Falls, Canada: A History of the City and the World Famous Beauty Spot: An Anthology.* Niagara Falls: Centennial History Project, 1967.
4526. Krueger, Ralph R. "Urbanization of the Niagara Fruit Belt." *Can Geogr* 22 (1978):179-84.
4527. Lloyd, Donald. "Land Use Trends of the Niagara Peninsula." M.A. thesis, Western Ontario, 1959.

4528. **Lorriman, F. R.; Thompson, E.; Bartle, T. F.** *Town of Thorold, 1850-1950:Centennial History.* Thorold, 1950.
4529. **Moss, Michael R.** "Forest Regeneration in the Rural-Urban Fringe: A Study of Secondary Succession in the Niagara Peninsula." *Can Geogr* 20 (1976):141-57.
4530. **Nelles, H. V.** "Loyalism and Local Power in the District of Niagara, 1792-1837." *OH* 58 (1966):99-114.
4531. *Niagara Falls through the Years.* Niagara Falls: Lundy's Lane Historical Society, 1967.
4532. **Niagara Historical Society.** *Images of Yesterday.* Niagara-on-the-Lake: Niagara Historical Society Museum, 1977.
4533. **Ontario Department of Economics and Development, Special Research and Surveys Branch.** *Economic Survey of the Niagara Region.* Toronto, 1963.
4534. **Ontario Department of Treasury and Economics, Regional Development Branch.** *Design for Development: Niagara (S. Ontario) Region. Phase 1: Analysis.* Toronto, 1970.
4535. **Parker, B. A.** "The Street-Clark Business of Niagara to 1844: A Study of a Commercial Dynasty." M.A. thesis, Western Ontario, 1978.
4536. **Phelps, Oliver S.** *St. Catharines A to Z.* 1856. Rev. ed. St. Catharines: St. Catharines and Lincoln Historical Society, 1967.
4537. **Read, D. B.** "Newark in 1792." *Proceedings Can Institute* 1 (1890):72-76.
4538. **Scott, D. C.** "Notes on the Meeting Place of the First Parliament of Upper Canada and the Early Buildings at Niagara." RSC, *Trans,* 7 (1913):175-91.
4539. **Steel, R. C.** "The Industrial Evolution of Merritton." B.A. essay, Brock, 1970.
4540. **Stokes, Peter J.** *Old Niagara-on-the-Lake.* Toronto: UTP, 1971.
4541. **Tweed, E.** "Evolution of St. Catharines, Ontario." M.A. thesis, McMaster, 1960.
4542. **Vernon, F.** "Some Aspects of the Development of Public Education in the City of St. Catharines." M.Ed. thesis, Toronto, 1960.
4543. **Walker, Susan, and Herod, Don.** *Exploring Niagara-on-the-Lake.* Toronto: Greey de Pencier, 1977.
4544. **Warnick, Paul C.** "The Development of Transportation in Canada West with Particular Reference to the Niagara Peninsula, 1845-1865." M.A. thesis, McMaster, 1954.
4545. **Watson, John Wreford.** "Urban Development in the Niagara Peninsula." *CJEPS* 9 (1943):463-86.
4546. _____. "The Changing Industrial Pattern of the Niagara Peninsula." OHS, *PR* 37 (1945):49-58.
4547. **White, Robert.** *Port Colborne—History.* Port Colborne: Greater Port Colborne Chamber of Commerce, 1969.
4548. **Wilson, Bruce.** "The Struggle for Wealth and Power at Fort Niagara, 1775-1783." *OH* 68 (1976):137-52.
4549. **Yeigh, Frank.** "Niagara and Thereabouts." *CGEJ* 4 (1932):348-58.
4550. **Young, Richard.** "The Economic and Social Development of Welland, 1905-1939." M.A. thesis, Guelph, 1976.

26. Stratford

4551. **Belden, H.** *Illustrated Historical Atlas of Perth County, Ontario.* 1879. Reprint. Owen Sound: Richardson, Bond and Wright, 1972.
4552. **Johnston, Hugh.** "Stratford and Goderich in the Days of the Canada Company." *OH* 63 (1971):71-85.
4553. **Johnston, W. S., and Johnston, J. M.** *History of Perth County to 1867.* Stratford: County of Perth, 1967.
4554. **Leach, James D.** "The Workers' Unity League and the Stratford Furniture Workers. The Anatomy of a Strike." *OH* 60 (1968):39-48.

4555. Morley, E. L. *A Perth County Bibliography.* Milverton: Milverton Sun, 1948.
4556. Stafford, Ellen. *Stratford Around and About.* Stratford: Fanfare Books, 1973.
4557. Thomas, Christopher. "Architectural Image for the Dominion: Scott Fuller and the Stratford Post Office." *J Can Art Hist* 3 (1976):83-94.

27. St. Thomas

4558. Brierly, J. S. *1881 and Onwards, Reminiscences of St. Thomas and Elgin County Half a Century Ago.* Montreal, 1931.
4559. Clark, K. L. "Social Relations and Urban Change in a Late Nineteenth Century South-western Ontario Railway City: St. Thomas, 1868 to 1890." M.A. thesis, York, 1976.
4560. Locke, P. R. *The History of Hydro-Electric Power in St. Thomas.* St. Thomas: Public Utilities Commission, 1966.
4561. Low, David. *St. Thomas, Ontario, Canada, a Centre of Influence in Elgin County.* St. Thomas: St. Thomas *Times-Journal*, 1960.
4562. Miller, Warren C., ed. *Vignettes of Early St. Thomas: An Anthology of the Life and Times of Its First Century.* St. Thomas: Sutherland, 1967.
4563. St. Thomas Board of Trade. *The Progressive Industrial and Railway Centre.* St. Thomas, 1913.

28. Sudbury

4564. Allen, Martha I. G. "History of the Finnish People of the Sudbury District." M.A. thesis, Western Ontario, 1954.
4565. Baine, R. P. "The Settlement of the Sudbury Region." M.A. thesis, Toronto, 1952.
4566. Barlow, Alfred E. "The Nickel and Copper Deposits of Sudbury." *Can Mining and Mechanical Rev* 10 (1891):150-53.
4567. Barnett, A. N. "Potential Homogenous Social Bonds in Metropolitan Sudbury." *Laurentian Univ Rev* 3 (February 1971):71-100.
4568. Battelle Memorial Institute. *Summary Report on Economic Development Opportunities for the Sudbury Area, Ontario.* Columbus, OH: Battelle Memorial Institute, 1959.
4569. Beach, Noel. "Nickel Capital: Sudbury and the Nickel Industry, 1905-1925." *Laurentian Univ Rev* 6, no. 3 (1974):55-74.
4570. Bell, Robert. *Sudbury Mining District.* Ottawa: Dawson, 1891.
4571. Blais, Gérald. "Le Collège du Sacre Coeur, Sudbury, Ontario." Thèse de M.A., Ottawa, 1968.
4572. Bouvier, Emile. "L'Université Laurentienne de Sudbury." *Relations* 233 (1960):120-23.
4573. Brandt, Gail Cuthbert. " 'J'y suis, j'y reste': The French Canadians of Sudbury, 1883-1913." Ph.D. thesis, York, 1976.
4574. _____. "The Development of French-Canadian Social Institutions in Sudbury, Ontario, 1883-1920." *Laurentian Univ Rev* 11, no. 2 (1979):5-22.
4575. Brouillette, Benoît. "La région minière de Sudbury." *Ac Ec* 12 (1937):227-52.
4576. Bush, E. R. "The Sudbury Nickel Region." *Engineering Mining J* 57 (1894):245-46.
4577. Cadieux, Lorenzo. *Frédéric Romanet du Caillaud, 'Comte' de Sudbury (1847-1919).* Montréal: Bellarmin, 1971.
4578. Cook, W. Rupert. *Survey of Freight Transportation Services in the Sudbury Area.* Toronto: Ontario Dept. of Treasury and Economics, 1969.
4579. Courteau, Guy. *Le docteur J.-Raoul Hurtubise, M.D., M.P., 1882-1955; 40 ans de vie française à Sudbury.* Montréal: Bellarmin, 1971.

4580. **Dembek, Klemens.** *Land Use and Municipal Finance in Sudbury.* Sudbury: Sudbury Planning Board, 1962.
4581. **Dorion, C.** *The First 75 Years: A Headline History of Sudbury.* Devon: Stockwell, 1959.
4582. **Dubinski, Walter.** "History of Ukrainians in the Sudbury Basin." M.A. thesis, Western Ontario, 1962.
4583. **Geldhart, Winston J.** *For Want of a Nail: The Story of Cochrane-Dunlop Hardware Ltd.* Toronto, 1966.
4584. **Havel, J. E.** "Some Effects of the Introduction of a Policy of Bilingualism in the Polyglot Community of Sudbury." *Can Rev Soc Anth* 9 (1972):57-71.
4585. _____, and **Keir, Robert.** *Politics in Sudbury. A Survey of Mass Communications, Behavior and Political Parties in Sudbury.* Sudbury: Laurentian University, 1967.
4586. **Heroux, Louis.** "Aperçu sur les origines de Sudbury, 1883-1904." *Documents historiques de la société historique du Nouvel-Ontario,* no. 2 (1943).
4587. **Howey, Florence.** *Pioneering on the C.P.R.* Ottawa: Mutual, 1938.
4588. **Knowles, John D.** *Sudbury-Copper Cliff Electric Railway Co.* Toronto: Upper Canada Railway Society, 1952.
4589. **Kon, William E.** "Boom Town into Company Town: The Story of Sudbury." *New Frontier* 1, no. 7 (1936):6-9.
4590. **Lang, John.** "A Lion in the Den of Daniels: A History of the International Mine, Mill and Smelter Workers Union in Sudbury, 1942-1962." M.A. thesis, Guelph, 1969.
4591. **Le Bourdais, D. M.** *Sudbury Basin: The Story of Nickel.* Toronto: Ryerson, 1953.
4592. **McArton, A. W.** "Impact of Railway Expansion on Economic Growth of the Sudbury, Ontario, Area." M.A. thesis, Oklahoma, 1966.
4593. **McCharles, Aeneas.** *Bemocked of Destiny: The Actual Struggles and Experiences of a Canadian Pioneer.* Toronto: William Briggs, 1908.
4594. **Manners, E.** "The Impact of Ukrainian Settlement in Sudbury: A Case Study." B.A. essay, Laurentian, 1971.
4595. **Martin, J. P.** "Sudbury. Etude économique et humaine de la ville et de son basin." Thèse de Ph.D., Paris, 1971.
4596. **Nickerson, R.** *Inventory of the Papers of Sudbury Mine, Mill and Smelter Union, Local 598.* Toronto: Manuscripts Section, Dept. of Public Records and Archives, 1970.
4597. **Peters, E. D.** "The Sudbury Mines and Works." *CAMJ* 8 (1889):123-26.
4598. **Plante, Albert.** "Ecoles bilingues d'Ontario: Ecoles bilingues de Sudbury." *Documents historiques de la Société Historique du Nouvel-Ontario,* no. 28 (1954).
4599. **Regimbal, R.** "Labour Conditions at the International Nickel Co. of Canada, Ltd., Sudbury, 1944-45." M.A. thesis, Montreal, 1946.
4600. **Richard, T. A.** "Nickel of Sudbury. An Historical Account." *CAMJ* 58 (1942):785-92.
4601. **Rumney, G. R.** "Population Trends in the Sudbury Area." Royal Canadian Institute, *Trans* 29 (1951):3-21.
4602. **Saarinen, Oiva W.** "Regional Planning in the Sudbury Area." M.A. thesis, Western Ontario, 1966.
4603. _____. "Planning and Other Developmental Influences on the Spatial Organization of Urban Settlement in the Sudbury Area." *Laurentian Univ Rev* 3, no. 3 (1971):38-70.
4604. **St. Amant, Jean-Claude.** *Répertoire des élections fédérales dans la ville du Sudbury, 1887-1972.* Sudbury: Université Laurentienne, 1974.
4605. **Stelter, Gilbert A.** "The Origins of a Company Town: Sudbury in the Nineteenth Century." *Laurentian Univ Rev* 3, no. 3 (1971):3-37.
4606. _____. "The Concept of Community in Sudbury." In *A Harmony of Cultures: Report of the Northern Ontario Conference for Ethnic Groups and Community Development,* edited by James Chacko and K. C. Alexander, pp. 23-27. Toronto: Ontario Dept. of the Provincial Secretary and Citizenship, 1971.

4607. _____. "Community Development in Toronto's Commercial Empire: The Industrial Towns of the Nickel Belt, 1883-1931." *Laurentian Univ Rev* 6, no. 3 (1974):3-54.
4608. **Stock, George.** "The Irish Catholics of Sudbury, Ontario, 1883-1930." M.A. thesis, Western Ontario, 1962.
4609. **Sudbury and District Chamber of Commerce.** *The Housing Problem of Sudbury, Ontario.* Sudbury: Chamber of Commerce, 1968.
4610. **Thompson, J. F., and Beasley, N.** *For the Years to Come, a Story of International Nickel of Canada.* Toronto: Longmans, 1960.
4611. **Winter, J. Ralph.** *Sudbury. An Economic Survey.* Sudbury: Laurentian University, 1967.
4612. **Wotherspoon, W. L.** "Nickel Ore Mining in Sudbury District." *CAMJ* 41 (1920):118-22.

29. Thunder Bay

4613. **Arthur, Elizabeth.** "Le Père Frémiot à Thunder Bay, de 1848 à 1852." *RHAF* 25 (1971):205-24.
4614. _____. "Inter-urban Rivalry in Port Arthur and Fort William, 1870-1907." In *Western Canada Past and Present,* edited by A. W. Rasporich, pp. 58-68. Calgary: University of Calgary and M&S, 1975.
4615. _____, ed. *Thunder Bay District, 1821-1892: A Collection of Documents.* Toronto: Champlain Society, Ontario Series, vol. 9, 1972.
4616. **Brown, W. Russell.** "Ships at Port Arthur and Fort William." *Inland Seas* 1 (October 1945):45-51.
4617. **Carthy, H. E.** "Port Arthur, Ontario: Its Industrial Development." Thunder Bay Historical Society, *AR* 16 (1926):39-51.
4617A. **Chochla, Mark.** "Port Arthur's Waverly Park: An Attempt at City Beautification." TBHMS, *PR* 5 (1977):24-31.
4618. **Dawson, I.** "Port Arthur/Fort William." *Habitat* 10, nos. 3-6 (1967):98-103.
4618A. **Donovan, Michael J.** "The Establishment of Roman Catholic Separate Schools in Port Arthur in the 1880s." TBHMS, *PR* 3 (1975):9-15.
4619. **Emery, George.** "Adam Oliver of Ingersoll and Thunder Bay." *OH* 68 (1976):25-43.
4620. **Fort William Hydro Electric Commission.** *Electricity and Fort William: History of the Development of Electricity in the City of Fort William, 1898-1967.* Fort William, 1967.
4620A. **Green, W. L. C.** "The Fort William Water Supply, 1905-09." TBHMS, *PR* 2 (1974): 1-3.
4621. **Harrington, Lyn.** "Thunder Bay: The Lakehead City." *CGEJ* 80 (1970):2-9.
4622. **Kouhi, Christine.** "Labour and Finnish Immigration to Thunder Bay, 1876-1914." *Lakehead Univ Rev* 9 (1976):17-40.
4623. **Lumby, J. R.** "The Port of Western Canada [Fort William]." *Can Mag* 28 (1906):33-39.
4624. **MacDonald, M.** "An Examination of Protestant Reaction toward the Non-English-Speaking Immigrant in Port Arthur and Fort William, 1903-1914." M.A. thesis, Lakehead, 1976.
4625. **Metsaranta, M. M.** "Ethnic Residential Concentration and Succession in a Section of the Former City of Port Arthur." B.A. essay, Lakehead, 1972.
4626. **Morrison, Jean F.** "Labour in Fort William and Port Arthur, 1903-1913." TBHMS, *PR* (1973):23-30.
4626A. _____. "Community and Conflict: A Study of the Working Class at the Canadian Lakehead, 1903-1913." M.A. thesis, Lakehead, 1974.
4627. _____. "Ethnicity and Class Consciousness: British, Finnish and South European Workers at the Canadian Lakehead before World War I." *Lakehead Univ Rev* 9 (1976):41-54.
4628. _____. "Ethnicity and Violence: The Lakehead Freight Handlers before World War I." In *Essays in Canadian Working Class History,* edited by Gregory S. Kealey and Peter Warrian, pp. 143-60. Toronto: M&S, 1976.

4628A. Piovesma, Ray H. "The Establishment of Fort William Municipal Airport, 1928-39." TBHMS, *PR* 4 (1976):24-35.
4629. Pucci, Antonio. "The Italian Community in Fort William's East End in the Early Twentieth Century." M.A. thesis, Lakehead, 1977.
4629A. ———. "Community in the Making: A Case of a Benevolent Society in Fort William's 'Little Italy.' " TBHMS, *PR* 6 (1978):16-27.
4630. Rankin, R. A. "Bibliography of Materials in Fort William Public Library Relating to Fort William, Port Arthur, and Northwestern Ontario." *Ont Lib Rev* 43 (1959):140-46.
4631. Rasmussen, M. A. "The Geographic Impact of Finnish Settlement on the Thunder Bay Area of Northern Ontario." M.A. thesis, Alberta, 1978.
4632. Rasporich, A. W. "A Boston Yankee in Prince Arthur's Landing: C. D. Howe and His Constituency." *Canada: An Historical Magazine* 1, no. 2 (1973):21-40.
4632A. ———. "Faction and Class in Modern Lakehead Politics." *Lakehead Univ Rev* 7 (Summer 1974):31-65.
4633. Russell, A. L. "Fort William in the Middle of the 19th Century." Thunder Bay Historical Society, *AR* 6 (1915):11-16.
4634. ———. "Brief History of Port Arthur Harbour." Thunder Bay Historical Society, *AR* 6 (1915):21-26.
4635. Slipper, M. A. "Women of the Twin Cities." *Canada West Monthly* 6 (1909):241-49.
4636. Tamminen, B. E. "The Rural-Urban Fringe of the City of Thunder Bay." B.A. essay, Lakehead, 1973.
4637. Vickers, W. W. "The Lakehead Cities of Thunder Bay." Thunder Bay Historical Society, *AR* 18-19 (1926-27, 1927-28):95-105.

30. Timmins

4638. Brown, L. Carson. "The Golden Porcupine." *CGEJ* 74 (1967):4-17.
4639. Bucksar, Richard G. "Timmins, the Porcupine and Gold." *Habitat* 12 (March-April 1969):7-12.
4640. Hanson, H. "Reminiscences of Early Days at Porcupine." *CAMJ* 62 (1941):226-32.
4641. Hare, R. E. "Porcupine: Premier Gold District of Northern Ontario." *Engineering Mining J* 115 (1923):359-63.
4642. William Lougheed Associates. *The Gold Mining Community: A Study of the Problems of Economic Growth.* Timmins: Industrial Commission, 1958.
4643. York, W. Milton. *Tales of the Porcupine Trails.* Toronto: Musson, 1911.

31. Toronto and Environs

a. General

4644. Adam, Graeme Mercer. *Toronto: Old and New.* 1891. Reprint. Toronto: Coles, 1972.
4645. Anderson, H. B. "An Historical Sketch of the Medical Profession of Toronto." *Can Medical Assoc J* 23 (1926):446-52.
4646. Arthur, Eric. *Toronto: No Mean City.* 2d ed. Toronto: UTP, 1974.
4646A. ———. *From Front Street to Queen's Park: The History of the Ontario Parliament Buildings.* Toronto: M&S, 1979.
4647. Ashworth, E. M. *Toronto Hydro Recollections.* Toronto: UTP, 1955.
4648. Baine, R. P., and McMurray, A. L. *Toronto: An Urban Study.* Toronto: Clarke, Irwin, 1970.

4649. **Baird, George.** "999 Queen [Toronto]: A Collective Failure of Imagination." *City Mag* 2, nos. 3-4 (1976):34-59.
4650. **Bean, Gordon A.** "The Archives of the Archdiocese of Toronto." CCHA, *Study Sessions* 37 (1970):97-100.
4651. **Beatty, J. David.** "History of Medical Education in Toronto." *UT Med J* 47 (1970):152-57.
4652. **Bissell, Claude T.** *University College: A Portrait 1853-1953.* Toronto: UTP, 1954.
4653. **Blair, J. W.** "Components of Population Change in the Toronto Region." M.A. thesis, York, 1975.
4654. **Bo, Lao.** "Hostages in Canada: Toronto's Chinese (1880-1947)." *Asianadian* 1, no. 2 (1978):11-14.
4655. **Bonis, Robert R.,** ed. *A History of Scarborough.* Scarborough: Scarborough Public Library, 1965.
4656. **Boyle, David.** *The Township of Scarborough, 1796-1896.* Toronto: Briggs, 1896.
4657. **Boylen, J. C.** *York Township, 1850-1954.* Toronto: Township of York and Board of Education of the Township of York, 1954.
4658. **Braithwaite, Max.** *Sick Kids: The Story of the Hospital for Sick Children, 1875-1975.* Toronto: M&S, 1974.
4659. **Brebner, J.** "University of Toronto: Its Expansion and Prospects." *Westminster* 11 (1907):67-74.
4660. **Burton, C. L.** *A Sense of Urgency. Memoirs of a Canadian Merchant.* Toronto: Clarke, Irwin, 1952.
4661. **Burwash, N.** "Review of the Founding and Development of the University of Toronto as a Provincial Institution." RSC, *Trans,* 11 (1905):37-98.
4662. _____. *The History of Victoria College.* Toronto: Victoria College Press, 1927.
4663. **Campbell, Dorothy.** *Toronto: Cabin to Highrise.* Toronto: Grant, 1977.
4664. **Card, Dorothy E.** "History of Direct Relief in Toronto." M.S.W. thesis, Toronto, 1938.
4665. **Cassels, Hamilton, Jr.** "York Mills, 1800-1955." *OH* 47 (1955):180-93.
4666. **Chamberlain, A. D.** "Colored Citizens of Toronto." Women's Canadian Historical Society of Toronto, *Trans* 8 (1914):10-15.
4667. **Chapman, H. D.** *Alfred Chapman, Architect, 1879-1949.* Toronto: Architectural Conservancy of Ontario, 1978.
4668. **Christie, Howard A.** "The Function of the Tavern in Toronto, 1834 to 1875, with Special Reference to Sport." M.P.E. thesis, Windsor, 1974.
4669. **Clarke, Charles.** *A History of the Toronto General Hospital.* Toronto: Briggs, 1913.
4670. **Cochrane, Honora M.,** ed. *Centennial Story: The Board of Education for the City of Toronto, 1850-1950.* Toronto: Nelson, 1950.
4671. **Collard, K. B.** "Montreal and Toronto." In *Great Cities of the World,* edited by W. A. Robson, pp. 353-82. New York: Macmillan, 1957.
4672. **Corelli, Rae.** *The Toronto That Used to Be.* Toronto: Toronto *Star,* 1964.
4673. **Cosbie, W. G.** *Toronto General Hospital, 1819-1965: A Chronicle.* Toronto: Macmillan, 1974.
4674. **Cummins, Captain J. F.** "Notes on the Military History of Toronto." *Canadian Defence Q* 5 (1928):478-85.
4675. **Dale, Allan.** "Toronto of Long Ago." *CGEJ* 9 (1934):49-55.
4676. **Davidson, T., et al.** *The Golden Years of East York.* Toronto: Centennial College Press, 1976.
4677. **Davies, Blodwen.** *Storied York, Toronto Old and New.* Toronto: Ryerson, 1931.
4678. **Deacon, Nadine A. H.** "Geographical Factors and Land Use in Toronto." *CGEJ* 29 (1944):80-99.

4679. **Deacon, William Arthur.** "Toronto." *CGEJ* 2 (1931):335-75.
4680. **Dendy, William.** *Lost Toronto.* Toronto: OUP, 1978.
4681. _____. *Walking Tours of Old Toronto.* Toronto: Macmillan, 1978.
4682. **Denison, Merrill.** *Harvest Triumphant. The Story of Massey-Harris. A Footnote to Canadian History.* Toronto: M&S, 1948.
4683. _____. *The People's Power. The History of Ontario Hydro.* Toronto: M&S, 1960.
4684. **De Visser, John.** *Toronto.* Toronto: OUP, 1975.
4685. **De Volpi, C. P.** *Toronto: A Pictorial Record, 1813-1882.* Montreal: Dev-Sco, 1965.
4686. **Dhar, Meena.** "Emergence of Land Use Planning in Ontario: With Special Emphasis on Planning in the City of Toronto." M.A. thesis, Waterloo, 1980.
4687. **Dickson, George, and Adam, Graeme Mercer.** *A History of Upper Canada College, 1829-1892.* Toronto: Rowsell and Hutchinson, 1893.
4688. **Douglas, K.** "The Northern Irish Immigrants of Metropolitan Toronto." B.A. essay, Queen's (Belfast), 1971.
4689. **T. Eaton Co.** *The Story of a Store. A History of the T. Eaton Company Limited, from 1869 to the Present Day.* Toronto, 1932.
4690. **Eaton, Flora M.** *Memory's Wall.* Toronto: Clarke, Irwin, 1956.
4691. **Falconer, Robert.** "University Federation in Toronto." *Dal Rev* 3 (1923):279-85.
4692. **Filey, Michael.** *A Toronto Album: Glimpses of the City That Was.* Toronto: UTP, 1970.
4693. _____. *Toronto: Reflections of the Past.* Toronto: Nelson, Foster, and Scott, 1974.
4694. _____. *Toronto: The Way We Were: A Collection of Photos and Stories about North America's Greatest City.* Toronto: Nelson, Foster and Scott, 1974.
4695. _____. *Trillium and Toronto Island.* Toronto: Peter Martin, 1976.
4696. _____. "Toronto's 'Ex': The Ever-Young Centenarian." *York Pioneer* 73 (1978):1-5.
4697. _____. *Toronto City Life: Old and New.* Toronto: Nelson, Foster and Scott, 1979.
4698. _____; **Howard, R.;** and **Weyerstroth, N.** *"Passengers Must Not Ride on Fenders." A Look at Toronto: Its People, Its Places, Its Streetcars.* Toronto: Green Tree, 1974.
4699. **Fillmore, Stanley, and Newfeld, Frank.** *The Pleasure of the Game: A History of the Toronto Cricket, Skating and Curling Club, 1827-1977.* Toronto: Toronto Cricket, Skating and Curling Club, 1977.
4700. **Fleming, Marie.** *100 Years: Evolution of the Ontario College of Art.* Toronto: Art Gallery of Ontario, 1976.
4701. **French, William.** *A Most Unlikely Village: An Informal History of the Village of Forest Hill.* Forest Hill: Corporation of the Village of Forest Hill, 1964.
4702. **Friedman, S. G.** "Social Geography of Toronto's Public Schools." M.A. thesis, Toronto, 1979.
4703. **Gagan, David.** "The Historical Identity of the Denison Family of Toronto." CHA, *HP* (1971):124-37.
4704. _____. *The Denison Family of Toronto, 1792-1925.* Toronto: UTP, 1973.
4705. **Gillen, M.** *The Masseys. Founding Family.* Toronto: Ryerson, 1966.
4706. **Given, Robert A.** *The Story of Etobicoke.* Islington: Etobicoke Historical Society, 1973.
4707. **Glazebrook, G. P. de T.** *The Story of Toronto.* Toronto: UTP, 1971.
4708. **Greenhill, Ralph, and Gowans, Alan.** *The Face of Toronto.* Toronto: OUP, 1960.
4709. **Guillet, Edwin C.** *Toronto—From Trading Post to Great City.* Toronto: Ontario Pub. Co., 1934.
4710. _____. "Toronto's 150 Years." *CGEJ* 28 (1944):204-11.
4711. **Hambly, W. B.** "Cabbage Town." *York Pioneer* 64 (1969):33-44.
4712. **Hardy, Eric.** "Montreal and Toronto." In *Great Cities of the World,* edited by W. A. Robson and D. E. Regan, pp. 985-1038. London: Allen and Unwin, 1972.

4713. **Harney, Robert F.** "A Note on Sources in Urban and Immigrant History [in Toronto]." *CES* 9, no. 1 (1977):60-76.
4714. _____, **and Troper, Harold.** *Immigrants: A Portrait of the Urban Experience.* Toronto: Van Nostrand Reinhold, 1975.
4715. _____, eds. "Immigrants in the City." Special Issue. *CES* 9, no. 1 (1977):1-76.
4716. **Hart, Patricia W.** *Pioneer Life in North York: A History of the Borough.* Toronto: General Publishing, 1968.
4717. **Henderson, J.L.H.** "The Founding of Trinity College, Toronto." *OH* 44 (1952):7-14.
4718. **Henderson, John,** ed. *The Book of Toronto.* Toronto: Southern Press, 1926.
4719. **Heyes, Esther.** *Etobicoke: From Furrow to Borough.* Etobicoke: Borough of Etobicoke Civic Centre, 1974.
4720. **Hill, Daniel.** "Negroes in Toronto." Ph.D. thesis, Toronto, 1960.
4721. **Hooper, N. A.** "Toronto: A Study in Urban Geography." M.A. thesis, Toronto, 1941.
4722. **James, R. Scott.** "The City of Toronto Archives." *UHR* 3-73 (February 1974):2-9.
4723. **Jameson, Spruce.** "One Hundred Years Ago and Since." *Can Bank* 52 (1945):102-37.
4724. **Jarvis, S.** "Sketch of the History of Toronto." *Ont Lib Rev* 35 (1951):5-7.
4725. **Jolliffe, R.** "A History of the Children's Aid Society of Toronto, 1891-1947." M.S.W. thesis, Toronto, 1952.
4726. **Jones, Elwood, and McCalla, Douglas.** "Toronto Waterworks, 1840-77: Continuity and Change in Nineteenth-Century Toronto Politics." *CHR* 60 (1979):300-323.
4727. **Kayfetz, Ben.** "The Evolution of the Jewish Community in Toronto." In *A People and Its Faith,* edited by A. Rose, pp. 14-29. Toronto: UTP, 1959.
4728. **Kelner, M.** "The Elite Structure of Toronto: Ethnic Composition and Patterns of Recruitment." M.A. thesis, Toronto, 1969.
4729. **Kerr, Donald P., and Spelt, Jacob.** "Some Aspects of Industrial Location in Southern Ontario." *Can Geogr* 15 (1960):12-25.
4730. _____. *The Changing Face of Toronto: A Study in Urban Geography.* Ottawa: Queen's Printer, 1965.
4731. _____. "The Growth of Toronto." In *Canada's Changing Geography,* edited by R. L. Gentilcore, pp. 163-81. Scarborough: Prentice-Hall, 1967.
4732. **Kilbourn, William,** ed. *The Toronto Book: An Anthology of Writings Past and Present.* Toronto: Macmillan, 1976.
4733. **Konrad, Victor A.** "The Past in the Present: Pre-Historical Resource Appraisal in Metropolitan Toronto." Ph.D. thesis, McMaster, 1978.
4734. **Kyte, E. C.,** ed. *Old Toronto: A Selection of Excerpts from "Landmarks of Toronto" by John Ross Robertson.* Toronto: Macmillan, 1978.
4735. **Lachapelle, Claire.** *La vie française à Toronto.* Documents historique no. 13. Sudbury: Société-historique du Nouvel-Ontario, 1974.
4736. **Lamont, G.** *Toronto and York County: A Sample Study.* Toronto: Dent, 1970.
4737. **Lappin, Adah.** *The Story of the Jewish Community of Toronto, 1856-1957.* Toronto: Bureau of Jewish Education, 1957.
4738. **Lorimer, James.** *The Ex: A Picture History of the Canadian National Exhibition.* Toronto: James Lewis and Samuel, 1973.
4739. _____, **and Phillips, M.** *Working People: Life in a Downtown City Neighbourhood.* Toronto: James Lewis and Samuel, 1971.
4740. **Macnab, Alan.** "The Toronto Dominion Bank." *Can Paper Money J* 12 (1976):84-88.
4741. **MacNab, John E.** "Toronto's Industrial Growth to 1891." *OH* 47 (1955):59-80.
4742. **Macpherson, M. E.** *Shopkeepers to a Nation. The Eatons.* Toronto: M&S, 1963.
4743. **Makler, Anita C.** "Coloured Brick in Yorkville." *J Can Art Hist* 4 (1977-78):98-110.
4744. **Mann, W. E.,** ed. *The Underside of Toronto.* Toronto: M&S, 1970.

4745. **Martin, G. M.** "Toronto, étude de population urbaine." Thèse de Ph.D., Paris, 1972.
4746. **Martyn, Lucy B.** *Toronto: 100 Years of Grandeur: The Inside Stories of Toronto's Great Homes and the People Who Lived There.* Toronto: Pagurian, 1978.
4747. _____. *Aristocratic Toronto: 19th Century Grandeur.* Toronto: Gage, 1979.
4748. **Massey-Harris Co.** *An Historical Sketch, 1847-1920.* Toronto, 1920.
4749. **Meirovich, Harvey.** "The Rise and Decline of a Toronto Synagogue: Congregation Beth Am." *Can Jewish Historical Society J* 1 (1977):97-113.
4750. **Meyer, François.** "A Toronto. Cinquante ans de Bauhaus." *Vie des arts* 57 (hiver 1969-70):29-33.
4751. **Middleton, Jesse Edgar.** *The Municipality of Toronto: A History.* 3 vols. Toronto: Dominion, 1923.
4752. _____. *Toronto's 100 Years.* Toronto: Centennial Committee [Southam Press], 1934.
4753. **Mika, Nick, and Mika, Helma.** *Toronto: Magnificent City.* Belleville: Mika, 1967.
4754. **Mulvany, C. Pelham.** *Toronto, Past and Present.* 1884. Reprint. Toronto: Coles, 1971.
4755. **Myers, Jay.** *The Great Canadian Road: A History of Yonge Street.* Toronto: Red Rock Publishing, 1977.
4756. **Nagata, Judith.** "Adaptation and Integration of Greek Working Class Immigrants in the City of Toronto, Canada: A Situational Approach." *International Migration Rev* 4 (1969):44-70.
4757. **Neal, Carolyn.** *Eden Smith, Architect, 1858-1949.* Toronto: Architectural Conservancy of Ontario, 1976.
4758. **Neilson, W. A.** "Upper Canada College." *Can Mag* 1 (1893):451-59.
4759. *North York in Pictures, 1889-1912.* Toronto: Toronto Public Library, 1974.
4760. **O'Neill, Nora.** "A Partial History of the Royal Alexandra Theatre, Toronto, 1907-1939." Ph.D. thesis, Louisana State, 1976.
4761. **Ontario Educational Communications Authority.** *Landmarks: Early Canadian Architecture in Toronto.* Toronto: OECA, 1971.
4762. **Parks, Judith.** "The Reverend Henry Scadding, 1813-1901. An English Victorian in Canada." M.A. thesis, Guelph, 1969.
4763. **Pearson, W. H.** *Recollections of Toronto of Old.* Toronto: Briggs, 1914.
4764. **Petroff, Lillian.** *The Macedonian Community in Toronto to 1930: Women and Emigration.* Canadian Women's History Series no. 5. Toronto: OISE, 1977.
4765. _____. "Macedonians: From Village to City." *CES* 9, no. 1 (1977):29-41.
4766. _____. "Macedonians in Toronto: From Encampment to Settlement." *UHR* 2-78 (October 1978):58-73.
4767. **Pirie, Margaret C.** "Patterns of Mobility and Assimilation: A Study of the Toronto Jewish Community." Ph.D. thesis, Yale, 1957.
4768. **Pitsula, James.** "The Emergence of Social Work in Toronto." *J Can St* 14, no. 1 (1979):35-42.
4769. **Price, Gifford A.** "A History of the Ontario Hospital, Toronto." M.S.W. thesis, Toronto, 1950.
4770. **Punter, J. V.** "Urbanities in the Country Side—Case Studies of the Impact of Exurban Development on the Landscape in the Toronto-Centred Region." Ph.D. thesis, Toronto, 1974.
4771. **Purdy, A. W.** "Toronto." *Habitat* 10, nos. 3-6 (1967):76-81.
4772. **Quinn, George.** "The Impact of European Immigration on the Elementary Schools of Central Toronto, 1815-1915." M.A. thesis, Toronto, 1968.
4773. **Reed, T. A.** "Buildings That Tell of Toronto's Development in Construction." *ENCR* 48 (1934):578-83.
4774. _____. "Toronto's Early Architects." *JRAIC* 27 (1950):46-51.
4775. _____, ed. *A History of the University of Trinity College, Toronto, 1852-1952.* Toronto: UTP, 1952.

4776. **Reitsma, H. J. A.** "North York: The Development of a Suburb." M.A. thesis, Toronto, 1962.
4777. **Roberts, V. M.** "Toronto Harbour." *CGEJ* 15 (1937):87-104.
4778. **Roberts, William.** *Houses of Old Toronto.* Toronto: Pagurian, 1977.
4779. **Robertson, John Ross, ed.** *Landmarks of Toronto.* 6 vols. Toronto: J. R. Robertson, 1894-1914. Vols. 1 and 3 Reprinted by Mika Publishing, Belleville, 1976 and 1978.
4780. **Robinson, Percy J.** "More about Toronto." *OH* (1953):123-27.
4781. **Ross, Alexander M.** *Toronto Guidebook.* Toronto: Greey de Pencier, 1979.
4781A. **Ross, M. G.** "The Toronto Y.M.C.A. in a Changing Community, 1864-1940." M.A. thesis, Toronto, 1947.
4782. **Ross, Victor A., and Trigge, A. St. L.** *History of the Canadian Bank of Commerce, with an Account of Other Banks Which Now Form Part of Its Organization.* Vols. 1 and 2. Toronto: OUP, 1921, 1922; Vol. 3. Toronto: Canadian Bank of Commerce, 1934.
4783. **Scadding, Henry.** "Toronto of Old: A Series of Collections and Recollections." *Can J Industry, Science, and Art* 10 (1869):149-74.
4784. _____. *Toronto of Old.* Abridged and edited by F. H. Armstrong. Toronto: OUP, 1966.
4785. _____, **and Dent, Charles.** *Toronto Past and Present.* Toronto: Hunter Rose, 1884.
4786. **Schull, J. J.** *100 Years of Banking in Canada, a History of the Toronto-Dominon Bank.* Toronto: Copp Clark, 1948.
4787. **Shapiro, Linda, ed.** *Yesterday's Toronto.* Toronto: Coles, 1979.
4788. **Simmons, James W., and Bourne, L. S.** "Toronto: Focus of Growth and Change." In #3475, pp. 83-106.
4789. **Skelton, O. D.** *The Dominion Bank, 1871-1921. Fifty Years of Banking Service.* Toronto: Dominion Bank, 1922.
4790. **Slaight, A., ed.** *Exploring Toronto.* Toronto: Toronto Chapter of Architects, 1972.
4791. **Smith, Elspeth.** *Recording Toronto: A Catalogue of Selected Pictures of Early Building and Street Scenes in the Town of York and the City of Toronto from the John Ross Robertson Historical Collection and Other Picture Collections of the Toronto Libraries.* Toronto: Toronto Public Libraries, 1960.
4792. **Souster, R.** "My Two Torontos." *Habitat* 10, nos. 3-6 (1967):74-75.
4793. **Speisman, Stephen.** *The Jews of Toronto: A History to 1937.* Toronto: M&S, 1979.
4794. **Spelt, Jacob.** *Toronto.* Toronto: Collier-Macmillan, 1973.
4795. **Stanford, G. H.** *To Serve the Community: The Story of Toronto's Board of Trade.* Toronto: UTP, 1974.
4796. **Stephenson, William.** *The Store That Timothy Built.* Toronto: M&S, 1969.
4797. **Tancock, Elizabeth.** "North Toronto's Past." *York Pioneer* 72 (1977):35-36; 73 (1977):18-24; 73 (1978):29-31.
4798. **Teefy, L.** "Historical Notes on Yonge Street." *OHS, PR* 5 (1904):53-60.
4799. **Timberlake, J.** *Illustrated Toronto. Past and Present.* Toronto: Gross, 1877.
4800. **Toronto Area Archivists Group.** *Guide to Archives in the Toronto Area.* Toronto: Toronto Area Archivists Group, 1975.
4801. **Toronto Board of Education.** *Centennial Story. The Board of Education for the City of Toronto, 1850-1950.* Toronto: Nelson, 1950.
4802. **Toronto City Planning Board.** *A Bibliography of Major Planning Publications: 1942-1977.* Toronto: Information Services, City of Toronto Planning Board, 1977.
4803. **Toronto Harbour Commissioners.** *The Port and Harbour of Toronto, 1834-1934.* Toronto: Hunter Rose, 1934.
4804. **Toronto Transit Commission.** *Transit in Toronto, 1849-1967.* Toronto, 1967.
4805. **Toronto Transportation Commission.** *Wheels of Progress. A Story of the Development of Toronto and Its Public Transportation Services.* 5th ed. Toronto, 1953.

4806. **Troper, Harold.** "Images of the 'Foreigner' in Toronto, 1900-1930: A Report." *UHR* 2-75 (October 1975):1-8.
4807. **Tucker, F. J., comp.** *75th Birthday, 1843-1923. The Consumers' Gas Company of Toronto.* Toronto: Consumers' Gas, 1923.
4808. **Utting, Gerald.** *Toronto the Good: An Album of Colonial Hogtown.* Toronto: Macmillan, 1979.
4809. **Vass, B.** *Toronto: A Photo Study of Urban Development.* Toronto: McGraw-Hill Ryerson, 1971.
4810. **Venditti, M. P.** "The Italian Ethnic Community of Metropolitan Toronto: A Case in Intra-Urban Network." M.A. thesis, York, 1975.
4811. **Walker, E. K.** *The Story of the Women Teachers' Association of Toronto.* Vol. 2: *1931-1963.* Toronto: Copp Clark, 1963.
4812. **Walker, Frank Norman.** *Sketches of Old Toronto.* Don Mills: Longmans, 1965.
4813. **Wallace, Archer.** "History of Socialism in Toronto." M.A. thesis, Western Ontario, 1917.
4814. **Wallace, Elisabeth.** "The Grange and Its Occupants: The Boultons and Goldwin Smith." *York Pioneer* 64 (1969):56-68.
4815. **Wallace, J. K.** "A Spatial Analysis of Crime Distributions in Metropolitan Toronto." M.A. thesis, York, 1975.
4816. **Wallace, W. S.** *A History of the University of Toronto, 1827-1927.* Toronto: University of Toronto, 1927.
4817. **Weller, J. P.** "The Evolution of Toronto: A Geographic Study." M.A. thesis, Ohio State, 1963.
4818. **West, Bruce.** *Toronto.* Toronto: Doubleday, 1979.
4819. **White, William Alan.** "Chicago and Toronto: A Comparative Study in Early Growth." Ph.D. thesis, Northwestern, 1974.
4820. **Whiteside, J.** "The Toronto Stock Exchange to 1900: Its Membership and the Development of the Share Market." M.A. thesis, Trent, 1979.
4821. **Wilson, Robert.** "Early Public Health in Toronto." *PHEJ* 14 (1923):210-24.
4822. **Woadden, A. R. N.** "The Growth of Toronto." *York Pioneer* 67 (1972):61-68.
4823. **Woodsworth, James Shaver.** "Toronto." *Can For* 19 (1940):352.
4824. **Wright, C. H. C.** "The University of Toronto." *JRAIC* 2 (1925):5-16.
4825. **Yeigh, Frank.** "Historic Landmarks of Toronto." *Westminster* 4 (1904):9-14.
4826. **Young, A. H.** "Trinity University, Toronto." *Can Mag* 7 (1896):395-405.
4827. **Young, W. H.** *Upper Canada College, Toronto, 1829-1929.* Toronto, 1929.
4828. **Zerker, Sally F.** "A History of the Toronto Typographical Union, 1832-1925." Ph.D. thesis, Toronto, 1972.
4829. _____. "The Development of Collective Bargaining in the Toronto Printing Industry in the Nineteenth Century." *Industrial Relations* 30 (1975):83-96.
4830. **Zucchi, John.** "*Paesani* in a Toronto Neighbourhood: The Italian Immigrants of the 'Ward,' 1870-1949." M.A. thesis, Toronto, 1979.

b. *Pre-1850*

4831. **Acheson, T. W.** "John Baldwin: Portrait of a Colonial Entrepreneur." *OH* 61 (1969):153-66.
4832. _____. "The Nature and Structure of York Commerce in the 1820s." *CHR* 50 (1969):406-28.
4833. **Andre, John.** *William Berczy: Co-Founder of Toronto.* Toronto: Borough of York, 1967.
4834. _____. *Infant Toronto as Simcoe's Folly.* Toronto: Centennial Press, 1971.

4835. **Angrave, John.** "John Strachan and Scottish Influence in the Character of King's College, York, 1827." *J Can St* 11 (1976):60-68.
4836. **Armstrong, Frederick H.** "The First Great Fire of Toronto, 1849." *OH* 53 (1961):201-21.
4837. ———. "The Rebuilding of Toronto after the Great Fire of 1849." *OH* 53 (1961):233-50.
4838. ———. "The Carfrae Family: A Study in Early Toronto Toryism." *OH* 54 (1962):161-81.
4839. ———. "Toronto in Transition: The Emergence of a City, 1828-1838." Ph.D. thesis, Toronto, 1965.
4840. ———. "Metropolitanism and Toronto Re-examined, 1825-1850." In #85, pp. 37-50.
4841. ———. "Toronto in 1834." *Can Geogr* 10 (1966):172-83.
4842. ———. "Reformer as Capitalist: William Lyon Mackenzie and the Printers' Strike of 1836." *OH* 59 (1967):187-96.
4843. ———. "William Lyon Mackenzie, First Mayor of Toronto: A Study of a Critic in Power." *CHR* 48 (1967):309-31.
4844. ———. "The Toronto Directories and the Negro Community in the Late 1840s." *OH* 61 (1969):111-19.
4845. ———. "Capt. Hugh Richardson: First Harbour Master of Toronto." *Inland Seas* 31 (1975):34-42, 49-50.
4846. **Bains, Yashdip Singh.** "Theatre and Society in Early Nineteenth Century Toronto." *Nineteenth Century Theatre Research* 3 (1975):83-96.
4847. **Berchem, F. R.** *The Yonge Street Story: 1793-1860*. Toronto: McGraw-Hill, Ryerson, 1977.
4848. **Burns, Florence.** *William Berczy*. Don Mills: Fitzhenry and Whiteside, 1977.
4849. **Burns, R. J.** "God's Chosen People: The Origins of Toronto Society." CHA, *HP* (1973):213-28.
4850. ———. "The First Elite of Toronto: An Examination of the Genesis, Consolidation and Duration of Power in an Emerging Colonial Society." Ph.D. thesis, Western Ontario, 1976.
4851. **Careless, J. M. S.** *Brown of the Globe*. Vol. 1: *The Voice of Upper Canada*. Toronto: Macmillan, 1959.
4852. **Cross, Michael S.** "The Stormy History of the York Roads, 1833-1865." *OH* 54 (1962):1-24.
4853. **Dyster, Barrie.** "Toronto, 1840-1860: Making It in a British Protestant Town." Ph.D. thesis, Toronto, 1970.
4854. **Ewart, Alan C., and Jarvis, J.** "Personnel of the Family Compact, 1791-1841." *CHR* 7 (1926):209-26.
4855. **Firth, Edith G.** "Alexander Wood, Merchant of York." *York Pioneer* 53 (1958):5-29.
4856. ———, ed. *Early Toronto Newspapers, 1793-1867*. Toronto: Baxter Pub. Co. in co-operation with the Toronto Public Library, 1961.
4857. ———, ed. *The Town of York, 1793-1815: A Collection of Documents of Early Toronto*. Toronto: Champlain Society, Ontario Series, vol. 5, 1962.
4858. ———, ed. *The Town of York, 1815-1934: A Further Collection of Documents of Early Toronto*. Toronto: Champlain Society, Ontario Series, vol. 8, 1966.
4859. **Guillet, Edwin C.** "Pioneer Banking in Ontario—The Bank of Upper Canada, 1822-1826." *Can Paper Money J* 14 (1978):9-18.
4860. **Hathway, Ernest Jackson.** "Early Schools of Toronto." OHS, *PR* 23 (1926):312-27.
4861. ———. *Jesse Ketchum and His Times*. Toronto: M&S, 1929.
4862. ———. *The Story of the Old Fort at Toronto*. Toronto: Macmillan, 1934.
4863. **Hayward, Robert J.** "Content Analysis in Historical Geography: A Case Study in Immigration in Toronto in 1847." M.A. thesis, Queen's, 1973.
4864. ———, **and Osborne, Brian S.** "The British Colonist and the Immigration to Toronto of 1847: A Content Analysis Approach to Newspaper Research in Historical Geography." *Can Geogr* 17 (1973):391-402.

4865. Hill, Daniel. "Negroes in Toronto, 1793-1865." *OH* 55 (1963):73-91.
4866. Hounson, Erik W. *Toronto in 1810.* Toronto: Ryerson, 1970.
4867. Johnson, J. K. "The Social Composition of the Toronto Bank Guards, 1837-1838." *OH* 64 (1972):95-104.
4868. _____. "The U.C. Club and the Upper Canadian Elite, 1837-1840." *OH* 69 (1977):151-68.
4869. Johnson, Leo A. "Land Policy, Population Growth and Social Structure in the Home District, 1793-1851." *OH* 63 (1971):41-60.
4870. Jones, James Edmund. *Pioneer Crimes and Punishments in Toronto and the Home District.* Toronto: Morang, 1924.
4871. Jukes, Mary. *A Visit to Early Toronto.* Toronto: Architectural Conservancy of Toronto, 1965.
4872. Kerr, W. B. "The Occupation of York (Toronto), 1813." *CHR* 5 (1924):9-21.
4873. Kilbourn, William. *The Firebrand: William Lyon Mackenzie and the Rebellion in Upper Canada.* Toronto: Clarke, Irwin, 1964.
4874. Malone, Tom. "Jesse Ketchum II in Upper Canada: The Birthright of Esau." M.A. thesis, Guelph, 1977.
4875. Miller, Audrey S. "Yonge Street Politics, 1828 to 1832." *OH* 62 (1970):101-18.
4876. _____, ed. *The Journals of Mary O'Brien, 1828 to 1838.* Toronto: Macmillan, 1968.
4877. O'Neill, Patrick B. "A History of Theatrical Activity in Toronto: From Its Beginnings to 1858." Ph.D. thesis, Louisiana, 1973.
4878. Robinson, Percy J. *Toronto during the French Régime: A History of the Toronto Region from Brulé to Simcoe, 1615-1793.* Toronto: Ryerson, 1933.
4879. _____. "Yonge Street and the North West Company." *CHR* 24 (1943):253-65.
4880. Romney, Paul. "The Ordeal of William Higgins." *OH* 67 (1975):69-89.
4881. _____. "William Lyon Mackenzie as Mayor of Toronto." *CHR* 56 (1975):416-36.
4882. Saunders, Audrey Murton. "Studies in Yonge Street Settlement Based on the O'Brien Diary." M.A. thesis, Toronto, 1944.
4883. Scadding, Henry. *Memories of Four Decades of York, Upper Canada.* Toronto: Hunter Rose, 1884.
4884. Shea, D. S. "The Irish Immigrant Adjustment to Toronto, 1840-1860." CCHA, *Study Sessions* 39 (1972):53-60.
4885. Thompson, Austin S. *Spadina: A Story of Old Toronto.* Toronto: Pagurian, 1975.
4886. Vaughan, Carol L. "The Bank of Upper Canada in Politics, 1817-1840." *OH* 60 (1968):185-204.

c. 1850-1921

4887. Aikens, J. R. "The Rival Operas: Toronto Theatre, 1874-84." Ph.D. thesis, Toronto, 1975.
4888. Amyot, John A. "Water Conditions in Toronto—A Plea for Filtration." *Can J Medicine and Surgery* 21 (1907):287-91.
4889. Armstrong, Christopher, and Nelles, H. V. *The Revenge of the Methodist Bicycle Company: Sunday Streetcars and Municipal Reform in Toronto, 1888-1897.* Toronto: Peter Martin, 1977.
4890. Armstrong, Frederick H. "The Second Great Fire of Toronto, 19-20 April, 1904." *OH* 70 (1978):39-62.
4891. Arnold, B. J. "The Street Railway Situation in Toronto." Canadian Club of Toronto, *Proceedings* 11 (1913):94-115.
4892. Ashley, S. M. "The Salvation Army in Toronto, 1882-1896." M.A. thesis, Guelph, 1969.

4893. **Bammen, Haley P.** "Patterns of School Attendance in Toronto, 1844-1878: Some Spatial Considerations." *Hist Educ Q* 12 (1972):381-410.
4894. **Banks, Margaret A.** "Toronto Opinion of French Canada during the Laurier Regime, 1896-1911." M.A. thesis, Toronto, 1950.
4895. **Bator, Paul A.** " 'Saving Lives on the Wholesale Plan': Public Health Reform in the City of Toronto, 1900-1930." Ph.D. thesis, Toronto, 1979.
4896. _____. " 'The Struggle to Raise the Lower Classes': Public Health Reform and the Problem of Poverty in Toronto, 1910-1921." *J Can St* 14, no. 1 (1979): 43-49.
4897. **Beer, G. Frank.** "Work of the Toronto Housing Company." In Canada, Commission of Conservation, *Report of the Fifth Annual Meeting Held at Ottawa, January 1914*, pp. 116-20. Toronto: Bryant, 1914.
4898. _____. "Housing Experience in Toronto." *Cn L* 3, no. 2 (1917):25-28.
4899. **Bell, Margaret.** "Toronto's Melting Pot." *Can Mag* 41 (1913):234-42.
4900. **Boultbee, Horace.** "Toronto: A City of Homes." *Can Mag* 32 (1909):299-306.
4901. **Bowker, Alan.** "Truly Useful Men: Maurice Hutton, George Wrong, James Mavor and the University of Toronto, 1880-1927." Ph.D. thesis, Toronto, 1975.
4902. **Bruce, J.** "The Toronto *Globe* and the Manpower Problem, 1914-1917." M.A. thesis, Queen's, 1967.
4903. **Campbell, K.** "Residential Mobility in Toronto, 1880-1910." M.A. thesis, Toronto, 1971.
4904. **Careless, J. M. S.** "The Toronto Globe and Agrarian Radicalism, 1850-1867." *CHR* 29 (1948):14-39.
4905. _____. *Brown of the Globe*. Vol. 2: *Statesman of Confederation, 1860-1880*. Toronto: Macmillan, 1963.
4906. **Carter-Edwards, Dennis.** "Toronto in the 1890s: A Decade of Challenge and Response." M.A. thesis, British Columbia, 1973.
4907. **Clark, C. A.** *Of Toronto the Good: A Social Study* 1898. Reprint. Toronto: Coles, 1970.
4908. **Clark, L. H.** "Putting a New Front on Toronto." *Can Mag* 42 (1913):205-15.
4909. **Clark, L. J.** "Formation of Toronto Island." *Proc Can Institute* 1 (1890):239-45.
4910. **Cleveland, F. A.** "Toronto's Financial Administration." Canadian Club of Toronto, *Proceedings* 12 (1914):211-26.
4911. **Coatsworth, E.** "Toronto's Government." League for American Municipalities, *Bulletin* 9 (February 1908):52-54.
4912. **Colgate, William.** *The Toronto Art Students' League 1886-1904*. Toronto: Ryerson, 1954.
4913. **Coombs, David Grosvenor.** "Changes in the Occupational Structure of Toronto, 1861-1911." M.A. thesis, York, 1975.
4914. _____. "The Emergence of a White Collar Workforce in Toronto, 1895-1911." Ph.D. thesis, York, 1978.
4915. **Craik, W. A.** "The Linking of Montreal and Toronto." *Can Mag* 28 (1906):40-44.
4916. **Davis, Donald F.** "Mass Transit and Private Ownership: An Alternative Perspective on the Case of Toronto." *UHR* 3-78 (February 1979):60-98.
4917. **Denison, S. A.** *Memoirs of a Police Magistrate*. Toronto: Best, 1927.
4918. **Doucet, Michael J.** "Mass Transit and the Failure of Private Ownership: The Case of Toronto." *UHR* 3-77 (February 1978):3-33.
4919. **T. Eaton Co.** *Golden Jubilee 1869-1919. A Book to Commemorate the Fiftieth Anniversary of the T. Eaton Co., Ltd*. Toronto: 1919.
4920. **Feeley, James.** "A Library in Crisis. The University of Toronto Library, 1890-1892." *OH* 62 (1971):220-34.
4921. **Forsey, Eugene A.** "The Toronto Trades Assembly, 1871-1878." *Canadian Labour* 10, no. 6 (1965):17-19. [continued in subsequent issues].
4922. **Galvin, M. A.** "The Jubilee Riots in Toronto, 1875." CCHA, *Report* 26 (1959):93-107.

4923. Goheen, Peter G. *Victorian Toronto, 1850-1900: Pattern and Process of Growth.* Chicago: University of Chicago, Dept. of Geography, Research Paper no. 127, 1970.

4924. Grant, Mrs. W. F. "Bygone Days in Toronto." *Can Mag* 42 (1914): 311-15.

4925. Gregory, W. D. "Municipal Toronto." *Outlook* 58 (1898):351-57.

4926. Hann, Russell. "Brainworkers and the Knights of Labor: E. E. Sheppard, Phillips Thompson, and the Toronto *News*, 1883-1887." In *Essays in Canadian Working Class History,* edited by Gregory S. Kealey and Peter Warrian, pp. 35-57. Toronto: M&S, 1976.

4927. Harney, Robert F. "Chiaroscuro: Italians in Toronto, 1885-1915." *Italian Americana* 1 (Spring 1975):142-67.

4928. _____. "The Commerce of Migration [Italians in Toronto]." *CES* 9, no. 1 (1977):42-53.

4929. _____. "Boarding and Belonging: Thoughts on Sojourner Institutions." *UHR* 2-78 (October 1978):8-37.

4930. Harrington, G. M. "Toronto and Its Early Theatrical Entertainments." *Can Mon* 8 (1882):600-613.

4931. Hocken, H. C. "Hydro-Electric System in Toronto." *Ann Am Ac Pol Soc Sci* 57 (1915):246-53.

4931A. Homel, Gene H. "James Simpson and the Origins of Canadian Social Democracy (Socialism in Toronto, 1910-1914)." Ph.D. thesis, Toronto, 1978.

4932. Houston, Susan E. "Social Reform and Education: The Issue of Compulsory Schooling, Toronto, 1851-1871." In *Egerton Ryerson and His Times,* edited by Neil McDonald and Alf Chaiton, pp. 254-76. Toronto: Macmillan, 1978.

4933. Jarrett, Gordon. *Metropolitan Toronto, Past and Present: Serial Photos.* Willowdale: Kirkup, 1973.

4934. Jarvis, Eric. "Municipal Compensation Cases: Toronto in the 1860s." *UHR* 3-76 (February 1977):14-22.

4935. _____. "Mid-Victorian Toronto: A Social and Administrative History, 1857-1873." Ph.D. thesis, Western Ontario, 1978.

4936. Johnston, Charles M. *McMaster University.* Vol. 1: *The Toronto Years.* Toronto: UTP, 1976.

4937. Johnston, Hugh. *A Merchant Prince. Life of the Hon. Senator John Macdonald.* Toronto: University of Toronto Library, 1893.

4938. Kealey, Gregory S. "Artisans Respond to Industrialism: Shoemakers, Shoe Factories and the Knights of St. Crispin in Toronto." *CHA, HP* (1973):137-57.

4939. _____. *Hogtown: Working Class Toronto at the Turn of the Century.* Toronto: New Hogtown Press, 1974.

4940. _____. " 'The Honest Workingman' and Workers' Control: The Experience of Toronto Skilled Workers, 1860-1892." *Labour* 1 (1976):32-68.

4941. _____. "The Orange Order in Toronto: Religious Riot and the Working Class." In *Essays in Canadian Working Class History,* edited by Gregory S. Kealey and Peter Warrian, pp. 13-34. Toronto: M&S, 1976.

4942. _____. *Toronto Workers Respond to Industrial Capitalism, 1867-1892.* Toronto: UTP, 1980.

4943. Kelso, J. J. "The Play Spirit and Playgrounds in Toronto." Empire Club of Canada, Toronto, *Addresses* (1907-1908):178-87.

4944. Klein, Alice, and Roberts, David Wayne. "Beseiged Innocence: The 'Problem' and Problems of Working Women, Toronto, 1896-1914." In *Women at Work: Ontario, 1850-1930,* edited by Janice Acton, Penny Goldsmith, and Bonnie Shepard, pp. 211-60. Toronto: Canadian Women's Educational Press, 1974.

4945. Knappe, C. F. "The Development of Planning in Toronto, 1893-1922: A Survey." M.A. thesis, Toronto, 1974.

4946. Kutcher, Stan. "J. W. Bengough and the Millenium in Hogtown: A Study of Motivation in Urban Reform." *UHR* 2-76 (October 1976):30-49.

4947. **Latimer, Elspeth A.** "Methods of Child Care as Reflected in the Infants Home of Toronto, 1875-1920." M.S.W. thesis, Toronto, 1953.
4948. **Leach, Edith E.** "Board and Lodging Conditions in Toronto." *To Pl Cn L* 6, no. 2 (1920):41-44.
4949. **Lewis, Victor George.** "Earlscourt, Toronto: A Descriptive, Historical, and Interpretive Study in Urban Class Development." M.A. thesis, Toronto, 1920.
4950. **Lighthall, William D.** "Toronto and Town Planning." Empire Club of Canada, *Speeches* 8 (1910-11):232-37.
4951. **Lindstrom-Best, Varpu.** *The Finnish Immigrant Community of Toronto, 1887-1913*. Occasional Papers in Ethnic and Immigration Studies. Toronto: Multicultural History Society of Ontario, 1979.
4952. **Lochhead, Douglas.** "John Ross Robertson, Uncommon Publisher for the Common Reader: His First Years as a Toronto Book Publisher." *J Can St* 11 (1976):19-26.
4953. **Long, W. A.** "Attitudes toward the Poor in Toronto, 1880-1911." M.A. thesis, Waterloo, 1977.
4954. **Looy, Anthony J.** "The Toronto *Daily Globe* and Church-State Relations, 1869-1878." M.A. thesis, Queen's, 1971.
4955. **McCalla, Douglas.** "The Commercial Politics of the Toronto Board of Trade, 1850-1860." *CHR* 50 (1969):51-67.
4956. **McGee, Robert.** "The Toronto Irish Catholic Press and Fenianism, 1863-1866." M.A. thesis, Ottawa, 1969.
4957. **McKenzie, B. A.** "The Impact of Social Change on the Organization of Welfare Services in Ontario, 1891-1921: Care of the Poor in Toronto." M.S.W. thesis, Toronto, 1966.
4958. **Maclean, W. F.** "A Greater Toronto." Empire Club of Canada, *Speeches* 6 (1907-1908):81-90.
4959. **McMann, Robert.** " 'A Kind of Monument to a Time When the World Ran on Steel Rails': Union Station, Railways and the City." In *The Open Gate, Toronto Union Station*, edited by Richard Bébout, pp. 21-52. Toronto: Peter Martin, 1972.
4960. **Mallon, Mary F.** "Musical Toronto in the Eighteen Nineties." *York Pioneer* 73 (1978):1-9.
4961. **Masters, D. C.** "Toronto vs. Montreal: The Struggle for Financial Hegemony." *CHR* 22 (1941):133-46.
4962. _____. *The Rise of Toronto, 1850-1890*. Toronto: UTP, 1947.
4963. **Mellen, Frances N.** "The Development of the Toronto Waterfront during the Railway Expansion Era, 1850-1912." Ph.D. thesis, Toronto, 1974.
4964. **Morrison, Terrence R.** "The Child and Urban Social Reform in Late Nineteenth-Century Toronto." Ph.D. thesis, Toronto, 1971.
4965. **Morton, Desmond.** *Mayor Howland: The Citizens' Candidate*. Toronto: Hakkert, 1973.
4966. **Naismith, George.** *Timothy Eaton*. Toronto: M&S, 1923.
4967. **Nicolson, Murray.** "The Irish Catholics and Their Church in Victorian Toronto, 1850-1900." Ph.D. thesis, Guelph, 1980.
4968. **Patterson, N.** "A Typical Canadian City: Historical Sketch of the City of Toronto." *Can Mag* 22 (1903):107-20.
4969. _____. "Toronto's Great Fire." *Can Mag* 23 (1904):128-35.
4970. **Paupst, K.** "A Note on Anti-Chinese Sentiment in Toronto before the First World War." *CES* 9, no. 1 (1977):54-59.
4971. **Pitsula, James.** "The Relief of Poverty in Toronto, 1880-1930." Ph.D. thesis, York, 1979.
4972. **Piva, Michael J.** *The Condition of the Working Class in Toronto, 1900-1921*. Ottawa: University of Ottawa Press, 1979.
4973. _____. "The Toronto District Labour Council and Independent Political Action: Factionalism and Frustration, 1900-1921." *Labour* 4 (1979):115-30.

4974. **Poulton, Ron.** *The Paper Tyrant: John Ross Robertson of the Toronto Telegram.* Toronto: Clarke, Irwin, 1971.
4975. **Purseley, Louis H.** *Street Railways of Toronto, 1861-1921.* Los Angeles: Electric Railway Publ., 1958.
4976. **Reed, T. A.** "The Observatory at Toronto, 1840-1908." *CGEJ* 55 (1957):234-43.
4977. **Richardson, Douglas,** ed. *Beaux Arts Toronto, Permanence and Change.* Toronto: Toronto Historical Board, 1973.
4978. **Risk, Margaret McNeill.** "A Study of the Origins and Development of Public Health Nursing in Toronto, 1890-1918." M.Sc. thesis, Toronto, 1973.
4979. **Roberts, David Wayne.** "Artisans, Aristocrats and Handymen: Politics and Unionism among Toronto Skilled Building Trades Workers, 1896-1914." *Labour* 1 (1976):92-121.
4980. _____. *Honest Womanhood: Feminism, Femininity, and Class Consciousness among Toronto Working Women, 1893-1914.* Toronto: New Hogtown Press, 1976.
4981. _____. "The Last Artisans: Toronto Printers, 1896-1914." In *Essays in Canadian Working Class History,* edited by Gregory S. Kealey and Peter Warrian, pp. 125-42. Toronto: M&S, 1976.
4982. _____. "Labour and Reform in Toronto, 1896-1914." Ph.D. thesis, Toronto, 1978.
4983. **Rohold, S. B.** "Glimpse of Toronto's Ghetto." *Westminster* 17 (1910):345-52.
4984. **Rotinberg, Lori.** "The Wayward Worker: Toronto's Prostitutes at the Turn of the Century." In *Women at Work: Ontario, 1850-1930,* edited by Janice Acton, Penny Goldsmith, and Bonnie Shepard, pp. 33-70. Toronto: Canadian Women's Educational Press, 1974.
4985. **Sangster, Joan.** "The 1907 Bell Telephone Strike: Organizing Women Workers." *Labour* 3 (1978):109-30.
4985A. **Shaw, A.** "Toronto as a Municipal Object Lesson." *Review of Reviews* 10 (August 1894):165-73.
4986. **Shaw, C. L.** "Fire-Fighters of Toronto." *Can Mag* 20 (1903):37-45.
4987. **Sheard, Charles.** "City of Toronto Disposal of Sewage and Water Filtration." Empire Club of Canada, *Speeches* 5 (1907-8):66-80.
4988. **Shostack, Hannah.** "Business and Reform: The Lost History of the Toronto Housing Company." *City Mag* 3, no. 7 (1978):24-31.
4989. **Smith, Goldwin.** "Toronto: A Turn in Its History." *Can Mag* 28 (1906-7):523-25.
4990. **Smith, R. H.** "Our Present Duty towards Toronto's Future." Canadian Club of Toronto, *Proceedings* 10 (1913):81-88.
4991. **Spalding, G. C.** "The Toronto *Daily Star* as a Liberal Advocate, 1899-1911." M.A. thesis, Toronto, 1954.
4992. **Speisman, Stephen.** "Munificent Parsons and Municipal Parsimony." *OH* 65 (1973):33-49.
4993. **Spencer, Stephen.** "The Good Queen of Hogs: Toronto, 1850-1914." *UHR* 1-75 (June 1975):38-42.
4994. **Spragge, Shirley C.** "The Provision of Workingmen's Housing: Attempts in Toronto, 1904-1920." M.A. thesis, Queen's, 1974.
4995. _____. "A Confluence of Interests: Housing Reform in Toronto, 1900-1920." In #29, pp. 247-67.
4996. **Stortz, Gerald J.** "John Joseph Lynch, Archbishop of Toronto: A Biographical Study of Religious, Political and Social Commitment." Ph.D. thesis, Guelph, 1980.
4997. **Sylvain, Robert.** "Séjour mouvementé d'un révolutionnaire italien à Toronto et à Québec." *RHAF* 13 (1959):183-229.
4998. **Tennant, G. R.** "The Policy of the *Mail,* 1882-1892." M.A. thesis, Toronto, 1946.
4999. **Tepperman, Lorne.** "Effects of the Demographic Transition upon Access to the Toronto Elite." *Can Rev Soc Anth* 14 (1977):285-93.

5000. **Thurston, Catharine.** "A Look at Early Toronto Theatre, 1860-1869." *York Pioneer* 71 (1976):22-26.
5001. **Weaver, John C.** "The Meaning of Municipal Reform: Toronto, 1895." *OH* 66 (1974):89-100.
5002. _____. "Order and Efficiency: Samuel Morley Wickett and the Urban Progressive Movement in Toronto, 1900-1915." *OH* 69 (1977):218-34.
5003. _____. "The Modern City Realized: Toronto Civic Affairs, 1880-1915." In #**29**, pp. 39-72.
5004. **Wickett, S. Morley.** "Municipal Government of Toronto." In #**895**, pp. 35-58.
5005. **Wilson, D.** "Toronto of Old." *Can Mon* 4 (1873):89-96.
5006. **Zerker, Sally F.** "The Development of Collective Bargaining in the Toronto Printing Industry in the Nineteenth Century." *Industrial Relations* 30 (1975):83-96.

d. Post-1921

5007. **Adamson, Anthony.** "The Unplanned Metropolis." *Can Wel* 36 (1960):15-18.
5008. **Akpara, E. E.** "The Journey to Work in Metropolitan Toronto and Region: An Aggregative Temporal and Cross-sectional Analysis." M.A. thesis, York, 1977.
5009. **Alexander, J. D.** "Popularity of Recreation Sites in the Metropolitan Toronto and Regional Conservation Authority." M.A. thesis, Western Ontario, 1972.
5010. **Anderson, Grace.** *Networks of Contact: The Portuguese and Toronto.* Waterloo: Wilfrid Laurier UP, 1974.
5011. **Archer, D. B.** "Public Housing in Toronto." *Canadian Labour* 2 (March 1966):13-16.
5012. **Atwal, A. S.** "The City of Toronto: A Study of Spatial and Temporal Residential Density Patterns in the Context of Planning Policy, 1956-1966." M.A. thesis, Waterloo, 1970.
5013. **Barrett, F. A.** "Post-War European Immigrants in Metropolitan Toronto: A Social Geography." M.A. thesis, Minnesota, 1963.
5014. **Bernard, A.; Léveillé, J.; and Lord, G.** *Profile: Toronto. The Political and Administrative Structures of the Metropolitan Region of Toronto.* Ottawa: MSUA, 1975.
5015. **Blair, J. W.** "Components of Population Change in the Toronto Region 1951-1971." M.A. thesis, York, 1975.
5016. **Blumenfeld, Hans.** "Hamburg and Toronto: A Comparison." *Plan Canada* 11, no. 1 (1970):39-54.
5017. **Bordessa, Ronald.** "Real Estate Salesmen and Residential Relocation Decisions." *Can Geogr* 22 (1978):334-39.
5018. **Borins, Sandford F.** "Pricing and Investment in a Transportation Network: The Case of Toronto Airport." *CJE* 11 (1978):680-700.
5019. **Bourne, L. S.** *Private Redevelopment of the Central City: Spatial Processes of Structural Change in the City of Toronto.* Chicago: University of Chicago, Dept. of Geography, Research Paper no. 112, 1967.
5020. _____. *Spatial Patterns and Determinants of Land Use Change in Metropolitan Toronto.* Research Paper #80. Toronto: CUCS, 1976.
5021. _____. "Urban Structure and Land Use Decisions [:The Case of Toronto]." *AAAG* 66 (1976):531-47.
5022. _____, **and Doucet, Michael J.** *Dimensions of Metropolitan Physical Growth: Land Use Change, Metropolitan Toronto.* Research Paper #38. Toronto. CUCS, 1970.
5023. **Bourne, L. S., and Maher, Christopher A.** *Comparative Explorations of City-Size Distributions: The Ontario-Quebec Urban System.* Research Paper #27. Toronto: CUCS, 1970.
5024. **Bourne, L. S., and Murdie, Robert A.** "Interrelationships of Social and Physical Space in the City: A Multivariate Analysis of Metropolitan Toronto." *Can Geogr* 16 (1972):211-29.

5025. **Brody, P. E. H.** "What Have We Learned from South Regent Park?" *CPR* 11, no. 2 (1961):2-6.
5026. **Bromley, John F.** *TTC'28: The Electric Railway Services of the Toronto Transportation Commission in 1928.* Toronto: Upper Canada Railway Society, 1978.
5027. _____, **and May, Jack.** *Fifty Years of Progressive Transit: A History of the Toronto Transit Commission.* New York: Electric Railroader's Association, 1973.
5028. **Brown, Philip.** *Some Perspectives on the Toronto Housing Market: A Review of Recent Studies.* Major Report Series #8. Toronto: CUCS, 1977.
5029. **Bruce, H. A.** *Report of the Lieutenant-Governor's Committee on Housing Conditions in Toronto.* Toronto: Hunter Rose, 1934.
5030. **Budden, Sandra, and Ernst, Joseph.** *The Moveable Airport: The Politics of Government Planning.* Toronto: Hakkert, 1973.
5031. **Bunting, T. E.** "An Empirical Analysis of Symbolic Urban Imagery: A Case Study of the New City Hall in Toronto." M.A. thesis, Western Ontario, 1967.
5032. **Bureau of Municipal Research.** "Regional Government: The Key to Genuine Local Autonomy." *Civic Affairs* (May 1968):9-33.
5033. _____. "The 101 Governments of Metro Toronto." *Civic Affairs* (October 1968):6-19.
5034. **Burton, Lydia, and Morley, David.** "Neighbourhood Survival in Toronto." *Landscape* 23 (1979):33-40.
5035. **Campbell, B. A.** "Retailing of Fruits and Vegetables by Four Chain Stores in Toronto." *Econ Annalist* 7 (August 1937):59-62.
5036. **Canadian Youth Council.** *Report on Slums and Re-Housing in Toronto.* Toronto, 1936.
5037. **Caulfield, J.** *The Tiny Perfect Mayor: David Crombie and Toronto's Reform Aldermen.* Toronto: Lorimer, 1974.
5038. **Chown, W. F.** "The Toronto Wholesale Fruit and Vegetable Trade." *Econ Annalist* 7 (February 1937):4-8.
5039. _____, **and Hopper, W. C.** *Wholesale Marketing of Fresh Fruits and Vegetables in the City of Toronto.* Ottawa: Dept. of Agriculture, 1937.
5040. **Ciccocelli, Joseph.** "Italian Immigration in Toronto." M.A. thesis, Western Ontario, 1977.
5041. **Civic Advisory Council of Toronto.** *Municipal Finance: A Report Prepared by the Civic Advisory Council of Toronto.* Toronto: UTP, 1950.
5042. **Clarkson, Stephen.** "The New City Politics—A Reply to Old Cliches." In #925, pp. 62-65.
5043. _____. "Barriers to Entry of Parties into Toronto's Civic Politics: Towards a Theory of Party Penetration." *CJPS* 4 (1977):206-23.
5044. **Coffey, William.** "Income Relationships in Boston and Toronto: A Tale of Two Countries?" *Can Geogr* 22 (1978):85-111.
5046. **Cook, Gail C. A.** "Effect of Federation of Education Expenditures in Metropolitan Toronto." Ph.D. thesis, Michigan, 1968.
5047. **Cooke, Henry R.** "Transportation for Metropolitan Toronto." *CPR* 21, no. 1 (1971):23-30.
5048. **Cotter, Evelyn, and Cotter, Graham.** "The Family Downtown." *Can Wel* 40 (1964):100-105.
5049. **Couzons, H. H.** "Town Planning from a Transportation Viewpoint." *TPICJ* 3, no. 1 (1924):12.
5050. **Crouch, W. W.** "Metropolitan Government in Toronto." *Pub Admin Rev* 14, no. 2 (1954):85-95.
5051. **Dagenais, Pierre.** "La Métropole du Canada: Montréal ou Toronto?" *Rev géogr Mtl* 23 (1969):27-37.
5052. **Dakin, A. J.** "Metropolitan Toronto Planning." *Town Plan Rev* 40 (1969):3-24.

5054. _____. *Toronto Planning: A Planning Review of the Legal and Jurisdictional Contexts from 1912 to 1970*. Toronto: University of Toronto, Dept. of Urban and Regional Planning, 1974.

5055. _____. "Toronto: A Federated Metro." In *World Capitals: Toward Guided Urbanization*, edited by H. Wentworth Eldridge, pp. 207-45. New York: Anchor, 1975.

5056. _____. *Historical Instrument for Considering Toronto Planning*. Papers on Planning and Design, no. 16. Toronto: University of Toronto, Dept. of Urban and Regional Planning, 1978.

5057. _____, and **Manson-Smith, P.** *Toronto Urban Planning: A Selected Bibliography*. Monticello, IL: CPL Exchange Bibliography no. 670, 1974.

5058. **Davis, R. A.** "The Mississauga Corridor: A Study of the Special Arrangement of Central Places in the Southern Part of the Province of Ontario." Ph.D. thesis, Clark, 1960.

5059. **Davison, A. M.** "An Analysis of the Significant Factors in the Patterns of Toronto Chinese Family Life as a Result of the recent Changes in Immigration Laws Which Permitted the Wives of Canadian Citizens to Enter Canada." M.S.W. thesis, Toronto, 1952.

5060. **Dawson, J. N.** "Rapid Transit and Changing Land Use in the Central City: The Example of Toronto." M.A. thesis, Georgia, 1968.

5061. **Del Guidice, Dominic, and Azcks, Steven M.** "The 101 Governments of Metro Toronto." In #870, pp. 219-29.

5062. **Dineen, Janice.** *The Trouble with Co-ops: The Political History of a Non-Profit Co-operative Housing Project*. Toronto: Green Tree, 1974.

5063. **Doucet, Michael J.** *Trends in Metropolitan Land Use and Land Consumption: Metropolitan Toronto, 1963-1968*. Research Paper #35. Toronto: CUCS, 1970.

5064. **Dudycha, D. J.** "Computer Mapping of Socio-Economic Patterns in Metro Toronto." *Can Cart* 15 (1978):23-24.

5065. **Dukhan, H.** "The Development of the Junior High School and the Senior High School in Metropolitan Toronto." M.Ed. thesis, Toronto, 1959.

5066. **Duncan, Lewis.** *Report of Housing for City of Toronto*. Toronto: Board of Control, 1942.

5067. **Dworaczek, M.** *Minority Groups in Metropolitan Toronto: A Bibliography*. Toronto: Ontario Ministry of Labour, 1973.

5068. **Ellwood, W. F.** "A Comparison of Location for the Dispersal of Projected Population Growth: Toronto Central Region." M.A. thesis, Carleton, 1972.

5069. **Faludi, E. G.,** ed. *Land Development in the Metropolitan Area of Toronto*. Toronto: Toronto Real Estate Board, 1952.

5071. **Ferguson, G. H.** "Decentralization of Industry and Metropolitan Control." *TPICJ* 2, no. 4 (1923):5-12.

5072. **Fetherling, Douglas.** "Toronto's Cultural Ferment, 1978-style." *CGEJ* 96, no. 2 (1978):28-35.

5073. **Field, N. C., and Kerr, Donald P.** *Geographical Aspects of Industrial Growth in the Metropolitan Region*. Toronto: Regional Development Branch, 1968.

5074. **Fisher, David.** "Montreal Regional Industrial Pattern as Compared with That of Toronto." M.A. thesis, McGill, 1940.

5075. **Franson, J. D.** "Employment Experience and Economic Position of a Selected Group of Indians in Metropolitan Toronto." M.S.W. thesis, Toronto, 1964.

5076. **Fraser, Graham.** *Fighting Back: Urban Renewal in Trefann Court*. Toronto: Hakkert, 1972.

5077. **Freedman, H. A.** "Intra-Urban Mobility in Toronto: A Study in Micromigration Analysis." M.A. thesis, Pennsylvania, 1967.

5078. **Gad, Gunter.** "Toronto's Central Office Complex: Growth, Structure, and Linkages." Ph.D. thesis, Toronto, 1975.

5079. **Gardiner, F. G.** "Metropolitan Toronto." *INCA* 54 (July 1953):89, 91-93.

5080. **Garner, H.** "Cabbagetown Revisited—The Story of a Slum." *Saturday Night* 72 (November 1957):10-11, 31.

5081. **Gathercole, C. E.** "The City of Toronto in Depression and Recovery, 1929-1939: A Study in Public Finance." M.A. thesis, Toronto, 1945.
5082. _____. "The Toronto Plan: An Experiment in Metropolitan Government." *Can Tax J* 1 (1953):366-73.
5083. **Gera, Surenda, and Kuhn, Peter.** "Occupation and Job Location Patterns: An Analysis of the Toronto Census Metropolitan Area." *Can Geogr* 23 (1979):266-76.
5084. **Glogowski, S. M.** "Metropolitan Toronto Planning: A Study in Transportation with Particular Reference to the Use of Traffic Simulation Models." M.Sc.Pl. thesis, Toronto, 1967.
5085. **Goldenberg, H. Carl.** *Royal Commission on Metropolitan Toronto: Report.* Toronto: Queen's Printer, 1965.
5086. **Goldrick, Michael D.** "The Anatomy of Urban Reform in Toronto." *City Mag* 3, nos. 4-5 (1978):29-39.
5087. **Gourlay, R. S.** "Basic Principles of Waterfront Development as Illustrated by the Plans of the Toronto Harbour Commissioners." *Proceedings of the Sixth National Conference on City Planning* (Toronto, 1914):17-53.
5088. **Granatstein, J. L.** "The York South By-Election of February 9, 1942. A Turning Point in Canadian Politics." *CHR* 48 (1967):142-58.
5089. _____. *Marlborough Marathon: One Street against a Developer.* Toronto: Hakkert, 1971.
5090. _____. "A Reply to Stephen Clarkson." In **#925**, pp. 66-67.
5091. **Gray, C.** *The St. Lawrence Neighbourhood in Toronto: An Analysis of Municipal Housing Policy.* Papers on Planning and Design, no. 22. Toronto: University of Toronto, Dept. of Urban and Regional Planning, 1979.
5092. **Grayson, John Paul.** "Neighbourhood and Voting: The Social Basis of Conservative Support in Broadview." Ph.D. thesis, Toronto, 1972.
5093. **Greenberg, Kenneth, and Merrens, H. Roy.** "A Map of Toronto's Waterfront." *Can Cart* 8 (1971):41-45.
5094. **Greenberg, Zeev.** "Israeli Immigrants in Toronto." M.A. thesis, York, 1971.
5095. **Grumm, J. G.** *Metropolitan Area Government: The Toronto Experience.* Lawrence, KS: University of Kansas, Governmental Research Center, 1959.
5096. **Grunier, R.** "The Hebrew-Christian Mission in Toronto." *CES* 9, no. 1 (1977):18-28.
5097. **Guerra, I. L.** "A Study of the Factors Affecting Water Use in Metropolitan Toronto." M.Sc. thesis, Toronto, 1971.
5098. **Haggart, Ron.** "'Are They Going to Give Us a Station or Not?': The Politics of Union Station." In *The Open Gate, Toronto Union Station,* edited by Richard Bébout, pp. 15-20. Toronto: Peter Martin, 1972.
5099. **Hancock, Macklin L.** "Flemingdon Park, A New Urban Community." In **#563**, pp. 205-28.
5100. **Harkness, Ross.** *J. E. Atkinson of the Star.* Toronto: UTP, 1963.
5101. **Harney, Robert F.** "The New Canadians and Their Life in Toronto." *CGEJ* 96, no. 2 (1978):20-27.
5102. **Harper, P. D.** "The Lowry Model of Urban Structure: A Review and Toronto Example." M.A. thesis, Toronto, 1972.
5103. **Harris, R. C.** "The City Planning Project." Empire Club of Canada, *Speeches* 27 (1929):336-49.
5104. **Heidenreich, Conrad E.** "The Junction of West Toronto: An Industrial Survey." B.A. essay, Toronto, 1961.
5105. **Helling, Rudolph A.** "A Comparison of the Acculturation of German Immigrants in Toronto, Ontario and Detroit, Michigan." Ph.D. thesis, Wayne State, 1961.
5106. **Henry, G. S.** "The Establishment of a Metropolitan County around Toronto." Canadian Club of Toronto, *Proceedings* 21 (1923-24):217-27.
5107. **Herman, Harry V.** *Men in White Aprons: A Study of Ethnicity and Occupation* [Macedonian Restauranteurs]. Toronto: Peter Martin, 1978.

5108. **Hill, Frederick I.** *Spatio-Temporal Trends in Population Density: Toronto, 1932-1966.* Research Paper #34. Toronto: CUCS, 1970.

5109. ———. "The Integration of Peripheral Towns into an Urban Field: The Toronto-Centred Region." Ph.D. thesis, Toronto, 1976.

5110. **Hitchcock, J.**, ed. *Case Studies of Neighbourhood Planning in Toronto.* Papers on Planning and Design, no. 1. Toronto: University of Toronto, Dept. of Urban and Regional Planning, 1973.

5111. **Hodge, Gerald.** *Theory and Reality of Industrial Location in the Toronto Region.* Toronto: University of Toronto, 1970.

5112. **Horton, J. T.** "The Municipality of Toronto: A Case Study of the Problems Related to Municipal Services in Expanding Metropolitan Areas." Ph.D. thesis, Northwestern, 1963.

5113. **Hough, M.** *The Urban Landscape: A Study of Open Space in Urban Metropolitan Areas.* Toronto: Conservation Council of Ontario, 1971.

5114. **Hutner, Florence.** "A Community Service Group [The United Jewish Welfare Fund of Toronto]." *Can Wel* 34 (1958):117-19.

5115. **Ingram, D. R.** "Migration and Population Change within Metropolitan Toronto, 1966-1971." *Can Geogr* 19 (1975):340-46.

5116. **Jacobson, Jerry.** "The Employment-Residence Structure in Two Selected Canadian New Communities [Don Mills and Bramalea]." M.A. thesis, Ottawa, 1977.

5117. **Jain, N. P.** "Aspects of Juvenile Justice in Toronto." LL.M. thesis, York, 1974.

5118. **Jansen, Clifford J.** "The Italian Community in Toronto." In *Immigrant Groups*, edited by Jean Leonard Elliott, pp. 207-15. Scarborough: Prentice-Hall, 1971.

5119. **Jarvis, Robert.** "Acting for a Developer." In *The Changing Face of Land Use and Development.* Special Lectures of the Law Society of Upper Canada, pp. 225-44. Toronto: Richard De Vov, 1974.

5120. **Jaschke, George.** "Jarvis Street, a Study in Urban Geography." M.A. thesis, Toronto, 1941.

5121. **Jones, Murray V.** "Housing in Metropolitan Toronto." *CPR* 5, no. 1 (1955):16-19.

5122. **Kaplan, Harold.** "Politics and Policy-Making in Metropolitan Toronto." *CJEPS* 31 (1965):538-51.

5123. ———. "Toronto Transit Commission: A Case Study of the Structural-Functional Approach to Administrative Organizations." *CJEPS* 33 (1967):171-79.

5124. ———. *Urban Political Systems: A Functional Analysis of Metro Toronto.* New York: Columbia UP, 1967.

5125. ———. "Electoral Politics in the Metro Area." In **#925,** pp. 145-52.

5126. ———. "Central City Politics." In **#925,** pp. 182-91.

5127. **Kay, Barry J.** "Voting Patterns in a Non-Partisan Legislature: A Study of Toronto City Council." *CJPS* 4 (1971):224-42.

5128. ———. "Decision-Making Patterns in an Urban Legislature. An Issue, Time and System Level Study of Toronto City Council." Ph.D. thesis, Rochester, 1976.

5129. **Kerr, Donald, and Spelt, Jacob.** "Overseas Trade at the Port of Toronto." *Can Geogr* 8 (1956):70-79.

5130. ———. "Manufacturing in Downtown Toronto." *Geogr Bull* 10 (1957):5-21.

5131. ———. "Manufacturing in Suburban Toronto." *Can Geogr* 10 (1958):11-19.

5132. **Kerwin, P.** "Citizen Participation in Urban Renewal: Evolution in Citizen Participation in Toronto." M.S.W. thesis, Toronto, 1968.

5133. **Kilbourn, William.** "The New Toronto: A Great Modern City." *CGEJ* 96, no. 2 (1978):10-19.

5134. **Kirkup, D. B.** *Boomtown: Metropolitan Toronto.* Toronto: Metro Toronto News, 1969.

5135. **Kling, S.** "Rural-Urban Relations in Vaughn, Whitchurch, Markham and King Townships." M.A. thesis, Toronto, 1949.

5136. Lai, Vivien Wai-Ying. "The Assimilation of Chinese Immigrants in Toronto." M.A. thesis, York, 1970.
5137. _____. "The New Chinese Immigrants in Toronto." In *Immigrant Groups*, edited by Jean Leonard Elliott, pp. 120-40. Scarborough: Prentice-Hall, 1971.
5138. Laidlaw, John. "What Toronto Can Do to Relieve Its Depression." Canadian Club of Toronto, *Proceedings* 33 (1935-36):269-97.
5139. Lascelles, G. A. "Financing Metropolitan Toronto." *Can Tax J* 3 (1955):16-24.
5140. Latham, R. F. "Urban Population Densities and Growth with Special Reference to Toronto." M.A. thesis, Queen's, 1967.
5141. Laurence, L. "Finances municipales comparées de Montréal, Toronto, et Vancouver." Thèse de M.A., Montréal, 1957.
5142. Law, R. C. "Distribution of Accessibility in Metropolitan Toronto, 1964-1969." M.A. thesis, Toronto, 1973.
5143. Lawson, M. B. M. "Neighbourhood Planning in Toronto." In #563, pp. 229-334.
5144. Le May, T. D. "Town Planning Problems in Toronto." *Can Engineer* 57 (1929):779-81.
5144A. Lemon, James T. "Environment, Residents' Groups and Political Parties." *Alternatives* 5, nos. 3-4 (1976):31-35.
5144B. _____. "Toronto: Is It a Model for Urban Life and Citizen Participation?" In *Citizen Participation and the Form of the City*, edited by David Ley. Vancouver: Tantalus, 1974.
5144C. _____. "The Urban Community Movement: Moving towards Public Households." In *Perspectives in Humanistic Geography*, edited by David Ley and M. Samuel, pp. 319-37. Chicago: Maaroufa, 1978.
5145. Li, Peter S. "The Stratification of Ethnic Immigrants: The Case of Toronto." *Can Rev Soc Anth* 15 (1978):31-40.
5146. McCaskill, Donald N. "The Urbanization of Native People in Toronto, Winnipeg, Edmonton, and Vancouver: A Comparative Analysis." Ph.D. thesis, York, 1979.
5147. McCordic, Wm. J. "Metro's Dilemma in Public Education." *Can Pub Admin* 7 (1964):464-78.
5148. McDougall, Harry. "Toronto's Waterfront Plan." *CGEJ* 84 (1972):2-15.
5149. Mclaren, Jack. *Let's All Hate Toronto*. Toronto: Kingswood House, 1956.
5150. McLeod, B. A. "Residential Preferences in Metropolitan Toronto." M.A. thesis, York, 1973.
5151. Macleod, Catherine. "Women in Production: The Toronto Dressmakers' Strike of 1931." In *Women at Work: Ontario, 1850-1930*, edited by Janice Acton, Penny Goldsmith, and Bonnie Shepard, pp. 309-30. Toronto: Canadian Women's Educational Press, 1974.
5152. Maher, Christopher A. "Residential Change and the Filtering Process: Central Toronto, 1953-1971." Ph.D. thesis, Toronto, 1972.
5153. _____. "Spatial Patterns in Urban Housing Markets: Filtering in Toronto, 1953-1971." *Can Geogr* 18 (1974):108-24.
5154. Makabe, Tomoko. "Ethnic Identity and Social Mobility: The Case of the Second Generation Japanese in Metropolitan Toronto." *CES* 10 (1978):106-23.
5155. Mann, W. E. "The Social System of a Slum: The Lower Ward, Toronto." In *Urbanism and the Changing Canadian Society*, edited by S. D. Clark, pp. 39-69. Toronto: UTP, 1961.
5156. Markusen, J. R., and Scheffman, D. T. *Speculation and Monopoly in Urban Development: Analytical Foundations with Evidence for Toronto*. Toronto: UTP, 1977.
5157. Marston, W. G. "Social Class Segregation within Ethnic Groups in Toronto." *Can Rev Soc Anth* 6, no. 2 (1969):65-79.
5158. Martin, Larry R. G. "Land Dealer Behaviour on the Toronto Urban Fringe." *Ont Geogr* 10 (1976):4-14.
5159. Mavor, James. *Niagara in Politics. A Critical Account of the Ontario Hydro-Electric Commission*. New York: Dutton, 1925.

5160. **Maxwell, Thomas R.** "La population d'origine française de l'agglomération métropolitaine de Toronto. Une étude sur la participation et l'identité ethnique." *Rech soc* 12 (1971):319-44.

5161. _____. *The Invisible French: The French in Metropolitan Toronto*. Waterloo: Wilfrid Laurier UP, 1977.

5162. **Milner, James B.** "The Metropolitan Toronto Plan." *Univ Pennsylvania Law Rev* 105 (1957):570-87.

5163. **Miron, John R.** *Changing Patterns of Household Formation in the Toronto CMA: 1951-1976*. Toronto: CUCS, 1979.

5164. **Moore, Peter W.** "Zoning and Neighbourhood Change in the Annex in Toronto, 1900-1970." Ph.D. thesis, Toronto, 1978.

5165. _____. "Zoning and Planning: The Toronto Experience, 1904-1970." In #29, pp. 316-41.

5166. **Morantz, A. L.** "Ethnic Voting in Toronto." M.A. thesis, Toronto, 1962.

5167. **Murdie, Robert A.** *Factorial Ecology of Metropolitan Toronto, 1951-1961*. Chicago: University of Chicago, Dept. of Geography, Research Paper no. 116, 1968.

5168. **Murphy, M. P.** "Toronto Transit." *Can Rail* 315 (1978):100-121.

5169. **Myles, J. S.** "The Organization and Administration of Industrial Recreation in Toronto." M.S.W. thesis, Toronto, 1957.

5170. **Nagata, Judith.** "Adaptation and Integration of the Greek Working Class Immigrants in the City of Toronto: A Situational Approach." *International Migration Rev* 4 (1969):44-70.

5171. **Nagler, Mark.** *Indians in the City: A Study of the Urbanization of Indians in Toronto*. Ottawa: Canadian Research Centre for Anthropology, 1970.

5172. **Neumann, Brigette; Mezoff, Richard; and Richmond, Anthony H.** *Immigrant Integration and Urban Renewal in Toronto*. The Hague: Nijhoff, 1973.

5173. **Njau, G. J.** "The Change in Population Distribution in Metropolitan Toronto: 1941-1961." M.A. thesis, Toronto, 1967.

5174. **O'Mara, James.** *Shaping Urban Waterfronts: The Role of Toronto's Harbour Commissioners, 1911-1960*. Downsview: York University, Geography Dept., Discussion Paper Series, March 1976.

5175. **Ossenberg, R. J.** "The Social Integration and Adjustment of Post-War Immigrants in Montreal and Toronto." *Can Rev Soc Anth* 1, no. 4 (1964):202-15.

5176. **O'Toole, Roger Laurence.** "The Sociology of Political Sects: Four Sects in Toronto in 1968-69." Ph.D. thesis, Toronto, 1972.

5177. **Paterson, N. R.** "The Manipulation of Technical Planning for Political Purposes: The 'Toronto II' Project." M.A. thesis, Western Ontario, 1976.

5178. **Phillips, Nathan.** *Mayor of All the People*. Toronto: M&S, 1967.

5179. **Pill, Juri.** *Planning and Politics: The Metropolitan Toronto Planning Review*. Cambridge, MA: MIT Press, 1979.

5180. "Planning the Village of Forest Hill-Greater Toronto Region." *TPICJ* 10, no. 3 (1931):57-59.

5181. **Plewes, J. C.** "The Urban Rush Hour: An Analysis of the Yonge Street Subway System." M.A. thesis, Queen's, 1970.

5182. **Polyzoi, Elouessa.** "The Greek Communal School and Cultural Survival in Pre-War Toronto." *UHR* 2-78 (October 1978):74-95.

5183. **Ramcharan, Subhas.** "The Economic Adaptation of West Indians in Toronto, Canada." *Can Rev Soc Anth* 13 (1976):295-304.

5184. **Ramlalsingh, R. D.** *A Study of the Decline of Trade at the Port of Toronto*. Downsview: York University, Geography Dept., Discussion Paper Series, August 1975.

5185. **Repo, Satu.** "The Big Shop: Finnish Immigrant Tailors in Toronto." *This Magazine* 9, no. 5-6 (1975):31-33.

5186. **Rice. R. G.** *Transportation in Toronto: Problems, Policies and Solutions.* Research Paper #87. Toronto: CUCS, 1977.
5187. **Richardson, Douglas.** " 'A Blessed Sense of Civic Excess': The Architecture of Union Station." In *The Open Gate, Toronto Union Station,* edited by Richard Bébout, pp. 67-96. Toronto: Peter Martin, 1972.
5188. **Richmond, Anthony H.** *Immigrants and Ethnic Groups in Metropolitan Toronto.* Toronto: York University, 1967.
5189. _____. *Ethnic Residential Segregation in Metropolitan Toronto.* Toronto: York University, Institute for Behavioural Research, 1972.
5190. _____. *Immigrants and Ethnic Groups in Metropolitan Toronto.* Toronto: York University, Institute for Behavioural Research, 1972.
5191. **Rose, Albert.** "Slum Clearance Will Continue in Toronto." *CPR* 5, no. 3 (1955):112-115.
5192. _____. *Regent Park: A Study in Slum Clearance.* Toronto: UTP, 1958.
5193. _____. "A Changed City." *Can Wel* 39 (1963):6-11.
5194. _____. "Services for the Changed City." *Can Wel* 39 (1963):64-71.
5195. _____. *Governing Metropolitan Toronto: A Social and Political Analysis, 1953-1971.* Berkeley and Los Angeles: Institute of Governmental Studies, University of California Press, 1972.
5196. **Rosenberg, Louis.** *Population Characteristics of the Jewish Community of Toronto.* Montreal: Canadian Jewish Congress, 1955.
5197. **Rossier, Henry.** *The New City, a Prejudiced View of Toronto.* Toronto: Macmillan, 1961.
5198. **Rudin, J. R.** *The Changing Structure of the Land Development Industry in the Toronto Area.* Major Report Series #13. Toronto: CUCS, 1978.
5199. **Schliewinsky, F. G.** *A Systems Approach to Neighbourhood Change: Metropolitan Toronto, 1951-1971.* Major Report Series #5. Toronto: CUCS, 1975.
5200. **Scott, F. R.** "The Trial of the Toronto Communists," *QQ* 39 (1932):512-27.
5201. **Sewell, John.** *Up against City Hall.* Toronto: James Lewis and Samuel, 1974.
5202. _____. "Don Mills: E. P. Taylor and Canada's First Corporate Suburb." *City Mag* 2 (1977):28-38.
5203. **Sharpe, Christopher A.** "New Construction and Housing Turnover: Vacancy Chains in Toronto." *Can Geogr* 22 (1978):130-44.
5204. **Sidlofsky, Samuel.** "Post-War Immigrants in the Changing Metropolis with Special Reference to Toronto's Italian Population." Ph.D. thesis, Toronto, 1969.
5205. **Silcox, Peter.** "The Metropolitan Council and Toronto's Metropolitan Problem." M.A. thesis, Toronto, 1962.
5206. **Simard, Jacques.** "Waterfront Countdown." *CPR* 12, no. 3 (1962):2-9.
5207. **Simmons, James W.** *Toronto's Changing Retail Complex.* Chicago: University of Chicago, Dept. of Geography, Research Paper no. 104, 1966.
5208. _____. *Patterns of Residential Movement in Metropolitan Toronto.* Toronto: University of Toronto, Dept. of Geography, 1974.
5209. _____. "How Much Growth Can Toronto Afford?" *CGEJ* 92, no. 2 (1976):4-11.
5210. **Skebo, Suzanne.** "Liberty and Authority: Civil Liberties in Toronto, 1929-1935." M.A. thesis, British Columbia, 1968.
5211. **Smallwood, F.** *Metro Toronto: A Decade Later.* Toronto: Bureau of Municipal Research, 1963.
5212. **Smith, G. J. A.** "Transportation and Urban Design: A Systems Approach to Toronto's Future Transportation Network." M.A. thesis, Toronto, 1970.
5213. **Spelt, Jacob.** "The Development of the Toronto Conurbation." *Buffalo Law Rev* 13 (1964):557-73.

5214. **Spencer, Byron G.** "Determinants of the Labour Force Participation of Married Women: A Micro-Study of Toronto Households." *CJE* 6 (1973):222-38.
5215. **Stapleford, F. N.** *After Twenty Years. A Short History of the Neighbourhood Workers Association, 1918-1938.* Toronto: The Association, 1938.
5216. **Starbird, Ethel A.** "Canada's Dowager Learns to Swing." *Nat Geogr Mag* 148 (1975):190-215.
5217. **Steed, Guy P. F.** "Standardization, Scale, Incubation, and Inertia: Montreal and Toronto Clothing Industries." *Can Geogr* 20 (1976):298-309.
5218. **Stein, David Lewis.** *Toronto for Sale: The Destruction of a City.* Toronto: New Press, 1972.
5219. **Stocks, Anthony Howard.** "Some Problems in the Finance and Organization of Metropolitan Government with Particular Reference to the Toronto Federation." Ph.D. thesis, New York (Buffalo), 1963.
5220. **Sturino, Franc.** "A Case Study of a South Italian Family in Toronto, 1935-1960." *UHR* 2-78 (October 1978):38-57.
5221. **Susman, Robert M.** "The Toronto Experiment: A New Concept in Local Government." M.A. thesis, Columbia, 1964.
5222. **Thomas, P. F.** "Rexdale: A Case Study in Suburban Industry." M.A. thesis, Waterloo, 1968.
5223. **Toronto Transportation Commission.** *Rapid Transit in Toronto.* Toronto, 1945.
5224. **Tsukada, N.** "Toronto's Chinatown: A Study of Changing Use." B.A. essay, York, 1968.
5225. **Vendetti, M. P.** "The Italian Ethnic Community of Metropolitan Toronto: A Case Study in Intra-Urban Networks." M.A. thesis, York, 1975.
5226. **Walker, Gerald.** "Social Perspectives on the Countryside: Reflections on the Territorial Farm North of Toronto." *Ont Geogr* 10 (1976):54-63.
5227. **Walker, Howard V.** "Toronto: The Architect and Urban Action." *CPR* 21, no. 2 (1971):18-20.
5228. **Walsh, Annmarie Houck.** *The Urban Challenge to Government: An International Comparison of Thirteen Cities.* New York: Praeger, 1969.
5229. **Wangenheim, E. D.** "The Social Organization of the Japanese Community in Toronto: A Product of Crisis." M.A. thesis, Toronto, 1956.
5230. **Wasteneys, H. C. F.** "A History of the University Settlement of Toronto, 1910-1958: An Exploration of the Social Objectives of the University Settlement and of Their Implementation." D.S.W. thesis, Toronto, 1975.
5231. "Why Toronto Housing Was Held Up." *TPICJ* 9, no. 2 (1930):34-36.
5232. **Williams, T. R.** "Some Facts and Fantasies Concerning Local Autonomy in the Metropolitan Toronto School System." *Can Pub Admin* 17 (1974):274-88.
5233. **Williamson, E. L. R.** "Impact upon Local Government [Scarborough] of a Rapid Increase in Population." M.A. thesis, Carleton, 1959.
5234. **Wilson, Norman D.** "Sunnyside Beach Development at Toronto." *TPICJ* 1, no. 12 (1922):7-9.
5235. **Wilson, Robert.** *A Retrospect, a Short Review of the Steps Taken in Sanitation to Transform the Town of Muddy York into the Queen City of the West.* Toronto: Dept. of Public Health of the City of Toronto, 1934.
5236. **Winnicki, W. R.** "Chinatown in Transition: The Impact of the New City Hall and Court House in Toronto's Chinatown." B.A. essay, Waterloo, 1969.
5237. **Winter, J. O.** "The Centre of a City: An Examination into the Fringe of Toronto's Central Business District." M.A. thesis, Toronto, 1966.
5238. **Wynne-Roberts, R. O.** "Town and Regional Planning in Relation to Sanitation." *TPICJ* 1, no. 11 (1922):4-8.
5239. **Young, C. R.** "The Structural Requirements of the Toronto Building By-Law." *Can Engineer* 26 (1914):383-88.

5240. **Zieber, George H.** "Toronto's Central Business District." M.A. thesis, Toronto, 1961.
5241. **Ziegler, Suzanne G.** "The Adaptation of Italian Immigrants to Toronto: An Analysis." Ph.D. thesis, Colorado, 1971.

32. Windsor

5242. "The Automobile Industry's Growth in Fifty Years." *INCA* 50 (1950):112-24.
5243. **Bezaire, P. J.** "Political Participation in Local Government, a Case Study of Extension Students in Windsor and Chatham." M.A. thesis, Laval, 1975.
5244. **Botsford, David P.** "Amherstburg." *W Ont Hist N* 1 (1943):12-15.
5245. **Cako, S. C.** "Labour's Struggle for Union Security. The Ford of Canada Strike, Windsor, 1945." M.A. thesis, Guelph, 1971.
5246. **Connely, M.** "Sandwich, Detroit and Gabriel Richard, 1798-1832." CCHA, *Report* (1951):25-37.
5247. **Cross, W. R.** "The Redevelopment Area of Windsor to 1900." M.A. thesis, Windsor, 1961.
5248. **Cusson, M.** "Windsor: Ville industrielle traditionelle." Thèse de L. ès L., Laval, 1973.
5249. **Dewar, D.** "Locational Patterns of Residential Building Activity in Windsor, Ontario 1961-1971." M.A. thesis, Windsor, 1974.
5250. **Douglas, R. Alan.** "The Battle of Windsor." *OH* 61 (1969):137-52.
5251. **Dzus, Roman.** "Residential Construction, Vacancy Chains and Mobility through Intra-Urban Space: A Case Study of the Windsor Metropolitan Area." M.A. thesis, Windsor, 1975.
5252. _____, and **Romsa, Gerald.** "Housing Construction, Vacancy Chains, and Residential Mobility in Windsor." *Can Geogr* 21 (1977):223-36.
5253. **Fuller, Robert M.** *Windsor Heritage.* Windsor, 1972.
5254. **Gardner, W. H.**, ed. *Windsor, Ontario, Canada, 1913, including Walkerville, Ford, Sandwich and Ojibway: An Authentic Compilation Embracing in Word and Pictorial Representation the Growth and Expansion of These Municipalities.* Windsor: *Evening Record,* 1913.
5255. **Green, Reuben.** "The Wage Structure in Windsor, Ontario, 1955-1965." M.A. thesis, Windsor, 1966.
5256. **Gross, W. R.** "The Redevelopment Area of Windsor to 1900." M.A. thesis, Windsor, 1961.
5257. **Hall, Frederick A.** "Musical Life in Windsor: 1875-1901." *Univ Windsor Rev* 9, no. 2 (1974):76-92.
5258. **Hartford, Jerome.** "Labour Unions and Windsor." *Commonweal* 50 (1949):262-65.
5259. **Havran, Martin J.** "Windsor—Its First Hundred Years." *OH* 46 (1954):179-86.
5260. **Hill, O. M.** "A City Looks at Itself." *Can Bus* 25 (1952):26-29, 156-58.
5261. **Hoskins, Ronald G.** "A Historical Survey of the Town of Walkerville, Ontario, 1858-1922, Including an Evaluation of the Influence of Hiram Walker and His Sons on the Growth and Development of the Town until 1922." M.A. thesis, Windsor, 1964.
5262. _____. "Hiram Walker and the Origins and Development of Walkerville, Ontario." *OH* 64 (1972):123-31.
5263. **Jarvi, Edith.** *Bibliography of Windsor and Essex Counties.* Windsor: Windsor Public Libraries, 1955. Supplement, 1960.
5264. **Lajeunesse, Ernest J.**, ed. *The Windsor Border Region: A Collection of Documents.* Toronto: Champlain Society, Ontario Series, vol. 4, 1960.
5264A. **Lebel, E. C.** "History of Assumption, The First Parish in Upper Canada." CCHA, *Report* (1954):23-28.
5265. **Markovich, R.** "The Evolution of Public Transport Networks in Windsor and London, 1872-1968." M.A. thesis, Windsor, 1971.

5266. **Mercer, W. M.** "The Windsor French: Study of an Urban Community." M.A. thesis, Windsor, 1974.
5267. **Moore, K. V.** "Episodes of Early Protestant Church History." *W Ont Hist N* 10 (1952):87-92.
5268. **Morrison, Neil F.** *Garden Gateway to Canada: 100 Years of Windsor and Essex County, 1854-1954*. Toronto: Ryerson, 1954.
5269. **Nixon, Peter G., and Campbell, Maurice A.** *Four Cities, Part Two: Windsor—A Study of Urban Problems*. Toronto: M&S, 1971.
5270. **Oliver, L. H. R.** "The Identification of Poverty Pockets in the City of Windsor, 1971." M.A. thesis, Windsor, 1977.
5271. **Perry, Charlotte Bronte.** *The History of the Coloured Canadian in Windsor, Ontario, 1867-1967*. Windsor: Summer Printing, 1967.
5272. **Price, Trevor.** "City-Manager Government in Windsor: A Study of Its Evolution and Mode of Operation." Ph.D. thesis, Queen's, 1975.
5273. **Robinson, J. Lewis.** "Windsor, Ont., A Study in Urban Geography." *CGEJ* 27 (1943):106-21.
5274. **Short, George D.** "Sport and Economic Growth in the Windsor Area, 1919 to 1939." M.P.E. thesis, Windsor, 1973.
5275. **Stinson, M. M.** "Strong are the Ties [relations between Detroit and Windsor]." *Inland Seas* 8 (1952):83-89.
5276. **Veres, Louis Joseph.** "History of the United Automobile Workers in Windsor, 1936-1955." M.A. thesis, Western Ontario, 1956.
5277. **Williams, G. P.** "An Analysis of Locational Factors of Wholesaling Functions in Windsor, Ontario with Emphasis upon Grocery Wholesale." M.A. thesis, Windsor, 1974.
5278. "Windsor City Hall." *JRAIC* 36 (1959):237-39.
5279. **Windsor, Rotary Club of.** *Historic Windsor, Ontario, Canada: A Sketch of a Dynamic Canadian City*. Windsor, 1947.

33. Other Centres

5280. **Adams, Thomas.** "Planning New Towns in Canada: Ojibway." *Cn L* 4, no. 4 (1918):73-80.
5281. **Agnew, Nelson Glenn.** "Social and Economic Change in Lindsay, under Metropolitan Impact, 1915-1930." M.A. thesis, Trent, 1971.
5282. **Arathoon, D.** "The Impact of Industrialization on Saltfleet Township, 1964-1971." M.A. thesis, Waterloo, 1973.
5283. **Armitage, Andrew.** *Once upon a Time in Owen Sound*. Cheltenham: Boston Mills, 1978.
5284. **Barker, Kent.** "Ajax: Planning a New Town in Ontario." *CPR* 1, no. 1 (1951):6-15.
5285. **Barr, Elinor, and Dyck, Betty.** *Ignace: A Saga of the Shield*. Winnipeg: Prairie Publishing, 1979.
5286. **Bender, I. C.** "A Case Study of the Social and Economic Development of a New Frontier Town: Atikokan, Ontario." B.A. essay, Western Ontario, 1968.
5287. **Bleasdale, Ruth E.** "Irish Labourers on the Cornwall, Welland, and Williamburg Canals." M.A. thesis, Western Ontario, 1976.
5288. **Boyer, Robert J.** *A Good Town Grew Here: The Story of Bracebridge, Ontario, 1860-1914*. Bracebridge: *Herald-Gazette*, 1975.
5289. **Brown, L. Carson.** "The Red Lake Gold Field." *CGEJ* 70 (1965):114-25.
5290. **Brown, Lewis.** *A History of Simcoe, 1829-1929*. Simcoe: Pearce, 1929.
5291. **Campbell, Isabelle.** *From Forest to Thriving Hamlets*. [Huron County]. Seaforth: Huron *Expositor*, 1968.

5293. **Clarkson, Marion E.** *Credit Valley Gateway: The Story of Port Credit.* Port Credit: Port Credit Public Library, 1967.
5294. **Collingwood Centennial Committee.** *The Story of Collingwood, 100 Years, 1858-1958.* Collingwood: Enterprise-Bulletin, 1958.
5295. **Cramm, E. W. R.** "An Analysis of the Urban Process in Pickering Township." M.A. thesis, Toronto, 1963.
5296. **Craven, Edna.** *In the Beginning: The Story of New Liskeard.* New Liskeard: Temiskaming Print Co., 1977.
5297. **Crichton, Vincent.** *Pioneering in Northern Ontario [Chapleau].* Belleville: Mika, 1976.
5298. **Cromien, P. B.** "Non-resident Landownership in the County of Lennox and Addington, 1951 to 1971." M.A. thesis, York, 1975.
5299. **Davidson, T. Arthur.** *A New History of the County of Grey and the Many Communities within Its Boundaries and the City of Owen Sound.* Owen Sound: Grey County Historical Society, 1972.
5300. **Duquemin, C. K.** "Sequent Occupance in the Lower Valley of Twenty Mile Creek, Lincoln County, South Township, Ontario: 1800-1905." M.A. thesis, New York, 1968.
5301. **Eadie, James A.** "The Napanee Mechanics' Institutes: The Nineteenth-Century Ontario Mechanics' Institute Movement in Microcosm." *OH* 68 (1976):209-21.
5302. **Farrell, John K. A.** "The History of the Negro Community in Chatham, Ontario, 1787-1865." Ph.D. thesis, Ottawa, 1965.
5303. **Fremelin, G.** "Historical Geography of Urban Development in Huron County." M.A. thesis, Western Ontario, 1958.
5304. **Germain, Dorie.** "L'évolution de la langue des travailleurs de la forêt de la région de Hearst." *Bulletin du Centre de recherche en civilisation canadienne-française* 14 (1977):22-26.
5305. **Goltz, E.** "Espanola: The History of a Pulp and Paper Town." *Laurentian Univ Rev* 6, no. 3 (1974):75-104.
5306. **Greaves, S. M.** "Severance Development: A Micro Study of Albion Township." M.A. thesis, Waterloo, 1975.
5307. **Guénette, R.** "L'histoire de Sturgeon Falls." Thèse de M.A., Laval, 1966.
5308. **Hall, D. J.** "Economic Development in Elgin County 1850-1880." M.A. thesis, Guelph, 1971.
5308A. **Harkness, John Graham.** *Stormont, Dundas, and Glengarry. A History 1784-1945.* Oshawa: Mundy-Goodfellow, 1946.
5309. **Ireland, John.** "Andrew Drew and the Founding of Woodstock." *OH* 60 (1968):230-45.
5310. **James, C. C.** "Origin of 'Napanee.' " *OHS, PR* 6 (1905):47-49.
5311. **Kauffman, Carl.** *Logging Days in Blind River, a Review of the Events That Established a Town.* Sault Ste. Marie: Sault *Star,* 1970.
5312. **Lee-Whiting, Brenda.** "An Energy Crisis in 1905 Ruined the Boomlet Ontario Town of Osceola." *CGEJ* 93, no. 2 (1976):32-37.
5313. **Lyons, Marjorie Eleanor.** "Elizabethtown: A Typical St. Lawrence River Township; Some Phases of Its Settlement and Development to 1850." M.A. thesis, Queen's, 1935.
5314. **MacDonald, J. E.** *This Point of Land, an Account of the Early History of Thessalon and the Surrounding Farming Community.* Sault Ste. Marie: Sault *Star,* 1977.
5315. **McFarlane, Leslie.** *A Kid in Haileybury.* Cobalt: Highway Book Shop, 1975.
5316. **MacKenzie, N. H.** "The Economic and Social Development of Muskoka, 1855-1888.' M.A. thesis, Toronto, 1943.
5317. **Marmick, Alice.** *Northland Post: The Story of the Town of Cochrane.* Cochrane, 1950.
5318. **Mathews, Hazel.** *Oakville and the Sixteen: The History of an Ontario Port.* 1953. Rev. ed. Toronto: UTP, 1971.

5319. **Mika, Nick, and Mika, Helma.** *Trenton, Past and Present: An Illustrated Glimpse into History.* Belleville: Mika, 1967.
5320. **Morris, John Alfred.** *Prescott, 1810-1967.* Prescott: Prescott *Journal*, 1967.
5321. **Mutambirwa, Christopher C.** "An Analytical Model of a Small Urban Community: The Case of the City of Woodstock." *Ont Geogr* 6 (1971):29-46.
5322. **Neal, Carolyn.** *Paris and Wolverton: A Tour.* Toronto: Architectural Conservancy of Ontario, 1975.
5323. **Norris, Darrell.** "Business Location and Consumer Behaviour, 1882-1910: Eastern Grey County, Ontario." Ph.D. thesis, McMaster, 1976.
5324. **Parrott, Donald F.** *The Second Gold Rush to Red Lake, 1945-1946.* Red Lake, 1976.
5325. **Rees, R.** "Brampton, Ontario—An Urban Study." M.A. thesis, Toronto, 1960.
5326. **Robertson, J. K.** "Tayville: Sketches of an Ontario Town in the Nineties." *QQ* 37 (1930):711-23; 38 (1931):667-77.
5327. **Roulston, P. J.** "The Urbanization of Nineteenth-Century Orangeville, Ontario: Some Historical and Geographical Aspects." M.A. thesis, Toronto, 1974.
5328. **Smallfield, W. E.** *The Story of Renfrew from the Coming of the First Settlers about 1820.* Renfrew: Smallfield, 1919.
5329. **Smith, Donald.** *At the Forks of the Grand: 20 Historical Essays on Paris, Ontario.* Paris: Paris Centennial Committee, 1956.
5330. **Smith, W. Randy.** *The Early Development of Three Upper Canadian Towns: Barrie, Holland Landing, and Newmarket.* Toronto: York University, Dept. of Geography, 1977.
5331. "The Storm after the Flood: The Fight for Port Hope." *Canadian Heritage* (June 1980):7-9.
5332. **Stymeist, David H.** *Ethnics and Indians: Social Relations in a Northwestern Ontario Town.* Toronto: Peter Martin, 1975.
5333. **Tait, Terence D.** "Haileybury: The Early Years." *OH* 55 (1963):194-204.
5334. **Walker, Gerald.** "Social Networks and Territory in a Commuter Village, Bond Head, Ontario." *Can Geogr* 21 (1977):329-50.
5335. **Walker, John A.** "Municipal Government in the County of Kent." Kent Historical Society, *Papers and Addresses* 2 (1915):19-29.
5336. **Walton, J. W.** "Blacks in Buxton and Chatham, Ontario: Did the 49th Parallel Make a Difference?" Ph.D. thesis, Princeton, 1979.
5337. **Whitebread, K.** "Historical Urban Development: The City of Brampton 1780-1875." B.A. essay, York, 1975.
5338. **Wice, George.** *Carved from the Wilderness. The Intriguing Story of Dryden, 1867-1967.* Dryden: Wilson, 1967.
5339. **Wills, Harold A.** *The Public Utilities of Cochrane, Ontario, 1910-1970.* Cochrane: Public Utilities Commission, 1970.
5340. **Wood, Harold A.** "The St. Lawrence Seaway and Urban Geography, Cornwall-Cardinal, Ont." *GEOR* 45 (1955):509-30.
5341. ———. "The Influence of the St. Lawrence Seaway upon the Cornwall-Prescott Area, Ontario." *Can Geogr* no. 7 (1956):31-34.
5342. **Yamazuchi, Takashi.** "The Single Enterprise Town of Wawa and Algoma Ore Properties." M.A. thesis, Toronto, 1960.

IX

Western Canada

1. General

5343. **Allan, D. D.** "The Effect of the Panama Canal on Western Canada." M.A. thesis, British Columbia, 1938.
5344. **Anderson, James D.** "The Municipal Government Reform Movement in Western Canada, 1880-1920." In #29, pp. 73-111.
5345. **Appana, M.** "An Analysis of Factors Influencing the Location of Manufacturing Industries in the Prairies." M.A. thesis, Manitoba, 1975.
5346. **Appelton, John.** "After War Financial Problems of Western Municipalities." *J Can Bank Assoc* 27 (1920): 162-67.
5347. **Armstrong, H. J.** "Municipal Problems in Western Canada." *Cn L* 3, no. 3 (1917):59-63.
5348. **Artibise, Alan F. J.** *Western Canada Since 1870: A Select Bibliography and Guide.* Vancouver: UBCP, 1978.
5349. _____. "Continuity and Change: Elites and Prairie Urban Development, 1914-1950." In #29, pp. 130-54.
5350. _____. "The Urban West: The Evolution of Prairie Towns and Cities to 1930." *Prairie For* 4 (1979):237-62.
5351. _____. "Boosterism and the Development of Prairie Cities, 1871-1913." In #5352, pp. 209-35.
5352. _____, ed. *Town and City: Aspects of Western Canadian Urban Development.* Regina: Canadian Plains Research Center, 1981.
5353. **Boddy, Trevor.** "Boomtown Urban Design: Prairie Architecture Examined." *Can Arch* 24 (October 1979):38-41.
5354. **Careless, J. M. S.** "Aspects of Urban Life in the West, 1870-1914." In #85, pp. 125-41.
5355. **Clark, A. B.** *An Outline of Provincial and Municipal Taxation in British Columbia, Alberta, and Saskatchewan.* Winnipeg: University of Manitoba, 1920.
5356. **Clark, S. D.** "The Prairie Wheat-Farming Frontier and the New Industrial City." In *The Developing Canadian Community,* edited by S. D. Clark, pp. 99-114. Toronto: UTP, 1962.
5357. **Dale, Edmund H.** "The General Problems of Western Canada's Small Rural Towns." *Regina Geogr Stud* 1 (1977):87-100.
5358. **Dalzell, A. G.** "New Lamps for Old in Western Canada." *TPICJ* 10, no. 2 (1931):44-50.
5359. **Davies, W. K. D., and Barrow, G. T.** "A Comparative Factoral Ecology of Three Canadian Prairie Cities." *Can Geogr* 17 (1973):327-53.
5360. **Davis, Arthur K.** "Urban Indians in Western Canada: Implications for Social Theory and Social Policy." *RSC, Trans,* 4th ser. 1 (1968):217-28.

5361. **Duncan, Albert S.** "Unemployment Relief in the Prairie Provinces, 1930-1937." M.A. thesis, McGill, 1938.

5362. **Galbraith, J. S.** "Land Policies of the Hudson's Bay Company, 1870-1913." *CHR* 32 (1951):1-21.

5363. **Gold, N. L.** "American Migration to the Prairie Provinces of Canada, 1890-1933." Ph.D. thesis, California, 1933.

5364. **Gracie, B. A.** "The Agrarian Response in Prairie Canada to Industrialization and Urbanization: 1900-1935." Ph.D. thesis, McMaster, 1976.

5365. **Gray, James H.** *Red Lights on the Prairies.* Toronto: Macmillan, 1971.

5366. ———. *Booze: The Impact of Whisky on the Prairies.* Toronto: Macmillan, 1972.

5367. **Hanson, Eric J.** "The Future of Western Canada: Economic, Social, and Political." *Can Pub Admin* 18 (1975):104-20.

5368. **Higgs, Robert Larry.** "Location Theory and the Growth of Cities in the Western Prairie Region, 1870-1900." Ph.D. thesis, Johns Hopkins, 1968.

5369. **Hodge, G. F.** "Branch Line Abandonment: Death Knell for Prairie Towns?" *Canadian Journal of Agricultural Economics* 16 (1968):54-70.

5370. **Howard, Henry.** *Canada, The Western Cities: Their Borrowings and Assets.* London: Investor's Guardian, 1914.

5371. **Innis, H. A.** "Industrialism and Settlement in Western Canada." In *Report of the International Geographical Congress,* pp. 369-76. Cambridge: Cambridge UP, 1928.

5372. **Ironside, R. G., et al.** "Frontier Development and Perspectives on the Western Canadian Frontier." In *Frontier Settlement,* edited by R. G. Ironside, V. B. Proudfoot, E. N. Shannon, C. J. Tracie, pp. 1-45. Edmonton: University of Alberta, Studies in Geography, 1974.

5373. **Jones, David C.; Sheehan, Nancy M.; and Stamp, Robert M., eds.** *Shaping the Schools of the Canadian West.* Calgary: University of Calgary, Dept. of Educational Foundations, 1979.

5374. **Kinsley, B. L.** "Social Conflict and Religious Reform: A Protestant Church in a Prairie Province Mining Town." M.A. thesis, Calgary, 1968.

5375. **Lenz, Karl.** "Large Urban Places in the Prairie Provinces: Their Development and Location." In *Canada's Changing Geography,* edited by R. L. Gentilcore, pp. 199-211. Scarborough: Prentice-Hall, 1967.

5376. **Lier, John.** "The Impact of the Rural Economy on Urban Structure and Form in the Canadian Wheat Belt." Ph.D. thesis, California (Berkeley), 1968.

5377. **Liggett, W. D.** "Planned Shopping Centres in the Prairie Provinces." M.A. thesis, Calgary, 1974.

5378. **McCann, L. D.** "Urban Growth in Western Canada, 1880-1960." *Alta Geogr* 5 (1969):65-74.

5379. **McCormack, A. Ross, and MacPherson, Ian, eds.** *Cities in the West: Papers of the Western Canada Urban History Conference—University of Winnipeg, October 1974.* Ottawa: National Museum of Man, Mercury Series, History Division Paper No. 10, 1975.

5380. **Mitchell, E. B.** *In Western Canada before the War: A Study of Communities.* London: Murray, 1915.

5381. **Morton, W. L.** "The Significance of Site in the Settlement of the American and Canadian West." *Ag Hist* 25 (1951):97-109.

5382. **Mozersky, K. A.** "Structure Differentiation of Community: An Analysis of Western Canadian Communities Undergoing Change." Ph.D. thesis, Cornell, 1970.

5383. **Murray, Olin B.** "Urban Growth and Population Shifts in the Prairie Region." *Can Lib J* 28 (1971):344-50.

5384. **Nader, G. A.** "Some Aspects of the Recent Growth and Distribution of Apartments in the Prairie Metropolitan Areas." *Can Geogr* 15 (1971):307-17.

5385. **Neilsen, M.** "The R.C.M.P. in Small Communities: A Question of Policy Style." M.A. thesis, Calgary, 1979.
5386. **Osborne, Kenneth, ed.** *The Prairies: Selected Historical Sources.* Toronto: M&S, 1969.
5387. **Peel, Bruce.** *A Bibliography of the Prairie Provinces to 1953, with Biographical Index.* 1956. 2d ed. Toronto: UTP, 1973.
5387A. **Perks, W. T.** "Canadian Planning: The View from the West." *Plan Canada* 20 (1980):69-72.
5388. **Phillips, Paul A.** "Structural Change and Population Distribution in the Prairie Region, 1911-1961." M.A. thesis, Saskatchewan, 1963.
5389. _____. "The Prairie Urban System, 1911-1961: Specialization and Change." In #5352, pp. 7-30.
5390. **Pickersgill, T. B.** "The Vanishing Prairie Village." *Habitat* 4, no. 3 (1961):16-20.
5391. **Poulin, Guy.** *Index to the Township Plans of the Canadian West/Index de plans des cantons de l'ouest canadien.* Ottawa: PAC, 1974.
5392. **Rasporich, A. W.** "Uptopian Ideals and Community Settlements in Western Canada, 1880-1914." In *The Canadian West,* edited by Henry C. Klassen, pp. 37-62. Calgary: University of Calgary and Comprint Publishing, 1977.
5393. **Regehr, T. D.** "Historiography of the Canadian Plains after 1870." In *A Region of the Mind,* edited by Richard Allen, pp. 87-102. Regina: Canadian Plains Research Center, 1973.
5394. **Reid, A. N.** "Local Government in the North-West Territories: The Villages." *Sask Hist* 4 (1951):41-56.
5395. _____. "Urban Municipalities in the North-West Territories: Their Development and Machinery of Government." *Sask Hist* 9 (1956):41-62.
5396. _____. "Functions of Urban Municipalities in the North-West Territories: Public Works and Public Utilities." *Sask Hist* 10 (1957):81-96.
5397. **Selwood, H. J., and Baril, Evelyn.** "The Hudson's Bay Company and Prairie Town Development, 1870-1888." In #5352, pp. 61-94.
5398. **Smith, Peter J.** "Changing Forms and Patterns in the Cities." In *The Prairie Provinces,* edited by Peter J. Smith, pp. 99-117. Toronto: UTP, 1972.
5399. **Spencer, L. O.** "Development and Planning of the Small Prairie Community in an Era of Rural Change." M.C.P. thesis, Manitoba, 1974.
5400. **Stabler, A.** *Taxation of Land Values in Western Canada.* History and Economics, No. 4. Montreal: McGill University, 1914.
5401. **Stabler, Jack C.** "The Future of Small Communities in the Canadian Prairie Region." *Contact* 9 (1977):145-73.
5402. **Taylor, John H.** "The Urban West: Public Welfare and a Theory of Urban Development." In #5379, pp. 286-313.
5403. **Thompson, Roderick Ross.** "Commodity Flows and Urban Structure: A Case Study in the Prairie Provinces." Ph.D. thesis, Calgary, 1977.
5404. **Voisey, Paul.** "The Urbanization of the Canadian Prairies, 1871-1916." *HS* 15 (1975):77-101.
5405. **Wade, F. C.** *Experiments with the Single Tax in Western Canada.* Denver: National Tax Association, 1914.
5406. **Warkentin, John H.** "Western Canada in 1886." H.S.S.M. *Trans,* ser. 3, 20 (1963-64):85-116.
5407. **Weir, Thomas K.** "Road back from the Prairie: Canadian Pioneers Settle in Cities." *Geogr Mag* 45 (1973):506-11.
5408. **Welling, Steven Lawrence.** "A Socio-Economic Classification of Prairie Towns in 1971." M.A. thesis, Calgary, 1977.

5409. **Whetten, N. L.** "The Social and Economic Structure of the Trade Centre in the Canadian Prairie Provinces with Special References to Its Change, 1910-1930." Ph.D. thesis, Harvard, 1932.
5410. **Whiteley, A. S.** "The Peopling of the Prairie Provinces of Canada." *AJS* 38 (1932):240-52.
5411. **Wickett, S. Morley.** "Municipal Government in the North-West Territories." *Can Mag* 26 (1905):67-69.
5412. _____. "Municipal Government in the North-West Territories." In **#895,** pp. 149-64.
5413. **Zimmerman, C. C., and Moneo, G. W.** *The Prairie Community System.* Ottawa: Agricultural Economics Research Council of Canada, 1971.

X

Manitoba

1. General

5414. **Donnelly, M. S.** *The Government of Manitoba.* Toronto: UTP, 1963.
5415. **Elias. P. D.** *Metropolis and Hinterland in Northern Manitoba.* Winnipeg: Manitoba Museum of Man and Nature, 1975.
5416. **Ewart, Alan C.** "Municipal History of Manitoba." In **#895,** pp. 131-48.
5417. **Fisher, Murray.** "Local Government Reorganization." H.S.S.M. *Trans,* ser. 3, 17 (1960-61):15-23.
5418. **Friesen, G. A.** *A Guide to the Study of Manitoba Local History.* Winnipeg: University of Manitoba Press, 1980.
5419. **Friesen, J.** "Expansion of Settlement in Manitoba, 1870-1890." H.S.S.M. *Trans,* ser. 3, 20 (1963-64):35-48.
5420. **H.S.S.M.** *Local History in Manitoba: A Key to Places, Districts, Schools and Transport Routes.* Winnipeg, 1976.
5421. **Hutchings, C. J.** "Municipal Taxation in Manitoba." M.A. thesis, Manitoba, 1927.
5422. **King, T. P.** "Taxation in Manitoba: Provincial and Municipal." M.A. thesis, Manitoba, 1926.
5423. **Lagasse, J. H.** "Community Development in Manitoba." *Human Organization* 20 (1961-62):232-37.
5424. **Loveridge, D. M.** *Historical Directory of Manitoba Newspapers, 1859-1978.* Winnipeg: University of Manitoba Press, 1980.
5425. **Manitoba.** Royal Commission on Local Government Organization and Finance. *Report [The Michener Report].* Winnipeg: Queen's Printer, 1964.
5426. **Merrill, Lesley I.** "Population Distribution in the Riding Mountains and Adjacent Plains of Manitoba and Saskatchewa, 1870-1946." M.A. thesis, McGill, 1953.
5427. **Morley, Marjorie.** *A Bibliography of Manitoba from Holdings in the Legislative Library of Manitoba.* 1953. Rev. ed. Winnipeg: Manitoba Legislative Library, 1970.
5428. **Phillips, A. D.** "The Development of Municipal Institutions in Manitoba to 1886." M.A. thesis, Manitoba, 1948.
5429. **Rich, S. George.** "Manitoba: Planning Assistance to Communities outside the Greater Winnipeg Area." *CPR* 8, no. 1 (1958):16-18.
5430. **Richtik, James M.** "A Historical Geography of the Interlake Area of Manitoba, 1871-1921." M.A. thesis, Manitoba, 1964.
5431. _____. "Manitoba Service Centres in the Early Settlement Period." *J Minnesota Academy of Science* 34 (1967):17-21.

5432. Sarbit, L. "Central Place Structure ana Change in Southern Manitoba Communities, 1961-1971." M.A. thesis, York, 1977.
5433. Scott, M. M. *A Bibliography of Western Canadian Studies Relating to Manitoba.* Winnipeg: Western Canada Research Council, 1967.
5434. Sinclair, Gordon. "Cities and Towns of Manitoba." *CGEJ* 81 (1970):54-63.
5435. Walker, David, ed. *Urban Growth: Choices for Manitobans.* Winnipeg: Institute of Urban Studies, 1976.
5436. Warkentin, John H., and Ruggles, Richard I. *Historical Atlas of Manitoba: A Selection of Facsimile Maps, Plans and Sketches from 1612 to 1969.* Winnipeg: H.S.S.M., 1970.
5437. Watts, William John. "A Central Place Hierarchy in Manitoba, Based on Hydro Consumption." M.A. thesis, Manitoba, 1968.
5438. Wong, W. H. "A Statistical Analysis of Selected Population Characteristics for Ninety Settlements in Manitoba." M.A. thesis, Manitoba, 1971.
5439. Young, Dennis A. "The Report of the Manitoba Royal Commission on Local Government Organization and Finance." *Can Pub Admin* 8 (1965):24-35.

2. Brandon

5440. *Brandon, Manitoba, Canada, and Her Industries.* Winnipeg: Steen and Boyce, 1882.
5441. Brown, G. W. "Unemployment in the City of Brandon." M.A. thesis, McMaster, 1932.
5442. Carter, Thomas Sydney. "A Rationalization of School Catchment Areas and Future School Locations: A Case Study of the City of Brandon." M.A. thesis, Saskatchewan, 1970.
5443. Clark, W. L. R. "Politics in Brandon City, 1899-1949." Ph.D. thesis, Alberta, 1976.
5444. Coleman, MacDonald. *The Face of Yesterday: The Story of Brandon, Manitoba.* Brandon: Junior Chamber of Commerce, 1957.
5445. Csversko, R. P. "The Urban Fringe of Brandon." B.A. essay, Brandon, 1971.
5446. MacDonald, Donald Ian. "A Study of the Financial Problems of an Urban Municipality in Manitoba: The City of Brandon." M.A. thesis, Toronto, 1938.
5447. Monu, E. D. "Rural Migrants in an Urban Community: A Study of Migrants from the Interlake Region of Manitoba in Winnipeg and Brandon." M.A. thesis, Manitoba, 1969.
5448. Rowe, Kaye. "Brandon: The Wheat City." *CGEJ* 78 (1969):159-63.
5449. Stadel, C. "Service Areas of a Non-Primate City in the Canadian Prairies: The Case of Brandon, Manitoba." In *Southern Prairies Field Excursion: Background Papers,* edited by A. H. Paul and E. H. Dale, pp. 77-104. Regina: University of Regina, 1972.

3. Churchill

5450. Campbell, A. C. "Churchill: Northern Metropolis." *Can Unionist* 6 (March 1933):167-70.
5451. Kingsmille, Roden. "The Back Door to the Northwestern Wheat Fields." *Can Mag* 31 (1908):549-52.
5452. Koolage, William Warren. "Adaptation of Chipewyan Indians and Other Persons of Native Background in Churchill, Manitoba." Ph.D. thesis, North Carolina, 1971.
5453. Pritchard, F. B. "A Development Plan for Churchill, Manitoba." M.C.P. thesis, Manitoba, 1970.
5454. Ridout, Dengil G. "Port Churchill." *CGEJ* 3 (1931):105-28.
5455. Saskatchewan. Department of Railways, Labour and Industries. *The Hudson Bay Route and the Port of Churchill in the Centre of Canada.* Regina: King's Printer, 1933.
5456. Turnbull, Thomas G. "A Functional View of Churchill, Manitoba." M.A. thesis, Southern Illinois, 1958.
5457. Williams, M. Y. "Churchill, Manitoba." *CGEJ* 39 (1949):122-33.

4. Dauphin

5458. Dauphin Historical Society. *Dauphin Valley Spans the Years.* Dauphin: The Society, 1970.
5459. Stewart, A. "The Dauphin District." M.A. thesis, Manitoba, 1932.
5460. Warkentin, John H. "Geography of the Dauphin Area." M.A. thesis, Toronto, 1954.
5461. _____. "The Dauphin Area—An Example of Regional Differentiation in the Canadian West." *Can Geogr* 1, no. 5 (1954):71-84.

5. Minnedosa

5462. Brown, E. J. "Early Days of Minnedosa." H.S.S.M. *Trans,* ser. 3, 21 (1964-65):7-12.
5463. Potyondi, Barry. "Country Town: The History of Minnedosa, Manitoba, 1879-1922." M.A. thesis, Manitoba, 1978.
5464. _____. "In Quest of Limited Urban Status: The Town Building Process in Minnedosa, 1879-1906." In #5352, pp. 121-46.
5465. Rose, W. J. "Early Minnedosa: The Crossing, the Town, and the Railway." H.S.S.M. *Trans,* ser. 3, 15 (1960):69-79.

6. Portage la Prairie

5466. Bell, M. J. "Portage la Prairie from Earliest Times to 1907." M.A. thesis, Manitoba, 1926.
5467. Collier, Anne M. *A History of Portage la Prairie and Surrounding District.* Portage la Prairie: City Council, 1969.
5468. Hecht, Alfred. "An Investigation into Central Place Aspects of Portage la Prairie." M.Sc. thesis, Manitoba, 1968.
5469. Metcalfe, J. H., ed. *The Tread of the Pioneers.* Toronto: Ryerson, 1932.
5470. Metcalfe, William H. "Portage la Prairie." *CGEJ* 76 (1968):64-71.
5471. *Portage la Prairie, Manitoba, and Her Industries.* Winnipeg: Steen and Boyce, 1882.
5472. Williamson, Norman J. "Some Settlement Patterns in the Area of Portage la Prairie." *Manitoba Pageant* 22 (Spring 1977):1-4.

7. St. Boniface

5473. Belton, G. S. "A History of the Origin and Growth of Schools in the City of St. Boniface." M.Ed. thesis, Manitoba, 1959.
5474. Donnelly, M. S. "Ethnic Participation in Municipal Government: Winnipeg, St. Boniface and the Metro Corporation of Greater Winnipeg." In #870, pp. 61-70.
5475. Driedger, Leo. "Maintenance of Urban Ethnic Boundaries: The French in St. Boniface." *Sociological Q* 20 (1979):89-108.
5476. LaPierre, Laurier. "Joseph-Israël Tarte et les évêques de Saint-Boniface." CCHA, *Study Sessions* 37 (1970):173-95.
5477. Turnbull, I. D. "Local Autonomy and Municipal Re-organization: A Study of Ethnic Influence on the Local Politics of St. Boniface." M.A. thesis, Manitoba, 1967.

8. The Pas

5478. Robinson, M. E., and Robinson, A. C. "The Pas—Crossroads of the New North." *CGEJ* 45 (1952):54-63.

5479. **Sim, Victor W.** "The Pas, Manitoba." *Geogr Bull* 8 (1956):1-21.
5480. **Wilton, Sidney.** *The Pas: A History.* The Pas: Chamber of Commerce, 1970.

9. Winnipeg

a. General

5481. **Anderson, J. C.** "Winnipeg: Golden Boy of the West." *Can Bus* 28 (September 1955):24-29.
5482. **Artibise, Alan F. J.** "Researching Winnipeg." *UHR* 2-72 (June 1972):14-18.
5483. ———. "An Urban Economy: Patterns of Economic Change in Winnipeg, 1873-1971." *Prairie For* 1 (1976):163-88.
5484. ———. "Patterns of Population Growth and Ethnic Relationships in Winnipeg, 1874-1974." *HS* 9 (1976):297-335.
5485. ———. "Winnipeg's City Halls, 1876-1965." *Manitoba Pageant* 22 (Spring 1977):5-10.
5486. ———. *Winnipeg: An Illustrated History.* History of Canadian Cities Series, vol. 1. Toronto: Lorimer and NMM, 1977.
5487. ———, **and Dahl, Edward H.** *Winnipeg in Maps/Winnipeg par les cartes, 1816-1972.* Ottawa: PAC, 1975.
5488. ———. "Maps in the Study of Winnipeg's Urban Development." In #**5379,** pp. 139-57.
5489. **Avent, R. H.** "The Winnipeg Town Planning Situation." *TPICJ* 7, no. 5 (1928):140-43.
5490. **Baker, Ralph C.** "Historic Flood Profile: City of Winnipeg." *Manitoba Pageant* 24 (Summer 1979):8-13.
5491. **Bellan, R. C.** "Relief in Winnipeg: The Economic Background." M.A. thesis, Toronto, 1941.
5492. ———. "The Development of Winnipeg as a Metropolitan Centre." Ph.D. thesis, Columbia, 1958.
5493. ———. *Winnipeg First Century: An Economic History.* Winnipeg: Queenston House, 1978.
5494. **Blake, H. W.** *The Era of Streetcars in Winnipeg, 1881-1955.* Winnipeg: Hignell Printing, 1971.
5495. ———. *The Era of Interurbans in Winnipeg, 1902-1939.* Winnipeg: Bishop Printing, 1971.
5496. **Bradley, W. E.** "History of Transportation in Winnipeg." H.S.S.M. *Trans,* ser. 3, 15 (1960):7-38.
5497. **Cannell, S.** "Forty Years Ago: Reminiscences of Winnipeg." *Can Bank* 51 (1955):122-41.
5498. **Champion, G.** "The Parks and Boulevards of Winnipeg." *Can Engineer* 20 (1911):167-71.
5499. **Church, Glenn Robert.** "An Investigation of Selected Urban Recreation Variables: Winnipeg's Assiniboine Park." M.A. thesis, Manitoba, 1972.
5500. **Dingwall, C. W.** "Winnipeg and the Needle Trades." *W Bus Indus* 20 (January 1946):18-21.
5501. **Douglas, William.** "Winnipeg Parks." H.S.S.M. *Trans,* ser. 3, 14 (1959):61-65.
5502. **Duncan, Lottie Jane Chapman.** "Cost of Living in Winnipeg." M.A. thesis, Manitoba, 1925.
5503. **Durkin, Douglas.** *The Magpie.* 1923. Reprint, with an introduction by Peter E. Rider. Social History of Canada, vol. 23. Toronto: UTP, 1974.
5504. **Fraser, W. J.** *St. John's College, Winnipeg: 1866-1966.* Winnipeg: Wallingford, 1966.
5505. **Fung, Yu-Han.** "Intra-Urban Mobility in Winnipeg: A Study of Geographic Elements." M.A. thesis, Manitoba, 1972.
5506. **Goldstein, Joy.** "National Identification in Winnipeg: An Analysis of School Naming Events, 1881-1976." *Prairie For* 3 (1978):117-30.

5507. **Good, Trent Leigh.** "A Planning Analysis of Outdoor Recreation in the Winnipeg Region." M.C.P. thesis, Manitoba, 1970.
5508. **Gordon, Anna.** "The Winnipeg Jewish Community: Patterns of Leadership in an Ethnic Subcommunity." M.A. thesis, Manitoba, 1972.
5509. **Graham, J. W.** *Winnipeg Architecture, 1821-1960.* Winnipeg: Manitoba Press, 1960.
5510. **Gray, James H.** *The Boy from Winnipeg.* Toronto: Macmillan, 1970.
5511. **Harris, George.** "Cars of the Winnipeg Electric Railway, 1904-1955." *Can Rail* 220 (1970):107-17.
5512. **Hay, Elizabeth.** "The City of Winnipeg." *Empire Digest* 5 (1948):53-61.
5513. **Hayley, W. T.** "A Study of the Population of Greater Winnipeg." Manitoba Society of Regional Studies. *Regional Rev* 2 (1964):1-14.
5514. **Henderson, David Gordon.** "A Study of Housing and Environmental Conditions in the City of Winnipeg." M.Arch. thesis, Manitoba, 1952.
5516. **Herstein, Harvey H.** "The Growth of the Winnipeg Jewish Community and the Evolution of Its Educational Institutions." M.Ed. thesis, Manitoba, 1964.
5517. ———. "The Growth of the Winnipeg Jewish Community and the Evolution of Its Educational Institutions." H.S.S.M. *Trans*, ser. 3, 22 (1965-66):27-66.
5518. **Hobbs, W. E.** "The Suburban Problem of Greater Winnipeg." *TPICJ* 1, no. 10 (1922):22-32.
5519. **Hood, M. L.** "Winnipeg—From Fort Garry to 1949." *W Bus Indus* 23 (May 1949):42-44, 182-84.
5520. **Hutchison, R.** *A Century of Service: A History of the Winnipeg Police Force, 1874-1974.* Winnipeg: City of Winnipeg, 1974.
5521. **Huzel, B.** "The Interurbans of Winnipeg." *Manitoba Pageant* 21 (Winter 1976):10-11.
5522. **Johnson, T. A.** "The Needle Trades in Winnipeg: A Study in Trade Unions." M.A. thesis, Manitoba, 1948.
5523. **Kerri, James N.** "Urban Native Canadians: The Adjustment of Amerindians to the City of Winnipeg," Ph.D. thesis, Washington, 1973.
5524. **Kirkconnell, Watson.** *The Golden Jubilee of Wesley College, Winnipeg, 1888-1938: The Story of Fifty Years of Service in Preparing Young Men and Women for Life and Its Needs.* Winnipeg: Columbia Press, 1938.
5525. **Koch, E.** *Winnipeg: Gateway to the West.* Toronto: Holt, Rinehart and Winston, 1967.
5526. **Krawchuk, P.** *The Ukrainians in Winnipeg's First Century.* Toronto: Kobzar Publishing, 1974.
5527. **Kuz, T. J., ed.** *Winnipeg, 1874-1974: Progress and Prospects.* Winnipeg: Manitoba Department of Industry and Commerce, 1974.
5528. **Ling, P. T.** "An Analysis of Commercial Structure along a Major Traffic Artery in Winnipeg: A Case Study of Portage Avenue." M.A. thesis, Manitoba, 1974.
5529. **Lucow, W. H.** "The Origin and Growth of the Public School System in Winnipeg." M.Ed. thesis, Manitoba, 1959.
5530. **Lunty, A. J., and Harley, K. C.** *Armstrong's Point: An Historical Survey.* Winnipeg: Provincial Archives of Manitoba, 1969.
5531. **McArton, D.** "75 Years in Winnipeg's Social History." *Can Wel* 25 (October 1949):11-29.
5532. **McCaskill, Donald.** "The Urbanization of Native People in Toronto, Winnipeg, Edmonton, and Vancouver: A Comparative Analysis." Ph.D. thesis, York, 1979.
5533. **Marlyn, John.** *Under the Ribs of Death.* Toronto: M&S, 1957.
5534. **Medovy, Harry.** *A Vision Fulfilled: The Story of the Children's Hospital of Winnipeg, 1909-1973.* Winnipeg: Peguis, 1979.
5535. **Mitchell, George, and Benham, M. L.** *Winnipeg.* Winnipeg: City of Winnipeg, 1974.
5536. **Morton, W. L.** *One University: A History of the University of Manitoba, 1877-1952.* Toronto: M&S, 1957.

5537. **O'Malley, M.** "How Ontario Supplies Winnipeg's Water." *CGEJ* 91, no. 3 (1975):28-31.
5538. **Page, John Edward.** "Catholic Parish Ecology and Urban Development in the Greater Winnipeg Region." M.A. thesis, Manitoba, 1958.
5539. **Parr, John,** ed. *Speaking of Winnipeg.* Winnipeg: Queenston House, 1974.
5540. **Paskievich, John, and Grace, Gregory.** *A Place Not Our Own: North End Winnipeg.* Winnipeg: Queenston House, 1978.
5541. **Ramsay, A.** "Winnipeg: City of Contrast and Beauty." *CGEJ* 26 (1943):44-47.
5542. **Rea, J. E.** "How Winnipeg Was Nearly Won." In #5379, pp. 74-87.
5543. **Robertson, Thomas B.** "Winnipeg—The Prairie Capital." *CGEJ* 7 (1933):133-42.
5544. **Rosenberg, Louis.** *The Jewish Community in Winnipeg.* Montreal: Canadian Jewish Congress, 1946.
5545. _____. *A Population Study of the Winnipeg Jewish Community.* Montreal: Canadian Jewish Congress, 1946.
5546. **Rostecki, Randy R.** "The Decline and Rise of the Warehouse District of Winnipeg." *Heritage Canada* 2 (Summer 1976):28-31.
5547. **Rowe, P. A.** "The Needle Trades in Winnipeg." *W Bus Indus* 23 (November 1949):52-71.
5548. _____. "Winnipeg's Fur Trade." *W Bus Indus* 24 (May 1950):64-69.
5549. **Rudnychyj, J. B.** *Mosaic of Winnipeg Street Names.* Winnipeg: University of Manitoba, 1979.
5550. **Russenholt, E. S.** "The Power of a City." Unpublished manuscript (City of Winnipeg Hydro Office).
5551. **Selwood, H. J.** *The Winnipeg Townscape: A Survey Guide.* Winnipeg: Manitoba Environmental Council, Study No. 7, 1976.
5552. **Shipley, Nan.** *Road to the Forks: A History of the Community of Fort Garry.* Winnipeg, 1970.
5553. **Short, R. B.** "The Wholesale Function in Winnipeg." M.A. thesis, Manitoba, 1973.
5554. **Simpson, E. G.** "City of Winnipeg." *JRAIC* 30 (1961):66-68.
5555. **Sisler, W. J.** *Peaceful Invasion.* Winnipeg: Ketchum Printing, 1944.
5556. **Sloane, P. L.; Rosender, J. M.; and Hernandez, M. J.** *Winnipeg: A Centennial Bibliography.* Winnipeg: Manitoba Library Association, 1974.
5557. **Stinson, Lloyd.** *Political Warriors: Recollections of a Social Democrat.* Winnipeg: Queenston House, 1975.
5558. **Thompson, William, and Kalen, Henry.** *Winnipeg Architecture.* Winnipeg: Queenston House, 1977.
5559. **Traverso, Peter.** "The Second Time Around: An Assessment of Recycling Warehouse Structures in Winnipeg." M.C.P. thesis, Manitoba, 1977.
5560. **University of Manitoba.** *From Rural Parkland to Urban Centre:.One Hundred Years of Growth at the University of Manitoba, 1877-1977.* Winnipeg: Hyperion, 1978.
5561. **Vincent, D. B.** *The Indian-Métis Urban Probe.* Winnipeg: Institute of Urban Studies, 1971.
5562. **Weir, Thomas R.** "Winnipeg: A City in the Making." In *Western Perspectives I,* edited by David J. Bercuson, pp. 21-32. Toronto: Holt, Rinehart and Winston, 1974.
5563. _____. *Atlas of Winnipeg.* Toronto: UTP, 1978.
5564. **Wichern, P. H.,** ed. *The Development of Urban Government in the Winnipeg Area.* Background Papers on Winnipeg Government and Politics. Vol. I. Winnipeg: Dept. of Urban Affairs, Province of Manitoba, 1975.
5565. _____. *Studies in Winnipeg Politics.* Background Papers on Winnipeg Government and Politics. Vol. II. Winnipeg: Dept. of Urban Affairs, Province of Manitoba, 1976.
5566. **Will, E. J. S.** "An Economic Land Use Analysis of South Point Douglas, Winnipeg." M.C.P. thesis, Manitoba, 1966.

5567. **Winnipeg Parks and Recreation Department.** *The History and Development of Assiniboine Park and Zoo in Winnipeg, Manitoba, Canada.* Winnipeg, 1972.
5568. _____. *Kildonan Park: History and Development.* Winnipeg, 1972.
5569. _____. *St. Vital Park: History and Development.* Winnipeg, 1973.

b. Pre-1921

5570. **Arnold, A. J.** "Earliest Jews in Winnipeg, 1874-1882." *Beaver,* Outfit 305 (1974):4-11.
5571. **Artibise, Alan F. J.** "Advertising Winnipeg: The Campaign for Immigrants and Industry, 1874-1914." H.S.S.M. *Trans,* ser. 3, 27 (1970-71):75-106.
5572. _____. "An Urban Environment: The Process of Growth in Winnipeg, 1874-1914." CHA, *HP* (1972):109-34.
5573. _____. "Mayor Alexander Logan of Winnipeg." *Beaver,* Outfit 304 (1974):4-12.
5574. _____. "Winnipeg and the City Planning Movement, 1910-1915." In *Western Perspectives I,* edited by David J. Bercuson, pp. 10-20. Toronto: Holt, Rinehart and Winston, 1974.
5575. _____. "Winnipeg, 1874-1914." *UHR* 1-75 (June 1975):43-50.
5576. _____. "The Origins and Incorporation of Winnipeg." In **#5379**, pp. 5-25.
5577. _____. *Winnipeg: A Social History of Urban Growth, 1874-1914.* Montreal: McGill-Queen's UP, 1975.
5578. _____. "Divided City: The Immigrant in Winnipeg Society, 1874-1921." In **#85**, pp. 300-36.
5579. _____, ed. *Gateway City: Winnipeg in Documents, 1873-1913.* Manitoba Record Society, vol. 5. Winnipeg: University of Manitoba Press, 1979.
5580. **Avery, Donald.** "The Radical Alien and the Winnipeg General Strike of 1919." In *The West and the Nation: Essays in Honour of W. L. Morton,* edited by Carl Berger and Ramsay Cook, pp. 209-31. Toronto: M&S, 1976.
5581. **Begg, Alexander, and Nursey, W. R.** *Ten Years in Winnipeg.* Winnipeg: Times Publishing House, 1879.
5582. **Bellan, R. C.** "Rails across the Red—Selkirk or Winnipeg." H.S.S.M. *Trans,* ser. 3, 18 (1961-62):69-77.
5583. _____. "Winnipeg, 1873-1914." Manitoba Society of Reginal Studies. *Regional Rev* 6 (1963):14-21.
5584. **Bercuson, David J.** *Confrontation at Winnipeg: Labour, Industrial Relations, and the General Strike.* Montreal: McGill-Queen's UP, 1974.
5585. **Bryce, George.** "The Five Forts of Winnipeg." RSC, *Trans,* 3 (1885):134-45.
5586. **Bryce, M. S.** *Historical Sketch of the Charitable Institutions of Winnipeg.* Winnipeg: Manitoba *Free Press,* 1899.
5587. **Careless, J. M. S.** "The Development of Winnipeg Business Community." RSC, *Trans,* 4th ser. 8 (1970):230-54.
5588. **Chapman, G. F.** "Winnipeg: The Melting Pot." *Can Mag* 33 (1909):409-16.
5589. _____. "Winnipeg: The Refining Process." *Can Mag* 33 (1909):548-59.
5590. **Chisick, Ernest.** "The Origins and Development of the Marxist Socialist Movement in Winnipeg: 1904-1922." M.A. thesis, Manitoba, 1970.
5591. **Cooper, Joy.** "Red Lights of Winnipeg." H.S.S.M. *Trans,* ser. 3, 27 (1970-72):61-74.
5592. **Cowan, Anna M.** "Memories of Upper Fort Garry." *Beaver,* Outfit 266 (1935):25-30.
5593. **Craig, Irene.** "Grease Paint on the Prairies: An Account of the Theatres, the Plays, and the Players of Winnipeg, 1866-1921." H.S.S.M. *Trans,* ser 3, 3 (1947):38-53.
5594. **Dafoe, John W.** "Early Winnipeg Newspapers." H.S.S.M. *Trans,* ser. 3, 3 (1946-47):14-24.

5595. **Douglas, William.** "The Forks Become a City." H.S.S.M. *Trans,* ser. 3, 1 (1944-45):51-80.
5596. **Dupuis, Michael.** "The *Toronto Daily Star* and the Winnipeg General Strike of 1919." M.A. thesis, Ottawa, PAST. Now, however, "workm1973.
5597. **Elliot, G. B.** *Winnipeg as It Is in 1874; And as It Was in 1860.* Ottawa: *Free Press* Office, 1875.
5598. **Greening, W. E.** "The Winnipeg Strike Trials." *Industrial Relations* 20 (1965):77-86.
5599. **Grenke, Arthur.** "The Formation and Early Development of an Urban Ethnic Community: A Case Study of the Germans in Winnipeg, 1872-1919." Ph.D. thesis, Manitoba, 1975.
5600. **Harris, George.** "Cars of the Winnipeg Electric Railway, 1881-1903." *Can Rail* 212 (1969):191-97.
5601. **Healey, W. J.** *Winnipeg's Early Days: A Short Historical Sketch.* Winnipeg: Stovel Printing, 1927.
5602. _____. "Early Days in Winnipeg." *Beaver,* Outfit 280 (1949):22-25.
5603. **Henderson, A. M.** "From Fort Douglas to the Forks." H.S.S.M. *Trans,* ser. 3, 23 (1966-67):15-32.
5604. **Hislop, Mary.** *The Streets of Winnipeg.* Winnipeg: Taylor, 1912.
5605. **Hossé, Hans A.** "The Areal Growth and Functional Development of Winnipeg from 1870-1913." M.A. thesis, Manitoba, 1956.
5606. **Kerr, Donald P.** "Wholesale Trade on the Canadian Plains in the Late Nineteenth Century: Winnipeg and Its Competition." In *The Settlement of the West,* edited by Howard Palmer, pp. 130-52. Calgary: University of Calgary and Comprint Publishing, 1977.
5607. **Lavallée, Omer.** "John M. Egan, A Railway Officer in Winnipeg, 1882-1886: An Account of the Canadian Pacific's First Years in the Manitoba Capital." H.S.S.M. *Trans,* ser. 3, 33 (1976-77):35-47.
5608. **Lowe, P.** "All Western Dollars [Alloway & Champion, Bankers]." H.S.S.M. *Trans,* ser 3, 2 (1945-46):10-25.
5609. **Lucas, Fred G.** *An Historical Souvenir Diary of the City of Winnipeg.* Winnipeg: Cartwright and Lucas, 1923.
5610. **McCormack, A. Ross.** "Radical Politics in Winnipeg, 1899-1915." H.S.S.M. *Trans,* ser. 3, 29 (1972-73):81-97.
5611. **MacFarlane, R. O.** "Winnipeg in the Seventies—As Seen through the Local Press." *Man Arts Rev* 2 (1940):5-14.
5612. **MacLeod, Margaret Arnett.** "The Company in Winnipeg." *Beaver,* Outfit 271 (1940):6-11.
5613. _____. "Winnipeg and the H.B.C." *Beaver,* Outfit 280 (1949):3-7.
5614. _____. "The City That Never Was." *Beaver,* Outfit 281 (1950):12-15.
5615. **McNaught, Kenneth, and Bercuson, David J.** *The Winnipeg Strike: 1919.* Toronto: Longman, 1974.
5616. **Mitchell, R.** "How Winnipeg Waged War on Typhoid." *Man Medical Rev* 49 (1969):166-67.
5617. **Morton, W. L.** "Winnipeg and Manitoba, 1874-1922." *Man Arts Rev* (Winter 1939):29-41.
5618. **Mott, Morris K.** "The 'Foreign Peril': Nativism in Winnipeg, 1916-1923." M.A. thesis, Manitoba, 1970.
5619. **Painchaud, Robert.** *Les francophones dans le monde des affaires de Winnipeg, 1870-1920.* Saint-Boniface: La Société Historique de Saint-Boniface, 1974.
5620. **Penner, Norman, ed.** *Winnipeg 1919: The Strikers' Own History of the Winnipeg General Strike.* Toronto: James Lewis and Samuel, 1973.
5621. _____. " 'Recollections of the Early Socialist Movement in Winnipeg' by Jacob Penner." *HS* 14 (1974):366-78.

5622. **Phillips, Paul A.** " 'Power Politics': Municipal Affairs and Seymour James Farmer, 1909-1924." In **#5370**, pp. 139-57.
5623. **Pratt, D. F.** "Williams Ivens and the Winnipeg Labour Church." B.D. thesis, St. Andrew's College, Saskatoon, 1962.
5624. **Prodan, C. S.** "The Building of the Winnipeg Aqueduct." *Manitoba Pageant* 24 (Winter 1979):1-4.
5625. **Ransom, E. J.** *Winnipeg, 1905: A Metropolis in the Making.* Winnipeg: Bulman, 1905.
5626. **Rea, J. E.**, ed. *The Winnipeg General Strike.* Canadian History through the Press Series. Toronto: Holt, Rinehart and Winston, 1973.
5627. **Reynolds, G. F.** "The Man Who Created the Corner of Portage and Main." H.S.S.M. *Trans,* ser. 3, 26 (1969-70):5-40.
5628. **Rostecki, Randy R.** "Some Old Winnipeg Buildings." H.S.S.M. *Trans,* ser. 3, 29 (1972-73):5-22.
5629. _____. "The Early History of the Cauchon Block, Later the Empire Hotel." *Manitoba Pageant* 21 (Spring 1976):10-17.
5630. _____. "The Growth of Winnipeg, 1870-1886." M.A. thesis, Manitoba, 1980.
5631. **Selwood, H. J.** "Urban Development and the Streetcar: The Case of Winnipeg, 1881-1914." *UHR* 3-77 (February 1978):34-41.
5632. _____, **and Baril, Evelyn.** "Land Policies of the Hudson's Bay Company at Upper Fort Garry, 1869-1879." *Prairie For* 2 (1977):101-19.
5633. **Spector, David.** "Winnipeg's First Labour Unions." *Manitoba Pageant* 21 (Summer 1976):13-15.
5634. _____. "The 1884 Financial Scandals and the Establishment of Business Government in Winnipeg." *Prairie For* 2 (1977):167-78.
5635. _____. "From Frivolity to Purposefulness: Theatrical Development in Late Nineteenth Century Winnipeg." *Can Drama* 4 (1978):40-51.
5636. **Steen, J. E.** *Winnipeg: A Historical Sketch of Its Wonderful Growth, Progress and Prosperity.* Winnipeg: Martel, 1903.
5637. **Sutcliffe, J. H.** "The Economic Background of the Winnipeg General Strike: Wages and Working Conditions." M.A. thesis, Manitoba, 1972.
5638. **Thompson, W. T.**, ed. *The City of Winnipeg: The Capital of Manitoba and the Commercial, Railway, and Financial Metropolis of the Northwest: Past and Present Development and Future Prospects.* Winnipeg: The Commercial, 1886.
5639. **Thorarinson, S. A.** "Early Icelandic Builders in Winnipeg." *Icelandic Canadian* 25 (Spring 1967):24-30.
5640. **Tuttle, C. R.** *The Civic Situation, Including a Brief History of the Corporation of Winnipeg from 1874 to the Present Time.* Winnipeg, 1883.
5641. **Usiskin, Roz.** "The Winnipeg Jewish Community: Its Radical Elements, 1905-1918." H.S.S.M. *Trans,* ser. 3, 33 (1976-77):5-33.
5642. _____. "Winnipeg Jewish Community: Its Radical Elements, 1905-1918." *Can Jewish Outlook* 15 (January 1977):11-13; 15 (February 1977):9-11.
5643. _____. "Toward a Theoretical Reformulation of the Relationship between Political Ideology, Social Class, and Ethnicity: A Case Study of the Winnipeg Jewish Radical Community, 1905-1920." M.A. thesis, Manitoba, 1978.
5644. *Winnipeg, Manitoba, and Her Industries.* Chicago: Steen and Boyce, 1881.

c. Post-1921

5645. **Axworthy, Lloyd.** *The Citizen and Neighbourhood Renewal.* Winnipeg: Institute of Urban Studies, 1972.

5646. _____, ed. *The Future City: A Selection of Views on Government in Greater Winnipeg*. Winnipeg: Institute of Urban Studies, 1971.
5647. _____, and Cassidy, J. *Unicity: The Transition*. Winnipeg: Institute of Urban Studies, 1971.
5648. **Axworthy, T.** *The Future City: The Politics of Innovation*. Winnipeg: Institute of Urban Studies, 1972.
5649. **Barrow, G. T.** "A Factoral Ecology of Three Cities: Edmonton, Regina and Winnipeg, 1961." M.A. thesis, Calgary, 1972.
5650. **Baxter, R. S.** "The Use of Diagnostic Variables in Urban Analysis with Particular Reference to Winnipeg." M.A. thesis, Manitoba, 1968.
5651. **Bernard, A.; Léveillé, J.; and Lord, G.** *Profile: Winnipeg. The Political and Administrative Structures of the Metropolitan Region of Winnipeg*. Ottawa: MSUA, 1975.
5652. **Bickel, Ralph Paul.** "Lord Selkirk Park, Winnipeg: An Urban Renewal Project." M.C.P. thesis, Manitoba, 1966.
5653. **Bloxom, William R.** "The Residential Land Conversion Process in Winnipeg." M.A. thesis, Manitoba, 1977.
5654. **Bonnycastle, R. H. G.** "Metro Comes to Winnipeg." *Habitat* 4 (1961):2-7.
5655. **Bossen, M.** "Rental Property Management in an Older Winnipeg Neighbourhood." *Urb For* 2 (Summer 1976):34-39.
5656. **Buduban, Cleto M.** "An Urban Village: The Filipino Garment Workers in Winnipeg." M.A. thesis, Manitoba, 1972.
5657. **Cook, Gail, and Feldman, Lionel D.** "Approaches to Local Government Reform in Canada: The Case of Winnipeg." *Can Tax J* 19 (1971):216-25.
5658. **Driedger, Leo.** "Toward a Perspective on Canadian Pluralism: Ethnic Identity in Winnipeg." *CJS* 2 (1977):77-95.
5659. _____. "Ukrainian Identity in Winnipeg." In *Ethnic Canadians*, edited by Martin L. Kovacs, pp. 147-66. Regina: Canadian Plains Research Center, 1978.
5660. **Earl, L.** "Winnipeg Moves Ahead." *W Bus Indus* 35 (November 1961):28-40.
5661. **Farrugi, John Joseph.** "An Urban Renewal Scheme in Winnipeg." M.Arch. thesis, Manitoba, 1960.
5662. **Flanagan, William Francis.** "Redevelopment of Abandoned Railway Yards in the Ukrainian Neighbourhood: Planning Proposals for the Canadian National Railways Fort Rouge Yards, Winnipeg." M.C.P. thesis, Manitoba, 1972.
5663. **Fromson, R. D.** "Acculturation or Assimilation: A Geographic Analysis of Residential Segregation of Selected Ethnic Groups, Metropolitan Winnipeg, 1951-1961." M.A. thesis, Manitoba, 1965.
5664. _____. "Planning in a Metropolitan Area: The Experiment in Greater Winnipeg." M.C.P. thesis, Manitoba, 1970.
5665. **Fung, Yu-Han.** "Intra-urban Mobility in Winnipeg: A Study of Geographic Elements." M.A. thesis, Manitoba, 1972.
5666. **Gallagher, James.** "The Economic Impact of High Rise Apartment Buildings on the Central Business District of Winnipeg." M.C.P. thesis, Manitoba, 1975.
5667. **Gerry, A. C.** "A Study of Urban Recreation with Particular Emphasis on Unicity Winnipeg." M.Arch. thesis, Manitoba, 1972.
5668. **Goldenberg, H. Carl.** *Report of the Royal Commission on Municipal Finances and Administration of the City of Winnipeg*. Winnipeg: King's Printer, 1939.
5669. **Good, Trent Leigh.** "A Planning Analysis of Outdoor Recreation in the Winnipeg Region." M.C.P. thesis, Manitoba, 1970.
5670. **Henderson, David Gordon.** "A Study of Housing and Environment Conditions in the City of Winnipeg." M.Arch. thesis, Manitoba, 1952.
5671. **Hunter, A. A., and Latiff, A. H.** "Stability and Change in the Ecological Structure of Winnipeg: A Multi-Method Approach." *Can Rev Soc Anth* 10 (1973):308-34.

5672. **Kent, R. H.** "The Dissonant Decade: A Study of Conflict between the City of Winnipeg and the Metropolitan Corporation of Greater Winnipeg." M.B.A. thesis, Manitoba, 1970.
5673. **Kerri, James N.** "Indians in a Canadian City [Winnipeg]: Analysis of Social Adaptive Strategies." *Urban Anthr* 5 (1976):143-56.
5673A. _____. "The Economic Adjustment of Indians in Winnipeg." *Urban Anthr* 5 (1976):351-65.
5674. **Laing, G. A.** *A Community Organizes for War: The Story of the Greater Winnipeg Co-ordinating Board for War Services and Affiliated Organizations, 1939-1946.* Winnipeg: The Board, 1948.
5675. "Land and City Politics in Winnipeg." *City Mag* 2, no. 8 (1977):21-29.
5676. **Levin, Earl A.** "Winnipeg Uni-City." *CPR* 21, no. 2 (1971):4-5.
5677. **Lightbody, James W.** "Adapting Urban Institutions: The Reform of Winnipeg, 1971." Ph.D. thesis, Queen's, 1977.
5678. _____. "Electoral Reform in Local Government: The Case of Winnipeg." *CJPS* 11 (1978):307-32.
5679. _____. "The Reform of a Metropolitan Government: The Case of Winnipeg, 1971." *Can Public Policy* 4 (1978):489-504.
5680. **McCracken, Melinda.** *Memories Are Made of This: What It Was Like to Grow Up in the Fifties.* Toronto: Lorimer, 1975.
5681. **McKillop, A. B.** "Citizen and Socialist: The Ethos of Political Winnipeg, 1919-1935." M.A. thesis, Manitoba, 1970.
5682. _____. "The Socialist as Citizen: John Queen and the Mayoralty of Winnipeg, 1935." *H.S.S.M. Trans,* ser. 3, 30 (1973-74):61-80.
5683. _____. "A Communist [Jacob Penner] in City Hall." *Can Dimension* 10, no. 1 (1974):41-50.
5684. _____. "The Communist as Conscience: Jacob Penner and Winnipeg Civic Politics, 1934-1935." In #5379, pp. 181-209.
5685. **MacPherson, L. G.** "Report of the Royal Commission on the Municipal Finances and Administration of the City of Winnipeg, 1939." *CJEPS* 6 (1940):68-72.
5686. **Manitoba.** *Proposals for Urban Reorganization in the Greater Winnipeg Area.* Winnipeg, 1970.
5687. **Masters, D. C.** "The English Communities in Winnipeg and in the Eastern Townships of Quebec." In *Regionalism in the Canadian Community, 1867-1967,* edited by Mason Wade, pp. 130-59. Toronto: UTP, 1969.
5688. **Matwijiw, Peter.** "Ethnicity and Urban Residence: Winnipeg, 1941-1971." *Can Geogr* 23 (Spring 1979):45-61.
5689. **Metropolitan Corporation of Greater Winnipeg.** *The Place of Winnipeg in the Economy of Manitoba.* Winnipeg, 1971.
5690. **Morris, R. Geoffrey.** "An Evaluation of the Functions and Characteristics of a Regional Shopping Centre: Polo Park, Winnipeg." M.A. thesis, Manitoba, 1968.
5691. **Nicholson, T. G.** "The Structure of Socio-Economic Areas and Housing Types in Winnipeg, 1961." M.A. thesis, Queen's, 1968.
5692. _____, and **Yeates, Maurice H.** "The Ecological and Spatial Structure of the Socio-Economic Characteristics of Winnipeg." *Can Rev Soc Anth* 6 (1969):162-79.
5694. **Pelletier, J. A.** "Growth Pattern of Apartment Development in Metropolitan Winnipeg." M.A. thesis, Manitoba, 1975.
5695. **Pereira, Cecil Patrick.** "East Indians in Winnipeg: A Study of the Consequences of Immigration for an Ethnic Group in Canada." M.A. thesis, Manitoba, 1971.
5696. **Plunkett, Thomas J.** *Unicity: A New Form of Unified Municipal Government in Greater Winnipeg.* Winnipeg: City of Winnipeg, 1972.
5697. **Rea, J. E.** "The Politics of Conscience: Winnipeg after the Strike." *CHA, HP* (1971):276-87.

5698. ———. "The Politics of Class: Winnipeg City Council, 1919-1945." In *The West and the Nation: Essays in Honour of W. L. Morton,* edited by Carl Berger and Ramsay Cook, pp. 232-49. Toronto: M&S, 1976.

5699. ———. *Parties and Power: An Analysis of Winnipeg City Council, 1919-1975.* Appendix IV. Report and Recommendations, Committee of Review, City of Winnipeg Act. Winnipeg: Dept. of Urban Affairs, 1976.

5700. ———. "Political Parties and Civic Power: Winnipeg, 1919-1975." In #29, pp. 155-65.

5701. **Rich, S. George.** "Planning in Metropolitan Winnipeg." *CPR* 12, no. 12 (1962):21-28.

5702. ———. "Metropolitan Winnipeg, 1943-1961." In #5379, pp. 237-68.

5703. ———. "Floodway Prevents 1974 Winnipeg Flood." *CGEJ* 88, no. 6 (1974):20-29.

5704. **Richtik, James M., and Selwood, H. J.** "Metropolitan Winnipeg: An Introduction." In *Southern Prairies Field Excursion: Background Papers,* edited by A. H. Paul and E. H. Dale, pp. 3-20. Regina: University of Regina, 1972.

5705. **Robinson, B. W.** "Leisure: A Suburban Winnipeg Study." M.A. thesis, Manitoba, 1968.

5706. **Romanowski, M. E.** "Stability and Change in the Ecological Structure and Pattern of Winnipeg, 1951-1971." B.A. essay, Winnipeg, 1975.

5707. **Rowley, Gwyn.** " 'Plus ça change . . .': A Canadian Skid Row." *Can Geogr* 22 (1978):211-24.

5708. **Shackleton, Doris.** "The Indian as Newcomer [in Winnipeg]." *Can Wel* 45, no. 4 (1969): 7-9.

5709. **Sheikh, Z. A.** "Housing Environment for Downtown Winnipeg." M.Arch. thesis, Manitoba, 1968.

5710. **Siamandas, George.** "Public Policy for Downtown Redevelopment in Winnipeg." M.A. thesis, Manitoba, 1971.

5711. **Slater, Ronald William.** "A Rapid Transit System for Winnipeg." M.C.P. thesis, Manitoba, 1970.

5712. **Talbot, L. D.** "A Study of the Development of Winnipeg's Planned Shopping Centres and an Analysis of Selected Planned Shopping Centre Characteristics." M.A. thesis, Manitoba, 1974.

5713. **Taraska, Peter.** *Committee of Review, City of Winnipeg Act: Report and Recommendations.* 2 vols. Winnipeg: Government of Manitoba, 1976.

5714. **Taylor, K. W.** "Class and Ethnic Voting in Winnipeg: The Case of 1941." *Can Rev Soc Anth* 14 (1977):174-87.

5715. **Theron, J. D.** "The Redevelopment of the City Core of Winnipeg." M.C.P. thesis, Manitoba, 1968.

5716. **Thompson, John Herd.** "The Political Career of Ralph H. Webb." *Red River Valley Historian* (Summer 1976):1-7.

5717. **Thraves, Bernard.** "Urban Delphi: Methodological Considerations in Forecasting the Growth of Winnipeg." *Alta Geogr* 13 (1977):69-89.

5718. **Turnbull, Kenneth Franklin.** "A Factor Analysis of Social Area Space: Metropolitan Winnipeg, 1951-1961." M.A. thesis, Manitoba, 1974.

5719. **Vincent, D. B.** "The Development of the High-Rise Apartment Complex in the Roslyn Road Area of Winnipeg." M.A. thesis, Manitoba, 1974.

5720. **Wagner, Jonathan F.** "The *Deutsche Zeitung Für Canada:* A Nazi Newspaper in Winnipeg." H.S.S.M. *Trans,* ser. 3, 33 (1976-77):49-59.

5721. **Walker, David.** "Winnipeg and Trizec." *City Mag* 2, nos. 3 and 4 (1976):24-32.

5722. ———. *The Great Winnipeg Dream* [*:Redevelopment in Downtown Winnipeg*]. Oakville and Ottawa: Mosaic Press/Valley Editions, 1979.

5723. **Weir, Thomas R.** "Land Use and Population Characteristics of Central Winnipeg." *Geogr Bull* 9 (1956):5-21.

5724. ———. "A Survey of the Daytime Population of Winnipeg." *QQ* 67 (1961):654-62.

5725. **West, George E.** "The Relevance of Structural Reform of Local Government to the Solution of Metropolitan Problems: A Case Study of Greater Winnipeg." M.A. thesis, Waterloo, 1974.

5726. **Wichern, P. H.** *Winnipeg's Unicity after Two Years: Evaluation of an Experiment in Urban Government.* Winnipeg: University of Manitoba, Dept. of Political Studies, 1974.

5727. **Wilmot, Fred.** *"Call 320": A Documentary Record of the 1950 Manitoba Flood and Red Cross Activities in the Disaster.* Winnipeg: Canadian Red Cross Society, c. 1950.

5728. **Wiseman, N., and Taylor, K. W.** "Ethnic vs. Class Voting: The Case of Winnipeg, 1945." *CJPS* 7 (1974):314-28.

5729. _____. "Class and Ethnic Voting in Winnipeg during the Cold War." *Can Rev Soc Anth* 16 (1979):60-76.

5730. **Yauk, T. B.** "Residential and Business Relocation from Urban Renewal Areas: A Case Study, the Lord Selkirk Park Experience." M.C.P. thesis, Manitoba, 1973.

10. Other Centres

5731. **Abra, Marion.** *A History of the Municipality of Birtle, the Town of Birtle, and the Villages of Foxwarren and Solsgirth, 1894-1974.* Birtle: History Committee of the Municipality of Birtle, 1974.

5732. **Bock, J.** "An Analysis of the Educational Effort of a Single Enterprise Community: Flin Flon, Manitoba." M.Ed. thesis, Manitoba, 1970.

5733. **Brown, T. O., and Everitt, J. C.** "Carberry and Its Search for Industry." *Manitoba Pageant* 24 (Spring 1979):11-17.

5734. **Carlson, W. E.** *History of Emerson.* Emerson: *Journal,* 1950.

5735. **Chaiko, R. M.** "An Analysis of the Educational Effort of a Single Enterprise Community: Pinawa, Manitoba." M.Ed. thesis, Manitoba, 1970.

5736. **Dawson, Colleen.** *St. Vital: Past, Present and Future.* St. Vital: Gleenwood School, 1973.

5737. *Emerson, Manitoba, and Her Industries: The Gateway City to the Golden Northwest.* Winnipeg: Steen and Boyce, 1882.

5738. **Falconer, Don.** "Social Impact of Industrial Development in a Small Town: Winkler, Manitoba." In *The Human Dimension in Industrial Development,* edited by David F. Walker, pp. 69-101. Waterloo: University of Waterloo, Dept. of Geography Publication Series No. 16, 1980.

5739. **Ferguson, M. M.** *A History of St. James.* Winnipeg, 1967.

5740. **Green, W. A.** "History of Development and Organization at Flin Flon Mine." Canadian Institute of Mining and Metallurgy, *Bulletin* 33 (1930):214-21.

5741. **Hambley, George H.** *Historical Records and Accounts of the Early Pioneers of the District of Swan Lake, Manitoba, 1873-1950.* Altona: Friesen, 1953.

5742. **Harrington, Lyn.** "Thompson, Manitoba—Suburbia in the Bush." *CGEJ* 81 (1971):154-63.

5743. **Heeney, Isabelle B.** "Grand Valley: A Boom Town, 1878-1885." *Manitoba Pageant* 24 (Summer 1979):1-4.

5744. **Landa, M. J.** "Easterville: A Case Study in the Relocation of a Manitoba Native Community." M.A. thesis, Manitoba, 1969.

5745. **Lauder, Kathleen S.** "Planning for Quality of Life in New Resource Communities [Mackenzie, B.C. and Leaf Rapids, Manitoba]." M.A. thesis, Waterloo, 1977.

5746. **McFadden, C. R.** "Souris City." *Manitoba Pageant* 17, no. 3 (1972):15-18.

5747. **McLeod, F. C. J.** "Recollections of Virden, 1882." *Manitoba Pageant* 22, no. 1 (1976):6-10.

5748. **Mertz, J. P.** "The Planning of Pine Falls, Manitoba: A Model Industrial Town." *TPICJ* 8, no. 3 (1929):47-48.

5749. **Mott, Morris K.** "One Town's Team: Souris and Its Lacrosse Club, 1887-1906." *Manitoba History* 1 (Spring 1980):10-16.
5750. **Neufeld, W.** "The Growth of Steinbach, 1873-1970." B.A. essay, Winnipeg, 1971.
5751. **Phelan, R. E.** "History of Flin Flon Mine up to Construction." Canadian Institute of Mining and Metallurgy, *Bulletin* 38 (1935):55-70.
5752. **Phillips, Gordon C.** *The Rise and Fall of a Prairie Town: A History of Lauder, Manitoba.* 2 vols. Ottawa, 1974.
5753. **Redekopp, Harold I.** "An Analysis of the Social and Economic Problems of Four Small Communities in Northern Manitoba: Wabouden, Thicket Portage, Norway House and Oxford House." M.A. thesis, Manitoba, 1968.
5754. **Rowan, M. L.** "Saint-Claude, Manitoba: A Demographic Analysis." M.A. thesis, Manitoba, 1973.
5755. **Sander, Lois Anne.** "History of an Icelandic Settlement [Gimli, Manitoba]." *Icelandic Canadian* 30, no. 3 (1972):17-19.
5756. **Sealey, Margaret, and Sealey, Bruce, eds.** *Six Métis Communities.* Winnipeg: Manitoba Métis Federation Press, 1974.
5757. **Taylor, James.** "The Church in Leaf Rapids: A Model for Isolated Communities?" *United Church Observer* 43 (December 1979):14-16.
5758. **Théoret, Anatole E.** *Sainte-Rose-du-Lac.* Winnipeg: Murray, 1948.
5759. **Venables, Alex.** *Muskeg to Metropolis: Thompson, Manitoba, 1957-1970.* Thompson: Thompson Centennial Committee, 1970.
5760. **Waddell, J. M.** *Dominion City: Facts, Fiction and Hyperbole.* Dominion City: Friesen, 1970.
5761. **Winkler, H. W.** "Early Environs of Morden." *Manitoba Pageant* 16 (Spring 1971):8-10.

XI

Saskatchewan

1. General

5762. **Abramson, J. A.** *Rural to Urban Adjustment.* Ottawa: Queen's Printer, 1968.
5763. **Alty, S. W.** "The Influence of Climate and Other Geographic Factors on the Growth and Distribution of Population in Saskatchewan." *Geogr* 24 (1939):10-33.
5764. **Arora, Ved P.** *Saskatchewan History: A Bibliography.* Regina: Provincial Library, 1973.
5765. **Atcheson, James W.** "Urban and Regional Patterns in Northern Saskatchewan." M.A. thesis, Saskatchewan, 1972.
5766. **Bohi, Charles W., and Grant, H. Roger.** "The Standardized Railroad Station in Saskatchewan: The Case of the Canadian National System." *Sask Hist* 29 (1976):81-102.
5767. _____. "The Standardized Railroad Station in Saskatchewan: The Case of the Canadian Pacific." *Sask Hist* 31 (1978):81-96.
5768. **Dale, Edmund H.** "The Urban Centres of Southern Saskatchewan: Current Trends (1951-1971) and Prospects." In *Southern Prairies Field Excursion: Background Papers,* edited by A. H. Paul and Edmund H. Dale, pp. 267-310. Regina, 1972.
5769. **Dawson, G. F.** *The Municipal System of Saskatchewan.* 1947. Rev. ed. Regina: Dept. of Municipal Affairs, 1952.
5770. **Ewert, William Alfred.** "A Study of Factors Related to the Reorganization of Municipal Boundaries in Saskatchewan." M.Sc. thesis, Saskatchewan, 1945.
5771. **Ingram, D. R.** "Patterns of Urban Places in Southern Saskatchewan." M.A. thesis, McMaster, 1968.
5772. **Institute for Northern Studies.** *Settlements of Northern Saskatchewan.* Saskatoon: University of Saskatchewan, 1976.
5773. **Kovach, J. J.** "Regional Development Planning for Saskatchewan." M.C.P. thesis, Manitoba, 1970.
5774. **Kristjanson, L. F.** *Population Trends in the Incorporated Centres of Saskatchewan, 1921-1961.* Saskatoon: University of Saskatchewan, 1962.
5775. **Lamont, G., and Proudfoot, V. B.** "Recent Changes [1961-1971] in Population in Northern Saskatchewan and Alberta." In *Frontier Settlement,* edited by R. G. Ironside, V. B. Proudfoot, E N. Shannon, and C. J. Tracie, pp. 93-112. Edmonton: University of Alberta, Studies in Geography, 1974.
5776. **Lawton, Alma.** "Urban Relief in Saskatchewan during the Years of Depression, 1930-39." M.A. thesis, Saskatchewan, 1969.
5777. **MacDonald, C.** *Publications of the Governments of the North-West Territories, 1876-1905, and the Province of Saskatchewan, 1905-1952.* Regina: Legislative Library, 1952.

5778. **McLarty, R. A.** "Tracking down the Saskatchewan Budget Bureau and Planning Board of 1964." *Can Pub Admin* 22 (1979):115-23.
5779. **Matheson, Marion H.** "Townsites and Urban Land Use in Southwestern Saskatchewan." *Can Geogr* 2-4, no. 11 (1958):9-16.
5780. **Mellis, Glen Wallace.** "Mobility of Commercial Services and Their Impact on the Strength of Urban Communities in Saskatchewan: A Comparative Study Based on 1954 and 1967 Data." M.A. thesis, Saskatchewan, 1971.
5781. **Moneo, G. W.** "The Major Trade Centre Communities of Saskatchewan, 1936-1966." M.A. thesis, Calgary, 1970.
5782. **Muir, Roland E.** "Local Government Reorganization in Saskatchewan." M.A. thesis, Minnesota, 1960.
5783. **Murray, Jean E.** "The Provincial Capital Controversy in Saskatchewan." *Sask Hist* 5 (1952):81-105.
5784. ———. "The Contest for the University of Saskatchewan." *Sask Hist* 12 (1959):1-30.
5785. **Murray, W. D.** "Regional Theory and Its Practical Application in the Province of Saskatchewan." M.A. thesis, Carleton, 1965.
5786. **Nader, G. A., and Watkins, R. C.** "The Delineation of Planning Regions: A Case Study of the Province of Saskatchewan." *Plan Canada* 16 (1976):15-24.
5787. **Nasim, Shaukat Ali.** "Leadership Consequences of Urban Decline: An Analysis of the Conceptions of the Role of Local Government Held by Municipal Leaders in the Growing and Declining Communities of Saskatchewan." Ph.D. thesis, Saskatchewan, 1979.
5788. **Pohorecky, Zenon.** *Saskatchewan People: A Brief Illustrated Guide to Their Ethnocultures.* Saskatoon: Saskatchewan Dept. of Culture and Youth, 1978.
5789. **Powell, T. J. D.** "Northern Settlement, 1929-1935." *Sask Hist* 30 (1977):81-98.
5790. **Rees, Ronald.** "The Small Towns of Saskatchewan." *Landscape* 18 (1969):29-33.
5791. **Richards, J. H., ed.** *Atlas of Saskatchewan.* Saskatoon: University of Saskatchewan, 1969.
5792. **Saskatchewan Department of Industry and Commerce.** *People at Work in Saskatchewan: Small Town Industry in Saskatchewan.* Regina, 1977.
5793. *Saskatchewan Homecoming '71: A Bibliography.* Regina: Bibliographic Services Division, Provincial Library, 1971. [Reprinted with supplement in 1972].
5794. **Smiley, Donald V.** "Local Autonomy and Central Administrative Control in Saskatchewan." *CJEPS* 26 (1960):299-313.
5795. **Tracie, C. J.** "Ethnicity and Settlement in Western Canada: Doukhobor Village Settlement in Saskatchewan." In *Western Canada Research in Geography: The Lethbridge Papers,* edited by Brenton M. Barr, pp. 51-66. Vancouver: B.C. Geographical Series, No. 21, 1975.
5796. **White, C. O.** *Power for a Province: A History of Saskatchewan Power.* Regina: Canadian Plains Research Center, 1976.
5797. **Williams, P. R.** "Dynamic Aspects of a Central Place System in Southern Saskatchewan." M.A. thesis, Saskatchewan, 1972.
5798. **Young, Stewart.** "Planning Programs in Saskatchewan." *TPICJ* 10, no. 1 (1931):5-8.
5799. **Zides, Murray.** "Saskatchewan Community Planning." *CPR* 5, no. 3 (1955):106-11.
5800. **Zwack, Robert Joseph.** "The Criteria for Selecting Consulting Engineers by Urban Municipal Government in Saskatchewan." M.B.A. thesis, Saskatchewan, 1972.

2. Battleford and North Battleford

5801. **Macdonald, R. H.** "Fort Battleford, Saskatchewan." *CGEJ* 68 (1963):54-61.
5802. **McPherson, Arlean.** *The Battlefords: A History.* Saskatoon: Modern Press, 1967.
5803. **Wetton, Cecilia.** *Historic Battleford through the Years, 1875-1955.* Battleford: Board of Trade, 1955.

3. Lloydminster

5804. **Dykstra, T. L., and Ironside, R. G.** "The Effects of the Division of the City of Lloydminster by the Alberta-Saskatchewan Inter-Provincial Boundary." *Cah géogr Q* 16 (1972):261-83.
5805. **McCormick, James Hanna.** *Lloydminster, or Five Thousand Miles with the Barr Colonists.* London: Dranes, 1924.
5806. **Oliver, E. H.** "The Coming of the Barr Colonists." CHA, *AR* (1926):65-87.
5807. **Rendell, Alice.** "Letters from a Barr Colonist." *Alta HR* 11 (Winter 1963):12-27.

4. Moose Jaw

5808. **Andrews, Garry Roy.** "The National Policy and the Settlement of Moose Jaw, Saskatchewan, 1882-1914." M.A. thesis, Bemidji State, 1977.
5809. **Brennan, J. William.** "Business-Government Co-operation in Townsite Promotion in Regina and Moose Jaw, 1882-1903." In #**5352**, pp. 95-120.
5810. **Foster, Keith A.** "Moose Jaw: The First Decade, 1882-1892." M.A. thesis, Regina, 1978.
5811. **Pascoe, J. E.,** ed. *Moose Jaw, Saskatchewan, Golden Jubilee: 1903-1953.* Moose Jaw: Times-Herald, 1953.
5812. **Smith, Pamela J.** "The City of Moose Jaw Debenture Default, 1937-1945: A Case Study of Community Power." M.A. thesis, Regina, 1974.
5813. **White, C. O.** "Moose Jaw Opts for Private over Municipal Ownership of its Electrical Utility." In #**5379**, pp. 88-115.

5. Prince Albert

5814. **Abrams, Gary William David.** "A History of Prince Albert, Saskatchewan to 1914." M.A. thesis, Saskatchewan, 1965.
5815. ———. *Prince Albert: The First Century, 1866-1966.* Saskatoon: Modern Press, 1966.
5816. **Courtney, John C.** "Mackenzie King and Prince Albert Constituency: The 1933 Redistribution." *Sask Hist* 29 (1976):1-13.
5817. **Friesen, Victor Carl.** "The Old Trail from Fort Carlton to the Prince Albert Settlement." *CGEJ* 82 (1971):12-21.
5818. **Rodwell, L.** "Lands Claims in the Prince Albert Settlement." *Sask Hist* 19 (1966):1-23.
5819. ———. "Prince Albert River Lots." *Sask Hist* 19 (1966):100-110.
5820. **Turner, Norman William.** "An Explanation of Land Use in the Prince Albert Area of Saskatchewan." M.A. thesis, Saskatchewan, 1968.
5821. **Young, Stewart.** "The Prince Albert Zoning Bylaw." *TPICJ* 10, no. 1 (1931):25-27.

6. Regina

5822. **Adams, Donald Lyall.** "Floods and Flood Management in the City of Regina, 1882-1974." M.A. thesis, Calgary, 1974.
5823. **Anderson, F. W.** *Regina's Terrible Tornado.* Calgary: Frontiers Unlimited, 1964.
5824. **Barbour, Cameron Robert.** "Land Use Changes in a Central District of Regina." B.A. essay, Regina, 1973.
5825. **Barrow, G. T.** "A Factoral Ecology of Three Cities: Edmonton, Regina and Winnipeg, 1961." M.A. thesis, Calgary, 1972.
5826. **Begg, W. A.** "Town Planning in Regina." *Construction* 8 (1915):26-28.

5827. **Brennan, J. William.** "Introduction: Historical." In #**5837**, pp. 1-34.
5828. _____, ed. *Regina before Yesterday: A Visual History, 1882-1945*. Regina: City of Regina, 1978.
5829. **Brennan, Patrick H.** "Unemployment and Public Works Relief: The Regina Experience, 1929-1932." B.A. Hons. essay, Regina, 1978.
5830. **Carter, David J.** "The Railway Mission—Regina." CCHS, *Journal* 10 (1968):202-17.
5831. **Caviedes, Cesar.** "The Functional Structure of Regina." In #**5837**, pp. 53-96.
5832. **Clarke, R. S.** "Planning in Regina: Post World War II." In #**5837**, pp. 217-36.
5833. **Clements, Montagu.** "Storm Clouds over Regina." *Sask Hist* 6 (1953):17-23.
5834. **Complin, Margaret.** "Floreat Regina." *CGEJ* 9 (1934):305-12.
5835. **Cullimore, D. R.** "Water Problems of a Growing City in a Semi-Arid Area." In #**5837**, pp. 135-62.
5836. **Dale, Edmund H.** "The Wascana Centre, Regina: Innovation in the Provision and Development of Open Space." In #**5837**, pp. 97-134.
5837. _____, ed. *Regina: Regional Isolation and Innovative Development*. Western Geographical Series, vol. 18. Victoria: University of Victoria, 1980.
5838. **Davies, Kent Blair.** "Parking in Regina: Its Distribution, Form, and Impact on the Morphology of the City." B.A. essay, Regina, 1971.
5839. **Deane, R. B.** *Mounted Police Life in Canada: A Record of Thirty-One Years' Service*. London: Cassell, 1916.
5840. **Donkin, John G.** *Trooper and Redskin in the Far North-West: Recollections of Life in the North-West Mounted Police, Canada, 1884-1888*. London: Sampson, Low, Marston, Searle and Rivington, 1889.
5841. **Drake, Earl G.** "Regina, 1882-1955." *CGEJ* 50 (1955):2-17.
5842. _____. "Regina in 1895: The Fair and the Fair Sex." *Sask Hist* 8 (1955):56-63.
5843. _____. *Regina: The Queen City*. Toronto: M&S, 1955.
5844. **Forward, Charles N.** "Regina and Saskatoon as Retirement Centres." *UHR* 1-78 (June 1978):9-17.
5845. **Hatcher, Colin K.** *Saskatchewan's Pioneer Streetcars: The Story of the Regina Municipal Railway*. Montreal: Railfare Enterprises, 1971.
5846. **Heimark, H.** "A Study of the City Centre for Regina, Saskatchewan." M.C.P. thesis, Manitoba, 1968.
5847. **Hughes, Margaret.** "The Functional Hierarchy of Business Centres in Regina." M.A. thesis, Regina, 1972.
5848. **Kadaali, Stephen James.** "The *Leader-Post* and the Natural Hazards of 1929-1939: A Content Analysis." M.A. thesis, Regina, 1977.
5849. **Kasymyra, Bohdan Z.** *Early Ukrainian Settlement in Regina, 1890-1920*. Winnipeg: Progress Publishing, 1977.
5850. **Kjellander, M. V.** "Regina, Saskatchewan: Profile of a Prairie Service Center." M.A. thesis, Pittsburgh, 1950.
5851. **Luscombe, B. W.** "Social Distance and Spatial Distance: Segregation and Dispersion of Social Classes in Regina, Saskatchewan." M.A. thesis, Regina, 1977.
5852. **McAra, Peter.** *Sixty-Two Years on the Saskatchewan Prairies*. Regina, 1945.
5853. **Mackay, N.** "Study of the Local Council of Women of Regina, 1929-1933." Unpublished paper, Archives of Saskatchewan, Regina, 1973.
5854. **Mahon, W. C.** *Real Estate Highlights, 1912-1972*. Regina: Regina Real Estate Board, 1972.
5855. **Martin, Mayor.** "Regina—Parks and Playgrounds." *Construction* 8 (1915):37-39.
5856. **Matravolgyi, T. A.** "Wascana Centre." *CGEJ* 82 (1971):60-65.
5857. **Mawson, Thomas H.** *Regina: A Preliminary Report on the Development of the City*. London, 1921.

5858. **Moser, John Lucas.** "The Impact of City Council's Decisions between 1903 and 1930 on the Morphological Development of Regina." M.A. thesis, Regina, 1978.
5859. _____. "Regina: Development by Controls—Prelude to Town Planning, 1930-1946." In #5837, pp. 187-216.
5860. **Neal, M. W.** *Regina, "Queen City of the Plains," 1903-1953.* Regina: Western Printers, 1953.
5861. **Neely, Byron Robert George.** "The Growth and Development of the Regina Educational System from Its Beginning to 1944." M.Ed. thesis, Saskatchewan, 1946.
5862. **O'Neill, Patrick B.** "Regina's Golden Age of Theatre: Her Playhouses and Players." *Sask Hist* 28 (1975):29-37.
5863. **Powers, J. W.** *The History of Regina.* Regina: *Leader,* 1887.
5864. **Reese, N. A.** "Regina: Her Development." *Construction* 8 (1915): 29-33.
5865. **Reid, A. N.** "Informal Town Government in Regina, 1882-1883." *Sask Hist* 6 (1953):81-88.
5866. **Richan, Donald.** "Social Structure and Social Change in Regina during the First World War." B.A. Hons. essay, Regina, 1977.
5867. **Robinson, M. E.** *History of Wascana Creek.* Regina: Government of Saskatchewan, 1975.
5868. **Rosenberg, Louis.** "The History of the Regina Jewish Community." *Jewish Post* (1923). Copy in Provincial Archives of Saskatchewan, Regina.
5869. **Roset, Lauretta.** "The Student View from Regina." In #5837, pp. 35-52.
5870. **Ross, Donald George.** "Crime in Regina: A Spatial Analysis." B.A. essay, Regina, 1976.
5871. _____. "Population Growth: The Catalyst of Spatial Changes in Regina, 1945-1975." M.A. thesis, Regina, 1979.
5872. **Ross, M.** "Development in Regina." *Construction* 8 (1915):33-35.
5873. **Sinton, Robert.** *Looking Backward from the Eightieth Milestone, 1935-1854.* Regina: Paragon Business College, 1935.
5874. **Steele, S. B.** *Forty Years in Canada.* London: Jenkins, 1915.
5875. **Stinson, Arthur.** "The Non-Movable Airport—Regina." *CPR* 24, no. 6 (1974):3-6.
5876. **Stone, Gladys May.** "The Regina Riot, 1935." M.A. thesis, Saskatchewan, 1967.
5877. **Swenarchuk, Janet,** ed. *From Dreams to Reality: A History of the Ukrainian Senior Citizens of Regina and District, 1896-1976.* Winnipeg: Trident, 1977.
5878. **Tangjerd, Lorne D.** "Innovation in Transportation: The Regina Telebus System." In #5837, pp. 163-86.
5879. **Thomas, Lewis H.** "The Saskatchewan Legislative Building and Its Predecessors." *JRAIC* 32 (1955):248-52.
5880. **Trotter, B.** *A Horseman and the West.* Toronto: Macmillan, 1925.
5881. **Turner, Allan R.,** ed. "Documents of Western History: Wascana Creek and the 'Pile o' Bones.' " *Sask Hist* 19 (1966):111-18.
5882. **Tyre, Robert.** "The Changing Face of Regina." *W Bus Indus* 35 (April 1961):30-34.
5883. **Ward, Norman.** "Davin and the Founding of the *Leader.*" *Sask Hist* 6 (1953):13-16.
5884. **Weaver, Emily P.** "Regina: The Capital of Saskatchewan." *Can Mag* 39 (1912):173-81.
5885. **Weidner, Harvey George.** "A Review of Planning Acts in Saskatchewan and Their Effects on the Urban Morphology of Regina." B.A. essay, Regina, 1978.
5886. **Young, Walter D.** "M. J. Coldwell: The Making of a Social Democrat." *J Can St* 9, no. 3 (1974):51-60.

7. Saskatoon

5887. **Anderson, G. W.,** and **Anderson, R. N.,** eds. *Two White Oxen: A Perspective of Early Saskatoon, 1874-1905.* Saskatoon: Anderson, 1972.

5888. **Archer, John Hall.** "The History of Saskatoon to 1914." M.A. thesis, Saskatchewan, 1948.
5889. _____. *Historic Saskatoon: A Concise Illustrated History of Saskatoon.* Saskatoon: Junior Chamber of Commerce, 1948.
5890. **Barber, Clarence Lyle.** "Unemployment Relief in Saskatoon." M.A. thesis, Saskatchewan, 1940.
5891. **Buckley, K. A. H.** *Growth and Housing Requirements: Report on Economic and Social Aspects of the Housing Problem in Saskatoon.* Saskatoon: University of Saskatchewan, 1958.
5892. **Bury, Duncan, and Piper, John.** "Saskatoon: How Do You Make a Land Bank Work?" *City Mag* 2, no. 7 (1977):28-34.
5893. **Clubb, S. P.** *Saskatoon: The Serenity and the Surge.* Saskatoon: Midwest, 1966.
5894. _____, and **Sarjeant, W. A. S.** *Saskatoon's Historic Buildings and Sites: A Survey and Proposals.* Saskatoon: Saskatoon Environmental Society, 1973.
5895. **Courtney, John C., and Smith, David E.** "Voting in a Provincial General Election and a Federal By-Election: A Constituency Study of Saskatoon City." *CJEPS* 32 (1966):338-53.
5896. **Creighton, Pauline R.** "Taxation in Saskatoon: A Study of Municipal Finance." M.A. thesis, Saskatchewan, 1925.
5897. **Crone, Ray.** "How Bold the Airborne: The First Commercial Aerial Venture in Saskatoon." *Sask Hist* 23 (1970):59-69.
5898. **Delainey, W. P., and Sarjeant, W. A. S.** *Saskatoon, the Growth of a City. Part I: The Formative Years, 1882-1960.* Saskatoon: Saskatoon Environmental Society, 1974.
5899. **Field, A. J.** "The Saskatoon Jewish Community, 1905-1962." Saskatoon: University Library, Shortt Collection, 1963.
5900. **Gyuse, Timothy T. I.** "Service Centre Change in Metropolitan Hinterlands: A Case Study of Calgary and Saskatoon, 1951-1971." M.A. thesis, Calgary, 1974.
5901. **Haynes, Anthony William.** "Nature and Growth of Villages and Small Towns Adjacent to Saskatoon, 1971-76, as Influenced by the City." M.Sc. thesis, Saskatchewan, 1979.
5902. **Kerr, D. C.** "Saskatoon: Boom and Bust on Third Avenue." *Next Year Country* 3, no. 1 (1975):19-24.
5903. _____. "Saskatoon, 1910-1913: Ideology of the Boomtime." *Sask Hist* 32 (1979):16-28.
5904. **Knowles, Eric.** "A 'Boomer' Settled in Saskatoon and Built: When John East Came West." *W Bus Indus* 20 (January 1946):60-64, 87.
5905. **Kuzmicz, Benedict Joseph.** "An Exploratory Analysis of Life Cycle and Social Class Concepts in Predicting Some of the Demand Determinants for Apartment Dwellings in Saskatoon." M.B.A. thesis, Saskatchewan, 1970.
5906. **Lainsbury, John Michael.** "The Implications of Railway Relocation in Western Canadian Cities: Saskatoon, A Case Study." M.Sc. thesis, British Columbia, 1968.
5907. **Lawton, Alma.** "Relief Administration in Saskatoon during the Depression." *Sask Hist* 22 (1969):41-59.
5908. **Li, Peter S.** "Prejudice against Asians in a Canadian City." *CES* 11, no. 2 (1979):70-77.
5909. **Lim, Hon-seng.** "Selected Characteristics of Population Distribution in the City of Saskatoon." M.A. thesis, Saskatchewan, 1969.
5910. **Luk, Lordson Wai-chung.** "The Assimilation of the Chinese in Saskatoon." M.A. thesis, Saskatchewan, 1971.
5911. **Men of the City** [Historical Association of Saskatoon]. *Narratives of Saskatoon, 1882-1912.* Saskatoon: University Book Store, 1927.
5912. **Morgenroth, Kasper G.** "The Development of the Organization and Administration of the Saskatoon School System, 1884-1947." M.Ed. thesis, Saskatchewan, 1949.
5913. **Morton, A. S.** *Saskatchewan: The Making of a University.* Toronto: UTP, 1959.
5914. **Nichol, John L.** *Through the Years with Knox.* Saskatoon: Knox Church, 1950.

5915. **Olm, Sharon Joan.** "Urban Fringe Development on the Southern Edge of Saskatoon." M.A. thesis, Saskatchewan, 1977.
5916. **Pattison, M.** *Cory in Recall.* Saskatoon: Rural Municipality of Cory, 1967.
5917. **Peel, Bruce, and Knowles, Eric.** *The Saskatoon Story, 1882-1952.* Saskatoon: East, 1952.
5918. **Piper, John.** "Saskatoon Robs the Bank." *City Mag* 1, no. 1 (1974):16-20.
5919. _____. "Lots for Lots in Hub City: Land Development in Saskatoon." *Next Year Country,* no. 2 (1974):18-22.
5920. **Quddus, M. Abdul.** "Environmental Influences in Changing Consumption Pattern: A Case Study of Bengalee Residents in Saskatoon." M.B.A. thesis, Saskatchewan, 1972.
5921. **Raby, S., and Richards, T.** "The Saskatoon Southeast Water Supply Project." *CGEJ* 81 (1970):92-101.
5922. **Ravis, Don.** *Advanced Land Acquisition by Local Government: The Saskatoon Experience.* Saskatoon: City of Saskatoon, 1972.
5923. **Rees, Ronald.** "The Magic City on the Banks of the Saskatchewan: The Saskatoon Real Estate Boom of 1910-13." *Sask Hist* 27 (1974):51-59.
5924. **Russell, E. T. P., ed.** *Streets and Roads of Saskatoon.* Saskatoon: Saskatoon Public Board of Education, 1973.
5925. "Saskatoon Zoning and Preliminary Town Plan." *TPICJ* 10, no. 3 (1931):55-57.
5926. **Siddique, M.** "Patterns of Familial Decision-Making and Division of Labour: A Study of the Immigrant Indian-Pakistani Community of Saskatoon." M.A. thesis, Saskatchewan, 1974.
5927. **Slobodin, Richard.** " 'Welcome to Saskatoon': A Late Depression Glimpse." *Sask Hist* 32 (1979):74-78.
5928. **Steck, Warren F., and Sarjeant, W. A. S.** "The History and Achievements of the Saskatoon Environmental Society." *UHR* 2-77 (October 1977):33-54.
5929. **Thomas, Lewis H.** "Saskatoon, 1883-1920: The Formative Years." In #5352, pp. 237-58.
5930. **Tiessen, Hugo.** "Saskatoon, Saskatchewan." *CGEJ* 86 (1973):54-61.
5931. **Tyre, Robert.** "The Changing Face of Saskatoon." *W Bus Indus* 35 (April 1961):38-42.
5932. **Williams, Albert Ronald.** "A Survey of the Professional and Major Amateur Theatre Presentations in Saskatoon from 1912 to 1930." M.A. thesis, Saskatchewan, 1967.
5933. **Willmott, Donald E.** *Industry Comes to a Prairie Town.* Saskatoon: University of Saskatchewan, Centre for Community Studies, 1962.

8. Swift Current

5934. **Belbeck, Dave, and Belbeck, Alice, eds.** *Golden Furrows: An Historical Chronicle of Swift Current.* Swift Current: Local Council of Women, 1954.
5935. **Greenblat, J.** *Those Were the Days in Swift Current.* Saskatoon: Modern Press, 1971.
5936. **Laporte, Rodney.** "The Legacy of Boosterism: Swift Current and the First World War." B.A. Hons. essay, Regina, 1979.
5937. **McGowan, D. C.** *Grassland Settlers: The Swift Current Region during the Era of the Ranching Frontier.* Regina: Canadian Plains Research Center, 1975.

9. Other Centres

5938. **Auclair, Elie J.** "Introduction générale à l'histoire de Gravelbourg." *CF* 19 (1931):249-57.
5939. **Broadbridge, Arthur Frederick.** "The History of Rosetown, 1904-1939." M.A. thesis, Saskatchewan, 1949.
5940. **Garrett, A. W.** *History of Milestone, 1893-1910.* Milestone, 1946.
5941. **Grant, Robert W.** *The Humboldt Story, 1903-1953.* Humboldt: Board of Trade, 1959.

5942. **Hébert, G.** *Les débuts de Gravelbourg.* Gravelbourg, 1966.
5943. **King, A.** *Estevan: The Power Centre.* Saskatoon: Modern Press, 1967.
5944. **King, Gillian Mary.** "A Geographical Analysis of the Settlement of La Ronge, Saskatchewan." M.Sc. thesis, Saskatchewan, 1968.
5945. **Levin, Earl A.** "Lanigan—A New Town for Saskatchewan." *CPR* 14, no. 4 (1964):13-19.
5946. **McCracken, J. W.** "Yorkton during the Territorial Period, 1882-1905." M.A. thesis, Saskatchewan, Regina, 1972.
5947. _____. "Yorkton during the Territorial Period, 1882-1905." *Sask Hist* 28 (1975):95-110.
5948. **McCutcheon, M. K., and Young, R. C.** "The Development of Uranium City." *Can Geogr* 1, no. 5 (1954):57-62.
5949. **Nebel, M.** "Rev. Thomas Johnson and the Insinger Experiment." *Sask Hist* 11 (1958):1-17.
5950. **Person, Lloyd H.** *Growing Up in Minby.* Saskatoon: Western Producer Prairie Books, 1977.
5951. **White, C. O.** "The Humboldt Municipal Electrical Utility: A Grassroots Feature of the Saskatchewan Power Corporation." *Sask Hist* 29 (1976):103-13.
5952. **Willmott, Donald E.** "Ethnic Solidarity in the Esterhazy Area, 1882-1940." In *Ethnic Canadians,* edited by Martin L. Kovacs, pp. 167-76. Regina: Canadian Plains Research Center, 1978.

XII

Alberta

1. General

5953. Anderson, Barrie James. "A Study of Rural to Urban Migration in the Province of Alberta." M.A. thesis, Calgary, 1971.

5954. Anderson, J. "Change in a Central Place System: Trade Centres and Rural Services in Central Alberta." M.A. thesis, Alberta, 1967.

5955. Betke, Carl F. "Farm Politics in an Urban Age: The Decline of the United Farmers of Alberta after 1921." In *Essays on Western History,* edited by Lewis H. Thomas, pp. 175-92. Edmonton: University of Alberta Press, 1976.

5956. Bettison, David G.; Kenward, John K.; and Taylor, Larrie. *Urban Affairs in Alberta.* Edmonton: University of Alberta Press, 1975.

5957. Breen, David H. "The Cattle Compact: The Ranch Community in Southern Alberta, 1881-1896." M.A. thesis, Calgary, 1969.

5958. Crawford, M. E. "A Geographic Study of the Distribution of Population Change in Alberta, 1931-1961." M.A. thesis, Alberta, 1962.

5959. Davies, W. K. D., and Welling, W. L. "The Socio-Economic Differentiation of Alberta Towns in 1971." In *Research Studies by Western Canadian Geographers: The Edmonton Papers,* edited by Brenton M. Barr, pp. 77-98. Vancouver: B.C. Geographical Series, No. 24, 1977.

5960. Dawson, John Brian. "Chinese Urban Communities in Southern Alberta, 1885-1925." M.A. thesis, Calgary, 1975.

5961. den Otter, A. A. "Social Life of a Mining Community: The Coal Branch." *Alta HR* 17, no. 4 (1969):1-11.

5962. Dew, I. F. *Bibliography of Material Relating to Southern Alberta Published to 1970.* Lethbridge: University of Lethbridge, 1975.

5963. Forsyth, J. *Government Publications Relating to Alberta: A Bibliography of Publications of the Government of Alberta from 1905 to 1968, and of Publications of the Government of Canada Relating to the Province of Alberta from 1867 to 1968.* High Wycombe: University Microfilms, 1972.

5964. Fryer, Harold. *Ghost Towns of Alberta.* Langley: Stagecoach, 1976.

5965. Gertler, Leonard O. "Some Economic and Social Influences on Regional Planning in Alberta." In #563, pp. 84-94.

5966. Grayson, John Paul, and Grayson, L. M. "The Social Base of Interwar Political Unrest in Urban Alberta." *CJPS* 7 (1974):289-313.

5967. Hanson, Eric J. "Local Government Reorganization in Alberta." *CGEPS* 16 (1950):53-62.

5968. _____. "A Financial History of Alberta." Ph.D. thesis, Clark, 1952.
5969. _____. *Local Government in Alberta*. Toronto: M&S, 1956.
5970. _____. "The Changing Structure of Local Government in Alberta." *Can Pub Admin* 1 (1958):26-36.
5971. _____. *Dynamic Decade: The Evolution and Effects of the Oil Industry in Alberta*. Toronto: M&S, 1958.
5972. Hanus, F. "Economic Analysis of Demand and Supply of Water in Alberta Municipalities." M.Sc. thesis, Alberta, 1974.
5973. Healy, Mary Darina. "Comparative Factorial Ecology of Large Albertan Cities, 1961-1971." M.A. thesis, Calgary, 1976.
5974. Holmgren, Eric J., and Holmgren, Patricia M. *Over 2000 Place Names of Alberta*. 3d ed. Saskatoon: Western Producer Prairie Books, 1976.
5975. Jones, Stephen B. "Mining and Tourist Towns in the Canadian Rockies." *Econ Geogr* 9 (1933):368-78.
5976. Keys, C. L. "Spatial Reorganization in a Central Place System: An Albertan Case." Ph.D. thesis, Alberta, 1975.
5977. Kilpatrick, Alexander Bruce. "A Lesson In Boosterism: The Contest for the Alberta Provincial Capital, 1904-1906." *UHR* 8 (February 1980):47-109.
5978. Lamont, G., and Proudfoot, V. B. "Recent Changes [1961-1971] in Population in Northern Saskatchewan and Alberta." In *Frontier Settlement,* edited by R. G. Ironside, V. B. Proudfoot, E. N. Shannon, and C. J. Tracie, pp. 93-112. Edmonton: University of Alberta, Studies in Geography, 1974.
5979. Laux, F. A. "The Zoning Game: Alberta Style." *Alta Law Rev* 9 (1971):268-308; 10 (1972):1-37.
5980. Lucas, Alastair R. "Municipal Councillors—Disqualification for Interest—Application of the Rule in Keech v. Sanford—Rex Rel Anderson v. Hawrelak; Starr v. City of Calgary." *Alta Law Rev* 5 (1966-67):330-35.
5981. McFarland, John R. "The Administration of the Alberta New Towns Program." *Duquesne U Law Rev* 3 (1966-67):377-91.
5982. McIntosh, R. G., and Housego, I. E., eds. *Urbanization and Urban Life in Alberta*. Edmonton: Alberta Human Resources Council, 1970.
5983. McMillan, M. L., and Plain, R. H. M. *The Reform of Municipal-Provincial Relationships in the Province of Alberta*. Edmonton: Alberta Urban Municipalities Association, 1979.
5984. Masson, Jack K. "The Ebb and Flow of Municipal Party Politics in Alberta." In *Society and Politics in Alberta: Research Papers,* edited by Carlo Caldarola, pp. 356-68. Toronto: Methuen, 1979.
5984A. Murchie, Graham; Skolfsky, Jack; and Stuart, David. "Evaluating Alberta's Regional Planning System Using 'Action Research.' " *Plan Canada* 20 (1980):113-18.
5985. Norton, D. G. "Provincial Grants to Alberta Municipalities: Review Assessment and Alternative Unconditional Grant Formulae." M.A. thesis, Alberta, 1979.
5986. Parkinson, Anna. "Growth Analysis of Small Urban Centres in Alberta, 1971-1976." M. Environmental Design thesis, Calgary, 1978.
5986A. _____, and Detomasi, D. D. "Planning Resource Towns for the Alberta Tar Sands." *Plan Canada* 20 (1980):91-102.
5987. Patterson, H. S. "Single Tax in Alberta." *Dal Rev* 6 (1926):362-66.
5988. Richards, L. "Community Development in Alberta." Ph.D. thesis, Toronto, 1974.
5989. Seymour, Horace L. "Town Planning in Alberta." *TPICJ* 9, no. 4 (1930):73-74.
5990. _____. "Town Planning in Alberta, 1930." *TPICJ* 10, no. 1 (1931):9-12.
5991. _____. "Town Planning Progress in Alberta up to December 31, 1931." Unpublished manuscript, Provincial Archives of Alberta, Edmonton.
5992. Snider, Earl Lawrence, and Kupfer, G. *Urbanization in Alberta: A Sociological Perspective*. Population Reprints No. 9. Edmonton: University of Alberta, 1974.

5993. Smith, Peter J. "The Principle of Utility and the Origins of Planning Legislation in Alberta, 1912-1975." In #**29**, pp. 196-225.
5994. _____, **and Johnson, Denis B.** *The Edmonton-Calgary Corridor.* Edmonton: University of Alberta, Studies in Geography, 1978.
5994A. Smith, Phyllis. "The New Planning Act in Alberta." *Plan Canada* 20 (1980):120-23.
5995. Task Force on Urbanization. *Index of Urban and Regional Studies, Province of Alberta.* Issue #1: "Regional Planning Commissions and Non-Metropolitan Cities of Alberta." Issue #2: "City of Calgary and City of Edmonton." Issue #3: "Private Consultants." Issue #4: "Government of Alberta Departments and Agencies." Issue #5: "Alberta Universities." Edmonton: Alberta Municipal Affairs Dept., 1973-1975.
5996. Torhjelm, Gary Douglas. "The Urban Hierarchy in Alberta." M.A. thesis, Calgary, 1972.
5997. Voisey, Paul. "Two Chinese Communities in Alberta: An Historical Perspective." *CES* 2, no. 2 (1970):15-30.
5998. _____. "Boosting the Small Prairie Town, 1904-1931: An Example from Southern Alberta." In #**5352**, pp. 147-76.

2. Calgary

a. General

5999. Baine, R. P. *Calgary: An Urban Study.* Toronto: Clarke, Irwin, 1973.
6000. Baureiss, G. A. "The City and the Sub-Community: The Chinese of Calgary." M.A. thesis, Calgary, 1971.
6001. _____. "The Chinese Community of Calgary." *CES* 3, no. 1 (1971):43-56.
6002. _____. "The Chinese Community in Calgary." *Alta HR* 22, no. 2 (1974):1-8.
6003. Carter, David J. *Where the Wind Blows: A History of the Anglican Diocese of Calgary.* Calgary: Kyle Printers, 1968.
6004. _____. *Calgary's Anglican Cathedral.* Calgary: Kyle Printers, 1973.
6005. Century Calgary Historical Series. Vol. 1: *Past and Present: People, Places and Events in Calgary.* Vol. 2: *Communities of Calgary: From Scattered Towns to a Major City.* Vol. 3: *Young People of All Ages: Sports, Schools and Youth Groups in Calgary.* Vol. 4: *The Search for Souls: Histories of Calgary Churches.* Vol. 5: *At Your Service, Part One: Calgary's Library, Parks Department, Military, Medical Services and Fire Department.* Vol. 6: *At Your Service, Part Two: Calgary's Police Force, Navy Base, Post Office, Transit System and Private Service Groups.* Photographic Collections. Vol. 1: *A Walk Through Old Calgary: Early Buildings Extant in 1975.* Vol. 2: *Be It Ever So Humble: A Photoessay of Calgary's Old Homes.* Calgary: Calgary Historical Series, 1975.
6006. Corbet, Elise A. "Woman's Canadian Club of Calgary." *Alta Hist* 25, no. 3 (1977):29-36.
6007. Cunniffe, Richard. *Calgary in Sandstone.* Calgary: Historical Society of Alberta, 1969.
6008. Daniels, L. A. "The History of Education in Calgary." M.A. thesis, Washington, 1954.
6009. Diemer, H. L. "Annexation and Amalgamation in the Territorial Expansion of Edmonton and Calgary." M.A. thesis, Alberta, 1975.
6010. Foran, M. L. *Calgary: An Illustrated History.* History of Canadian Cities Series, vol. 2. Toronto: Lorimer and NMM, 1978.
6011. _____. "Land Development Patterns in Calgary, 1884-1945." In #**29**, pp. 293-315.
6012. _____. "Four Faces of Calgary." *Alta Hist* 27, no. 1 (1979):1-9.
6013. Fraser, W. B. *Calgary.* Toronto: Holt, Rinehart and Winston, 1967.
6014. Gibson, John S. "The Impact of the Railroad on Urban Patterns: An Alberta Example." *Alta Geogr* 1 (1964-65):41-46.
6015. _____. "An Evaluation of the Role of Physical Factors in the Evolution of Land Use in the Bow River Valley in Calgary." M.A. thesis, Alberta, 1965.

6016. **Gray, James H.** "Calgary Celebrates." *Beaver,* Outfit 281 (1950):6-11.
6017. **Harrington, Lyn.** "The Calgary Stampede." *CGEJ* 48 (1954):222-28.
6018. **Hatcher, Colin K.** *Stampede City Streetcars: The Story of the Calgary Municipal Railway.* Montreal: Railfare Enterprises, 1975.
6019. **Jameson, Sheilagh S.** "The Archives of the Glenbow-Alberta Institute (Calgary)." *UHR* 3-77 (February 1978):69-79.
6020. **Johnson, Denis Bruce.** "Application of Central Place Theory to the Retail Structure of the City of Calgary." M.A. thesis, Calgary, 1963.
6021. **Levin, Arthur.** "A Soviet Jewish Family Comes to Calgary." *CES* 6, nos. 1 and 2 (1974):53-66.
6022. **Linder, Alice Dorothy.** "Ethnic Strategies of Three Minority Groups in the City of Calgary." M.A. thesis, Calgary, 1975.
6023. **MacEwan, Grant.** *Calgary Cavalcade: From Fort to Fortune.* Saskatoon: Western Producer Book Service, 1975.
6024. **McNeill, Leishman.** *Tales of the Old Town: Calgary 1875-1950.* Calgary: *The Herald,* 1951.
6025. **Morrison, E. C., and Morrison, P. N. R., eds.** *Calgary, 1875-1950: A Souvenir of Calgary's Seventy-Fifth Anniversary.* Calgary: Calgary Publishing Co., 1950.
6026. **Morrow, E. Joyce.** *'Calgary, Many Years Hence': The Mawson Report in Perspective.* Calgary: City of Calgary and University of Calgary, 1979.
6027. **Newinger, Scott.** "The Street Cars of Calgary." *Alta HR* 22, no. 3 (1974):8-12.
6028. **Peach, John S.** "Calgary—The Foothill City." *CGEJ* 53 (1956):168-81.
6029. **Peudie, R.** "Urban Parks and Planning in Calgary." M.A. thesis, Calgary, 1968.
6030. **Smith, Peter J.** *A Study of Calgary's Past and Probable Future Population Growth.* Calgary: City Planning Dept., 1959.
6031. _____. "Calgary: A Study in Urban Pattern." *Econ Geogr* 38 (1962):315-29.
6032. _____. "Change in a Youthful City: The Case of Calgary, Alberta." *Geogr* 56 (1971):1-14.
6033. **Snider, Earl Lawrence.** "Level of Living for an Urban Area: Calgary." M.A. thesis, Calgary, 1967.
6034. **Stamp, Robert M.** *School Days: A Century of Memories.* Calgary: Calgary Board of Education and M&S West, 1975.
6035. **Stanley, George F. G.** "From New Brunswick to Calgary—R. B. Bennett in Retrospect." In #**6084**, pp. 242-66.
6036. **Stead, Robert J. C.** "Calgary—City of the Foothills." *CGEJ* 36 (1948):154-71.
6037. **Stokes, Ernest B.** "The Development and Evaluation of an Urban Growth Model for Calgary." M.A. thesis, Calgary, 1973.
6038. **Strom, T.** "With the Eau Claire in Calgary." *Alta HR* 12, no. 3 (1964):1-11.
6039. **Weston, Phyllis E.** "The History of Education in Calgary." M.A. thesis, Alberta, 1951.
6040. _____. "A University for Calgary." *Alta HR* 11, no. 3 (1963):1-11.
6041. **Youe, Christopher.** "Eau Claire, the Company and the Community." *Alta Hist* 26, no. 3 (1979):1-6.

b. Pre-1921

6042. **Braden, Thomas B.** "When the *Herald* Came to Calgary." *Alta HR* 9, no. 3 (1961):1-4.
6043. **Bussard, Lawrence H.** "Early History of Calgary." M.A. thesis, Alberta, 1935.
6044. _____. "The Establishment of Fort Calgary." *Alta HR* 3, no. 1 (1955):34-41.
6045. **Byrne, M. B.** "The Early History of the Catholic Church in Calgary." In #**6084**, pp. 169-80.

6046. **Carter, David J.** "Calgary's Early Anglicans." In **#6084,** pp. 190-202.
6047. **Christenson, R. A.** "The Calgary and Edmonton Railway and the *Edmonton Bulletin.*" M.A. thesis, Alberta, 1967.
6048. **Coats, Douglas.** "Calgary: The Private Schools, 1900-1916." In **#6084,** pp. 141-52.
6049. **Coppock, K.** "Calgary and the Company." *Beaver,* Outfit 271 (1941):42-47.
6050. **Dawson, John Brian.** "The Chinese Experience in Frontier Calgary: 1885-1910." In **#6084,** pp. 124-40.
6051. **Dempsey, Hugh A.** "Calgary's First Stampede." *Alta HR* 3, no. 3 (1955):3-13.
6052. _____. "Calgary-Edmonton Trail." *Alta HR* 7, no. 4 (1959):16-21.
6053. _____. "Brisebois: Calgary's Forgotten Founder." In **#6084,** pp. 28-40.
6054. _____, ed. *The Best of Bob Edwards.* Edmonton: Hurtig, 1975.
6055. **Elliott, G. B.** *Calgary, Alberta, Canada: Her Industries and Resources.* Calgary: Burns and Elliott, 1885.
6056. **Evans, Simon.** "Spatial Aspects of the Cattle Kingdom: The First Decade, 1882-92." In **#6084,** pp. 41-56.
6057. **Foran, M. L.** "The Calgary Town Council, 1884-1895: A Study of Local Government in a Frontier Environment." M.A. thesis, Calgary, 1970.
6058. _____. "The Travis Affair and the Town of Calgary, 1885-1886." *Alta HR* 19, no. 4 (1971):1-7.
6059. _____. "Urban Calgary, 1884-1895." *HS* 9 (1972):61-76.
6060. _____. "Bob Edwards and Social Reform." *Alta HR* 21, no. 3 (1973):13-17.
6061. _____. "Land Speculation and Urban Development in Calgary, 1884-1912." In **#6084,** pp. 203-20.
6062. _____. "Early Calgary, 1875-1895: The Controversy Surrounding the Townsite Location and the Direction of Town Expansion." In **#5379,** pp. 26-45.
6063. _____. "The Boosters in Boosterism: Some Calgary Examples." *UHR* 8 (October 1979):77-82.
6064. _____. "The Making of a Booster: Wesley Fletcher Orr and Nineteenth Century Calgary." In **#5352,** pp. 289-307.
6065. **Jameson, Sheilagh S.** "The Social Elite of the Ranch Community and Calgary." In **#6084,** pp. 57-70.
6066. **Kennedy, N. J.** "The Growth and Development of Music in Calgary, 1875-1920." M.A. thesis, Alberta, 1952.
6067. **Klassen, Henry C.** "Social Troubles in Calgary in the Mid-1890s." *UHR* 3-74 (February 1975):8-16.
6068. _____. "The 'Bond of Brotherhood' and Calgary Workingmen." In **#6084,** pp. 267-71.
6069. _____. "Life in Frontier Calgary." In *Western Canada Past and Present,* edited by A. W. Rasporich, pp. 42-57. Calgary: University of Calgary and M&S West, 1975.
6070. _____. "Bicycles and Automobiles in Early Calgary." *Alta Hist* 24, no. 2 (1976):1-8.
6071. _____. "In Search of Neglected and Delinquent Children: The Calgary Children's Aid Society, 1909-1920." In **#5352,** pp. 375-91.
6072. **MacEwan, Grant.** *Eye Opener Bob.* Edmonton: Hurtig, 1957.
6073. _____. "The Town-Country Background at Calgary." In **#6084,** pp. 1-5.
6074. _____. *Pat Burns: Cattle King.* Saskatoon: Western Producer Prairie Books, 1979.
6075. **McGinnis, J. P. Dickin.** "Birth to Boom to Bust: Building in Calgary 1875-1914." In **#6084,** pp. 6-19.
6076. _____. "A City Faces an Epidemic [Calgary, 1918-19]." *Alta Hist* 24, no. 4 (1976):1-11.
6077. **MacLeod, H. L.** "Properties, Investors and Taxes: A Study of Calgary Real Estate Investment, Municipal Finances and Property Tax Arrears, 1911-1919." M.A. thesis, Calgary, 1977.

6078. McLeod, N. L. "Calgary College, 1912-1915: A Study of an Attempt to Establish a Privately Financed University in Alberta." Ph.D. thesis, Calgary, 1970.
6079. Mawson, Thomas H. *Calgary: A Preliminary Scheme for Controlling the Economic Growth of Calgary.* Calgary: City Planning Commission, 1914.
6080. May, E. G. "A British Bride-To-Be Comes to Calgary." *Alta HR* 6, no. 1 (1958):19-24.
6081. Perry, J. Fraser. "Central Methodist Church before World War One." In #6084, pp. 181-89.
6082. Philip, C. R. "The Women of Calgary and District, 1874-1914." M.A. thesis, Calgary, 1975.
6083. Pratt, J. "Calgary: A Study in Optimism." *Can Mag* 35 (1910):483-90.
6084. Rasporich, A. W., and Klassen, Henry C., eds. *Frontier Calgary: Town, City and Region, 1875-1914.* Calgary: University of Calgary and M&S West, 1975.
6085. Reeves, B. O. K. "'Kootsisaw': Calgary before the Canadians." In #6084, pp. 20-27.
6086. Stamp, Robert M. "The Response to Urban Growth: The Bureaucratization of Public Education in Calgary, 1884-1914." In #85, pp. 282-99.
6087. Stanley, George F. G. "The Naming of Calgary." *Alta Hist* 23, no. 3 (1975):7-9.
6088. Taraska, Elizabeth A. "The Calgary Craft Union Movement, 1900-1920." M.A. thesis, Calgary, 1975.
6089. Thomas, Lewis G. "The Rancher and the City: Calgary and the Cattlemen, 1883-1914." RSC, *Trans,* 4th ser. 6 (1968):203-15.
6090. Thorner, T. "The Not-So-Peaceable Kingdom—Crime and Criminal Justice in Frontier Calgary." In #6084, pp. 100-113.
6091. Voisey, Paul. "In Search of Wealth and Status: An Economic and Social Study of Entrepreneurs in Early Calgary." In #6084, pp. 221-41.
6092. Ward, Tom. *Cowtown: An Album of Early Calgary.* Calgary: M&S, 1975.
6093. Weadick, Guy. "Origins of the Calgary Stampede." *Alta HR* 14, no. 4 (1966):20-24.

c. Post-1921

6094. Alberta. Royal Commission on the Metropolitan Development of Calgary and Edmonton. *Report.* Edmonton: Queen's Printer, 1956.
6095. Anderson, Frank. "Calgary's Crazy Corrections Association." *Can Wel* 36 (1960):107-9.
6096. Atwell, P. H. "Kinship and Migration among Calgarian Residents of Indian Origin." M.A. thesis, Calgary, 1969.
6097. Barr, B. M. "The Importance of Regional Inter-Industry Linkages to Calgary's Manufacturing Firms." In #6098, pp. 1-51.
6098. _____, ed. *Calgary: Metropolitan Structure and Influence.* Western Geographical Series, vol. 11. Victoria: University of Victoria, 1975.
6099. Baskett, Harold Kenneth. "Concepts of Neighbourhood: Perspectives of Planners and High Rise Dwellers in Calgary." M.A. thesis, Calgary, 1970.
6100. Bernard, A.; Léveillé, J.; and Lord, G. *Profile: Calgary. The Political and Administrative Structures of the Metropolitan Region of Calgary.* Ottawa: MSUA, 1975.
6101. Bibby, R. W. "The Secular and the Sacred: A Study of Evangelism as Reflected in Membership Additions to Calgary Evangelical Churches, 1966-70." M.A. thesis, Calgary, 1971.
6102. Boal, F. W., and Johnson, Denis Bruce. "The Functions of Retail and Service Establishments on Commercial Ribbons." *Can Geogr* 9 (1965):154-69.
6103. Breen, David H. "Calgary: The City and the Petroleum Industry since World War Two." *UHR* 2-77 (October 1977):55-71.
6104. Davies, W. K. D. "A Multivariate Description of Calgary's Community Areas." In #6098, pp. 231-69.

6105. _____. "Alternative Factoral Solutions and Urban Social Character: A Data Analysis of Calgary in 1971." *Can Geogr* 22 (1978):273-97.
6106. _____, **and Gyuse, Timothy T. I.** "Changes in the Central Place System around Calgary, 1951-1971." In **#6098,** pp. 123-56.
6107. Davies, W. K. D., and Healey, D. M. "Consistency and Change in the Ecological Patterns of Calgary: 1961-1971." In *Research Studies by Western Canadian Geographers: The Edmonton Papers,* edited by B. M. Barr, pp. 99-120. Vancouver: B.C. Geographical Series, No. 24, 1977.
6108. Gyuse, Timothy T. I. "Service Centre Change in Metropolitan Hinterlands: A Case Study of Calgary and Saskatoon, 1951-1971." M.A. thesis, Calgary, 1974.
6109. Harasym, D. G. "The Planning of New Residential Areas in Calgary, 1944-1973." M.A. thesis, Alberta, 1975.
6110. Hemingway, Peter. "Downtown Calgary: A Series of Urban Lesions." *Can Arch* 20 (1975):20-31.
6111. Homenuck, H. P. M. *Locational Pattern of Civic Decision-Making: Calgary, 1948-1968.* Toronto: York University, Institute of Behavioural Research, 1971.
6112. Houghton, J. R. "The Calgary Public School System, 1939-1969: A History of Growth and Development." M.Ed. thesis, Calgary, 1971.
6113. House, J. D. *The Last of the Free Enterprisers: The Oilmen of Calgary.* Toronto: Macmillan, 1980.
6114. Johnson, Denis Bruce. "Food Store-Dwelling Linkages in Selected Areas of Calgary." In **#6098,** pp. 193-230.
6115. Johnston, P. A., and Nodwell, L. M. *Metropolitan Calgary Population: Historical Review, 1946-1970.* Calgary: City of Calgary, 1970.
6116. Lawrence, M. C. "U.S. Expatriates in Calgary and Their Problems." M.S.W. thesis, Calgary, 1972.
6117. Legare, Leo Joseph. "An Exploratory Analysis of Life and Social Class Concepts as Demand Determinants for Mobile Homes in Calgary." M.B.A. thesis, Saskatchewan, 1972.
6118. MacEwan, Grant. *Poking into Politics.* Edmonton: Institute of Applied Art, 1966.
6119. McEwen, Alice, and Barr, B. M. "Some Aspects of Calgary's Role in the Intra-Industry Manufacturing Linkages of Southern Alberta: The Case of the Mobile Home Industry." In **#6098,** pp. 52-76.
6119A. McKellar, James. "The Calgary Civic Centre: An Art of Illusion." *Plan Canada* 20 (1980):73-80.
6120. Melland, John F. "Redevelopment in Central Calgary: A Study of Change." M.A. thesis, Montana, 1969.
6121. Mohan, Elizabeth Marilyn. "Aspects of Intra-Urban Mobility: Calgary, 1963-1968." M.A. thesis, Calgary, 1971.
6122. Morah, Benson Chukwuma. "The Assimilation of Uganda Asians in Calgary." M.A. thesis, Calgary, 1974.
6123. Pearce, William. "Reservation of Land at Calgary [c. 1925]." *Alta Hist* 27, no. 2 (1979):22-28.
6124. Peitchinis, Stephen. "Why Should Anyone in Calgary Need Aid?" *Can Wel* 45, no. 3 (1969):6-13.
6125. Saarinen, Thomas Frederick. "The Changing Office Functions in Calgary's Central Business District, 1942-1962." M.A. thesis, Chicago, 1963.
6126. Smith, Peter J. "Edmonton and Calgary: Growing Together." *CGEJ* 92, no. 3 (1976):26-33.
6127. _____, **and Harasym, D. G.** "Planning for Retail Services in New Residential Areas since 1944." In **#6098,** pp. 157-92.
6128. Stokes, Ernest B. "The Development and Evaluation of an Urban Growth Model for Calgary." M.A. thesis, Calgary, 1973.

6129. **Takia, Emile F.** "Changes in Land Use Patterns in Downtown Calgary, 1953-1969." M.A. thesis, Calgary, 1971.
6130. **Walker, I.** "Neighbourhood Development at Calgary." *CPR* 20, no. 2 (1970):24-25.
6131. **Whitehead, J.** "County Residential Growth in the Calgary Region: A Study of Exurbanization." M.A. thesis, British Columbia, 1968.
6132. **Wong, C. S. J.** "Assimilation and Education: A Study of Post-War Immigrants in Edmonton and Calgary." M.A. thesis, Alberta, 1972.
6133. **Woo, H. M.** "Relationship between Stores and Population in Northwest Calgary, 1948-1968." M.A. thesis, Calgary, 1969.
6134. **Zieber, George H.** "Inter- and Intra-city Location Patterns of Oil Offices for Calgary and Edmonton, 1950-1970." Ph.D. thesis, Alberta, 1971.
6135. _____. "The Dispersed City Hypothesis with Reference to Calgary and Edmonton." *Alta Geogr* 9 (1973):4-13.
6136. _____. "Calgary as an Oil Administrative and Oil Operations Centre." In #6098, pp. 77-122.

3. Edmonton

a. General

6137. **Batey, W. L.** "The Location Requirements and Spatial Organization of Federal Services: The Case of Edmonton." M.A. thesis, Alberta, 1976.
6138. **Bedford, Elaine.** "An Historical Geography of Settlement in the North Saskatchewan River Valley, Edmonton." M.A. thesis, Alberta, 1976.
6139. **Caldarola, Carlo, and Paul, G. S.** "Voting in Edmonton [in Provincial and Federal Elections]." In *Society and Politics in Alberta: Research Papers,* edited by Carlo Caldarola, pp. 322-55. Toronto: Methuen, 1979.
6140. **Cashman, A. W.** *The Edmonton Story.* Edmonton: Institute of Applied Art, 1956.
6141. _____. *The Best Edmonton Stories.* Edmonton: Hurtig, 1976.
6142. _____. *Edmonton Exhibition: The First Hundred Years.* Edmonton: Edmonton Exhibition Association, 1979.
6143. **Crowston, M. A.** "The Growth of the Metal Industries in Edmonton." M.A. thesis, Alberta, 1971.
6144. **Dale, Edmund H.** "The Role of Successive Town and City Councils in the Evolution of Edmonton, Alberta, 1892-1966." Ph.D. thesis, Alberta, 1969.
6145. _____. "Decision-Making in Edmonton: Planning without a Plan, 1913-1945." *Plan Canada* 11 (1971):134-47.
6146. **Diemer, H. L.** "Annexation and Amalgamation in the Territorial Expansion of Edmonton and Calgary." M.A. thesis, Alberta, 1975.
6147. **Duggan, D. M.** *Review of Municipal Government Organization.* Edmonton: City of Edmonton, 1923.
6148. **Edmonds, W. E.** *Edmonton Past and Present: A Brief History.* Edmonton: Douglas, 1943.
6149. **Edmonton Journal.** "Roots: The Ethnic History of Edmonton." Edmonton, 1976. [Reprint of articles in *Journal*].
6150. **Eliasoph, H. P.** "Edmonton's Impact on Surrounding Urban Centres." M.A. thesis, Alberta, 1978.
6151. **Evans, David.** *A History of the City Council of Edmonton, 1892-1977.* Edmonton: City of Edmonton, 1978.

6152. **Hamilton, Sally Anne.** "An Historical Geography of Coal Mining in the Edmonton Area." M.A. thesis, Alberta, 1971.
6153. **Hanson, Eric J.** *An Economic Base Study of the Edmonton Metropolitan Area.* Edmonton: Alberta, 1957.
6154. **Hart, E. J.** "The History of the French-Speaking Community of Edmonton, 1795-1935." M.A. thesis, Alberta, 1971.
6155. **Hutton, Charles L. A.** "Functional Differentiation among Small Towns in the Edmonton Area." M.A. thesis, Alberta, 1965.
6156. **Ironside, R. G., and Hamilton, Sally Anne.** "Historical Geography of Coal Mining in the Edmonton District." *Alta HR* 20, no. 3 (1972):6-16.
6157. **Jones, O. D.** "The Historical Geography of Edmonton, Alberta." M.A. thesis, Toronto, 1962.
6158. **Jordan, Mabel E.** "Edmonton—Old and New." *CGEJ* 51 (1955):244-47.
6159. **Lai, H.** "Evolution of the Railway Network of Edmonton and Its Land Use Effect." M.A. thesis, Alberta, 1967.
6160. **LaRose, Helen.** "The City of Edmonton Archives." *UHR* 3-74 (February 1975):2-7.
6161. **Lee, T. R.** "A Manufacturing Geography of Edmonton." M.A. thesis, Alberta, 1963.
6162. **McCann, L. D.** *Neighbourhoods in Transition: Processes of Land Use and Physical Change in Edmonton's Residential Areas.* Edmonton: University of Alberta, Studies in Geography, 1975.
6163. **McCaskill, Donald.** "The Urbanization of Native People in Toronto, Winnipeg, Edmonton, and Vancouver: A Comparative Analysis." Ph.D. thesis, York, 1979.
6164. **McConnell, R. S.** "Planning in Edmonton, Alberta." *TPICJ* 44 (1957-58):39-43.
6165. **Macdonald, John.** *The History of the University of Alberta, 1908-1958.* Edmonton: University of Alberta, 1958.
6166. **MacGregor, James G.** *Edmonton: A History.* 1967. 2d ed. Edmonton: Hurtig, 1975.
6167. **Maclean, R. A.** "The History of the Roman Catholic Church in Edmonton." M.A. thesis, Alberta, 1958.
6168. **Marlyn, F., and Lash, H. N.** "The Edmonton District, A City Centred, Multiple-Resource Region." In *Regional and Resource Planning in Canada,* edited by Ralph R. Krueger, pp. 47-52. Toronto: Holt, Rinehart and Winston, 1963.
6169. **Martin, John.** "Geographic Inequalities in Property Tax Levels: A Study of Urban Municipalities in the Edmonton Regional Planning District." M.A. thesis, Alberta, 1971.
6170. **Nicoll, Ian M.** "Urban Municipal Finance in a Period of Expansion: A Study of the City of Edmonton." M.A. thesis, Alberta, 1950.
6171. **Peterson, D. D.** "Wholesale Trade between Edmonton and Selected Northern Communities." M.A. thesis, Alberta, 1978.
6172. **Poetschke, T. R.** "Reasons for Immigration and Ethnic Identity: An Exploratory Study of German Immigrants in Edmonton, Alberta." M.A. thesis, Alberta, 1978.
6173. **Rees-Powell, Alan Thomas.** "Differentials in the Integration Process of Dutch and Italian Immigrants in Edmonton." M.S.W. thesis, Alberta, 1964.
6174. **Snider, Howard Mervin.** "Variables Affecting Immigrant Adjustments: A Study of Italians in Edmonton." M.A. thesis, Alberta, 1966.
6175. **Suski, Julian G.** *Edmonton: Short History.* Edmonton: City of Edmonton, 1965.
6176. **Watt, A. B.** "Edmonton." *CGEJ* 33 (1946):242-51.
6177. **Weaver, John C.** "Edmonton's Perilous Course, 1904-1929." *UHR* 2-77 (October 1977):20-32.
6178. **Wonders, William C.** "River Valley City—Edmonton on the North Saskatchewan." *Can Geogr* 3, no. 14 (1959):8-16.

b. Pre-1921

6179. **Askin, W. R.** "Labor Unrest in Edmonton and District and Its Coverage by the Edmonton Press, 1918-1919." M.A. thesis, Alberta, 1973.
6180. **Babcock, Douglas R.** *A Gentleman of Strathcona: Alexander Cameron Rutherford.* Edmonton: Historic Sites Service, Occasional Paper No. 8, 1980.
6181. **Betke, Carl F.** "The Original City of Edmonton: A Derivative Prairie Urban Community." In #5352, pp. 309-45.
6182. **Blower, James.** *Gold Rush: A Pictorial Look at the Part Edmonton Played in the Gold Era of the 1890s.* Toronto: Ryerson, 1971.
6183. _____. "Matthew McCauley [First Mayor of Edmonton]." *Alta HR* 20, no. 1 (1972):11-17.
6184. **Burry, S.** "Edmonton to the Klondike." *Alta HR* 21, no. 2 (1973):20-25.
6185. **Cameron, B.** "The City on the Saskatchewan." *Can Mag* 15 (1900):99-107.
6186. **Christenson, R. A.** "The Calgary and Edmonton Railway and the *Edmonton Bulletin.*" M.A. thesis, Alberta, 1967.
6187. **Corbett, E. A.** *McQueen of Edmonton.* Toronto: Ryerson, 1934.
6188. **Day, J. R.** "Edmonton Civic Politics, 1891-1914." *UHR* 3-77 (February 1978):42-68.
6189. **Dunn, J. T.** "To Edmonton in 1892." *Beaver,* Outfit 281 (1950):3-5.
6190. **Gilpin, John F.** "The City of Strathcona, 1891-1912." M.A. thesis, Alberta, 1978.
6191. _____. "Failed Metropolis: The City of Strathcona, 1891-1912." In #5352, pp. 259-88.
6192. **Holmgren, Eric J.** "Edmonton's Remarkable High Level Bridge." *Alta Hist* 26, no. 1 (1978):1-9.
6193. **Jamieson, F. C.** "Edmonton Courts and Lawyers in Territorial Times." *Alta HR* 4, no. 1 (1956):3-9.
6194. **Jamieson, Heber C.** "The Early Medical History of Edmonton." *CMAJ* 30 (1933):431-37.
6195. **Kendal, Elaine.** *The Development of Edmonton and Its Buildings to 1914.* Manuscript Report Series. Ottawa: Historic Sites, Parks Canada, 1977.
6196. **MacGregor, James G.** *Edmonton Trader: The Story of John A. McDougall.* Toronto: M&S, 1963.
6197. _____. *The Klondike Rush through Edmonton, 1897-1898.* Toronto: M&S, 1970.
6198. **Niddrie, J. G.** "The Edmonton Boom of 1911-1912." *Alta HR* 13, no. 2 (1965):1-6.
6199. **Ockley, B. A.** "A History of Early Edmonton." M.A. thesis, Alberta, 1932.
6200. **Oliver, Frank.** "The Founding of Edmonton." *QQ* 37 (1930):78-94.
6201. **Orrell, John.** "Edmonton Theatres of Alexander W. Cameron." *Alta Hist* 26, no. 2 (1978):1-10.
6202. **Parnell, C.** "The Founding of Fort Edmonton." *Beaver,* Outfit 276 (1945):3-4.
6203. **Peake, Frank A.** "The Beginnings of the Diocese of Edmonton, 1875-1913." M.A. thesis, Alberta, 1952.
6204. _____. "Anglican Beginnings in and about Edmonton." *Alta HR* 3, no. 2 (1955):15-32.
6205. **Sheremata, J. D.** "Entertainment in Edmonton before 1914." M.A. thesis, Alberta, 1970.
6206. **Thomas, Lewis G.** "Mission Church in Edmonton: An Anglican Experiment in the Canadian West." *PNQ* 49 (1958):55-60.
6207. **Williams, J. D.** "A History of the Edmonton, Dungevan and British Columbia Railway, 1907-1919." M.A. thesis, Alberta, 1956.

c. Post-1921

6208. **Alberta. Royal Commission on the Metropolitan Development of Calgary and Edmonton.** *Report.* Edmonton: Queen's Printer, 1956.

6209. **Anderson, James.** "Economic Base Measurement and Changes in the Base of Metropolitan Edmonton, 1951-1961." *Alta Geogr* 4 (1968):4-9.
6210. **Bannon, Michael Joseph.** "The Evolution of the Central Area of Edmonton, Alberta, 1946-1966." M.A. thesis, Alberta, 1967.
6211. **Barrow, G. T.** "A Factoral Ecology of Three Cities: Edmonton, Regina, and Winnipeg, 1961." M.A. thesis, Calgary, 1972.
6212. **Bernard, A.; Léveillé, J.; and Lord, G.** *Profile: Edmonton, The Political and Administrative Structures of the Metropolitan Region of Edmonton.* Ottawa: MSUA, 1974.
6213. **Betke, Carl F.** "The Social Significance of Sport in the City: Edmonton in the 1920s." In #**5379**, pp. 211-35.
6214. **Betts, George Michael.** "The Edmonton Aldermanic Election of 1962." M.A. thesis, Alberta, 1963.
6215. **Brown, Sheila A.** "Shopper Attitudes towards Competitive Regional Centres as a Factor in Patronage Choice." In #**6258**, pp. 93-118.
6216. **Carter, T. S.** "A Profile of Tenants in Central Edmonton: Their Characteristics and Housing Preferences." M.A. thesis, Alberta, 1978.
6217. **Chan, Wah May Minnie.** "The Impact of the Technical Planning Board on the Morphology of Edmonton." M.A. thesis, Alberta, 1969.
6218. **Chivers, Batya.** "Friendly Games: Edmonton's Olympic Alternative." *City Mag* 1, nos. 5 and 6 (1975):48-54.
6219. **Curtis, P. J.** "Some Aspects of Industrial Linkages in Edmonton's Oil Industry." M.A. thesis, Alberta, 1972.
6220. **Dale, Edmund H.** "Civic Centre—Edmonton." *CPR* 20, no. 2 (1970):2-9.
6221. **Dant, Noel.** "Edmonton: Practical Results of Planning Measures since 1950." *CPR* 4 (1954):31-40.
6222. **Davies, W. K. D.** "A Social Taxonomy of Edmonton's Community Areas in 1971." In #**6258**, pp. 161-98.
6223. **Edmonton. City Planning Department.** *Metropolitan Edmonton Population: 1946-1970.* Edmonton: City of Edmonton, 1971.
6224. **Emanuel, L.** "Some Aspects of Ethnic Identity in an Edmonton Parish." *CES* 6, no. 2 (1974):87-96.
6225. **Fairburn, Kenneth J.** "Location Changes of Edmonton's High-Status Residents, 1937-1972." In #**6258**, pp. 199-232.
6226. _____, **and Barr, B. M.** "Edmonton's Manufacturing Economy: A Comparative Analysis." In #**6258**, pp. 29-58.
6227. **Giffen, N. B.** "The Mobile Home in the Edmonton Area." M.A. thesis, Alberta, 1976.
6228. **Gillese, J. P.** "Big Boom Town." *Can Bus* 26 (September 1953):22-24, 116-18.
6229. **Graden, R. R.** "The Planning of New Residential Areas in Edmonton, 1950-1976." M.A thesis, Alberta, 1979.
6230. **Haigh, R. J.** "Resident Characteristics of Six Urban Fringe Communities in the Edmonton Region." M.A. thesis, Alberta, 1978.
6231. **Hassbrung, M.** "A Geographical Analysis of Land Use in Edmonton's Rural-Urban Fringe Zone." M.Sc. thesis, Alberta, 1969.
6232. _____. "Land Use Diversity in the Rural-Urban Fringe Zone of Edmonton." *Alta Geogr* 6 (1970):59-64.
6233. **Hayter, J. G.** "Residential Mobility and the Function of Seven Selected High Rises in Central Edmonton." M.A. thesis, Alberta, 1973.
6234. **Hemingway, Peter.** "Downtown without Direction [Edmonton]." *Can Arch* 20 (1975):28-38.
6235. **Herscovitch, G.** "Industrial Water Use in Edmonton." M.Sc. thesis, Alberta, 1969.

6236. **Hodgson, M. C.** "The Fiscal Development of the City of Edmonton since 1946." M.A. thesis, Alberta, 1965.

6237. **Ironside, R. G.** "Locational Adjustment in Public Service Facilities." In #**6258,** pp. 233-62.

6238. **King, Mona F.** "Some Aspects of Post-War Migration to Edmonton, Alberta." M.A. thesis, Alberta, 1971.

6239. **McCann, L. D., and Smith, Peter J.** "The Residential Development Cycle in Space and Time." In #**6258,** pp. 119-60.

6240. **McCracken, Kevin W. J.** "Patterns of Intra-Urban Migration in Edmonton and the Residential Relocation Process." Ph.D. thesis, Alberta, 1973.

6241. **McDonald, D. N.** "Health Care and Community Development: The Inner City of Edmonton." M.A. thesis, Alberta, 1978.

6242. **McDonald, Hugh.** "Edmonton Is Booming Cautiously." *W Bus Indus* 23 (May 1949):106-10.

6243. **McGillivray, C. L.** "Mental Maps of a Canadian City: Edmonton, Alberta." *Alta Geogr* 10 (1974):30-42.

6244. **Martin, A.** "Selected Aspects of the Functional Relationship between Consumers and Commercial Ribbons: A Case Study of Whyte Avenue, Edmonton." M.A. thesis, Alberta, 1974.

6245. **Masson, Jack K.** "Decision-Making Patterns and Floating Coalitions in an Urban City Council [Edmonton]." *CJPS* 8 (1975):128-37.

6246. **Monanu, P. C.** "Journey to Work Patterns in Edmonton, 1971." M.A. thesis, Alberta, 1976.

6247. **Muller, Jean-Claude.** "The Mapping of Travel Time in Edmonton, Alberta." *Can Geogr* 22 (1978):195-210.

6248. **Plunkett, R. E.** "Central Business District Employment in Edmonton 1961-1967." M.A. thesis, Alberta, 1975.

6249. **Podmore, D. R.; McGlasken, S.; and Steen, P.** "Railway Relocation: The Edmonton Approach." *Contact* 9, no. 1 (1977):133-44.

6250. **Rose, R. T.** "Edmonton: Boom Town Plus." *Can Bus* 16 (July 1943):86-92.

6251. **Scott, W. G.** "Urban Growth Management: The Development of a Program for the Edmonton Area." M.Sc. thesis, British Columbia, 1976.

6252. **Seifried, Neil R. M.** "The Changing Economy of Edmonton, 1961-1971." In #**6258,** pp. 1-28.

6253. _____. "The Expanding Urban Economy of a Spontaneous Growth Centre: Edmonton, Alberta." *Alta Geogr* 14 (1978):105-21.

6254. **Smith, Benjamin George.** "An Activity Systems Impact Analysis of the Edmonton Transit System Strike, 1973-1974." M.Sc. thesis, Alberta, 1975.

6255. **Smith, Peter J.** "Edmonton and Calgary: Growing Together." *CGEJ* 92, no. 3 (1976):26-33.

6256. _____, **and Bannon, Michael Joseph.** "The Dimensions of Change in the Central Area of Edmonton." In *The Geographer and Society,* edited by W. R. Derrick Sewell and Harold D. Foster, pp. 184-99. Western Geographical Series, Vol. 1. Victoria: University of Victoria, 1970.

6257. **Smith, Peter J., and Diemer, H. L.** "Equity and the Annexation Process: Edmonton's Bid for the Strathcona Industrial Corridor." In #**6258,** pp. 263-89.

6258. **Smith, Peter J., ed.** *Edmonton: The Emerging Metropolitan Pattern.* Western Geographical Series, vol. 15. Victoria: University of Victoria, 1978.

6259. **Soderstrom, R. W.** "An Analysis of the Edmonton Social Planning Council." M.A. thesis, Alberta, 1975.

6260. **Stevens, George R.** *A City Goes to War.* Brampton: Charter Publishing, 1964.

6261. **Walchuk, W.** "Planning Edmonton's Future." *CPR* 18, no. 1 (1968):5-9.
6262. **Wass, Keith, and Goard, Alan.** "People First in Edmonton." *Can Wel* 47, no. 2 (1971):16-17.
6263. **Windsor, R. F.** "The Campus Fringe of the University of Alberta." M.A. thesis, Alberta, 1964.
6264. **Wonders, William C.** "Edmonton, Alberta: Some Current Aspects of Its Urban Geography." *Can Geogr* 2-4, no. 9 (1957):7-20.
6265. _____. "Repercussions of War and Oil on Edmonton, Alberta." *Cah géogr Q* 3 (1959):343-51.
6266. **Wong, C. S. J.** "Assimilation and Education: A Study of Post-War Immigrants in Edmonton and Calgary." M.A. thesis, Alberta, 1972.
6267. **Woychuk, J. K.** "Tax-Exempt Property: City of Edmonton, 1970." M.A. thesis, Alberta, 1972.
6268. **Zieber, George H.** "The Dispersed City Hypothesis with Reference to Calgary and Edmonton." *Alta Geogr* 9 (1973):4-13.

4. Lethbridge

6269. **Carpenter, J. H.** *The Badge and the Blotter: A History of the Lethbridge Police.* Lethbridge: Whoop-Up Country Chapter, Historical Society of Alberta, 1975.
6270. **den Otter, A. A.** "Irrigation and the Lethbridge *News.*" *Alta HR* 18, no. 4 (1970):17-25.
6271. _____. "Sir Alexander T. Galt and the Northwest: A Case Study of Entrepreneurialism on the Frontier." Ph.D. thesis, Alberta, 1975.
6272. _____. "Coal Town in Wheat Country: Lethbridge, Alberta, 1885-1905." *UHR* 1-76 (June 1976):3-5.
6273. _____. "Urban Pioneers of Lethbridge." *Alta Hist* 25, no. 1 (1977):15-23.
6274. _____. "Lethbridge: Outpost of a Commercial Empire, 1885-1906." In #5352, pp. 177-202.
6275. **McGrath, C. A.** *The Galts, Father and Son: Pioneers in the Development of Southern Alberta.* Lethbridge: *Herald,* [c. 1937].
6276. **Mallett, Robin B.** "Settlement Process and Land Use Change: Lethbridge-Medicine Hat Area." M.A. thesis, Alberta, 1971.
6277. **Mowers, Cleo W.** "Lethbridge, Alberta." *CGEJ* 84 (1972):140-51.
6278. **Sponchia, C. R. E.** "Public Accounting in Lethbridge: An Industry Study." M.A. thesis, Alberta, 1975.

5. Medicine Hat

6279. **Bristol, Samuel.** "The City That Was Born Lucky." *Can Mag* 41 (1913):124-26.
6280. **Common, R.** "Early Settlement about Medicine Hat, Alberta." *Geogr Bull* 9, no. 3 (1967):284-93.
6281. **Harrington, Lyn.** "Medicine Hat—'The Town that was Born Lucky.'" *CGEJ* 80 (1970):126-33.
6282. **Kipling, Rudyard.** "The Town that was Born Lucky [Medicine Hat]." *Alta HR* 9, no. 1 (1961):5-7.
6283. **Mallett, Robin B.** "Settlement Process and Land Use Change: Lethbridge-Medicine Hat Area." M.A. thesis, Alberta, 1971.
6284. **Morrow, J. W.** *Early History of the Medicine Hat Country.* Medicine Hat: *News,* 1923.

6. Red Deer

6285. **Baker, Alan Maurice.** "The Red Deer Region: An Economic and Regional Geography." M.A. thesis, Alberta, 1962.
6286. **Dawe, R. W.** "The Development of the Red Deer Community in Relation to the Development of Western Canada." M.A. thesis, Alberta, 1954.
6287. _____. *History of Red Deer, Alberta.* Red Deer: Kiwanis Club, n.d.
6288. **Gaetz, A. L.** *Park Country: A History of Red Deer and District.* Vancouver: Wrigley, 1948.
6289. **Meeres, E. L.** *The Homesteads That Nurtured a City: The History of Red Deer, 1880-1905.* Red Deer, 1978.
6290. **Paul, L. J.** "Spatial Differentiation among Residential Districts in Red Deer." M.A. thesis, Alberta, 1968.
6291. **Stephenson, A. T.** "Red Deer's System of Government by Commission." *Western Municipal News,* Vol. 6 (January 1911), pp. 15-16.
6292. **Watson, Kenneth F.** "Landbanking in Red Deer." M.A. thesis, British Columbia, 1974.

7. Other Centres

6293. **Bagley, R.** "Lacombe in the Nineties." *Alta HR* 10, no. 3 (1962): 18-27.
6294. **Barclay, Harold.** "An Arab Community in the Canadian Northwest: A Preliminary Discussion of the Lebanese Community in Lac La Biche, Alberta." *Anthropologica* 10 (1968):143-56.
6295. _____. "A Lebanese Community in Lac La Biche, Alberta." In *Immigrant Groups,* edited by Jean Leonard Elliott, pp. 66-83. Scarborough: Prentice-Hall, 1971.
6296. **Bhajan, Edward R.** "Community Development Programs in Alberta: Analysis of Development Efforts in Five Communities [Indians in Fort McMurray, Fort Chipewyan, Hinton, Slave Lake, Wabasco]." M.A. thesis, Alberta, 1972.
6297. **Brown, Edward C.** "A Small Town Plans [Hinton, Alberta]." *CPR* 15, no. 3 (1965):10-16.
6298. **Burnet, Jean.** "Town-Country Relations and the Problem of Rural Leadership [A Case Study of Hanna, Alberta]." *CJEPS* 13 (1947):395-409.
6299. **Burpee, Lawrence J.** "Where Rail and Airway Meet [Fort McMurray]." *CGEJ* 10 (1935):230-46.
6300. **Donaldson, R. M.** "The Economic Base of Camrose." M.A. thesis, Alberta, 1965.
6301. **Drouin, Emeric O.** *Joyau dans la plaine: Saint-Paul, Alberta, colonie métisse, 1896-1909, paroisse blanche, 1909-1951.* Québec: Ferland, 1968.
6302. **Gregg, R. C.** "The Star of the West [Edson, Alberta]." *CPR* 13 (1963):2-10.
6303. **Hurt, Leslie J.** *The Victoria Settlement, 1862-1922.* Edmonton: Historic Sites Service, Occasional Paper No. 7, 1979.
6304. **Jensen, B. J.** "The County of Mountain View, Alberta: A Study in Community Development, 1890-1925." M.A. thesis, Alberta, 1975.
6305. **Kerri, James N.** "Fort McMurray: One of Canada's Resource Frontier Towns." M.A. thesis, Manitoba, 1970.
6306. **McCarty, R. F.** "Fort Assiniboine, Alberta, 1823-1914: Fur Trade Post to Settled District." M.A. thesis, Alberta, 1976.
6307. **Pépin, Cornélie L.** *Histoire de St-Paul, Alberta, 1896-1951.* Trois-Rivières: Bien Public, 1952.
6308. **Ream, P. T.** *The Fort on the Saskatchewan: A Resource Book on Fort Saskatchewan and District.* Edmonton: Metropolitan Printing, 1974.

Alberta 243

6309. _____. *The Fort on the Saskatchewan.* Fort Saskatchewan: Fort Saskatchewan Historical Society, 1975.
6310. **Rendall, Harold A.** "Trade Areas of Camrose, Wetaskiwin, and Ponoka." M.A. thesis, Alberta, 1962.
6311. **Reynolds, A.** *'Siding 16': An Early History of Wetaskiwin to 1930.* Wetaskiwin: Alberta RCMP Centennial Committee, 1975.
6312. **Scace, R. C.** "Banff Townsite: Evolution of a National Park Community." M.A. thesis, Alberta, 1967.
6313. _____. *An Annotated Bibliography of the Banff National Park Area.* Ottawa: National and Historic Parks Branch, Dept. of Indian Affairs and Northern Development, 1970.
6314. _____. *Banff, Jasper, Kootenay and Yoho: An Initial Bibliography of the Contiguous Canadian Rocky Mountains National Parks.* Ottawa: National and Historic Parks Branch, Dept. of Indian Affairs and Northern Development, 1973.
6315. **Smith, Peter J.** "Fort Saskatchewan: An Industrial Satellite of Edmonton." In **#563**, pp. 250-65.
6316. **Tetreault, A.** "Historic St. Albert: Transformation and Highlights, 1890-1954." *Alta HR* 5, no. 1 (1957):25-29.
6317. **Thirnbeck, A. R.** "An Analysis of a Group of Prairie Settlements North-east of Calgary, Alberta." M.A. thesis, Calgary, 1971.
6318. **Thomas, Lewis G.** "Four Foothills Communities: An Introduction." In *Our Foothills*, edited by R. H. King, pp. 9-26. Calgary: Millarville, Kew, Priddis, and Bragg Creek Historical Society, 1975.
6319. _____. "Okotoks: From Trading Post to Suburb." *UHR* 8 (October 1979):3-22.
6320. **West, Karen.** "Cardston: The Temple City of Canada." *CGEJ* 71, no. 5 (1965):162-69.
6321. **Woywitka, A. B.** "Drumheller Strike of 1919." *Alta HR* 21, no. 1 (1973):1-7.

XIII

British Columbia

1. General

6322. **Akrigg, G. Philip V., and Akrigg, Helen B.** *1001 British Columbia Place Names.* 1969. Rev. 3d ed. Vancouver: Discovery Press, 1973.
6323. **Anderson, Ian Douglas.** "Discrimination Patterns with Change in Population Size of Urban Centres: A Case Study of Indians in Southwestern British Columbia." M.A. thesis, Simon Fraser, 1971.
6324. **Aylsworth, J. A.** "Transport Development and Regional Economic Growth in Northeastern British Columbia." M.A. thesis, British Columbia, 1974.
6325. **Bancroft, Clifford.** *Mining Communities in British Columbia: Social Infrastructure Analysis.* Victoria: British Columbia Dept. of Mines and Petroleum Resources and University of British Columbia, 1975.
6326. **Barlee, N. L.** *Gold Creeks and Ghost Towns.* Summerland: *Canada West Magazine,* 1970.
6327. **Beattie, Roderick Norman.** "Banking in Colonial British Columbia." B.A. essay, British Columbia, 1939.
6328. **Bradbury, John H.** "Instant Towns in British Columbia, 1965-1972." Ph.D. thesis, Simon Fraser, 1977.
6329. _____. "Class Structures and Class Conflicts in 'Instant' Resource Towns in British Columbia: 1965-1972." *BC Studies* 37 (1978):3-18.
6330. _____. "New Settlements Policy in British Columbia." *UHR* 8 (October 1979):47-76.
6331. _____. "The Instant Towns of British Columbia: A Settlement Response to the Metropolitan Call on the Productive Base." In #6510, pp. 117-33.
6332. _____. "Instant Resource Towns Policy in British Columbia, 1965-1972." *Plan Canada* 20 (1980):19-38.
6333. **Cantwell, Eugenie A.** "The Development of the Ports and Harbours of British Columbia." B.Comm. essay, British Columbia, 1935.
6334. **Carlsen, A. E.** "Major Developments in Public Finance in British Columbia, 1920-1960." Ph.D. thesis, Toronto, 1961.
6335. **Clark, A. B.** *An Outline of Provincial and Municipal Taxation in British Columbia, Alberta and Saskatchewan.* Winnipeg: University of Manitoba, 1920.
6336. **Clark, S. D.** "Mining Society in British Columbia and the Yukon." In *The Social Development of Canada,* edited by S. D. Clark, pp. 308-79. Toronto: UTP, 1942.
6337. _____. "The Gold-Rush Society of British Columbia and the Yukon." In *The Developing Canadian Community,* edited by S. D. Clark, pp. 81-98. Toronto: UTP, 1962.
6338. **Collier, R. W.** "The Evolution of Regional Districts in British Columbia." *BC Studies* 15 (1972):29-39.

6339. **Crerar, Alistair Donald.** "Planning in the Lower Mainland of British Columbia." *Can Geogr* 1, no. 4 (1953):21-26.
6340. **Edwards, M. H., and Lort, J. C. R.** *A Bibliography of British Columbia: Years of Growth 1900-1950.* Victoria: University of Victoria, Social Sciences Research Centre, 1975.
6341. **Farley, A. L.** "A Regional Study of Southeastern Vancouver Island." M.A. thesis, British Columbia, 1949.
6342. _____. *Atlas of British Columbia: People, Environment, and Land Use.* Vancouver: UBCP, 1979.
6343. **Floyd, P. D.** "The Human Geography of Southeastern Vancouver Island, 1842-1891." M.A. thesis, Victoria, 1970.
6344. **Forrester, Elizabeth A. M.** "The Urban Development of Central Vancouver Island." M.A. thesis, British Columbia, 1966.
6345. _____. "The Urban Hierarchy of Central Vancouver Island." In *Research Studies by Western Canadian Geographers: The Edmonton Papers,* edited by B. M. Barr, pp. 121-34. Vancouver: B.C. Geographical Series, No. 24, 1977.
6346. **Gamble, Ellsworth Paul.** "The British Columbia Railway and Regional Development." M.A. thesis, British Columbia, 1972.
6347. **Gibson, Edward M. W.** *The Urbanization of the Strait of Georgia Region.* Geographical Paper No. 57. Ottawa: Environment Canada, 1976.
6348. **Goldenberg, H. Carl.** *Provincial-Municipal Relations in British Columbia.* Victoria: King's Printer, 1947.
6349. **Grimmer, Dennis McLean.** "The Expansion of Urban Fringe Communities: A Case Study of the Lower Mainland Region of British Columbia." M.A. thesis, British Columbia, 1965.
6350. **Hardwick, Walter G.** "The Georgia Strait Urban Region." In *British Columbia,* edited by J. Lewis Robinson, pp. 119-34. Toronto: UTP, 1972.
6351. **Hayter, Roger.** "Labour Supply and Resource-Based Manufacturing in Isolated Communities: The Experience of Pulp and Paper Mills in North Central British Columbia." *Geoforum* 10 (1979):163-77.
6352. **Holdsworth, Deryck William, and Bailey, P.** *B.C. Urban History: Discovering the Past in the Present.* Vancouver: University of British Columbia, 1974.
6353. **Holmes, Marjorie C.** *Royal Commissions and Commissions of Inquiry in British Columbia, 1872-1942.* Victoria: King's Printer, 1945.
6354. _____. *Publications of the Government of British Columbia, 1871-1947.* Victoria: King's Printer, 1950.
6355. **Howell-Jones, Gerald I.** "A Century of Settlement Change: A Study of the Evolution of Settlement Patterns in the Lower Mainland of British Columbia." M.A. thesis, British Columbia, 1966.
6356. _____. "The Urbanization of the Fraser Valley." In *Lower Fraser Valley: Evolution of a Cultural Landscape,* edited by A. H. Siemens, pp. 139-62. Vancouver: B.C. Geographical Series, No. 9, 1968.
6357. **Humphries, Charles W.** "The Writing of Local History: A Review Article." *BC Studies* 22 (1974):71-75.
6358. **Hutchinson, R. Gordon, ed.** *Western Canadian Ports.* Vancouver: University of British Columbia, Centre for Transportation Studies, 1977.
6359. **Jackson, John J.** "Geography and Planning in British Columbia: The Publications of the Lower Mainland Regional Planning Board." *Can Geogr* 8 (1964):92-96.
6360. **Kaliski, Stephen Felix.** "The Growth and Development of the Manufacturing Industry in British Columbia." B.A. essay, British Columbia, 1952.
6361. **Keary, W. H.** *Report of the Royal Commission on Municipal Government, 1912.* Victoria: King's Printer, 1913.
6362. **Kennedy, Sharon.** "The Differential Growth of Urban Centres in British Columbia, 1951-1961." B.A. essay, British Columbia, 1970.

6363. **Kitto, Robert Henry.** "The Settlement of the Lower Fraser Valley, British Columbia." M.A. thesis, Southern California, 1932.

6364. **Lowther, Barbara J.** *A Bibliography of British Columbia: Laying the Foundations 1849-1899.* Victoria: University of Victoria, Social Sciences Research Centre, 1968.

6365. **MacDonald, K. J.** "Sources of Electoral Support for Provincial Political Parties in Urban British Columbia." *BC Studies* 15 (1972):40-52.

6366. **McDonald, Robert A. J.** "Victoria, Vancouver, and the Evolution of British Columbia's Economic System, 1886-1914." In #**5352**, pp. 31-55.

6367. **Mikkelsen, P. M.** "Land Settlement Policy on the Mainland of British Columbia, 1858-1874." M.A. thesis, British Columbia, 1950.

6368. **Moffat, Robert Y.** "Urban and Rural Voting in British Columbia, 1906-1930." M.A. thesis, Washington, 1947.

6369. **Nesbitt, James George.** "Regional Differences in the Structure and Growth of Manufacturing in British Columbia." M.A. thesis, British Columbia, 1973.

6370. **Nicholson, T. J.** "The Regional Districts of British Columbia." M.A. thesis, British Columbia, 1974.

6371. **Oberlander, H. Peter.** "The 'Patron Saint' [Colonel Moody] of Town Planning in British Columbia." In #**563**, pp. 36-41.

6372. **Palmer, Bernard C.** "Development of Domestic Architecture in British Columbia." *JRAIC* 5 (1928):405-16.

6373. **Paterson, T. W.** *Ghost Towns of Vancouver Island.* Langley: Stagecoach, 1975.

6374. _____. *Encyclopedia of Ghost Towns and Mining Camps of British Columbia.* Langley: Stagecoach, 1979.

6375. **Porteous, J. Douglas.** "Urban Social Geography." In *Vancouver Island: Land of Contrasts,* edited by Charles N. Forward, pp. 309-28. Western Geographical Series, vol. 17. Victoria: University of Victoria, 1979.

6376. **Ramsey, Arthur Bruce.** *Ghost Towns of British Columbia.* Vancouver: Mitchell Press, 1963.

6377. **Rizui, A. A. B.** "Urbanization Trends in British Columbia, Canada." *Pakistan Geogr Rev* 22 (1967):9-24.

6378. **Robinson, Ira M.** "Planning for Small Communities in British Columbia." *CPR* 5, no. 1 (1955):10-15.

6379. _____. "Urbanization in British Columbia." Vancouver: University of British Columbia, 1957. [Unpublished paper.]

6380. **Rumsey, F.** "The Metropolitan-Hinterland Relationship in British Columbia." B.A. essay, British Columbia, 1973.

6381. **Smith, Allan.** "The Writing of British Columbia History." *BC Studies* 45 (1980):73-102.

6382. **Smith, Charles W.** *Pacific Northwest Americana: A Checklist of Books and Pamphlets Relating to the History of the Pacific Northwest.* New York: Wilson, 1921.

6383. **Sproule-Jones, Mark, and Van Klaversen, Adrie.** "Local Referenda and Size of Municipality in British Columbia: A Note on Two of Their Interrelationships." *BC Studies* 8 (1970-71):47-50.

6384. **Stanbury, W. T.** *Success and Failure: Indians in Urban Society [in British Columbia].* Vancouver: UBCP, 1975.

6385. _____. "Reserve and Urban Indians in British Columbia." *BC Studies* 26 (1975):39-64.

6386. _____; **Fields, D. B.; and Stevenson, D.** "B.C. Indians in an Urban Environment: Income, Poverty, Education and Vocational Training." *Manpower Review, Pacific Region* 5 (1972):11-33.

6387. **Tennant, Paul.** "Bylaws and Setbacks: The Oil Industry and Local Government in British Columbia." *BC Studies* 9 (1971):3-14.

6388. **Todd, Eric C. E.** "Municipal Control of Air Pollution in British Columbia." *UBC Law Rev* 6 (1971):261-70.

6389. **Ward, W. Peter.** "Class and Race in the Social Structure of British Columbia, 1870-1939." *BC Studies* 45 (1980):17-36.
6390. **Welch, Ruth Lilian.** "The Growth and Distribution of Population in British Columbia, 1951-61." M.A. thesis, British Columbia, 1964.
6391. **White, George Brooks.** "A History of the Eastern Fraser Valley since 1885." M.A. thesis, British Columbia, 1937.
6392. **Wickett, S. Morley.** "Local Government in British Columbia." In #**895,** pp. 213-20.
6393. **Willmott, W. E.** "Some Aspects of Chinese Communities in British Columbia Towns." *BC Studies* 1 (1968-69):27-36.
6394. **Wilson, James W.** "Regional Planning in British Columbia." *CPR* 2, no. 4 (1952):102-4.
6395. **Wilson, J. Donald, and Jones, David C.,** eds. *Schooling and Society in Twentieth Century British Columbia.* Calgary: University of Calgary, Dept. of Educational Foundations, 1980.
6396. **Woodward, Frances M.** "Bibliography of British Columbia." *BC Studies* 1 (1968-69). [A continuing feature.]
6397. _____. "Fire Insurance Plans and British Columbia Urban History." *BC Studies* 42 (1979):13-26.
6398. _____. "British Columbia Fire Insurance Plans: A Union List." *BC Studies* 42 (1979):27-50.

2. Esquimalt

6399. **Jordan, Mabel E.** "H.M.C. Dockyard, Esquimalt." *CGEJ* 50 (1955):124-32.
6400. **Longstaff, F. V.** *Esquimalt Naval Base: A History of Its Work and Defences.* Victoria: Victoria Book and Stationery Co., 1941.
6401. **MacKinnon, C. S.** "The Imperial Fortresses in Canada: Halifax and Esquimalt, 1871-1906." Ph.D. thesis, Toronto, 1965.
6402. **Roberts, Joseph.** "The Origins of the Esquimalt and Nanaimo Railroad: A Problem in British Columbia Politics." M.A. thesis, British Columbia, 1937.
6403. **Robinson, Leigh Burpee,** *Esquimalt: 'Place of Shoaling Waters.'* Esquimalt, 1947.
6404. **Schurman, D. M.** "Esquimalt: Defence Problem, 1865-1887." *BCHQ* 19 (1955):57-70.

3. Fort Langley

6405. **Curtis, Charles K.** *Fort Langley: An Historical Study.* Vancouver: University of British Columbia, Dept. of Education, 1960.
6406. **Inkster, Tom H.** "Fort Langley: Mainland B.C.'s Big Town, 1827-58." *CGEJ* 95, no. 1 (1977):48-53.
6407. **Murphy, Paul.** "The History of Fort Langley." B.A. essay, British Columbia, 1929.
6408. **Nelson, Denys.** *Fort Langley, 1827-1927: A Century of Settlement.* 1927. Reprint. Vancouver: Art, Historical, and Scientific Association, 1947.
6409. **Smith, D. B.** "The First Capital of British Columbia: Langley or New Westminster?" *BCHQ* 21 (1957-58):16-50.

4. Kamloops

6410. **Artibise, Alan F. J.** "Electoral Reform in the City of Kamloops: A Background Paper." In *Report on Local Government,* Appendix. Kamloops: City of Kamloops, 1975.
6411. **Balf, Mary.** *Kamloops: A History of the District up to 1914.* Kamloops: Kamloops Museum Association, 1969.

6412. _____. *The Mighty Company: Kamloops and the H.B.C.* Kamloops: Kamloops Museum Association, 1975.
6413. **Balf, R.** *Kamloops, 1914-1945.* Kamloops: Kamloops Museum Association, 1975.
6414. **Black, J. A.** "Kamloops: A City in the Southern Intermountain Region of B.C." M.A. thesis, Kent State, 1965.
6415. **Clemson, Donovan.** "Kamloops: City in the Sage." *CGEJ* 74 (1967):18-27.
6416. **Harvey, A. G.** "David Stuart: Okanagan Pathfinder and Founder of Kamloops." *BCHQ* 9 (1945):277-89.
6417. **Hoppenrath, I.** "Brocklehurst: Fragment of the Canadian Mosaic." *B.C. Perspectives* 3 (1973):3-14.
6418. **McPhail, L. R.** "Local Government in British Columbia: A Case Study [of Kamloops]." In *Malaspina Papers: Studies in Human and Physical Geography,* edited by R. Leigh, pp. 51-56. Vancouver: B.C. Geographical Series, No. 17, 1973.
6419. **Miller, Donna.** "Residential Location and Expansion: Kamloops, British Columbia, 1950-1966." B.A. essay, British Columbia, 1969.

5. Kitimat

6420. **Baxter, J. Russell.** "Kitimat: The First Five Years." *Can Arch* 1 (1956):20-23.
6421. **Endersby, Stanley Alfred.** "Kitimat, British Columbia: An Evaluation of Its Physical Planning and Development." M.Sc. thesis, British Columbia, 1965.
6422. **McGuire, B. J., and Wild, Roland.** "Kitimat—Tomorrow's City Today." *CGEJ* 59 (1959):142-61.
6423. **Meldrum, Pixie.** *Kitimat: The First Five Years.* Kitimat: Corporation of the District of Kitimat, 1958.
6424. **Richardson, Nigel H.** "A Tale of Two Cities [Prince Rupert and Kitimat]." In #563, pp. 269-84.

6. Nanaimo

6425. **Carroll, Harry.** *History of Nanaimo Pioneers.* Nanaimo: Herald Presses, 1935.
6426. **Gidney, Norman.** "From Coal to Forest Products: The Changing Resource Base of Nanaimo, B.C." *UHR* 1-78 (June 1978):18-47.
6427. **Johnson, Patricia M.** *A Short History of Nanaimo.* Nanaimo: Centennial Committee, 1958.
6428. **Jordan, Mabel E.** "The Century Old Bastion at Nanaimo." *CGEJ* 49 (1954):18-19.
6429. **McKelvie, B. A.** "The Founding of Nanaimo." *BCHQ* 8 (1944):169-88.
6430. **Matheson, Marion H.** "Some Effects of Coal Mining upon the Development of the Nanaimo Area." M.A. thesis, British Columbia, 1950.
6431. **Norcross, E. Blanche, ed.** *Nanaimo Retrospective: The First Century.* Nanaimo: Historical Society, 1979.
6432. **Roberts, Joseph.** "The Origins of the Esquimalt and Nanaimo Railroad: A Problem in British Columbia Politics." M.A. thesis, British Columbia, 1937.
6433. **Robinson, J. Lewis.** "Nanaimo, B.C." *CGEJ* 70 (1965):162-69.
6435. **Smith, Brian Ray Douglas.** "Some Aspects of the Social Development of Early Nanaimo." B.A. essay, British Columbia, 1956.
6436. **Strongitharm, Bryan Deane.** "Local Government Reorganization: A Case Study in Local Government in Nanaimo, B.C." M.A. thesis, British Columbia, 1975.

7. New Westminster

6437. **Chambers, Lucy B.** *The Court House of New Westminster.* New Westminster: Heritage Preservation Foundation of New Westminster and the B.C. Heritage Trust, 1980.

6438. **Firmaling, Tito Castro.** "Citizen Participation in Selected Planning Programs: A Case Study of New Westminster." M.A. thesis, British Columbia, 1968.

6439. **Ireland, W. E.** *New Westminster: The Royal City—The First 100 Years.* New Westminster: Columbian Co., 1960.

6440. **Kennedy, J. J.** "New Westminster, 1861-1869: A Disappointed Metropolis." *B.C. Hist N* 2 (1969):8-17.

6441. **McDonald, Margaret Lillooet.** "New Westminster, 1859-1871." M.A. thesis, British Columbia, 1947.

6442. **Mather, Barry.** *New Westminster: The Royal City.* Vancouver: Dent and City of New Westminster, 1958.

6443. **St. John, R. Monro.** "New Westminster on the Fraser." *CGEJ* 9, no. 5 (1934):247-55.

6444. **Smith, D. B.** "The First Capital of British Columbia: Langley or New Westminster?" *BCHQ* 21 (1957-58):16-50.

6445. **Weir, Thomas R.** "A Geographical Study of New Westminster and Its Regional Relationship." M.A. thesis, Syracuse, 1945.

6446. _____. "New Westminster, B.C." *CGEJ* 36 (1948):22-38.

6447. **Woodland, Alan.** *New Westminster: The Early Years, 1858-1898.* New Westminster: Nunaga, 1973.

8. Penticton

6448. **Atkinson, Reginald Noel.** *Historical Souvenir of Penticton, B.C., 1869-1967.* Penticton: Okanagan Historical Society, 1967.

6449. **Rosenthal, H. M.** "Penticton Profile: A Case Study in Community Involvement." M.A. thesis, Simon Fraser, 1972.

6450. **Wahl, E.** "Penticton and Its Region." M.A. thesis, British Columbia, 1955.

9. Prince George

6451. **Harrington, Robert F.** "Prince George: Western White Spruce Capital of the World." *CGEJ* 77 (1968):72-83.

6452. **Holmes, Neil Bradford.** "The Promotion of Early Growth in the Western Canadian City: A Case Study of Prince George, B.C., 1909-1915." B.A. essay, British Columbia, 1974.

6453. **Runnalls, F. E.** "Boom Days in Prince George." *BCHQ* 8 (1944):281-306.

6454. _____. *A History of Prince George.* Vancouver: Wrigley, 1946.

6455. **Young, Cy.** "Prince George: Hub of British Columbia." *W Bus Indus* 27 (August 1953):28-29, 65-68.

10. Prince Rupert

6456. **Adams, John Q.** "Prince Rupert, British Columbia." *Econ Geogr* 14 (1938):167-83.

6457. **Bell, Ann.** "Youth in our Town [Prince Rupert]." *Can Wel* 39 (1963):50-54.

6458. **Bell, David Seymour.** "A History of Real Estate Development in Prince Rupert." B.Comm. essay, British Columbia, 1968.

6459. **Bowman, P.** *Prince Rupert: The City of Muskeg, Rocks and Rain.* Prince Rupert, 1973.
6460. **Cadell, H. M.** "The New City of Prince Rupert." *Scottish Geogr Mag* 30 (1914):237-50.
6461. **Clief, Eugene Van.** "Prince Rupert: An Error in Location." *JOGG* 58 (1959):127-32.
6462. **Crerar, Alistair Donald.** "Prince Rupert, British Columbia: The Study of a Port and Its Hinterland." M.A. thesis, British Columbia, 1951.
6463. **Dobie, Sheila,** "Prince Rupert, B.C.: Adjusting to Peace after World War II." *B.C. Hist N* 13, no. 1 (1979):10-18.
6464. **Grand Trunk Pacific Railway Company.** *Prince Rupert, B.C.: The Pacific Coast Terminus of the Grand Trunk Pacific Railway.* Montreal, 1912.
6465. **Large, Richard G.** *Prince Rupert: A Gateway to Alaska.* Vancouver: Mitchell Press, 1960.
6466. **Richardson, Nigel H.** "A Tale of Two Cities [Prince Rupert and Kitimat]." In #**563**, pp. 269-84.
6467. **Warman, C.** "Prince Rupert." *Can Mag* 30 (1908):395-401.
6468. **Weaver, Emily P.** "Keeping up with Prince Rupert." *Can Mag* 38 (1912):357-65.

11. Vancouver and Environs

a. General

6469. **Adam, Robert D.** "Myth and Realities of Vancouver's Oriental Trade, 1886-1942." M.A. thesis, Victoria, 1980.
6470. **Appelbe, Frank.** *The Community Arts Council of Vancouver through the Years.* Vancouver: Community Arts Council, 1979.
6471. **Ashlee, Ted.** *Gabby, Ernie and Me: A Vancouver Boyhood.* Vancouver: Douglas, 1976.
6472. **Ashworth, Mary.** "The Settlement of Immigrants in Greater Vancouver." *Can Wel* 53 (1977):9-12.
6473. **Astles, A. R.** "The Role of Historical and Architectural Preservation in the Vancouver Townscape." In *Peoples of the Living Land: Geography of Cultural Diversity in British Columbia,* edited by J. V. Minghi, pp. 145-62. Vancouver: B.C. Geographical Series, No. 15, 1972.
6474. **Bannerman, Gary W.** *Gastown: The 107 Years.* North Vancouver: The *Times,* 1974.
6475. **Barclay, Herbert Richmond.** "A Review of the Finance of the City of Vancouver." B.Comm. essay, British Columbia, 1935.
6476. **Barford, Jerome C.** "Vancouver's Interurban Settlements: Their Early Growth and Functions—The Change and Legacy Today." B.A. essay, British Columbia, 1966.
6477. **Barker, Mary L.** "Recreation Hinterlands: A Metropolitan Call on the Environmental Base." In #**6510**, pp. 135-56.
6478. **Basi, R. S.** "The Vancouver Board of Trade: A Study of Its Organization and Role in the Community." M.A. thesis, British Columbia, 1953.
6479. **Bissley, Paul L.** *The History of the Vancouver Club.* Vancouver: Vancouver Club, 1971.
6480. **Bottomley, John.** "Ideology, Planning and the Landscape: The Business Community, Urban Reform and the Establishment of Town Planning in Vancouver, British Columbia, 1900-1940." Ph.D. thesis, British Columbia, 1977.
6481. **Bower, R.** *Stanley Park: An Island in the City.* Vancouver: November House, 1972.
6482. **Broadfoot, Barry.** *The City of Vancouver.* Vancouver: Douglas, 1976.
6483. **Brouillette, Benoît.** "Le port de Vancouver (comparé au port de Montréal)." *Ac Ec* 29 (1953):448-80.
6484. **Brown, John A.** "The Historical Geography of South Surrey, British Columbia." M.A. thesis, Western Washington State College, 1971.
6485. **Buckley, Alfred.** "Planning the British Columbia University Endowment Lands: A Great Town Planning Scheme for Western Canada." *TPICJ* 5, no. 6 (1926):2-4.

6486. **Cain, Louis P.** "Water and Sanitation Services in Vancouver: An Historical Perspective." *BC Studies* 30 (1976):27-43.
6487. **Campbell, Michael G.** "The Sikhs of Vancouver: A Case Study in Minority-Host Relations." M.A. thesis, British Columbia, 1977.
6488. **Chao, M.** "Chinatown, Vancouver." M.U.P. thesis, Oregon, 1971.
6489. **Cho, George C. H.** "Residential Patterns of the Chinese in Vancouver, British Columbia." M.A. thesis, British Columbia, 1970.
6490. _____, **and Leigh, R.** "Patterns of Residence of Chinese in Vancouver." In *Peoples of the Living Land: Geography of Cultural Diversity in British Columbia,* edited by J. V. Minghi, pp. 67-84. Vancouver: B.C. Geographical Series, No. 15, 1972.
6491. **Collier, R. W.** "Downtown: Metropolitan Focus." In #**6510,** pp. 159-78.
6492. _____, ed. *The Port of Vancouver.* Vancouver: University of British Columbia Extension Dept., 1966.
6493. **Collins, Barbara Rose.** "Indians in Vancouver." M.S.W. thesis, British Columbia, 1966.
6494. **Cooper, Marion Gibb Struthers.** "Residential Segregation of Elite Groups in Vancouver, British Columbia." M.A. thesis, British Columbia, 1971.
6495. **Cornwall, Ira Hugh Brooke.** "A Geographical Study of the Port of Vancouver in Relation to Its Coastal Hinterland." M.A. thesis, British Columbia, 1952.
6496. **Cran, G. A., and Hacking, N.** *Annals of the Royal Vancouver Yacht Club, 1903-1965.* Vancouver: R.V.Y.C., 1965.
6497. **Crerar, Alistair Donald.** "Population Density and Municipal Development—The Vancouver, B.C., Metropolitan Area." *Can Geogr* 2-4, no. 9 (1957):1-6.
6498. **Cromwell, J.** "Perceptual Differences between Established and New Residents in the Urban-Rural Fringe: Surrey, B.C." In *Peoples of the Living Land: Geography of Cultural Diversity in British Columbia,* edited by J. V. Minghi, pp. 229-42. Vancouver: B.C. Geographical Series, No. 15, 1972.
6499. **Cummings, D. E.** "Railway Entrances to Vancouver, 1887-1969." *Can Rail* 221 (1970):143-63.
6500. **Dalzell, A. G.** "Housing: The Relation of Housing and Town Planning in Cities Such as Vancouver." *TPICJ* 6, no. 3 (1927):102-6.
6501. _____. "Town Planning Problems in Vancouver." *Can Eng* 52 (1927):616-18.
6502. **Daniels, C. H.** *A Narrative History of the Terminal City Club.* Vancouver: Terminal City Club, 1936.
6503. **Davis, Chuck.** *Guide to Vancouver.* Vancouver: Douglas, 1973.
6504. _____. *The Vancouver Book.* Vancouver: Douglas, 1976.
6505. **Denike, K. G.** "Financial Metropolis of the West." In #**6510,** pp. 43-56.
6506. **Douhaniuk, William.** "Indians in Vancouver." M.S.W. thesis, British Columbia, 1966.
6507. **Ecroyd, L. G.** "Greater Vancouver—Metropolis and Gateway." *W Bus Indus* 35 (July 1961):38-53.
6508. **Elsammy, A. M.** "The Past and Present of Robson Street." M.Arch. thesis, British Columbia, 1976.
6509. **Evenden, L. J.** "Shaping the Vancouver Suburbs." In #**6510,** pp. 179-200.
6510. _____, ed. *Vancouver: Western Metropolis.* Western Geographical Series, Vol. 16. Victoria: University of Victoria, 1978.
6511. **Foreman, A. E.** "A Major Street Plan for Greater Vancouver." *TPICJ* 6, no. 4 (1927):128-31.
6512. **Forster, Victor Wadham.** *Vancouver through the Eyes of a Hobo.* Vancouver: McCormick, 1934.
6513. **Forward, Charles N.** "The Functional Characteristics of the Geographic Port of Vancouver." In #**6510,** pp. 57-78.

6514. **Francis, R. A.** "Victoria-Vancouver: A Study in Contrasts on the West Coast." *Can Bus* 30 (1957):30-33.
6515. **Freer, Katherine M.** *Vancouver: A Bibliography Compiled from Material in the Vancouver Public Library and the Special Collections of the University of British Columbia Library.* Vancouver: Vancouver Public Library, 1962.
6516. **Gibson, Edward M. W.** "The Impact of Social Belief on Landscape Change: A Geographical Study of Vancouver." Ph.D. thesis, British Columbia, 1972.
6516A. _____. "Lotus Eaters, Loggers, and the Vancouver Landscape." In *Cultural Discord in the Modern World,* edited by L. J. Evenden and F. F. Cunningham, pp. 57-74. Vancouver: B.C. Geographical Series, No. 20, 1974.
6517. **Graham, David; Yesaki, Arthur; and Yuen, Ronald.** "An Investigation of the Japanese Presence in Vancouver." B.Arch. essay, British Columbia, 1970.
6518. **Grant, K. F.** "Food Habits and Food Shopping Patterns of Greek Immigrants in Vancouver." In *Peoples of the Living Land: Geography of Cultural Diversity in British Columbia,* edited by J. V. Minghi, pp. 125-44. Vancouver: B.C. Geographical Series, No. 15, 1972.
6519. **Green, George.** *History of Burnaby and Vicinity.* North Vancouver: Shoemaker, McLean and Veitch, 1947.
6520. **Griggs, Neil John Francis.** "The Urban Growth and Transportation Implications in Port Development: A Case Study, Vancouver, British Columbia." M.A. thesis, British Columbia, 1970.
6521. **Gunn, Angus M.** *Vancouver, B. C.: Profile of Canada's Pacific Metropolis.* Richmond: Smith Lithograph, 1968.
6522. **Gutstein, Donald.** *Vancouver Ltd.* Toronto: Lorimer, 1975.
6523. **Habinski, A. A.** "The Jews in Vancouver: Industrial Location, Assimilation, and Residential Location." M.A. thesis, Simon Fraser, 1973.
6524. **Hardwick, Walter G.** "The Persistence of Vancouver as the Focus for Wood Processing in British Columbia." *Can Geogr* 9 (1965):92-96.
6525. _____. *Vancouver.* Don Mills: Collier-Macmillan, 1974.
6526. **Harker, Douglas E.** *Saints: The Story of St. George's School for Boys, Vancouver.* Vancouver: Mitchell, 1979.
6527. **Hayter, Roger.** "Forestry in British Columbia: A Resource Basis of Vancouver's Dominance." In #**6510**, pp. 95-116.
6528. **Holdsworth, Deryck William.** "Vernacular Form in an Urban Context: A Preliminary Investigation of Façade Elements in Vancouver Housing." M.A. thesis, British Columbia, 1971.
6529. _____. "House and Home in Vancouver: Images of West Coast Urbanism, 1886-1929." In #**85**, pp. 186-211.
6530. **Howard, Irene.** *Vancouver's Svenskar: A History of the Swedish Community in Vancouver.* Vancouver: Historical Society, 1970.
6531. **Huel, Raymond.** *Vancouver's Past.* Vancouver: Soules, 1974.
6532. **Indra, D. M.** "South Asian Stereotypes in the Vancouver Press." *Ethnic and Racial Studies* 2 (1979):166-89.
6533. **Kalman, Harold.** *Exploring Vancouver: Ten Tours of the City and Its Buildings.* Vancouver: UBCP, 1974.
6534. _____. *Exploring Vancouver 2.* Vancouver: UBCP, 1978.
6536. **Kennedy, W.** *Vancouver Tomorrow: A Search for Greatness.* Vancouver: Mitchell, 1975.
6537. **Kerr, Donald P.** "Vancouver—A Study in Urban Geography." M.A. thesis, Toronto, 1943.
6538. **Kidd, Thomas.** *History of Richmond Municipality.* 1927. Reprint. Richmond: Richmond Printers, 1973.
6539. **Kloppenborg, Anne, ed.** "Almost Vancouver: Plans and Proposals That Never Left the Drawing Board." *Urban Reader* 3, no. 8 (1975):18-20.

6540. _____; Niwinski, Alice; Johnson, Eve; and Gruetter, Roberts, eds. *Vancouver's First Century: A City Album, 1860-1960.* Vancouver: Douglas, 1977.
6541. **Kuthan, G., and Stainsby, D.** *Vancouver Sights and Insights.* Toronto: Macmillan, 1962.
6542. **Lambrou, Yianna.** "The Greek Community of Vancouver: Social Organization and Adaptation." M.A. thesis, British Columbia, 1975.
6543. **Laurence, L.** "Finances municipales comparées de Montréal, Toronto, et Vancouver." Thèse de M.A., Montréal, 1957.
6544. **Leggett, John C.** "The Persistence of Working-Class Consciousness in Vancouver." In *Visible Minorities and Multiculturalism: Asians in Canada,* edited by K. Victor Ujimoto and Gordon Hirabayashi, pp. 241-62. Toronto: Butterworths, 1980.
6545. **Le Neveu, Allan Henry.** "Vancouver as a Pacific Port." B.A. essay, British Columbia, 1922.
6546. **Lewis, Alfred H.** *South Vancouver, Past and Present.* Vancouver: Western Publishing Bureau, 1920.
6547. **Logan, Harry T.** *Tuum Est: A History of the University of British Columbia.* Vancouver: University of British Columbia, 1958.
6548. **Lopatin, Ivan Alexis.** "The Geography of Vancouver." M.A. thesis, British Columbia, 1929.
6549. **McCaskill, Donald N.** "The Urbanization of Native People in Toronto, Winnipeg, Edmonton, and Vancouver: A Comparative Analysis." Ph.D. thesis, York, 1979.
6550. **MacDonald, Norbert.** "Population Growth and Change in Seattle and Vancouver, 1880-1960." *PHR* 39 (1970):279-321.
6551. **McGeer, Gerald C.** "Vancouver's Golden Jubilee." *CGEJ* 13 (1936):11-24.
6552. **McGill, Alan S.** "The Theory of Property Taxation and Its Application in the City of Vancouver." B.A. essay, British Columbia, 1948.
6553. **McGovern, Peter D.** "Industrial Development in the Vancouver Area." *Econ Geogr* 37 (1961):189-206.
6554. **McGregor, D. A.** "Adventures of Vancouver Newspapers, 1892-1926." *BCHQ* 10 (1946):89-142.
6555. **MacInnes, Tom.** "The Port of Vancouver." *CGEJ* 2 (1931):289-309.
6556. **McKee, William C.** "The History of the Vancouver Park System, 1886-1929." M.A. thesis, Victoria, 1976.
6557. _____. "The Resources of the Vancouver City Archives." *UHR* 2-77 (October 1977):3-9.
6558. _____. *Portholes and Pilings: A Retrospective Look at the Development of Vancouver Harbour up to 1933.* Occasional Paper No. 1. Vancouver: City of Vancouver Archives, 1978.
6559. _____. "The Vancouver Park System, 1886-1929: A Product of Local Businessmen." *UHR* 3-78 (February 1979):33-49.
6560. **McPherson, H. L.** "The Planning of the University Endowment Lands, Vancouver." *TPICJ* 5, no. 6 (1926):5-18.
6561. **Marlatt, Daphne, and Itter, Carole,** eds. "Opening Doors: Vancouver's East End." *Sound Heritage* 8, no. 1-2 (1979):1-186.
6562. **Matheson, Harold Kenneth.** "Indians in Vancouver." M.S.W. thesis, British Columbia, 1966.
6563. **Mayhew, Barry W.** *A Regional Atlas of Vancouver.* Vancouver: United Community Services of the Greater Vancouver Area, 1967.
6564. **Mitchell, N., and Forster, S.** *The Symphony Story.* Vancouver: Women's Committee, Vancouver Symphony Society, 1971.
6565. "Modern Town Planning Underway in British Columbia: Planning the Vancouver Lands." *TPICJ* 4, no. 6 (1925):1-7.
6566. **Moodie, Robert James.** "Gastown: Past, Present and Future." M.A. thesis, British Columbia, 1971.

6567. **Moogk, Peter N.** *Vancouver Defended: A History of the Men and Guns of the Lower Mainland Defences, 1859-1949.* Surrey: Antonson, 1978.
6568. **Morley, Alan.** *Vancouver: From Milltown to Metropolis.* Vancouver: Mitchell, 1961.
6569. **Nicol, Eric.** *Vancouver.* 1970. 2d ed. Toronto: Doubleday, 1978.
6570. **Nilson, Deborah.** "The 'Social Evil': Prostitution in Vancouver." B.A. essay, British Columbia, 1976.
6571. **Ogden, R. Lynn.** "Vancouver City Archives: A New Resource." *UHR* 1-74 (June 1974):20-23.
6572. **Ohannesian, P. B.** "Deco Revisited: An Architect's Tour of Vancouver." *Western Living* 7, no. 1 (1977):22-26.
6573. **Patillo, R. W.** *The West End of Vancouver: A Social Profile.* Vancouver: United Community Services, 1969.
6574. **Patterson, Frederick Jenkins.** "A Financial History of the Corporation of West Vancouver." M.A. thesis, British Columbia, 1928.
6575. **Patterson, James G.** *The Greeks in Vancouver: A Study in the Preservation of Ethnicity.* Canadian Centre for Folklore Studies, Paper 18. Ottawa: National Museums of Canada, 1976.
6576. "A Plan for South Vancouver." *TPICJ* 9, no. 1 (1930):6-10.
6577. **Porter, Richard P. R.** "Vancouver: The Role of Ethnic Origin in Population Distribution." B.A. essay, British Columbia, 1965.
6578. **Richmond Centenary Council.** *Report on Local Government.* Richmond, 1968.
6579. **Robinson, J. Lewis.** "How Vancouver Has Grown and Changed." *CGEJ* 89, no. 4 (1974):40-48.
6580. **Ross, Leslie J.** *Richmond: Child of the Fraser.* Richmond: Richmond Centennial Society, 1979.
6581. **Rothery, Agnes.** *The Ports of British Columbia: The Story of Canada's Great Pacific Seaport Cities, Vancouver and Victoria.* Toronto: M&S, 1943.
6582. **Roy, Patricia E.** "Railways, Politicians and the Development of the City of Vancouver as a Metropolitan Centre, 1886-1929." M.A. thesis, Toronto, 1963.
6583. _____. "The British Columbia Electric Railway Company, 1897-1928: A British Company in British Columbia." Ph.D. thesis, British Columbia, 1970.
6584. _____. "The Fine Art of Lobbying and Persuading: The Case of the B.C. Electric Railway." In *Canadian Business History: Selected Studies,* edited by D. S. Macmillan, pp. 125-43. Toronto: M&S, 1972.
6585. _____. "Protecting Their Pocketbooks and Preserving Their Race: White Merchants and Oriental Competition." In #5379, pp. 116-38.
6586. _____. *Vancouver: An Illustrated History.* History of Canadian Cities Series, vol. 3. Toronto: Lorimer and NMM, 1980.
6587. _____. "Vancouver: 'The Mecca of the Unemployed,' 1907-1929." In #5352, pp. 393-413.
6588. **Sage, Walter N.** "Vancouver: The Rise of a City." *Dal Rev* 17 (1937):47-54.
6589. _____. "Vancouver: 60 Years of Progress." *J Commerce Year Book* (1947):95-116.
6590. **Sandison, James.** *Schools of Old Vancouver.* Vancouver: Vancouver Historical Society, 1971.
6591. **Seebaran, R. B.** "The Migration of the Sons of Freedom into the Lower Mainland of British Columbia: The Vancouver Experience." M.S.W. thesis, British Columbia, 1965.
6592. **Sinclair, Sylvia.** "Vancouver, B.C., and Sydney, Australia: A Comparison." *CGEJ* 68 (1964):28-37.
6593. **Smith, A. G.** "The British Columbia Town Planning Act." *TPICJ* 5, no. 1 (1926):7-10.
6594. **Smith, Andrea B.** "Mount Pleasant: A Neighbourhood History." Vancouver Historical Society, *Newsletter* 15 (February 1976):7-11.

6595. **Soules, Gordon.** *Vancouver at Your Feet.* Vancouver: Soules, 1971.
6596. **Stevens, Leah.** "Rise of the Port of Vancouver, British Columbia." *Econ Geogr* 12 (1936):61-70.
6597. ———. "The Grain Trade of the Port of Vancouver, British Columbia." *Econ Geogr* 12 (1936):185-96.
6598. **Stevenson, J., and Gervin, J. K.** "Labour's Growth in Vancouver." *American Federationist* 58 (1951):122-23.
6599. **Tarasoff, Koozma John.** "A Study of Russian Organizations in the Greater Vancouver Area." M.A. thesis, British Columbia, 1963.
6600. ———. "Russians in the Greater Vancouver Area." In *Slavs in Canada,* pp. 138-47. Edmonton: Inter-University Committee on Canadian Slavs, 1966.
6601. **Tassie, Peter.** "The Urban Growth and Transportation Implications in Port Development: A Case Study, Vancouver, British Columbia." M.A. thesis, British Columbia, 1970.
6602. **Thom, William Wylie.** "The Fine Arts in Vancouver, 1886-1936: An Historical Survey." M.A. thesis, British Columbia, 1969.
6603. **Treleaven, G. Fern.** *The Surrey Story.* 3 vols. Surrey: Surrey Museum and Historical Society, 1969-1972.
6604. **Vancouver, City Planning Department.** *Vancouver's Heritage: Twenty-Two Buildings and Two Historic Areas.* Vancouver: Vancouver Heritage Advisory Committee, 1974.
6605. **Vancouver Exhibition Association.** *1886-1936: Fifty Years of Progress.* Vancouver, 1936.
6606. **Waites, K. A., ed.** *The First Fifty Years: Vancouver High Schools, 1890-1940.* Vancouver, 1942.
6607. **Walden, Phyllis Sarah.** "A History of West Vancouver." M.A. thesis, British Columbia, 1947.
6608. **Walhouse, F.** "The Influence of Minority Ethnic Groups on the Cultural Geography of Vancouver." M.A. thesis, British Columbia, 1961.
6609. **Watt, Robert D.** "Art Glass Window Design in Vancouver: The Role of the Pattern Book." *Mat Hist Bull* 6 (1978):74-114.
6610. ———. *Rainbows in Our Walls: Art and Stained Glass in Vancouver, 1890-1940.* Vancouver: Vancouver Museums and Planetarium Association, 1979.
6611. **Weaver, John C.** "The Property Industry and Land Use Controls: The Vancouver Experience, 1910-1945." *Plan Canada* 19 (1979):211-26.
6612. **Weightman, Barbara Ann.** "The Musqueam Reserve: A Case Study of the Indian Social Milieu in an Urban Environment." Ph.D. thesis, Washington, 1972.
6613. **Wickberg, Edgar.** "Chinese and Canadian Influences on Chinese Politics in Vancouver, 1900-1947." *BC Studies* 45 (1980):37-55.
6614. **Wilson, J. W.** "Electric Power Development in British Columbia: A Case of Metropolitan Dominance?" In #**6510**, pp. 79-94.
6615. **Woodsworth, James Shaver.** *On the Waterfront: With the Workers on the Docks at Vancouver.* Ottawa: Mutual Press, 1928.
6616. **Woodward-Reynolds, Kathleen Marjorie.** "A History of the City and District of North Vancouver." M.A. thesis, British Columbia, 1943.
6617. **Yarham, E. R.** "Vancouver's Romance: From Log Huts to 'Queen of the Pacific Shore.'" *United Empire* 27 (1936):180-83.

b. Pre-1921

6618. **Adams, Thomas.** "The Planning of Greater Vancouver." *Cn L* 1, no. 3 (1915):57-60.
6619. **Andrews, Margaret W.** "Epidemic and Public Health: Influenza in Vancouver, 1918-1919." *BC Studies* 34 (1977):21-44.

6620. _____. "Medical Attendance in Vancouver, 1886-1920." *BC Studies* 40 (1978-79):32-56.
6621. _____. "Medical Services in Vancouver, 1886-1920: A Study in the Interplay of Attitudes, Medical Knowledge, and Administrative Structures." Ph.D. thesis, British Columbia, 1979.
6622. Barrett, John. "What the Panama Canal and Pan-American Trade Means to Vancouver and Canada." Canadian Club of Vancouver, *Speeches, 1910-1911,* pp. 43-49.
6623. Bennet, Morton L. "Vancouver and the Company." *Beaver,* Outfit 270 (1940):32-37.
6624. Boutilier, Helen R. "Vancouver's Earliest Days." *BCHQ* 10 (194):151-70.
6625. Brooks, F. G. H. "Vancouver's Origins." B.A. essay, British Columbia, 1952.
6626. Burnes, John Rodger. *North Vancouver: Saga of a Municipality in Its Formative Days, 1891-1907.* North Vancouver: Carson Graham School, 1972.
6627. Dawson, W. J. "The Building of a City." Canadian Club *Addresses* (Vancouver), 1909-10, pp. 39-45.
6628. Durham, Julian. "Vancouver." *Can Mag* 12 (1898):109-14.
6629. Flynn, James E. "Early Lumbering on Burrard Inlet, 1862-1891." B.Sc. thesis, British Columbia, 1942.
6630. Fripp, R. M. "Speculations on the Problem of Housing and the Working Classes in Vancouver." *ENCR* 28 (1914):1276-78.
6630A. Gallois, Robert. "Social Structure of Space: Vancouver, 1886-1901." M.A. thesis, Simon Fraser, 1980.
6631. Godenrath, P. F. "Advertising a City." *Westward Ho! Mag* 5 (1909):555-58.
6632. Gomery, Darrel. "A History of Early Vancouver." B.A. essay, British Columbia, 1936.
6633. Gordon, W. R. "Industrial Vancouver." *B.C. Mag* 7 (1911):626-29.
6634. Grant, J. H. "Burrard Inlet in Early Times." *B.C. Mag* 7 (1911):487-97.
6635. Grant, Roland D. "The Future of Vancouver, and Why." Canadian Club of Vancouver, *Speeches, 1909-1910,* pp. 65-73.
6636. Hayball, G. "A History of the Vancouver Public Library, 1869-1900." *B.C. Hist N* 10, no. 4 (1977):21-30.
6637. Hillman, W. A. "The Magic of the Single Tax." *B.C. Mag* 7 (1911):303-5.
6638. Howay, F. W. "Early Shipping in Burrard Inlet, 1863-1870." *BCHQ* 1 (1937):3-20.
6639. _____. "Early Settlement on Burrard Inlet." *BCHQ* 1 (1937):101-14.
6640. Kenvyn, R. "Vancouver's Harbour and Shipping." *B.C. Mag* 7 (1911):474-86.
6641. Lamb, Bessie. "From 'Tickler' to 'Telegram': Notes on Early Vancouver Newspapers." *BCHQ* 12 (1948):175-99.
6642. Lamb, W. Kaye. "The Pioneer Days of the Trans-Pacific Service, 1887-1891." *BCHQ* 1 (1937):143-69.
6643. McCann, L. D. "Urban Growth in a Staple Economy: The Emergence of Vancouver as a Regional Metropolis, 1886-1914." In #**6510**, pp. 17-42.
6644. MacDonald, Norbert. "Seattle, Vancouver, and the Klondike." *CHR* 49 (1968):234-46.
6645. _____. "Vancouver in the Nineteenth Century." *UHR* 1-75 (June 1975):51-54.
6646. _____. "A Critical Growth Cycle for Vancouver, 1900-1914." In #**85**, pp. 142-59.
6647. _____. "The Canadian Pacific Railway and Vancouver's Development to 1900." *BC Studies* 35 (1977):3-35.
6648. McDonald, Robert A. J. "Business Leaders in Early Vancouver, 1890-1914." Ph.D. thesis, British Columbia, 1977.
6649. _____. "City-Building in the Canadian West: A Case Study of Economic Growth in Early Vancouver, 1886-1893." *BC Studies* 43 (1979):3-28.
6650. _____. "Victoria, Vancouver, and the Evolution of British Columbia's Economic System, 1886-1914." In #**5352**, pp. 31-55.
6651. McDougall, R. J. "Vancouver Real Estate for Twenty-Five Years." *B.C. Mag* 7 (1911):597-607.

6652. McGregor, D. A. "The Marvel of Vancouver." *B.C. Mag* 7 (1911):457-72.
6653. Makovski, L. W. "The Rise of the Merchant Princes." *B.C. Mag* 7 (1911):542-50.
6654. _____. "The Rock on Which Vancouver Is Built: Financial Growth." *B.C. Mag* 7 (1911):588-96.
6655. Matters, Diane L. "The Development of Public Welfare Institutions in Vancouver, 1910-1920." B.A. essay, Victoria, 1973.
6656. _____. "A Chance to Make Good: Juvenile Males and the Law in Vancouver, B.C., 1900-1915." M.A. thesis, British Columbia, 1978.
6657. _____. "Public Welfare Vancouver Style, 1910-1920." *J Can St* 14, no. 1 (1979):3-15.
6658. Mawson, Thomas H. "Vancouver: A City of Optimists." *Town Plan Rev* 4 (1913):7-12.
6659. Paton, J. A. "The Inside Story of Point Grey." *B.C. Mag* 7 (1911):735-37.
6660. Pethick, Derek. *Vancouver Recalled: A Pictorial History to 1887.* Saanichton: Hancock House, 1974.
6661. Playfair, W. "Vancouver and the Railways." *B.C. Mag* 7 (1911):498-504, 537-41.
6662. Roberts, Sheila. *Shakespeare in Vancouver, 1889-1918.* Occasional Paper No. 3. Vancouver: Vancouver Historical Society, 1971.
6663. Robertson, Angus E. "The Pursuit of Power, Profit, and Privacy: A Study of Vancouver's West End Elite, 1886-1914." M.A. thesis, British Columbia, 1977.
6664. Rosenthal, Star. "Union Maids: Organized Women Workers in Vancouver, 1900-1915." *BC Studies* 41 (1979):36-55.
6665. Roy, Patricia E. "Regulating the British Columbia Electric Railway: The First Public Utilities Commission in B.C." *BC Studies* 11 (1971):3-20.
6666. _____. "The British Columbia Electric Railway and Its Street Railway Employees: Paternalism in Labour Relations." *BC Studies* 16 (1972-73):3-24.
6667. _____. "The Preservation of the Peace in Vancouver: The Aftermath of the Anti-Chinese Riot of 1887." *BC Studies* 31 (1976):44-59.
6668. Sugimoto, Howard H. "Japanese Immigration, the Vancouver Riots and Canadian Diplomacy." M.A. thesis, Washington, 1966.
6669. _____. "The Vancouver Riots of 1907: A Canadian Episode." In *East Across the Pacific,* edited by H. Conroy and T. S. Miyakawa, pp. 92-126. Santa Barbara: American Bibliographical Center, 1972.
6670. _____. "The Vancouver Riot and Its International Significance." *PNQ* 64 (1973):163-74.
6671. Taylor, L. D. "What Single Tax Has Done for Vancouver." *B.C. Mag* 6 (1910):411-15.
6672. Timms, P. T. *Vancouver: The Golden Years, 1900-1910.* Vancouver: Vancouver Museums Association, 1971.
6673. Todd, Robert B. "The Organization of Professional Theatre in Vancouver, 1886-1914." *BC Studies* 44 (1979-80):3-24.
6674. Vancouver Museum and Planetarium. *The Golden Years, 1900-1910.* Vancouver, 1971.
6675. Weston, G. "Vancouver City Police." *B.C. Mag* 7 (1911):558-61.
6676. Wynne, Robert E. "American Labor Leaders and the Vancouver Anti-Oriental Riot." *PNQ* 57 (1966):172-80.
6677. Young, David John. "The Vancouver City Police Force, 1886-1914." B.A. essay, British Columbia, 1976.
6678. Young, E. M. "The Hospitals and Charities of Vancouver City." *B.C. Mag* 7 (1911):608-11.

c. Post-1921

6679. Armstead, L. D. "Spatial Changes in Land Use at Seattle, Tacoma and Vancouver International Airports." M.A. thesis, Western Washington, 1969.

6680. **Ball, B. K.** "The Ownership of Vancouver's C.B.D., 1951-1971." M.Sc. thesis, British Columbia, 1974.
6681. **Bartholomew, H.** *A Plan for the City of Vancouver, B.C., Including Point Grey and South Vancouver and a General Plan of the Region.* Vancouver: Town Planning Commission, 1929.
6682. **Bernard, A.; Léveillé, J.; and Lord, G.** *Profile: Vancouver. The Political and Administrative Structures of the Metropolitan Region of Vancouver.* Ottawa: MSUA, 1975.
6683. **Bjonback, Ralph Derek.** "The Factors of Growth in Manufacturing Employment in Metropolitan Vancouver, 1949-1958." M.A. thesis, British Columbia, 1971.
6684. **Bland, John, and Spruce-Sales, Harold.** "Physical Planning in Vancouver's Government." *CPR* 2 (1952):18-26.
6685. **Bradbury, Bettina.** "The Road to Receivership: Unemployment and Relief in Burnaby, North Vancouver City, North Vancouver District, and West Vancouver." M.A. thesis, Simon Fraser, 1976.
6686. **Brittain, Horace L.** *An Investigation and Survey into the Municipal Organization of Burnaby, B.C.* Vancouver: Burnaby Broadcast, 1933.
6687. **Brodie, Steve.** *Bloody Sunday, Vancouver, 1938.* Vancouver: Young Communist League, 1974.
6688. **Churchill, Dennis Michael.** "False Creek Development: A Study of the Actions and Interactions of the Three Levels of Government as They Affected Public and Private Development of the Waterway and Its Land Basin." M.A. thesis, British Columbia, 1954.
6689. _____. *Local Government and Administration in the Lower Mainland Metropolitan Communities.* Vancouver: Metropolitan Joint Committee, 1959.
6690. "City Plan for Vancouver Now Complete." *TPICJ* 10, no. 2 (1931):29-32.
6691. **Corbett, D. C., and Toren, E. R.** *A Survey of Metropolitan Governments.* Vancouver: University of British Columbia, 1958.
6692. **Desjardins, E. J.** "A Community Rehabilitation Centre." *Can Wel* 32 (1957):277-81.
6693. **Easton, Robert, and Tennant, Paul.** "Vancouver Civic Party Leadership: Background Attitudes and Non-Civic Party Affiliations." *BC Studies* 2 (1969):19-29.
6694. _____. "Vancouver Civic Party Leadership." In #**925**, pp. 110-23.
6695. **Fitzpatrick, Anne L.** "Volunteer Bureau of Greater Vancouver." *Can Wel* 31 (1955):128-34.
6696. **Forward, Charles N.** *Waterfront Land Use in Metropolitan Vancouver.* Ottawa: Queen's Printer, 1968.
6697. _____. "Relationships between Elderly Population and Income Sources in the Urban Economic Bases of Victoria and Vancouver." *BC Studies* 36 (1977-78):34-46.
6698. **Fountain, G. F.** "Zoning Administration in Vancouver." *Plan Canada* 2 (1961):115-24.
6699. **Gale, Donald T.** "The Impact of Canadian Italians on Retail Functions and Façades in Vancouver, 1921-1961." In *Peoples of the Living Land: Geography of Cultural Diversity in British Columbia,* edited by J. V. Minghi, pp. 107-24. Vancouver: B.C. Geographical Series, No. 15, 1972.
6700. **Gayler, H. J.** "Private Residential Redevelopment in the Inner City: The West End of Vancouver, Canada." *TPICJ* 57 (1971):15-20.
6701. _____. "Consumer Spatial Behaviour and Its Relation to Social Class and Family Status in Metropolitan Vancouver, Canada." Ph.D. thesis, British Columbia, 1974.
6702. **Gutstein, Donald.** "The Developers' TEAM: Vancouver's 'Reform' Party in Power." *City Mag* 1, no. 2 (1975):13-28.
6703. **Hamilton, S. W.** "The Land Market in Metropolitan Vancouver." In #**6510,** pp. 201-18.
6704. **Hardwick, Walter G.** "Vancouver: The Emergence of a 'Core-Ring' Urban Pattern." In *Geographical Approaches to Canadian Problems,* edited by R. L. Gentilcore, pp. 112-19. Toronto: Prentice-Hall, 1971.

6705. **Horsman, A. L., and Raynor, P.** "Citizen Participation in Local Area Planning: Two Vancouver Cases." In #**6510**, pp. 239-54.
6706. **Ioannon, Gregory P.** "Parties and Participation in Vancouver, 1964-1976." M.A. thesis, British Columbia, 1977.
6707. **Jamieson, William Sinclair.** "Analysis of Growth of Vancouver's Central Business District." M.B.A. thesis, British Columbia, 1972.
6708. **Klenke, M.** "Economic Revitalization of the Gastown Historic Site, 1966-1974." *Urban Reader* 3 (October 1975):20-23.
6709. **Laponce, J. A.** *People vs. Politics: A Study of Opinions, Attitudes and Perceptions in Vancouver-Burrard, 1963-1965.* Toronto: UTP, 1969.
6710. **Lioy, Michele.** *Social Trends in Greater Vancouver: A Study of a North American Metropolis.* Vancouver: Soules, 1975.
6711. **Lower Mainland Regional Planning Board of British Columbia.** *Manufacturing Industry in the Lower Mainland Region in British Columbia, 1931-1976: A Study of Past Trends and Future Prospects.* New Westminster, 1960.
6712. **McAfee, Ann.** "Evolving Inner-City Residential Environments: The Case of Vancouver's West End." In *Peoples of the Living Land: Geography of Cultural Diversity in British Columbia*, edited by J. V. Minghi, pp. 163-82. Vancouver: B.C. Geographical Series, No. 15, 1972.
6713. _____. "Defining Housing Problems, Policy and Programmes in a Canadian City: The Case of Vancouver." In #**6510**, pp. 219-38.
6714. **McCandless, Richard.** "Vancouver's 'Red Menace' of 1935: The Waterfront Situation." *BC Studies* 22 (1974):56-70.
6715. **Marcus, Robert J.** "Youth Services Can Be Relevant." *Can Wel* 45, no. 5 (1969):13-14.
6716. **Miller, Fern.** "Vancouver Civic Political Parties." Ph.D. thesis, Yale, 1972.
6717. _____. "Vancouver Civic Political Parties: Developing a Model of Party-System Change and Stabilization." *BC Studies* 25 (1975):3-31.
6718. **Minghi, Julian V., and Rumley, Dennis.** "Toward a Geography of Campaigning: Some Evidence from a Provincial Election in Vancouver, British Columbia." *Can Geogr* 22 (1978):145-62.
6719. **Moore, Helen Margaret.** "Contemporary Church Architecture, Vancouver, 1953-63." B.A. essay, British Columbia, 1964.
6720. **Morris, J. E.** "Empirical Analysis of Business Location in Greater Vancouver." M.B.A. thesis, British Columbia, 1974.
6721. **Namm, R.** "Relocation of Vancouver's Chinatown Residents under Urban Renewal." *J Soc Social Welfare* 3 (1975):125-30.
6722. **Northey, John Laird.** "The Influence of Airports on the Location of Non-Aviation Industry. A Case Study: The Vancouver Metropolitan Area, British Columbia." M.A. thesis, British Columbia, 1963.
6723. **Patterson, J. M.** "The Factorial Urban Ecology of Greater Vancouver: Characteristics of the Data Base." M.A. thesis, British Columbia, 1974.
6724. **Pendakur, V. Setty.** *Cities, Citizens and Freeways.* Vancouver: Transportation Development Agency, 1972.
6725. "A Plan for the City of Vancouver, B.C." *TPICJ* 8, no. 4 (1929):80-84.
6726. **Price, Edmund Van Sandford.** "The Housebuilding Industry in Metropolitan Vancouver." M.B.A. thesis, British Columbia, 1970.
6727. **Rankin, Harry.** *A Socialist Perspective for Vancouver.* Vancouver: Progress Books, 1974.
6728. _____. *Rankin's Law: Recollections of a Radical.* Vancouver: November House, 1975.
6729. **Raynor, Ashley E.** "A Study of Development Control in Burnaby, B.C." M.Sc. thesis, British Columbia, 1977.

6730. **Rees, M. H. W.** "Factors Affecting the Utilization of Indian Reserve Lands: A Comparative Study of Two Indian Bands within Metropolitan Vancouver." B.A. essay, Simon Fraser, 1968.

6731. **Rumley, Dennis.** "Stability and Change in Electoral Patterns: The Case of the 1972 B.C. Provincial Election in Vancouver." Ph.D. thesis, British Columbia, 1975.

6732. **Seymour, Horace L.** "The Progress of Town Planning in Vancouver and Point Grey." *TPICJ* 6, no. 6 (1927):215-16.

6733. **Sharpe, Robin.** "A Study in the Voting Behaviour of the Chinese Community in Vancouver-Centre." B.A. essay, British Columbia, 1956.

6734. **Steed, Guy P. F.** "Intrametropolitan Manufacturing: Spatial Distribution and Locational Dynamics in Greater Vancouver." *Can Geogr* 17 (1973):235-58.

6735. **Stobie, Peter W.** "Private Inner City Redevelopment in Vancouver: A Case Study of Kitsilano." M.A. thesis, British Columbia, 1979.

6736. **Straaton, Karin Vivian.** "The Political System of the Vancouver Chinese Community: Associations and Leadership in the Early 1960s." M.A. thesis, British Columbia, 1974.

6737. **Stratton, P. R. V.** "Public Housing Experience in Vancouver." *Habitat* 3 (March-April 1960):20-23.

6738. **Symonds, D.** "Some Insights into the Changing Nature of Suburbs on Commercial Centres in Vancouver, 1920-1950." B.A. essay, British Columbia, 1968.

6739. **Tanqueray, J. F. D.** "The Vancouver Civic Centre and English Bay Development Scheme." *TPICJ* 8, no. 1 (1929):2-5.

6740. **Tennant, Paul, and Zirnhelt, D.** "The Emergence of Metropolitan Government in Greater Vancouver." *BC Studies* 15 (1972):3-28.

6741. _____. "Metropolitan Government in Vancouver: The Strategy of Gentle Imposition." *Can Pub Admin* 16 (1973):124-38.

6742. **Tse, M.-L.** "Urban Population Density Distribution: A Contribution from the Vancouver Case." M.A. thesis, British Columbia, 1976.

6743. **Ulmer, A. L.** "A Comparison of Land Use Changes in Richmond, B.C. [1930-1958]: A Study of Urban Expansion upon an Agricultural Area in a Rural-Urban Fringe." M.A. thesis, British Columbia, 1964.

6744. **Umbach, J. E.** "Planning a Government Subdivision in Point Grey Municipality." *TPICJ* 4, no. 6 (1925):7-9.

6745. **Walker, J. Alexander.** "Quilchena Park, B.C." *TPICJ* 6, no. 2 (1927):74-76.

6746. _____. "A Plan for the City of Vancouver, B.C." *TPICJ* 10, no. 2 (1931):35-43.

6747. **Weightman, Barbara Ann.** "Indian Social Space: A Case Study of the Musqueam Band of Vancouver, British Columbia." *Can Geogr* 20 (1976):171-86.

6748. **Whetter, David.** *Forever Deceiving You: The Politics of Vancouver Development.* Vancouver: Urban Research Group, 1972.

6749. **Wong, S. T.** "Urban Redevelopment and Rehabilitation in the Strathcona Area: A Case Study of an East Vancouver Community." In #**6510**, pp. 255-70.

6750. **Wood, Marjorie R.** "Hinduism in Vancouver: Adjustments in the Home, the Temple and the Community." In *Visible Minorities and Multiculturalism: Asians in Canada,* edited by K. Victor Ujimoto and Gordon Hirabayashi, pp. 277-88. Toronto: Butterworths, 1980.

6751. **Young, G. A.** "The Municipal Subdivision Approval Process in Metropolitan Vancouver." M.Sc. thesis, British Columbia, 1974.

6752. **Young, R. E.** "Street of T'ongs: Planning in Vancouver's Chinatown." M.A. thesis, British Columbia, 1975.

12. Vernon

6753. **Gabriel, Theresa.** *Vernon, B.C.: A Brief History.* Vernon: Okanagan Historical Society, 1958.

6754. **Hurst, Theresa.** *An Illustrated History of Vernon and District.* Vernon: Okanagan Historical Society, 1967.
6755. **Kilvert, Barbara.** "Vernon, Okanagan Valley." *Beaver,* Outfit 291 (1960):48-53.
6756. **Stevens, H. H.** "Vernon and the Okanagan in 1894." Okanagan Historical Society, *Report* 32 (1968):35-41.

13. Victoria

6757. **Abraham, Dorothy E. A.** *Romantic Vancouver Island: Victoria, Yesterday and Today.* Victoria: Acme Press, 1947.
6758. **Armstrong, C. L.** "Victoria: The City of Certainties." *B.C. Mag* 7 (1911):651-60.
6759. **Artibise, Alan F. J.; Segger, Martin; Brown, Marian; and Gibson, Beth.** *Civic Archival Survey of Greater Victoria.* Victoria: University of Victoria, 1979.
6760. **Barber, Irene Teresa.** "A History of the Bastion Theatre." M.A. thesis, Victoria, 1976.
6761. **Bentick, Brian Leslie.** "Saving, Investment, and the Land Market: Victoria, 1872-93." Ph.D. thesis, Yale, 1969.
6762. **Bissley, Paul L.** *Early and Late Victorians: A History of the Union Club of British Columbia.* Sidney: Review Printing and Publishing, 1969.
6763. "British Columbia's Capital City." *West Shore* 15 (1889):291-300.
6764. **Brooks, G. W. S.** "Edgar Crow Baker: An Entrepreneur in Early British Columbia." *BC Studies* 31 (1976):23-43.
6765. **Burns, F. H.** "Victoria in the 1850s." *Beaver,* Outfit 280 (1949): 36-39.
6766. **Capital Region Planning Board.** *Retirement in the Capital Region of British Columbia.* Victoria, 1969.
6767. **Careless, J. M. S.** "The Lowe Brothers, 1852-1870: A Study in Business Relations on the North Pacific Coast." *BC Studies* 2 (1969):1-18.
6768. _____. "The Business Community in the Early Development of Victoria, B.C." In *Canadian Business History: Selected Readings,* edited by D. S. Macmillan, pp. 104-23. Toronto: M&S, 1972.
6769. **Cauthers, Janet, ed.** "A Victorian Tapestry: Impressions of Life in Victoria, B.C., 1880-1914." *Sound Heritage* 7, no. 3 (1978):1-76.
6770. **Clack, C.** *The Best of Victoria, Yesterday and Today: A Nostalgic 115 Years Pictorial History of Victoria.* Victoria: Victoria Weekly, 1973.
6771. **Clack, Roderick D.** "Victoria's Downtown Improvement Plan." *CPR* 9, no. 3 (1959):73-78.
6772. **Cotton, Peter.** "A Little of What You Fancy: Some Notes on the Transport of Architectural Ideas to Victoria, British Columbia." *BC Lib Q* 31 (July 1967):23-28.
6773. **Crystal Garden Preservation Society.** *The Crystal Gardens: West Coast Pleasure Palace.* Victoria, 1977.
6774. **Curtis, Lynn H.** *The War Is Over! A Study of Labour-Management Relations at St. Joseph s Hospital, Victoria, B.C.* Victoria: Social Science Research, 1970.
6775. **Diespecker, Richard Allan.** "The Jewel of Juan de Fuca." *CGEJ* 11 (1935):239-48.
6776. **Durham, Julian.** "Victoria." *Can Mag* 12 (1899):207-13.
6777. **Eaton, Leonard K.** *The Architecture of Samuel Maclure.* Victoria: Art Gallery of Greater Victoria, 1971.
6778. **Elliott, Craig C.** "Legitimate Theatre in Early Victoria, B.C." *B.C. Hist N* 3, no. 3 (1970):6-14.
6779. **England, Robert.** "A Victoria Real Estate Man; The Enigma of Sir Arthur Currie." *QQ* 65 (1958):210-21.
6780. **Everett, T. Thomson.** *Victoria Illustrated: A Brief History of Victoria from 1842.* Toronto: Victoria Publishing, 1892.

6781. **Farley, A. L.** "A Regional Study of Southeastern Vancouver Island." M.A. thesis, British Columbia, 1949.
6782. **Fawcett, Edgar.** *Some Reminiscences of Old Victoria.* Toronto: Briggs, 1912.
6783. **Ferris, Ray.** "Amalgamation of Social Services in Victoria." *Can Wel* 50, no. 5 (1974):10-12.
6784. **Floyd, P. D.** "The Human Geography of Southeastern Vancouver Island, 1842-1891." M.A. thesis, Victoria, 1970.
6785. **Forward, Charles N.** *Land Use in the Victoria Area, British Columbia.* Geographical Paper No. 43. Ottawa: Geographical Branch, 1969.
6786. _____. "A Comparison of Waterfront Land Use in Four Canadian Ports: St. John's, Saint John, Halifax and Victoria." *Econ Geogr* 45 (1969):155-69.
6787. _____. "Parallelism of Halifax and Victoria." *CGEJ* 90, no. 3 (1975):34-43.
6788. _____. "The Physical Geography of Victoria, circa 1860, as Perceived by Colonists, Mapmakers, and Visitors." In #**6792**, pp. 1-44.
6789. _____. "Relationships between Elderly Population and Income Sources in the Urban Economic Bases of Victoria and Vancouver." *BC Studies* 36 (1977-78):34-46.
6790. _____. "The Evolution of Victoria's Functional Character." In #**5352**, pp. 347-70.
6791. _____, ed. *Residential and Neighbourhood Studies in Victoria.* Western Geographical Series, vol. 5. Victoria: University of Victoria, 1973.
6792. **Foster, Harold D.**, ed. *Victoria: Physical Environment and Development.* Western Geographical Series, vol. 12. Victoria: University of Victoria, 1976.
6793. **Francis, R. A.** "Victoria-Vancouver: A Study in Contrasts on the West Coast." *Can Bus* 30 (1957):30-33.
6794. **Gallacher, Daniel Thomas.** "City in Depression: The Impact of the Years 1929-1939 on Greater Victoria, British Columbia." M.A. thesis, Victoria, 1969.
6795. **Gregson, H.** *A History of Victoria, 1842-1970.* Victoria: Observer Publishing, 1970.
6796. **Hearn, George R., and Wilkie, David.** *The Cordwood Limited: A History of the Victoria and Sidney Railway.* 1966. Rev. 3d ed. Victoria: B.C. Railway Historical Society, 1973.
6797. **Holloway, Godfrey F.** *The Empress of Victoria.* 1968. 2d ed. Victoria: Empress Publications, 1976.
6798. **Ireland, W. E.** "Gold Rush Days in Victoria, 1858-1859." *BCHQ* 12 (1948):231-46.
6799. **Jupp, Ursula.** *From Cordwood to Campus in Gordon Head, 1852-1959.* Victoria, 1975.
6800. **Kerr, Alastair W.** "The Architecture of Victoria's Chinatown." *Datum* 4, no. 1 (1979):8-11.
6801. **Klenman, A.** "Victoria Was First B.C. Jewish Centre." *Jewish Western Bulletin* (April 1971):49-56.
6802. **Lai, Chuen-Yan David.** "The Chinese Consolidated Benevolent Association in Victoria: Its Origins and Functions." *BC Studies* 15 (1972):53-67.
6803. _____. "Chinese Attempts to Discourage Emigration to Canada: Some Findings from the Chinese Archives in Victoria." *BC Studies* 18 (1973):33-49.
6804. _____. "The Demographic Structure of a Canadian Chinatown [Victoria] in the Mid-Twentieth Century." *CES* 11, no. 2 (1979):49-62.
6805. _____. "The Population Structure of North American Chinatowns in the Mid-Twentieth Century: A Case Study." In *Visible Minorities and Multiculturalism: Asians in Canada*, edited by K. Victor Ujimoto and Gordon Hirabayashi, pp. 13-22. Toronto: Butterworths, 1980.
6806. **Laing, F. W., and Lamb, W. Kaye.** "The Fire Companies of Old Victoria." *BCHQ* 10 (1946):43-75.
6807. **Lamb, W. Kaye.** "The Founding of Fort Victoria." *BCHQ* 7 (1943):71-92.
6808. **Lee, Barrie.** *Victoria on Foot: Walking Tours of Victoria's Old Town.* Victoria: Terrapin, 1979.

6809. **Lee, Christopher Lockhart.** "The Effect of Planning Controls on the Morphology of the City of Victoria, British Columbia." M.A. thesis, Victoria, 1970.
6810. **Lines, K.** "A Bit of Old England: The Selling of Tourist Victoria." M.A. thesis, Victoria, 1972.
6811. **Lort, J. C. R.** "Victoria Public Library." *BC Libr Q* 31 (1967):3-22.
6812. **Lort, R.** "On Samuel Maclure, MRAIC." *JRAIC* 35 (1948):114-15.
6813. **McCaffey, E.** "Victoria—The Beautiful." *Westward Ho! Mag* 6 (1910):188-91.
6814. _____. "Victoria: A Metropolis in the Making." *Man to Man* 6 (1910):1060-69.
6815. _____. "The Commercial Progress and Future of Victoria." *B.C. Mag* 8 (1912):374-80.
6816. **McCann, L. D.** "The Structure and Patterning of Manufacturing in the Victoria Metropolitan Area." B.A. essay, Victoria, 1966.
6817. **McDonald, Robert A. J.** "Victoria, Vancouver, and the Evolution of British Columbia's Economic System, 1886-1914." In #5352, pp. 31-55.
6818. **Myers, Thomas R.** *90 Years of Public Utility Service on Vancouver Island, 1869-1950: A History of the B.C. Electric.* Victoria: British Columbia Electric Railway, 1954.
6819. **Oak Bay Anniversary Committee.** *Golden Jubilee, 1906-1956: Fifty Years of Growth.* Oak Bay: Corporation of the District of Oak Bay, 1956.
6820. **Pethick, Derek.** *Victoria: The Fort.* Vancouver: Mitchell Press, 1968.
6821. **Pilton, James William.** "Early Negro Settlement in Victoria." B.A. essay, British Columbia, 1949.
6822. **Pullen, Henry F.** "Chinatown in Victoria." *Can Mag* 30 (1908):537-41.
6823. **Reeves, John H.** "Transport Costs and the Location of Industry in Victoria." *Econ Record* 27 (1951):231-36.
6824. **Reksten, Terry.** *Rattenbury [:A Victoria Architect].* Victoria: Sono Nis, 1978.
6825. **Robinson, M. E.** "A Method for Investigating the Effects of Tourism on the Functional and Morphological Development of a City: As Applied to Greater Victoria, B.C." Ph.D. thesis, Northwestern, 1957.
6826. **Rome, David.** "Early British Columbia Jewry: A Reconstructed Census." *CES* 3 (1971):57-62.
6827. **Rothery, Agnes.** *The Ports of British Columbia: The Story of Canada's Great Pacific Seaport Cities, Vancouver and Victoria.* Toronto: M&S, 1943.
6828. **Roy, Patricia E.** "The Illumination of Victoria: Late Nineteenth-Century Technology and Municipal Enterprise." *BC Studies* 32 (1976-77):79-92.
6829. **Ruzicka, Stanley Edward.** "The Decline of Victoria as the Metropolitan Centre of British Columbia, 1885-1901." M.A. thesis, Victoria, 1974.
6830. **Sedgwick, Charles Peter.** "The Context of Economic Change and Continuity in an Urban Overseas Chinese Community." M.A. thesis, Victoria, 1973.
6831. **Segger, Martin.** *Walking Tour: Old Town, Victoria.* Victoria: Heritage Map Tours, 1974.
6832. _____. *House Beautiful: Style in Decorative and Applied Arts, 1860-1920: An Exhibition.* Victoria: British Columbia Provincial Museum, 1974.
6833. _____, **and Franklin, Douglas.** *Victoria: A Primer for Regional History in Architecture, 1843-1929.* Watkins Glen, NY: American Life Foundation and Study Institute, 1979.
6834. **Sherrin, P. M.** "Spanish Spies in Victoria." *BC Studies* 36 (1977-78):23-33.
6835. **Shortt, Adam.** *Report of Dr. Adam Shortt Investigating the Financial Condition of the City of Victoria, B.C.* Victoria: Victoria Printing and Publishing Co., 1922.
6836. **Smyly, C.** "Heritage Lost: The Vanished Landmarks of Victoria." *Western Living* 6, no. 10 (1976):22-26, 109.
6837. _____. "Heritage Saved [Victoria]." *Western Living* 6, no. 12 (1976):40-48.
6838. **Sorby, Thomas C.** *The Harbour and City of Victoria: The Port of Vancouver Island, B.C.* Victoria: Victoria Inner Harbour Association, 1916.

6839. **Victoria, Corporation of the City of.** *Victoria Illustrated.* Victoria: Ellis, 1891.
6840. **Victoria Trades and Labour Council.** *Official Labour Review and Book of Reference.* Victoria: Trades and Labour Council, 1912.
6841. **Walden, Frederick Ellsworth.** "The Social History of Victoria, British Columbia, 1858-1871." B.A. essay, British Columbia, 1951.
6842. **Walker, M.** "Victoria: City of Many Facets." *Dal Rev* 24 (1945):399-401.
6843. **Warburton, T. R.** "Religious and Social Influences on Voting in Greater Victoria." *BC Studies* 10 (1971):3-25.
6844. **Weber, Ralph E.** "Riot in Victoria, 1860." *J Negro Hist* 56 (1971):141-48.
6845. **Willison, Marjory.** *Victoria, B.C.: City of Enchantment in Canada's Evergreen Playground.* Victoria: Canadian Pacific Railway for the Empress Hotel, 1933.
6846. **Wilson, James W.** *Report on a Planning Program for the Capital Region of British Columbia.* New Westminster: Lower Mainland Regional Planning Board, 1952.
6847. **Woodcock, George, and Woodcock, I.** *Victoria.* Victoria: Morriss, 1971.
6848. **Wright, J. M.** "The Settlement of the Victoria Region, British Columbia." M.A. thesis, McGill, 1956.

14. Other Centres

6849. **Akrigg, Helen B.** "History and Economic Development of the Shuswap Area." M.A. thesis, British Columbia, 1964.
6850. **Ala, L. G.** "Ladner, British Columbia." M.A. thesis, British Columbia, 1961.
6851. **Andrew, F. W.** *The Story of Summerland.* Penticton: Penticton *Herald,* 1945.
6852. **Andrews, Craig.** *Bay Ave., Trail, 1897-1910.* Castlegar: Continneh Books, 1973.
6853. **Apps, M. J.** "From Isolation to Suburbia: The Urbanization of Bowen Island." B.A. essay, British Columbia, 1973.
6854. **Asante, Nadine.** *The History of Terrace.* Terrace: Terrace Public Library Association, 1973.
6855. **Barlee, N. L.** "The Vanished City—Phoenix." *Canada West Mag* 5, no. 3 (1975):5-15.
6856. **Bilsland, William W.** "Atlin, 1898-1910: The Story of a Gold Rush." *BCHQ* 16 (1952):121-79.
6857. _____. "The History of Revelstoke and the Big Bend." M.A. thesis, British Columbia, 1955.
6858. _____, **and Ireland, W. E.** *Atlin, 1898-1910: The Story of a Gold Boom.* Atlin: Centennial Committee, 1971.
6859. **Booth, Michael R.** "Gold Rush Theatre: The Theatre Royal, Barkerville, British Columbia." *PNQ* 51 (1960):97-102.
6860. **Botting, P. J.** "The Village of Clinton." B.A. essay, British Columbia, 1972.
6861. **Brougham, W. F.** "A Typical Mining Town—Nelson, B.C." *Can Mag* 14 (1899):19-27.
6862. **Buckland, Frank M.** *Ogopogo's Vigil: A History of Kelowna and the Okanagan.* Kelowna: Okanagan Historical Society, 1966.
6863. **Chambers, Edith D.** *History of Port Coquitlam.* Port Coquitlam: Thompson, 1973.
6864. **Cherrington, John.** *Mission on the Fraser: Patterns of a Small City's Progress.* Vancouver: Mitchell Press, 1974.
6865. **Connolly, Phyllis H.** "A Geographical Analysis of Historical Events in the Maple Ridge District." B.A. essay, British Columbia, 1953.
6866. **Cook, Norman A., and Shea, C.** *Population Growth and Trends in the Dewdney-Alouette Regional District, 1921-1974.* Maple Ridge: Dewdney-Alouette Regional District, 1975.
6867. **Cottingham, Mollie E.** "History of the West Kootenay District in British Columbia." M.A. thesis, British Columbia, 1947.

6868. **Cromwell, J.** "Social Space in the Rural-Urban Fringe: A Study of Fleetwood, B.C." M.A. thesis, Simon Fraser, 1970.
6869. **Currie, Laurie.** *Princeton: 100 Years*. Princeton: Similkameen Spotlight Publishing, 1967.
6870. **Daem, Mary, and Dickey, E. E.** *A History of Early Revelstoke*. Revelstoke: City of Revelstoke, 1962.
6871. **Dahl, Erwin.** *Gateway to the Interior: A Brief History of Hope*. Chilliwack: Chilliwack Progress, 1971.
6872. **Davis, Isabelle F.** "Forty-Ninth Parallel City: An Economic History of Ladysmith." B.A. essay, British Columbia, 1953.
6873. **Doe, Ernest.** *History of Salmon Arm, 1885-1912*. Salmon Arm: *Observer*, 1947.
6875. **Ecroyd, L. G.** "Main Trading Centres: The Alberni Valley, Nanaimo, Courtenay, Cumberland, Comox, Duncan, Campbell River, Victoria." *W Bus Indus* 29 (April 1955):71-72, 74-86.
6876. **Elliott, Gordon Raymond.** *Quesnel: Commercial Centre of the Cariboo Gold Rush*. Quesnel: Cariboo Historical Society, 1958.
6877. **Gray, Arthur W.** *Kelowna: Tales of Bygone Days*. Kelowna: Kelowna Print, 1968.
6878. **Gung, Janice Sui-Ching.** "The Development of Resource-based New Towns in British Columbia: A Community Study of Gold River." M.A. thesis, British Columbia, 1970.
6879. **Harris, Lorraine.** *Half-way to the Goldfields: A History of Lillooet*. Vancouver: J. J. Douglas, 1975.
6880. "Industry and Humanity: The New Town of Powell River, B.C." *TPICJ* 6, no. 5 (1927):163-68.
6881. **Ivanisko, Henry.** "Changing Patterns of Residential Land Use in the Municipality of Maple Ridge, 1930-1960." M.A. thesis, British Columbia, 1964.
6883. **Lauder, Kathleen S.** "Planning for Quality of Life in New Resource Communities [Mackenzie, B.C., and Leaf Rapids, Manitoba]." M.A. thesis, Waterloo, 1977.
6884. **Lozovsky, N.** "Goals and Their Realization in Planning and Building an Instant Town: Gold River." M.A. thesis, British Columbia, 1970.
6885. **Ludditt, W.** *Barkerville*. Vancouver: Mitchell Press, 1974.
6886. **Mackintosh, C. H.** "British America's Golden Gateway to the Orient [Rossland, B.C.]." *Can Mag* 8 (1897):305-18.
6887. **Mercer, William M.** *Growth of Ghost Towns: The Decline of Forest Activity in the East Kootenay*. Victoria: Royal Commission on Forestry, 1944.
6888. **Moore, John Phillip.** "Residents' Perceptions of Quality of Life in Vanderhoof and Mackenzie, Two Northern British Columbia Resource Communities." M.B.A. thesis, Simon Fraser, 1976.
6889. **Oberlander, H. Peter, and Cave, R. J.** *A Study for Urban Renewal in Trail, B.C.* Trail: Corporation of the City of Trail, 1959.
6890. **Oberlander, H. Peter, and Oberlander, Cornelia.** "Critique: Canada's New Towns [Powell River]." *Progres Arch* 8 (1956):113-19.
6891. **Osing, Olga.** "Canada's Volcanic City: Rossland, B.C." *CGEJ* 73 (1966):166-71.
6892. **Parsons, Alberta, and Lawrence, Barbara.** "Keremeos: A History." Okanagan Historical Society, *Report* 36 (1972):50-58.
6893. **Pogue, Basil Gregory.** "Some Aspects of Settlement, Land-Use and Vegetation Change in the Revelstoke Area, B.C., 1885-1962." M.A. thesis, Calgary, 1970.
6894. **Porteous, J. Douglas.** "Gold River: An Instant Town in British Columbia." *Geogr* 55 (1970):317-22.
6895. **Pym, Harold, ed.** *Port Hardy and District: The Historical Story of Northernmost Vancouver Island*. Port Hardy: North Vancouver Island Medical Society, 1967.
6896. **Ramsey, Arthur Bruce.** *Rain People: The Story of Ocean Falls*. Ocean Falls: Ocean Falls Centennial Committee, 1971.

6897. **Riis, Nelson A.** "Settlement Abandonment—A Case Study of Walhachin, B.C." *UHR* 2-72 (June 1972):19-23.
6898. _____. "The Walhachin Myth: A Study in Settlement Abandonment." *BC Studies* 17 (1973):3-25.
6899. **Roberts, A.** "Impact Study of the Effect of the Craigmont Mine on the Town of Merritt, British Columbia." B.A. essay, British Columbia, 1968.
6900. **Sanmarco, Sebastian Ricardo.** "Resource Towns in British Columbia: A Study of the Physical Environment of Gold River and Golden." M.Arch. thesis, British Columbia, 1971.
6901. **Scott, David, and Henie, Edna.** *Nelson: Queen City of the Kootenays—An Historical Profile.* Vancouver: Mitchell Press, 1972.
6902. **Serra, J.** *The History of Armstrong, B.C.* Armstrong: Okanagan Historical Society, 1967.
6903. **Silverman, Peter Guy.** "Military Aid to Civil Power in British Columbia: The Labor Strikes at Wellington and Steveston, 1890-1900." *PNQ* 61 (1970):156-61.
6904. **Sloan, W. A.** "The Crowsnest Pass during the Depression: A Socio-Economic History of Southeastern British Columbia, 1918-1939." M.A. thesis, Victoria, 1968.
6905. **Stewart, J., and Monk, H. A. J.** *A History of Coquitlam and Fraser Mills, 1858-1958.* Coquitlam: District of Coquitlam, 1958.
6906. **Taylor, Henry Edwin.** *Powell River's First 50 Years.* Powell River: *News*, 1960.
6907. **Terris, Edward M.** "Ladner: A Pioneer Study." M.A. thesis, Western Washington, 1973.
6908. **Thomas, David.** "The Company Town: Britannia." B.A. essay, British Columbia, 1975.
6909. **Thrupp, S. L.** "A History of the Cranbrook District in the East Kootenay." M.A. thesis, British Columbia, 1929.
6910. **Trade Union Research Bureau.** *The Mackenzie Story: A Study in the History and Development of a Forest Industry Town at Mackenzie, British Columbia.* Mackenzie: Citizens Committee of Mackenzie, 1974.
6911. **Trail Board of Trade.** *Trail, B.C., A Brief Story of the History and Development of the Most Important Industrial Centre in Interior of British Columbia.* Trail, 1931.
6912. **Trail Golden Jubilee Society.** *Trail, B.C.: A Half Century, 1901-1951.* Trail: Golden Jubilee Society, 1951.
6913. **Turnbull, Elsie G.** "Forgotten Towns of the West Kootenay." *Canada West Mag* 6, no. 5 (1976):28-35.
6914. **Wamboldt, Beryl.** "Enderby and District: From Wilderness to 1914." Okanagan Historical Society, *Report* 33 (1969):30-48.
6915. **White, Brian P.** "Tahsis: Preliminary Investigations of a British Columbia Company Town." B.A. essay, Simon Fraser, 1969.
6916. **Yerbury, J. C.** "Nineteenth Century Kootenay Settlement Patterns." *W Can J Anth* 4 (April 1975):23-35.

XIV

The North

1. General

6917. **Adams, John Q.** "Settlements of the Northeastern Canadian Arctic." *Geogr Rev* 31 (1941):112-26.
6918. **Armstrong, Graham T.** "Railways in the North." *North* 16, no. 3 (1969):24-29.
6919. **Balikci, Asen, and Cohen, Ronald.** "Community Patterning in Two Northern Trading Posts." *Anthropologica* 5, no. 1 (1963):33-45.
6920. **Bennett, Gordon.** *Yukon Transportation: A History.* Ottawa: Dept. of Indian and Northern Affairs, 1978.
6921. **Bethune, William C.** *Canada's Eastern Arctic: Its History, Resources, Population, and Administration.* Ottawa: Dept. of the Interior, 1934.
6922. _____. *Canada's Western Northland: Its History, Resources, Population, and Administration.* Ottawa: Dept. of Mines and Resources, 1937.
6923. *Bibliography of McGill Northern Research, 1887-1975.* Montreal: McGill University, Centre for Northern Studies and Research, 1976.
6924. **Bladen, V. W.** *Canadian Population and Northern Colonization.* Toronto: UTP, 1962.
6925. **Bone, R. M.** "The Canadian Northland: A Study of Its Economic Development, with Observations of the Comparative Development of the Siberian Northland." Ph.D. thesis, Nebraska, 1953.
6926. **Bovey, John A.** "The Attitudes and Policies of the Federal Government towards Canada's Northern Territories, 1870-1930." M.A. thesis, British Columbia, 1967.
6927. **Bowdler, M. C.** "An Architecture for the North." *North* 8, no. 6 (1961):1-8.
6928. **Brown, J. N. Elliott.** "Evolution of Law and Government in the Yukon Territory." In *#895*, pp. 195-212.
6929. **Bruce, Jean.** "Arctic Housing." *North* 16, no. 1 (1969):1-9.
6930. **Bucksar, Richard G.** "The Frontiers Recede." *North* 8, no. 6 (1961):16-23.
6931. **Carter, F. A. G., and Phillips, R. A. J.** "Organizing for Northern Administration: A Practical Problem in Decentralization." *Can Pub Admin* 5 (1962):104-16.
6932. **Chance, Norman A., and Trudeau, John.** "Community Adjustment to Rapid Change among the Eskimo and Cree." *North* 11, no. 1 (1964):34-39.
6933. **Clark, S. D.** "Mining Society in British Columbia and the Yukon." In *The Social Development of Canada,* edited by S. D. Clark, pp. 308-79. Toronto: UTP, 1942.
6934. _____. "The Gold-Rush Society of British Columbia and the Yukon." In *The Developing Canadian Community,* edited by S. D. Clark, pp. 81-98. Toronto: UTP, 1962.
6935. **Coutts, Robert.** *Place Names of the Yukon: Their Origins and History.* Vancouver: Gray's, 1979.

6936. **Dear, Michael.** "Planning Community Health Services in Arctic Canada." *Musk-Ox* 19 (1976):28-36.
6937. **Department of Northern Affairs.** *The Population of the Northwest Territories and the Yukon, 1951-1961.* Ottawa: Northern Coordination and Research Centre, 1962.
6938. **Duerden, Frank.** *The Evolution and Nature of the Contemporary Settlement Pattern in a Selected Area of the Yukon Territory.* Winnipeg: University of Manitoba, Centre for Settlement Studies, 1971.
6939. _____. "The Development of the Non-Native Settlement Pattern of the Yukon Territory." *CI* 2, no. 2 (1978):11-32.
6940. **Erskine, Ralph.** "Architecture and Town Planning in the North." *Polar Record* 14 (1968):165-71.
6941. **Francis, J. W.** "Garden Cities in the North." *North* 17, no. 2 (1970):1-6.
6942. **Fried, Jacob.** "Settlement Types and Community Organization in Northern Canada." *Arctic* 16 (1963):93-100.
6943. _____. "White-dominant Settlements in the Canadian Northwest Territories." *Anthropologica* 5 (1963):56-67.
6944. **Grainge, Jack W., and Royle, John C.** "How Arctic Community Life Has Changed." *CGEJ* 91, no. 6 (1975):38-45.
6945. **Green, Jerry Edward.** "A Functional Analysis of the Populated Places in Canada's Yukon Territory and the Mackenzie District of the Northwest Territories, 1898-1971: A Study in Settlement Persistence." Ph.D. thesis, North Carolina (Chapel Hill), 1976.
6946. **Heinke, G. W.** *Report on Municipal Services in Communities of the Northwest Territories.* Ottawa: Information Canada, 1974.
6947. **Hemstock, C. A.** *Yukon Bibliography.* Edmonton: University of Alberta, Boreal Institute of Northern Studies, 1973.
6948. _____. *Yukon Bibliography Update to 1973.* Edmonton: University of Alberta, Boreal Institute for Northern Studies, 1975.
6949. _____, and **Cooke, G. A.** *Yukon Bibliography Update, 1963-1970.* Edmonton: University of Alberta, Boreal Institute for Northern Studies, 1975.
6950. **Honigmann, John, and Honigmann, Irma.** *Eskimo Townsmen.* Ottawa: University of Ottawa, Canadian Research Centre for Anthropology, 1965.
6951. **Hughes, C. C.** "Observations on Community Change in the North: An Attempt at a Summary." *Anthropologica* 5 (1963):69-79.
6952. **Jacobsen, George.** "Canada's Northern Communities." *North* 15, no. 6 (1968):34-37.
6953. **Laatsch, W. G.** "Yukon Mining Settlement: An Examination of Three Communities." Ph.D. thesis, Alberta, 1972.
6954. **Lidster, E. L. R.** "Community Adult Education Centres in the Northwest Territories of Canada." *The Northian* 11 (1975):7-11.
6955. **Lotz, J. R.** *Yukon Bibliography.* Ottawa: Northern Co-ordination and Research Centre, 1964.
6956. _____. "Northern Settlements and the Squatter Problem." *North* 11, no. 6 (1964):24-33.
6957. _____. "Resources Development and Settlement Patterns in the Yukon Territory." In *Science in Alaska,* Proceedings of the 16th Alaskan Science Conference (1965):300-309.
6958. **Mayne, Robert E.** "Community Planning in the Arctic Environment." M.A. thesis, Manitoba, 1968.
6959. **Mills, Thora McIlroy.** "The Contribution of the Presbyterian Church to the Yukon during the Gold Rush, 1897-1910." Committee on Archives of The United Church of Canada, *Bulletin* 25 (1976):1-94.
6960. **Morton, W. L.** "The North in Canadian History." *Northern Affairs Bull* 7, no. 1 (1960):26-29.
6961. _____. "The North in Canadian Historiography." RSC, *Trans,* 4th ser. 8 (1970):31-40.

6962. **Neville, F. J.** "Social Welfare in the Northwest Territories." *North* 11, no. 3 (1964):52-54.
6963. **Nordland, R. V.** "Settlement Planning in the Arctic." M.C.P. thesis, Manitoba, 1972.
6964. **Paterson, T. W.** *Ghost Towns of the Yukon.* Langley: Stagecoach, 1977.
6965. **Petrie, Ian.** "Territorial Land Use Regulations." *North* 19, no. 3 (1972):1-5.
6966. **Pickard, M. K.** "Administration for Development in Northern Canada: How It Looks to a Private Citizen." *Can Pub Admin* 3 (1960):367-71.
6967. **Rae, G. W.** "Settlement of the Great Slave Lake Frontier." Ph.D. thesis, Michigan, 1964.
6968. *Répertoire des travaux sur le nord, publiés par le centre d'études nordiques et l'Institut de géographie de l'Université Laval, 1953-1964.* Québec: Université Laval, Centre d'études nordiques, 1965.
6969. **Richardson, M.C.** "Community Development in the Canadian Eastern Arctic: Aspects of Housing and Education." M.A. thesis, Alberta, 1976.
6970. **Ridge, F. G.** "General Principles for Planning Sub-Arctic Settlements." Ph.D. thesis, McGill, 1953.
6971. **Ridge, M. F.** *Yukon Bibliography Update to 1975.* Edmonton: University of Alberta, Boreal Institute for Northern Studies, 1977.
6972. **Roberts, L. W.** "Wage Employment and Its Consequences in Two Eastern Arctic Communities." Ph.D. thesis, Alberta, 1977.
6973. **Robertson, Gordon.** "Administration for Development in Northern Canada: The Growth and Evolution of Government." *Can Pub Admin* 3 (1960):354-62.
6974. **Robertson, R. G.** "The Future of the North." *North* 8, no. 2 (1961):1-13.
6975. **Robinson, I. M.** *New Industrial Towns on Canada's Resource Frontiers.* Chicago: University of Chicago Press, 1962.
6976. **Rowley, G. W.** "Settlement and Transportation in the Canadian North." *Arctic* 7 (1954):336-42.
6977. **Sivertz, B. G.** "Administration for Development in Northern Canada: Development of Human and Material Resources." *Can Pub Admin* 3 (1960):363-66.
6977A. **Stabler, Jack C., and Olfert, M. Rose.** "Development Planning in the Northwest Territories." *Plan Canada* 20 (1980):103-12.
6978. **Taylor, C. D. N.** "The Construction and Operation of Mining Camps in the North." *Northern Affairs Bull* 7, no. 1 (1960):9-15.
6979. **Usher, Peter.** "The Canadian Western Arctic: A Century of Change." *Anthropologica* 13 (1971):169-83.
6980. **Van Ginkel, Blanche.** "New Towns in the North." In #337, pp. 298-308.
6981. **Willmott, W. E.** "Organization and Authority in an Eskimo Community." *North* 8, no. 5 (1961):7-11.
6982. _____. "Household and Family." *North* 8, no. 5 (1961):25-36.
6983. **Wonders, William C.** "Transportation and the Settlement Frontier in the Mackenzie Valley Area." *North* 13, no. 1 (1966):34-38.
6984. _____, ed. *Canada's Changing North.* Toronto: M&S, 1971.
6985. **Zaslow, Morris.** "A History of Transportation and Development of the Mackenzie Basin, 1870-1921." M.A. thesis, Toronto, 1948.
6986. _____. "The Development of the Mackenzie Basin, 1920-1940." Ph.D. thesis, Toronto, 1957.
6987. _____. *The Opening of the Canadian North, 1870-1914.* Toronto: M&S, 1971.

2. Dawson City

6988. **Baldwin, W. W., and Heinke, G. W.** *Evaluation of Municipal Services at Dawson and Old Crow, Yukon Territory.* Toronto, 1973.

6989. **Burg, A.** "Along the Yukon Trail." *Nat Geog Mag* 104 (1953):395-416.
6990. **Bush, Edward F.** *The Dawson Daily News: Journalism on Canada's Last Frontier.* Ottawa: Dept. of Indian Affairs and Northern Development, 1971.
6991. _____. *Banking in the Klondike, 1898-1968.* Ottawa: Dept. of Indian and Northern Affairs, 1973.
6992. **Clark, S. D.** "Voices from the Past." *North* 9, no. 3 (1962):1-11.
6993. **Fuller, O. T.** "Bright Lights under Midnight Dome: The Story of Arizona Charley Meadows and the Palace Grand." *North* 9, no. 3 (1962):35-41.
6994. **Garrett, R. M., and Rogatnick, A.** "The Grand Palace Theatre." *JRAIC* 39, no. 4 (1966):61-66.
6995. **Guest, Hal.** *Dawson City: San Francisco of the North.* Manuscript Report Series. Ottawa: Historic Sites, Parks Canada, 1978.
6996. **Gutsell, Barbara.** "Dawson City." *Geogr Bull* 3 (1953):23-35.
6997. **Hamulik, B.** "This Is My Town: Dawson City." *Alaska* 39, no. 5 (1973):13-14.
6998. **Jeffares, C. A.** "Dawson City, Yukon Territory: An Evaluation of Factors Contributing to Its Renewed Viability." M.A. thesis, Alberta, 1977.
6999. **Lotz, J. R.** *Dawson City, Yukon Territory.* Ottawa: Dept. of Northern Affairs, 1962.
7000. _____. *The Dawson Area: A Regional Monograph.* Ottawa: Northern Co-ordination and Research Centre, 1965.
7001. **Martin, Brian R.** "The Ghosts of Dawson." *North* 18, no. 3 (1971):30-33.
7002. **Sack, D.** *A Brief History of Dawson City and the Klondike.* Whitehorse: Yukon News, 1974.
7003. **Wade, F. C.** "The Klondike: Four Year Retrospect." Royal Colonial Institute, *Proceedings* 33 (1902):292-99.
7004. **Warner, Iris.** "A Museum for Dawson City." *North* 10, no. 4 (1963):13-16.
7005. _____. "Pioneer Banking at Dawson." *Alaska J* 1 (1971):41-48.
7006. **Woodside, H. J.** "City of Dawson." *Can Mag* 17 (1901):403-13.

3. Whitehorse

7007. **Bain, D.** "Future Bright for Yukon Capital." *Trade and Commerce* 72, no. 4 (1977):32-39.
7008. **Boyle, H.** "Whitehorse." *Habitat* 10, nos. 3-6 (1967):162-65.
7009. **Brekke, D. T.** "A Descriptive Survey of Outdoor Education in Whitehorse, Yukon." M.Ed. thesis, Alberta, 1977.
7010. **Bucksar, Richard G.** "The Problem of Squatters in the Northland." *Habitat* 13, no. 1 (1970):24-27.
7011. _____. "Canada's Emerging Northern Metropolis." *Habitat* 16, nos. 5-6 (1973):39-43.
7012. **Connelly, Alan.** "Dancing in the Streets." *Northern Affairs Bull* 6, no. 4 (1959):26-28.
7013. **Denis, Paul Yves.** "Whitehorse: Esquisse de géographie urbaine." Thèse de M.A., Montréal, 1955.
7014. _____. "Les facteurs géographiques de la situation et du site de Whitehorse." *RCGG* 9 (1955):161-78.
7015. **Erlam, Rusty.** "Getting to the Heart of the Matter [:Juvenile Problems in Whitehorse]." *North* 14, no. 4 (1967):2-5.
7016. **Institute of Local Government, Queen's University.** *The City of Whitehorse.* Kingston: Queen's University, 1960.
7017. **Kellett, George.** "The Houses of Whitehorse." *North* 15, no. 1 (1968):18-23.
7018. **Koroscil, Paul M.** "The Changing Landscape of the Yukon Territory and the Settlement of Whitehorse." Ph.D. thesis, Michigan, 1970.

7019. _____. "The Changing Landscape of Whitehorse, Yukon Territory: A Historical Perspective." In *Peoples of the Living Land: Geography of Cultural Diversity in British Columbia*, edited by J. V. Minghi, pp. 183-212. Vancouver: B.C. Geographical Series, No. 15, 1972.

7020. **Lambert, Carmen.** "Identification et intégration ethnique à l'intérieur d'une ville nordique, Whitehorse, Yukon." Thèse de Ph.D., McGill, 1974.

7021. _____. "To Be or Not to Be: A Question Concerning Indian Cultural Identity in Whitehorse, Yukon." In *Ethnic Canadians*, edited by Martin L. Kovacs, pp. 177-88. Regina: Canadian Plains Research Center, 1978.

7022. **Lotz, J. R.** *Whitehorse, Yukon Territory: A General Introduction.* Ottawa: Dept. of Northern Affairs, 1961.

7023. _____. *The Squatters of Whitehorse, Yukon Territory.* Ottawa: Dept. of Northern Affairs and National Resources, 1961.

7024. _____. "The Squatters of Whitehorse: A Study of the Problems of New Northern Settlements." *Arctic* 18, no. 3 (1965):172-88.

7025. _____. "The Squatters of Whitehorse: A Study of the Problems of New Northern Settlements." In *The People Outside: Studies of Squatters, Shack Town and Shanty Residents and Others Dwelling on the Fringe of Canada*, edited by J. R. Lotz, pp. 113-28. Ottawa: Canadian Research Centre for Anthropology, 1971.

7026. **Rimes, L.** "Busy, Modern Capital: Vital Heart of Yukon." *Trade and Commerce* 69, no. 5 (1974):36-44.

7027. **Wilhelm, G., and Wilhelm, T.** "Squatter Relocation: Whitehorse, Yukon Territory." In *The People Outside: Studies of Squatters, Shack Town and Shanty Residents and Others Dwelling on the Fringe in Canada*, edited by J. R. Lotz, pp. 130-57. Ottawa: Canadian Research Centre for Anthropology, 1971.

7028. **Wilkinson, Henry.** "Boom or Bust in Whitehorse?" *North* 25, no. 2 (1978):24-29.

4. Yellowknife

7029. **Black, J. M., and Boxer, A. J.** "Bridging the Gap at Yellowknife [:Eskimo Students in the City]." *Northern Affairs Bull* 6, no. 3 (1959):28-31.

7030. **Bourne, L. S.** "The Urban and Regional Economy of Yellowknife, N.W.T." M.A. thesis, Alberta, 1963.

7031. _____. *Yellowknife, N.W.T.: A Study of Its Urban and Regional Economy.* Ottawa: Dept. of Northern Affairs and National Resources, 1963.

7032. **Bredin, Pearl E.** "Yellowknife Goes to the Dogs [:The 1960 Carnival]." *Northern Affairs Bull* 7, no. 3 (1960):40-42.

7033. **Cranna, Mona.** "An Art Gallery for the North." *North* 11, no. 4 (1964):28-30.

7034. **Inglis, George Erskine.** "Yellowknife: Capital of the Northwest Territories." *CGEJ* 80 (1970):38-45.

7035. **Koroscil, Paul M.** "Urbanization in the Canadian North: Yellowknife, N.W.T." *CI* 1 (1975):115-37.

7036. **Leitch, Adelaide.** "Yellowknife: Town of Air Age." *CGEJ* 48 (1954):168-77.

7037. **Ostergaard, P.** "Quality of Life in a Northern City: A Social Geography of Yellowknife, N.W.T." M.A. thesis, British Columbia, 1976.

7038. **Parker, Helen.** "Yellowknife's Museum of the North." *North* 10, no. 6 (1963):31-34.

7039. **Price, Ray.** *Yellowknife.* Toronto: Peter Martin, 1967.

7040. **Stavely, Michael.** "The Population Geography of Yellowknife, N.W.T." *Alta Geogr* 2 (1965-66):12-24.

7041. **Sullivan, Michael.** "The Heart of the Last Frontier." *Northern Affairs Bull* 6, no. 4 (1959):19-23.

5. Other Centres

7042. Alderman, Tom. "Norman Wells—Way Out Town." *North* 12, no. 4 (1965):12-16.

7043. Alford, M. E. "Old Crow." *Alaska Sportsman* 30 (1964):22-24.

7044. Barger, Walter K. "Great Whale River: Adaptation to Modern Town Life in the Canadian North." Ph.D. thesis, North Carolina, 1974.

7045. _____, **and Daphne, E.** "Differential Adaptation to Northern Town Life by the Eskimos and Indians of Great Whale River." *Human Organization* 30 (1971):25-30.

7046. Berton, Pierre. "Fortymile: American Outpost on the Yukon." *UTQ* 22 (1958):413-23.

7047. Bond, Courtney C. J. "Two Communities in the Eastern Arctic." *CGEJ* 81 (1970):184-93.

7048. Courval, Michel de. "L'éducation des adultes à Frobisher Bay." *North* 16, no. 2 (1969):16-17.

7049. Dunning, A. D. W. "Townsite and Town-Planning [at Pine Point]." *North* 11, no. 3 (1964):42-47.

7050. Pritchard, Gordon B. "New Town [Inuvik] in the Far North." *Geogr Mag* 37 (1964):344-57.

7051. Rensaa, E. M. "Building at Inuvik." *Northern Affairs Bull* 6, no. 5 (1959):5-9.

7052. Stevenson, Alex. "Baker Lake." *North* 12, no. 2 (1965):1-6.

7053. Sullivan, Michael. "Hay River Story." *Northern Affairs Bull* 7, no. 2 (1960):15-18.

7054. Zarchikoff, W. W. "The Development of Settlement Patterns in Hay River, Northwest Territories, 1892-1971." M.A. thesis, Simon Fraser, 1975.

A Guide to Canadian Urban Studies

I. Introduction	275
II. Newsletters and Journals	276
1. Urban History Review	
2. Urban Reader	
3. Urban Focus	
4. Plan Canada	
5. Urban Forum	
6. Contact: Journal of Urban and Environmental Affairs	
7. Urban Canada Index	
8. Urban History Yearbook	
9. Journal of Urban History	
10. Urbanism—Past and Present	
11. Planning History Bulletin	
12. Urban Affairs Quarterly	
13. City Magazine	
III. Canadian Housing Information Centre	278
IV. Public Archives of Canada	280
1. Public Records and Manuscripts	
2. National Map Collection	
3. National Photography Collection	
4. Paintings, Drawings and Print Section, Picture Division	
V. Provincial and Territorial Archives	287
1. Newfoundland	
2. Prince Edward Island	
3. Nova Scotia	
4. New Brunswick	
5. Quebec	
6. Ontario	
7. Manitoba	
8. Saskatchewan	
9. Alberta	
10. British Columbia	
11. Yukon	

VI. Municipal Archives, Specialized Libraries, and   303
Urban Information Centres
 1. Newfoundland Planning Library
 2. St. John's City Archives
 3. Prince Edward Island Heritage Foundation
 4. Prince Edward Island Planning Library
 5. Nova Scotia Development Library
 6. Moncton Museum
 7. Quebec Urban Community
 8. City of Quebec Archives
 9. City of Montreal Archives
 10. Montreal Municipal Library
 11. Regional History Society of Trois-Rivières
 12. City of Trois-Rivières Archives
 13. City of Toronto Archives
 14. Toronto Planning Board Library
 15. Metropolitan Toronto Municipal Reference Library
 16. City of Ottawa Archives
 17. National Capital Commission Library
 18. City of Kingston Archives
 19. London Urban Resource Centre
 20. Urban Documentation Centre, McMaster University
 21. Sault Ste. Marie Public Library
 22. Sudbury Public Library
 23. Thunder Bay Historical Museum
 24. Manitoba Department of Urban Affairs
 25. City of Winnipeg Planning Library
 26. City of Winnipeg Archives
 27. Saskatchewan Department of Municipal Affairs Library
 28. Saskatoon Public Library
 29. Moose Jaw Public Library
 30. Alberta Department of Municipal Affairs Library
 31. City of Calgary Planning Library
 32. Glenbow Archives (Calgary)
 33. City of Edmonton Archives
 34. Medicine Hat Historical Foundation
 35. Red Deer Archives
 36. City of Vancouver Archives
 37. Greater Vancouver Regional District Planning Library
 38. Vancouver Planning Library
 39. Simon Fraser University Archives
 40. Kamloops Museum and Archives
 41. Victoria City Archives

VII. Audio-Visual Resources   309
   1. Films
   2. Slides
   3. Canada's Visual History Series
   4. Urban Profile Slide Series
   5. Audiotapes

VIII. Other Resources   313
   1. Urban Profile Series
   2. Urban Prospects Series
   3. Urban Studies Series
   4. Parks Canada Reports
   5. Western Geographical Series
   6. History of Canadian Cities Series
   7. Facsimiles of Canadian City Plans
   8. Urban History Committee of the Canadian Historical Association
   9. Institute of Local Government
   10. Institute of Urban Studies
   11. Canadian Council on Urban and Regional Research
   12. Bureau of Municipal Research
   13. Centre for Urban and Community Studies
   14. The Federation of Canadian Municipalities
   15. The Canadian Social History Project
   16. Research Group on Montreal Society in the Nineteenth Century
   17. Toronto Area Archivists Group

I. *INTRODUCTION*

This guide is a comprehensive listing and critique of sources available for the teaching and study of Canada's urban past and present. Since the study of Canadian urban development has developed so swiftly in the last decade, teachers and students can no longer approach the field confident that they are aware of all the available material. It is our hope that this guide will both provide immediate information on a wide variety of journals, archives, and organizations and direct readers to the publications or agencies that can provide more detailed data on related subjects.

This guide was prepared with the co-operation of many people, and their assistance is gratefully acknowledged. In particular, the various provincial archives responded to our requests for information on their holdings in the urban area, as did archivists in the Public Archives of Canada and in several city archives. Many other individuals also assisted in this compilation by providing summaries or by answering detailed questions. It should also be noted that some of the material in this guide was drawn from other publications including the *Directory of*

Canadian Urban Information Sources (Ottawa: MSUA, 1977), the *Directory of Canadian Records and Manuscript Repositories* (Ottawa: Association of Canadian Archivists, 1977), and the "Urban Studies Issue" of *Communique: Canadian Studies* 3 (April 1977).

II. NEWSLETTERS AND JOURNALS

The rapid growth of urban studies is nowhere more apparent than in the increasing number of periodicals devoted to urban themes. The following selective list of journals and newsletters contains only those devoted almost exclusively to urban topics. Specialists should be familiar with all of them, but other journals should not be neglected since they often contain relevant items. An examination of the entries in the bibliography section of this volume indicates those journals that do carry urban material.

1. *Urban History Review* (1972-   )
   Publisher: National Museums of
                Canada
                Ottawa, Ontario K1A 0M8
   Editor: Alan F. J. Artibise
   Frequency: 3 issues per year.
   Comments: This bilingual journal is the best single source of information on urban studies in Canada. The *Review* contains information on a variety of subjects regarding urban development in articles, reviews, research notes, thesis abstracts, archival notes, conference information, notes on photographic collections, and so on. Despite its title, the *Urban History Review* is not restricted to historians, and it carries material on developments in other countries, especially the United States and Great Britain. Occasionally, the *Review* publishes special theme issues, such as "The Canadian City in the Nineteenth Century" (June 1975); "Urban Reform in Canada" (October 1976); "The Urban Immigrant" (October 1978); "Fire, Water, and Disease in the Nineteenth Century City" (June 1979); and "Aspects of Urban Heritage" (October 1980).

2. *Urban Reader* (1973-   )
   Publisher: Social Planning
                Department
                Vancouver City Hall
                453 West 12th Avenue
                Vancouver, B.C.
                V5Y 1V4

   Editor: Alice Niwinski
   Frequency: 9 issues per year.
   Comments: The *Urban Reader* is a review of urban news and opinion intended to present outlines of subjects rather than thorough studies. Although the *Urban Reader* is of particular interest to residents of the lower mainland of British Columbia, it is highly recommended for anyone interested in urban studies. Its features include an up-to-date look at the urban scene, classroom material, research sources, book reviews, and historical features. Also noteworthy are a series of historical photo-essays on Vancouver which have been published as special editions.

3. *Urban Focus:* (1972-   )
   Publisher: Institute of Local
                Government
                Queen's University
                99 University Avenue
                Kingston, Ontario
                K7L 3N6
   Editor: T. J. Plunkett
   Frequency: 5 issues per year.
   Comments: *Urban Focus* provides a vehicle for the discussion and development of viewpoints regarding the problems of urban government in a federal system. It has a newsletter format, usually 6-10 pages consisting of short articles, notes, and comments. Recent issues have also contained items on the historical development of urban Canada.

4. *Plan Canada* (1959-   )
   Publisher: Canadian Institute of
                 Planners
                 Suite 30, 46 Elgin
                 Street
                 Ottawa, Ontario
                 K1P 5K6
   Editor: Henry Hightower
   Frequency: 4 issues per year.
   Comments: Most of the articles carried in the journal deal with planning and related areas, but *Plan Canada* also includes topics broadly connected with urban development. Regular features are a book review section, lists of recent Canadian municipal documents, listing of articles in other journals, and an historical section entitled "From the Past." *Plan Canada* has also produced a number of special issues, including "Urban Surveying and Mapping" (May 1971), "Planning Education for Urban and Regional Planning in Canada" (April 1964), "Land Use Classification and Coding in Canada: An Appraisal" (June 1968), and "Canadian Resource Towns" (March 1978).

5. *Urban Forum* (1975-   )
   Publisher: Canadian Council on
                 Urban and
                 Regional Research
                 251 Laurier West
                 Ottawa, Ontario K1P 5J6
   Editor: Vernon Lang
   Frequency: 4-6 issues per year.
   Comments: The bilingual *Urban Forum* superseded the six-year-old *Urban Research Bulletin*. Besides feature articles, it contains interviews, book reviews, a calendar of events, and a section on studies in progress. Recent articles have dealt with land use, planning, architecture, conservation, taxation, and urban growth.

6. *Contact: Journal of Urban and Environmental Affairs* (1968-   ).
   Publisher: Faculty of Environ-
                 mental Affairs
                 University of Water-
                 loo
                 Waterloo, Ontario
                 N2L 3G1
   Editor: N. E. P. Pressman
   Frequency: 3 issues per year.
   Comments: The aim of *Contact,* which is affiliated with the School of Urban and Regional Planning at Waterloo, is to provide current information on urban and environmental problems. Issues include feature articles, reviews, a section on international developments, and reports on other journals, conferences, and symposia. Occasional special issues are also published.

7. *Urban Canada Index* (1977-   )
   Publisher: Micromedia Limited
                 Box 502, Station S
                 Toronto, Ontario
                 M5M 4L8
   Editor: Linda Pethevick
   Frequency: Quarterly, with
                 annual cumulation.
   Comments: The *Urban Canada Index* covers publications issued in Canada in the field of urban and regional planning and development. The *Index* includes government and non-government monographs and serial publications. The *Index* began with monographs issued in 1976 and serials issued from January 1977.

8. *Urban History Yearbook* (1974-   )
   Publisher: Leicester University Press
                 University of Leicester
                 Leicester, England
                 LE1 7RH
   Editor: David Reeder
   Frequency: Annual.
   Comments: The *Yearbook* is a more formal and extensive elaboration of the *Urban History Newsletter* begun more than a decade ago by the late H. J. Dyos. It includes articles, notes on urban history meetings, synopses of experiments in urban history, reviews of books on the urban past, an extensive current bibliography, and a detailed annual survey and register of research in progress. The *Yearbook* has correspondents around the world and deals with developments in the field on an international scale. The Canadian correspondent is Gilbert A. Stelter, Department of History, University of Guelph, Guelph, Ontario, N1G 2W1.

9. *Journal of Urban History* (1974-   )
   Publisher: Sage Publications
                 P.O. Box 776
                 Beverly Hills, CA 90212
                 U.S.A.
   Editor: Blaine A. Brownell
   Frequency: Quarterly.
   Comments: The *Journal of Urban History*

is the major scholarly journal in the field, and it contains articles on specific cities, the relationship of cities to broader regions, new research techniques and methodologies, interdisciplinary approaches, comparative studies, and historiography. The *JUH* also has an excellent book review section that encompasses works done in the field of urban history throughout the world. Members of the editorial board include representatives of many countries; the Canadian member is Alan F. J. Artibise, Department of History, University of Victoria, Victoria, B.C. V8W 2Y2.

10. *Urbanism—Past and Present* (1974-   )
    Publisher: Department of History
                 University of Wisconsin-
                 Milwaukee
                 Box 413
                 Milwaukee, WN 53201
                 U.S.A.
    Editor: Bruce Fetter
    Frequency: Biannual.
    Comments: This journal supersedes the Urban History Group *Newsletter* which was published between 1954 and 1975. It contains topical analyses of basic urban problems, theoretical interpretations of urbanism, and the results of specific urban-related research. A major objective of *UPP* is to establish a dialogue among the social sciences and humanities through a regular commentary on articles by various specialists. Each issue also contains an international bibliography of urban studies.

11. *Planning History Bulletin* (1979-   )
    Publisher: Centre for Urban and
                 Regional Studies
                 University of
                 Birmingham
                 P.O. Box 363
                 Birmingham, England
                 B15 2TT
    Editor: Michael Naslas
    Frequency: Biannual.
    Comments: The *Bulletin* supersedes the Planning History Group *Newsletter*. It contains a current bibliography, a register of research in progress, full reports of Planning History Group meetings, information concerning other meetings and conferences, news and announcements, correspondence, book reviews, information on books and articles received, and occasional short articles.

12. *Urban Affairs Quarterly* (1964-   )
    Publisher: Sage Publications
                 P.O. Box 5024
                 Beverly Hills, CA 90212
                 U.S.A.
    Editor: Louis H. Masotti
    Frequency: Quarterly.
    Comments: This journal is aimed at those engaged in basic or applied urban research and those responsible for formulating and implementing public policy. Since the journal's inception, it has pursued comparative and cross-cultural studies and welcomed critiques of existing policies and programmes. Research notes and review essays on new publications in the field are featured, and there are periodic guest-edited theme issues.

13. *City Magazine* (1974-79)
    Publisher: James Lorimer and
                 Company
                 35 Britain Street
                 Toronto, Ontario
                 M5A 1R7
    Comments: City Magazine ceased publication in 1979, but beginning in 1980, a *City Magazine Annual* will be published. For those teaching in urban studies and related fields, *City Magazine's* first five years constitute an invaluable source of information on Canadian issues. As an independent publication, it was closely associated with the citizen movement and the urban reformers who played an important role in urban Canada since the early 1970's.
    Volumes I to III of *City Magazine* (32 issues) are still available from the publisher, as is an index in a separate volume.

III. CANADIAN HOUSING INFORMATION CENTRE

In 1979 the federal Ministry of State for Urban Affairs was disbanded. Nevertheless, the *Directory of Canadian Urban Information Sources*, produced by the MSUA in 1977, is still of use to urban researchers.

The Canadian Housing Information Centre is an amalgamation of the former Information Resource Service of the MSUA, the Central Mortgage and Housing Corporation's National Office Library, and a small technical library of CMHC's professional standards and technology directorate, now located within CMHC. Requests for information on federal government activities and publications should be directed to:

> Canadian Housing Information Centre
> C.M.H.C. Annex
> Montreal Road
> Ottawa, Ontario K1A 1P7

The centre's objectives are: to provide an integrated and comprehensive library and documentation service on housing, community planning and development; to direct clients to the most appropriate external source for information when required; and to provide access to the final reports of research projects and activities supported by either CMHC or other government departments or agencies.

The CHIC services are available to federal government staff and to the public, including officials of other governments, academic and non-profit institutions, business enterprises, individuals, and professionals.

The specific services of the CHIC include:

A. *Reference*
   The centre provides general information on all its holdings; referral to other sources; information on key personnel, programmes, and policies of various governmental and non-governmental organizations (the centre maintains over 500 vertical files on organizations); and access to bibliographic information on particular topics.

B. *Publications*
   The centre produces and distributes publications such as an acquisition list; a quarterly conference calendar; a directory of officials in provincial and territorial departments of housing, municipal and urban affairs; and documentation on human settlements received from international organizations.

C. *Periodicals*
   The centre subscribes to approximately 600 periodicals and newsletters, and some of these are available on interlibrary loan.

D. *Special Collections*
   The centre holds a number of special collections, including research reports; municipal information (official plans, master plans, financial reports, neighbourhood studies, land use plans, and urban renewal reports); maps (land use maps and street plans); a professional standards and technology collection; the papers and national reports from the conference on Human Settlements

held in Vancouver in 1976; international documents; external research reports of the MSUA; and papers, theses, and reports resulting from the CMHC Scholarship Programme.

IV. PUBLIC ARCHIVES OF CANADA

395 Wellington Street
Ottawa, Ontario K1A 0N3

Teachers and researchers in urban studies should not overlook the rich resources of the PAC. Those interested may write to the PAC generally or to its separate divisions: Manuscripts; Public Records; National Map Collection; Archives Library; National Photography Collection; Pictures; National Film, Television, and Sound Archives; and Machine Readable Archives. Though the staff can do only limited research in response to inquiries, they can provide useful information to those unable to visit the PAC.

Reproductions of most documents are available, as is a price list for reproduction services. Microfilm copies of some materials from the Manuscripts and Public Records divisions are obtainable on interlibrary loan. The PAC also has numerous brochures and guides which will be sent on request.

The following sections, based on material provided by PAC staff, report on those divisions of particular interest to urban specialists.

1. *Public Records and Manuscripts*

The Manuscripts Division contains nationally significant and historically valuable private manuscripts, corporate records, and non-federal public records. The Public Records Division is the official repository for the historical records of the Government of Canada. Together, the two divisions contain much material related to Canadian urban development.

The standard source for urban specialists is the census rolls. The PAC has a relatively complete set of these records for the decades between 1851 and 1881, including the industrial census of 1871. There are scattered returns before 1851, and it is possible to supplement these with statistical records compiled periodically by the various colonial governments. As well, there are extensive files in the Department of Immigration which help establish settlement patterns and detail many aspects of urban growth in later periods. While census rolls after 1881 are still not open, Statistics Canada does release some records on a periodic basis.

Other government records also provide insights. For the period before Confederation, there are land records, petitions, reports, police records, and public health files for Canada East and Canada West. The bulk of this material appears in the records of the Executive Council and the Civil and Provincial Secretaries. After 1867, the records of the Privy Council, the National Capital Commission,

National Parks, Royal Commissions, and departments like Railways and Canals, Transport, Interior (Dominion Lands Branch), Public Works, and Labour provide much information. Also useful are the records of CMHC and the files of the Canadian National Railways.

These records include far more than the routine business of policy appraisal and implementation. Often they contain large caches of correspondence with individuals, organizations, and corporations. The records of the C.N.R., for example, provide a valuable source for examining the intimate connection of railroad construction and operation with urban growth. The C.N.R. records are comprised of the records of smaller lines which were at one time or another absorbed by the parent system.

The large collection of business records in the Manuscripts Division also provides excellent sources. Among them are the records of the Canadian Manufacturer's Association and the Toronto Board of Trade, the Van Horne letterbooks, the Sir John Willison Papers, and the records of Kerry and Chace Limited. Using such papers, it is possible to investigate trade patterns, factory life, entrepreneurial elites, and wage scales. And these business records can be complemented by the records of various labour associations and organizations, such as the papers of the Toronto District Labour Council and the Toronto Typographical Union. These collections document important social conditions such as unemployment, working conditions, ethnic tensions, and the apprenticeship system. The records of social and moral reform groups like the National Council of Women and the Canadian Welfare Council are also important. These organizations were established on a city and town basis and offer interesting comments on a great many urban areas.

The PAC has also traditionally acted as the regional repository for the Ottawa Valley and has acquired a large collection of documents referring to Ottawa and Hull.

Finally, in co-operation with the Humanities Research Council of Canada, the PAC publishes the *Union List of Manuscripts in Canadian Repositories*. Besides listing the manuscript material held in the PAC, the *Union List* provides a guide to the location of the papers of individuals and organizations in over 170 participating archives. The *Union List* is available in most major libraries.

2. *National Map Collection*

The National Map Collection contains over 20,000 maps, plans, charts, and other related materials on Canadian urban centres. The sixteen-volume *Catalogue of the National Map Collection, Public Archives of Canada* reproduces the almost 100,000 cards in the Map Collection's catalogue.

The number of items for various cities gives some idea of the extent of the collection's holdings. For Quebec, Montreal, Kingston, Ottawa, and Toronto, there are more than 1,000 maps each, ranging from maps of individual lots to large scale maps showing all streets, major buildings and other features.

Military activity in these cities is largely responsible for this profusion. For other centres such as St. John's, Halifax, Winnipeg, and Vancouver, there are approximately 300 maps each. Maps of each city's environs are also available and are useful in studies of cities in their larger context.

The National Map Collection also holds more than 50,000 architectural and engineering drawings of buildings, bridges, wharves, and so on designed and constructed by the federal government and its agencies as well as by architects and engineers in private practice.

The general nature of the collection can best be described by discussing the various types or groupings of maps. Most of the maps of Canadian urban centres before 1800 are transcripts or photographic copies of maps produced predominantly by the military, and the originals are held by French and British repositories. In the early decades of this century, the PAC had copyists in London and Paris transcribing documents relating to Canada. In recent years, microfilm and other photographic means of reproduction have replaced these copyists.

Topographic maps produced originally by the Department of Militia and Defence, and currently part of the National Topographic System, are a principal source for the study of twentieth-century Canadian urban development. The scale of approximately one inch to the mile is sufficiently large to permit accurate study of the territorial expansion of a city and the construction of railways, hydro-electric power lines, factories, and major buildings. For some cities, many revised sheets were printed. For example, the first Ottawa sheet was printed in 1906, and there have been more than a dozen revisions.

The collection of panoramic maps or bird's-eye views of Canadian cities consists of more than 100 items. This type of map is a non-photographic depiction of a city as if viewed from above at an oblique angle. Although not generally drawn at scale, they are reasonably accurate visual representation of street patterns, individual buildings and major landscape features. The technique flourished in the period 1870-1910, and several editions are available for most major Canadian cities.

Fire insurance atlases also constitute a rich source of historical information. These atlases were used by insurance companies from approximately 1870 to the present day to determine insurance premiums on structures. As a rule, each sheet covers several city blocks and shows all existing structures. Various symbols and colours are used to indicate the type of material used in construction, the number of stories, the type of roofing, and other details. The National Map Collection has approximately 30,000 sheets, documenting about 1,400 places. In 1977, the National Map Collection published a valuable catalogue to this material (Robert J. Hayward, *Fire Insurance Plans in the National Map Collection*). The history of fire insurance cartography in Canada given in the introduction to the volume is interesting and helpful.

Real estate maps produced by Nirenstein's for several Canadian cities in 1929 and 1955 are similar in nature to insurance plans. Buildings are identified with dimensions, number of floors, type of construction material used, and the city's assessment of the land and its building valuation. Further information about these maps, with a list of the cities included, appears in *UHR* 2-77 (October 1977): 91-95.

A number of other types of maps should be mentioned. Maps of individual townships on the prairies are invaluable in a study of the early years of urban development. British admiralty charts and Canadian hydrographic charts often locate such features as mills and breweries. And useful bits of information are sometimes found on maps produced by the Geological Survey of Canada, in county maps and atlases, and in the extensive fortification surveys carried out just after the middle of the nineteenth-century.

The National Map Collection has published two bilingual guides to maps of individual cities: Thomas L. Nagy, *Ottawa in Maps: A Brief Cartographical History of Ottawa, 1825-1973* (Ottawa, 1974), and A. F. J. Artibise and E. H. Dahl, *Winnipeg in Maps, 1816-1972* (Ottawa, 1975).

Finally, the large collection of original historical atlases and recently produced facsimiles contains hundreds of town plans useful for comparative studies. And the Foreign Section of the National Map Collection holds a large collection of current foreign topographic maps and modern town plans of large cities outside Canada.

3. *National Photography Collection*

Much photographic documentation of nineteenth-century Canadian cities has been destroyed, but surprising riches remain and active steps are being taken to locate and preserve them. The PAC's National Photography Collection, with more than six million photographs, represents the largest and probably the most accessible collection in Canada. The following remarks indicate only the range of material and the contents of some of the larger collections. The staff of the Photography Collection can often direct urban specialists to other institutions and individuals having important photographic material. Also, researchers should consult the *Guide To Canadian Photographic Archives* (Ottawa, 1979), which lists and describes the collection of photographic documents in more than 110 Canadian archival repositories. It contains an alphabetical list of titles and a cross-reference list of personal names, organizations, geographical names and subjects. The *Guide* is available from the Canadian Government Publishing Centre, Supply and Services Canada, Hull, Quebec, K1A 0S9.

The William J. Topley Collection is one of the largest and most comprehensive in the National Photography Collection and is second only to the Notman Collection in Montreal as a record of 19th-century Canada. Topley came to Ottawa in 1868 as manager of the new Notman studio there and later purchased the business. During the fifty-eight years of his career, Topley was recognized as one of the leading photographers in Ottawa. In addition to portraits of many of Canada's most prominent politicians, the pictures contain extensive coverage of

Ottawa. One can trace its growth from a crude lumbering town in 1865 to a bustling and relatively wealthy city in 1900.

A good record of Toronto has been preserved as well. Some of the earliest photographs of Toronto are found in a book of original prints entitled *Toronto in the Camera,* published in 1867. The 1870's are represented by about twenty negatives of downtown Toronto taken by the same photographer but found in two different collections—Alexandra Studio and Mike Filey. Frank Micklethwaite came to Toronto from Ireland and set up his own studio in 1878. He soon gained prominence as a photographer, but most of his negatives were lost or destroyed over the years. What remains of his work are about 500 negatives of Toronto from 1890 to 1910. These photos depict the busy downtown streets, the stately residences of the upper middle class, the churches, for which the city was famous, and the major buildings. They are therefore of interest to the historian of architecture as well as to the more general urban historian.

All of these collections were published in various forms. Late in the nineteenth century, when reproduction of photos in books became practical, many cities produced pamphlets of half-tone reproductions extolling their virtues. Both Topley's and Micklethwaite's photos presented such idealized visions.

A different outlook is presented in the Toronto Transit Collection. Here the changes in the city are reflected in the increasing need for more, and more efficient, transportation. Of particular interest in this context is a series of photos taken in the 1930's showing extreme traffic congestion in downtown Toronto, which hampered the movements of buses and street cars. Another section shows the amount of labour involved in laying and repairing streetcar lines.

The coming of the electric streetcar in the 1890's helped to extend the boundaries of the city dweller. Consequently, amusement parks like those in Aylmer, Quebec, and Britannia Beach outside of Ottawa became practical and enjoyed great popularity. The William Harmer Collection shows some aspects of this form of entertainment.

Since Daguerre first announced his invention in 1839, amateurs have played an important role in photography. As might be expected, their work presents a totally different perspective on city life than does that of the professional. John Boyd, who worked for the Grand Trunk Railway, began photographing in 1888, taking his equipment with him on his travels. What resulted was a personal view of the cities and towns he visited showing city growth, industrial pollution, recreation, transportation, and middle class life over a period of fifty years.

The H. J. Woodside Collection contains the work of another amateur. While Woodside was neither as discerning nor as capable a photographer as Boyd, the large body of material on Dawson City and the Klondike mines at the height of the 1898 Gold Rush and shortly afterwards adds another dimension to the coverage of the professionals. Woodside took his camera into the houses of Dawson away from the garish and celebrated hotels on the river front. What emerges is a picture of ordinary men and women living ordinary lives under difficult conditions. This is certainly a far cry from the often sensational photographs of E. A. Hegg found in the National Museum Collection. Hegg captured the excitement of the mines, the dance halls, the gold and the boom days of Dawson; Woodside shows how life was after the excitement died down.

Many aspects of modern urban life have been covered by press photographers, and there are a number of excellent press collections in the PAC which are added to on a monthly basis. The largest and most comprehensive at present is the *Montreal Gazette* Collection which covers the Montreal scene from 1938 to 1968. In Toronto the Alexandra Studio Collection gives similar coverage though in less detail for the years 1920 to 1950. Both the *Globe and Mail* and *Toronto Star* Collections present a total view of Toronto, but they only go back to 1968. The *Dominion Wide* and the *Capital Press* Collections cover events in Ottawa.

The Centennial Commission and EXPO '67 Collections are specialized but very thorough, the former encompassing the whole of Canada. The National Film Board Collection brings together photographers on a wide variety of subjects all across Canada. Much of this collection bears directly on city life from the 1940's to the early 1960's.

4. *Paintings, Drawings and Print Section, Picture Division*

The collection of the Paintings, Drawings and Prints Section contains a great wealth of information for urban studies in the early development period of Canadian towns and cities. However, a word of caution is in order for those who will use this pictorial documentation. The first known view of a settlement in Canada is the famous woodcut of Hochelaga (1556) from Ramusio's *Terzo Volume della Navigazione e Viagge*. . . . Although it is accompanied by a detailed legend, the depiction appears to be almost totally imaginary. This tendency to present the New World in a dramatic or picturesque fashion was characteristic of the seventeenth and eighteenth centuries and also of the nineteenth century as the Romantic period intensified Europe's taste for views of distant and exotic lands and unusual and curious phenomena. A further source of distortion was the printing process. The printing plate was usually engraved from a drawing made especially for that purpose from the original drawing or painting. As a result, most prints were two steps away from the original.

For the years prior to 1755, the collection includes views of Québec, Montréal, Trois-Rivières, Louisbourg, and of a certain number of forts, all of which served to illustrate books and atlases of the period. In these early views, there is a tendency to highlight the tower points of the main buildings. Perspective is poor, but individual buildings are often very detailed as if they had been sketched separately at close range. The general appearance is similar to the city views of Hartmann Schedel's *Nuremberg Chronicle,* 1493. The New World being far away, European engravers copied one another profusely with the result that almost identical views were printed in several different countries such as France, England, Germany, and Italy.

The taking of New France by the British brought a new type of artist to Canada. The military topographer recorded in pencil and watercolour views of cities, forts, and landscape. These amateur artists followed the route of garrison towns and fortified places: St. John's, Halifax, Québec, the forts of the Richelieu River, Montréal, Kingston, York (Toronto), London, Chatham and Amherstburg. The building of the Rideau Canal (1825-29) provided a new route from Montreal to Kingston. Ottawa, then a small picturesque lumber town, received its share of artistic attention, particularly from the military engineers responsible for the canal's construction.

The earliest views in the collection are those of the small Acadian hamlets of Annapolis Royal and Fort Cumberland sketched in 1755 by Captain John Hamilton. Other noted artists who worked in Canada in the eighteenth and early nineteenth centuries were Thomas Davies, James Hunter, James Peachey, George Heriot, Sempronius and Severus Stretton, and Alexander C. Mercer. The town most often depicted was Québec. In particular, the works of James Pattison Cockburn constitute an important record of the city's streets and buildings. Other towns to be frequently depicted were Halifax, Montréal, Kingston, and York.

With the arrival of British troops, important series of city views were printed. Paramount among these were Richard Short's engraved views of Halifax and Québec. During the nineteenth century, the development of lithography allowed for pictures to be drawn directly on stone and to be reproduced in large quantities. Views of cities published as series became popular. The new technique of lithography was well suited to the printing of large formats such as panoramic views, bird's-eye views and other large prints illustrating the main buildings for industries found in the larger cities. Edwin Whitefield's panoramic views of Québec, Montréal, Ottawa, Hamilton, Toronto, Kingston, and London are well known.

Important illustrated publications also appear in the nineteenth century: N. P. Willis', *Canadian Scenery* (1842), illustrated with engravings after Bartlett; the *Illustrated London News* (1843-90) which contains many important views of Canadian cities; Grant's *Picturesque Canada* (1882); *The Canadian Illustrated News* (1869-83); *The Canadian Pictorial and Illustrated War News* (1885); and *The Dominion Illustrated News* (1889-91). These volumes contain illustrations of such events as fires and other disasters and of more prosaic occurrences such as the installation of new waterworks in a particular city.

Beyond the Great Lakes, the paintings, drawings, and prints of the PAC contain little useful information for the study of urban growth. When the first artists accompanied settlers and explorers into the West, towns hardly existed. By the time communities came into existence, photography was already replacing the pencil (or pen) and brush as a means of accurately recording scenery. However, there are some early views of Winnipeg, Prince Albert, and Victoria.

It should also be noted that since 1975 the Picture Division has made available to the public portions of its collection in microfiches and slide series. One slide set, for example, includes forty slides of Quebec City during the period 1826-32. For further information, contact Archives Canada Microfiches, Picture Division, PAC.

V. PROVINCIAL AND TERRITORIAL ARCHIVES

Under the terms of the British North America Act, all Canadian municipalities fall under the purview of provincial governments. Accordingly, all provincial archives contain a wealth of material pertaining to urban development. Indeed, in some provinces, provincial archives are the official repository of city records. The following descriptions of material provide a succinct guide to these collections, but researchers and teachers should also contact the various archives for detailed information. As well, all provincial archives have detailed listings of their holdings in the *Union List of Manuscripts*.

1. *Newfoundland and Labrador*
   Provincial Archives
   Colonial Building
   Military Road
   St. John's, Newfoundland A1C 2C9

While specific municipal records are virtually non-existent until 1949, insight into the urban evolution of Newfoundland can be derived from a variety of sources. The Archives holds plans of the city of St. John's for the period 1847-92 and Insurance Atlases for 1880 and 1893. And since St. John's was the administrative centre of the island, the Governors' records are useful. Life in the city can also be examined in numerous St. John's newspapers, including the *Royal Gazette* which dates back to 1810. The Archives holds voting lists for several larger centres for the late nineteenth century and directories beginning in 1864-65.

Data on the economy of urban settlements is limited, but the *Newfoundland Census* (eight of which are available for the period 1836-1901) includes data on population, occupations, dwellings, fishing boats and gear, etc.

The Archives has a good collection of parish registers of the major religious denominations of St. John's and the larger towns such as Harbour Grace, Carbonear, and Placentia. These date back to c.1790 and end at 1890. Land grants, court records, and individual business records are also available for some towns.

The Archives holds a photograph collection of some 5,000 items that have been catalogued and are readily available. Most of these are of St. John's, but a few detail activities in smaller centres.

There are a number of private collections among the Archives' holdings which are related to urban development. These include the papers of Governors Duckworth and Cochrane and the papers of various lawyers, politicians, and businessmen.

During the twentieth century, and particularly since 1949, there has been a rapid increase in the number of communities with local governments. The Archives holdings for the recent past are consequently much richer. They contain, for example, a good collection of local newspapers.

2. *Prince Edward Island*
    Public Archives
    Box 1000
    Charlottetown, P.E.I. C1A 7M4

The principal holdings of the P.E.I. Public Archives in the local government and urban areas are the extensive collection of material relating to Charlottetown (RG 20). The records of the city were transferred to the Public Archives in 1977. The records date from 1855, the year of the first incorporation act of the city, and include data on the city corporation, the sewer and water commission, police and city courts, and the board of school trustees. A detailed finding aid to the Charlottetown records has been prepared and is available on request.

The Public Archives also has a map collection which contains material on Charlottetown, Summerside, and several smaller towns. This collection is indexed. The photographic collection, which includes many prints of urban areas, is unindexed.

3. *Nova Scotia*
    Public Archives
    Coburg Road
    Halifax, N.S. B3H 1Z9

A detailed guide to the records of the Public Archives of Nova Scotia was published in 1976 *(Inventory of Manuscripts in the Public Archives of Nova Scotia)*.

Important urban related records held in the Archives include the following: RG 23, Department of Municipal Affairs—these records date from 1935 when the department was created to regulate municipal finances; RG 27, Department of Public Works—papers regarding the maintenance and construction of all provincial public buildings; RG 28, Railways—a collection of 61 volumes of correspondence, reports, and accounts for the period 1845-1950; RG 30, Department of Trade, Commerce, and Industry—which includes such records as surveys of incorporated communities; RG 59, Nova Scotia Housing Commission—eight volumes of material from 1970-75; and RG 35, Elective Municipal Government—covering the period since 1879, when non-elective courts of general sessions of the peace and grand juries were replaced with elected municipal councils.

Of particular importance is RG 35, which contains records of cities and towns. The material in the City of Halifax Collection (RG 35-102) includes city council records and the papers of the mayor, city manager, city clerk, police department, assessment office, city treasurer, city engineer, and so on. The Town of Wolfville Collection (RG 35-200) includes assessment records, financial papers, town clerk's correspondence, proceedings of town council, tax records, school board reports, and papers relating to the administration of justice.

The Nova Scotia Archives has an extensive collection of photographs and prints, paintings, and drawings. Most of this collection has been indexed. One major collection of photographs contains 12,000 prints taken for publication in the Halifax *Chronicle-Herald* and the *Mail-Star,* covering the period c.1950-67. Also noteworthy is the Notman Studio Collection, which contains 4,500 prints of Halifax and other Nova Scotia communities during the period c.1869-c.1920.

4. *New Brunswick*
   Provincial Archives
   P. O. Box 6000
   Fredericton, N.B. E3B 5H1

A detailed guide to the records of the Provincial Archives of New Brunswick was published in 1977 (Ann Rigby, *A Guide to the Manuscript Collections in the Provincial Archives of New Brunswick).*

The New Brunswick Archives holds a wide variety of materials pertinent to the study of urban history and local government. These include the records of the Department of Municipal Affairs (available for each of the province's fifteen counties), village and town records (including such places as Nashwaaksis, Newcastle, St. Andrews, Sackville, St. Stephen, Silverwood, Edmundston, Marysville, Milltown, and Dalhousie); and extensive material on the major centres of Fredericton, Saint John, and Moncton.

The Fredericton records include council minutes, assessment books, real estate valuations, property books, water and sewage registers, almshouse accounts, correspondence, and miscellaneous accounts and reports. An inventory is available.

The Saint John records include the papers of the Common Council of Saint John, which contain minutes, petitions, reports of committees, vouchers and accounts, communications and letters, etc. A calendar of holdings is being prepared.

The Moncton records include council and committee minutes, police committee minutes, correspondence of the city clerk, accounts, assessments, civic election material, and miscellaneous material.

There are as well a number of major collections which cover all aspects of New Brunswick history and therefore contain relevant material on urban areas. In particular, the papers of the House of Assembly and the Executive Council both contain material on urban subjects since these bodies received petitions and reports regarding cases where individuals, groups, or communities desired the provincial authorities to take some action on their behalf.

Holdings in maps, plans, drawings, and photographs also have potential for those studying the urban past. The Archives possesses photographs of nearly every major community in the province and is actively adding to these holdings. In the map section a collection of prime importance is the Mott, Myles and Chatwin Collection of architectural plans and drawings. In addition, the Archives has several bird's-eye views of New Brunswick towns and cities, usually dated c.1880. Maps which are also valuable to the researcher are the surveys which laid out the original network of streets for each town and city.

For researchers interested in demography, the PANB is the official repository for wills, court records, and municipal records such as assessment rolls, although the latter are not plentiful. The Archives does have copies of the census records from 1851 to 1881. The Archives also holds microfilm copies of all land records in New Brunswick.

The list of available publications in the PANB series can be obtained by writing the Archives.

5. *Quebec*
    Archives nationales du Québec
    C.P. 10450
    Sainte-Foy, Québec G1V 4N1

    Archives nationales du Québec à Montréal
    85, rue Sainte-Thérèse
    Montréal, Québec H2Y 1E4

    Archives nationales du Québec à Trois-Rivières
    140, rue St.-Antoine
    Trois-Rivières, Québec G9A 5N6

The Archives nationales du Québec holds a wide variety of materials pertaining to urban history at its various repositories. Moreover, its holdings on urban-related subjects date from c.1635. A guide was published in 1968 and is now being updated *(Etat général des archives publiques et privées du Québec).*
Researchers will find in RG E 1, Intendants, several ordinances on building

materials, hygiene, and other urban-related topics (see, Pierre-Georges Roy, *Inventaire des ordonnances des intendants de la Nouvelle-France*). RG E 2, Grands Voyers, contains valuable information on street layouts and various by-laws in seventeenth-century Quebec City (see, Pierre-Georges Roy, *Inventaire des procès-verbaux des grands voyers*). Records of the grands voyers, which are also deposited in the Montréal and Trois-Rivières repositories, cover the years 1668 to 1855.

RG E 21, Terres et Forêts, contains material on land grants in Quebec City from the seventeenth to the nineteenth century. It also includes records of the Jesuit Estates and of other seigneuries.

Most of the correspondence exchanged between municipalities and the provincial government from Confederation to 1918 may be found in RG E 4, Secrétariat provincial. This record group also contains various lists of potential value to the urban historian (craftsmen, inns, taverns before 1850) and poll books (1820's and 1830's), as well as petitions addressed to the legislative assembly after 1867.

The Department of Municipal Affairs, which took over the Provincial Secretary's responsibilities for municipalities in 1918, has been slow in transferring its records to the Archives nationales. Nevertheless, RG E 7, Affaires municipales, offers to the researcher files of the Service provincial d'urbanisme (1940's and 1950's), Contentieux, Direction générale de la prévention des incendies (1960's), and of some "closed-up" municipalities in the Gaspé and North Shore regions. RG E 7 also includes the records of agencies with particular responsibilities in the improvement of public health and hygiene and the approval of waterworks and sewer installations: the Conseil supérieur d'hygiène de la province du Québec and its successors the Service provincial d'hygiène and the Service de génie sanitaire, 1887-1963.

For the researcher interested in unemployment and welfare services during the Depression, relevant material can be consulted in RG E 24, Travail, and E 25, Travaux publics. Research on urban criminal patterns is, on the other hand, facilitated by the records of the Prison de Québec which run from 1813 to 1967 and constitute part of RG E 17, Justice.

Valuable information can also be found in RG E 26, Commissions d'enquête et comités d'étude. Several commissions and committees are especially concerned with urban-related subjects. They are: Commission royale d'enquête sur l'administration des affaires de la Cité de Montréal par son conseil de ville, 1909; Comité d'enquête relative à la question des tramways de Montréal, 1943; Commission royale d'enquête sur les activités dans le district de Montréal de la police provinciale, etc., 1944; Commission d'enquête sur les problèmes du logement, 1949-52; Commission d'enquête sur l'administration de la justice à la Cour municipale de Québec, 1965; Commission chargée d'estimer l'effet financier du regroupement municipal sur la rive sud [of Montreal], 1968. Though most of its records (public audiences, memoranda) are in the Library of the National Assembly, the Archives nationales holds the correspondence and several studies of the Commission royale d'enquête sur les problèmes constitutionnels, 1954.

Finally, the Archives nationales also has records of various boards and commissions involved in urban-related areas: Commission des Transports du Québec, E 28; Commission du salaire minimum, E 29; Régie des loyers, E 34, and Régie des services publics, E 35. Records of E 28, however, have still not been arranged.

The Archives nationales' most important holdings in the area of local government records consists of the City of Trois-Rivières archives, kept in its Trois-Rivières repository. The Quebec City repository's holdings are more modest. They consist of 90 linear feet of records coming from 13 municipalities, mostly rural, and including minute-books, by-law-books, assessment rolls, accounting registers, census and electoral lists. Local government records are also deposited in the Hull regional centre.

On 21 May 1980 the Department of Municipal Affairs issued a ministerial decree regulating the transfer of local government records to the Archives nationales. This measure should considerably improve the availability of municipal records to researchers in urban history.

The Archives nationales possesses judicial archives of the French regime in its Québec, Montréal, and Trois-Rivières repositories. Since courts also had administrative duties at that time, their records contain useful information. This is the case for the Conseil supérieur, T 1. Pierre-Georges Roy has published an index of the published *Jugements et délibérations du Conseil supérieur* from 1663 to 1716 as well as the *Inventaire des jugements et délibérations du Conseil supériéur de la Nouvelle-France de 1717 à 1760*. Furthermore, the Archives nationales will accession shortly the judicial archives accumulated in the Québec region from 1772 to 1946. The Archives nationales also has in its custody notarial minutes, vital records, and land surveyors' procès-verbaux from the 1600's up to 1875. Some of the land surveyors' records are even more recent.

Researchers interested in urban cultural history will find valuable information in the following manuscripts kept in Québec: Club musical des dames, 1908-c. 1960; and a collection entitled Théâtre à Québec, 1640-1962. Other records of interest include: Société Saint-Vincent de Paul; Quebec Board of Trade; S.-N. Parent (Mayor of Québec in the late 1800's); and Sir George Garneau (Mayor of Québec in the early 1900's).

The Archives nationales' holdings in maps, plans, and photographs are significant both in quality and quantity. It possesses maps of all the main cities of Québec, several of them dating back to the eighteenth century. It also possesses insurance plans of most Québec cities from 1875 to 1972. Plans of land surveyors are also available for the seventeenth- to nineteenth-century period.

The Archives nationales puts at the disposal of researchers a great number of photographs of many areas of the province, many more than a century old. The majority of photographs are concentrated in Québec City and Montréal repositories.

6. *Ontario*
   Archives of Ontario
   77 Grenville Street
   Queen's Park
   Toronto, Ontario M7A 2R9

Of the many record groups which contain material of value to the urban history researcher, two in particular, RG 19 and RG 21, merit considerable attention. RG 19 consists of the records of the former Department of Municipal Affairs, primarily for the period 1934-72. Various facets of the Ontario government's involvement with municipalities are documented in these files. The major records series include ministers' files, deputy ministers' files, the records of the Community Planning Branch, the Law Branch, the Municipal Assessment Branch, the Municipal Finance Branch, the Municipal Organization and Administration Branch, the Municipal Research Branch, and the Municipal Subsidies Branch. One significant series in this record group predates 1934 and consists of the municipal financial statements acquired by the former Bureau of Industries. This series contains municipal financial statements from virtually every municipality in the province from 1884-1968.

RG 21 consists of both microfilm copies and original records which the Archives has acquired from Ontario municipalities, including minutes, by-laws, and assessment rolls. Virtually all of this material relates to municipalities in southern Ontario. Apart from these, the Archives has also acquired correspondence and financial, election, and committee records from a substantial number of cities and towns.

Two record groups which document the early interaction of the provincial government with Ontario's cities and towns are RG 8 and RG 49. RG 8, the Records of the Provincial Secretary, contains two series which are particularly noteworthy. The general correspondence files for the period 1867-1909 contain a wealth of material relating to requests from municipalities for incorporation and changes in status. RG 8 also contains the records of the Bureau of Municipal Affairs (1918-33), the predecessor of the Department of Municipal Affairs. RG 49, the records of the Office of the Clerk of the Legislative Assembly contains petitions on various issues from municipalities to the legislative assembly for the period 1867-1957.

The financial relationship between the province, its treasury, and towns is well documented in the records of the Department of Treasury and Economics (RG 6). Those areas which are especially well covered include municipal finance, municipal financial planning, and provincial grants to municipalities. More recent provincial-municipal records are located in the Ministry of Treasury, Economics and Intergovernmental Affairs (RG 50). Provincial approval of certain specific programmes and projects of urban municipalities is recorded by the orders and decisions of the Ontario Municipal Board found in RG 37, for the period 1906-63. RG 37 also includes the files of various former chairmen of the OMB for the period, 1906, 1907, and 1950-72. Provincial orders-in-council approving certain municipal by-laws are available in RG 3 for the period 1867-1970. The province's involvement in urban housing and development is documented by two record groups. RG 43, Ministry of Housing, and RG 44, Ontario Housing Corporation, contain records dealing with all facets of the Ontario government's involvement in urban housing for 1964-78. The industrial surveys contained in RG 9 (Industry and Tourism) provide a wealth of statistical data for each municipality for the period 1960-79.

The records of RG 18, Commissions and Committees, reflect the provincial government's continual interest in municipal issues, particularly involving urban municipalities. Among the more significant commissions represented in this record group are the Royal Commission on Municipal Institutions, 1888; the Commission on Municipal Taxation, 1893; the Commission on Border Cities Amalgamation, 1935; and the Royal Commissions on Metro Toronto in 1965 and 1977. Also included are the records of commissions which carried out investigations into financial affairs of municipalities as well as municipal election irregularities. RG 18 also contains the records of the legislature's Standing Municipal Committee for 1873-1936 and of various select committees which studied municipal related issues.

The Archives' map collection holds maps of the province's cities and towns as well as insurance plans for the period 1880-1970.

Miscellaneous records of interest to urban researchers include the following: the Frank Beer Papers (material on Toronto urban reform and housing, c.1918); the Thomas L. Church Papers (Mayor of Toronto, 1915-21); the Niagara Historical Society Collection (municipal records of Niagara Town and District, 1793-1899); Toronto City Council Papers, 1834-1880's; the John A. McPhail Papers (Mayor of Sault Ste. Marie, 1915-16); and the Sir William H. Hearst Papers (concerning housing during World War I).

7. *Manitoba*
   Provincial Archives
   200 Vaughan Street
   Winnipeg, Manitoba R3C 0P8

The holdings of the Provincial Archives are divided into five sections by type of material—manuscripts, public records, maps, audio-visual, photographs, and paintings.

The manuscript section contains private manuscripts, corporate records, church records, and papers of associations. The holdings are divided into sixteen groups. Manuscript Groups 10, 11, 14, and 15, containing the papers of associations, business firms, individuals, city and municipal records, would be of primary interest to researchers seeking information on local government and urban-related records. Examples of specific units in these groups are the records of the Winnipeg Board of Trade; the Manitoba Restaurant Association; Winnipeg Economic Development Board, Inc.; Eastern Manitoba Development Bureau; the Winnipeg Construction Association; and the papers of various trade unions, which contain minutes, annual reports, publications, membership lists, etc.

The records of social and moral reform groups such as the Provincial Council of Women, Winnipeg Council of Women, Women's Christian Temperance Union, Manitoba Provincial Organization of Business and Professional Women's Clubs, Children's Aid Society, Social Planning Council of Winnipeg, Margaret Scott Nursing Mission, and the Canadian Red Cross Society (Manitoba Division) offer interesting comments on social problems in larger cities and towns of the province.

The papers of various real estate agents and firms are of interest to students of urban history. The papers of David Macarthur have extensive documentation on the Winnipeg real estate boom and bust of 1881-83 in the Parish of St. John and also contain many half-breed land assignments for the years 1877-82. The papers of the firm of Campbell, Hay, Boddy, and Conner reflect the boom-bust in Portage la Prairie real estate for the years 1881-85. The records of the Marshall R. Grant Realty Company of Winnipeg, consisting of real estate listings, sales, ledgers, journals, and correspondence for the years 1903-18, reflect the increased immigration and demand for housing in Winnipeg in the first decade of this century and the slower market of the second decade.

Original or microfilm copies of the Red River Settlement and Manitoba census returns are available for the years 1832, 1833, 1838, 1840, 1843, 1847, 1849, 1856, 1870, and 1881. A nominal index has been prepared for the returns from 1832 to 1856, and work is almost complete on the returns for 1870. A useful supplement is church registers. The Church of England registers for the early Red River parishes are available on microfilm for 1820 to 1900 and have been indexed up to 1870. A microfilm of the Catholic Parish of St. Boniface church registers for 1825 to 1904 is also available.

Autobiographies, such as those with the papers of Michael Harris, who covered labour for the *Winnipeg Free Press,* and memoirs and biographical sketches of school inspectors and teachers can also be found in the manuscript collection. The papers of W. J. Sisler contain much material on the teaching of children of recent immigrants in north-end Winnipeg in the period before World War I and into the 1920's.

The Provincial Archives is the repository for the manuscript holdings of the Jewish Historical Society of Western Canada. In its holdings are several units relating to labour, cultural, social welfare, loan and fund raising associations, individuals in the business community, and extensive papers of the Jewish Immigrant Aid Society. These papers relate primarily to immigrants settling in rural communities, but many of them later returned to urban areas.

The Provincial Archives has a small collection of records relating to the City of Winnipeg, including council minutes and early records of the health and engineering departments. The City of Winnipeg has recently established its own archives under the jurisdiction of the City Clerk, inventoried in 1979.

The holdings of provincial government public records are not extensive, but they do contain material from a number of government departments, boards, and agencies as well as records of some Royal Commissions and non-continuing commissions of inquiry. The most extensive unit is that of the Department of Public Works, which was responsible for many functions carried on by the province in its formative years, such as the construction and maintenance of jails, court houses, asylums, government offices, public buildings, roads, and bridges. Until 1931 the department administered the Bureau of Labour and was responsible for factory inspection, building trades inspectors, fair wages, etc. When the Branch was transferred to the Department of Labour, it continued to be one of the agencies responsible for unemployment relief, and the files contain much correspondence with the Employment Service of Canada.

The photograph section contains approximately 75,000 catalogued items relating to Manitoba cities, towns, events, industries, and personalities. For larger centres such as Winnipeg, Brandon, Portage la Prairie, and Flin Flon, there are extensive holdings with separate files on bridges, buildings, churches, homes, hospitals, hotels, parks, railway stations, streets, and general views. There are several separate collections of special interest to urban historians. The photograph collection of the former Department of Industry and Commerce dates from the late 1940's and includes material on all industries in the province. The *Winnipeg Free Press* collection dates from 1959 and consists of all staff photographers' negatives. The L. B. Foote Collection, nationally known for its coverage of the Winnipeg General Strike, is a valuable source for the social history of Winnipeg from 1910 to 1930.

The architectural and historical building collection consists of approximately 10,000 items relating to buildings of architectural or historical significance in southern Manitoba. Downtown Winnipeg, especially that area vulnerable to reconstruction, was photographed in considerable detail. The students working on this project also compiled information on architects, builders, construction detail, and vulnerability. The book *Early Buildings of Manitoba* is based on this collection.

Other special collections include those relating to the New Iceland area of the province and record the story of the growth of such centres as Gimli and Riverton and the commercial fishery and lumber industry in the Lake Winnipeg area. The Jewish Historical Society Collections contain about 2,700 photographs relating to Jewish immigration, farming activities, business ventures, and associations. The Canadian Airways Limited Collection has many items from the 1920's and

1930's of interest to urban historians, such as aerial views of cities, mining communities, and airports.

The map collection has fire insurance atlases of the major cities and towns in the province for the years 1917-19, and for Winnipeg only for 1955 with partial revisions in 1963 and 1973. The *Historical Atlas of Manitoba* by Warkentin and Ruggles gives a commentary on the collection and reproduces several of the more representative items, as does *Winnipeg in Maps,* by Artibise and Dahl.

The Provincial Archives has few municipal records, but this important source is not in danger of being lost. Provincial legislation has set retention schedules for the various types of municipal records and makes provision for their deposit in the Provincial Archives if the municipality does not wish to keep records designated for permanent retention.

8. *Saskatchewan*

Saskatchewan Archives Office
5th Floor, Library Building
University of Regina
Regina, Saskatchewan S4S 0A2

Saskatchewan Archives Office
Murray Memorial Library Building
University of Saskatchewan
Saskatoon, Saskatchewan S7N 0W0

Since its formation in 1945, the Saskatchewan Archives has been actively involved in seeking out, preserving, and encouraging the use of documentary evidence on all aspects of provincial history. These activities have resulted in extensive collections in both Saskatoon and Regina of official records of provincial government departments, private papers of residents of Saskatchewan prominent in all walks of life, the records of organizations and voluntary associations, business records, photographs, maps, architectural drawings, pamphlets, published local histories, and oral history interviews.

Saskatchewan's urban growth and development over the years has been reasonably well-documented in the holdings of the Provincial Archives, but much remains to be done to ensure the preservation of the complete archives of the province's urban municipalities. For the urban historian, municipal records are of primary interest, but there are other urban-related records created by Saskatchewan government agencies and private organizations which give a different perspective.

The following general description of archival sources highlights the variety of source material which must be examined by those conducting research in this field.

In acquiring local government records, the legislated responsibility of the Saskatchewan Archives Board is discretionary. Under Section 13 of the Archives Act, municipalities may with the consent of the Board deposit any non-current records for preservation in the Archives. As a result, limited series of council minutes, by-laws, assessment and tax rolls have been deposited in the original or borrowed for microfilming by the Saskatchewan Archives Board. More extensive series of records for the cities of Regina, Saskatoon, and Prince Albert have been deposited in the original or on microfilm with the Archives.

Non-current records created by government departments, boards, commissions, agencies and crown corporations are transferred to the Saskatchewan Archives Board if they are judged to be of long-term historical value. This ongoing process has allowed the Archives to acquire a vast quantity of documentary evidence dating back to the Territorial period and containing a wealth of information on the development and implementation of government policies.

Holdings of the Department of Municipal Affairs include municipal corporation files, municipal financial statements, municipal inspection files, and community planning files which describe the establishment and expansion or contraction of municipal corporations. The Local Government Board was established in 1913 to supervise the borrowing arrangements and loan expenditures of municipalities, school districts, and rural telephone companies. Its records relate to various aspects of borrowing and spending by cities, towns, villages, rural municipalities, school districts, and rural telephone companies. The Archives also contains the correspondence, reports, and briefs of the Commission of Inquiry into Provincial and Municipal Taxation (Jacoby Commission) established during the mid-1930's to study and make recommendations on a suitable taxation structure for local and provincial government.

Personal papers and correspondence also contain information of value to urban history studies. Through inventories or other finding aids, the researcher may locate files of relevant material in the following collections: Walter Scott (1867-1938), Premier of Saskatchewan; W. Norman McGillivray, member of Saskatchewan Municipal Advisory Commission; William Melville Martin (1876-1970), Premier of Saskatchewan; Meyer Brownstone, Deputy Minister of Municipal Affairs.

The records of private organizations are another useful source. Records from the following organizations have been acquired by the Saskatchewan Archives Board for permanent preservation: Regina Chamber of Commerce; Association of Professional Community Planners of Saskatchewan; Melfort Board of Trade; Saskatchewan Municipalities Association; Retail Merchants' Association of Canada (Saskatchewan) Inc.; Prince Albert Chamber of Commerce.

Illustrative material in the Archives include topographical, soil, forestry, survey, township, municipal, and school district maps. There are some plans and drawings for villages and towns showing the location of buildings. At present the photograph collection houses nearly 150,000 photographs catalogued under a variety of names and subject headings. For entries, researchers may look at the alphabetical card index under the names of communities, organizations, and individuals.

To consult these archival sources, researchers should write to determine location of material, access limitation, and extent.

9. *Alberta*
   Provincial Archives
   12845-102nd Avenue
   Edmonton, Alberta T5N 0M6

The Provincial Archives is responsible for the preservation of the records of the provincial government and most departments have some connection with the developing urban fabric of the province. Of particular note are the papers of the Premier's Office, which are available to researchers for 1921 to 1959. The Department of Municipal Affairs has deposited records of the Provincial Planning Branch, Municipal Inspection Branch, and Local Authorities Board, as well as the files of the 1956 Royal Commission on the Metropolitan Development of Calgary and Edmonton (McNally Commission). Researchers interested in crime and law enforcement have access to inquest and criminal case files, court records, and administrative records from the Attorney-General's department.

The Provincial Archives also preserves papers from private individuals and organizations, many of which provide insights into aspects of urban history. The Archives has the minutes and financial records of a number of smaller communities in the province, including the town of Athabasca, long the base of the Athabasca-Mackenzie River transportation system. Some town and village records are included with the records of the counties and municipal districts of which they form a part.

Records of churches in the province held by the Provincial Archives include those of the Anglican Dioceses of Edmonton, Athabasca, and Mackenzie River; the Alberta Conference of the United Church; the Western Canada Synod, Lutheran Church in America; and the Oblates, Redemptorists, and Sisters of the Assumption, all of the Roman Catholic Church. For labour inquiries, the records of the Edmonton Trades and Labour Council, Alberta Union of Public Employees, and a number of other unions are available. Information on the social role of urban women is available through records of the Women's Canadian Club, Local Council of Women, University Women's Club of Edmonton, and Imperial Order Daughters of the Empire. Business and private papers of individuals and organizations are also of potential value.

The extensive photographic holdings of the Provincial Archives provide excellent visual coverage of Calgary and Edmonton and some record of other Alberta communities. Six collections of commercial photographs provide an overlapping record of Edmonton's history from the 1880's to the 1970's. In addition, two sets of political cartoons offer editorial comment on the civic affairs of Calgary.

The archives map collection contains a good chronology of street plans for Calgary and Edmonton and a selection of maps for other communities. There are also fire insurance maps for Edmonton and Strathcona from 1899 to 1914. Two sets of fire insurance maps provide sheets for many of the major centres in Alberta from the early 1900's to the 1970's. Other items, such as an atlas of the Edmonton-area coal mine locations, provide valuable data on urban growth.

10. *British Columbia*
    Provincial Archives
    655 Belleville Street
    Victoria, B.C. V8V 1X4

Urban-related records in the Provincial Archives of British Columbia can be found in five different portions of the collection.

The Manuscript and Government Records Division holdings include the records of individuals and corporate bodies active in the political, economic, and social life of B.C.'s urban communities. Manuscript collections are indexed by personal, corporate, and place names to facilitate locating records related to individuals, corporate bodies, or specific geographical locations.

As a matter of policy, the Provincial Archives does not collect and preserve the records of municipal corporations, except those of disincorporated municipalities whose records fall by law to the care of the provincial government. Hence, for example, the Archives has the records of Sandon and Phoenix.

The records of the Ministry of Municipal Affairs, though not extensive, are a valuable source for urban studies. In addition, the records of several commissions of inquiry, notably those on municipal government (1912) and property assessment and taxation (1975), will be of particular interest. A wide range of other government records, including extensive holdings of the colonial governments of Vancouver Island and British Columbia, document the relationship between the municipalities and the senior government. In the Premier's Papers, records of the Legislative Assembly, and Provincial Secretary's records may be found petitions, correspondence, and other submissions to government from municipalities and citizens on the subject of urban needs and development.

The Map Division of the Provincial Archives collects all maps relating to the Pacific Northwest in general and British Columbia in particular, from earliest times to the present, as well as other cartographic material of interest to students and researchers of Pacific Northwest history. A reference collection consists of general atlases, gazetteers, maps of Canada, the provinces, and adjacent western U.S. States. Other material includes architectural plans of public and private buildings, railway location plans, historic fort site plans, ship plans, Royal Engineers' maps and sketches, British Admiralty and Canadian Hydrographic charts, and related federal and provincial government cartographic material. Fire Insurance plans for various B.C. centres together with street maps and cadastral maps are additional source material useful in tracing the urban and regional development of the province. A very complete copying service is provided for the varying needs of the user.

Historical photographs are arranged according to geographical location. Large urban areas are subdivided into many subject categories. The photographic division has a good representation of images relating to all towns and cities in British Columbia, though Victoria is most heavily documented. The collection is particularly strong in nineteenth- and early twentieth-century photographs. Major collections relating to urban history include those of Richard and Hannah Maynard and J. H. A. Chapman, which document Victoria and, to a lesser extent, the province from 1865 to 1940.

The Aural History Division holds over 17,000 hours of contemporary records and retrospective interviews that provide a rich source of narrative, descriptive, and anecdotal material on urban history. The majority of the tapes focus on the experiences of individuals and groups rather than on political and economic development as such, but they are a useful source for anyone interested in the largely undocumented history of so-called ordinary people. The collection has information on elites, ethnic groups, economic groups, and communities within many cities and towns. Only 2,000 hours of tapes are fully catalogued and even fewer transcribed, but all materials can be researched at the Archives.

The Library of the Provincial Archives holds the Northwest Collection of books, pamphlets, and other printed materials. This library is perhaps the richest source of published items found anywhere for the history of British Columbia. The *Dictionary Catalogue of the Library of the Provincial Archives* (1971) may be found in most libraries.

11. *Yukon*
    Yukon Archives
    Box 2703
    Whitehorse, Yukon Y1A 2C6

Prior to the 1950's, the Territorial Government was responsible for the administration of the towns and cities of the Yukon (Dawson had been incorporated briefly, 1902-4). The Central Registry files of the Territorial Government contain administrative material on such subjects as schools, fire departments, townsites, land titles, churches, parks, garbage disposal, sanitation, waterfront, post office, cemeteries, R.N.W.M.P., airports and air travel, public library, roads, hospitals, tax sales, and incorporation. The files deal mainly with Whitehorse and Dawson but also include material on the gold creeks, Stewart Crossing, Mayo, Carcross, Hootalinqua, Fort Selkirk, Granville, and Carmacks. The records of the Economic Research and Planning Unit of the Territorial Government contain 200 completed survey forms of tourist impressions of Dawson City.

The Dawson City records are divided into four series. Series 1 is also divided into four parts: Series 1-A contains Assessment and Tax Records, 1902-59; Series 1-B, Assessment of Land Improvement Register, 1948; Series 1-C, Revenue and Expenditure Records and Series 1-D, Vouchers and Invoices, 1902-25. The remaining series are Series 2—Correspondence and Registry Files, 1950-66;

Series 3—City Council Minutes 1962-69; and Series 4—Miscellaneous Records, 1898-1962. In addition to these records, the Archives also holds Dawson City By-laws, 1950-75, and records of the Dawson Fire Department, 1907-72, which include Daily Reports, 1907-72, and Inspection Reports, 1903-11. The Faro By-Laws 1971-76 are held in the Archives.

The City of Whitehorse has deposited its inactive records in the Archives. The records are divided into four main series: Series A—Central Registry Files, 1947-73; Series B—City Council Minutes, 1950-74; Series C—City Financial Records, 1950-74; and Series D—Tax and Assessment Ledgers and Voter's Lists, 1950-77. In addition to the above, the Archives also contains City of Whitehorse By-Laws, 1950-73 and Cemetery Records, 1904-79. School registers for several communities are also available.

There are a number of collections contained within Corporate Records that relate to urban topics. Among them are the records of the Whitehorse Chamber of Commerce, 1945-74; Whitehorse Board of Trade; Whitehorse Drama Club, 1946-72; Whitehorse Golf and Country Club, 1955-56; I.O.D.E., containing files on Whitehorse Public Library, 1916-62, and the Yukon Sourdough Rendezvous, 1963-78. Of more general interest are the Royal Mail Service and Canadian Development Company, 1899-1907, the United Church of Canada Alberta Conference, and the Iris Warner Collection. The White Pass and Yukon Route records contain material on cost-shared community development funds, the company's land holdings, river records from Whitehorse to Dawson, and water sewers in Whitehorse and Keno. In addition there is the Cahill Collection, which deals with the banning of public drinking in Whitehorse, the Canadian Coachways Ltd. Collection relating to a transportation study for Whitehorse in 1961, and the Woodall Collection, which contains information on the establishment of a post office at Old Crow.

There are a number of diaries within the manuscript collection that depict life in Yukon communities from the time of the Gold Rush. Examples of these are the Israel Albert Lee diary about Dawson, 1898-1901, and the diary of Georgia White, 1898. In addition there are Capt. T. V. Fleming's memories of Whitehorse c.1900 and some materials in the Otto Nordling Collection.

Many of the films in the Archives collection contain scenes of Yukon communities. There are gold rush footage and travelogues which feature Dawson and Whitehorse in addition to the other communities along the Trail of '98 and the Yukon River. In addition there are films depicting the building of the Alaska Highway and Canol Pipeline, the burning of the riverboats, the move of the *S.S. Klondike*, the last voyage of the *Keno,* and the burning of the Bonanza Hotel in Dawson.

The Archives' photograph collections are accessible by means of an integrated visual finding aid, which consists of a xerox copy of the reference print and the relevant catalogue card. It is arranged alphabetically by subject. In addition to this, specific collections may be of interest to a researcher studying Yukon communities. For example, Dawson is well represented in the Vogee Collection, 1897-1903; Public Archives of Canada Collection, 1898-1940; National Museums of Canada, 1898-1951; Martz Collection, 1905; Provincial Archives of B.C. Collection, 1894-1941; University of Washington Collection, 1897-1922; T. R. Lane Collection, 1898; C. Haines Collection, 1935-1944; Vancouver Public Library Collection, 1897-1900; J. Hunston Collection, 1905-56; Bartsch Collection, 1899-1900; Anchorage Historical and Fine Art Museum Collection, 1898-1907; University of Alaska Collection, 1895-1948; Martha Louise Black Collection, 1898-1935; MacBride Museum Collection, 1897-1956; Alaska Historical Library Collection, 1897-1960; Gillis Collection, 1898-1924; H. C. Barley Collection, 1898-1912; and W. A. Chisholm Collection, 1899-1909. Whitehorse is represented in the Vogee Collection, 1897-1903; Ernest Brown Collection, 1895-1907; J. Hunston Collection, 1905-6; Bartsch Collection, 1899-1907; Martha Louise Black Collection, 1898-1935; MacBride Museum Collection, 1897-1956; James Collection, 1914-15; Macpherson Collection, 1941-45; Atlin Historical Society Collection, 1898-1937; and H. C. Barley Collection, 1898-1912.

In addition to these, the Vogee Collection, 1897-1903, features Dyea, Skagway, and Bennett; the R. A. Carter Collection, 1942, depicts communities along the Alaska Highway; Martha Louise Black Collection, 1898-1935, contains scenes of Mayo; the MacBride Museum Collection includes views of Carcross; the Alaska Historical Library features Fortymile, Mayo, and Tagish; the James Collection, 1914-15, Atlin Historical Society Collection, 1898-1937, and the Barley Collection, 1898-1912, contain photographs of Atlin; and the H. C. Barley Collection, 1898-1912, includes views of Carcross and Selkirk.

Most of the urban related maps in the Yukon Archives map collection are townsite and lot plans. There are plans for some of the Dawson government buildings, zoning and electoral maps for Whitehorse and plans for the Mayo hospital and airport. The following communities are represented in the Map Collection: Bennett City, 1898; Carcross, 1900-1907; Carmacks, 1936; Dawson, 1898-1975; Fortymile, 1899; Klondike City, 1904; Mayo, 1903-38; Selkirk, 1900; Watson Lake and Whitehorse, 1899-1969.

VI. MUNICIPAL ARCHIVES, SPECIALIZED LIBRARIES, AND URBAN INFORMATION CENTRES

A growing number of Canadian cities are recognizing the need for organizing, cataloguing, and preserving urban sources. The following list of city archives, specialized libraries, and urban information centres gives some idea of this trend, but urban researchers and teachers of urban studies courses should check in their own locality since new archives and centres are still being established. Developments in this area are also regularly reported in such journals as the *Urban His-*

tory Review and *Archivaria*. For a complete archives listing, as of 1977, see the *Directory of Canadian Records and Manuscript Repositories* (Ottawa: Association of Canadian Archivists, 1977). For a complete libraries listing, see the useful guides to the collections of Canadian research and special libraries in the following series: *Research Collections in Canadian Libraries. 1. Universities* (Ottawa: Information Canada, 1972), 5 vols.; *Research Collections in Canadian Libraries. II. Special Studies* (Ottawa: Printing and Publishing, Supply and Services, 1976), 5 vols.; *Canadian Library Directory* (Ottawa: Supply and Services, 1974-76), 2 vols.

1. *Newfoundland Planning Library*
   Department of Municipal Affairs and Housing
   Confederation Building
   St. John's, Newfoundland A1C 5R7
   Holdings: Newfoundland community development plans, regulations, planning and other community studies; urban and rural planning; Atlantic region economic development; land use, housing, urban affairs. *Access:* Collection for use of staff; access by arrangement.

2. *St. John's City Archives*
   City Hall
   New Gower Street
   St. John's, Newfoundland
   Holdings: Records of the City of St. John's. *Access:* By appointment only.

3. *Prince Edward Island Heritage Foundation*
   2 Kent Street
   P.O. Box 902
   Charlottetown, P.E.I. C1A 7L9
   Holdings: Local business papers, photographs, minute books, letter-books, diaries, pamphlets, maps, and genealogical material. *Access:* Open weekdays and Thursday evening.

4. *Prince Edward Island Planning Library*
   P.O. Box 2000
   Charlottetown, P.E.I. C1A 7N8
   Holdings: 7,000 books; 300 periodicals. Contains some material on urban affairs, urban planning and renewal, land use and planning, regional development, housing, and transportation. *Access:* Inter-library loans; open to the public.

5. *Nova Scotia Development Library*
   5151 George Street
   P.O. Box 519
   Halifax, Nova Scotia B3J 2R7
   Holdings: 5,000 books; 200 periodicals. Contains material relating to urban planning, associated studies, directories of manufacturing, industry proposals, studies, and reviews. *Access:* Inter-library loans.

6. *Moncton Museum*
   20 Mountain Road
   Moncton, New Brunswick E1C 2J8
   Holdings: Municipal records, photographs, and newspapers. *Access:* Open weekdays.

7. *Quebec Urban Community*
   Centre de documentation de la communauté urbaine de Québec
   930, chemin Ste-Foy
   Québec, Québec G1S 2K9
   Holdings: 8,000 books and pamphlets; 2,000 microfiche; 150 periodicals. The collection reflects the particular services supplied by the Quebec Urban Community: administration, industrial and tourist promotion, and land management. *Access:* Inter-library loans. Researchers should make an appointment.

8. *City of Quebec Archives*
   Archives
   Ville de Québec
   Case Postale 37
   Hôtel de Ville
   Québec, Québec G1R 4S9
   Holdings: Official documents from the time of municipal incorporation in 1833 to the present; maps and blueprints (approx. 2,000) from the nineteenth century to the present; building permits (approx. 25,000) from 1928 to the present; photographs (7,200) from 1890 to the present; microfilm of minutes and debates of council and committees, assessment roles, and departmental records from 1833. The Archives Library has 3,000 catalogued volumes. Directories have been compiled for almost all documents held. *Access:* Archival material is for

reference only. Library material is available on inter-library loan.
Publications: The archives has seven publications available:
#1. *La ville de Québec.* 1971.
#2. *Guide de la cartothèque.* 1975.
#3. *Etat sommaire des Archives de la ville de Québec.* 1976.
#4. *Répertoire numérique détaillé de la série CC.* 1978.
#5. *Répertoire numérique détaillé de la série FF.* 1978.
#6. *L'hôtel de ville avant 1929.* 1978.
#7. *Rapport annuel 1978-1979.* 1979.
Further Information: See Murielle Doyle-Frenière, "Les archives de la ville de Québec," *UHR* 1-77 (juin 1977):33-37.

9. *City of Montreal Archives*
   Archives municipales
   Ville de Montréal
   275 est, rue Notre-Dame
   Pièce 16
   Montréal, Québec H2Y 1C6
Holdings: The Archives is the legal depository for all official city documents from 1832 to the present. Records of decisions taken by the administration as well as the Executive Council and City Council are maintained at the Archives. Minutes and proceedings of Council, its committees, and the Executive Committee are now on microfilm. Assessment rolls from 1847 are in the collection. Press clippings from newspapers dated to the 1920's are classed by subject headings. There is a small specialized library of works on the City of Montréal. *Access:* Archival material is for reference only.
Further Information: See Henri Gérin-Lajoie, "Les archives municipales de la ville de Montréal," *UHR* 2-74 (octobre 1974):2-4.

10. *Montreal Municipal Library*
    Bibliothèque Municipale de Montréal
    Salle Gagnon
    1210 est, rue Sherbrooke
    Montréal, Québec H2L 1L9
Holdings: Archives of individuals and families, photographs, maps, and plans. Material dates from 1610. *Access:* Open six days a week.

11. *Regional History Society of Trois-Rivières*
    Societé d'histoire régionale des Trois-Rivières (Archives)
    190, rue Bonaventure
    Trois-Rivières, Québec G9A 2B1
Holdings: Municipal archives, maps, and plans, 1764-1976. *Access:* Open weekdays.

13. *City of Toronto Archives*
    City Hall
    Toronto, Ontario M5H 2N2
Holdings: Records of City Council, committees, commissions, boards and departments; by-laws and assessment rolls from 1834 to the present; city voters lists for 1924-26 and 1957 to the present; building permits from 1882 onwards; building plans from 1917 to the present; 25,000 photographs and 1,500 maps. Also the city art collection; politicians' personal papers; surviving records of former municipalities of Yorkville, Brockton, Parkdale, East Toronto, West Toronto, North Toronto, West Hill, and Swansea. *Access:* Archival materials are for reference only.
Further Information: See R. Scott James, "The City of Toronto Archives," *UHR* 3-73 (February 1974):2-9.

14. *Toronto Planning Board Library*
    20th Floor, East Tower
    City Hall
    Toronto, Ontario M5H 2N2
Holdings: 9,000 books; 36 periodicals. Specialties include planning board reports with emphasis on land use, planning, transportation, urban renewal, and civic design. The library also has an extensive collection of slides, newspaper clippings, and photographs. *Access:* Staff reference library; open to public by appointment only.

15. *Metropolitan Toronto Municipal Reference Library*
    City Hall
    Toronto, Ontario M5H 2N1
Holdings: 42,000 books; 450 periodicals; 30,000 microfilms. Specialties: housing, municipal finance, municipal government; municipal services; pollution; urban planning and renewal; urban geography; urban sociology, and urban transportation. The library has a collection of Toronto material from city, borough, and metropolitan governments and from outside agencies. Voters lists are collected from Toronto area. Extensive newspaper files and pamphlets are available for consultation. *Access:* Open to the public.

16. *City of Ottawa Archives*
    City Hall
    111 Sussex Drive
    Ottawa, Ontario K1A 5A1
Holdings: Council minute books (1847-   );
By-Laws (1850-   ); Minute books for Waterworks Commission (1872-79), the Board of Health (1890-1968), Parks Management Board (1893-1904); records of old municipalities of Ottawa East (1898-1905) and New Edinburgh (1867-82); city directories; photograph collection. *Access:* Open to the public.
Further Information: See Edwin Welch, "The City of Ottawa Archives," *UHR* 1-76 (June 1976):10-13.

17. *National Capital Commission Library*
    48 Rideau Street
    Ottawa, Ontario K1N 8K5
Holdings: 6,000 books; 250 periodicals. Specialties: urban and regional planning, land use, architecture, transportation and recreation. *Access:* Interlibrary loans. Members of the public may use the collection of official N.C.C. documents.

18. *City of Kingston Archives*
    Douglas Library
    Queen's University
    Kingston, Ontario K7L 5C4
Holdings: In 1972 the university arranged with the city to provide storage and research facilities for municipal records which date back to the incorporation of the city in 1838 through to the present. The Archives collection includes: Minutes of Council (1838-   ); minutes and reports of committees; assessment rolls (1843-1934); court of revision records (1847-1942); records of the Public Utilities Commission, Board of Education, Board of Health, Old House of Industry, and many others. *Access:* Archival material is for reference only.
Further Information: See Anne MacDermaid, "The City of Kingston Archives," *UHR* 1-78 (June 1978):3-8.

19. *London Urban Resource Centre*
    322 Queens Avenue
    London, Ontario N6B 1X4
Holdings: Government documents relating to community and urban affairs; reports, unpublished research papers, monographs and research relating to London; community development library; indices of materials of other agencies. *Access:* Open to public.

20. *Urban Documentation Centre, McMaster University*
    Room 415
    General Sciences Building
    McMaster University
    1200 Main Street
    Hamilton, Ontario L8S 4K1
Holdings: The centre is a specialized library collection on urban and regional affairs. The collection of 12,000 items concentrates on government documents, university discussion papers, conference proceedings, planning reports, briefs from housing associations and community groups, and series publications from 75 university research centres. Special features are extensive files of Hamilton area data and documentation and newspaper clippings on local issues. *Access:* All citizens of Hamilton have full borrowing privileges.

21. *Sault Ste. Marie Public Library*
    50 East Street
    Sault Ste. Marie, Ontario P6A 3C3
Holdings: Private papers, books, photographs, slides, microfilm, maps, and audio tapes relating to Sault Ste. Marie and the Algoma district. *Access:* Open to the public.

22. *Sudbury Public Library*
    74 Mackenzie Street
    Sudbury, Ontario P3C 4X9
Holdings: Private papers, maps, and photographs relating to Sudbury and area. *Access:* Open to the public.

23. *Thunder Bay Historical Museum*
    219 S. May Street
    Thunder Bay, Ontario P7E 1B5
Holdings: Papers relating to the Thunder Bay area. *Access:* Open to the public.

24. *Manitoba Department of Urban Affairs*
    Urban Research and Information System
    505-352 Donald Street
    Winnipeg, Manitoba R3B 2H8
Holdings: 2,000 volumes, 65 periodicals. Specialties: housing, municipal, urban, environment, recreation, transportation. A complete bibliography of urban material contained in the Winnipeg government, public, and local community libraries is maintained for reference purposes. An *Urban Research and Information Catalogue* is also maintained and sent to subscribers. *Access:* Library open to public; no loans.

25. *City of Winnipeg Planning Library*
    Room 206
    100 Main Street
    Winnipeg, Manitoba R3C 1A5
Holdings: 7,000 books; 60 periodicals. Specialties: city planning, local government, sociology, urban economics, urban geography, housing, pollution, and transportation. Collection includes 3,000 theses and planning studies. *Access:* Open to the public; interlibrary loans.

26. *City of Winnipeg Archives*
    City Clerk's Department
    Council Building
    Civic Centre
    Winnipeg, Manitoba R3B 1B9
Holdings: The archives is in its infancy since it was established only in 1979. One of the first tasks of the Records Control and Archives Branch of the City Clerk's Department is to centralize the records of the former cities, towns, and municipalities which were subsumed when Unicity was created in 1971. To date such records as minutes of councils and committees, tax rolls, vital statistics records, committee reports, and general journals have been assembled and work is proceeding on building permits and plans. *Access:* Material is for reference only.

27. *Saskatchewan Department of Municipal Affairs Library*
    Westman Chambers Building
    1791 Rose Avenue
    Regina, Saskatchewan S4P 1Z5
Holdings: 500 books; 200 periodicals, pamphlets, etc. Specialties: planning, urban affairs, administration, economics, architecture, and landscape design. *Access:* Interlibrary loans.

28. *Saskatoon Public Library*
    Local History Room
    23rd Street and 4th Avenue
    Saskatoon, Saskatchewan S7K 0J6
Holdings: Photographs and printed material relating to Saskatoon and the surrounding area. *Access:* Open to the public.

29. *Moose Jaw Public Library (Archives Department)*
    461 Langdon Crescent
    Moose Jaw, Saskatchewan S6H 0X6
Holdings: Photographs, memoirs, private papers, books, pamplets, and clippings relating to Moose Jaw and area. *Access:* Open to the public.

30. *Alberta Department of Municipal Affairs Library*
    Jarvis Building
    9925-107th Street
    Edmonton, Alberta T5K 2H9
Holdings: 10,000 books; 150 periodicals. Major subject areas are urban and regional planning, municipal finance and administration, assessment, and taxation. Collection also includes microfiche, statutes and regulations, directories, annual reports, Alberta planning documents, and Alberta municipal statistics from 1972. The library also produces an annual publication: *Urban and Regional Studies in Alberta*. *Access:* Open to general public.

31. *City of Calgary Planning Library*
    P.O. Box 2100
    Calgary, Alberta T2P 2M5
Holdings: 6,500 volumes; 200 periodicals. Collection includes material on land use and controls, transportation, engineering and planning, architecture, parks and recreation planning, land economics, housing, community renewal, local government, city and regional planning, urban affairs, and citizen participation. There is also a special collection of Canadian general (official) plans and zoning by-laws. Also holds City of Calgary publications. *Access:* Open to public by appointment only.

32. *Glenbow Archives*
    9th Avenue and 1st Street, S.E.
    Calgary, Alberta T2G 0P3
Holdings: The Archives holds both official and private material relating to Calgary. Private material includes company records, papers of societies and organizations, church records, and individual papers. Other records include material relating to schools, board of trade papers, labour records, and a mass of miscellaneous items relating to early events, individuals and general happenings in the life of Calgary.

Glenbow became the official archives for the City of Calgary in 1973 and now holds the following official papers: city clerk's papers; city commissioner's papers; planning commission minutes; tax and assessment rolls; and a number of other items.

Glenbow also holds a great deal of material relating to the history of smaller cities and towns in Southern Alberta, both private manu-

scripts and public documents. *Access:* Open to the public.
Further Information: See S. S. Jameson, "The Archives of the Glenbow-Alberta Institute (Calgary)," *UHR* 3-77 (February 1978):69-79.

33. *City of Edmonton Archives*
10105-112 Avenue
Edmonton, Alberta T5G 0H1
Holdings: 2,500 books, periodicals, and reports. Reports include those of city administration and city departments. Also holds photographs, maps, plans, and documents relating to development of Edmonton. *Access:* Open to the public.
Further Information: See Helen LaRose, "The City of Edmonton Archives," *UHR* 3-74 (February 1975):2-7.

34. *Medicine Hat Historical Foundation*
1302 Bomford Crescent
Medicine Hat, Alberta T1A 5E6
Holdings: Collections relating to the Medicine Hat area, including the Cypress Hills. *Access:* Open to the public.

35. *Red Deer Archives*
4818-49 Street
Red Deer, Alberta T4N 1T8
Holdings: Records of City Council and other groups, including local companies; maps, photographs, private papers, etc. All relating to Red Deer and District. *Access:* Open to the public.

36. *City of Vancouver Archives*
1150 Chestnut Street
Vancouver, B.C. V6J 3J9
Holdings: The collection includes privately donated manuscripts; civic departmental records (1886 to present); maps; building plans; charts; historical photographs; books; pamphlets and periodicals; microfilms; audio and computer tapes. The collection concentrates on documenting the history of Vancouver and the Lower Mainland. *Preliminary Inventories* (4 vols.) describing the private manuscript holdings are available. *Access:* Open to the public.
Further Information: See Bill McKee, "The Resources of the Vancouver City Archives," *UHR* 2-77 (October 1977):3-9.

37. *Greater Vancouver Regional District Planning Library*
2034 West 12th Avenue
Vancouver, B.C. V6J 2G2
Holdings: Publications of the Greater Vancouver Regional Planning District and its predecessor, the Lower Mainland Planning Board; approximately 3,500 reports from other agencies on various aspects of urban and regional planning; approximately 110 periodicals; B.C. statutes, bills, votes, and debates; selected Statistics Canada publications (census and general); newspaper clippings; pamphlet material; and air photographs. *Access:* Open to the public.

38. *Vancouver Planning Library*
453 West 12th Avenue
Vancouver, B.C. V5Y 1V4
Holdings: 5,000 books and documents; 100 periodicals. The collection includes municipal, regional, provincial, and federal government publications; Vancouver by-laws; selected B.C. legislation; as well as reference and general planning works. *Access:* Open to the general public.

39. *Simon Fraser University Archives*
Burnaby, B.C. V5A 1S6
Holdings: Municipal records of Burnaby and Port Coquitlam. *Access:* Open to the public.

40. *Kamloops Museum and Archives*
207 Seymour Street
Kamloops, B.C. V2C 2E7
Holdings: Records pertaining to the Kamloops district; indexed newspapers; city assessment rolls; letters, diaries, maps, and photographs. *Access:* Open to the public.

41. *Victoria City Archives*
613 Pandora Street
Victoria, B.C. V8W 1P6
Holdings: Minutes, annual reports, and assessment records of the City of Victoria; private papers, diaries, commercial business records, maps, and photographs. *Access:* Open to the public.

VII. AUDIO-VISUAL RESOURCES

This area of urban studies is one of the most difficult to outline since there is so much material being produced. Moreover, many communities have had visual materials (slides, films, and photographs) gathered together and made available for use. Readers should check local libraries and museums for information on these collections.

The following data thus deal with major sources of audio-visual resources on urban studies. More detailed information can be obtained from catalogues prepared for users by such agencies as the National Film Board. Also, two specialized catalogues are worthy of mention. The first is James E. Page, *Seeing Ourselves: Films for Canadian Studies* (Ottawa: National Film Board, 1979). This 200-page volume contains detailed synopses of productions and detailed ordering information. All teachers will find it an indispensable guide. Copies can be obtained from the Publications Division, The Canadian Film Institute, 75 Albert Street, Ottawa K1P 5E7. The second is John W. Auld, *Human Settlements: Audio-Visual Catalogue* (Guelph: Office for Educational Practice, University of Guelph, 1978). This catalogue is an annotated and indexed collection of films, filmstrips, and audio-video tapes which have been assembled from more than forty producers/distributors in North America. Among the list of key works are topics such as architecture, design, planning, housing, and the environment. The catalogue can be ordered from the University of Guelph.

1. *Films*

The following is a select list of films available for urban studies. All films listed are 16 mm, sound/colour films, unless otherwise indicated. The major distributors are:

National Film Board of Canada (NFB)
Distribution Branch
P.O. Box 6100
Montreal, Quebec H3C 3H5

Central Mortgage and Housing Corporation (CMHC)
Information and Communications
373 Sussex Drive
Ottawa, Ontario K1A 0P6

Canadian Filmmakers' Distribution Centre (CFDC)
Suite 430-144 Front Street
Toronto, Ontario M5J 1G2

Canadian Film Institute (CFI)
303 Richmond Road
Ottawa, Ontario K1X 6X3

Bleeker Street. An account of the battle between a developer and the population of a downtown Toronto neighbourhood which the developer won. 25 mins., CFDC.

Boomsville. An ironic view of town planning, or rather the lack of it, and what has happened to cities as a result. 10 mins., 35 mm, NFB.

To Build a Better City. Urban renewal in Vancouver. 14 mins., NFB.

The Changing City. An examination of the National Housing Act. 27 mins., NFB.

Citizen Harold. An animated film about one man's attempt to bring about change in his community. 8 mins., NFB.

A City Is. A multi-image look at the conglomerate city. 17 mins., NFB.

The City. A study of housing, transporation, suburban growth, and the importance of green spaces in the modern city. 14 mins., NFB.

City Limits. A critical analysis of North American cities by Jane Jacobs, a New Yorker who chooses to live in Toronto. 28 mins., NFB.

City under Pressure. A case study of municipal government in Edmonton. 17 mins., NFB.

Colonel By's Town. A description of early Ottawa, narrated by Charlotte Whitton. 17 mins., CMHC.

Day after Day. An analysis of life in a small paper mill town in Quebec. 27 mins., NFB.

Design Innovations in Canadian Settlements. Suggestions for effective use of land and energy. 17 mins., CMHC.

Encounter on Urban Environment. An examination of the Halifax/Dartmouth community. 108 mins., black and white, NFB.

Halifax Neighbourhood Centre Project. A description of a campaign to protest the problems of poverty in the central core. 33 mins., black and white, NFB.

Heritage Kingston. Using documents from each major period, this film traces Kingston's evolution since 1673. 27 mins., CFDC.

High River. A description of how the people of this Alberta town have maintained their community's identity despite the proximity of Calgary. 14 mins., CMHC.

Inner City. A portrayal of four processes—massive redevelopment, stability, revitalization, and decline—in Canada's inner-city areas. 17 mins., CMHC.

In Old Toronto. The contrasts of old and new in Toronto's core, narrated by former mayor Nathan Phillips. 17 mins., CMHC.

Little Burgundy. The story of the fight by residents of this Montreal district to prevent redevelopment. 30 mins., black and white, NFB.

The Liveable Region Plan. The approach to metropolitan planning in the Greater Vancouver Regional District. 7 mins., CMHC.

Louisbourg. A detailed account of the reconstruction and refurbishing of the fortress and city. 20 mins., NFB.

Management of Urban Growth and Land Use. Discussion of regional economic development programmes, legislative control of land use, and public ownership of land. 21 mins., CMHC.
Montreal: The Neighbourhood Revived. Montreal is used as a case study of urban renovation and restoration through government grants and subsidies. 57 mins., NFB.
Neighbourhoods. A description of the various neighbourhoods that make up Toronto. 14 mins., CMHC.
Saint John Design. Traces the renovation of the city core and shows the degree of public participation in the process. 14 mins., CMHC.
Saskatoon—Land and Growth Control. Shows the effective use of zoning and controlled growth. 56 mins., NFB.
Sir John's Home Town. Narrated by John Diefenbaker. The development of Kingston from its position as capital to 1975. 17 mins., CFI.
Steeltown. A portrait of Hamilton, the Pittsburgh or Birmingham of Canada. 55 mins., NFB.
There Goes the Neighbourhood. Centring on the St. Louis district of downtown Montreal. This film proposes solutions of co-operative ownership and management to the threat of demolition of neighbourhoods. 13 mins., CFDC.
There Is Still Time. Barbara Ward uses Quebec City as an example of the possibilities of living in a still largely unspoiled city, but one which is threatened by pollution, land speculation, and unplanned growth. 26 mins., NFB.
Ville-Marie. A study of early Montreal and of what survives of Ville-Marie in the Montreal of today. 27 mins., NFB.
Warsaw/Quebec. By using two historically preserved cities, this film asks whether it is possible to provide modern amenities without destroying the past. 56 mins., NFB.

2. *Slides*

The following is a select list of slide sets available for purchase from the National Film Board. In all cases the sets contain ten slides. *Canadian Cities: Part 1; Canadian Cities: Part 2; Montreal: Part 1; Montreal: Part 2; Montreal: Part 3; Toronto: Cultural Aspects; Toronto: The Harbour; Toronto: Physical Features; Old Montreal: Part 1; Old Montreal: Part 2; Old Victoria; History of Canada in Maps: Urban Development.* The NFB *Media Catalogue* also lists a number of other audio-visual aids for urban studies, including filmstrips, 8 mm film loops, media kits, and overhead projectuals. The catalogue is available, free of charge, from the NFB.

3. *Canada's Visual History Series*

Canada's Visual History series is a co-operative venture of the National Film Board and the National Museum of Man (National Museums Canada). This on-going project is designed to meet two specific needs. First, it provides the teacher with the most recent research on a variety of topics relating to the social and economic history of Canada, combining these insights with many rare illustrations gleaned from collections not readily accessible to teachers and students. Second, it presents this information in a dramatic format, carrying the student back in time with all the impact that the camera provides.

Each volume of *Canada's Visual History* comprises 30 slides (both colour and black and white) and a comprehensive bilingual manual. The manuals include background essays, a discussion of the significance of each slide, a recommended reading list and suggested extension activities.

Volumes in the series can be ordered from:

> McIntyre Educational Media Ltd.
> 30 Kelfield Street
> Rexdale, Ontario M9W 9Z9

The following is a list of volumes dealing with urban topics that are available: Alan F. J. Artibise, *Winnipeg: The Growth of a City, 1874-1914;* Terry Copp, *Poverty in Montreal, 1897-1929;* J. M. S. Careless, *Urban Development in Central Canada to 1850;* Norbert MacDonald, *Vancouver's Early Development;* Gregory and Linda Kealey, *Poverty and the Working Class in Toronto;* John Taylor, *Cities in Crisis: The Great Depression;* David Sutherland, *Halifax, 1749-1849: Garrison into Metropolis;* Jean Morrison, *Thunder Bay: Gateway between East and West;* Paul-André Linteau and Jean-Claude Robert, *Pre-Industrial Montreal, 1760-1850;* Frederick H. Armstrong and Daniel J. Brock, *London, Ontario: A Case Study in Metropolitan Evolution.*

4. Urban Profile Slide Series

This series is produced by and available from:

> Canadian Association of Geographers
> Burnside Hall
> McGill University
> 805 Sherbrooke Street
> Montreal, Quebec H3A 2K6

Each "kit" contains 20 slides and a booklet with descriptions of the slides and a short essay. This is an on-going series and the following list contains only those sets now available. Sets on Ottawa, Regina, and Victoria are in preparation. *Montreal—Transport Centre; Hamilton—Steel City; Halifax—Changing Waterfront Uses; Toronto—A Complex Metropolis; Winnipeg—A Prairie Transport Centre; Thunder Bay—City in the Middle; Calgary—Planned Growth and Change; Central Toronto—Diversity in the Downtown Area; Sherbrooke—Regional Centre; St. John's—The Fragile Inner City; Vancouver—Urban Diversity.*

5. *Audiotapes*

The following is a select list of audiotapes available from:

    C.B.C. Learning Systems Publications
    P.O. Box 500
    Toronto, Ontario M5N 1E6

Can the Urb Be Planned Anew? An interview with town planning authority Hans Blumenfeld about the extent to which planning can be effective in developing cities. 30 mins.

Cities—Designing Environments. A six-part series prepared by the Institute of Design at the University of Waterloo in which members of various disciplines discuss functions and theories of urban planning, design philosophy, and related topics. 30 mins. each.

Decisions in the Big City. A discussion on the nature of decision-making, with material drawn from Toronto, Montreal, and Winnipeg. 60 mins.

Ideology and Utopia. Hans Blumenfeld contrasts Western and Marxist approaches to city planning. 30 mins.

Mental and Physical Pollution of the Contemporary Canadian City. Daniel Cappon, psychiatrist, and Leon Kumore, urban consultant, discuss the impact of highrise and high-density living on mental well-being. 30 mins.

New Towns. Jane Jacobs and others at the Stratford seminar on urban design in 1969. 30 mins.

Pollution in the City. Jane Jacobs and others discuss air, water, and noise pollution and their economic costs. 30 mins.

Transportation in Theory. Interview with Hans Blumenfeld on transportation strategies in some of the world's large cities. 30 mins.

The Urb is Orbing. Discussion between Canadian and commonwealth participants on city life, present and future. 60 mins.

What is a City? A discussion among several urban planners in Montreal. 30 mins.

VIII. OTHER RESOURCES

There are a wide variety of organizations, institutes, series publications, and programmes devoted either entirely or partially to some aspect of Canadian urban studies. The following list is designed to indicate the wide range of such resources; it is not a complete listing. More detailed information on the on-going activities of organizations, and data on series publications, can best be obtained from the newsletters and journals listed in Section II above.

1. *Urban Profiles Series*

In 1973 the Ministry of State for Urban Affairs provided a research grant to a group from the Université du Québec à Montréal for a factual study of ten Canadian urban regions. The ten regions were chosen on the basis of 1971 census data. The common thread to the governing of these ten centres is the presence of some two-tier form of government, ranging from the urban community model in Montreal and Quebec, to the regional planning commissions of Alberta, to the regional government system introduced in Ontario over the past few years.

Publication of the *Profiles* was prompted by the enthusiasm and recommendations of those local elected and administrative officials who assisted the research team as well as by the recognized need to make municipal information more generally available. The series was published between November 1974 and July 1975.

The ten volumes published in the *Profiles* series are in the bibliography and cover the following cities: Halifax-Dartmouth, Québec, Montréal, Ottawa-Hull, Toronto, Hamilton-Wentworth, Winnipeg, Calgary, Edmonton, and Vancouver. All were compiled by a team consisting of André Bernard, Jacques Léveillé, and Guy Lord. All titles are available in English and French editions.

2. *Urban Prospects Series*

The *Urban Prospects* series, published by Macmillan of Canada for the former Ministry of State for Urban Affairs, was intended to provoke discussions and debate on important urban issues. As the name implies, the series focused primarily on current issues facing Canadian urban society, and the volumes were prospective, concerned with the future rather than the past. The goal of the series was to provide an opportunity for authors to present their views on the wide range of urban issues of concern to decision makers and policy planners in Canadian government.

The series contains twelve volumes which were published in separate French and English editions.

Jackson, C. I., ed. *Canadian Settlements—Perspectives* (1975; 126 pp.).
Burke, C. D. *The Parasites Outnumber the Hosts: A Review of Some Economic Trends and Their Impact on Public Policy for Urban, Regional and National Economic Development* (1975; 48 pp.).
Coleman, A. *Canadian Settlement and Environmental Planning* (1976; 64 pp.).
Burke, C. D., and Ireland, D. J. *An Urban/Economic Development Strategy for the Atlantic Region* (1976; 92 pp.).
Coopersmith, P., and Hall, R. C. *Heritage by Design* (1976; 51 pp.).
Nelson, R. F. W. *The Illusions of Urban Man* (1976; 76 pp.).
Lash, H. *Planning in a Human Way: Personal Reflections on the Regional Planning Experience in Greater Vancouver* (1976; 96 pp.).
Hamilson, S., and Maffini, G. *The Superior Oracle* (1976; 56 pp.).
Burke, C. J., and Ireland, D. J. *Holding the Line: A Strategy for Canadian Development* (1976; 80 pp.).
Rawson, M. *Ill Fares the Land: Land-Use Management at the Urban/Rural Resource Edges: The British Columbia Land Commission* (1976; 45 pp.).

Kettle, J. *Hindsight on the Future* (1976; 91 pp.).

Thompson, R. *People Do It All the Time: How Community-Based Enterprises across Canada Are Successfully Meeting the Needs of Their Communities* (1976; 80 pp.).

3. *Urban Studies Series*

Clarke, Irwin and Company has published three volumes and a teacher's guide in this series. The published volumes are:

Baine, R. P., and McMurray, A. L. *Toronto: An Urban Study* (1970; 126 pp., maps, illustrations).

Harvey, E. Roy. *Sydney, Nova Scotia: An Urban Study* (1971; 94 pp., maps, illustrations).

Baine, R. P. *Calgary: An Urban Study* (1973; 128 pp., maps, illustrations).

Baine, R. P.; McMurray, A. L.; and Harvey, E. Roy. *Urban Studies Series Teacher's Guide* (1974; 41 pp.).

According to the general editor of the series, Richard P. Baine, the format followed by these urban studies is a "a major departure from the format of a standard textbook." Designed for intensive use in urban studies courses, the volumes are compilations of selected material in the form of photographs, maps, charts, diagrams, and statistics. There is little expository writing.

4. *Parks Canada Reports*

Historians should be aware that the research reports of the historians, architectural historians, and archeologists who work for Parks Canada are available to the public in three separate formats. Two of these, *Canadian Historic Sites: Occasional Papers in Archaeology and History/Lieux historiques canadiens: cahiers d'archéologie et d'histoire* and *History and Archaeology/Histoire et Archéologie*, are publications containing one or more reports. These are sold by the Department of Supply and Services and by some bookstores. They are also on deposit in the National Library and in the Public Archives Library.

Less well known is the third source of Parks Canada reports, the Manuscript Report Series/Travail inédit (MRS). This collection of printed, unedited reports contained 259 volumes by the end of 1978. The subjects of the reports reflect the full range of Parks Canada's historic site activities, which are as diverse as the following titles suggest: *The Development of Edmonton and Its Buildings to 1914; Fouilles archéologiques d'un bloc domestique aux Forges du Saint-Maurice en 1974 (25G51); A History of the Structure and Use of Province House, Prince Edward Island 1837-1977; Grubstake to Grocery Store: The Klondike Emporium, 1897-1907.*

Content is based on excavation reports and on primary and secondary material obtained from private individuals and from a wide variety of private and public institutions in Canada, the United States, Britain, and France. The scope of the project determines both the size of the report and the depth of analysis required.

MRS is not a publication, and therefore it is not available from Parks Canada or the Department of Supply and Services. Copies are deposited for the use of the public with the National Library and the Public Archives of Canada. The latter repository places copies in its own Public Records Division and in the Public Archives Library and distributes one copy of each volume to each of the provincial and territorial archives. Any restriction on the use of this material is imposed by the repository in question. MRS is covered by Canadian copyright laws, and Parks Canada asks that normal scholarly acknowledgement be observed.

Researchers can become familiar with the MRS title listing by consulting the Public Archives inventory for Record Group 84.

5. *Western Geographical Series*

Published by the Department of Geography of the University of Victoria, this series has produced several volumes of interest to urban specialists and has plans for others. Published volumes include:

Forward, C. N., ed. *Residential and Neighbourhood Studies in Victoria* (1973).
Barr, B. M., ed. *Calgary: Metropolitan Structure and Influence* (1975).
Foster, H. D., ed. *Victoria: Physical Environment and Development* (1976).
Smith, P. J., ed. *Edmonton: The Emerging Metropolitan Pattern* (1978).
Evenden, L. J., ed. *Vancouver: Western Metropolis* (1978).
Dale, E. H., ed. *Regina: Regional Isolation and Innovative Development* (1980).

Teachers of urban studies courses might also find C. J. B. Wood, *Handbook of Geographical Games* (Vol. 7) a major asset in the classroom. This volume describes in detail several geographical simulation games, invented by the author, which are designed to give participants a greater understanding of decision-making and its impact on the landscape. The games allow players to take part in pioneer settlement, compete for land in an urban fringe area, design new towns, be involved in the transportation of oil, and determine the location of an airport. Participation in a variety of differing roles allows players to become more keenly aware of the complexities and stresses of decision-making and its role in modifying the landscape.

In addition to volumes devoted entirely to urban themes, several chapters in other volumes in the series contain material of interest to those studying the history, growth, and future prospects of cities. For example, in W. R. D. Sewell and H. D. Foster, eds., *The Geographer and Society* (Vol. 1), there are articles on "Park Awareness and Park Use in Cities"; "The Dimensions of Change in the Central Area of Edmonton"; and "The Future of Cities and the Future of Urban Research."

6. *History of Canadian Cities Series*

In response to a continuing demand for more popular publications, the History Division of the National Museum of Man has undertaken to publish a series of books on Canadian cities under the general editorship of Alan F. J. Artibise, University of Victoria. The purpose of this series is to offer a stimulating insight into Canada's urban past. During the next several years, the Museum plans to publish volumes dealing with such varied communities as Montreal and Vancouver, Chicoutimi and Brandon, London and Sydney. While the series is primarily designed to meet the Museum's commitment to provide informative and attractive publications for the general public, the projected volumes in the series will fill needs at the university and college levels in urban history and urban studies and will also be useful for high school students working on their own community or on urban Canada in general.

To date, three volumes have been published. They are Alan F. J. Artibise, *Winnipeg: An Illustrated History* (1977); M. Foran, *Calgary: An Illustrated History* (1978); and P. E. Roy, *Vancouver: An Illustrated History* (1980). The volumes are co-published by the National Museum of Man and James Lorimer. Other volumes either in press or being prepared include: Toronto (2 vols.), Montreal (2 vols.), Halifax, Saint John, Whitehorse, Quebec, Kitchener, Fredericton, Ottawa, Regina, Charlottetown, Hamilton, Kingston, and Windsor.

7. Facsimiles of Canadian City Plans

The Historical Maps Committee of the Association of Canadian Map Libraries has produced inexpensive facsimiles of early Canadian city plans. They are: Halifax (1750), Quebec City (1777), Toronto (1851 and 1857), Montreal (1859), Ottawa (1874), Vancouver (1902), and Edmonton (1907). All the plans are printed in dark brown ink on durable off-white paper measuring 17 by 22 inches and are suitable for framing as well as for research and classroom use.

The ACML has also reproduced a large number of non-urban maps, and a number of these are of use to urban researchers wishing to study cities in their larger context. These include Smyth's *Map of . . . Upper Canada Describing All the New Settlements . . .* (1813); a detailed topographical map, *Niagara Frontier,* by R. H. Strotherd and others (1865); and Westmacott's map of *Manitoba in 1876 "Shewing the Townships and Settlements."*

In addition to maps already reproduced, individuals or institutions may sponsor the reproduction of a map. The sponsorship fee is $150.00, for which the sponsor receives 100 copies of the print run of 500. The remaining 400 are retained by the ACML for sale to raise funds for the association's activities.

For future information about this programme, possible sponsorship, or bulk orders at reduced rates, contact:

>Serge Sauer
>Chairman, Historical Maps Committee
>c/o Department of Geography
>University of Western Ontario
>London, Ontario N6A 5C2

8. *Urban History Committee of the Canadian Historical Association*

This committee was established in 1971, and since that time it has been actively involved in the organization of urban history sessions for the C.H.A. annual meetings, advising the editors of the *Urban History Review,* and organizing conferences. In May 1977, the committee was involved in the organization of the "Canadian Urban History Conference" which was held at the University of Guelph. A "North American Urban History Conference" is now being planned for Guelph in August 1982.

The Urban History Committee holds two meetings per year open to everyone interested in the historical development of urban Canada. Persons interested in the activities of the committee can obtain more information from the "notes and comments" section of the *Urban History Review.*

9. *Institute of Local Government*
   Queen's University
   99 University Avenue
   Kingston, Ontario K7L 3N6

The Institute of Local Government was established in 1945 as a centre for research, education, and publication on urban local governments. Current and future programmes of the institute focus on the following: (1) development of continuing education for individuals concerned with local government, politics, and administration; (2) development of a continuing programme of research and publication with particular emphasis on an inter-disciplinary approach; (3) participation in programmes of instruction by agreement with any department or faculty which considers an understanding of urban government essential to its requirements; and (4) counselling students interested in a career in urban government and assisting in course selections.

In recent years these broad objectives have been met through such activities as annual week-long seminars for municipal administrators; three-year correspondence courses for municipal officials in Ontario; and seminars for selected groups to deal specifically with urban policy and management issues. The institute has also published a number of occasional papers on specific topics in urban local government, and it publishes *Urban Focus* on a regular basis.

10. *Institute of Urban Studies*
    University of Winnipeg
    515 Portage Avenue
    Winnipeg, Manitoba R3B 2E9

The Institute was established in 1969. It conducts research in a number of areas: policy research in housing and urban affairs, planning in older neighbourhoods, new housing initiatives, performance of the new scheme of local government in Winnipeg, citizen participation, urban growth, senior citizen housing, and social housing management training.

The Institute also supports citizen-based organizations such as the People's Committee for a Better Neighbourhood and Winnipeg Home Improvement Project and encourages local neighbourhood institutions. It has undertaken various contract studies which include evaluation of Winnipeg Meals on Wheels Service and other social service delivery organizations; a study of women's concerns about the quality of life in the city; studies on para-professionalism and the community policing programme; two reports on Winnipeg's core area published in 1975 and 1979; an inner-city housing study; a Winnipeg rental market study; and native studies.

The Institute also organizes community education seminars and provides teaching services for the University of Winnipeg Urban Studies Program. A list of the Institute's programmes and publications is available on request.

11. *Canadian Council on Urban and Regional Research*
    251 Laurier Avenue West
    Ottawa, Ontario K1P 5J6

The Council has three major objectives. They are: (1) to identify gaps in knowledge in urban and regional affairs and encourage research in these areas; (2) to facilitate the flow of research information; and (3) to bring together concerned organizations, administrations, elected officials, and the academic community to identify issues and areas requiring further research.

The Council also publishes the bilingual journal *Urban Forum/Colloque urbain*.

12. *Bureau of Municipal Research*
    2 Toronto Street
    Suite 306
    Toronto, Ontario M5C 2B6

The Bureau's objectives are to inform the public about governmental policy-making, to stimulate public debate, and to provide constructive evaluation of programmes. To this end, it undertakes research in such areas as planning, land use, transportation, urban development, housing, government organization and staffing, taxation, assessment, municipal finance, intergovernmental relations, and environment.

Besides publishing special studies and monographs, the Bureau publishes *Topic,* an occasional newsletter, and *Civic Affairs*. The latter is published about three times per year and provides in-depth analyses of key issues.

13. *Centre for Urban and Community Studies*
    University of Toronto
    150 St. George Street
    Toronto, Ontario M5S 1A1

The Centre, established in 1964, has an active programme of research and publication in the following areas: comparative urban systems; theory and analysis; urban housing markets and public policy; demographic change; recent trends in urban development and economic growth; the implications of declining urban growth rates; the inner city; the physical environment as attraction and determinant; social effects in housing; urban social networks and contact systems; communities and neighborhood change; land-use structure and change; land policy review; children in the city; co-operative housing; and urban data systems. The Centre has published more than twelve books and bibliographies and well over 130 major reports and research papers. A complete list of publications is available on request.

The Centre also has an on-going programme of seminars, lectures, and visiting speakers.

For further information on the Centre, see L. S. Bourne, "The Centre for Urban and Community Studies," *UHR* 2-78 (October 1978):100-104.

14. *The Federation of Canadian Municipalities*
    Suite 1318, Tower B
    Place de Ville
    112 Kent Street
    Ottawa, Ontario K1P 5P2

This federation of approximately 250 municipalities and regional governments and 18 provincial municipal associations is concerned with all areas affecting municipalities, including finance, economics, social planning, transportation and communication, environmental protection, community development, cultural affairs, recreation and leisure. The FCM organizes an annual conference; distributes and exchanges federal reports and information, municipal statistics, and research reports; and co-ordinates and supports research on municipal affairs. The FCM also publishes a monthly information bulletin called *FCM FORUM*.

15. *The Canadian Social History Project*
    Department of History and Philosophy of Education
    The Ontario Institute for Studies in Education
    252 Bloor Street West
    Toronto, Ontario M5S 1V6

The Canadian Social History Project, sometimes referred to as the "Hamilton Project," was a pioneering study in the field of Canadian Social History. It has ceased to function as an active project but continues to exert an influence on Canadian social and urban historians. A large collection of data, stored on computer tapes and microfilm, remains in the Department and can be consulted by researchers by arrangement.

The original goal of the project was the examination of the effects of industrialization, urbanization, and modernization on social life in nineteenth-century Canada, using Hamilton as a case study. Under the direction of its founder, Michael B. Katz, the project began generating a large data base containing complete censuses, assessment rolls, and city directories, as well as various school, marriage, welfare, and newspaper records.

The specific concerns of the project included questions of wealth, occupational structure, family, household, class, life-cycle, age and sex relationships, ethnicity, race, religion, spatial and home-ownership patterns, literacy, schooling, marriage and social mobility.

The general goals of the project were to make contributions (1) to knowledge about nineteenth-century urban society and its relation to education; (2) to important questions in sociology and social theory; (3) to the development and refinement of new techniques in historiography; and (4) to the technology of record linkage in general.

The work of the project can be followed in a series of reports available from OISE. The first four Interim Reports, dating from 1969 to 1973, are available on microfilm. A selection of papers from the modestly circulated Reports No. 5 and 6 is available in: Edward Jackson and Ian Winchester, eds., *Records of the Past: Exploring New Sources in Social History,* Informal Series No. 13, Ontario Institute for Studies in Education (Toronto, 1979).

The project is now under the direction of Ian Winchester and has moved in several new directions. Now it is involved in the study of small towns and rural areas in Ontario. Using the village of Orillia and two rural and culturally diverse eastern Ontario townships as case studies, some of the hypotheses developed about urban Hamilton were tested to see if they were equally suitable for explaining small towns and rural life. One paper which resulted from this study is Chad Gaffield and David Levine, "Dependency and Adolescence on the Canadian Frontier: Orillia, Ontario in the Mid-Nineteenth Century," *History of Education Quarterly 18* (Spring 1978):35-47.

The project was also involved in the area of curriculum assistance and the development of instructional materials. A prototype set of materials, called the "Orillia Kit," was developed which contained resource material selected to illustrate significant aspects of social life in the nineteenth-century Canadian small town.

16. *Research Group on Montreal Society in the Nineteenth Century*
    Groupe de recherche sur la société Montréalaise au 19e siècle
    Departement d'histoire
    Université du Québec à Montréal
    Montréal, Québec H3C 3P8

Founded in 1972, the "Montreal Society Project" has as its objective the study of society in Montreal during the period 1815 to 1914. Among the diverse issues being examined by the research group are: the change from an artisan to an industrial society; the nature of industrial society in the second half of the nineteenth century; the composition of the bourgeoisie, its activities and means of controlling the economy and institutions of the society; and the place of French

Canadians in the spatial and social make-up of Montreal society. Directors of the project are Paul-André Linteau, Jean-Claude Robert, and Jean-Paul Bernard.

A full description of the work of the group can be found in the numerous publications which are available on request.

17. *Toronto Area Archivists Group*

Founded in 1973, TAAG is an association open to all individuals and institutions interested in archives and related fields. The Group holds ten general meetings each year, produces a newsletter, maintains an advisory service on archives-related problems, conducts educational courses, and has a publications programme. Enquiries should be addressed to:

>Mr. Lee Brebner
>TAAG Chairman
>Regional Municipality of Peel Archives
>Brampton, Ontario

Publications:

Guide to Archives in the Toronto Area. First published in 1975, this well-received volume was updated and expanded and republished in 1978. Each entry consists of the name of the repository, date of establishment, address, telephone number, and name of the head of the institution, opening hours, restrictions (if any), facilities, and a summary of the nature and extent of the holdings.

Ontario's Heritage. TAAG has begun a programme of co-ordinating a systematic survey of local records in Ontario which will include not only all existing municipal records, but also the records of local educational, religious, and private organizations. For the purposes of the survey, the province has been divided into 15 regions, and regional survey teams are being recruited. Upon completion, TAAG plans to publish the findings in fifteen volumes under the title *Ontario's Heritage: A Guide to Archival Resources.* Section I of the *Guide* includes entries for all existing municipal structures in the region and a locator index provides researchers with up-to-date information should they wish to contact the municipality directly. To supplement the volume, important local records held by agencies outside the specific region are listed in an appendix. At present two volumes of *Ontario's Heritage* have been published: Volume One (Peterborough Region: Peterborough, Haliburton and Victoria Counties); and Volume Seven (Region of Peel: Regional Municipality of Peel). At least three more volumes are scheduled for 1980, including one volume for Northern Ontario and one for Metropolitan Toronto. For further information see Victor L. Russell, "Municipal Records in Ontario," *UHR* 3-78 (February 1979):122-124.

Author Index

Aass, C., 819
Abra, Marion, 5731
Abraham, Dorothy E. A., 6757
Abrams, Garry William David, 5814, 5815
Abrams, Percy, 3760
Abramson, J. A., 5762
Acheson, T. W., 459, 460, 1098, 1099, 1623, 1707, 1708, 4831, 4832
Acland, J. H., 2945
Adair, Edward Robert, 2439
Adam, Graeme Mercer, 4644, 4687
Adam, Richard, 2484
Adam, Robert D., 6469
Adams, Cleophus, 3302
Adams, Donald Lyall, 5822
Adams, J. Gordon, 1548, 1768, 1769
Adams, John Q., 6917, 6456
Adams, John S., 789
Adams, Robert M., 3855
Adams, Thomas, 95, 481, 482, 483, 484, 485, 486, 487, 488, 489, 490, 491, 492, 493, 494, 495, 496, 497, 498, 635, 714, 715, 716, 717, 718, 719, 720, 721, 722, 723, 724, 790, 833, 1391, 1917, 2560, 3295, 3394, 4234, 4501, 5280, 6618
Adamson, Anthony, 549, 662, 3535, 5007
Adler, G. M., 3395
Adshead, S. D., 499
Agnew, Nelson Glenn, 5281
Agocs, Carol, 403
Aikens, J. R., 4887
Aikins, T., 1220
Aitchison, J. H., 931, 3396, 3397
Aitken, Barbara B., 3398
Aitken, Hugh G., 223
Aitken, R. M., 1519
Akian, Gail G., 445
Akpara, E. E., 5008
Akrigg, G. Philip V., 6322
Akrigg, Helen B., 6322, 6849
Ala, L. G., 6850
Alberta Royal Commission on the Metropolitan Development of Calgary and Edmonton, 6094, 6208
Alcorn, Richard S., 1918
Alderman, Tom, 7042
Alexander, David, 1520, 1521, 1770, 1771
Alexander, J. D., 5009
Alford, M. E., 7043

Allaire, Emilia-B., 3084
Allan, D. D., 5343
Allen, Edwin G., 1549
Allen, Martha I. G., 4564
Allison, D., 1100
Allston, J. T., 1772, 1835
Allyn, Nathaniel Constantine, 404
Alman, Albert, 1433, 1434
Alty, S. W., 5763
Ambrose, Peter J., 461
Amery, A. D., 4362
Ames, Herbert Brown, 932, 933, 2561
Amy, W. Lacey, 1836
Amyot, John A., 4888
Anderson, Allan J., 3890
Anderson, Amos McIntyre, 1599
Anderson, B., 3033
Anderson, B. L., 1
Anderson, Barrie James, 5953
Anderson, C. E., and Co., 3399
Anderson, F. W., 5823
Anderson, Frank, 6095
Anderson, G. W., 5887
Anderson, George, 857
Anderson, Grace, 5010
Anderson, Grant, 500
Anderson, H. G., 4645
Anderson, I. B., 350
Anderson, Ian Douglas, 6323
Anderson, J., 5954
Anderson, J. C., 5481
Anderson, James, 6209
Anderson, James D., 897, 898, 925, 5243
Anderson, Nels, 1551
Anderson, Robert, 407
Anderson, R. N., 5887
Anderson, Ross Cardwell, 2946
Anderson, W. J., 89
Andras, Robert, 934
Andres, James M., 993
Andress, D. D., 4176
Andrew, Caroline, 2185, 2228
Andrew, F. W., 6851
Andrews, A., 1552, 1709
Andrews, Craig, 6852
Andrews, Garry Ray, 5808
Andrews, Gwenyth, 1341
Andrews, Margaret W., 6619, 6620, 6621
Angers, Bernard, 858

Angers, Lorenzo, 2141, 2142
Angers, Majella, 1919
Angrave, John, 4835
Angus, A. D., 2947
Angus, Fred F., 1624
Angus, Margaret, 3891, 3892, 3972, 3973, 3974, 3975
Annan, Ernest, 4363
Antoft, Kell, 1141
Appana, M., 5345
Appelbe, Frank, 6470
Appleton, John, 5346
Apps, M. J., 6853
Arathoon, D., 5282
Arber, Ross D., 3976
Archer, D. B., 5011
Archer, H., 313
Archer, John Hall, 5888, 5889
Archibald, B., 1101
Archibald, Stephen, 1222
Arès, Richard, 2660, 2661
Argaez, G., 1553
Armitage, Andrew, 5283
Armond, Y., 4236
Armstead, L. D., 6678
Armstrong, Alan H., 501, 834
Armstrong, C. L., 6758
Armstrong, Christopher, 967, 1392, 4889
Armstrong, Frederick H., 97, 98, 3400, 3611, 3806, 4099, 4100, 4135, 4136, 4836, 4837, 4838, 4839, 4840, 4841, 4842, 4843, 4844, 4845, 4890
Armstrong, G. H., 3401
Armstrong, G. M., 4502
Armstrong, Graham T., 6918
Armstrong, H. J., 5347
Armytage, W. H. G., 502
Arnell, J. C., 1102
Arnold, A. J., 5570
Arnold, B. J., 4891
Arora, Ved P., 5764
Arsenault, Bona, 1435
Arthur, Elizabeth, 4613, 4614, 4615
Arthur, Eric, 4646, 4646A
Artibise, Alan F. J., 2, 29, 84, 85, 99, 180, 345, 346, 503, 5348, 5349, 5350, 5351, 5352, 5482, 5483, 5484, 5485, 5486, 5487, 5488, 5571, 5572, 5573, 5574, 5575, 5576, 5577, 5578, 5579, 6410, 6759
Asante, Nadine, 6854
Ashlee, Ted, 6471
Ashley, S. M., 4892
Ashton, Patrick, 636
Ashworth, E. M., 4647
Askin, W. R., 6179
Asling, S. E., 3761
Assaly, L. C. W., 4177

Asselin, Maurice, 3296
Association des guides historiques de Québec, 2948
Association of Canadian Archivists, 3
Astles, A. R., 664, 6473
Atcheson, James W., 5765
Atherton, William Henry, 1057, 2229, 2230
Atkinson, Reginald Noel, 6448
Atlantic Development Board, 1103
Atwal, A. S., 5012
Atwell, P. H., 6096
Aubin, Henry, 637, 2231
Aubin, V. P., 2186
Aubry, Pierre, 3231
Auclair, Elie-J., 2232, 2232A, 2233, 2234, 3226, 5938
Aucoin, P. C., 1430
Audet, Francis J., 2485, 3085, 3307, 4236, 4310
Audet, Louis-Philippe, 3035, 3036
Audet, Lucille, 2662
Audet, P. H., 2486
Augustine, H. A., 4503
Auyang, Antonio C., 2663
Avent, R. H., 5489
Avery, Donald, 5580
Axworthy, Lloyd, 30, 899, 5645, 5646, 5647
Axworthy, T., 5648
Aylsworth, J. A., 6324
Azard-Malaurie, Marie Madeleine, 2949
Azcks, Steven M., 5061

Babcock, Douglas R., 6180
Babcock, Robert H., 1625
Bachand, Benoît, 3249
Bacon, E. N., 665
Baehre, R. K. F., 4137
Bagley, R., 6293
Baglole, Harry, 1735, 1736
Bailey, Alfred G., 1105
Bailey, P., 6352
Bailey, Thomas M., 3762
Baillargeon, Georges, 2235
Baillargeon, H.-P., 2236
Baillargeon, Noël, 3037, 3038
Baillie, Murray, 1393
Bailly, A. S., 3152
Bain, D., 7007
Bain, Ian, 3401A
Baine, R. P., 4565, 4648, 5999
Baines, James, 3893
Bains, Yashdip Singh, 1342, 1343, 4846
Baird, Bonnie, 791
Baird, Francis, 1576
Baird, George, 4649
Baird, K. A., 4040

Baker, Alan Maurice, 1939, 3419, 6285
Baker, H. R., 1058
Baker, J., 505
Baker, John F., 1106
Baker, Melvin, 1837, 1838
Baker, Ralph C., 5490
Balakrishnan, T. R., 380, 409
Balcer, Georges, 3308
Balciumas, T., 3402
Baldwin, Douglas, 3362, 3363, 3364, 3365, 3366
Baldwin, M., 100
Baldwin, W. W., 6988
Balf, Mary, 6411, 6412
Balf, R., 6413
Balharrie, Watson, 4364
Balikci, Asen, 6919
Ball, B. K., 6680
Ball, Jean, 1839
Ball, N. R., 3403
Ballahan, Maurice Bernard, 1921
Ballantyne, C. C., 2562
Bammen, Haley P., 4893
Bancroft, Clifford, 6325
Banfield, E. C., 587
Banks, Margaret A., 4894
Banks, W. J., 4365
Bannerman, Gary W., 6474
Bannister, J. A., 3404
Bannon, Michael Joseph, 6210, 6256
Barbeau, Marius, 2950, 2951
Barbeau, Victor, 2237, 2238
Barber, Clarence E., 994
Barber, Clarence Lyle, 5890
Barber, G. M., 9122, 3405
Barber, Irene Teresa, 6760
Barbour, Cameron Robert, 5824
Barcelo, Michel, 351, 2664
Barclay, Harold, 6294, 6295
Barclay, Herbert Richmond, 6475
Barford, Jerome C., 6476
Barger, Walter K., 7044, 7045
Baril, Evelyn, 5397, 5632
Barker, G. M., 798
Barker, Kent, 5284
Barker, Mary L., 6477
Barlee, N. L., 6326, 6855
Barlow, Alfred E., 4566
Barnes, Michael, 4031, 4032
Barnett, A. N., 4567
Barnett, Robert F. J., 4015
Barovick, B. M., 1142
Barr, B. M., 6097, 6098, 6119, 6226
Barr, Elinor, 5285
Barrett, F. A., 5013
Barrett, John, 6622
Barron, F. L., 3406

Barrow, G. T., 5359, 5649, 5825, 6211
Barss, Peter, 1529
Barthe, J.-B.-M., 3309
Bartholomew, H., 6681
Bartholomew, Harland, 638
Bartle, T. F., 4528
Basevi, Vincent, 859
Basi, R. S., 6478
Baskerville, Peter, 3677
Baskett, Harold Kenneth, 6099
Bassett, John M., 1223
Bater, James H., 3625
Bates, Gordon, 1059
Bates, Hilary, 3407
Batey, W. L., 6137
Bator, Paul A., 4895, 4896
Battelle Memorial Institute, 4568
Baureiss, G. A., 6000, 6001, 6002
Bawtinheimer, R., 3708
Baxter, David, 31
Baxter, J. Russell, 6420
Baxter, R. S., 5650
Bayley, C. M., 2665
Bazin, Jules, 2487
Beach, Noel, 4569
Bean, Gordon A., 4650
Beasley, N., 4610
Beaton, Wallace, 764
Beattie, Kim, 1829
Beattie, R. N., 3408
Beattie, Roderick Norman, 6327
Beatty, J. David, 4651
Beauchamp, Pierre, 1965
Beaudet, Colette, 3153
Beaudet, L., 3039
Beaudin, François, 2239, 2488, 2952
Beaudoin, Marie-Louise, 2440
Beaudry, Françoise, 3232
Beaudry, G., 2666
Beaudry, René, 3040
Beaudry, Yvon, 3280
Beaulieu, André, 1923, 1924, 1925, 1926
Beaulieu, Claude, 2240, 2667
Beauregard, Ludger, 2217, 2241, 2242, 2243, 2668, 2877, 3233, 3250, 3281, 3310
Beauregard, Robert A., 835
Bechard, Auguste, 3041
Beck, C. W., 1486
Beck, M. J., 1143, 1144
Becker, J. Richard, 1751
Bédard, Robert-J., 1927, 3409
Bédard, Roland, 2982, 3154
Bedford, Elaine, 6138
Beecroft, Eric, 860, 936, 937, 938
Beedle, A., 995
Beer, G. Frank, 506, 725, 3410, 4897, 4898
Beeson, Louis, 4484

Begg, Alexander, 5581
Begg, W. A., 5826
Bégin, Benoît-J., 3251, 3311
Bélanger, B., 3342
Bélanger, Claude, 2669
Bélanger, Gérard, 996
Bélanger, Joseph, 3343
Bélanger, Léonidas, 2129
Bélanger, Marcel, 1928, 1954, 2244, 2670
Bélanger, Noël, 2671
Bélanger, R., 2672
Bélanger, René, 2143
Belbeck, Alice, 5934
Belbeck, Dave, 5934
Belcher, Jonathan, 1145
Belden, H., 4551
Belding, A. M., 1626
Belhumeur, David, 3234
Belkin, Simon, 410
Bell, Ann, 6457
Bell, David Seymour, 6458
Bell, F. H., 1146, 1224
Bell, Fannie C., 1711
Bell, Geoffrey, 1578
Bell, J. Jones, 2489, 3894
Bell, M. J., 5466
Bell, Margaret, 4899
Bell, Robert, 4570
Bell, W. J., 3709
Bellan, R. C., 32, 5492, 5493, 5582, 5583
Bellemare, J.-E., 3344
Belliveau, Hector, 1579
Belliveau, John E., 1600
Bellman, David, 2245
Bellows, G., 1840
Belton, G. S., 5473
Bender, I. C., 5286
Bender, Thomas, 101
Benevelo, L., 507
Benham, M. L., 5535
Benjamin, J., 2673
Bennet, Martin L., 6623
Bennett, Edward H., 4330
Bennett, Gordon, 6920
Bennett, M. B., 3763
Benoist, Emile, 3204
Bensley, Edward Horton, 2246, 2490
Bentick, Brian Leslie, 6761
Berchem, F. R., 4847
Bercuson, David J., 5584, 5614
Bergeron, Arthur, 3345
Bergeron, Cécile, 3312
Bergeron, Michel, 2149
Bergevin, B.-M., 1919
Bergevin, J. C., 3346
Berku, Dida, 2674
Berman, Alf, 2675

Bernard, A., 1394, 2676, 3155, 3857, 4366, 5014, 5651, 6100, 6212, 6682
Bernard, Jean-Paul, 2491
Bernier, Jacques, 2563, 2564, 3086, 3087
Bernier, Jean, 2247
Bernier, Paul-Etienne, 3156
Bernier, Réal, 3205
Berry, Brian J. L., 102
Berry, David B., 997
Berton, Pierre, 7046
Bertram, G. W., 224, 227
Bertrand, Camille, 2248, 2441
Bertrand, Jean-Pierre, 1930
Bérubé, A.-E., 2186
Best, J. Linden, 1225, 1395
Bethune, William C., 6922
Betke, Carl F., 5955, 6181, 6213
Bettison, David G., 900, 5956
Betts, George Michael, 970, 3977, 6214
Bezaire, P. J., 5243
Bezanson, T., 4367
Bhajan, Edward R., 5296
Biays, P., 3347
Bibby, R. W., 6101
Bice, C., 4101
Bickel, Ralph Paul, 5652
Biernacki, C. M., 726
Biggar, C. R. W., 4311
Bilodeau, B., 2187
Bilsland, William W., 6856, 6857, 6858
Bilson, Geoffrey, 1226, 1627
Bindon, Katryn M., 3978
Binford, Henry C., 103
Binns, M. A., 4178
Binns, Richard M., 2565
Birchall, G., 3779
Bird, J. Brian, 1107
Bird, R. M., 998
Bird, T. M., 3806A
Bird, Will R., 1204
Birkett, Patricia, 1147
Biron, Robert, 2173
Bishop, Olga B., 3412
Bissell, Claude T., 4652
Bissley, Paul L., 6479, 6762
Bisson, Margaret M., 2566
Bjonback, Ralph Derek, 6683
Black, A., 861
Black, J. A., 6414
Black, J. M., 7029
Blackburn, Clyde, 4368
Blackmer, Hugh A., 1208
Blackmore, Laura, 1901
Bladen, V. W., 6924
Blaine, W. E., 3807
Blair, Gladys, 4368
Blair, J. W., 4653, 5015

Blais, André, 2185
Blais, Gérald, 4571
Blaise, P., 3260
Blake, H. W., 5494, 5495
Blakeley, Phyllis R., 1148, 1227, 1228, 1344, 1397, 1398
Blanchard, Raoul, 2249, 2677, 2678, 2679, 2953, 3313
Blanchette-Lessard, Lucie, 2492
Bland, John, 508, 509, 2250, 2251, 2954, 6684
Bland, Warren R., 3413, 3414, 3415
Bleasdale, Ruth E., 3416, 5287
Blishen, Bernard R., 2680
Bliss, Michael, 4436
Bloomfield, Elizabeth, 4041
Bloomfield-Schachter, E., 2816
Blouin, A., 2681
Blower, James, 6182, 6183
Bloxom, William R., 5653
Blue, Charles S., 4311
Blumenfeld, Hans, 33, 282, 510, 639, 939, 4369, 5016
Bo, Lao, 4654
Boal, F. W., 6102
Bock, J., 5732
Bockus, Elton C., 3417
Boddy, Trevor, 5353
Boeckh, John L., 4437
Bogue, Margaret B., 3418
Bohi, Charles W., 5766, 5767
Boissevain, Jeremy, 2682
Boisvert, Jean-Jacques, 3252
Boisvert, Michel, 252
Boland, Edgar J., 4438
Bolduc, Roch, 940
Bolduc, Roger, 3348
Bolger, Francis W. P., 1737
Bollens, J. C., 34
Bolton, Robert J., 4439
Bond, Courtney Claude Joseph, 1449, 4237, 4238, 4239, 4240, 4312, 4331, 7047
Bone, R. M., 6925
Bonenfant, Jean-Charles, 1923, 3314
Bonis, Robert R., 4655
Bonnett, P. A., 792
Bonnier, L., 1932
Bonnycastle, R. H. G., 5654
Bonnycastle, Richard, 1773
Booth, Michael R., 6859
Booth, P. J., 793
Boothroyd, P. D., 1487
Borah, Woodrow, 35, 511
Bordeleau, B., 2188
Bordessa, Ronald, 5017
Borg, R., 4440
Borgfjord, M. R., 794

Borins, Sandford F., 5018
Borobé, P.-H., 4313
Borrett, William C., 1229, 1230
Borthwick, John Douglas, 2252, 2253, 2254
Bosher, John F., 3042
Bosquet, Jean-Claude, 4391
Bossen, M., 5655
Bosworth, N., 2493
Botsford, David P., 5244
Botting, P. J., 6860
Bottomley, John, 6480
Bouchard, Diana, 2683
Bouchard, Gaetan, 1933
Bouchard, Gérard, 2144, 2145, 2146, 2147, 2148, 2149
Bouchard, Louis-Marie, 2150, 2151, 2152
Boucher, Neil, 1530
Boucher, Réal, 3235
Bouchette, Joseph, 1935
Boudreault, M., 1936
Bougie, M., 2684
Boulet, J. A., 2936
Boulkind, Mabel, 2685
Boult, Jean-Claude, 2189
Boultbee, Horace, 4900
Bourassa, Guy, 941, 1937, 2255, 2687, 2688, 2689, 2690
Bourdon, Jean, 1938
Bourdon, Joseph-Pierre, 2256
Bourget, M., 3349
Bourguignon, J.-C., 2257, 2691
Bourinot, J. G., 862
Bourne, L. S., 192, 253, 254, 352, 640, 726, 795, 796, 797, 798, 836, 1939, 1940, 1996, 3419, 3481, 4788, 5019, 5020, 5021, 5022, 5023, 5024, 7030, 7031
Bourns, Brian, 4241
Boutet, Edgar, 2190
Boutilier, Helen R., 6624
Boutwell, W. D., 2955
Bouvier, Emile, 4572
Bovey, John A., 6926
Bowden, Martyn J., 799, 800
Bowdler, M. C., 6927
Bower, Peter John, 1436
Bower, R., 6481
Bowker, Alan, 4901
Bowland, James G., 999
Bowles, Roy T., 462, 463
Bowman, P., 6459
Bowsfield, H., 104
Boxer, A. J., 7029
Boyaner, Eli, 1628
Boyce, Gerald E., 3641
Boyer, Robert J., 5288
Boyle, David, 4656
Boyle, H., 7008

Boyle, John, 4103
Boyle, Terry, 3420
Boylen, J. C., 4657
Bradbury, Bettina, 2567, 6685
Bradbury, John H., 314, 6328, 6329, 6330, 6331, 6332
Braddock, John, 1629
Braden, Thomas B., 6042
Bradino, D., 3858
Bradley, W. H., 4242
Bradley, W. S., 5496
Bradshaw, Brian, 3710
Bradshaw, T., 3421
Braithwaite, Max, 4658
Brandon, K. F., 3422
Brandt, Gail Cuthbert, 4573, 4574
Brann, Esther, 3157
Brault, Lucien, 2191, 2192, 2568, 4243, 4244, 4245, 4246
Brazeau, Joseph, 2692, 2693
Brazer, Harvey E., 1000
Brebner, J., 4659
Bredimas-Assimopoulos, Nadia, 2694
Bredin, Pearl E., 7032
Breen, David H., 5957, 6103
Breithaupt, W. H., 4042
Brekke, D. T., 7009
Bremner, A., 4102
Bremner, Benjamin, 1752
Brennan, J. William, 5809, 5827, 5828
Brennan, Patrick H., 5829
Brenton, G. W., 1108
Breton, Raymond, 411, 445
Brevis, I. N., 193
Brewster, Winfield, 3654
Bridger, M. K., 2695, 2696
Bridle, Augustus, 727, 4332
Brien, G., 1941
Briere, J., 3252A
Brierly, J. S., 4558
Brink, A. W., 3764
Bristol, Samuel, 6279
Brittain, Horace L., 863, 864, 6686
Britton, John N. H., 225, 1922, 3405
Broadbridge, Arthur Frederick, 5939
Broadfoot, Barry, 6482
Brochu, M., 1942
Brock, Daniel J., 4099, 4136, 4138
Brock, R. W., 3859
Brodeur, Serge, 2182
Brodie, Steve, 6687
Brody, Hugh, 446
Brody, P. E. H., 5025
Bromley, John F., 5026, 5027
Bronson, H. L., 1399
Brookes, Alan A., 1109, 1554
Brooks, F. G. H., 6625
Brooks, G. W. S., 6764

Brougham, W. F., 6861
Brouillard, Pierre, 2258, 2569
Brouillette, Benoît, 1943, 2154, 2259, 2260, 2261, 2262, 2697, 3350, 4575, 6483
Brouillette, Normand, 3253
Brousseau, Jean D., 3222
Brousseau, Margo, 1944
Brown, C. A. B., 1060
Brown, Clement, 2956
Brown, D. M., 1531
Brown, E. J., 5462
Brown, Edward C., 6297
Brown, G. W., 5441
Brown, George Stanley, 1522
Brown, Graham, 381
Brown, Howard C., 1902, 1903
Brown, I. D., 3764
Brown, J. N. Elliott, 6928
Brown, John A., 6484
Brown, L. Carson, 3667, 3668, 3690, 4033, 4638, 5289
Brown, Lewis, 5290
Brown, Marian, 6759
Brown, Philip, 802, 5028
Brown, R. A., 105
Brown, Robert F., 3646
Brown, Robert Stewart, 4474
Brown, Roger David, 1481
Brown, Roger James, 2193
Brown, Ron, 3423
Brown, Sheila A., 6215
Brown, T. O., 5733
Brown, W. M., 1231
Brown, W. Russell, 4616
Brown, Wallace, 1110
Brown, Wilfrid Harold, 2698
Brozowski, Roman, 412, 3424
Bruce, H. A., 5029
Bruce, J., 4902
Bruce, Jean, 6929
Bruchési, Jean, 2263, 2957
Bruchési, L. P. N., 2570
Bruneau, A. A., 3282
Brunet, Michel, 3088
Brunger, Alan G., 4139, 4441
Brunnelle-Lavoie, L., 3261
Brunton, S., 4433
Bryan, Claude G., 3072
Bryan, Nancy, 283
Bryant, R. W. G., 641
Bryce, M. S., 5586
Bryce, Peter H., 413, 414, 415, 416, 728
Brydon, Dianne, 4442
Bryfogle, R. C., 4, 5, 36
Brym, Robert J., 1111
Buck, Frank E., 512
Buck, W. P., 194
Buckland, Frank M., 5862

Buckley, Alfred, 513, 514, 3262, 6485
Buckley, K. A. H., 729, 5891
Bucksar, Richard G., 4639, 6930, 7010, 7011
Budden, Sandra, 5030
Buduban, Cleto M., 5656
Buggey, Susan, 666, 1232
Buies, Arthur, 3126
Bunge, John Christian, 837
Bunting, T. E., 5031
Burant, James K. P., 1346, 1347
Burchard, J., 133
Burdett, Gillian M., 2699
Bureau of Municipal Research, 5032, 5033
Burg, A., 6989
Burgess, Joanne, 2571, 2572
Burghardt, Andrew F., 3758, 3861
Burke, Peter, 106
Burkholder, Mabel, 3765
Burley, David V., 1630
Burley, Kevin, 4140
Burnell, A. E. K., 3425, 3426
Burnes, John Roger, 6626
Burnet, Jean, 6298
Burnett, A. A., 1001
Burnett, Jean Robertson, 3427
Burns, F. H., 6765
Burns, Florence, 4848
Burns, J. E., 1347
Burns, R. J., 4849, 4850
Burns, R. M., 865
Burns, Terrence, 1233
Burpee, Lawrence J., 6299
Burrill, M. F., 2264
Burrows, Susan, 265, 3508
Burry, S., 6184
Burtniak, John, 4521
Burton, C. L., 4660
Burton, Lydia, 5034
Burwash, N., 4661, 4662
Bury, Duncan, 5892
Bush, E. R., 4576
Bush, Edward F., 284, 6990, 6991
Bussard, Lawrence H., 6043, 6044
Bussières, Roger, 1945
Butcher, P. J., 3886
Butcher, Wilfred F., 3158
Butler, A. N., 1400
Butler, George Frederick, 1234
Butler, Peter M., 1112
Byerly, A. E., 3711
Byrne, M. B., 6045
Byrnes, John Maclay, 1841
Byrnes, T. C., 3428

Cadwell, H. M., 6460
Cadieux, Lorenzo, 4577

Cain, Louis P., 6486
Cako, S. C., 5345
Caldarola, Carlo, 6139
Caldwell, H. G., 357
Callahan, W. R., 1830
Callard, K., 866
Callum, C., 1774
Calnan, D. M., 802, 3678
Calnek, William A., 1209
Calvin, Delano D., 3895
Cameron, B., 6185
Cameron, Christina, 3089
Cameron, James Malcolm, 1488, 3712, 3713, 3714
Cameron, John R., 1113
Cameron, Jean, 2700
Cameron, K. D., 942
Campbell, A. C., 5450
Campbell, B. A., 5035
Campbell, Bertha J., 1482, 1483
Campbell, C. T., 4141, 4142, 4143, 4144, 4145
Campbell, D. F., 1149
Campbell, Dorothy, 4663
Campbell, H. A., 4217
Campbell, Isabelle, 5291
Campbell, K., 4903
Campbell, M. F., 3766, 3767, 3768
Campbell, M. J., 3769
Campbell, Mary I., 3896
Campbell, Maurice A., 3429, 4199, 5269
Campbell, Michael G., 6487
Campbell, Roderick Calvin, 1631
Campbell, W. W., 4314
Campeau, Charles-Edouard, 195, 1946, 2265, 2266, 2701, 2702, 2703, 2704
Camu, Pierre, 285, 1947, 1948, 1949, 1950, 2267, 2705, 2706, 3159, 3315, 3430
Canada Commission of Conservation, 37, 3297
Canada Life Assurance Company, 3770
Canadian Chamber of Commerce, 4044
Canadian Council on Urban and Regional Research, 6
Canadian Federation of Mayors and Municipalities, 943, 944, 1002, 1003
Canadian Youth Council, 5036
Cannell, S., 5497
Canniff, W. D., 4504
Cantwell, Eugenie A., 6333
Capital Region Planning Board, 6766
Capling, A. J., 667
Caragianis, Eva M., 1712
Card, Dorothy E., 4664
Careless, J. M. S., 38, 39, 107, 108, 109, 255, 256, 257, 1114, 3431, 4851, 4904, 4905, 5354, 5587, 6767, 6768
Careless, William, 1951
Carle, Claude, 2958

Carlos, Serge, 828
Carlsen, A. E., 6334
Carlson, David, 838
Carlson, W. E., 5734
Carlyle, R., 3897
Carman, A. R., 2573
Carney, B., 839
Carnochan, Janet, 4505, 4506, 4507
Carol, H., 3432
Caron, J. C., 3161
Caron, J. P., 642
Caron, Marie Ange, 3205A
Caron, Roland, 2707
Carpenter, J. H., 6269
Carr, N., 4179
Carre, W. H., 1235
Carrel, Frank, 2959, 2960
Carr-Harris, B., 4247
Carrier, André, 3166
Carrière, Gaston, 2194, 2195, 2214, 4248, 4315, 4316, 4333
Carroll, Harry, 6425
Carry, J. H., 110
Carson, G. W., 1713
Carson, Terry M., 1904
Carswell, R. E., 286, 1004, 1061
Carter, C. N., 3762
Carter, David G., 2268
Carter, David J., 5830, 6003, 6004, 6046
Carter, F. A. G., 6931
Carter, Harold, 111, 112
Carter, J. Smyth, 3771
Carter, T. S., 6216
Carter, Thomas Sydney, 5442
Carter-Edwards, Dennis, 3679, 4906
Carthy, H. E., 4617
Cartwright, D. G., 3433
Carver, Humphrey, 113, 515, 516, 517, 518, 803
Casetti, Emilio, 353
Casey, Teresa, 1634
Casgrain, Henry Raymond, 2961
Cashman, A. W., 6140, 6141, 6142
Cassels, Hamilton, Jr., 4665
Cassels, W. L., 519
Cassidy, H. M., 3434
Cassidy, J., 5647
Castelli, Mireille D., 1952
Castells, Manuel, 40, 114
Castonguay, Charles, 2936
Cauchon, Noulan, 520, 521, 522, 523, 524, 525, 526, 527, 528, 529, 530, 531, 2154, 4371, 4372, 4373, 4374
Caulfield, J., 5037
Cauthers, Janet, 6769
Cave, R. J., 6889
Caviedes, Cesar, 5831

Cazalis, Pierre, 3264
Central Mortgage and Housing Corporation (CMHC), 731
Centre for Settlement Studies, 315
Century Calgary Historical Series, 6005
Cernushi-Salkoff, Serafin, 115
Cestre, Gilbert, 3090
Chabot, Marie-Emmanuel, 3043, 3091
Chadwick, Edward Marion, 3435
Chagon, Claude, 3351, 3352
Chaiko, R. M., 5735
Chamard, L., 3353
Chamberlain, A. D., 4666
Chamberlain, S. B., 730
Chambers, Debra, 3715
Chambers, Edith D., 6863
Chambers, Edward J., 226, 227
Chambers, Ernest J., 2270
Chambers, F. T. D., 3254
Chambers, Jack, 4103
Chambers, Lucy B., 6437
Champagne, F., 3283
Champion, G., 5498
Chan, David W., 2708
Chan, Wah May Minnie, 6217
Chance, Norman A., 6932
Chandler, David B., 3861
Chandonnet, Jean, 2962
Chanette, François, 1005
Chanteloup, R. E., 1551
Chao, M., 6488
Chapman, G. F., 5588, 5589
Chapman, H. D., 4667
Chapman, J. S., 4045
Chappell, C. H., 1006
Charbonneau, C., 3316
Charbonneau, Gaétan, 3160
Charbonneau, Hubert, 2098, 2422, 2709, 2710
Chard, Donald F., 1150, 1437
Charette, François, 1953
Charland, Thomas M., 2492
Charles, E., 382
Charlton, B. E., 3808
Charney, Melvin, 1954, 2711
Charpentier, Alfred, 1955, 2574
Charteris, J. F., 4334
Château, J. P., 1956
Chatters, Carl H., 947, 1011, 1012, 1062
Chaulk, A., 1842
Chausse, Gilles, 2495
Cherrington, John, 6864
Cherry, G. E., 532
Chevalier, Michel, 354
Chevrette, F., 2271
Chiarmonte, Louis J., 1775
Chickekian, Gars, 2712
Chicoine, René, 2378

Chimbos, Peter D., 3436
Chinnery, G. A., 116
Chipperfield, G. H., 945
Chisamore, Dale, 3651
Chisick, Ernest, 5590
Chivers, Batya, 6218
Cho, George C. H., 6489, 6490
Chochla, Mark, 4617A
Choko, Marc Henri, 2272, 2713
Choplin, Robert, 2443
Choquette, C.-P., 3236
Choquette, Fernand, 3264
Choquette, R., 2273
Chouinard, François-Xavier, 3044
Chouinard, H. J. J. B., 2963
Choukrou, Jean-Marc, 354
Chown, W. F., 5038, 5039
Christenson, R. A., 6047, 6186
Christiansen-Ruffman, Linda, 1408
Christie, Howard A., 4668
Christie, R., 3437
Chung, Joseph, 642
Church, Glenn Robert, 5499
Churchill, Dennis Michael, 6688, 6689
Ciccocelli, Joseph, 5040
Cimon, Jean, 383, 1957, 2964, 2965, 3364
Cinq-Mars, Eugène, 2196
Civic Advisory Council of Toronto, 5041
Clack, C., 6770
Clack, Roderick D., 6771
Clairmont, D. H., 1401
Clark, A. B., 5355, 6335
Clark, Andrew H., 1151, 1438, 1738
Clark, C. A., 4907
Clark, Douglas, 840
Clark, John, 141
Clark, K. L., 4559
Clark, L. H., 4908
Clark, L. J., 4909
Clark, Louisa, 3701
Clark, R. M., 1007, 1008
Clark, Robert, 3647
Clark, Ron, 533
Clark, S. D., 41, 355, 384, 385, 417, 804, 1115, 1958, 5356, 6336, 6337, 6933, 6934, 6992
Clark, W. Harold, 356
Clark, W. L. R., 5443
Clarke, B. Frank, 4104
Clarke, Charles, 4669
Clarke, John, 3438, 3439
Clarke, R. S., 5832
Clarkson, Marion E., 5293
Clarkson, Stephen, 5042, 5043
Clatworthy, S. J., 732
Clawson, Marion, 567
Clayton, F. A., 1009

Clements, Montagu, 5833
Clemson, Donovan, 6415
Cleveland, F. A., 4910
Clief, Eugene Van, 6461
Cloutier, Pierre, 3303
Cloutier, Raoul, 2967
Cloutier, St.-Georges, 3317
Clubb, S. P., 5893, 5894
Clunie, David, 3354
Coats, Douglas, 6048
Coatsworth, E., 4911
Cobb, Henri, 2714
Cochrane, Honora M., 4670
Cockburn, M. N., 1618
Code, Douglas, 3691
Coffey, William, 5044
Cohen, Anthony P., 1776
Cohen, Ronald, 6919
Coke, J., 1116
Cole, A. A., 3669
Cole, A.O.C., 4443
Cole, Frederick, 4335
Cole, W. H., 3651A
Coleman, A., 4376
Coleman, J., 4444
Coleman, MacDonald, 5444
Coleman, Romalis, 2715
Coleman, Thelma, 3716
Colgate, William, 4912
Collard, Edgar A., 2274, 2275, 2276, 2277, 2278
Collard, K. B., 2279, 4671
Collier, Anne M., 5467
Collier, R. W., 668, 6338, 6491, 6492
Collingwood (Ontario) Centennial Committee, 5294
Collins, A. B., 4485
Collins, Barbara Rose, 6493
Collins, Louis W., 1236
Collishaw, W., 4046
Colloton, F. W., 4486, 4487
Colthart, A. J., 258
Comité de rénovation et de mise en valeur du Vieux Québec, 2968
The Commercial Magazine Co. Ltd., 3127, 3237
Commission of Conservation, 37, 3297
Commission urbaine de Québec, 2969
Common, R., 6280
Compeau, C.-E., 386
Complin, Margaret, 5834
Condit, Carl W., 805
Condon, Ann K. Gordon, 1555
Conelly, M., 5246
Conklin, E. N., 2280
Connelly, Alan, 7012
Connolly, Phyllis H., 6865

Connon, John P., 3717
Conrod, W. Hugh, 1402
Conroy, Mary P., 2496
Conwell, Russell H., 1632
Conzen, M. R. G., 117
Conzen, Michael P., 259, 806, 807
Cook, Frederick, 4336
Cook, Gail, 5657
Cook, Gail C. A., 5046
Cook, George L., 118
Cook, Norman A., 6866
Cook, Ramsay, 260
Cook, W. Rupert, 4578
Cooke, Henry R., 5047
Coombs, Albert Ernest, 4508
Coombs, David Grosvenor, 4913, 4914
Cooper, I., 534, 733, 1063
Cooper, J. A., 868
Cooper, J. J., 2281
Cooper, John Irwin, 2282, 2283, 2284, 2497, 2498, 2575, 3128
Cooper, Joy, 5591
Cooper, Marion Gibb Struthers, 6494
Copeland, Mary, 1512
Copeland, Pat, 1237
Copes, Parzival, 1778, 1843
Copp, Terry, 2576, 2577, 2716, 2717, 3440, 4047
Coppock, K., 6049
Corbeil, Wilfrid, 2208
Corbet, Elise A., 6006
Corbett, D. C., 6691
Corbett, E. A., 6187
Corbett, Gail, 4445
Corelli, Rae, 4672
Corke, Charles, 3718
Corley, N. T., 2499
Cornish, F. J., 535
Cornwall, Ira Hugh Brooke, 6495
Corrivault, Claude, 3161
Cosbie, W. G., 4673
Costello, Evelyn Paula, 1633
Côté, Alphonse, 2718
Côté, Denise, 2197
Côté, Michelle, 3162
Côté, Y., 3355
Cotret, René de, 3318
Cotter, Evelyn, 5048
Cotter, Graham, 5049
Cottingham, Mollie E., 6867
Cotton, Peter, 6772
Couillard-Després, Abbé A., 3285
Couling, Gordon, 3719
Coulman, Donald E., 3720
Coulon, Jacques, 2719, 3319
Coupal, Michel, 1959
Courteau, Guy, 4579

Courtney, D. S., 1778
Courtney, J. L., 4377
Courtney, John C., 5816, 5895
Courval, Michel de, 7048
Cousineau, A., 1064, 2578
Cousineau, Aimé, 2720
Coutts, Robert, 6935
Couzons, H. H., 5049
Cowan, Anna M., 5592
Coward, Elizabeth Ruggles, 1532
Cowie, F. W., 2579, 2580
Craig, Irene, 5593
Craig, J. D., 536
Craig, Martha, 3772
Craigie, Cynthia Helen, 2198
Craik, W. A., 2581, 4915
Cramm, E. W. R., 5295
Cran, G. A., 6496
Cranna, Mona, 7033
Craven, Edna, 5296
Craw, G. Wilson, 4446
Crawford, Kenneth Grant, 869, 946, 1010, 3441, 3442, 4180
Crawford, M. E., 5958
Crawford, Patricia, 3443
Creasy, G. J., 4509
Creed, Catherine, 4510
Creighton, Donald Grant, 3898
Creighton, Pauline R., 5896
Crerar, Alistair Donald, 537, 643, 6339, 6462, 6497
Crichton, Vincent, 5297
Croil, James, 3773
Croll, David A., 841
Cromien, P. B., 5298
Cromwell, J., 6498, 6868
Crone, Kennedy, 2285
Crone, Ray, 5897
Cronin, James E., 119
Crook, Robert, 4077
Crosbie, John C., 1779, 1844
Cross, Dorothy Suzanne, 2582, 2583, 2584
Cross, H. F., 3979
Cross, Harold, 2286
Cross, K. J., 842
Cross, L. Doreen, 4337
Cross, Michael S., 4317, 4318, 4319, 4320, 4321, 4852
Cross, W. R., 5247
Crouch, W. W., 5050
Crowley, D. F., 730
Crowley, Ronald W., 46, 196, 464
Crowley, Terence Allan, 1439
Crowston, M. A., 6143
Crozier, M. J., 4447
Cruikshank, E. A., 4146, 4511, 4512
Cryderman, B., 1845

Crystal Garden Preservation Society, 6773
Csverko, R. P., 5445
Cuddy, S., 4147
Cudmore, S. A., 357
Culham, David John, 3444
Cullen, Mary C., 1755
Cullimore, D. R., 5835
Cullingworth, J. B., 3445
Culliton, John, 2287
Cumberland, R. W., 3980
Cumming, Marion, 1580
Cumming, Ross, 4048
Cummings, D. E., 6499
Cummings, H. R., 4249
Cummins, Captain J. F., 4674
Cunniffe, Richard, 6007
Curnoe, W. Glen, 4103, 4105
Currie, Laurie, 6869
Curtis, Charles K., 6405
Curtis, Clifford A., 947, 1011, 1012, 1062, 3446
Curtis, Lynn H., 6774
Curtis, P. J., 6219
Cushing, J. E., 1634
Cusson, M., 5248
Cutler, Maurice, 644
Cutts, A. B., 3721
Cyr, Georges, 1556

Daem, Mary, 6870
Dafoe, John W., 5594
Dagenais, Pierre, 2721, 2722, 5051
Dahl, Edward H., 7, 3092, 5487, 5488
Dahl, Erwin, 6871
Dahms, Frederick A., 3447, 3448, 3722, 3723, 3724, 3725, 3726, 3727
Daigneault-Saint-Denis, Nichole, 2492
Dakin, A. J., 5052, 5053, 5054, 5055, 5056, 5057
Dale, Allan, 2288, 4675
Dale, Edmund H., 5357, 5768, 5836, 6144, 6145, 6220
Dales, J. H., 228
Daley, Timothy T., 1238
Dalhousie College, Centenary Committee of, 1239
D'Allaire, Micheline, 3046, 3047
Daly, Margaret, 2723
Dalzell, A. G., 539, 540, 541, 542, 543, 645, 670, 734, 735, 736, 737, 738, 5358, 6500, 6501
Damphousse, R., 3265
Dandel, M. F., 261
Dandenault, Roch, 3356
Daneau, Jean-Jacques, 3286
Daniels, L. A., 6008

Dant, Noel, 901, 6221
D'Arcy, Kenneth Carl Ross, 465
Darroch, A. G., 466
Dauphin Historical Society, 5458
Davey, Ian E., 3809, 3810, 3811, 3828
Davey, P., 120, 191
David, Hélène, 2133
Davidson, J. R., 2724
Davidson, Mary, 2725
Davidson, N. M., 2289, 2726
Davidson, T., 4676
Davidson, W. A., 3774
Davies, Blodwen, 2970, 4250, 4251, 4677
Davies, Gordon W., 739
Davies, J. B., 1960, 3449
Davies, Kent Blair, 5839
Davies, P. G., 948
Davies, W. K. D., 5359, 5959, 6104, 6105, 6106, 6107, 6222
Davis, Arthur K., 5360
Davis, Bruce P., 3899
Davis, Carol L., 3899
Davis, Chuck, 6503, 6504
Davis, Donald F., 4916
Davis, Isabelle F., 6872
Davis, J. M., 1117
Davis, K., 42
Davis, R. A., 5058
Davis, Richard E., 2290
Davis, Ruth Helen, 4148
Davis, W. L., 4149
Davison, A. M., 5059
Davy, B. W., 3450
Dawe, R. N., 6286, 6287
Dawson, Carl A., 544, 2291
Dawson, Colleen, 5736
Dawson, G. F., 5769
Dawson, I., 4618
Dawson, J. N., 5060
Dawson, John Brian, 5960, 6050
Dawson, W. J., 6627
Day, J. R., 6188
Deacon, Nadine A. H., 3451, 4678
Deacon, P. A., 545
Deacon, William Arthur, 4679
Dean, W. G., 3452
Deane, R. B., 5839
Dear, Michael, 3861, 6936
De Bard, August A., 1240
De Boneville, Jean, 2585
Decarie, D., 3252A
Décarie-Audet, Louise, 2444
De Celles, A. D., 3129
Dechêne, Louise, 1961, 2445, 2446, 2447
Defoe, Deborah, 3900, 3901
De Grandmont, Eloi, 2292
De Guise, J.-G., 2727

De Jong, Nicolas J., 2728
Delâge, Jean, 2729
Delainey, W. P., 5898
Delaney, R. E., 1780
De la Roche, Mazo, 2971
Del Balso, Michael, 2640
Delfosse, Georges, 2293
Del Guidice, Dominic, 5061
Delise, A., 2156
Dell'Aniello, Paul, 2730
De Lorimier, François C., 3287
De Lorimier, Michel, 2500
De Lorme, Pierre, 2731
Delottinville, Peter, 1714
Delvaux, Paul-Henri, 3048
Dembek, Klemens, 4580
Demiers, Armand, 1962
Demers, Louis-Philippe, 3266
Demko, D., 3453
Dempsey, Hugh A., 121, 6051, 6052, 6053, 6054
Denault, Hayda, 3163
Dendy, J., 3981
Dendy, William, 4680, 4681
Denhez, 671, 1241
Denike, K. G., 6505
Denis, Paul-Yves, 1963, 2294, 2732, 2733, 3454, 7013, 7014
Denison, Merrill, 2295, 4682, 4683
Denison, S. A., 4917
Dennis, Michael, 740
Dennis, R. I., 808
den Otter, A. A., 5961, 6270, 6271, 6272, 6273, 6274
Dent, Charles, 4785
Denton, Frank T., 467, 468, 3812, 3813
Déom, André, 3357
Department of Northern Affairs, 6937
Department of Planning and Works, 4378
Derbyshire, Edward, 3244, 3245
Dersi, Louis-Antoine, 2734
Desbarats, Guy, 2735
Desbrisay, Mather Byles, 1533
Deschamp, Jean, 2736
Deschamps, Clement E., 1964
Desjardins, Bertrand, 1965
Desjardins, E. J., 6692
Desjardins, Edouard, 2296, 2297, 2448, 2449, 2737
Desjardins, M. A., 2199
Desjardins, Micheline, 1966, 2972
Desjardins, R., 3253A
Desloges, Yvon, 3049, 3093
Desmeules, Jean, 3164
Desrochers, Gilles, 1967
Des Rosiers, Rachel, 2185
Desrossiers, Lise, 1242

Detomasi, D. D., 5986A
Detwyler, T. R., 809
Deveau, J. Alphonse, 1534
Devine, P. K., 1846
De Visser, John, 4684
De Volpi, C. P., 2298, 2973, 3456, 4252, 4513, 4685
Dew, I. F., 5962
Dewar, D., 5349
Dewar, Kenneth, 3457
Dewey, Alex. G., 2501, 2502
DeWitt, Robert L., 1581, 1905
Dextraze, Pierre, 3206
Déziel, Julien, 2299
Dhar, Meena, 4686
Diamant, Claude, 3165
Diamond, Mrs. Clarence, 4049
D'Iberville-Moreau, Luc, 2300, 2301
Dickason, Olive Patricia, 1440
Dickey, E. E., 6870
Dickie, Robert, 1348
Dickinson, R. E., 43, 546
Dickson, F. W. R., 4050
Dickson, George, 4687
Diemer, H. L., 6009, 6146, 6257
Diespecker, Richard Allan, 6775
Dietz, S. H., 316
Dike, M. L., 4034
Dill, John, 741
Dillon, Willard Francis, 4150
Dinien, Janice, 5062
Dingman, R. G., 1013
Dingwall, C. W., 5500
Dionne, N. E., 2977
Divay, Gérard, 2738
Dixon, Louise, 1615
Dobbin, Francis H., 4448, 4449
Dobie, Sheila, 6463
Doe, Ernest, 6873
Dolan, George R., 3902
Dolbey, I. J., 3458
Dollier de Casson, François, 2450
Dolmat, Waclaw B., 2302
Dompierre, J., 2974
Donaldson, R. M., 6300
Donkin, John G., 5840
Donnellan, Brian, 4450
Donnelly, M. S., 5414, 5474
Doney, H. J., 4181
Donnison, D. V., 3652
Donohoe, E. F., 4051
Donovan, Michael J., 4618A
Dorion, C., 4581
Dorion, C.-N., 1968
Dorion, Henry, 3176
Dosman, E. J., 447
Doucet, Jean-Louis, 1969

Doucet, Michael J., 3811, 3814, 3815, 3816, 4918, 5022, 5063
Doucet, R., 3255
Douch, R., 122
Doughty, Arthur George, 2975, 2976, 2977, 3050
Douglas, J. M., 1014
Douglas, K., 4688
Douglas, Muriel H., 2303
Douglas, R. Alan, 5250
Douglas, W. A. B., 1349
Douglas, William, 5501, 5595
Douhaniuk, William, 6506
Douville, Raymond, 3320
Downey, Fairfax Davis, 1441
Downey, Terrence J., 3692
Doyle, Frank W., 1243
Doyle, James, 3903
Doyle, Kevin, 4451
Doyle, Trudy, 3903
Doyle-Frenière, Murielle, 2978
Doyon, Charles, 2304
Drake, Earl G., 5841, 5842, 5843
Drapeau, Julien, 1970
Draper, J. A., 902
Draper, William G., 3904
Drewery, Ellen M., 4182
Driedger, Leo, 418, 419, 420, 421, 5475, 5658, 5659
Drolet, Antonio, 3094, 3095, 3096
Drolet, Jean-Claude, 2157, 2158, 2159, 2160, 2161
Drouer, Glenn, 358
Drouin, Eneric O., 6301
Drouin-Lapointe, Denise, 3227
Drummond, Albert W., 3728
Dua, A. S., 1152
Dubé, Yves, 3207
Dubinski, Walter, 4582
Dubois, A., 2739
Dubreuil, G., 2740
Dubuc, Alfred, 1971, 2503, 2504
Ducharme, O., 2741
Duder, R., 1847
Dudley, J. G., 2584
Dudycha, D. J., 4052, 5064
Due, John F., 287
Duerden, Frank, 6938, 6939
Duffus, A. F., 1244
Duffy, Lise, 3166
Dufresne, Sylvie, 2389, 2586
Dugas, R., 1972
Duggan, D. M., 6147
Duggan, G. H., 1635
Duhamel, R., 4253
Dukhan, H., 5065
Dumais, Monique, 3208

Dumas-Rousseau, Michèle, 2587
Dumont, Fernand, 3228
Dumont, Y., 3229
Duncan, Albert S., 5361
Duncan, Dorothy, 3729
Duncan, Kenneth J., 3730
Duncan, Lewis, 903, 5066
Duncan, Lottie Jane Chapman, 5502
Duncan, M., 1973
Dunford, J. R., 3655
Dunham, Mabel, 4053
Dunlop, Allan C., 1468
Dunn, John A., 3666
Dunn, J. T., 6189
Dunning, A. D. W., 7049
Dupire, Jean, 2742
Dupont, Claude, 2742A
Dupont, Hébert Roger, 2589
Dupré, J. Stephen, 3459
Dupré, P., 3256
Dupuis, Aurore, 2451
Dupuis, Michael, 5596
Duquemin, C. K., 5300
Durand, Guy, 1974
Durham, Julian, 6628, 6776
Durkin, Douglas, 5503
Durocher, René, 1975, 2040
Durrand, Gilles, 1976
Durrant, D. A., 1636
Durst, H., 4054
Dusok, Watson, 359
Dutton, C. N., 288
Duval, André, 2979
Duval, Monique, 2980
Dworaczek, M., 5067
Dyck, Betty, 5385
Dyde, D. F., 3905
Dyde, S. W., 3942
Dykstra, T. L., 5804
Dyos, H. J., 44, 123, 124, 646
Dyster, Barrie, 4853
Dzus, Roman, 5251, 5252

Eadie, James A., 5301
Earl, L., 5660
Easterbrook, W. T., 229
Eastham, Francis, 3862
Easton, Robert, 6693, 6694
Eaton, Arthur W. H., 1245, 1350
T. Eaton Co., 4689, 4919
Eaton, Flora M., 4690
Eaton, Leonard K., 6777
Ebanks, G. E., 380
Eberts, E. H., 2130
Eby, Ezra, 4056
Echenberg, H. D., 4151

Ecroyd, L. G., 6507, 6875
Edgar, James D., 4338
Edmison, J. Alexander, 3906, 3907, 4452
Edmonds, W. E., 6148
Edmonton, City Planning Department, 6223
Edmonton Journal, 6149
Edwards, C. B., 4152
Edwards, Joseph Plimsoll, 1442, 1476, 1477
Edwards, M. H., 6340
Edwards, M. J., 2305
Eggleston, Wilfrid, 4254
Eisenhauer, Harry, 1578
Electa, Mary, 3908
Elford, Jean, 4475
Elias, P. D., 5415
Eliasoph, H. P., 6150
Elliot, Bruce S., 2200
Elliot, Una, 4183
Elliott, Craig C., 6778
Elliott, G. B., 5597, 6055
Elliott, Gordon Raymond, 6876
Elliott, Shirley B., 1351, 1352
Ellis, F., 1637
Ellis, W. S., 3909
Ells, Margaret, 1353
Ellwood, W. F., 5068
Elsammy, A. M., 6508
Emanuel, L., 6224
Emerson, Bruce E., 1015
Emery, Claire, 3775
Emery, George, 4619
Endersby, Stanley Alfred, 6421
England, Robert, 6779
English, John, 3460
Ennals, Peter M., 3680, 3776
Enos, Kathleen, 3288
Erickson, Arthur, 672, 673
Erlam, Rusty, 7015
Ernst, Joseph, 5030
Erskine, Ralph, 6940
Escojido, André, 3167
Espesset, H., 3092
Ethier, Jean-Marie, 2134
Evan-Perry, B., 547
Evans, David, 6151
Evans, J. A. S., 3461
Evans, L. C., 3777
Evans, Marjorie, 448
Evans, Reginald Dickey, 1153, 1154
Evans, Roger Albert, 1354
Evans, Simon, 6056
Evenden, L. J., 6509, 6510
Everett, T. Thomson, 6780
Everitt, J. C., 5733
Ewart, Alan C., 4854, 5416
Ewert, William Alfred, 5770
Ewing, James, 548, 2743, 2744, 2745, 2746

Fahos, J. G., 2590
Faillon, Etienne Michel, 2452
Fairburn, Kenneth J., 6225, 6226
Fairlie, Anne, 4453
Falardeau, Jean-Charles, 1977, 2023, 2981, 3168, 3169, 3170
Falconer, Don, 5738
Falconer, Robert, 4691
Falkenhagen, J. D., 3863
Falkner, Ann, 674, 675
Faludi, E. G., 549, 3864, 4488, 5069
Faris, R. E. L., 197
Farley, A. L., 6341, 6342, 6781
Farrell, David R., 2505
Farrell, John K. A., 4106, 4153, 5302
Farrugi, John Joseph, 5661
Faucher, Albert, 950, 1978, 1979, 1980, 3097, 3462
Fauteau, Joseph-Noël, 1981
Fawcett, Edgar, 6782
Fay, C. R., 1781, 1831, 1848, 1849
Fay, S. F. J., 1155, 1739
Fear, Jon, 4339
Feberdy, L. I., 2747
Fecteau, Nelson, 3305
Federal Publications Service, 810
Feeley, James, 4920
Feindel, Susan T., 2306
Feldman, Lionel D., 742, 870, 1065, 3464, 3465, 5657
Fellows, Robert F., 1557, 1582
Felt, Lawrence F., 1558
Felt, Paula C., 1558
Fenton, Charles Stephen, 3865
Ferguson, G. H., 550, 5071
Ferguson, Guy, 4454
Ferguson, M., 4057
Ferguson, M. M., 5739
Fergusson, Charles Bruce, 1156, 1157, 1158, 1246, 1247, 1248, 1249, 1355, 1356
Ferland, Yvan, 2748
Ferland-Angers, Albertine, 2307
Fernandez, Ray, 6783
Ferris, T. T. M., 4107
Fesenmaier, Daniel R., 4148
Fessenden, E. J., 4514
Fetherling, Douglas, 5072
Feld, A. J., 5899
Field, N. C., 3466, 5073
Fields, D. B., 6386
Filey, Michael, 4692, 4693, 4694, 4695, 4696, 4697, 4698
Fillmore, Charles L., 1535
Fillmore, Stanley, 4699
Filteau, Gerard, 3257
Finan, W. M., 8
Finberg, H. R. P., 125

Finestone, Harold, 3266
Fingard, Judith, 1066, 1118, 1119, 1159, 1357
Finley, A. Gregg, 1715, 1716
Finn, T. D., 4255
Finnis, F. H., 1016, 1017, 1018, 1019, 1020, 3467, 3468,
Firestone, Melvin M., 1782, 1905, 1906, 1906A
Firestone, O. J., 743
Firey, Walter, 647
Firth, Edith G., 4856, 4857, 4858
Firmaling, Tito Castro, 6438
Fischer, Lewis R., 1120, 1358, 1740, 1741
Fiset, Edouard, 2751, 2983
Fish, Susan, 740
Fisher, David, 2752, 5074
Fisher, Gerald, 1121
Fisher, Murray, 5417
Fisher, Val, 4515
Fitch, James M., 676
Fitzpatrick, Anne L., 6695
Fizet, Edouard, 1982, 2982
Flaman, Richard, 4185
Flanagan, William Francis, 5662
Flanders, D., 4186
Fleisch, Sylvia, 92
Fleming, A. Grant, 551
Fleming, C. E. B., 2753
Fleming, David, 4516
Fleming, Jane I., 4187
Fleming, Marie, 4700
Fleming, P. W., 1638
Flemming, H. A., 1250
Floyd, P. D., 6343, 6784
Flynn, James E., 6629
Flynn, Louis J., 3910, 3911, 3912, 3913, 4016
Fogarty, Donald William, 1251
Foggin, Peter M., 2754, 2755, 2756
Fontaine, Gabriel, 2183
Fontaine, H., 4397
Fontaine, L., 2219
Foote, Raymond Leslie, 1583
Foran, Edward B., 1850, 1851
Foran, M. L., 6010, 6011, 6012, 6057, 6058, 6059, 6060, 6061, 6062, 6063, 6064
Forbes, James A., 3448, 3727, 3731
Ford, Barbara, 3775
Ford, George B., 552
Foreman, A. E., 6511
Forêtier, Pierre, 2506
Forrester, Elizabeth A. M., 6344, 6345
Forrester, J., 3778, 3779
Forsey, Eugene A., 1160, 4921
Forster, S., 6564
Forster, Victor Wadham, 6512
Forsyth, J., 5963
Fortier, John, 1443

Fortier, Margaret, 1444
Fortin, Berthe, 2757
Fortin, Gérald, 1982A, 1983, 1984, 3228
Fortin, I., 2758
Fortin, Jacinthe, 2162
Fortin, Marc, 3230
Fort William Hydro Electric Commission, 4620
Forward, Charles N., 45, 811, 1122, 1403, 1639, 1783, 1852, 1853, 5844, 6513, 6696, 6697, 6785, 6786, 6787, 6788, 6789, 6790, 6791
Foster, Harold D., 6792
Foster, Josephine, 2507
Foster, Keith A., 5810
Foster, Mark, 289
Foster, Matthew James, 3866
Foucault, E. A., 3469
Foulché-Delbosc, Isabel, 3321
Fountain, G. F., 6698
Fournier, Jocelyn, 2175
Fournier, Laval, 1985
Fournier, Pierre, 2759
Fowke, V. C., 3470
Fowler, E. P., 904
Fox, Arthur, 1784
Fox, M. F., 677, 4380
Francis, J. W., 5941
Francis, R. A., 6514, 6793
Francoeur, Jean, 3238
Frank, David, 1490, 1491, 1492
Franklin, Douglas, 6833
Franson, J. D., 5075
Fraser, A., 1854
Fraser, Alexander, 4108
Fraser, D. G., 1359
Fraser, Derek, 905
Fraser, F. W., 4188
Fraser, Graham, 290, 2986, 5076
Fraser, James A., 1717
Fraser, Mary, 3471
Fraser, W. B., 6013
Fraser, W. J., 5504
Frederickson, Mary, 1123
Fredericton Central Area Concept Plan, 1584
Freedman, H. A., 5077
Freeman, Bill, 3780, 3867
Freer, Katherine M., 6515
Frei, John W., 2760
Freitag, Michel, 360
Fremelin, G., 5303
French, J. R., 951
French, R. de L., 291
French, William, 4701
Frenette, J.-V., 3209
Frenette, Marcel, 3358
Frey, M. W., 696
Friar, J., 3868

Fried, Jacob, 6942, 6943
Friedman, S. G., 4702
Friesen, G. A., 5418
Friesen, J., 5419
Friesen, Victor Carl, 5817
Fripp, R. M., 6630
Frisch, Michael, 126
Fromson, R. D., 5663, 5664
Froom, James D., 1124, 1404
Frowd, W. A., 1405
Fry, Henry, 3171
Fryer, Harold, 5964
Fukushima, M., 744
Fuller, O. T., 6993
Fuller, Paul G., 4154
Fuller, Robert M., 5253
Fullerton, Douglas, H., 4381
Fulton, D., 553
Fung, Yu-Han, 5505, 5665
Furry, C. G., 3781
Fyfe, Stewart, 230, 952, 1550

Gabeline, D., 2761
Gabriel, Teresa, 6753
Gad, Gunter, 5078
Gaetz, A. L., 6288
Gaffield, Chad M., 3472, 4224
Gagan, David, 4704, 4705
Gagne, Jean-A., 3099
Gagné, Raymond, 3161
Gagnon, Antoine, 1987, 3359, 3360
Gagnon, Eugene, 2592
Gagnon, F. E. A., 3100
Gagnon, Gabriel, 3172, 3173
Gagnon, Gilbert, 2761
Gagnon, R., 1988
Gagnon-Lacasse, Francine, 2763
Galarneau, Claude, 1989
Galarneau, France, 2508, 2602
Galbraith, J. S., 5362
Gale, Donald T., 6699
Gale, George, 3130
Gallacher, Daniel Thomas, 6794
Gallagher, James, 5666
Gallant, Susan, 1601
Gallois, Robert, 6630A
Galt, George, 678
Galvin, M. A., 4922
Galvin, Martin J., 3473
Gamache, J. Charles, 3131
Gamble, Ellsworth Paul, 6346
Ganong, W. F., 1559
Gard, Anson, 3670, 4218, 4340, 4341
Gardiner, F. G., 5079
Gardiner, J., 554
Gardner, W. H., 4155, 4156, 5254

Gariépy, Gérard, 2764
Gariépy, Wilfrid, 1990
Garigue, Philippe, 1991, 1992, 3246
Garner, H., 5080
Garnett, N. G., 1640
Garrett, A. W., 5940
Garrett, R. M., 6994
Garry, Robert, 3361
Garvey, John, 4109
Gathercole, C. E., 5081, 5082
Gaumond, Michel, 2984
Gauthier, Paul, 2765
Gauthier, Raymonde, 3051, 3052, 3322
Gauvin, D., 2176
Gauvin, Michel, 2593, 2594
Gayler, H. J., 6700, 6701
Geiger, Dorothy, 3914
Geldhart, Winston J., 4583
Gellert, Judith, 2766
Genest, Nicole, 2453, 3053
Gentilcore, R. Louis, 1161, 3475, 3476
George, M. V., 422
George, Peter J., 467, 3812, 3813
Gera, Surenda, 5083
Geraghty, E., 4110
Gerecke, Kent, 555, 556, 557
Gérin, Léon, 3915
Gérin-Lajoie, Henri, 2308
Germain, Annick, 1993
Germain, Claude, 2767, 2768, 2769
Germain, Denis, 745, 746, 2770, 2771, 2772
Germain, Dorie, 5304
Germano, J., 2309
Gerry, A. C., 5667
Gertler, Leonard O., 46, 361, 558, 559, 560, 561, 562, 563, 564, 843, 5965
Gervais, Gaetan, 1994
Gervin, J. K., 6598
Gesner, Claribel, 1445
Gibbard, Harold A., 2310, 2773
Gibbon, J. M., 2311
Gibbon, K. M., 906
Gibbs, J. P., 127
Gibbs, Phillip F., 2312
Gibson, Beth, 6759
Gibson, Edward M. W., 6347, 6516, 6516A
Gibson, James A., 4342, 4343
Gibson, John S., 6014, 6015
Gibson, Thomas, 3982
Gidney, Norman, 6426
Gidney, R. E., 3477
Giffard, Ann, 1742
Giffen, N. B., 6227
Giguère, Georges-Emile, 2509
Gilbert, Beth, 1641
Gillen, M., 4705
Gillese, J. P., 6228

Gillespie, W. I., 198
Gillis, Allison Ronald, 1252, 1253
Gillis, J. M., 30, 747
Gillis, Robert Peter, 4256, 4344, 4345
Gilmour, Gillian M., 2774
Gilmour, James M., 225, 3478
Gilpin, John F., 6190, 6191
Given, Robert A., 4706
Glaab, Charles N., 128
Glazebrook, G. P. de T., 3479, 3480, 4707
Glenday, D., 231
Glendenning, B. G. S., 1718
Glogowski, S. M., 5084
Goad, C.-E., 2594A, 2594B
Goard, Alan, 6262
Godbout, Jacques, 748, 3174
Godenrath, P. F., 6631
Godin, J., 1995
Goheen, Peter G., 199, 232, 4923
Golant, S., 1996, 3481
Gold, N. L., 5363
Goldberg, J., 749
Goldberg, S. A., 1997
Goldenberg, H. Carl, 1022, 1023, 5058, 5668, 6348
Goldfield, D. R., 129
Golding, P., 1998
Goldrick, Michael D., 200, 870, 904, 5086
Goldstein, Joy, 5506
Goldthorpe, Harry, 2985
Goltz, E., 5305
Gomery, Darrel, 6632
Good, Trent Leigh, 5507, 5669
Good, W. G., 387
Goodchild, Michael F., 4184
Gordon, David, 233
Gordon, Ian A., 3732
Gordon, James D., 1254
Gordon, W. R., 6633
Gorham, Raymond P., 1586
Goshan, D., 1642
Goshorn, Warner S., 2313
Gosling, S. M., 2314
Gosselin, Auguste, 2454
Gosselin, E., 3268
Gosselin, Emile, 1999
Gouett, Paul M., 1360
Gouin, Paul, 2986
Goulet, Elie, 3269
Gourd, Benoît-Beaudry, 3215, 3215A, 3296
Gourdeau-Côté, Suzanne, 2315
Gourlay, Robert F., 3482
Gourlay, R. S., 5087
Gouvernement du Québec, 2000
Gowans, Alan, 679, 680, 681, 2001, 2002, 4708
Gracie, B. A., 5364

Graden, R. R., 6229
Graff, Harvey J., 130, 3817
Graham, David, 6517
Graham, F. T., 2316
Graham, Gerald Sandford, 292
Graham, J. E., 4111
Graham, J. W., 5509
Graham, John F., 1024, 1163
Grainge, Jack W., 6944
Granatstein, J. L., 9, 907, 5088, 5089, 5090
Granbois, A., 2775
Grand Trunk Pacific Railway Company, 6464
Grandt, F. R., 844
Grant, George M., 2003
Grant, H. Roger, 5766, 5767
Grant, H. T., 3671
Grant, J. H., 6634
Grant, John N., 1125, 1536
Grant, K. F., 6518
Grant, Marguerite H. L., 1361
Grant, Mrs. W. F., 4924
Grant, Robert W., 5941
Grant, Roland D., 6635
Grant, W. L., 3916
Graser, Otto, 2776
Grassner, C., 234
Grattan, Patricia, 1855
Gratton, Valmore, 2777, 2778
Gravel, Albert, 3270
Gravel, L., 4257
Gray, Arthur W., 6877
Gray, C., 5091
Gray, Clayton, 2317
Gray, D. M., 3779
Gray, F. W., 1493
Gray, Helen M., 1494
Gray, James H., 5365, 5366, 5510, 6016, 6017
Grayson, John Paul, 5092, 5966
Grayson, L. M., 5966
Greaves, S. M., 5306
Gréber, Jacques, 4382, 4383, 4384
Green, Alan G., 4017
Green, George, 6519
Green, Jerry Edward, 6945
Green, Reuben, 5255
Green, W. A., 5740
Green, W. L. C., 4620A
Greenberg, Kenneth, 5093
Greenberg, Zeev, 5094
Greenblat, J., 5935
Greenhill, Basil, 1742
Greenhill, Ralph, 3483, 4517, 4708
Greenhous, Brereton, 1560
Greening, W. E., 2004, 3271, 3324, 4258, 4259, 5598
Greenough, John Joseph, 1255, 1362
Greenway, H. F., 750

Greenwood, Frank M., 2005
Greenwood, J. L., 1537
Greer, Allan, 1446
Greer-Wootten, Bryn, 812, 2696, 2779, 2780
Gregg, Marjorie Wyeth, 751
Gregg, R. C., 6301
Gregory, Grace, 5540
Gregory, W. D., 4925
Gregson, H., 6795
Grenier, Fernand, 3175, 3176
Grenke, Arthur, 5599
Grenon, Hector, 2781
Griffin, J. A., 3782
Griggs, Neil John Francis, 6520
Grimble, L. G., 293
Grimmer, A. K., 317, 3298
Grimmer, Dennis McLean, 6349
Grimsby Historical Society, 3783
Grindstaff, C. F., 380
Gross, W. R., 5256
Groulx, Adélard, 2782
Groulx, Lionel, 2318, 4347
Groupe de recherche en art populaire (GRAP), 2319
Groupe de recherche sur la société Montréalaise au XIXe siècle (GRSM), 2320
Groupe de travail sur l'urbanisation, 2006
Gruetter, Robert, 6540
Grumm, J. G., 5095
Grunier, R., 5096
Guay, Michèle, 2595
Gubbay, Aline, 2321
Guénette, R., 5307
Guérette, Fernand, 3362
Guérette, G., 1561
Guérette, Réal, 3210
Guérin, Marc-Aimé, 2783
Guerra, I. L., 5097
Guértin, Pierre-S., 2201
Guest, Hal, 6995
Guillet, Edwin C., 3681, 3682, 4260, 4455, 4709, 4710, 4859
Guimond, Lionel, 2510
Guimond, Paul-Henri, 3210
Guimont, A., 2187
Guindon, H., 231
Guitard, Michèle, 2322
Gundy, H. Pearson, 3917, 3918, 3919, 3983
Gung, Janice Sui-Ching, 6878
Gunn, Angus M., 6521
Gunton, Thomas I., 565
Gurstein, Michael, 449
Gutsell, Barbara, 6996
Gutstein, Donald, 648, 682, 6522, 6702
Gutwirth, J., 2784
Guy, R. M., 1164, 1469
Gwyn, Julian, 1447

Gwynne-Timothy, John, 4112
Gyuse, Timothy T. I., 5900, 6106, 6108

Haak, L. A., 3869
Habinski, A. A., 6523
Hacking, J. H., 3734
Hacking, N., 6496
Hagarty, W. G., 3984
Haggard, H. Rider, 388
Haggart, Ron, 5098
Hague, Ernest W. J., 752
Hahn, H., 908
Haig, R. B., 4261
Haig, R. M., 1025
Haigh, R. J., 6230
Haldane, Elizabeth, 4058
Haldeman, B. A., 566
Halifax, City of, 1256, 1257
Hall, Alfred V., 3887
Hall, C. J., 3483A
Hall, Carl A. S., 3483
Hall, D. J., 5308
Hall, Frederick A., 5257
Hall, G. E., 871
Hall, Oswald, 3693, 3694
Hall, Peter, 131, 567
Hall, Thomas, 47
Hallam, W. T., 1259
Hallé, Robert, 3304
Halliday, H. A., 2327
Hallsworth, A. G., 4026
Hallwa, T. L., 4113
Hambly, George H., 5741
Hambly, W. B., 4711
Hamdami, D., 1785
Hamel, P., 2007
Hamelin, Jean, 1923, 1924, 1925, 3054
Hamelin, Louis-Edmond, 2008, 2220, 3363, 3364
Hamil, Fred C., 4114, 4157
Hamilton, John R., 1643
Hamilton, Raphael N., 4489
Hamilton, S. W., 6703
Hamilton, Sally Anne, 6152, 6156
Hamilton, W., 201
Hamilton, William B., 10, 132, 1126
Hammerström, Ingrid, 47
Hammond, M. O., 4348
Hauliki, B., 6997
Hancock, Maclin L., 5099
Hancock, W. G., 1786
Handelman, Donald, 1787, 2785
Handlin, O., 133
Hann, Russell, 3485
Hanna, David B., 2596, 2597
Hannay, J., 1644

Hansford, G. R., 1165
Hanson, Eric J., 5367, 5967, 5968, 5969, 5970, 5971, 6153
Hanson, H., 4640
Hanus, F., 5972
Harasym, D. G., 6109, 6127
Hardoy, Jorge E., 35, 568
Hardwick, Walter G., 6350, 6524, 6525, 6704
Hardy, Eric, 1026, 1027, 4712
Hardy, Jean-Pierre, 3055, 3101
Hardy, René, 3102, 3132
Hare, John E., 2511, 3103, 3104
Hare, R. E., 4641
Hareven, Tamara, 1067
Harker, Douglas E., 6526
Harkness, John Graham, 5308A
Harkness, Ross, 5100
Harley, K. C., 5530
Harnett, Ken O., 1260
Harney, Moses, 1856
Harney, Robert F., 423, 2787, 4713, 4714, 4715, 4927, 4928, 4929, 5101
Harper, J. Russell, 1645, 2598, 3088
Harper, P. D., 5102
Harrington, A. R., 1261
Harrington, G. M., 4930
Harrington, Lyn, 3486, 4621, 5742, 6017, 6281
Harrington, Michael Francis, 1857, 1858
Harrington, Robert F., 6451
Harris, Donald, 1448
Harris, G. M., 872
Harris, George, 5511, 5600
Harris, John E., 1262
Harris, Lorraine, 6879
Harris, R. C., 5103
Harris, R. V., 1263, 1264
Harris, R. Colebrook, 134
Harrison, P., 202
Hart, E. J., 6154
Hart, G. E., 1363
Hart, Patricia W., 4716
Hartford, Jerome, 5258
Hartland, Penelope, 235
Hartling, Philip L., 1538
Hartman, Chester, 845
Hartman, Edward T., 569
Hartwick, J. M., 196
Harvey, A. G., 6416
Harvey, D. C., 135, 1166, 1167, 1168, 1265, 1266, 1267, 1268, 1269, 1270, 1756
Harvey, David, 48
Harvey, Fernand, 2009, 2010, 2011
Harvey, Jacqueline, 2163
Harvey, Janice, 2512, 2599
Harvey, Pierre, 2788
Harvey, R., 1495

Hasan, Nino, 570
Hassbrung, M., 6231, 6232
Hastings, C. H., 1068
Hastings, Charles J., 753, 754
Hatcher, Colin K., 5845, 6018
Hathaway, Ernest Jackson, 4860, 4861, 4862
Hatton, Beth, 2600
Hatton, Joseph, 1788
Hatton, Warwick, 2600
Hauser, P. N., 136, 137
Havel, J., 755, 4584, 4585
Havran, Martin J., 5259
Hawco, J. R., 1789
Hawkins, Alfred, 3105
Haworth, Kent M., 11
Hay, Alan K., 4385
Hay, Elizabeth, 1646, 5512
Hayball, G., 6636
Haydu, G., 4189
Hayley, W. T., 5513
Haynes, Anthony William, 5901
Haynes, E. Russell, 1647
Hays, Samuel P., 909
Hayter, J. G., 6233
Hayter, Roger, 6351, 6527
Hayward, Robert J., 12, 13, 14, 4863, 4864
Head, Clifford Grant, 1790
Healey, D. M., 6107
Healey, Denis, 1406
Healey, W. J., 5601, 5602
Healy, Mary Darina, 5973
Heap, Margaret, 2601, 2602
Hearn, George R., 6796
Heath, Francis M., 4490
Hébert, G., 5942
Hébert, Gérard, 2326
Hébert, Jean-Claude, 3056
Hébert, Jean-Pierre, 2789
Hébert, N. T., 2455
Hébert, Serge, 2012
Hecht, Alfred, 5468
Heeney, Isabelle B., 5743
Heffernan, Jean D., 1484
Hefferton, S. J., 1791
Heick, Welf H., 4059, 4060
Heidenreich, Conrad E., 3487, 5104
Heimark, H., 5846
Heinke, G. W., 6946, 6988
Heintz, Gladys J., 4061
Heit, M., 4518
Helling, Rudolph A., 5105
Hellyer, Paul, 756
Hellyer Task Force Report, 757
Hemingway, Peter, 6110, 6234
Hemmean, Douglas, 1127
Hemstock, C. A., 6947, 6948, 6949
Henderson, A. M., 5603

Henderson, David Gordon, 5514, 5670
Henderson, J. L., 4158
Henderson, J. L. H., 4717
Henderson, John, 4718
Hendrie, Lillian M., 2327
Henie, Edna, 6901
Henripin, Jacques, 389, 2013, 2710, 2790, 2791
Henry, Frances, 1169
Henry, G. S., 5106
Henson, Guy, 1407
Hepburn, A. C., 138
Heritage Ottawa, 4262, 4263
Heritage Trust of Nova Scotia, 1271
Herman, Harry V., 5107
Hernandez, M. J., 5556
Herod, Don, 4543
Heron, Craig, 3488
Heroux, J.-P., 2328
Heroux, Louis, 4586
Herrington, W. S., 3489
Hershberg, Theodore, 139
Herscovitch, G., 6235
Herstein, Harvey H., 5516, 5527
Hessel, R. H., 4190
Hessler, R., 845
Heubert, V. H., 4191
Hewett, G. T., 571
Hewitt, Marsha, 3780
Heyes, Esther, 4719
Hibbard, F. W., 1069
Hickey, Paul, 954, 3490, 3491, 3492
Hickman, George Albert, 1792
Hiess, A., 3365
Higgins, Brian E., 1859
Higgins, D. J. H., 873, 874, 955, 1408
Higgs, R. W., 2164
Higgs, Robert, 204
Higgs, Robert Larry, 5368
Hildebrand, Grant, 683
Hill, Daniel, 4720, 4865
Hill, Frederick I., 5108, 5109
Hill, George William, 1272, 1273, 1364
Hill, Hamnett P., 4264, 4322, 4349
Hill, Isabel Louise, 1587
Hill, O. M., 5260
Hillman, W. A., 6637
Hills, C. A., 3493
Hilton, D. K., 2014
Hilton, George W., 294
Hilton, Kenneth D., 3366
Himmelman, Melody, 1409
Hinds, Ann, 3735
Hines, F. R., 4159
Hinshelwood, N. M., 2329
Hislop, Mary, 5604
Historical and Scientific Society of Manitoba (H.S.S.M.), 5420

Hitchcock, J., 5110
Hitsman, J. Mackay, 1449, 2987
Hobbs, W. E., 5518
Hocken, H. C., 956, 957, 4931
Hodge, G. F., 5369
Hodge, Gerald, 205, 262, 263, 1743, 1744, 1749, 5111
Hodgetts, Charles A., 758, 759, 760, 761, 762
Hodgetts, J. E., 236, 3985
Hodgins, J. G., 3494
Hodgson, M. C., 6236
Hoffman, Andrew, 2792
Hogg, A. M., 3216
Holcomb, Briavel, 835
Holdsworth, Deryck William, 6352, 6528, 6529
Hollier, R., 2330
Hollingsworth, S., 1170
Holloway, Godfrey F., 6797
Holman, H. T., 1745
Holman, Lois C., 3495
Holmes, Marjorie C., 5353, 6354
Holmes, Neil Bradford, 6452
Holmgren, Eric J., 5974, 6192
Holmgren, Patricia M., 5974
Holt, Glen E., 295
Holt, H. S., 4350
Homel, Gene H., 4931A
Homenuck, H. P., 6111
Honigmann, Irma, 6950
Honigmann, John, 6950
Hood, M. L., 5519
Hood, M. M., 4230
Hooff, Sally, 2321
Hooper, N. A., 4721
Hopkins, Henry Whitmer, 2331
Hopkinson, M. W., 4160
Hoppenrath, I., 6417
Hopper, W. C., 5039
Horovitz, William B., 2603
Horseman, A. L., 49, 6705
Horsey, A., 4265
Horsey, E. E., 3986
Horton, J. T., 5112
Horwood, H., 1860
Horwood, Joan, 1410
Hosken, Fran P., 318
Hoskins, Ronald G., 5261
Hossé, Hans A., 911, 4386, 4387, 5605
Hough, M., 5113
Houghton, J. R., 6112
House, J. D., 6113
Housego, I. E., 5982
Housson, Erik W., 4866
Houston, Samuel, 3987
Houston, Susan E., 3496, 3497, 4932
Howard, Henry, 5370
Howard, Irene, 6530

Howard, R., 4698
Howard, Richard, 1450
Howard, W. H., 1274
Howay, F. W., 6638, 6639
Howell, David F., 1365
Howell-Jones, Gerald I., 6355, 6356
Howey, Florence, 4587
Hoyt, Homer, 649
Hubbard, Robert Hamilton, 684, 4266, 4267, 4268, 4269
Hubert, J., 2988
Huck, Marilyn Glynn, 4062
Huebert, Victor H., 657
Huel, Raymond, 6531
Hughes, C. C., 6951
Hughes, Everett C., 2015, 2016, 2177, 2793
Hughes, Gary, 1648
Hughes, J. E., 1060
Hughes, Margaret, 5847
Hughson, J. W., 4240
Hugo-Brunt, Michael, 572, 1128, 1129, 1793
Hulbert, F., 3178
Hulchanski, J. D., 534, 573, 574, 575, 576, 733, 1063
Hultin, Neil C., 3400
Humes, Samuel, 958
Humphries, Charles W., 6357
Humphrys, Graham, 3247
Hunt, T. A., 875
Hunter, A. A., 5671
Hunter, E. L., 4270
Hunter, James Jamison, Jr., 1171
Hurd, W. Burton, 424
Hurst, Theresa, 6754
Hurt, Leslie, 6303
Hurtubise, Luc, 2738
Hutchings, C. J., 5421
Hutchinson, R. Gordon, 6358
Hutchinson, Ruth Gillette, 1038
Hutchison, R., 5520
Hutchison, Thomas, 1794
Hutner, Florence, 5114
Hutton, Charles L. A., 813, 6155
Huzel, B., 5521
Hyde, F. D., 4226

Ibbotson, Leonard, 4115
Igartua, José E., 1918, 2513, 2514, 2515, 2516
Indra, D. M., 6532
Inglis, George Erskine, 7034
Ingram, D. R., 5115, 5771
Inkster, Tom H., 6406
Innis, F. C., 2332
Innis, H. A., 296, 5371
Institute for Northern Studies, 5772
Institute of Local Government, Queen's University, 319, 3498, 7016

Ioannon, Gregory P., 6706
Ireland, John, 5309
Ireland, W. E., 6439, 6798, 6858
Ironside, R. G., 5372, 5804, 6156, 6237
Irvine, Lorraine, 3647
Isaacs, I. J., 1649
Isbister, Alexander Fraser, 2135
Isbister, John, 3499
Isenberg, Seymour, 2794
Israël, Wilfrid Emerson, 2795
Itter, Carole, 6561
Ivanisko, Henry, 6881
Iverson, Noel, 1795

Jacek, Henry, 3870, 3871
Jacin, N. P., 5114
Jack, David Russell, 1619, 1650, 1652
Jack, L. B., 1029
Jackson, E. E., 1496
Jackson, J., 4161, 4162
Jackson, J. T., 685
Jackson, John D., 3500
Jackson, John J., 6359
Jackson, John N., 50, 4519, 4520, 4521, 4522
Jackson, W. A. D., 3501
Jacobs, Jane, 51, 206, 577
Jacobs, Philip, 207, 3239, 3325
Jacobsen, George, 6952
Jacobson, Jerry, 5116
James, C. C., 5310
James, E. M., 3785
James, F. C., 763
James, N. C., 4116
James, R. Scott, 4722
James, William, 3785
Jameson, Sheilagh S., 6019, 6065
Jameson, Spruce, 4723
Jamieson, F. C., 6193
Jamieson, Heber C., 6194
Jamieson, S. M., 2796
Jamieson, Walter, 686
Jamieson, William Sinclair, 6707
Janelle, Donald, 4117
Janin, G., 2604
Janisset, M.-F., 2332A
Jansen, Clifford J., 5118
Jansson, D. W., 1588
Jarrell, R. A., 3106
Jarrett, Gordon, 4933
Jarvi, Edith, 5263
Jarvis, Eric, 4934, 4935
Jarvis, J., 4854
Jarvis, Robert, 5119
Jarvis, S., 4724
Jarvis, W. H. P., 3673
Jaschke, George, 5120
Jean, Luce, 2989

Jeffares, C. A., 6998
Jefferson, R., 4271
Jenkins, Kathleen, 2333
Jensen, B. J., 6304
Jensen, L. B., 1275
Jewitt, A. R., 1366
Jobin, Albert, 2990
Johns, Anthony, 1603
Johnson, Arthur L., 1276, 3920
Johnson, C. H., 1367
Johnson, Dennis Bruce, 6020, 6102, 6114
Johnson, Eve, 6540
Johnson, H., 208
Johnson, I. C., 1030
Johnson, J. A., 1031
Johnson, J. H., 140
Johnson, J. K., 3921, 4867, 4868
Johnson, John, 1210
Johnson, John S., 2334
Johnson, L. L., 4271
Johnson, Leo A., 3737, 4869
Johnson, Nora, 3738
Johnson, Patricia M., 6427
Johnson, Peter Graham, 1172
Johnson, Rodrigue, 2797
Johnson, T. A., 5522
Johnston, Andrew J. B., 1173, 1277
Johnston, Charles M., 3648, 3786, 4936
Johnston, H. W., 1278
Johnston, Hugh, 3702, 4552, 4937
Johnston, J. M., 4553
Johnston, John A., 2605
Johnston, Keith L., 1411
Johnston, P. A., 6115
Johnston, R. J., 52, 814
Johnston, W. S., 4553
Jolliffe, R., 4725
Jones, C. F., 2798
Jones, David C., 5373, 6395
Jones, Ellwood, 4456, 4726
Jones, F. E., 3872
Jones, F. S., 470
Jones, George P., 1513
Jones, Howard, 1070
Jones, James Edmund, 4870
Jones, Murray V., 578, 2017, 5121
Jones, Murray V., and Associates Limited, 1279
Jones, O. D., 6157
Jones, R. W., 3695
Jones, Stephen B., 5975
Jones, V. C., 4523
Jordan, John A., 3107
Jordan, Mabel E., 6158, 6399, 6428
Jouandet-Bernadet, R., 642
Joy, John, 1861
Joyce, J. G., 910, 911

Jozsa, J. M., 1412, 3179
Judd, William W., 4163
Jukes, Mary, 4871
Jupp, G. A., 2335
Jupp, Ursula, 6799

Kadaali, Stephen James, 5848
Kaiser, T. E., 4231
Kalbach, Warren E., 362, 425, 431
Kalen, Henry, 5558
Kaliski, Stephen Felix, 6360
Kalman, Harold, 687, 688, 4272, 6533, 6534
Kaplan Harold, 53, 5122, 5123, 5124, 5125, 5126
Kardos, R., 2799
Kariel, H. G., 264
Karr, Clarence, 3739
Kasahara, Yashika, 363
Kasymyra, Bohdan Z., 5849
Katz, Michael B., 3819, 3820, 3821, 3822, 3823, 3824, 3825, 3826, 3827, 3828
Kauffman, Carl, 5311
Kaufman, Alvin, 4063
Kay, Barry J., 5127, 5128
Kayfetz, Ben, 4727
Kayser, Edmond, 2202
Kealey, Gregory S., 4938, 4939, 4940, 4941, 4942
Keane, Patrick, 1368
Keary, W. H., 6361
Keating, C., 2336
Keating, D., 2336
Keating, Donald R., 912
Keddie, Vincent, 3502
Keep, G. R. C., 2517, 2518, 2519
Keilhoffer, P., 819
Keir, Robert, 4585
Keirstead, W. C., 1589
Keith, Gerald, 1653
Keith, J. Clark, 3503, 3504
Keith-Lucas, B., 876
Kellett, George, 7017
Kellett, J. R., 237
Kellough, W. R., 764
Kelly, L. A., 28
Kelner, M., 4728
Kelso, J. J., 4943
Kemp, F. A., 4018
Kendal, Elaine, 6195
Kennedy, David, 3740
Kennedy, J. J., 6440
Kennedy, N. J., 6066
Kennedy, R., 1862
Kennedy, Sharon, 6362
Kennedy, W., 6536
Kennedy, W. J. V., 815
Kennedy, W. K. P., 4219

Kenney, J. E., 1523
Kent, D. M., 3922
Kent, R. H., 5672
Kent, W. J., 1863
Kentridge, Leon R., 2800
Kenvyn, R., 6640
Kenward, John K., 5956
Kerr, Alistair W., 6800
Kerr, D. C., 5902, 5903
Kerr, Donald P., 209, 3466, 3505, 4729, 4730, 4731, 5073, 5129, 5130, 5131, 5606, 6537
Kerr, James E., 3656
Kerr, Kenneth J., 1796
Kerr, W. B., 1174
Kerri, James N., 450, 5523, 5673, 5693, 6305
Kerwin, P., 5132
Kesteman, Jean-Pierre, 3272
Ketchum, C. J., 4388
Ketchum, J. D., 15
Keyfitz, Nathan, 390, 2018
Keys, C. L., 5976
Khor, Ean, 2801
Kidd, Martha Ann, 4457, 4458
Kidd, Thomas, 6538
Kilbourn, William, 3787, 4732, 4873, 5133
Kilpatrick, Alexander Bruce, 5977
Kilvert, Barbara, 6755
King, A., 5943
King, Edwin D., 1280
King, Gillian Mary, 5944
King, Leslie J., 2019, 3506
King, M. J., 2337, 2991
King, Margaret M., 3923
King, Mona F., 6238
King, T. P., 5422
Kingsmille, Roden, 5451
Kingston Historical Society, 3924
Kingston Social Planning Council, 3925
Kinniburgh, James, 4389
Kinsley, B. L., 5374
Kipling, Rudyard, 6282
Kirby, W., 4524
Kirjan, C., 3053
Kirk, D. W., 3507
Kirk, J. Michael, 4164
Kirkconnell, Watson, 3888, 3917, 5524
Kirkland, John S., 54, 4027
Kirkup, D. B., 5134
Kitchen, Harry M., 1071
Kitchen, John M., 579, 4390
Kitchener, Urban Renewal Committee, 4064
Kitto, Robert Henry, 6363
Kiwanis Club, Stamford, Ont., 4525
Kjellander, M. V., 5840
Klassen, Henry C., 2520, 6067, 6068, 6069, 6070, 6071, 6084

Klein, Alice, 4944
Klenke, M., 6708
Klenman, A., 6801
Klinck, George, 4065
Kling, S., 5135
Kloppenberg, Anne, 320, 6539, 6540
Klotz, Otto, 3657
Knappe, C. F., 4945
Knight, David B., 141, 142, 265, 3508, 4351, 4352, 4353, 4354
Knight, Rolf, 321
Knoff, L. L., 2338
Knott, Leonard L., 2339
Knowles, David C., 2521
Knowles, Eric, 5904, 5917
Knowles, John D., 4588
Knowles, M., 580
Knowles, Valerie, 2340
Knowlton, Isaac C., 1719
Koch, E., 5525
Koltun, Lilly, 689
Kon, William E., 4589
Konard, Victor A., 4733
Konarek, J., 4491
Koolage, William Warren, 5452
Koop, R. H., 3509
Koroscil, Paul M., 61, 7018, 7019, 7035
Kotseff, L. E., 3553
Kouhi, Christine, 4622
Kovach, J. J., 5773
Kovitz, M., 2802
Krause, E. R., 1452
Krawchuk, P., 5526
Krebs, H. H., 210
Kremenliev, Gregor, 3368
Krim, Arthur J., 297
Krishnamurti, U. K., 690
Kristjanson, L. F., 5774
Krohn, R. G., 2753
Krueger, Ralph R., 36, 581, 1072, 1562, 3510, 4066, 4192, 4526
Kugler-Gagnon, Marianne, 4306
Kuhn, Peter, 5083
Kunin, R., 471
Kunka, Gloria Mae, 959
Kupfer, G., 5992
Kurman, Louis A., 3788
Kurokawa, Minako, 4067
Kutcher, Stan, 4946
Kuthan, G., 6541
Kuwabara, B., 691
Kuz, A. J., 266
Kuz, T. J., 5527
Kyte, E. C., 4734

Laatsch, W. G., 6953
Labelle, Rhéal, 2203

Laberge, J. E., 1073
Laberge, L., 2020, 2021, 2803
La Branche, Bill, 4458
Labrèque, Lucille, 3064
Lacelle, Claudette, 3108
Lacey, Laurie, 1539
Lach, E., 4492
Lachance, André, 2456, 3057
Lachapelle, Claire, 4735
Lacoste, Norbert, 2341, 2342, 2804, 2805, 2806
Lacote, D. S., 3493
Lafferty, Louis W., 1757
La Flamme, A., 3024
Laflamme, H., 2204
Laforest, M., 2807
Laframboise, Yves, 3058
La France, Marc, 3059, 3060, 3092, 3109
Lagace, Anita, 1720
Lagasse, J. H., 5423
Laghaout, M., 3223
Lahaise, Robert, 2343, 2344
Lai, Chuen-Yan David, 6802, 6803, 6804, 6805
Lai, H., 6159
Lai, Vivien Wai-Ying, 5136, 5137
Laidlaw, John, 5138
Laing, F. W., 6806
Laing, G. A., 5674
Lainsbury, John Michael, 5906
Lajeunesse, Ernest J., 5264
Lajeunesse, J. M., 2345
Lajeunesse, Marcel, 2606
Lamarche, François, 211
Lamarche, Rodolphe, 4391, 4392
Lamarre, Nicole, 1797
Lamb, A. S., 1074
Lamb, Bessie, 6641
Lamb, W. Kaye, 6642, 6806, 6807
Lambert, Barbara, 1281
Lambert, Carmen, 7020, 7021
Lambert, Phyllis, 692, 2346, 2347, 2348, 2607, 2608, 2609
Lambert, R., 16, 650
Lambrou, Yianna, 6542
Lamonde, Yvan, 2022, 2349, 2350
Lamont, G., 4736, 5775, 5978
Lamontagne, G., 3180
Lamontagne, Léopold, 3988, 3989
Lamontagne, Maurice, 1980, 2023
Lamothe, J., 3326
Lamothe, J.-C., 2351
Lampard, Eric E., 55, 212, 364, 365, 582
Lampson, Réal, 2808
Lamy, R., 1205
Lanctôt, Gustave, 2024, 2352, 2457, 2458, 2459, 2460, 3224

Landa, M. J., 5744
Landon, Fred, 3511, 3512, 4165, 4166, 4167
Landry, Yves, 2098
Lane, Barbara M., 693
Lane, Richard B., 1282
Laneuville, André, 2025
Lang, John, 4590
Lang, V., 1864
Langdon, I., 238
Langelier, F., 3110
Langlois, Claude, 2809
Langlois, George, 2026
Langlois, Jean-Claude, 322, 323, 2353, 2354
Langman, R. C., 3513
Langmuir, J. W., 3514
Langral, Georges, 2810
Langston, W. J., 3327
Langton, W. A., 694
Lanken, D., 2761
Lapalme, Loretta, 3062
Lapierre-Adamcyk, Evelyne, 391
LaPierre, Laurier, 5476
Lapierre, Richard, 2811
Laplante, Jean de, 2812
Lapointe, Gérard, 2027, 3181
Lapointe, Laurent, 3240
Lapointe, Michelle, 2205
Lapointe, Pierre-Louis, 2214
Lapointe-Roy, Huguette, 2522
Laponce, J. A., 6709
Laporte, Pierre, 2028
Laporte, Rodney, 5936
Lapp, Ronald A., 3928
Lappin, Adah, 4737
Large, Richard G., 6465
Larivière, Claude, 2813
Laroque, Paul, 3133
LaRose, Helen, 6160
Larouche, Fernand, 324, 3217
Larouche, Léonidas, 3369
Larouche, Pierre, 2814
Larson, Peter, 765
Lascelles, G. A., 5139
Lash, H. N., 2815, 6168
Lasry, J.-C., 2816
Lasserre, F., 695
Latham, R. F., 5140
Latiff, A. H., 5671
Latimer, Elspeth A., 4947
Lauder, Kathleen S., 17, 325, 338, 5745, 6883
Laurence, L., 2817, 5141, 6543
Laurin, J.-E., 2029, 2355
Lauriston, V., 3703, 4476
Laux, F. A., 5979
Lavallée, André, 2609A
Lavallée, Jean, 2184, 2818
Lavallée, Laval, 16, 17, 650

Lavallée, Omer, 5607
Lavedan, Pierre, 2030
Laverdière, Camille, 3370
Lavergne, Gérald, 3259
Lavigne, Jacques, 2031
Lavigne, Marie, 2610, 2611, 2819, 2820
Lavigueur, H., 2338
Lavoie, Yolande, 2032
Law, R. C., 5142
Lawrence, Barbara, 6892
Lawrence, Joseph W., 1654
Lawrence, M. C., 6116
Lawson, J. Murray, 1283, 1542
Lawson, M. B. M., 5143
Lawton, Alma, 5776, 5907
Lazure, L., 3371
Lea, N. D., and Associates, 298
Leach, Edith E., 3515, 4948
Leach, James D., 4554
Leacock, Stephen, 2356, 4225
Leaning, John D., 816, 4273
Leary, R. M., 4393
Lebel, E. C., 5264A
Leblanc, André E., 2357
Le Blanc, E., 1604
Le Blant, Robert, 3063
Leblond de Brumath, A., 2358
Le Bourdais, D. M., 4591
Le Cavalier, Patricia F., 4394
Lechasseur, Antonio, 3211A
Leclerc, Gilberte, 3182
Leduc, Pierre, 2359, 2612
Lee, Barrie, 6808
Lee, Chun-Fen, 3516, 4068
Lee, Christopher Lockhart, 6809
Lee, Judith M., 3517
Lee, Robert C., 3741
Lee, T. R., 6161
Lees, Lynn, 143
Lee-Whiting, Brenda, 5312
Lefebvre, André, 2523
Lefebvre, Fernand, 2360, 2524
Lefebvre, Guy, 2821
Lefrançois, Pierre-C., 2822
Légaré, Anne, 2033
Légaré, Jacques, 1965, 2709, 2710, 3070
Légaré, Jean-Paul, 3211
Legare, Leo Joseph, 6117
Legault, Guy-R., 2823
Legendre, D., 3290
Léger, Albert-Ange, 337
Legge, Arthur E. E., 3328
Legge, Charles, 2613
Legget, John C., 6545
Legget, Robert F., 3373, 4274
Legros, Hector, 4275
Leigh, Amy, 1075, 1080

Leigh, R., 93, 817, 6490
Leitch, Adelaide, 7036
Lelièvre, A. B., 2206
Leman, A. B., 56
Leman, I. A., 56
Le May, T. D., 583, 5144
Le Messurier, Henry W., 1865, 1866
Lemieux, Marc, 3374
Lemieux, Vincent, 3183, 3184
Lemire, Robert, 2608, 2609
Lemoine, James M., 2992, 2993, 2994, 2995, 2996, 2997
Lemon, Donald P., 1605
Lemon, James T., 144, 145, 5144A, 5144B, 5144C
Lendray-Zwicki, Joseph B., 2207, 4395
Le Neveu, Allan Henry, 6545
Lenz, Carl, 5375
Leo, Christopher, 299
Léonard, Jean-François, 2824, 2825
Lepine, Y., 2826
Leroy, Vély, 2827
Lesage, J., 2828
Lessard, Claude, 3329
Lessard, Marc-André, 2034, 2035
Lessard, Michel, 2036
Letarte, Jacques, 2036A
Letendre, A., 2998
Létourneau, Hubert, 3064
Lett, W. P., 4276, 4323
Levac, Anne Carswell, 877
Levéillé, J., 1394, 2676, 3155, 3857, 4366, 5014, 5651, 6100, 6212, 6682
Léveillée, Jacques, 2829, 2830, 2831, 2832
Lévesque, J. R., 3518
Levesque, Robert, 2833
Levin, Arthur, 6021
Levin, Earl A., 651, 5676, 5945
Levine, David, 4224
Levine, G. J., 3929, 3990
Levinson, Harvey, 2834
Levitt, Alan, 4517A
Lewis, A. C., 2835
Lewis, Alfred H., 6546
Lewis, D. E., 1867
Lewis, D. S., 2361
Lewis, Paul, 3704
Lewis, Victor George, 4949
Li, Peter S., 5145, 5908
Li, Si-Ming, 818
Li, Ying H., 2836
Lidster, E. L. R., 6954
Liebbrandt, Gottlieb, 4069, 4070
Lieberson, S., 2837
Lieff, P. J., 2037
Lier, John, 5376
Liggett, W. D., 5377

Lightbody, James W., 913, 914, 5677, 5678, 5679
Lighthall, William D., 846, 915, 960, 1076, 2362, 2614, 4950
Lin, Hon-seng, 5909
Lim, J. L., 4071
Limoges, Thérèse, 2838
Linder, Alice Dorothy, 6022
Lindstrom-Best, Varpu, 4951
Lines, K., 6810
Ling, P. T., 5528
Linkletter, A. Z., 1284
Linteau, Paul-André, 1975, 2038, 2039, 2040, 2363, 2491, 2525, 2526, 2615, 2616, 2617, 2618, 2619, 2620
Lioy, Michele, 6710
Lister, Herbert, 3829
Lithwick, I., 366
Lithwick, N. H., 57, 58, 59, 213, 916, 961, 3519
Little, C. H., 1413
Little, Jack, 2044
Livermore, J. D., 4019
Livingston, Gordon, 1655
Lizars, Robina, 3705
Lloyd, Antony John, 60
Lloyd, Donald, 4527
Lloyd, Sheila, 4355
Lochhead, Douglas, 18, 4952
Locke, P. R., 4500
Logan, Harry T., 6547
Logan, J. W., 1285
Logan, R., 3789
Loiselle, Roland, 2364
Lomas, A. A., 1175
Londerville, John J. D., 4459
London Ontario Chamber of Commerce, 4118
Long, J. A., 917
Long, Norton E., 146
Long, R. S., 1176
Long, W. A., 4953
Longstaff, F. W., 6400
Longstreet, T. Morris, 2365, 2999, 4277
Loosley, E. W., 823
Looy, Anthony J., 4954
Lopatin, Ivan Alexis, 6548
Lord, G., 1394, 2676, 2839, 3155, 3185, 3857, 4366, 5014, 5651, 6100, 6212, 6682
Lord, Ian, 564
Lorimer, James, 652, 918, 919, 920, 921, 922, 4738, 4739
Lorriman, F. R., 4528
Lort, J. C. R., 6340, 6811
Lort, R., 6812
Lotz, J. R., 6955, 6956, 6957, 6999, 7000, 7022, 7023, 7024, 7025
Louder, Frederick, 2840

Loudon, J. D., 3674
Lovatt, Bill, 1656
Love, D. V., 3493
Lovell, Walter S., 3930, 3931
Lovendon, P., 392
Loveridge, D. M., 5424
Low, David, 4561
Lowden, James David, 847
Lowe, P., 5608
Lower, A. R. M., 267, 1657, 3932, 3933, 3934, 4278
Lower Mainland Regional Planning Board of British Columbia, 6711
Lowther, Barbara J., 6364
Lozovsky, N., 6884
Lubove, R., 147
Lucas, Alistair R., 5980
Lucas, Fred G., 5609
Lucas, G. C., 4279
Lucas, Rex A., 326
Lucas, Richard, 3830
Luciuk, Lubomyr Y., 3935
Lucow, W. H., 5529
Ludditt, W., 6885
Luk, Lordson Wai-chung, 5910
Lumby, J. R., 4623
Lundgren, J., 2332
Lundgren, R., 3696
Lunty, A. J., 5530
Luscombe, B. W., 5851
Lutman, John H., 4119, 4120, 4121
Lutz, Burkart, 148
Lynch, P., 1370
Lyons, Marjorie Eleanor, 5313
Lys-Cambridge, L., 268

McAfee, Ann, 6712, 6713
MacAllister, Edith, 1721
McAra, Peter, 5852
McArthur, Duncan, 3000
McArthur, N. M., 3520, 4122
McArton, A. W., 4592
McArton, D., 5531
McCabe, R. W., 3521
McCaffey, E., 6813, 6814, 6815
McCalla, Douglas, 3831, 3832, 3833, 4726, 4955
McCallum, John, 3521A
McCammon, Andrew, 3522
McCandless, Richard, 6714
McCann, L. D., 149, 327, 696, 1414, 5378, 6162, 6239, 6643, 6816
McCarthy, J. O., 368, 1077
McCarthy, Michael P., 962
McCarty, R. F., 6306

McCaskill, Donald N., 451, 453, 5146, 5532, 6163, 6549
McCharles, Aeneas, 4593
McClelland, Peter D., 1563
McConnell, R. S., 6164
McConniff, J., 2621
McCordic, Wm. J., 5147
McCormack, A. Ross, 5379, 5610
McCormick, James Hanna, 5805
McCracken, J. W., 5946, 5947
McCracken, Kevin W. J., 6240
McCracken, Melinda, 5680
McCready, J. E. B., 4356
McCullough, J. W. S., 766, 2042, 3523
McCurry, R. K., 3524
McCutcheon, Henry R., 1799
McCutcheon, M. K., 5948
MacDermaid, Anne, 3936, 4020
MacDermaid, M. A., 2527
McDermid, G. E., 1497
MacDermot, Hugh E., 2366, 2528
MacDonald, Bruce F., 1470
MacDonald, C., 5777
McDonald, D. N., 6241
McDonald, Donald, 4232
MacDonald, Donald Ian, 5446
McDonald, Hugh, 6242
McDonald, J. E., 5314
MacDonald, James S., 1371
Macdonald, John, 6165
MacDonald, K. J., 6365
MacDonald, M., 4624
McDonald, Margaret L., 2793
McDonald, Margaret Lillooet, 6441
McDonald, Mary L., 2529
MacDonald, Nancy K., 1286
MacDonald, Norbert, 6550, 6644, 6645, 6646, 6647
Macdonald, Norman, 426, 427
Macdonald, R. H., 5801
McDonald, Robert A. J., 6366, 6648, 6649, 6650, 6817
Macdonnell, G. M., 3937
McDonough, John, 3871
MacDougall, Alex, 3134
McDougall, D., 428
McDougall, Elizabeth A., 2530
McDougall, Harry, 3525, 5148
Macdougall, J. B., 3526
McDougall, R. J., 6651
McDougall, W., 2841
McDowall, Duncan L., 3991, 4021, 4493
McDowell, Laurel, 4035
MacEwan, Grant, 6023, 6072, 6073, 6074, 6118
MacEwan, Paul, 1498
McEwen, Alice, 6119

McFadden, C. R., 5746
Mcfarland, H. B. R., 963
McFarland, John R., 5981
Macfarlane, Alan, 151
McFarlane, Leslie, 5315
McFarlane, M., 1287
McFarlane, R. O., 5611
McGahan, Elizabeth M. W., 1658, 1659
McGaughey, Charles Eustace, 3527
McGee, Robert, 4956
McGee, Timothy J., 1288
McGeer, Gerald G., 6551
McGill, Alan S., 6552
MacGillivray, C. J., 1216
MacGillivray, C. L., 6243
Macgillivray, Donald W., 1499, 1500
McGinnis, J. P. Dickin, 6075, 6076
McGlasken, S., 6249
McGovern, Peter D., 6553
McGowan, D. C., 5937
MacGowan, D. F., 1722
McGrath, C. A., 6275
McGrath, P. T., 1868
McGraw, Donald, 2825, 2842
McGregor, D. A., 6554, 6652
MacGregor, James G., 6166, 6196, 6197
McGuire, B. J., 6422
Machar, Agnes M., 3939, 3940, 3941
McHoull, W. Donald, 3938
Machum, L. A., 1607
McIlwraith, Thomas, 3528
McInnes, J. R., 1032
MacInnes, Tom, 6555
McInnis, Marvin, 4022
McIntosh, R. G., 5982
MacIver, I., 3529
MacIver, John M., 964, 2367
McKay, Alexander G., 3834
McKay, Ian, 1289, 1290
McKay, K. W., 3530
MacKay, Michael, 1660
Mackay, N., 5853
MacKay, Robert W. S., 2368
McKean, F. K., 4434, 4435
McKee, D. L., 1564, 1800
McKee, William C., 6556, 6557, 6558, 6559
McKee-Allain, Isabelle, 1606
McKegney, Patricia, 4072
McKellar, James, 6119A
McKelvie, B. A., 6429
McKenna, Bruce, 3531
McKenzie, B. A., 4957
McKenzie, Grace M., 2136
Mackenzie, Lois, 3555
MacKenzie, N. H., 5316
MacKenzie, Ruth Heartz, 1758
McKillop, A. B., 5681, 5682, 5683, 5684

MacKinnon, C. I., 1415
MacKinnon, C. S., 6401
MacKinnon, Frank, 1746, 1759, 1760
MacKinnon, Fred R., 1078
MacKinnon, Ian F., 1177
MacKinnon, J. G., 1501
MacKinnon, John Stephen, 1661
MacKinnon, R. D., 254
MacKinnon, Wayne Emerson, 1747
Mackintosh, C. H., 6886
Mclaren, Jack, 5149
McLarty, R. A., 5778
McLean, Eric, 2369
McLean, F. H., 2370
MacLean, J., 4477
MacLean, John S., 2622
MacLean, M. C., 393
Maclean, R. A., 6167
Maclean, Raymond A., 1217
MacLean, T. D., 1457
Maclean, W. F., 4958
McLellan, A. G., 4073
MacLellan, O., 1130
McLemore, R., 819
McLennan, C. Prescott, 1291, 1292
MacLennan, H., 1293, 2371, 2372
MacLennan, Ian, 923
McLennan, John S., 1453
McLeod, B. A., 5150
Macleod, Catherine, 5151
McLeod, F. C. J., 5747
MacLeod, G. W., 1662
MacLeod, H. L., 6077
McLeod, Hugh, 151
McLeod, Judy, 3532
MacLeod, Malcolm, 3533
MacLeod, Margaret Arnett, 5612, 5613, 5614
McLeod, N. L., 6078
MacLeod, Paul G., 2531
McLeod, R. R., 1478
McMann, Robert, 4959
MacMechan, Archibald, 1294, 1295, 1296, 1297, 1298
McMenemy, John M., 3873
Macmillan, Arvo Arnold, 1178
Macmillan, Cyrus, 2373
Macmillan, David S., 239
McMillan, J. G., 4036
Macmillan, J. W., 394
Macmillan, James A., 767
McMillan, M. L., 5983
McMorine, J. K., 3992, 3993
McMullin, Stanley E., 61
McMurray, A. L., 4648
Mcnab, Alan, 4740
MacNab, John E., 4741
McNaught, Kenneth, 5615

McNeill, Leishman, 6024
MacNiett, W. S., 1372
MacPhail, Cathy, 4494
McPhail, J. G., 4280
McPhail, L. R., 6418
McPherson, Arlean, 5802
MacPherson, Charlotte H. G., 3001
McPherson, H. L., 6560
MacPherson, Ian, 5379
MacPherson, Ken, 3483
MacPherson, L. G., 5685
Macpherson, M. E., 4742
MacQuarrie, M. R., 1663
McRae, Edward Davidson, 328
McRae, K. D., 4396
MacRae, Marion, 3534, 3535, 3835
MacRossie, W., 653
MacSkimming, W. T., 4249
Mactaggart, H. I., 3536
MacTavish, Newton, 3135
McVey, Wayne W., 362
Macvicar, William M., 1211
McVittie, J. I., 878

Mackie, Joan, 4272
Mackie, John, 3942
Macri, Pamela, 741
Mage, Julius, 4074
Magill, D. W., 1179, 1401, 1502
Magill, Max, 3994
Magnan, A., 3330
Mahatty, R. V., 4281
Maher, Christopher A., 5023, 5152, 5153
Maheux, Arthur, 3111, 3136, 4397
Maheaux, Louis-Philippe, 2221
Mahon, W. C., 5854
Mahoney, T. D., 4517
Mailhiot, Bernard, 2843, 2844
Major, Marjorie, 1299
Makabe, Tomoko, 5154
Makler, Anita C., 4743
Makovski, L. W., 6653, 6654
Malcolmson, Patricia E., 3995
Mallach, Stanley, 300
Mallett, Robin B., 6276, 6283
Mallon, Mary F., 4960
Mallory, Enid, 4282
Mallory, James R., 2845
Malo, Roch, 2222
Malone, Tom, 4874
Manchur, S. W., 2846
Mandel, Eli, 62
Mandelle, Roméo, 2847
Mangala, M., 2043
Manitoba, Government of, 5686
Manitoba, Royal Commission on Local Government Organization and Finance, 5425

Manly, C. M., 4075
Mann, W. E., 4744, 5155
Manners, E., 4594
Manning, H. E., 1033
Mannion, John J., 1131, 1801
Manseau, H., 2044
Manson-Smith, P., 5057
Manula, Francis A., 452
Marani, F. H., 697
Marble, Allan E., 1383
Marchal, Léon, 2461
Marchand, Jean-René, 3375
Marcus, Robert J., 6715
Marett, Clara M., 3742
Marier, Claude, 3186
Marier, Georges, 2045
Marion, S., 2532, 2533
Mariyana, Soy, 848
Markovich, R., 5265
Markusen, Ann R., 1079
Markusen, J. R., 5156
Marlatt, Daphne, 6561
Marlyn, F., 6168
Marlyn, John, 5533
Marmick, Alice, 5317
Marois, Michèle R., 2056
Marple, David, 3537
Marquis, Georges-Emile, 3002, 3137
Marquis, H., 2036
Marsan, Jean-Claude, 2046, 2374
Marsh, Leonard, 19, 584
Marshall, A. H., 1034
Marshall, John U., 152, 240, 269, 2780, 3538, 3539
Marshall, M. V., 1525
Marsolais, Jean-Marc, 2223
Marston, Katherine A., 3743
Marston, W. G., 5157
Martel, J., 3273
Martel, Pierre-B., 2224
Martell, Eve, 2623
Martell, J. S., 1180, 1373, 1503
Martin, A., 6244
Martin, Ann, 3874
Martin, Brian R., 7001
Martin, Dan, 2848, 2849
Martin, Fernand, 2850
Martin, G. M., 4745
Martin, J.-M., 2047
Martin, Gérald, 2851
Martin, J.-P., 2048, 4595
Martin, Jacques, 2852
Martin, John, 6169
Martin, John Patrick, 1300
Martin, Larry R. G., 76, 5158
Martin, Mayor, 5855
Martin, Yves, 153, 369, 2013, 2049, 2050, 2051, 3207, 3229, 3364

Martineau, Paul G., 2624
Martin-Tard, Louis, 2292
Martyn, Lucy B., 4746, 4747
Marx, H., 2271
Masolf, L. D., 241
Mason, Philip, 2376
Massey, Georges, 2052
Massey-Harris Co. Ltd., 4748
Massicotte, E.-Z., 2376, 2462, 2463, 2464, 2465, 2466, 2467, 2468, 2469, 2470, 2471, 2472, 2473, 2474, 2534
Masson, Jack K., 924, 925, 5984, 6245
Massue, Huet, 2853
Masters, D. C., 301, 2053, 2625, 3003, 4961, 4962, 5687
Materazzi, F., 2208
Mather, Barry, 6442
Mather, C. A., 1940
Mather, Edith, 2377, 2378
Matheson, Harold Kenneth, 6562
Matheson, Marion H., 1664, 5779, 6430
Mathews, Hazel, 5318
Mathieu, Jacques, 3065, 3066, 3067, 3138, 3139
Matrovolgyi, T. A., 5856
Matte, E., 3376
Matte, Gilbert, 3212
Matters, Diane L., 6655, 6656, 6657
Matthews, Keith, 1132, 1802, 1803, 1804, 1869, 1870, 1871
Matthews, Ralph, 1795, 1805, 1806
Matwijiw, Peter, 429, 5688
Maurault, Olivier, 2379, 2380, 2381, 2382, 2383, 2384, 2475, 2476, 2626
Mavor, James, 3540, 5159
Mawson, Thomas H., 585, 5857, 6079, 6658
Maxwell, J. A., 879
Maxwell, J. W., 242, 270
Maxwell, Thomas R., 5160, 5161
May, Betty F., 20
May, E. G., 6080
May, Edward G., 2209
May, J., 4283
May, Jack, 5027
Maybee, Janet A., 1374
Mayell, J. F., 329
Mayer, Harold M., 154, 370
Mayhew, Barry W., 6563
Mayne, Robert E., 6958
Mayo, H. B., 586, 1807
Mayrand, Pierre, 2054
Meacham, J. H., 1748
Medam, Alain, 2385
Medjuck, Sheva, 1608, 1609, 3836
Medovy, Harry, 5534
Meekison, John Peter, 1035
Meen, Sharon P., 302

Meeves, E. L., 6289
Meirovich, Harvey, 4749
Melancon, J.-M., 2854
Meldrum, Pixie, 6423
Melland, John F., 6120
Mellen, Frances N., 4963
Mellis, Glen Wallace, 5780
Mellish, John T., 1762
Ménard, Denis, 2855
Ménard, G., 2055
Mennill, David C., 4193, 4194
Men of the City (Historical Association of Saskatoon), 5911
Mercer, John, 155, 2856, 3875
Mercer, W. M., 5266
Mercer, William M., 6887
Mercier, Bernard-E., 2385A
Merkel, Andrew, 1301
Merrens, H. Roy, 5093
Merrett, J. Campbell, 1665, 1666
Merrill, C. R., 2131
Merrill, Leslie I., 5426
Mertz, J. P., 5748
Messier, Camille, 2056
Metcalfe, Alan, 2627, 2628
Metcalfe, J. H., 5469
Metcalfe, William H., 5470
Metropolitan Corporation of Greater Winnipeg, 5689
Metsaranta, M. J., 4635
Metson, Graham, 1416
Metton, Alain, 2857
Metzler, N., 1301
Meyer, François, 4750
Meyer, John, 2858
Meyerson, M., 587
Mezoff, Richard, 5172
Michas, N. A., 1036
Michaud, C., 3274
Michaud, Laurent, 2057, 3378
Michaud, Marguerite, 1610
Michelson, William, 156, 395
Mechie, George, 3379
Middleton, Diana J., 194, 3790, 3837
Middleton, Jesse Edgar, 4751, 4752
Migner, Robert-Maurice, 2833, 2859, 2860
Migue, J. L., 1037
Mika, Helma, 3541, 3642, 3643, 3644, 4753, 5319
Mika, Nick, 3541, 3642, 3643, 3644, 3943, 3944, 4753, 5319
Mikel, W. C., 3645
Mikkelson, P. M., 6367
Milanson, Harold, 3542
Milde, G. T., 2590
Millen, Walter H., 2209
Miller, Audrey S., 4875, 4876

Miller, C. Warren, 4562
Miller, Donna, 6419
Miller, Emile, 2386
Miller, Evelyn, 2387
Miller, Fern, 6716, 6717
Miller, J. D., and Associates Ltd., 1212
Miller, Orlo, 3543, 4123, 4124, 4125, 4126, 4168
Miller, R. J., 3744
Millidge, J. W., 1667
Mills, David S., 1907
Mills, James C., 4495
Mills, John M., 3544, 3791
Mills, Richard E., 3745
Mills, Thora McIlroy, 6959
Millward, H. A., 588, 4195
Milner, James B., 589, 698, 5162
Milner, William C., 1616, 1668
Minghi, Julian V., 6718
Ministry of State for Urban Affairs (MSUA), 21
Minton, Eric, 4284, 4285
Minville, Esdras, 2861
Miquelon, Dale, 2058, 3068
Miron, John R., 214, 5163
Mitchell, C. H., 590
Mitchell, E. B., 5380
Mitchell, George, 5535
Mitchell, J. R., 1303
Mitchell, N., 6564
Mitchell, R., 5616
Mitchell, V. W., 1304
Miyao, Takahiro, 215
Moffat, Charles W., 1617
Moffat, Robert Y., 6368
Mohan, Elizabeth Marilyn, 6121
Mollenknopf, John H., 926
Mollmann, Albert Von, 2862
Monanu, P. C., 6246
Moneo, G. W., 5413, 5781
Monet, Jacques, 2536
Monk, H. A. J., 6905
Montminy, Jean-Paul, 2035
Montpetit, Raymond, 2388, 2389
Montréal, Que., Service d'urbanisme, 2863
Montreal Society of Architecture, 2390
Montreal Urban Community Transit Commission, 2391
Monu, E. D., 5447
Moodie, Robert James, 6566
Moogk, Peter N., 2059, 2060, 2061, 2477, 6567
Moon, Robert, 3004
Mooney, George S., 63, 216, 217, 965
Moore, Christopher, 1454, 1455, 1456
Moore, Dan, 3876
Moore, Helen Margaret, 6719

Moore, John Phillip, 6888
Moore, K. V., 5267
Moore, Marian F., 1305
Moore, Peter W., 5164, 5165
Moorhouse, Walter, 699
Morah, Benson Chukwuma, 6122
Morantz, A. L., 5166
Morgan, John S., 1080
Morgan, Robert, 1457, 1504
Morgenroth, Kasper G., 5912
Morin, Denis, 2062
Morin, L.-E., 2629
Morin, R., 2063, 3187
Morin, Victor, 2392, 2393, 2394
Morrisseau, H., 3380
Morley, Alan, 6568
Morley, David, 5034
Morley, E. L., 4555
Morley, Marjorie, 5427
Morley, William F. W., 1133, 1926, 3545
Morris, Janet, 4460
Morris, J. E., 6720
Morris, John Alfred, 5320
Morris, R. Geoffrey, 5690
Morrison, E. C., 6025
Morrison, G. E., 4461
Morrison, Jean F., 4626, 4626A, 4627, 4628
Morrison, K. Margaret, 1417
Morrison, N. M., 2064
Morrison, Neil F., 5268
Morrison, P. N. R., 6025
Morrison, Philip S., 768
Morrison, Sandra, 4184
Morrison, Terrence R., 3546, 4964
Morrisseau, H., 3380
Morrow, E. Joyce, 6026
Morrow, J. W., 6284
Morrow, Robert A. H., 1485
Morse, C., 880
Morse, Richard M., 271
Morse, Robert, 1181
Morse, Susan Langley, 1182
Morton, A. S., 5913
Morton, Desmond, 4865
Morton, W. L., 966, 5381, 5536, 5617, 6960, 6961
Mosdell, H. M., 1808
Moser, John Lucas, 5858, 5859
Moss, Michael R., 4529
Mott, H. Y., 1809
Mott, Morris K., 5618, 5749
Mowat, Grace Helen, 1620
Mowers, Cleo W., 6277
Moyer, William, 4076, 4077
Moyles, Robert Gordon, 1871, 1872
Mozersky, K. A., 5382
Muddiman, B., 2630, 4286

Muir, Doris J., 3547
Muir, Roland E., 5782
Muise, D. A., 22
Mullaly, Emmet J., 1763
Mullane, G., 1306
Muller, Edward K., 243
Muller, Jean-Claude, 6247
Mulvany, C. Pelham, 4462, 4754
Mumford, Lewis, 64
Muncaster, Russell W., 4196, 4197
Municipal Publishing Company, 881
Munro, Don, 3548
Munro, W. B., 882
Munske, R. R., 1810
Muntz, M., 3683
Murch, B., 4398
Murchie, Graham, 5984A
Murdie, Robert A., 74, 4074, 5024, 5167
Murphy, Achille, 3140
Murphy, Larry, 3549
Murphy, M. P., 5168
Murphy, Michael P., 1873, 1874
Murphy, Paul, 6407
Murphy, R., 157
Murray, A. L., 2632
Murray, J. A., 769
Murray, Jack, 1723
Murray, Jean E., 5783, 5784
Murray, John, 1505
Murray, Olin B., 5383
Murray, R., 1307
Murray, T. A., 1081, 1082
Murray, W. C., 1134, 1308
Murray, W. D., 5785
Murricane, K., 2864
Musée d'Art contemporain, Montréal, 2865
Mutambirwa, Christopher C., 3550, 5321
Mutswairo, Solomon M., 4399
Myers, Jay, 4755
Myers, Thomas R., 6818
Myles, J. S., 5169

Nablo, R. W., 1135
Nadeau, Jacques, 3275
Nadeau, Mireille, 3213
Nader, G. A., 5384, 5786
Nadon, Pierre, 3331
Naegele, Kaspar D., 1724, 3697
Nagata, Judith, 4756, 5170
Nagler, Mark, 5171
Nagy, T. L., 4287
Naismith, George, 4966
Namm, R., 6721
Nantel, Guillaume-Alphonse, 2633
Nasby, Judith M., 3746
Nasim, Shaukat Ali, 5787

Nason, R., 1621
National Capital Commission, 4288, 4324
Neal, Carolyn, 4757, 5322
Neal, M. W., 5860
Neary, Peter F., 1908
Neatby, Hilda, 3945, 4023
Nebel, M., 5949
Neely, Bryan Robert George, 5861
Neil, Edmund, 3188
Neilson, M., 5385
Neilson, W. A., 4758
Nelles, Douglas H., 4169
Nelles, H. V., 303, 967, 1392, 4530, 4889
Nelson, Denys, 6408
Nesbit, W. C., 1669
Nesbitt, James George, 6369
Neufeld, W., 5750
Neumann, Brigette, 5172
Neville, F. J., 6922
Nevitt, Adela Adam, 770
Newall, P. D., 4198
New Brunswick. Royal Commission on Finance and Municipal Taxation, 1565
Newcomer, Mabel, 1038
Newfeld, Frank, 4699
Newfoundland Historic Trust, 1875
Newinger, Scott, 6027
Ng, Che L., 2866
Nga, Nguyen Thuy, 4400
Niagara Historical Society, 4532
Nichol, Helen R., 2634
Nichol, John L., 5914
Nichols, C. M., 4226
Nichols, John W., 1876
Nicholson, Byron, 3005, 3141
Nicholson, N. L., 3551
Nicholson, T. G., 5691, 5692
Nicholson, T. J., 6370
Nickel, Edith, 767
Nickerson, R., 4596
Nicol, Eric, 6569
Nicoll, Ian M., 6170
Nicolls, F. W., 592
Nicolson, Murray, 4967
Niddrie, J. G., 6198
Niellon, Françoise, 2065
Nilson, Deborah, 6570
Nish, Cameron, 2395
Nitkin, D. A., 3552
Niwinski, Alice, 6540
Nixon, G. P., 4199
Nixon, Peter G., 3429, 5269
Njau, G. J., 5173
Nobbs, Percy E., 593, 654, 700, 701, 702, 2867
Noble, E. J., 4227
Noble, G. W., 472

Nodwell, L. M., 6115
Noppen, Luc, 3006, 3007, 3008, 3069, 3112, 3113
Norbert, Prosper, 3381
Norbert, Roland, 2066
Norcliffe, G. B., 3553, 4078
Norcross, E. Blanche, 6431
Nordland, R. V., 6963
Norris, Darrell, 5323
North Bay Board of Trade, 4220
Northey, John Laird, 6722
Northrup, D. A., 1670
Norton, D. G., 5985
Norton, J. T., 1309
Nova Scotia Association of Architects, 1310
Nova Scotia Steel and Coal Co. Ltd., 1506
Nursey, W. R., 5581
Nwala, V. E., 4401

Oak Bay Anniversary Committee, 6819
Oberlander, Cornelia, 6890
Oberlander, H. Peter, 66, 330, 594, 595, 596, 597, 6371, 6889, 6890
O'Brien, Allan, 3554
O'Brien, Michael, 2868
Obright, D. C., 4028
O'Carroll, Anthony Cecil, 245
Ockley, B. A., 6199
O'Connell, Martin P., 1039
O'Connor, K., 246
O'Dea, A. C., 1811
O'Dea, Shane, 1813, 1877, 1878
O'Flaherty, Patrick, 1812
O'Gallagher, Marianna, 3114, 3115
Ogden, R. Lynn, 23, 6571
Ohannesian, P. B., 6572
Oland, Sidney, 1375
O'Leary, M. Grattan, 4402
Olfert, M. Rose, 6977A
Oliver, E. H., 5806
Oliver, Frank, 6200
Oliver, J., 1040
Oliver, L. H. R., 5270
Oliver, Thomas J., 3009, 3010
Olivier, M., 2067
Olivier-Lacamp, Gael, 3070
Olm, Sharon Joan, 5915
Olmstead, Frederick Law, 2635
O'Malley, M., 5537
O'Mara, James, 5174
O'Meara, Henry, 1856
Ondaatje, Kim, 3555
O'Neil, Lynne E., 4463
O'Neil, Pierre, 3276
O'Neill, Nora, 4760
O'Neill, Patrick B., 4877, 5862

O'Neill, Paul, 1813, 1879, 1880, 1881
Onn, Gerald, 4127
Ontario, Department of Economics and Development, Special Research and Surveys Branch, 4534
Ontario, Department of Health, 3556
Ontario, Department of Municipal Affairs, 3557
Ontario, Department of Trade and Development, and the Ontario Development Corporation, 3558
Ontario, Department of Treasury and Economics, and the Department of Municipal Affairs, 3559
Ontario, Department of Treasury and Economics, Regional Development Branch, 3560, 4534
Ontario, Educational Communications Authority, 4761
Ornstein, M. D., 466
Orillia Historical Society, 4228
Orrell, John, 6201
Osborne, Brian S., 3947, 3996, 4864
Osborne, Kenneth, 5386
O'Shaughnessy, Katherine, 703
Osing, Olga, 6891
Ossenberg, R. J., 2869, 5175
Ostergaard, P., 7037
Ostiguy, Jean, 3241
Ostry, Sylvia, 468, 473
O'Toole, Roger Laurence, 5176
Ottawa Welfare Council, 4406
Ouellett, Fernand, 2068, 2069, 2070, 2071, 2537, 2538, 3011, 3116, 3117
Ouellet, J., 2072
Ouellet, M.-F., 2165
Outhet, R. A., 1083
Overton, David, 3561
Owen, David S., 849
Owens, G. B., 4200
Owens, H. T., 1041
Oxley, J. M., 1672, 4128

Pacey, Mary, 1590
Pacreau, C., 3382
Page, John Edward, 5538
Paillé, Michel-P., 3118
Pain, S. A., 4037
Painchaud, Robert, 5619
Paint, H. M., 2870
Palko, S., 4398
Palmer, Bernard C., 6372
Palmer, Bryan D., 3488, 3838, 3997
Palmer, Virginia, 3418
Pammett, H. T., 4464, 4465
Panabaker, D. N., 3658

Pando, Robert Ian, 4079
Panneton, G., 3330
Panting, Gerald, 1521, 1526
Pape, G., 2761
Papillon, Marthe, 3189
Paquet, Gilles, 59, 158, 159, 2073, 2539
Paradis, Wilfrid H., 3071
Paré, A., 2871
Paré, Simone, 3190
Parent, Gilles, 2074
Parent, Honoré, 598
Parenteau, Roland, 2075, 2076, 2872
Paris, Jacques, 1749
Parisella, John E., 2973
Parizeau, Gérard, 2077
Parker, B. A., 4535
Parker, Gilbert, 3072
Parker, Helen, 2038
Parker, Keith A., 247
Parker, L. J., 4221
Parker, Victor J., 331
Parker, W. H., 2078, 3119
Parkinson, Anna, 5986, 5986A
Parks, Judith, 4762
Parks, William T., 599
Parnall, M. B., 3747
Parnell, C., 6202
Parr, G. J., 3562
Parr, John, 5539
Parrisset, Marie-Françoise, 2874
Parrott, Donald F., 5324
Parsons, Alberta, 6892
Pascoe, J. E., 5811
Paskievich, John, 5540
Pasternak, Jack, 4080
Patenaude, J.-Z. Leon, 2875
Paterson, N. R., 5177
Paterson, T. W., 6373, 6374, 6964
Patillo, R. W., 6573
Paton, J. A., 6659
Patterson, Frederick Jenkins, 6574
Patterson, H. S., 5987
Patterson, J. M., 6723
Patterson, James G., 6575
Patterson, N., 4968, 4969
Pattison, M., 5916
Paul, G. S., 6139
Paul, L. J., 6290
Paulette, Claude, 3008
Paulin, Jean-Claude, 3305
Paumier, Cyril, 2876
Paupst, K., 4970
Payne, A. M., 1312
Payne, Hilary, 3563
Payne, Marilyn, 1673
Payzant, Joan, 1313
Payzant, Lewis, 1313

Peach, John S., 6028
Peake, Frank A., 6203, 6204
Pearce, William, 6123
Pearson, Norman, 67, 68, 272, 332, 371, 600, 655, 3564, 3698, 3699, 3877
Pearson, R. E., 1882
Pearson, W. H., 4763
Peck, Mary, 1591
Peck, T., 3659
Peebles, Elaine, 4517A
Peel, Bruce, 5387, 5917
Peet, Richard, 474
Peitchinis, Stephen, 6124
Pelletier, A. J., 396
Pelletier, J. A., 5694
Pelletier, Jean, 2877
Péloquin, Bonaventure, 2079
Pendakur, V. Setty, 6724
Pendergast, James A., 4233
Pendergast, R. A., 2540
Penner, Norman, 5620, 5621
Pense, Fred, 3948
Pentland, H. C., 160, 475, 476
Pépin, Cornélie L., 6307
Pépin, Fernand, 2137
Pépin, Pierre-Yves, 3383
Percival, Ray N., 3565, 3700
Percival, W. P., 2396
Pereira, Cecil Patrick, 5695
Perin, Robert, 2636
Perkins, Charlotte I., 1213
Perks, W. T., 2878, 5387A
Perley, M. E., 3949
Perlin, A. B., 1883
Perreault, Claude, 2397
Perreault, G., 3299
Perreault, Guy, 2958
Perreault, J.-A. Claude, 2478
Perreault, Louis, 2879
Perron, Linda, 4392
Perry, Charlotte Bronte, 5271
Perry, J. Fraser, 6081
Perry, J. Harvey, 1042, 1043
Perry, Margaret L., 1314
Perry, Robert L., 3660
Person, Lloyd H., 5950
Pésant, Yves, 2178
Pessen, Edward, 397
Peters, E. D., 4597
Petersen, G. B., 374
Petersen, J., 3566
Peterson, B. H., 968
Peterson, D. D., 6171
Peterson, Roger, 1137
Pethick, Derek, 6660, 6820
Petrie, Ian, 6965
Petroff, Lillian, 4764, 4765, 4766

Petryshyn, J., 3684, 3685, 3686
Peudie, R., 6029
Phaneuf, Georges-Etienne, 3242
Phelan, R. E., 5751
Phelps, Edward C., 24, 4100, 4478, 4479, 4480, 4483
Phelps, Oliver, 4536
Philbrook, T. V., 1814, 1909
Philip, C. R., 6082
Phillips, A. D., 5428
Phillips, D. A., 771
Phillips, F., 1592
Phillips, Fred H., 1593
Phillips, Gordon C., 5752
Phillips, M., 4739
Phillips, Nathan, 5178
Phillips, Paul A., 5388, 5389, 5622
Phillips, R. A. J., 3567, 6931
Phillips-Cleland, Jennifer, 1315
Philp, John, 3568
Philpott, Stuart Bowman, 430
Picard, François, 3013
Piché, Odessa, 2080
Pick, Alfred John, 2880
Pickard, M. K., 6966
Picker, A., 2881
Pickersgill, T. B., 5390
Pickett, James, 772
Pickford, Frank A., 3687
Pictou Heritage Society, 1471
Pierce, D. J., 3998
Pierce, Dixwell L., 1044
Pierre-Deschenes, Claudine, 2081
Piers, H., 1316
Pigeon, L. B., 4325
Pill, Juri, 5179
Pilton, James William, 6821
Pinard, Maurice, 411
Pinard, Yolande, 2611, 2637, 2637A
Pincombe, Charles Alexander, 1611
Pincombe, P. G., 4201
Pineault, Gilles, 3191
Pineault, Laval, 3191
Piovesma, Roy H., 4628A
Piper, John, 5892, 5918, 5919
Pirie, Margaret C., 4767
Pitcher, Rosemary, 3014
Pitsula, James, 4768, 4971
Pitt, David G., 1884
Piva, Michael, 3569, 4972, 4973
Plain, R. H. M., 5983
Plante, Albert, 4598
Playfair, W., 6661
Plewes, J. C., 5181
Ploegaerts, Léon, 4408
Plouffe, M., 3120
Plunkett, R. E., 6248

Plunkett, Thomas J., 69, 883, 884, 885, 969, 970, 1045, 1566, 1832, 5696
Podmore, D. R., 6249
Podoluk, J. C., 477
Poetschke, T. R., 6172
Pogue, Basil Gregory, 6893
Pohorecky, Zenon, 5788
Poirier, R., 2179
Poisson, Yves, 3192
Polèse, Mario, 828, 2082, 2756, 3152
Pollack, Gladys, 2638
Pollock, John W., 4038
Polyzoi, Elouessa, 5182
Poole, Thomas W., 4466
Poon, C. L., 850
Pope, William, 1514
Port, A. W., 333
Porteous, J. Douglas, 334, 335, 6375, 6894
Porter, John R., 2083, 3007
Porter, Richard P. R., 6577
Pothier, Bernard, 1458
Potrin, G., 1674
Potter, H. H., 2883
Potyondi, Barry, 5463, 5464
Pouleton, Ron, 4974
Poulin, Guy, 5391
Pouliot, Adrien, 3015
Pouliot, Léon, 2541
Powell, Alan, 70
Powell, C. W., 1046, 1815
Powell, Ken, 1419
Powell, M., 861
Powell, T. J. D., 5789
Powers, J. W., 5863
Pratley, P. L., 1675
Pratt, D. F., 5623
Pratt, J., 6083
Pred, Allan, 273
Pressman, N. E. P., 161, 336, 337, 338, 601, 602
Preston, B., 4046
Preston, Richard A., 162, 3950, 3951, 3952, 3953, 3958, 3999
Preston, Richard E., 71, 76, 218, 3570
Prézeau, Pierre, 2084, 2884
Price, Brian J., 3954
Price, Edmund Van Sandford, 6726
Price, Enid M., 2639
Price, Gifford A., 4769
Price, J., 453
Price, Mary J., 3571
Price, Ray, 7039
Price, S. R., 1676
Price, Trevor, 3572, 5272
Priddis, H., 4130
Prince Edward Island, Department of Industry and Commerce, Industrial Intelligence Unit, 1764

Prince, Samuel, 773
Prince, Samuel Henry, 1420
Prior, L. C., 4496
Pritchard, F. B., 5453
Pritchard, Gordon B., 7050
Pritchett, J. P., 3998
Proctor, F. B., 3573
Prodan, C. S., 5624
Pross, A. Paul, 1183, 1540
Prost, Robert, 2885
Proudfoot, V. B., 5775, 5978
Proulx, D., 3878
Proulx, Gilles, 1459
Proulx, Jean-Pierre, 1910
Provencher, Jean, 3054
Provost, Abbé, 3121
Provost, Honorius, 3016, 3017, 3384
Prowse, D. W., 1816
Prus, V., 2849
Pucci, Antonio, 4629, 4629A
Pullen, Henry F., 6822
Punch, Katherine, 4497
Punch, Terrence M., 1317, 1377, 1378, 1379, 1380, 1381, 1382, 1383
Punnett, R. J., 927
Punter, J. V., 4770
Punter, L. B., 3575
Purdy, A. W., 4771
Purdy, M. J., 4289
Purseley, Louis H., 4975
Purvis, Donald F., 304
Putnam, J. H., 4409
Puxley, Evelyn, 2398
Pym, Harold, 6895

Quddus, M. Abdul, 5920
Québec, Ministère des affaires municipales, Direction générale de la planification, 2085
Query, Jacques, 2542
Quigley, J. Gordon, 1280
Quinn, George, 4772

Rabottin, Maurice, 2543
Raby, S., 5921
Racine, Jean-Bernard, 2399, 2886
Racine, Lewis, 2887
Raddall, J. H., 1318
Radford, John P., 163
Rae, G. W., 6967
Raina, S. K., 2888
Rajotte, E. C., 2180
Rajotte, F., 3193
Ramcharan, Subhas, 5183
Ramirez, Bruno, 2640
Ramlasingh, R. D., 5184

Ramsay, A., 5541
Ramsay, Dean P., 3576
Ramsay, J. M., 454
Ramsey, Arthur Bruce, 6376, 6896
Randal, F. H., 4357
Raney, E. F., 1047
Rankin, Harry, 6727, 6728
Rankin, R. A., 4630
Ransam, E. J., 5625
Rashleigh, E. T., 72
Rasmussen, M. A., 4631
Rasporich, A. W., 4632, 4632A, 5392, 6084
Ravis, Don, 5922
Rawin, S., 2891
Rawlyk, George A., 1460, 1461
Ray, David Michael, 73, 74, 3577, 3578
Rayburn, J. A., 1677
Rayburn, W. O., 1678
Raymond, Raoul, 2479
Raymond, W. O., 1479
Raynault, Adhémar, 2891A
Raynault, André, 2086
Raynor, Ashley E., 6729
Raynor, P., 6705
Rea, J. E., 5542, 5626, 5697, 5698, 5699, 5700
Read, D. B., 4537
Ream, P. T., 6308, 6309
Redekopp, Harold I., 5753
Reed, H. R., Jr., 4081
Reed, M., 3579
Reed, T. A., 4773, 4774, 4775, 4976
Reeds, L. G., 3879
Rees, M. H. W., 6730
Rees, P., 1679, 5325
Rees, Ronald, 5790, 5923
Reese, N. A., 5864
Rees-Powell, Alan Thomas, 6173
Reeves, B. O. K., 6085
Reeves, John H., 6832
Regan, J. W., 1319
Regehr, T. D., 5393
Regimbal, R., 4599
Régnier, Michel, 2400
Reid, A. N., 5394, 5395, 5396, 5865
Reid, Allana Gertrude, 3073, 3074
Reid, F. L., 432
Reid, W. Stanford, 3748
Reilly, J. Nolan, 1206
Reilly, Sharon, 1527
Reimer, P., 28
Reitsma, H. J. A., 4776
Reive, T. G., 4082
Reksten, Terry, 6824
Remiggi, Frank W., 2597
Rempel, John, 3580, 3581
Remy, Jean, 219

Renaud, Charles, 2892
Rendall, Harold A., 6310
Rendell, Alice, 5807
Renfrew, Stewart, 603
Rennie, D. L. C., 2893
Rensaa, E. M., 7051
Repo, Satu, 5185
Reps, J. W., 604
Rettig, George, 605
Reville, Frederick D., 3649
Reynolds, A., 6311
Reynolds, G. F., 5627
Reynolds, Lloyd George, 2087, 2401
Reynolds, Reg, 25
Reynolds, Roy, 3582
Reynolds, T., 3955
Rheault, C., 2167
Rheault, Michel, 2210, 4411
Rhude, R., 1320
Ribordy, F.-X., 2895
Rice, James Richard, 1680, 1681
Rice, R. E., 248
Rice, R. G., 5186
Rich, Edwin Ernest, 2402
Rich, S. George, 5429, 5701, 5702, 5703
Richan, Donald, 5866
Richard, Camille, 1612, 3195
Richard, Louis, 3332
Richard, Mireille, 2896
Richard, T. A., 4600
Richards, Elva M., 3653
Richards, J. H., 3583, 5791
Richards, L., 5988
Richards, T., 3548, 5921
Richardson, A. J. H., 3018, 3019
Richardson, Boyce, 75
Richardson, Douglas, 688, 704, 3483, 3585, 4977, 5187
Richardson, Evelyn M., 1421
Richardson, George, 4024
Richardson, M. C., 6969
Richardson, Nigel H., 774, 2897, 6424, 6466
Richmond, Anthony H., 431, 5172, 5188, 5189, 5190
Richmond Centenary Council, 6578
Richmond, D. R., 3586
Richtik, James M., 5430, 5431, 5704
Ricker, Helen S., 1528
Ricom-Singh, Françoise, 372
Ricour, Françoise, 2403, 2404, 2405
Riddett, R. H., 3880
Ridge, F. G., 6970
Ridge, M. F., 6971
Ridler, Neil, 1567
Ridout, Dengil G., 5454
Riendeau, Roger, 1084
Riffel, J. A., 339

Riis, Jack, 1085
Riis, Nelson A., 6897, 6898
Rimes, L., 7026
Rioux, Jean Roch, 2544
Rioux, Marcel, 2088, 2740
Risk, Margaret McNeill, 4978
Ritchie, Thomas, 705, 706
Rivers, P. E., 4290
Rivet, Monique, 3142
Rizui, A. A. B., 6377
Robbins, M. C., 2641
Roberge, Roger A., 340
Robert, Georges, 2089, 2090, 2181, 3251, 3311
Robert, Jean-Claude, 1961, 2040, 2225, 2226, 2491, 2525, 2526, 2545, 2546
Robert, Lionel, 851
Robert, Percy A., 2898
Roberts, A., 6899
Roberts, David, 1682, 3122
Roberts, David Wayne, 3792, 4944, 4979, 4980, 4981, 4982
Roberts, James, 3839
Roberts, Joseph, 6402, 6432
Roberts, L. W., 6972
Roberts, Leslie, 2406, 2407, 3218
Roberts, Peter Job, 1911
Roberts, Richard D., 3840
Roberts, Sheila, 6662
Roberts, Theodore Goodridge, 1683
Roberts, V. M., 4777
Roberts, William, 4778
Robertson, Angus E., 6663
Robertson, Barbara, 2899
Robertson, Gordon, 6973
Robertson, Harold H., 1184
Robertson, J. K., 5326
Robertson, John Ross, 4779
Robertson, Monica, 1634
Robertson, R. G., 6974
Robertson, Thomas B., 5543
Robeye, Lactance, 1048
Robillard, Claude, 2408
Robins, R., 2091
Robinson, A. C., 5478
Robinson, Arthur S., 1613
Robinson, B. B., 775
Robinson, B. W., 5705
Robinson, Charlotte M., 1684
Robinson, Cyril, 1541
Robinson, Ira M., 341, 599, 6378, 6379
Robinson, J. Lewis, 5273, 6433, 6579
Robinson, Leigh Burpee, 6403
Robinson, M. E., 5478, 5867, 6825
Robinson, Percy J., 4780, 4878, 4879
Robitaille, André, 2092, 3385
Robitaille, René, 3364

Robson, Frederic, 3675
Robson, William A., 971
Rochan, A., 396
Roche, J. F., 3123
Rocher, Guy, 2409
Rockwood, Jim, 1885
Rodwell, L., 5818, 5819
Rogatnick, A., 6994
Roger, Charles, 4291
Rogers, George W., 1321
Rogers, Grace McLeod, 1462
Rogers, I. M., 972
Rogers, Jerry, 1725
Rogers, Joseph, 1384
Rohold, S. B., 4983
Romalis, Coleman, 2900
Romanowski, M. E., 5706
Rome, David, 6826
Romney, Paul, 4880, 4881
Romsa, Gerald, 5252
Ronish, Donna A., 2642, 2643
Roper, J. I., 1185
Roquebrune, R. de., 2901
Rose, Albert, 373, 852, 973, 974, 5191, 5192, 5193, 5194, 5195
Rose, R. T., 6250
Rose, W. J., 5465
Rosenberg, Louis, 2410, 2902, 2903, 5196, 5544, 5545, 5868
Rosender, J. M., 5556
Rosenfeld, R. C., 820
Rosenthal, H. M., 6449
Rosenthal, Star, 6664
Roset, Lauretta, 5869
Ross, A. H. D., 4292
Ross, Aileen, 2904
Ross, Alexander M., 3749, 4781
Ross, Donald George, 5870, 5871
Ross, Evelyn, 921, 922
Ross, G. A., 1422
Ross, Herman Russell, 2905
Ross, Ian C., 4170
Ross, Leslie J., 6580
Ross, M., 5872
Ross, M. G., 4781A
Ross, P. D., 4293
Ross, R. K., 3587
Ross, Victor A., 4782
Ross, W. G., 305
Ross, W. Gillies, 2138, 3386
Ross, Winnifred M., 1186
Rossier, Henry, 5197
Rossignol, Léo F., 2211, 2212, 2213, 2214
Rossignol, Martin, 4294
Rostecki, Randy R., 5546, 5628, 5629, 5630
Rothery, Agnes, 6581, 6827
Rotinberg, Lori, 4984

Rouillard, Jacques, 2093
Rouillard, O. E., 2168
Rouleau, Jean-Paul, 2169
Rouleau, P., 2007
Roulston, P. J., 5327
Rousseau, François, 3075, 3076
Rousseau, Louis, 2547
Routaboule, D., 2094
Routhier, Adolphe Basile, 3143
Routhier, François, 2132, 3387
Routley, H. T., 3588
Rowan, Jan C., 2906
Rowan, John, 3610
Rowan, M. L., 5754
Rowat, Donald Cameron, 606, 886, 887, 888, 906, 975, 976, 977, 1187, 1188, 1423, 4412, 4413, 4414, 4415
Rowe, C. Francis, 1886
Rowe, F. W., 1817
Rowe, Kaye, 5448
Rowe, K. C., 3388
Rowe, P. A., 5547, 5548
Rowe, R. C., 3219, 3220
Roweis, S. T., 607, 610, 656
Rowland, K., 608
Rowley, G. W., 6976
Rowley, Gwyn, 5707
Roy, Antoine, 4000
Roy, Camille, 3124, 3144
Roy, Gilles, 3196
Roy, J. A., 4001
Roy, Jean-Louis, 2095, 2096
Roy, Jean-Marie, 2097, 3197
Roy, Patricia E., 6582, 6583, 6584, 6585, 6586, 6587, 6665, 6666, 6667, 6828
Roy, Pierre-Georges, 3020, 3021, 3022, 3023, 3077, 3145
Roy, Raymond, 2098
Royle, John C., 6944
Rubin, K., 4416
Ruddell, David Thierry, 3055, 3092, 3101, 3109
Ruddick, S., 2411
Rudin, J. R., 5198
Rudin, Ronald, 2099, 3243, 3277
Rudnychyj, J. B., 5549
Ruff, Norman J., 1568
Rugg, Robert D., 2215, 4417, 4418
Ruggles, Richard I., 5436
Rumilly, Robert, 2412, 2413, 2414, 2415, 2416
Rumley, Dennis, 6718, 6731
Rumney, G. R., 4601
Rumsey, F., 6380
Runciman, J. Herbert, 1214
Runnalls, F. E., 6453, 6454
Russell, A. L., 4633, 4634

Russell, Daniel J., 2644
Russell, David, 3793
Russell, E. T. P., 5924
Russell, Edgar A., 1912
Russell, Hilary, 4295
Russell, M. E., 25
Russell, Paul G., 3650
Russenholt, E. S., 5550
Russwurm, L. M., 4090
Russwurm, Lorne H., 71, 76, 3589, 3590, 3750, 4083, 4090, 4202, 4203
Rutherford, J. G., 274
Rutherford, Paul F. W., 978, 979
Ruzicka, Stanley Edward, 6829
Ryan, Joan, 455
Ryan, William F., 2100
Ryder, N. B., 433

Saarinen, Eliel, 77
Saarinen, Oiva W., 342, 3301, 3591, 3889, 4602, 4603
Saarinen, Thomas Frederick, 6125
Sabourin, Bernard, 4419
Sabourin, Joanne M., 4296, 4297, 4420
Sack, D., 7002
Sacouman, R. James, 1111
Sage, Walter N., 6588, 6589
Sager, Eric W., 1120, 1887, 1888
St. Amant, Jean-Claude, 4604
Saint-Amour, Jean-Pierre, 2216
Ste. Croix, Lorne J., 2548
Saint-Cyr, J.-F., 2645
Saint-Cyr, Michel, 3198
St. David's Church, St. John's, Nfld., 1889
St.-Germain, G., 3291
Saint John Board of Trade, 1685
Saint John, N.B., 1688
Saint John, N.B., Common Council, 1687
St. John, R. Monro, 6443
Saint-Laurent, Jacques, 3199
Saint-Maurice, D., 2907
Sainte-Mesmin, Benique-Charles, 1385
Saint-Onge, C., 3278
St. Pierre, Jocelyn, 3200
Saint-Pierre, Ruth, 3213
St. Thomas Board of Trade, 4563
Saleh, M., 4204
Sales, Arnaud, 2101
Salvail, Narcisse, 3292
Sampson, B., 691
Samson, Denis, 3078
Sancton, Andrew B., 2417, 2908
Sander, Lois Anne, 5755
Sandham, Alfred, 2418, 2646
Sandison, James, 6590

Sandusky, Robert J., 1624
Sanford, Barbara, 609
Sangster, Joan, 4985
Sanmarco, Sebastian Ricardo, 6900
Santiago, A. M., 2909
Santos, B. R., 1049
Sarbit, L., 5432
Sarjeant, W. A. S., 5894, 5928
Sarty, L. I., 1189
Saskatchewan, Department of Industry and Commerce, 5792
Saskatchewan, Department of Railways, Labour and Industries, 5455
Saunders, Audrey Murton, 4882
Saunders, E. A., 1323
Saunders, J. M., 4205
Saunders, Stanley Alexander, 1138
Savard, Pierre, 3146, 3147, 3148
Savoie, Gerald, 2910
Saxton, P., 1190
Sawers, Larry, 87, 221
Saywell, John T., 776
Scace, R. C., 6312, 6313, 6314
Scadding, Henry, 4783, 4784, 4785, 4883
Scanlon, T. J., 980
Scatterly, P., 3688
Scheffman, D. T., 5156
Schliewinsky, F. G., 5199
Schmandt, H. J., 34
Schneider, Kenneth R., 822
Schnore, L. R., 137, 164, 164A, 374
Schoenauer, Norbert, 2421, 2911, 3389
Schouten, Jaap, 4421
Schull, J. J., 4786
Schurman, D. M., 4002, 4003, 4004
Schwartzman, David, 1507
Scollie, F. Brent, 3592
Scott, A. J., 619, 656
Scott, B. S., 4131, 4171
Scott, D. C., 4538
Scott, David, 6901
Scott, F. R., 5200
Scott, James, 3706, 4084
Scott, M., 611
Scott, M. M., 5433
Scott, M. O., 4358
Scott, Mary McKay, 4298
Scott, R. W., 4326, 4359
Scott, W. G., 6251
Scovil Brothers, Saint John, 1689
Scully, Vincent, 707
Seaborn, Edwin, 3593
Sealey, Bruce, 5756
Sealey, Margaret, 5756
Sealy, Nanciellen D., 1569, 1726, 1727
Searles, Jr., John R., 853
Sedgwick, Charles Peter, 6830

Seebaran, R. B., 6591
Seeley, J. R., 823
Segger, Martin, 6759, 6831, 6832, 6833
Séguin, Normand, 2102, 2148, 3390
Seidel, Judith, 2912
Seifried, Neil R. M., 3594, 6252, 6253
Selwood, H. J., 5397, 5551, 5631, 5632, 5704
Semple, Neil, 3596
Senior, Elinor, 2549, 2550, 2551
Sennett, Richard, 88
Serra, J., 6902
Seth, James, 1324
Seunath, M. A., 1086
Seurot, Paul, 306
Sewell, John, 307, 824, 5201, 5202
Sexton, F. H., 1191
Seymour, Horace L., 497, 616, 3596, 4085, 4086, 4087, 5989, 5990, 5991, 6732
Shackleton, Doris, 5708
Shadbolt, Douglas, 708
Shaffir, William, 2913
Shand, G. V., 1515, 1516
Shank, Wesley I., 2914
Shapiro, Linda, 4787
Sharma, Brajesh, 2915
Sharpe, Christopher A., 1892, 5203
Sharpe, Robin, 6733
Sharples, John, 165
Shaver, J. M., 434
Shaw, A., 4985A
Shaw, C. L., 4986
Shaw, Patrick Vincent, 1325
Shaw, R. E., 1326
Shaw, W. G. S., 343
Shay, Margaret E., 2139
Shea, C., 6866
Shea, D. S., 4884
Sheard, Charles, 4987
Sheehan, Nancy M., 5373
Sheehy-Casey, M. T., 2419
Sheikh, Z. A., 5709
Shepard, W. C., 2916
Shepherd, Francis J., 2420
Sheppard, E. S., 709
Sheremata, J. D., 6205
Sherk, A. B., 4088
Sherman, Max, 4206
Sherman, Robert, 3407
Sherrin, P. M., 6834
Sherwood, Roland H., 1472, 1473, 1474
Shimwell, Joseph, 4422
Shindman, B., 220
Shipley, Nan, 5552
Shockey, William J., 612
Shooner, Pierre, 2917
Short, A., 4004
Short, George D., 5274

Short, R. B., 5553
Shortt, Adam, 435, 613, 614, 3597, 6835
Shortt, George E., 2918, 2919
Shostack, Hannah, 4988
Shrimpton, Mark, 1890, 1891, 1892
Shumski, Gary, 3794
Shurt, Greta, 3751
Siamandas, George, 5710
Sibley, C., 2647
Siddique, M., 5926
Sidlofsky, Samuel, 5104
Siegel, J., 192
Siemens, L. B., 344
Siemiatycki, Myer, 3841
Sigouin, Alice, 2480
Silcox, Peter, 5205
Silver, Sheldon, 1050
Silverman, Peter Guy, 6903
Silzer, V. J., 854
Sim, R. A., 823
Sim, Victor W., 1818, 5479
Simard, André, 2170
Simard, Jacques, 5206
Simard, Réal, 2227
Simard, Sylvain, 2103
Simcoe, Elizabeth, 3599
Simmons, James W., 78, 79, 166, 192, 275, 276, 277, 278, 279, 352, 436, 437, 438, 478, 657, 797, 4788, 5207, 5208, 5209
Simmons, Robert, 79, 438
Simpson, E. G., 5554
Simpson, L., 777
Sinclair, A., 1424
Sinclair, A. M., 439
Sinclair, Gordon, 5434
Sinclair, M. H., 2422
Sinclair, Sylvia, 6592
Sinnot, J. Cyril, 1765
Sinton, Robert, 5873
Sirois, A., 2423
Sirois, F. B., 3024
Sise, Hazen, 710, 2920
Sisler, W. J., 5555
Sissons, C. B., 3660
Sitwell, O. F. G., 1475, 3601
Sivertz, B. G., 6977
Sizler, V. J., 778
Sjoberg, Gideon, 80
Skebo, Suzanne, 5210
Skelton, O. D., 4789
Skepple, Adolphus D., 4029
Skimuzu, Ronald, 3871
Skolfsky, Jack, 5984A
Skolnick, Michael L., 1819
Slack, Brian, 308, 2922
Slaight, A. D., 4790
Slater, David W., 221, 375, 615, 855, 1051

Slater, Ronald William, 5711
Slemko, B., 917
Slemon, P., 2648
Slipper, M. A., 4635
Sloan, W. A., 6904
Sloane, P. L., 5556
Slobodin, Richard, 5927
Small, F. L., 1087
Small, H. Beaumont, 4299
Smallfield, W. E., 5328
Smallwood, F., 5211
Smallwood, Joseph R., 1820
Smart, J. D., 3602
Smiley, Donald V., 5794
Smith, A. G., 616, 6593
Smith, A. R. G., 4089
Smith, Allan, 6381
Smith, André, 2315
Smith, Andrea B., 6594
Smith, Benjamin George, 6254
Smith, Brian F., 1690
Smith, Brian Ray Douglas, 6435
Smith, C. Ray, 617
Smith, Carl, 3842
Smith, Charles D., 2104
Smith, Charles W., 6382
Smith, D. B., 6409, 6444
Smith, David E., 5895
Smith, Donald, 5329
Smith, Doris Mae, 456
Smith, Douglas Frederick, 4467
Smith, Elspeth, 4791
Smith, F. N., 2105
Smith, F. P., 4005
Smith, G. J. A., 5212
Smith, George, 4481, 4482
Smith, Goldwin, 4989
Smith, J. F. C., 4423
Smith, J. H., 3843, 3844, 3845
Smith, James F., 1542
Smith, John F., 711
Smith, Leslie K., 4481, 4482
Smith, Margaret, 1821
Smith, Mary Elizabeth, 1691
Smith, Pamela J., 5812
Smith, Pemberton, 3149
Smith, Peter J., 167, 618, 5398, 5993, 5994, 6030, 6031, 6032, 6126, 6127, 6239, 6255, 6256, 6257, 6258, 6315
Smith, Phillip, 1913
Smith, Phyllis, 5994A
Smith, R. H., 4990
Smith, Rebecca L., 1766
Smith, T. Watson, 1480
Smith, W. Randy, 3539, 3603, 5330
Smith, W. Richmond, 1088
Smith, Willard Vandine, 3392

Smith, William, 1192
Smucker, Joseph, 249
Smyly, C., 6836, 3837
Sneddon, R., 4468
Snider, Earl Lawrence, 5992, 6033
Snider, Howard Mervin, 6174
Société Canadienne de Science Economique, 2424
Société historique de Montréal, 2425, 2425A
Société historique du Québec, 3025
Soderstrom, R. W., 6259
Soeder, R. R., 4090
Solomon, David N., 2426
Sommerville, M. M., 856
Sorby, Thomas C., 6838
Soucy-Roy, C., 2649
Soules, Gordon, 6595
Souster, R., 4792
Southam, Peter, 2106
Spalding, G. C., 4991
Spector, David, 3846, 5633, 5634, 5635
Speisman, Stephen, 4793, 4992
Speller, R. G., 1193
Spelt, Jacob, 3505, 3604, 4729, 4730, 4731, 4794, 5129, 5130, 5131, 5213
Spencer, Bryon G., 5214
Spencer, L. O., 5399
Spencer, Stephen, 4993
Spicer, Elizabeth, 4172
Spindel, Donna J., 1386
Sponchia, C. R. E., 6278
Spragge, G. W., 3605
Spragge, Godfrey L., 619
Spragge, Shirley C., 4994, 4995
Spray, W. A., 1728
Spreiregen, Paul D., 81, 712
Spricenieks, Alfred, 4091
Sprougate, G. P., 2923
Sproule-Jones, Mark, 6383
Spruce-Sales, Harold, 6684
Spurr, John W., 3956
Spurr, P., 658, 659
Squire, S. L., 1089
Stabler, A., 5400
Stabler, Jack C., 5401, 6977A
Stacey, C. P., 1327, 3079
Stacey, Robert, 3606
Stadel, C., 5449
Stafford, Ellen, 4556
Stafford, J. D., 376
Stainsby, D., 6541
Stamp, Robert M., 2107, 3607, 5373, 6034, 6086
Stanbury, W. T., 6384, 6385, 6386
Stanford, G. H., 4795
Stanislas, Frère, 2427
Stankovic, D., 3608

Stanley, George F. G., 3957, 3958, 4006, 4007, 4008, 6035, 6087
Stapleford, F. N., 5215
Starbird, Ethel A., 5216
Stave, Bruce M., 168, 169, 170, 171, 172
Stavely, Michael, 1822, 7040
Stead, Robert J. C., 6036
Steck, Warren F., 5928
Steed, Guy P. F., 2925, 5217, 6734
Steele, David A., 1207
Steele, Marion, 779, 780
Steele, R. C., 4539
Steele, S. B., 5874
Steen, J. E., 5636
Steen, P., 6249
Steeves, Helen I., 1614
Stein, David Lewis, 5218
Stelter, Gilbert A., 26, 29, 35, 82, 83, 84, 85, 99, 173, 174, 175, 176, 177, 178, 179, 180, 345, 346, 503, 3609, 3610, 4605, 4606, 4607
Stephens, D. E., 1543
Stephens, G. W., 2650
Stephens, Gary P., 1425
Stephenson, A. T., 6291
Stephenson, Gordon, 1426
Stephenson, William, 4796
Steppler, Glenn A., 3026
Steven, Paul, 9
Stevens, George R., 6260
Stevens, H. H., 6756
Stevens, J., 86
Stevens, Leah, 6596, 6597
Stevens, Thalia O., 1692
Stevenson, Alex, 7052
Stevenson, D., 6386
Stevenson, H. A., 3611
Stevenson, J., 6598
Stevenson, John A., 3661
Stevenson, M. A., 3612
Stewart, A., 5459
Stewart, Audrey, 564
Stewart, Bryce, 781
Stewart, C. M., 3125
Stewart, George, 1693
Stewart, Herbert Leslie, 1387
Stewart, J., 6905
Stewart, J. Douglas, 3959, 4009
Stewart, McLeod, 4327
Stinson, Arthur, 928, 5875
Stinson, Lloyd, 5557
Stinson, M. M., 5275
Stobie, Peter W., 6735
Stock, George, 4608
Stocks, Anthony Howard, 5219
Stoddart, Jennifer, 2610, 2611, 2819, 2820
Stoddart, P. J., 3613

Stokes, C. W., 3027
Stokes, Ernest B., 6037, 6128
Stokes, John, 3690
Stokes, Peter J., 3420, 4540
Stone, Gladys Mae, 5876
Stone, Ken, 3881
Stone, Leroy O., 377, 378, 440, 441, 479
Stone, Michael E., 782
Storey, Robert H., 3847
Stortz, Gerald J., 4996
Story, George M., 1893, 1894
Stoughton, Arthur Alexander, 713, 1052
Straaton, Karen Vivian, 6736
Stroh, Jacob, 4092
Strom, T., 6038
Strong-Boag, Veronica, 398
Strongitharm, Bryan Deane, 6436
Strothard, J., 3752
Stuart, David, 5984A
Sturino, Franc, 5220
Stymeist, David H., 5332
Sudbury and District Chamber of Commerce, 4609
Sugimoto, Howard H., 6668, 6669, 6670
Sullivan, Alan, 4498
Sullivan, G. V.; 4207
Sullivan, Genevieve, 4469, 4470
Sullivan, Michael, 7041, 7053
Sulte, Benjamin, 3080, 3333
Summers, F., 1823
Sunderland, Terry, 1508
Sundquist, K. E., 3536
Suski, Julian G., 981, 6175
Susman, Robert M., 5221
Sutcliffe, A. R., 620
Sutcliffe, J. H., 5637
Sutherland, David Alexander, 1328, 1388, 1389, 1427
Sutherland, Neil, 399
Sutton, S. B., 825
Swainson, Donald, 4025
Swanborough, R., 3849
Swanson, J. A., 204
Swartzen, Gordon W., 1729
Sweeney, Robert, 2428
Swenarchuk, Janet, 5877
Sylvain, Robert, 2651, 4997
Symonds, D., 6738
Symonds, H., 181
Synge, Jane, 3849

Tabb, William K., 87
Tait, Terence D., 5333
Takia, Emile F., 6129
Talbot, L. D., 5712
Talman, J. J., 4132, 4133

Tamblyn, W. F., 4173
Tamminen, B. E., 4636
Tancock, Elizabeth, 4797
Tanghe, Raymond, 2429, 2925, 2926, 2927, 2928
Tangjerd, Lorne D., 5878
Tangri, O. P., 309
Tanguay, C., 3306
Tanimura, H., 621
Tanner, T., 4208
Tanqueray, J. F. D., 6739
Taraska, Elizabeth A., 6088
Taraska, Peter, 5713
Tarasoff, Koozma John, 6599, 6600
Tardif, J. P. E., 622
Task Force on Urbanization (Alberta), 5995
Tassie, Peter, 6601
Tata, S. B., 2430
Tate, Alan, 4424, 4425
Taube, E., 4134
Taylor, C. D. N., 6978
Taylor, C. J., 3960
Taylor, Donald, 182
Taylor, Griffith, 2108, 3614, 3615
Taylor, H. W., 3439
Taylor, Henry Edwin, 6906
Taylor, I. C., 3616
Taylor, James, 5757
Taylor, John H., 142, 1090, 1091, 1092, 4300, 4301, 5402
Taylor, K. W., 5714, 5728, 5729
Taylor, L. D., 6671
Taylor, Larrie, 5956
Taylor-Vaisey, Robert D., 4471
Teefy, L., 4798
Temperley, Howard, 1570
Templin, Hugh, 3753
Tennant, G. R., 4998
Tennant, Paul, 6387, 6693, 6694, 6740, 6741
Tennant, R. D., 4426
Tennyson, Brian D., 1194, 1509, 1510
Tepperman, Lorne, 4999
Terrill, Frederick W., 2431
Terris, Edward M., 6907
Tessier, Albert, 3334, 3335
Tessier, J.-G., 3393
Tetrault, A., 6316
Tetrault, Martin, 2652
Thayer, Frederick C., 982
Théoret, Anatole E., 5758
Theriault, Yvan, 3336, 3337
Thernstrom, Stephan, 88, 183
Theron, J. D., 5715
Thibault, Claude, 27
Thibault, Henri-Paul, 1463, 1464, 3208
Thibault, Suzel, 3214
Thibodeau, J.-C., 2929

Thirnbeck, A. R., 6317
Thivierge, J., 2363
Thom, William Wylie, 6602
Thoman, R. S., 3617
Thomas, C. E., 1329
Thomas, Christopher, 4557
Thomas, David, 6908
Thomas, J. W. N., 1053
Thomas, John P., 480, 3618
Thomas, Lewis G., 6089, 6206, 6318, 6319
Thomas, Lewis H., 5879, 5929
Thomas, P. F., 5222
Thompson, A. Audley, 1330
Thompson, A. W., 3882, 4209
Thompson, Austin S., 4885
Thompson, E., 4528
Thompson, Ethel A., 1730
Thompson, F. D., 396
Thompson, F. F., 4010
Thompson, Fred, 1428
Thompson, J. F., 4610
Thompson, John Herd, 5716
Thompson, Marjorie, 1595
Thompson, Robert, 3754
Thompson, Roderick Ross, 5403
Thompson, W. A., 4201
Thompson, W. R., 222
Thompson, W. T., 5638
Thompson, Wilbur R., 280
Thompson, William, 5558
Thorarinson, S. A., 5639
Thorburn, C. H., 4302
Thorner, T., 6090
Thornton, Patricia A., 1914
Thornley, Betty, 1622
Thorpe, Wendy L., 1195
Thouez, Jean-Pierre, 2109, 3279
Thrall, Grant Ian, 3883
Thraves, Bernard, 5717
Thrift, Eric W., 4427, 4428
Thrupp, S. L., 184, 6909
Thurston, Catherine, 5000
Tiessen, Hugo, 5930
Tiessen, Paul, 4093
Timberlake, J., 4799
Timms, P. T., 6672
Tindal, C. R., 889, 983
Tindal, S. Nobes, 889
Tochon, Nelson, 4429
Tocque, Philip, 1824
Todd, E. W., 4039
Todd, Eric C. E., 6388
Todd, Fred G., 826
Todd, Robert B., 6673
Toker, Franklin, 2432
Tombs, L. C., 2433
Tomovcik, Vladimir, 4430

Toren, E. R., 6691
Torhjelm, Gary Douglas, 5996
Toronto Area Archivists Group, 4800
Toronto Board of Education, 4801
Toronto City Planning Board, 4802
Toronto Harbour Commissioners, 4803
Toronto Transit Commission, 4804
Toronto Transportation Commission, 4805, 5223
Torrance, Gordon V., 3795
Tourangeau, Rémi, 3029
Tousignant, Pierre, 2552
Tracey, W. R., 400
Tracie, C. J., 5795
Trade Union Research Bureau, 6910
Trail Board of Trade, 6911
Trail Golden Jubilee Society, 6912
Traquair, Ramsay, 2111, 2112, 2434
Tratt, Gertrude, 1196
Traverso, Peter, 5559
Treleaven, G. Fern, 6603
Tremaine, M., 1331
Tremblay, A., 2271, 2839, 2930, 3185
Tremblay, Louis, 4303
Tremblay, Louis-Marie, 3202
Tremblay, M., 2113
Tremblay, M. A., 89
Tremblay, Michel, 3008
Tremblay, Robert, 2553
Tremblay, Victor, 2171, 2172
Tremblay, Yves, 2554
Trépanier, Léon, 2435, 2931
Trépanier, M.-O., 2839, 3185
Tretheway, W. G., 3676
Tribble, S. P., 1731
Trigge, A. St. L., 4782
Triggs, Stanley, 2598
Trotier, Louis, 185, 2114, 2115, 2116, 2117, 2244
Troper, Harold, 423, 4714, 4715, 4806
Trotman, James, 4360
Trotter, B., 5880
Troughton, Michael, 4211
Trudeau, Joan, 457
Trudeau, John, 6932
Trudeau, Michelle, 2118, 2436
Trudeau, Pierre Elliott, 2140
Trudel, Jacques, 2119
Trudel, Jean, 3089
Trudel, Marcel, 2120, 2121, 2122, 2481, 2482, 3081, 3082, 3338, 3339
Trudelle, Joseph, 3030
Trueman, Stuart, 1694
Tse, M.-L., 6742
Tsukada, N., 5224
Tuck, Robert C., 1750
Tucker, F. J., 4807

Tucker, Walter B., 1915
Tufts, L. F., 1093
Tulchinsky, Gerald J. J., 2555, 2556, 2557, 3961
Tunbridge, T. E., 3962
Tupper, E. S., 1332
Turcot, Jean, 2932
Turcotte, Georges E., 2933
Turnbull, Elsie G., 6913
Turnbull, I. D., 5477
Turnbull, Kenneth Franklin, 5718
Turnbull, Thomas G., 5456
Turner, Allan R., 5881
Turner, Jonni, 1767
Turner, Norman William, 5820
Turner, Philip J., 2123
Turowetz, A., 231
Turpin, Pierre, 2082
Tuttle, C. R., 5640
Tweed, E., 4541
Tyre, Robert, 5882, 5931
Tyrrell, T. A. C., 3619
Tyrrell, W. G., 105

Uliana, J. A., 4094
Ulmer, A. L., 6743
Umbach, J. E., 6744
Underhill, Frank, 984
Union des municipalités de la province de Québec, 2124
University of Manitoba, 5560
Unwin, R., 623
Upton, Phyllis G., 2934
Uren, P. E., 3340
Usher, Peter, 6979
Usiskin, Roz, 5641, 5642, 5643
Utting, Gerald, 4808
Uttley, W. V., 4095, 4096

Vachon, A., 3083
Vaison, Robert, 1197, 1198
Vallières, M., 2125
Vance, James E., Jr., 90, 250, 660, 827
Vancouver, City Planning Department, 6604
Vancouver Exhibition Association, 6605
Vancouver Museum and Planetarium, 6674
Van Emery, M., 4499
Van Ginkel, Blanche, 6980
Van Klaversen, Adrie, 6383
Vannin, E., 1333
Van Nus, Walter, 624, 625, 626, 627
Van Steen, Marcus, 1429
Varson, R., 1430
Vass, B., 4809
Vaucrosson, Noel V., 2935
Vaughan, Carol, 4886

Vaughan, Edgar, 3755
Velloni, Pietro, 3203
Veltman, Calvin J., 2936
Venables, Max, 5759
Venditti, M. P., 4810, 5225
Veres, Louis Joseph, 5276
Verge, H., 1202, 1511
Vermette, Luce, 2483
Vernon, Charles W., 1334
Vernon, F., 4542
Versailles, Yvan, 2937
Vey, W. E., 4097
Viau, Jacques, 890
Viau, Pierre, 2126
Vickers, Elizabeth Smith, 3850
Vickers, W. W., 4637
Victoria, Corporation of the City of, 6839
Victoria Trades and Labour Council, 6840
Viger, Jacques, 2558
Villeneuve, Paul Y., 828
Vincelli, B. M., 2559
Vincent, D. B., 5561, 5719
Vincent, Patrick, 3884
Vincent, Rodolphe, 3031
Vincent, Roger, 3221
Vineberg, S., 1054
Vinton, Warren J., 783
Virak, Victor, 829
Vivian, Henry, 628, 784, 785
Voisey, Paul, 5404, 5997, 5998, 6091
Voisine, Nive, 3341

Waddell, J. M., 5760
Wadden, Brian, 1895
Wade, F. C., 5405, 7007
Wadel, Cato, 1825
Wagdin, G. A., 1055
Wagner, Jonathan F., 5720
Wagner, Michael J., 4472
Wahl, E., 6450
Wainwright, W. H., 629
Waite, Catherine Ann, 1431
Waites, K. A., 6606
Walchuk, W., 6261
Walden, Frederick Ellsworth, 6841
Walden, Phyllis Sarah, 6607
Waldron, Gordon, 3620
Walford, Dorice C., 830
Walhouse, F., 6608
Walkem, Richard T., 3963, 4011
Walker, Alexander, 347, 348
Walker, David, 194, 5435, 5721, 5722, 5735
Walker, David F., 3621, 3622, 3623, 3624, 3625, 3790, 3837
Walker, E. K., 4811
Walker, Frank Norman, 4812
Walker, Gerald, 5226, 5334

Walker, H. J. N., 4304
Walker, H. W., 349
Walker, Howard V., 3796, 5227
Walker, I., 6130
Walker, J. Alexander, 6745, 6746
Walker, John A., 5335
Walker, M., 6842
Walker, Susan, 4543
Wall, Geoffrey, 3626
Wallace, Archer, 4813
Wallace, Arthur W., 1199, 3797
Wallace, Carl M., 1695, 1696
Wallace, Dorothy, 3707
Wallace, Elisabeth, 4814
Wallace, F. W., 1697
Wallace, Frederick W., 310
Wallace, J. K., 4815
Wallace, Mrs. Ernest, 1545
Wallace, Robert C., 3964, 3965
Wallace, W. S., 4816
Wallot, Jean-Pierre, 158, 159, 2073, 2539
Walsh, Annmarie Houck, 5228
Walsh, Henry Cecil, 2653
Walton, J. W., 5336
Wamboldt, Beryl, 6914
Wangenheim, E. D., 5229
Warburton, T. R., 6843
Ward, Clarence, 1698
Ward, David, 186, 442
Ward, H. B., 3798
Ward, H. R., 4212
Ward, Norman, 5883
Ward, Tom, 6092
Ward, W. Peter, 6389
Warfe, Chris, 4361
Wargon, Sylvia T., 401
Wark, L., 630
Warkentin, John H., 5406, 5436, 5460, 5461
Warman, C., 6467
Warner, Iris, 7004, 7005
Warner, Sam Bass, Jr., 91, 92, 165, 187, 188, 661, 831
Warnick, Paul C., 3851, 4544
Warrian, Peter, 3627
Wass, Keith, 6262
Wassef, Nadia, 2938
Wassingham, D. G., 1571
Wasteneys, H. C. F., 5230
Waters, J. W., 4213
Waters, N. M., 4214
Waterston, Elizabeth, 3150, 3756
Watkins, Lyndon, 1335
Watkins, R. C., 5786
Watson, J., 3966
Watson, John Wreford, 1336, 3629, 3799, 4545, 4546
Watson, Joyce N., 3628
Watson, Kenneth F., 6292

Watson, R. G., 1732
Watt, A. B., 6176
Watt, John, 1546
Watt, Robert D., 6609, 6610
Watts, William John, 5437
Way, Ronald L., 3967
Weadick, Guy, 6093
Weaver, Emily P., 1699, 3032, 3630, 5884, 6468
Weaver, John C., 189, 190, 929, 985, 986, 987, 1432, 3800, 5001, 5002, 5003, 6177, 6611
Webb, Ross Allan, 1200
Weber, Ralph E., 6844
Webster, Donald H., 1094
Webster, G., 4030
Webster, J. Clarence, 1572
Webster, Jackie, 1700
Webster, John C., 1733
Webster, T. Stewart, 3968
Weekes, F. E., 3631
Weidner, Harvey George, 5885
Weightman, Barbara Ann, 6612, 6747
Weinmayr, M. V., 2590
Weir, R. Stanley, 2127, 2654
Weir, Thomas K., 5407
Weir, Thomas R., 5562, 5563, 5723, 5724, 6446
Weis, Eduardo, 1701
Welch, Edwin, 4305, 4328
Welch, Ruth Lillian, 6390
Wellbourne, Arthur J., 2939
Weller, J. P., 4817
Welling, Steven Lawrence, 264, 5408
Welling, W. L., 5959
Wellington County, Centennial Committee, 3757
Wellman, B., 930
Wells, Clayton W., 4098
Wells, E. P., 3852
Wells, W. D., 3853
Wentzells Ltd., 1337
Wenziong, Gao, 3885
Werthman, W. C., 1596
Wesche, Rolf, 4306
Wesley, George J., 2940
West, Bruce, 4818
West, George E., 5725
West, Karen, 6320
Westhues, Kenneth, 3632
Westland, S. I., 3801
Weston, D. R., 3294
Weston, G., 6675
Weston, Phyllis E., 6039, 6040
Wetton, Cecilia, 5803
Weyerstroth, N., 4698
Whalen, Hugh J., 891, 892, 1139, 1573
Whalen, James M., 1702

Whalley, George, 3969
Whebell, C. F. J., 3633, 3634, 3635, 3636
Whetten, N. L., 5409
Whetter, David, 6748
Whidden, David G., 1218, 1219
Whipp, C., 4483
Whitaker, J. P., 281, 4500
White, Brian P., 6915
White, C. O., 5796, 5813, 5951
White, Carole, 4522
White, G. A., 1338
White, George Brooks, 6391
White, James, 631
White, John, 1095
White, Robert, 4547
White, William Alan, 4819
White, William J., 1547
Whitebread, K., 5337
Whitehand, J. W. R., 832
Whitehead, J., 6131
Whitehead, Paul C., 1253
Whiteley, A. S., 5410
Whiteley, W. H., 1826
Whiteside, J., 4820
Whiteway, Louise, 1896, 1897
Whitman, J., 1339
Whitnall, G. Gordon, 632
Whitton, Charlotte, 4307
Wice, George, 5338
Wickberg, Edgar, 6613
Wickern, P. H., 5564, 5565, 5726
Wickett, S. Morley, 893, 894, 895, 988, 989, 5004, 5411, 5412, 6392
Wicks, René, 1827
Wickwar, W. H., 896
Wiesman, Brahm, 786
Wightman, W. R., 3439
Wild, Roland, 6422
Wilhelm, G., 7027
Wilhelm, T., 7027
Wilkinson, Henry, 7028
Will, E. J. S., 5566
Willett, J., 1703
William Lougheed Associates, 4642
Williams, Albert Ronald, 5932
Williams, David M., 3655
Williams, G. P., 5277
Williams, J. D., 6207
Williams, J. S., 1704
Williams, M. E., 1734
Williams, M. Y., 5457
Williams, P. R., 5797
Williams, T. R., 5232
Williamson, E. L. R., 5233
Williamson, J. G., 204
Williamson, Norman J., 5472
Willison, Marjory, 6845

Wilkie, David, 6796
Willmott, Donald E., 5933, 5952
Willmott, W. E., 6393, 6981, 6982
Willows, Maurice, 1096
Wills, Harold A., 5339
Willson, K., 788
Wilmot, Fred, 5727
Wilson, A. D., 787
Wilson, Andrew, 4329
Wilson, Bruce, 4548
Wilson, Charles, 4215
Wilson, D., 5005
Wilson, E. C., 1201
Wilson, E. L., 2437
Wilson, George H., 311
Wilson, Ian E., 3959
Wilson, J. Donald, 6395
Wilson, J. W., 6614
Wilson, James W., 6394, 6846
Wilson, Laurence M., 2438
Wilson, Norman D., 312, 5234
Wilson, R., 443
Wilson, R. D., 2369
Wilson, Robert, 4821, 5235
Wilson, S., 3033
Wilton, Sidney, 5480
Winchester, I., 191, 3802
Windsor Board of Trade, 1517
Windsor, R. F., 6263
Windsor, Rotary Club of, 5279
Wingfield, Alexander H., 3803
Winkler, H. W., 5761
Winks, Robin W., 1140
Winkworth, P. S., 2298
Winman, E., 402
Winnicki, W. R., 5236
Winnipeg Parks and Recreation Department, 5567, 5568, 5569
Winter, J. O., 5237
Winter, J. Ralph, 4611
Winton, A. C., 1898
Wise, S. F., 4012, 4013
Wiseman, N., 5728, 5729
Withers, J. W., 1899
Witty, David R., 617
Woadden, A. R. N., 4822
Wolfe, J. S., 3758
Wolfe, R. I., 3637
Wolff, M., 44
Wolforth, J., 93
Wonders, William C., 1828, 1833, 6178, 6264, 6265, 6983, 6984
Wong, C. S. J., 6132, 6266
Wong, S. T., 6749
Wong, W. H., 5438
Woo, H. M., 6133
Wood, C. E., 3638

Wood, Edward I., 4431
Wood, Frank, 3759
Wood, Harold A., 3804, 5340, 5341
Wood, J. David, 3476, 3639
Wood, J. T., 1340
Wood, J. W., 4473
Wood, K., 1202, 1511
Wood, Marjorie R., 6750
Wood, W. D., 28
Wood, William, 3034
Wood, William C. H., 1465, 3151
Woodcock, George, 6847
Woodcock, I., 6847
Woodcock, Judith Ann, 3547
Woodhead, K. H., 2128
Wood-Holt, B., 1705
Woodhouse, T. Roy, 3805, 3854
Woodland, Alan, 6447
Woodruff, C. R., 990
Woodside, H. J., 7006
Woodsworth, James Shaver, 1097, 4823, 6615
Woodward, Frances M., 6369, 6397, 6398
Woodward-Reynolds, Kathleen Marjorie, 6616
Woolcock, H. R., 4174
Wotherspoon, W. L., 4612
Woychuk, J. K., 6267
Woywitka, A. B., 6321
Wrenshall, C. M., 991
Wright, A. Jeffrey, 1390
Wright, C. H. C., 4824
Wright, Esther Clark, 1597, 1706
Wright, Frederick, 2941, 2942
Wright, J. M., 6848
Wright, John M., 4432
Wrigley, E. A., 251
Wusaty, N., 2943
Wynn, Graeme, 1574, 1575, 3640
Wynne, Robert E., 6676
Wynne-Roberts, R. O., 633, 5238

Yamazuchi, Takashi, 5342
Yarham, E. R., 6617
Yauk, T. B., 5730
Yelland, F. T., 4175

Yeates, Maurice H., 94, 5692
Yeigh, Frank, 3970, 4549, 4825
Yeamans, W. C., 379
Yerbury, J. C., 6916
Yesaki, Arthur, 6517
Yeung, Y. M., 4216
Yorath, C. J., 1056
York, W. Milton, 4643
You, A., 4308
Youe, Christopher, 6041
Young, A. H., 4309, 4826
Young, Anna G., 3971
Young, Brian J., 2656, 2657, 2658
Young, C. R., 5239
Young, Cy, 6455
Young, David John, 6677
Young, Dennis A., 992, 5439
Young, E. M., 6678
Young, Ewart, 1834, 1900, 1916
Young, G. A., 6751
Young, J. C., 1466
Young, Maurice H., 4014
Young, R. E., 6752
Young, Richard, 4550
Young, Stewart, 634, 5798, 5821
Young, W. H., 4827
Young, Walter D., 5886
Younge, E. R., 444
Younkin, Rebecca J., 1598
Yuen, Ronald, 6517

Zakuta, Leo, 2944
Zarchikoff, W. W., 7054
Zaslow, Morris, 6985, 6986, 6987
Zeitoun, L., 458
Zerker, Sally F., 4828, 4829, 5006
Zides, Murray, 5799
Zieber, George H., 5240, 6134, 6135, 6136, 6268
Ziegler, Suzanne G., 5241
Zimmerman, C. C., 5413
Zirnhelt, D., 6740, 6741
Zucchi, John, 4830
Zuk, Nancy, 3743
Zwack, Robert Joseph, 5800

Place Index

Abitibi-Témiskaming, Qué., 3215, 3215A
Acton, Ont., 3612
Adolphustown, Ont., 3980
Africville, N.S., 1401
Ajax, Ont., 5285
Albert Mines, Qué., 3386
Amherst, N.S., 1204-1207
Amherstburg, Ont., 5244
Annapolis Royal, N.S., 1208-1214
Antigonish, N.S. 1215-1219
Argyle, N.S., 1525
Armstrong, B.C., 6902
Arvida, Qué., 2129-2132
Asbestos, Qué., 2133-2140
Atikokan, Ont., 5286
Atlin, B.C., 6856, 6858

Badger, Nfld., 1916
Baie-Comeau, Qué., 3388
Baker Lake, N.W.T., 7052
Banff, Alta., 6312-6314
Barkerville, B.C., 6859, 6885
Barrie, Ont., 3448, 5330
Bathurst, N.B., 1710, 1734
Battleford, Sask., 5801-5803
Bay Roberts, Nfld., 1912
Beamsville, Ont., 3807
Beauport, Qué., 3181, 3190
Beaver Harbour, N.S., 1538
Belleville, Ont., 3641-3645
Bell Island, Nfld., 1908
Berlin, Ont., 4072, 4092, 4093. *See also* Kitchener-Waterloo
Birtle, Man., 5731
Bishop's Falls, Nfld., 1916
Black Lake, Qué., 3303
Blind River, Ont., 5311
Bond Head, Ont., 5334
Botwood, Nfld., 1916
Bowen Island, B.C., 6853
Bracebridge, Ont., 5288
Bramalea, Ont., 5116
Brampton, Ont., 5325, 5337
Brandon, Man., 5440-5449
Brantford, Ont., 3646-3650
Bridgeport, Ont., 4050, 4091
Bridgetown, N.S., 1532
Bridgewater, N.S., 1540

Britannia, B.C., 6908
Brocklehurst, B.C., 6417. *See also* Kamloops
Brockville, Ont., 3520, 3651-3653, 5292
Buckingham, Qué., 3392
Burlington, Ont., 3772, 3775
Burnaby, B.C., 6519, 6685, 6686, 6729. *See also* Vancouver
Buxton, Ont., 5336

Calgary, Alta., 5900, 5994, 5995, 5999-6136
Cambridge, Ont., 3654-3661. *See also* Galt; Hespeler; Preston
Campbell River, B.C., 6875
Camrose, Alta., 6300, 6310
Cap-de-la-Madeleine, Qué., 3349, 3383
Capelton, Qué., 3386
Carberry, Man., 5733
Cardinal, Ont., 3520, 5340
Cardston, Alta., 6320
Causapscal, Qué., 3362
Chambly, Qué., 3378
Chance Harbour, N.B., 1730
Chandler, Qué., 3368
Chapleau, Ont., 5297
Charlesbourg, Qué., 3007
Charlotte, N.B., 1707, 1708
Charlottetown, P.E.I., 1751-1767
Chateauguay, Qué., 2232, 2233, 2288
Chatham, N.B., 1717
Chatham, Ont., 5243, 5302, 5336
Chibougamau, Qué., 3361
Chicoutimi and the Saguenay Region, Qué., 2141-2172
Chicoutimi-Nord, Qué., 2167
Churchill, Man., 5450-5457
Churchill Falls, Nfld., 1913
Clifton, N.B., 1722
Clinton, B.C., 6860
Coaticook, Qué., 3356
Cobalt, Ont., 3547, 3662-3669
Cobourg, Ont., 3677-3689
Cochrane, Ont., 5317, 5339
Cod Cove, Nfld., 1909
Collingwood, Ont., 5294
Comox, B.C., 6875
Conception Bay, Nfld., 1908
Conestogo, Ont., 4057
Copper Cliff, Ont., 4588

Place Index 371

Coquitlam, B.C., 6863, 6905
Corner Brook, Nfld., 1829-1834
Cornwall, Ont., 3416, 3520, 5287, 5340, 5341
Courtenay, B.C., 6875
Cranbrook, B.C., 6909
Cumberland, B.C., 6875

Dartmouth, N.S. *See* Halifax-Dartmouth
Dauphin, Man., 5458-5461
Dawson City, Y.T., 6988-7006
Dipper Harbour, N.B., 1730
Dominion City, Man., 5760
Don Mills, Ont., 5116, 5202
Drumheller, Alta., 6321
Drummondville, Qué., 2173-2180
Dryden, Ont., 5338
Dufferin, Qué., 2898
Duncan, B.C., 6875
Dundas, Ont., 3764, 3771, 3773, 3774, 3796, 3805, 5308A
Duparquet, Qué., 3355

Easterville, Man., 5744
East Hants, N.S., 1545
East York, Ont., 4676
Ecum Secum, N.S., 1538
Edmonton, Alta., 3152, 5146, 5649, 5825, 5994, 5995, 6009, 6052, 6134, 6137-6268
Edson, Alta., 6302
Elizabethtown, Ont., 5313
Elliot Lake, Ont., 3690-3700
Elmira, Ont., 4065
Elora, Ont., 3717, 3743, 3745. *See also* Guelph
Emerson, Man., 5734, 5737
Enderby, B.C., 6914
Espanola, Ont., 5305
Esquimalt, B.C., 6399-6404. *See also* Victoria
Esterhazy, Sask., 5952
Estevan, Sask., 5943
Etobicoke, Ont., 549, 4706, 4719. *See also* Toronto
Eustis, Qué., 3386

Fergus, Ont., 3753. *See also* Guelph
Fermont, Qué., 3354, 3366, 3389
Fiber, Nfld., 1909
Fleetwood, B.C., 6868
Flin Flon, Man., 5732, 5740, 5751
Fogo, Nfld., 1905
Forest Hill, Ont., 4701, 5180. *See also* Toronto
Forestville, Qué., 3373
Fort Assiniboine, Alta., 6306

Fort Carleton, Sask., 5817
Fort Chipewyan, Alta., 6296
Fort Langley, B.C., 6405-6409
Fort McMurray, Alta., 6296, 6299, 6305
Fort Saskatchewan, Alta., 6308, 6309, 6315
Fort William, Ont. *See* Thunder Bay
Fortymile, Y.T., 7046
Foxwarren, Man., 5731
Fredericton, N.B., 1136, 1576-1598, 1655
Freeport, N.S., 1537
Frobisher Bay, N.W.T., 7048

Galt, Ont., 3656, 3659-3661, 3711
Georgetown, P.E.I., 1750
Gimli, Man., 5755
Glace Bay, N.S., 1541, 1547
Goderich, Ont., 3701-3707, 3738
Golden, B.C., 6900
Gold River, B.C., 6878, 6884, 6894, 6900
Granby, Qué., 2181-2184
Grand Falls, N.B., 1720
Grand Falls, Nfld., 1831, 1901, 1915, 1916
Grand'mère, Qué., 3249
Grand Valley, Man., 5743
Gravelbourg, Sask., 5938, 5942
Grimsby, Ont., 3783, 3789, 3807. *See also* Hamilton
Guelph, Ont., 3448, 3708-3759

Haileybury, Ont., 3547, 5315, 5333
Halifax-Dartmouth, N.S., 1119, 1220-1432, 1479, 1639, 3179
Hamilton, Ont., 549, 3589, 3760-3885, 4202
Hampton, N.B., 1713
Hanna, Alta., 6298
Harbour Breton, Nfld., 1904
Harbour Grace, Nfld., 1911
Harrigan Cove, N.S., 1538
Hay River, N.W.T., 7054
Haysville, Ont., 4089
Héberville, Qué., 3390
Hespeler, Ont., 3654, 3658
Hinton, Alta., 6296, 6297
Holland Landing, Ont., 5330
Hull, Qué., 2185-2216, 4246. *See also* Ottawa
Humboldt, Sask., 5941, 5951

Ignace, Ont., 5285
Ile Jésus, Qué., 2405. *See also* Montréal
Inner Placentia Bay, Nfld., 1902
Insinger, Sask., 5949
Inuvik, N.W.T., 7050, 7051
Iroquois, Ont., 3520

Jasper, Alta., 6314
Joliette, Qué., 2217-2227
Jonquière, Qué., 2132, 2167

Kamloops, B.C., 6410-6419
Kapuskasing, Ont., 3886-3889
Kelowna, B.C., 6862, 6877
Kénogami, Qué., 2132, 2167
Kenora, Ont., 549
Keremeos, B.C., 6892
Kingston, Ont., 1657, 3890-4030
Kipawa, Qué. See Témiskaming
Kirkland Lake, Ont., 3547, 4031-4039
Kitchener-Waterloo, Ont., 3711, 3750, 4040-4098, 4199
Kitimat, B.C., 2130, 6420-6424

Lachine, Qué., 2427, 2499, 2555. See also Montréal
Lachute, Qué., 3357, 3358
Lac La Biche, Alta., 6294, 6295
Lacombe, Alta., 6293
Ladner, B.C., 6850, 6907
Ladysmith, B.C., 6872
Langley, B.C., 6405-6409
Lanigan, Sask., 5945
La Ronge, Sask., 5944
La Salle, Qué., 2427. See also Montréal
Laterrière, Qué., 2146
Lauder, Man., 5752
Lauzon, Qué., 3374
Laval, Qué., 2818, 2666. See also Montréal
Lawrencetown, N.S., 1283. See also Halifax-Dartmouth
Leaf Rapids, Man., 3354, 5745, 5747
Lethbridge, Alta., 6269-6278
Lévis, Qué., 3020, 3021, 3127, 3143, 3145, 3183, 3184, 3196. See also Québec City
Lillooet, B.C., 6879
Lindsay, Ont., 5281
Liverpool, N.S., 1531
Lloydminster, Sask., 5804-5807
London, Ont., 3429, 3589, 3882, 4083, 4099-4216, 5265
Londonderry, N.S., 1543
Longueuil, Qué., 2415. See also Montréal
Louisbourg, N.S., 1433-1466, 3040
Lunenburg, N.S., 1381, 1529, 1533, 1539

McAdam, N.B., 1725
Mackenzie, B.C., 6888, 6910

Maces Bay, N.B., 1730
Maisonneuve, Qué., 2608, 2619, 2620. See also Montréal

Maple Ridge, B.C., 6865, 6881
Marysville, N.B., 1136, 1724
Matane, Qué., 3359, 3360
Medicine Hat, Alta., 6279-6284
Merritt, B.C., 6899
Merrittown, Ont., 4539. See also St. Catharines
Milestone, Sask., 5940
Millertown, Nfld., 1916
Milltown, N.B., 1719
Minby, Sask., 5950
Minnedosa, Man., 5462-5465
Mirabel, Qué., 3393
Mirimachi, N.S., 1479
Mission, B.C., 6864
Mississauga, Ont., 5058. See also Toronto
Moncton, N.B., 1136, 1599-1614, 3836
Montmagny, Qué., 3350
Montréal, Qué., 2003, 2029, 2228-2944, 2991, 2999, 3040, 3054, 3146, 3177, 3185, 4277, 4346, 4671, 4712, 4915, 4961, 5023, 5051, 5074, 5175, 5217
Montréal-Est, Qué., 2656, 2937. See also Montréal
Montréal-Nord, Que., 2854. See also Montréal
Moose Head, N.S., 1538
Moose Jaw, Sask., 5808, 5813
Morden, Man., 5761
Morrisburg, Ont., 3520
Moser River, N.S., 1538
Mountain View, Alta., 6304
Mount Royal, Qué., 2245, 2590, 2632, 2635, 2641, 2744, 2827, 2849, 2920. See also Montréal
Muskoka, Ont., 5316

Nanaimo, B.C., 6426-6436, 6875
Napanee, Ont., 5301, 5310
National Capital Region, 4257, 4288, 4350, 4368, 4369, 4371, 4374, 4379, 4382-4385, 4388, 4403, 4410, 4412, 4427, 4428. See also Hull; Ottawa
Necum Teuch, N.S., 1538
Nelson, B.C., 6861, 6901
Newark, Ont., 4537. See also Niagara-on-the-Lake
Newcastle, N.B., 1721
New Edinburgh, Ont., 4262. See also Ottawa
New Hamburg, Ont., 4049. See also Kitchener-Waterloo
New Liskeard, Ont., 3547, 5296
Newmarket, Ont., 5330
New Westminster, B.C., 6437-6447
Niagara Falls, Ont., 4518, 4525, 4531. See also St. Catharines

Niagara-on-the-Lake, Ont., 4506, 4509, 4511, 4514, 4516, 4524, 4532, 4540, 4543. *See also* St. Catharines
Nicolet, Qué., 3344
Norman Wells, N.W.T., 7042
North Battleford, Sask., 5801-5803
North Bay, Ont., 3547, 4217-4222
North Vancouver, B.C., 6616, 6626, 6685. *See also* Vancouver
North York, Ont., 4759, 4776. *See also* Toronto
Norway House, Man., 5753

Oakville, Ont., 3772, 5318
Ocean Falls, B.C., 6896
Ogdensburg, Ont., 3920
Ojibway, Ont., 5254, 5280
Okotoks, Alta., 6319
Old Crow, Y.T., 6988, 7043
Orangeville, Ont., 5327
Orillia, Ont., 4223-4229
Ore Blight, Nfld., 1909
Oromocto, N.B., 1712, 1729
Osceola, Ont., 5312
Oshawa, Ont., 3612, 4230-4233
Ottawa, Ont., 2003, 2207, 2210, 2215, 2365, 2999, 4234-4432. *See also* Hull; National Capital Region
Outremont, Qué., 2403, 2404, 2416. *See also* Montréal
Owen Sound, Ont., 3448, 5283, 5299
Oxford House, Man., 5753

Parent, Qué., 3382
Paris, Ont., 5322, 5329
Parry Sound, Ont., 4433-4435
Penticton, B.C., 6448-6450
Peterborough, Ont., 549, 3688, 4436-4473
Petrolia, Ont., 4477, 4478, 4480, 4483
Phoenix, B.C., 6855
Pickering, Ont., 5295
Pierreville, Qué., 3345
Pinawa, Man., 5735
Pine Falls, Man., 5748
Placentia, Nfld., 1910
Pocatière, Qué., 3353
Pointe-Claire, Qué., 2841. *See also* Montréal
Ponoka, Sask., 6310
Portage La Prairie, Man., 5466-5472
Port Arthur, Ont. *See* Thunder Bay
Port Colborne, Ont., 4547
Port Coquitlam, B.C., 6863, 6905. *See also* Vancouver
Port Credit, Ont., 5293

Port Dufferin, N.S., 1538
Port Hardy, B.C., 6895
Port Hawkesbury, N.S., 1540
Port Hope, Ont., 3680, 5331
Port Stanley, Ont., 4107
Powell River, B.C., 6880, 6890, 6906
Prescott, Ont., 3520, 5320, 5341
Preston, N.S., 1283
Preston, Ont., 3657
Prince Albert, Sask., 5814-5821
Prince George, B.C., 6451-6455
Prince Rupert, B.C., 6456-6468
Princeton, B.C., 6869
Pugwash, N.S., 1542

Québec City, Qué., 1412, 2003, 2324, 2337, 2365, 2537, 2538, 2710, 2786, 2839, 2945-3203, 4277, 4346, 4362, 4997
Queenston, Ont., 4505. *See also* St. Catharines
Quoddy, N.S., 1538

Red Deer, Alta., 6285-6292
Red Lake, Ont., 5289, 5324
Regina, Sask., 549, 5649, 5809, 5822-5886, 6211
Renfrew, Ont., 5328
Revelstoke, B.C., 6857, 6870, 6893
Rexdale, Ont., 5222
Richelieu, Qué., 2242, 2421, 2911
Richmond, B.C., 6538, 6580, 6743. *See also* Vancouver
Rimouski, Qué., 3204-3214
Rivière-du-Loup, Qué., 3343
Rosetown, Sask., 5939
Rossland, B.C., 6886, 6891
Rouyn-Noranda, Qué., 3215-3221

Saanich, B.C. *See* Victoria
Sackville, N.B., 1615-1617
Sainte-Agathe-des-Monts, Qué., 3351, 3352
St. Albert, Alta., 6316
Saint Andrews, N.B., 1618-1622
St. Boniface, Man., 5473-5477. *See also* Winnipeg
St. Catharines, Ont., 4501-4550
Saint-Claude, Man., 5754
St. Croix, N.B., 1534, 1714
Saint-Denis-sur-Richelieu, Qué., 3380
Ste-Foy, Qué., 3164, 3188, 3195. *See also* Québec City
Saint-Georges de Beauce, Qué., 3348
Saint-Hyacinthe, Qué., 3231-3243, 3325
St. James, Man., 5739. *See also* Winnipeg

374 *Canada's Urban Past*

St-Jean-de-Boischatel, Qué., 3346. *See also* Québec City
Saint-Jean D'Iberville, Qué., 3222-3225
St. Jérôme, Qué., 3226-3230
Saint John, N.B., 1119, 1623-1706, 3933
St. John's, Nfld., 1119, 1640, 1835-1900
St. Laurent, Qué., 2266, 2413, 2705, 2706, 2794, 2874, 3367. *See also* Montréal
St. Léonard, Qué., 2873. *See also* Montréal
Sainte-Marie de Beauce, Qué., 3342, 3363, 3364, 3384, 3385
St. Martin's, N.B., 1715, 1716
St. Mary's Bay, N.S., 1534
Saint Paul, Alta., 6301, 6307
Sainte-Rose-du-Lac, Man., 5758
St. Stephen, N.B., 1708, 1709, 1719
Sainte-Thècle, Qué., 3375
St. Thomas, Ont., 4212, 4558-4563
St. Vital, Man., 5736. *See also* Winnipeg
Salmon Arm, B.C., 6873
Sarnia, Ont., 3429, 4083, 4199, 4474-4483
Saskatoon, Sask., 5844, 5887-5933, 6108
Sault Ste. Marie, Ont., 4484-4500
Savage Cove, Nfld., 1906
Scarborough, Ont., 4655, 4656, 5233. *See also* Toronto
Schefferville, Qué., 3244-3248, 3366
Selkirk, Man., 5581
Senneterre, Qué., 3347
Sept-Iles, Qué., 3248, 3370, 3379, 3391
Shawinigan, Qué., 3249-3259
Shediac, N.B., 1711, 1733
Shelburne, N.S., 1476-1480
Sherbrooke, N.S., 1536
Sherbrooke, Qué., 2436, 3260-3279
Sillery, Qué., 3162. *See also* Québec City
Simcoe, Ont., 5290
Slave Lake, Alta., 6296
Solsgirth, Man., 5731
Sorel, Qué., 3277, 3280-3294
Souris City, Man., 5746, 5749
South Vancouver, B.C., 6546, 6576, 6681. *See also* Vancouver
Springhill, N.S., 1481-1485
Steinback, Man., 5750
Steveston, B.C., 6903
Stratford, Ont., 549, 3590, 4551-4557
Strathcona, Alta., 6190, 6191, 6257. *See also* Edmonton
Strathroy, Ont., 4147. *See also* London
Sturgeon Falls, Ont., 5307
Sudbury, Ont., 3547, 4564-4612
Summerland, B.C., 6851
Surrey, B.C., 6484, 6498, 6603. *See also* Vancouver
Swan Lake, Man., 5741

Swift Current, Sask., 5934-5937
Sydney, N.S., 1194, 1438, 1486-1511, 1546

Tadoussac, Qué., 3369, 3381
Tahsis, B.C., 6915
Tayville, Ont., 5326
Témiskaming, Qué., 3215, 3215A, 3295-3301
Terrace, B.C., 6854
Terrace Bay, Ont., 549
Terra Nova, Nfld., 1916
Thetford Mines, Qué., 3302-3306
Thessalon, Ont., 5314
Thicket Portage, Man., 5753
Thompson, Man., 5743, 5759
Thorold, Ont., 4528
Thunder Bay, Ont., 4613-4637
Timmins, Ont., 4638-4643
Toronto, Ont., 2279, 2325, 2581, 2625, 2722, 2752, 2817, 2853, 2881, 2887, 2917, 2924, 3590, 3612, 4186, 4644-5241, 5532
Tracy, Qué., 3290
Trail, B.C., 6852, 6889, 6911, 6912
Trenton, Ont., 5319
Trinity Bay, Nfld., 1907
Tri-Town, Ont., 3547
Trois-Rivières, Qué., 3239, 3307-3341
Truro, N.S., 1535, 1544

Uranium City, Sask., 5948

Valleyfield, Qué., 3371, 3372
Vancouver, B.C., 2261, 2817, 5141, 5146, 5532, 6366, 6469-6752
Vanderhoof, B.C., 6888
Verdun, Qué., 2299. *See also* Montréal
Vernon, B.C., 6753-6756
Victoria, B.C., 6366, 6757-6848, 6875
Virden, Man., 5747

Wabasca, Alta., 6296
Wabowden, Man., 5753
Walhachin, B.C., 6897, 6898
Walkerville, Ont., 5254, 5261, 5262. *See also* Windsor
Waterloo, Ont. *See* Kitchener-Waterloo
Wawa, Ont., 5342
Welland, Ont., 3416, 4503, 4519, 4550, 5287. *See also* St. Catharines
Wellington, B.C., 6903
Westmount, Qué., 2321, 2406, 2614. *See also* Montréal

West Vancouver, B.C., 6573, 6607, 6663, 6700, 6712. *See also* Vancouver
Wetaskiwin, Alta., 6310, 6311
Whitehorse, Y.T., 7007-7028
Willard, Ont., 3612
Williamsburg, Ont., 3416, 5287
Windsor, N.S., 1512-1518
Windsor, Ont., 549, 3429, 4199, 5242-5279
Winkler, Man., 5738

Winnipeg, Man., 5146, 5474, 5481-5730, 5825, 6211
Wolverton, Ont., 5322
Woodstock, N.B., 1136, 1723
Woodstock, Ont., 5309, 5321

Yarmouth, N.S., 1136, 1519-1528
Yellowknife, N.W.T., 7029-7041
Yorkton, Sask., 5946, 5947

Subject Index

Note to Users

Two guiding principles were used to organize the entries:

1. Material was categorized beginning with general (e.g. "Ornamental Aspects of Cities"), followed by material where a place was named (e.g. "Architecture in Ontario"), followed by material where a specific topic and place was named (e.g. "Residential Architecture in Vancouver"). An example is:

   Architecture: 662, 663
      General: North, 6927; B.C., 6372;
         Hamilton, 3844
      Specific: baroque revival, Que., 2002;
         classical tradition, Ont., 3461;
         Victorian, Hamilton, 3834, 3850

2. Within each entry, places are listed alphabetically beginning with large units (e.g. Maritimes), followed by provinces (e.g. N.B.), followed by parts of provinces (e.g. Southern Ont.), followed by specific cities or towns. For example:

   Industry: 224, 230, etc.
      General: Maritimes, 1099; B.C., 6711;
         Southern Ont., 3413; Brandon, 5440

Users should also note the following:

1. In complex and/or long entries, italics have been used in the category "Specific topics by place" to ease the task of locating material.
2. Unless otherwise noted, the entry sub-headings "General" and "Specific" mean "General by place" and "Specific topic by place."
3. Occasionally, sub-headings other than "General" and "Specific" are used, but these entries are self-explanatory.

Acadians: N.B., 1569, 1726, 1727; N.S., 1530; Fredericton, 1759; Moncton, 1606; Louisbourg, 1458. *See also* French-Canadians; Ethnicity

Adams, Thomas: Iroquois Falls, 3301; Kipawa, 3295; Ojibway, 5280; Montreal, 2560; Temiskaming, 3301; conservation, 501; housing, 714-724; planning, 481-497; slums, 833

Agrarian politics: Alta., 5955; Ont., 3485;

Western Canada, 5364; Hanna, 6298; Toronto, 4904. *See also* Agriculture; Rural

Aged, problems of: Regina and Saskatoon, 5844; St. John, 1641; Montreal, 2700; Quebec City, 3115; Vancouver and Victoria; 6697; Victoria, 6766. *See also* Social problems

Agriculture: 493, 537, 655; Canada, 4203; Central Canada, 3499; N.S., 1161; Que., 2101; Que. and Ont., 3521A; Annapolis Valley, 1208; Montreal, 2242; Saguenay, 2148; Toronto, 5226. *See also* Agrarian politics; Rural

Airports: Fort William, 4628A; Regina, 5875. *See also* Transportation

Aluminum: 2129, 2130, 2131, 2132. *See also* Staples; Mining

Americans: Calgary, 6116. *See also* Immigration; Ethnicity

Ames, H. B.: Montreal, 2561, 2573, 2644

Annexation: Que., 1927; Edmonton, 6146, 6257; Montreal, 2884. *See also* Growth, urban

Apartments: Prairie metropolitan areas, 5384; Calgary, 6099; Kitchener, 4071; Saskatoon, 5905; Winnipeg, 5694. *See also* Housing; House building

Archives: Calgary, 6019; Edmonton, 6160; Kingston, 3936, 3954; Montreal, 2239, 2269, 2308, 2395; Ottawa, 4305; Peterborough, 4471; Quebec City, 2952, 2978, 3064; Toronto, 4650, 4733, 4800; Trois-Rivières, 3329; Vancouver, 6551, 6557; Victoria, 6759. *See also* Indexes; Document collections; Guides

Architects: Toronto, 5227; Vancouver, 6572; Diamond & Myers, 691; Erickson, Arthur, 672, 673, 682; Kahn, Albert, 683; Thomas, William, 706. *See also* Building; Architecture; Planning

Architecture: 662, 663, 667, 672, 676, 677, 679, 680, 681, 683, 684, 687, 689, 690, 691, 692, 693, 694, 695, 696, 697, 698, 699, 701, 702, 705, 706, 708, 709, 710, 713

General: North, 6927; Prairie, 5333; B.C., 6372; Ont., 3486, 3534; Que., 1951, 2046, 2083, 2111, 2112, 2123; Hamilton, 3844, 3797; Kingston, 3916, 3932, 4009; Montreal, 2250, 2267, 2306, 2344, 2346, 2348, 2374, 2377, 2379, 2390, 2667; Ottawa, 4247, 4266, 4272; Peterborough, 4457; Quebec City, 2946, 2949, 2951, 2967, 3002, 3007, 3008, 3014, 3018, 3019, 3025, 3051, 3058, 3112, 3113, 3140; St. John, 1635, 1675; Stratford, 4557; Toronto, 4646, 4649, 4667, 4757, 4761, 4774, 4825; Vancouver, 6508, 6604, 6719; Victoria, 6772, 6777, 6824, 6833; Winnipeg, 5509, 5558

Specific: baroque revival, Que., 2002; classical tradition, Ont., 3461; *folk,* Trinity Bay, 1907; *Scottish,* Guelph, 3721; and *town planning,* North, 6940; and *urbanism,* Que., 1920, 1954, 2054; *Victorian,* Hamilton, 3834, 3850

See also Architects; Buildings; Church architecture; Preservation, architectural; Planning

Armenians: Montreal, 2712. *See also* Ethnicity; Immigration

Art: Fredericton, 1580; Guelph, 3746; Halifax, 1235; Joliette, 2218; Kingston, 3959; Montreal, 2319, 2487, 2612; Quebec City, 3089; St. John, 1673; Toronto, 4912, 4977; Vancouver, 6470, 6602, 6609, 6610; Yellowknife, 7033. *See also* Architecture: Building

Asians: 408; Calgary, 6122; Saskatoon, 5908, 5926; Vancouver, 6469, 6532, 6585, 6676; Winnipeg, 5695. *See also* Ethnicity; Japanese; Chinese; Indians (Asian); Immigration

Automobiles: 286, 290; Calgary, 6070; Windsor, 5242. *See also* Transportation

Banking: Maritimes, 1124; B.C., 6327; Charlottetown, 1751; Dawson City, 6991, 7005; Fredericton, 1577, 1578; Kingston, 3994; Montreal, 2295, 2497, 2559; Pictou, 1467; St. Hyacinthe, 3240; Toronto, 4740, 4782, 4786, 4789, 4859, 4886; Winnipeg, 5608. *See also* Finance

Bengalese: Saskatoon, 5920. *See also* Ethnicity; Indian (Asian); Immigration

Bicycles: Ottawa, 6070. *See also* Transportation

Bibliographies: 2, 4, 5, 6, 8, 9, 17, 18, 21, 26, 27, 28

General: Prairies, 5387; Western Canada, 5348; B.C., 6340, 6364, 6396; Man., 5427, 5433; Nfld., 1803, 1804, 1811; N.S., 1197, 1198; Que., 1975; Sask., 5764, 5793; Y.T., 6947, 6948, 6949, 6955, 6971; Abitibi-Temiskaming, 3215; Banff Park, 6313; Banff, Jasper, Kootenay, Yoho Parks, 6314; Cape Breton, 1194; Southern Alta., 5962; Lambton County and Sarnia, 4479; Perth County, 4555; Windsor and Essex County, 5263; Fort William and Port Arthur, 4630; Hull, 2189; Kingston, 3900, 3901, 3905, 3922;

Montreal, 2228, 2253, 2342, 2350; northern towns, 3547; Ottawa, 4245, 4270, 4288; Peterborough, 4470; Quebec City, 3208; Winnipeg, 5556; St. John's, 1837; Sault Ste. Marie, Ont., and Michigan, 4494; Vancouver, 6515
 Specific types: architectural history, 687; community network, 930; frontier communities, 315; housing, 726, 741; land issues, 741; municipal govt., 861, 894; northern research, 6923; public health, 1063; town planning, 534, 573, 620, 733, 1063
 Specific types by place: architectural conservation, Ont., 3443; *cities,* Que., 2034; *community development,* Northeastern Ont., 3610; *early settlers,* Waterloo Township, 4056; *govt. publications,* Alta., 5963; *local history,* Canada, 3545; Maritimes, 1133; *metropolitan,* Que., 1931; *minority groups,* Toronto, 5067; *Oblate Fathers,* Ottawa, 4248; *planning publications,* Toronto, 4802; *urbanization,* Montreal, 2244; *urban planning,* Toronto, 5057; *working class,* Hamilton, 3792
Blacks: Maritimes, 1125, 1140; N.S., 1169; Halifax, 1287, 1401; South Western Ont., 3552; Buxton and Chatham, 5336; Chatham, 5302; London, 4165; Montreal, 2795, 2883, 2923; Toronto, 4666, 4720, 4844, 4865; Victoria, 6821; Windsor, 5071. *See also* Ethnicity; Immigration
Blight, urban: 558; London, 4192. *See also* Renewal, urban
Boards of Trade: Halifax, 1427; Toronto, 4795, 4955; Vancouver, 6478. *See also* Chambers of Commerce
Boarding: Moncton and Hamilton, 3836; Toronto, 4929, 4948. *See also* Housing; Immigration; Working class
Board of Control: 980. *See also* Municipal government.
Boomtowns: N.S., 1543; Grand Valley, 5743; Edmonton, 6198, 6228, 6242, 6250; Osceola, 5312; Prince George, 6453; Saskatoon, 5903, 5904; Toronto, 5134; Whitehorse, 7028. *See also* New towns
Boosterism: Prairie Cities, 5351; Alta., 5977, 5998; Calgary, 6063, 6064; Halifax, 1384; Ottawa, 4351; Prince George, 6452; St. John, 1696; Swift Current, 5936; Vancouver, 6631. *See also* Growth; Planning; Entrepreneurs
Borough system: Montreal, 2941, 2942. *See also* Municipal Government; Urban growth
Bossism: 962; Montreal, 2860. *See also* Reform, urban

Bridges: Edmonton, 6192; Montreal, 2613. *See also* Transportation
Building: north, 3526; Ont., 3580; Calgary, 6075; Inuvik, 7051; Montreal, 2609; Toronto, 3580. *See also* Architecture; Buildings
Buildings: Nfld., 1813; N.S., 1199; Calgary, 6007; Edmonton, 6195; Fredericton, 1591, 1596; Guelph, 3744; Halifax, 1356; Kingston, 3972, 3974; Louisbourg, 1452, 1463; Moncton, 1600, 1610; Ottawa, 4267, 4269, 4298, 4357; Pictou, 1471; Quebec City, 3014, 3019; St. John, 1651; St. John's, 1873, 1875, 1877, 1878; Winnipeg, 5628. *See also* Building; Architecture
Business: 226; Southern Ont., 3487; Eastern Grey County, 5323; Charlottetown, 1757; Halifax, 1338; Kingston, 3921; Montreal, 2520, 2556; Quebec City, 3198; Regina, 5847; Toronto, Acton, Willard, Oshawa, 3612; Toronto, 5237; Vancouver, 6648, 6720; Victoria, 6767, 6768; Windsor, 1513; Winnipeg, 5587, 5634. *See also* Merchant; Commerce; Entrepreneur; Trade

Cabbagetown (Toronto): 4711, 5080
Canada Company: Guelph, 3712, 3713, 3714, 3716, 3739, 3741; Stratford and Goderich, 4552
Canals: Montreal, 2499, 2555; Ottawa, 4314; Welland, 4519. *See also* Transportation
Capital development: 233; N.B., 1558; St. John's, 1887. *See also* Finance; Economy
Capital cities: Ottawa, 4335, 4342, 4343, 4347, 4352, 4353, 4354, 4359, 4381, 4382, 4383, 4388, 4423, 4428; N.B., 1570; Kingston, 3998, 4007; Regina, 5783
Carnivals: Montreal, 2586; Quebec City, 3178; Yellowknife, 7032. *See also* Recreation; Entertainment
Census: N.B., 1554; Fredericton, 1582; Halifax, 1379; Louisbourg, 1451; Montreal, 2526; Quebec City, 3039, 3121; Saguenay, 2149. *See also* Demography; Population
Central business district: 799, 800; Edmonton, 6210, 6248, 6256; Hamilton, 3868; Hull, 2207; Montreal, 2877; Ottawa, 4297, 4420, 4422; Peterborough, 4468; Regina, 5846; Toronto, 5240; Vancouver, 6707. *See also* Economy
Central office complex: Toronto, 5078. *See also* Central business district
Central place system: Alta., 5954, 5976; Man., 5432; Ont., 3570; P.E.I., 1749; Sask.,

5797; Calgary, 6020, 6106; Guelph, Barrie, Owen Sound, 3448; Guelph, 3723, 3727, 3731; Portage la Prairie, 5468. *See also* Metropolitan areas

Chambers of Commerce: Lévis, 3145; Quebec City, 3011, 3186; St. John's, 1842, 1848. *See also* Boards of Trade

Children: English Canada, 399; Montreal, 2634; Ottawa, 4406. *See also* Child welfare; Orphans; Family

Child welfare: 1057; Nfld., 1787; N.S., 1186; Ont., 3401A, 3546, 3576; Calgary, 6071; Montreal, 2303; Toronto, 4725, 4947, 4964. *See also* Children; Orphans; Social problems

Chinatowns: Hamilton, 3885; Toronto, 5224, 5236; Vancouver, 6488, 6721, 6752; Victoria, 6800, 6804, 6805, 6822. *See also* Ethnicity; Chinese; Immigration

Chinese: Alta., 5960, 5997; B.C., 6393; Calgary, 6000, 6001, 6002, 6050; Montreal, 2662; Saskatoon, 5910; Toronto, 4654, 4970, 5059, 5136, 5137, 5224, 5236; Vancouver, 6488, 6489, 6490, 6613, 6667, 6721, 6733, 6736; Victoria, 6800, 6802, 6803, 6804, 6805, 6830. *See also* Asians; Ethnicity; Chinatowns; Immigration

Cholera: Halifax, 1226; Quebec City, 1961, 3107; St. John, 1627. *See also* Disease; Public health; Hospitals; Water

Church architecture: 668; Que., 2001; Upper Canada, 3535; Montreal, 2432; Quebec City, 3007; Vancouver, 6719. *See also* Architecture; Buildings; Churches and religion

Churches and religion: 151; Prairies, 5374; N.S., 1147, 1173, 1177; Cape Breton, 1497; Calgary, 6005; Charlotte, 1708; Halifax, 1291; Leaf Rapids, 5757; Quebec City, 3006; London, Toronto, 4186; Victoria, 6843; Windsor, 5267

Denominations: Anglican, N.S., 1159; Calgary, 6003, 6004, 6046; Dartmouth, 1334; Edmonton, 6204; Halifax, 1264, 1272, 1329; Hamilton, 3761; Kingston, 3890, 3992, 3993, 4002, 4003; London, 4125; Ottawa, 4242, 4264, 4268, 4271; Peterborough, 4456; St. John's, 1865; Toronto, 4762, Trois-Rivières, 3328; *Baptist*, Amherst, 1207; Halifax, 1280; *Christian*, Charlottetown, 1753; *Congregationalist*, St. John's, 1889; *Disciples of Christ*, Halifax, 1326; *Doukhobors*, Saskatchewan, 5795; Vancouver, 6591; *Evangelical*, Calgary, 6101; *Labour*, Winnipeg, 5623; *Lutheran*, Waterloo County, 4059, 4060;

Fredericton, 1581; *Mennonite*, 418, 419, 420; Waterloo County, 4067, 4074; *Methodist*, Central Canada, 3595; Calgary, 6081; Charlottetown, 1762; Kingston, 4010; St. John's, 1876; Toronto, 4436, 4889; *Mission*, Edmonton, 6206; *Mormon*, Cardston, 6320; *Presbyterian*, Y.T., 6959; Cape Breton, 1505; Carleton County, 4279; Guelph, 3748; Kingston, 3987; Montreal, 2521, 2530; Orillia, 4223; Ottawa, 4280; Quebec City, 3134; St. John, 1652; St. John's, 1847; Springhill, 1483; *Roman Catholic*, Nfld., 1789; Que., 2100, 2611, 3138; Eastern Townships, 2105; Calgary, 6045; Charlottetown, 1763; Chicoutimi, 2157, 2158, 2159, 2170; Edmonton, 6167, 6203; Halifax, 1347; Hull, 2194, 2195, 2205, 2209; Joliette, 2207; Kingston, 3908, 3911, 3912; London, 4106, 4153; Moncton, 1610; Montreal, 2236, 2283, 2309, 2341, 2362, 2379, 2380, 2382, 2449, 2451, 2452, 2488, 2527, 2541, 2547, 2570, 2595, 2626, 2636, 2806; Ottawa, 4275, 4313, 4315; Peterborough, 4438; Quebec City, 3015, 3030, 3043, 3045, 3046, 3071, 3091, 3102, 3132; Rimouski, 3208, 3211A; St. Boniface, 5476; St. Hyacinthe, 3235, 3242; St. Jerome, 3228; St. John's, 1886; Sault Ste. Marie, 4489; Sherbrooke, 3268; Thunder Bay, 4613; Toronto, 4967, 4996; Trois-Rivières, 3330, 3341; Windsor, 5264A; Winnipeg, 5538; *Salvation Army*, Toronto, 4892; *United*, Halifax, 1308, 1314; Kingston, 3893; St. John's, 1884, 1893; Saskatoon, 5914; Springhill, 1482

Protestant-Catholic relations, Ont., 3473; Kingston, 3942, 4019; Port Arthur and Fort William, 4624; Toronto, 4853, 4954

See also Education; Ethnicity; Immigration

Citizen action and participation: 828, 901, 902; Hull, 2197; New Westminster, 6438; St. John's, 1845; Toronto, 5144B; Vancouver, 6705; Winnipeg, 5646. *See also* Municipal government; Civil liberties

City Beautiful: 605, 626. *See also* Planning

City Efficient: 627. *See also* Planning

City hall: Kingston, 3944; Toronto, 5031; Windsor, 5278; Winnipeg, 5485. *See also* Architecture; Municipal government

City manager: 945, 951, 964, 975, 992; Halifax, 1240; Montreal, 2856; Windsor, 5272. *See also* Municipal Government

Civic Improvement League: 867

Civic centre: Calgary, 6119A; Edmonton, 6220; Quebec City, 2090; Vancouver, 6739. *See also* Architecture; Planning

Civic square: Hamilton, 3867. *See also* Architecture; Planning; Civic centre
Civil liberties: Toronto, 5210. *See also* Reform
Civil service: Kingston, 3985
Coal: Alta., 5961; N.S. and Cape Breton, 1490, 1491, 1492, 1493, 1503, 1506, 1507; Southern Ont., 3621; Edmonton, 6152, 6156; Halifax, 1398; Nanaimo, 6426, 6430; Springhill, 1481, 1485
Colleges. *See* Education
Commerce: Guelph, 3715; Hull, 2188; Montreal, 2729, 2789; Niagara, 4535; Toronto, 4832; Victoria, 6815
Commerical structure: Sask., 5780; Kitchener-Waterloo, 4045; London, 4216; Montreal, 2502, 2663, 2762, 2822, 2866; St. John's, 1852; Sherbrooke, 3264; Winnipeg, 5528. *See also* Business; Trade; Merchant; Entrepreneur
Commission government: 984, 989, 992; Red Deer, 6291. *See also* Municipal government
Committee of review: Winnipeg, 5713
Communication: telephone, London, 4110; Trans Pacific Service, Vancouver, 6642. *See also* Transportation; Metropolitanism
Community organization and development: 912; Eastern Arctic, 6969; North, 6951; Northern trading posts, 6919; Cape Breton, 1511; Alta., 5988; Man., 5423; Nfld., 1819; Calgary, 6104; Edmonton, 6222; Elliot Lake, 3695; Fogo, 1905; Harbour Breton, 1904; London, 4118, 4182; Montreal and Quebec City, 2839; Sudbury, 4606, 4607; Toronto, 5099
Company towns: 318, 319, 320, 321, 322, 328, 329, 330, 331, 332, 334, 338, 341, 344, 345, 346, 349; Britannia, 6908; Chandler, 3368; Fermont, 3389; Sudbury, 4589, 4605; Tahsis, 6915; Temiskaming, 3298. *See also* Resource towns; Mining; New towns; Pulp and paper towns; Single enterprise towns
Comparisons among/between places: Qué.-Ont., 1963; Birtle-Foxwarren-Solsgirth, 5731; Calgary-Edmonton, 5995; Chicago, U.S.A.-Toronto 4819; Detroit, U.S.A.-Windsor, 5275; Guelph-Galt-Kitchener, 3711; Halifax-Victoria, 1403, 6787; Hamburg, Germany-Toronto, 5016; Jonquière-Kenogami-Arvida, 3387; Calais, Maine-St. Stephen, 1719; Montreal -Louisiana, U.S.A., 2475; Montreal -Toronto, 4671, 4712, 4915, 5051; Prince Rupert-Kitimat, 6424, 6466; Quebec-Montreal-Ottawa, 4277; Sandwich, Upper Canada-Detroit, U.S.A., 5246; Seattle, U.S.A.-Vancouver -Klondike, 6644; Vancouver -Sydney, Australia, 6592; Victoria-Vancouver, 6514, 6793
Congestion: 521
Conservation: Ont., 3471; Quebec City, 2986. *See also* Ecology; Architecture
Construction: Montreal, 1930, 2675; Quebec City, 3086; Toronto, 4773
Conurbation: Toronto, 5213
Coordination boards: Winnipeg, 5674
Corridors: Ont., 3634; Edmonton to Calgary, 5994; Toronto to Stratford, 3590
Cost of living: Kingston, 4015; Toronto, 4972; Winnipeg, 5502. *See also* Occupations
Crime:
  General: Calgary, 6090; Montreal, 2895, 2910; Regina, 5870; Quebec City, 3057; Toronto, 4815, 4870
  Specific: crime, poverty, and ignorance, Ont., 3497; *Mafia,* Hamilton, 3780; *vandalism,* St. John's, 1891; *violence,* Toronto, 4880
  See also Social problems; Police; Justice

Decentralization:
  General: Ont., 3635; Calgary, Edmonton, 6135; Edmonton, 6268
  Specific: administration, North, 6931; *industry,* Toronto, 5071; *population and industry,* Que., 2055
Decline, urban: Nfld., 1795; Sask., 5787; Kingston, 3947. *See also* Growth
Demography: N.B., 1707; Montreal, 2442, 2767; Rimouski, 3210; St. Claude, 5754; Strait of Belle Isle, 1914. *See also* Population; Census; Immigration
Depression: Crowsnest Pass, 6904; Toronto, 5081, 5138; Victoria, 6794. *See also* Social problems
Developers: 648, 652; independent developers, Montreal, 2937; Toronto, 5089; Vancouver, 6702, 6739. *See also* Building
Development:
  General: Western Canada, 5352; Maritimes, 1108; Mackenzie Basin, 6986; Nfld., 1770 1810; Ont., 3617; Ont., 1939; P.E.I., 1743, 1744; Que., 2045, 2099; Que., Ont., 3419; Northeastern Ont., 3560, 3591; Northern Ont., 3542; South Central Ont., 3604; Southern Ont., 3432; Southwestern Ont., 3558; Vancouver Island, 6344; Niagara Peninsula, 4545; Niagara Region, 4534; Huron County, 5303; Brampton; 5337, Burnaby, 6729; Charlottetown, 1755; Guelph, 3724; Halifax, 1279; London, 4187, 4212; Montreal,

Subject Index   381

2294; Quebec City, 3073; Regina, 5857, 5864, 5872; St. Hyacinthe, 3231; St. John, 1647; St. John's, 1844; Toronto, 4770
Specific: controls, Regina, 5859; *innovation,* Regina, 5837; *modernization,* Placenta Bay, 1902; *planning,* N.W.T., 6977A; Churchill, 5433; *problems,* Montreal, 2854; *redevelopment,* Toronto, 5019; Vancouver, 6700, 6749; Windsor, 5247, 5256; *underdevelopment,* Maritimes, 1101, 1106, 1111
See also Planning; Developers; Growth
Directories:
General: Ont., 3399; Guelph 3734
Specific: community resources, St. John's, 1862; *newspapers,* Man., 5424; *street,* Montreal, 2584
See also Guides; Indexes; Archives
Disease: 1092; Ottawa, 4301. *See also* Public health; Cholera; Tuberculosis; Typhoid; Hospitals
Document collections: Kingston, 3999; Sudbury, 4586; Toronto, 4857, 4858; Windsor, 5264; Winnipeg, 5579. *See also* Guides; Indexes; Archives
Downtown, inner city: 794, 795, 799, 800, 801, 819, 827, 829, 830, 849
General: Edmonton, 6234; Kitchener, 4064; Ottawa, Hull, 4363; Peterborough, 4460; Montreal, 2840
Specific: decline, St. John's, 1892; *improvement,* Victoria, 6771; *metro focus,* Vancouver, 6491; *private development,* Vancouver, 6735; *redevelopment,* Winnipeg, 5710; *residential environment,* Vancouver, 6712
Drainage and water problems: Eastern Townships, 2109; Montreal, 2266, 2705
Dutch: Ont., 3436; Edmonton, 6173; London, 4183. *See also* Ethnicity; Religion; Education

Eaton's: Toronto, 4689, 4742, 4796, 4919, 4966
Ecology:
General: three cities, Western Canada, 5359; Alta. cities, 5973; Edmonton, Regina, Winnipeg, 5649, 5825, 6211; Vancouver, 6723
Specific: change, Kingston, 4029; *factorial,* Toronto, 5167; *land use,* Ont., 3493; *patterns,* 792, 798; Calgary, 6107; *spatial structure,* Winnipeg, 5671, 5692, 5706
Economic activity: 193, 216, 217; Alta., 5959; N.B., 1563; Nfld., 1799; N.S., 1142, 1352; Que., 1967; Niagara Region, 4533;
Edmonton, 6153, 6209, 6252, 6253; Granby, 2182; Halifax, 1412; Joliette, 2222, 2225; Kingston, 4022; Kingston-Quebec City, 1947, 3430; Kirkland Lake, 4034; Montreal, 2531; Placenta Bay, 1902; Quebec City, 3165, 3176, 3179; St. Jean, 3365; St. John's, 1843; Toronto, Montreal, Vancouver, 5141; Sudbury, 4611; Victoria, 6650; Victoria, Vancouver, 6817; Wabouden, Thisket, Portage, Norway House, Oxford House, 5753; Yellowknife, 7030, 7031
Economic change: N.B., 1552, 1709; Que., 2069; Kingston, 3991, 4021; Louisbourg, 1447, 1454; Winnipeg, 5483. *See also* Urban growth; Industry
Economic growth: 196, 198, 199, 200, 203, 204, 206, 208, 211, 212, 214, 218, 219, 222, 223, 231, 232, 233, 235, 238, 249, 251; North and Siberia, 6925; N.S., 1162; Elgin County, 5308; Calgary, 6079; Montreal, 2355; Muskoka, 5316; Quebec City, 3192; St. Andrews, 1621; St. John and Portland, Maine, 1625; Sorel, 3283, 3288, 3292; Sudbury, 4568; Vancouver, 6649; Welland, 4550
Economic history: Maritimes, 1138; Que., 2029, 2068; Belle Isle, 1908; Cap de la Madeleine, 3383; Causapscal, 3362; Lachute, 3358; London, 4171; Shawinigan, 3249, 3255; Thetford Mines, 3304; Winnipeg, 5493
Education and schools:
General: Canadian West, 5373; B.C., 6395; N.S., 1171; Nfld., 1792, 1817; Upper Canada, 3417, 3494; Bathurst, 1734; Calgary, 6005, 6008, 6034, 6039, 6086, 6112; Cobourg, 3678; Flin Flon, 5732; Guelph, 3747; Kingston, 4005; London, 4152; Montreal, 2271, 2689; Ottawa, 4249; Peterborough, 4439, 4459; Pinawa, 5735; Quebec City, 3035; Regina, 5861, 5869; St. Boniface, 5473; St. Catharines, 4542; St. John, 1669; Saskatoon, 5912; Toronto, 4702, 4860, 5147, 5232; Vancouver, 6526, 6590; Winnipeg, 5506, 5529
Specific: administration of, Brandon, 5442; Moncton, 1599; *adult,* N.W.T., 6954; Frobisher Bay, 7048; Halifax, 1368; *attendance,* 467; Hamilton, 3809, 3825, 3828; Toronto; 4893; *blind,* Halifax, 1251; *boards,* Toronto, 4670, 4801; *business,* Montreal, 2412, 2934; *colleges,* Bytown, 4316; Calgary, 6048; Guelph, 3742, 3749; Kingston, 3897, 3951, 3952, 3953; Montreal, 2349, 2605; Ottawa, 4303; Quebec

City, 3036; Saint Denis sur Richelieu, 3380; Sudbury, 4571; Toronto, 4700, 4827, 4687, 4758; Trois-Rivières, 3312, 3332; Winnipeg, 5504, 5524; *deaf,* Halifax, 1325; *expenditure,* Toronto, 5046; *immigration,* Toronto, 4772; *industrial,* N.S., 1191; *location model,* Kingston, 4030; *manual,* New France, 2061; *outdoor,* Whitehorse, 7009; *planning,* London, 4176; *poor,* Halifax, 1357; *reorganization,* Montreal, 2759; *secondary,* Guelph, 3751; Halifax, 1285, 1348; Kitchener, Waterloo, 4043; Montreal, 2699; St. John, 1638; Toronto, 5065; Vancouver, 6606; *seminary,* Chicoutimi, 2160, 2161; Montreal, 2509; Quebec City, 3016, 3037, 3038, 3081, 3111, 3129; Paris, France, 3017; *separate,* Halifax, 1233; Hull, 2192, 4246; Kingston, 3910; Montreal, 2873; Ottawa, 4246; Port Arthur, 4618A; *service,* Montreal, 2742; *social change,* Upper Canada, 3477, 3496; *social reform,* Toronto, 4932; *teacher,* Hamilton, 3872; Montreal, 2868; *universities,* Alta., 5995; Sask., 5784; Calgary, 6040, 6078; Edmonton, 6165, 6263; Fredericton, 1589; Halifax, 1239, 1265, 1266, 1267, 1268, 1301, 1406; Hamilton, 3852; Kingston, 3894, 3895, 3919, 3937, 3938, 3945, 3964, 3965, 3966, 4023; London, 4112, 4116, 4132, 4133, 4148, 4173; Montreal, 2313, 2315, 2372, 2373, 2384, 2434, 2490, 2587, 2643; Ottawa, 4248, 4333; Quebec City, 3124; St. John's, 1840; Saskatoon, 5913; Sudbury, 4572; Toronto, 4652, 4659, 4661, 4662, 4691, 4717, 4775, 4816, 4824, 4826, 4835, 4901, 4920, 4936; Vancouver, 6485, 6547, 6560; Victoria, 6799; Waterloo, 4084; Winnipeg, 5536, 5560; *women,* Montreal, 2642, 2643, 2685, 2699; Toronto, 4811

Egyptians: Montreal, 2938. *See also* Ethnicity; Immigration

Elections: Edmonton, 6214; Kamloops, 6410; Montreal, 2508, 2686; Vancouver, 6718, 6731; Winnipeg, 5678. *See also* Politics

Elites: 985; Western Canada, 5349; Alta., 5996; Nfld., 1796, 1809; Que., 2082; Calgary, 6065; Kingston, 4012, 4013, 4035; London, 4104, 4156; Montreal, 2245, 2555, 2904; Ottawa, 4318, 4325; Quebec City, 3150; Toronto, 4728, 4814, 4838, 4848, 4849, 4850, 4861, 4868, 4874, 4876; Saskatoon, 5911; Vancouver, 6345, 6663

Elite clubs: Union Club, B.C., 6762; Vancouver Club, Vancouver, 6479; Terminal City Club, Vancouver, 6502

Energy: fuel, power, and industry, 228; industrial location, Southern Ont., 3624; sources, Southern Ont., 3622. *See also* Hydro power; Oil

English: Lower Canada, 2005; Nfld., 1786; P.E.I., 1742; Eastern Townships, 2053; Montreal, 2724, 2725; Quebec City, 3158; Winnipeg and Eastern Townships, 5687. *See also* Ethnicity

Entertainment: Edmonton, 6201, 6205; Montreal, 2389; Winnipeg, 5705. *See also* Hotels; Exhibitions and fairs; Carnival; Theatre; Sport; Stampede; Recreation

Entrepreneurs: 194, 221, 229, 237; Maritimes, 1120; B.C., 6764; N.B., 1574, 1718; Nfld., 1814; Cape Breton, 1500; Calgary, 6091; Cobourg, 3666; Hamilton, 3790, 3826; Joliette, 2226; Lethbridge, 6271; Moncton, 1614; Montreal, 2504; Orillia, 4227; Petrolia, 4478; Pictou, 1468; Toronto, 4831

Environment, urban: 577, 582, 601, 809, 810; Que., 2119; Halifax, 1260

Eskimo: North, 6950; Yellowknife, 7029; Great Whale River, 7045; and Cree, northern communities, 6932; students, Yellowknife, 7029. *See also* Ethnicity

Ethnicity: 403, 424, 433
  General: Sask., 5788; Upper Canada, 3427; Edmonton, 6149, 6224; Hamilton, 3824, 3866; Quebec City, 3117; Vancouver, 6577, 6608; Winnipeg, 5658
  Specific: acculturation, 430, 431, 444; Whitehorse, 7020; Winnipeg, 5588; Toronto, 4899; *class,* B.C., 6389; Lakehead, 4627; *concentration,* Port Arthur, 4625; *culture,* Kirkland Lake, 4038; London, 4154; Toronto, 5072; *elite,* Toronto, 4728; *language,* Montreal, 2543, 2660, 2661, 2693, 2837, 2936; Ottawa and Hull, 4398; Sudbury, 4584, 4598; *nativism,* Toronto, 4806; Vancouver, 6585; Winnipeg, 5618; *occupation,* Montreal, 2538; Toronto, 5107; *relations,* Ont., 3500; Montreal, 2417, 2843, 2844; *French,* Toronto, 4970; Winnipeg, 5484; *residence,* Hamilton, 3860; Winnipeg, 5688; *segregation,* 409, 429; Toronto, 5157, 5189; Winnipeg, 5663; *strategy and solidarity,* Calgary, 6022; Esterhazy, 5952; *stratification,* Toronto, 5145; *trade unions,* 430; *violence,* Lakehead, 4628; *voting and politics,* Montreal, 2690; Toronto, 5166; St. Boniface, 5474, 5477; Winnipeg, 5714, 5728, 5729

Subject Index   383

See also Immigration; Education; Churches and religion
Exhibitions and fairs: Edmonton, 6142; Regina, 5842; Toronto, 4696, 4738. *See also* Carnivals; Sport; Recreation
Explosions: Dartmouth, 1402; Halifax, 1396, 1399, 1405, 1410, 1416, 1420, 1421, 1422

Fairs. *See* Exhibitions and fairs
Family:
  General: 1070; Canada, 396; Ont., 3435; Wentworth County, 3813; Hamilton, 3812; Kingston, 3973; Quebec City, 3169, 3189
  Specific: class, Hamilton, 3827; *economy,* Montreal, 2567; *fertility,* Canada, 380; *homes,* Southern Ont., 3420; Kingston, 3972; *household,* North, 6982; Moncton, 1609; *income,* Quebec City, 3160; *kinship,* Nfld., 1797; Que., 1991, 2088; *land and education,* Eastern Ont., 3472; *life,* Quebec City, 3084; *life cycle,* Que., 2023; *size,* Canada, 382; *structure,* Que., 1965; Laterriere, 2146
  See also Women; Marriage
Family Compact: Brockville, 3653; Toronto, 4854. *See also* Elite
Federal Capital: 888; Ottawa, 4374, 4379, 4412, 4414. *See also* Capital Cities
Financial hegemony: Toronto and Montreal, 2625, 4961
Financial institutions: Montreal, 2277, 2304, 2638
Finns: Sudbury, 4564; Toronto, 4951, 5185; Thunder Bay, 4622, 4631. *See also* Ethnicity
Fire: 1092; London, 4214; Montreal, 2455, 2465, 2474, 2489; Ottawa, 4301, 4339, 4348; Quebec City, 3100; St. John, 1632, 1693; St. John's, 1849, 1856, 1863, 1871; Toronto, 4836, 4837, 4890, 4969
Fire control: 1092; B.C., 6397, 6398; Calgary, 6005; Hamilton, 3848; Peterborough, 4448; Toronto, 4986; Victoria, 6806
Fiscal: *problems,* Ont., 3638; *development,* Edmonton, 6236
Floods: Port Hope, 5331; Regina, 5822; Winnipeg, 5490, 5703, 5727
Forests, urban: 791
Form and urban structure: 665, 789, 790, 796, 797, 805, 806, 807, 808, 812, 813, 814, 821, 822, 825, 836, 1712, 5398
Fortifications: Lake Ontario, 3525; Que. 2065; Halifax, 1255, 1282, 1316, 1362, 1415; Halifax and Esquimalt, 6401; Kingston, 3902, 3927, 3930, 3957, 3963, 3981, 4011; Louisbourg, 1444, 1448; Montreal, 2307, 2454, 2646; Quebec City, 2976, 2992, 3041, 3078, 3093, 3137; Toronto, 4862; Winnipeg, 5552, 5585; Victoria, 6807, 6820. *See also* Military

French-Canadians:
  General: Nfld., 1797; Edmonton, 6154; Hearst, 5304; Ottawa, 4235, 4308; Sudbury, 4573, 4574, 4577, 4579; Toronto, 4735, 4878, 5160, 5161; Windsor, 5266; Winnipeg, 5619
  Specific: colonization, Eastern Townships, 2074; *demography,* Montreal, 2710; *emigration,* Que., 1979; *heritage,* Kingston, 3988; *industrialization,* Que., 1958, 1997; *life,* Que., 2003; *opinion,* Toronto, 4894; *population,* Que., 1973; *question,* London, 4160; *settlement,* Eastern Ont., 3433; *society,* Qué., 2077; *urbanization,* Que., 2035
  See also Ethnicity; Education; Immigration
Fringe, urban: 832; B.C., 6349; Brandon, 5445; Saskatoon, 5915; Waterloo and Wellington County, 3750. *See also* Rural
Function and structure: 240, 242; N.W.T., 5396; Maritimes, 1122; Que., 2114; Wellington County, 3726; Chicoutimi, 2165; Y.T. and N.W.T., 6945; Regina, 5831; Victoria, 6790. *See also* Planning
Fur trade: Montreal, 2402; Winnipeg, 5548. *See also* Staples

Galt family: Lethbridge, 6271, 6275. *See also* Elites
Garden City: 493, 513, 514, 571, 628; North, 6941; Ont., 4515. *See also* Planning
Geography of Canada, 3475; N.S., 1151; Que., 1966, 2097; Man., 5430; Edmonton, 6138, 6157, 6264; Elliot Lake, 3691; Granby, 2184; Lauzon, 3374; London, 4169, 4213; Montreal, 2668, 2677, 2678, 2679, 2697; New Westminster, 6445; Peterborough, 4463; Quebec City, 2972, 3197; Red Deer, 6285; Rimouski, 3209; St. Hyacinthe, 3238; Salaberry de Valleyfield, 3372; Sault Ste. Marie, 4500; Shawinigan, 3252; South Surrey, 6484; Toronto, 4721, 4730; Vancouver, 6537, 6548; Victoria, 6788; Waterloo Township, 4058; Whitehorse, 7013, 7014; Windsor, 5273
Germans: Upper Canada, 4061; Waterloo County, 4097; Edmonton, 6172; Hamilton, 3865; Kitchener, Waterloo, 4069, 4070, 4088; Montreal, 2862; Toronto and

Detroit, Mich, 5105; Winnipeg, 5599. *See also* Ethnicity; Immigration
Ghetto: Toronto, 4983. *See also* Slums
Ghost towns: Alta., 5964; B.C., 6326, 6374, 6376; Ont., 3404, 3423; Y.T., 6964; Phoenix, 6855; Vancouver, 6373; West Kootenays, 6913
Gold mining: B.C. and Y.T., 6337, 6934; Atlin, 6856, 6858; Edmonton and Klondike, 6182, 6197; Porcupine, 4638, 4640, 4641, 4643; Red Lake, 5289, 5324; Timmins, 4639, 4642; Victoria, 6798. *See also* Staples; Mining
Grain trade: Hamilton, 3832, 3833; Montreal, 2798; Vancouver, 6597. *See also* Agriculture; Rural
Greeks: Canada, 3436; Montreal, 2694; Toronto, 4756, 5170, 5182, 5183; Vancouver, 6518, 6542, 6575. *See also* Ethnicity; Immigration
Greenbelt: Ottawa, 4386, 4387. *See also* Planning; Ecology
Growth, urban: 192, 205, 207, 208, 214, 215, 233, 243, 278, 280, 281, 361, 366, 374, 378, 497, 559, 946, 955, 973, 974, 1051; Canada, 218; Western Canada, 5368, 5378; Prairie Region, 5350, 5383; Alta., 5986; B.C., 6362; Man., 5435; Nfld., 1772; Ont., 3550; Ont., Que., 1940, 1960, 1996, 2019, 3449, 3454, 3506, 5023; Que., 1957, 2047, 2086; Northern Sask., 5765; Waterloo Township, 4054; Barrie, Holland Landing, Newmarket, 5330; Calgary, 6037, 6128; Calgary, Edmonton, 6009; Edmonton, 6251; Edmonton, Calgary, 6126, 6255; Hull, 2208; London, 4134, 4136, 4195; London to Hamilton, 3589; Montreal, 2353, 2421, 2447, 2863, 2886; Quebec City, 2956, 3059, 3118, 3168, 3191; St. Hyacinthe, 3239; Saskatoon, 5898, 5901; Sherbrooke, 3279; Toronto, 4731, 4817, 4822, 4923, 5209; Trois-Rivières, 3325; Vancouver, 6601, 6643, 6646; Winnipeg, 5572, 5577, 5605, 5636, 5717
Guides: Brantford and Brant County, 3646; London, 4121; Montreal, 2243, 2292, 2336, 2368, 2390, 2428; Niagara on the Lake, 4543; Halifax, 1310; Ottawa, 4238, 4262, 4263; Quebec City, 2000, 2022, 2948, 2960, 2969, 3009, 3010; Toronto, 4781, 4790; Winnipeg, 5551; Vancouver, 6503, 6533, 6534. *See also* Indexes; Walking tours

High rises: Montreal, 2888, 2914; Winnipeg, 5666, 5719. *See also* Building; Architecture
High schools. *See* Education
Hospitals: Charlottetown, 1765; Halifax, 1361; Hamilton, 3769; Kingston, 3891, 3982; Montreal, 2243, 2247, 2296, 2343, 2361, 2366, 2479, 2528; Quebec City, 2961, 3022, 3045, 3046, 3047, 3048, 3062, 3075, 3076; Toronto, 4658, 4669, 4673; Vancouver, 6678; Winnipeg, 5534. *See also* Public health
Hotels and inns: Guelph, 3735; London, 4204; Montreal, 2281, 2335, 2467, 2534; Quebec City, 3014; Toronto, 4668. *See also* Entertainment
Households: Nfld., 1778; Quebec City, 3070; Toronto, 5163. *See also* Family; Marriage
Housing: 716, 720, 722, 723, 731, 734, 738, 742, 743, 745, 746, 748, 750, 755, 765, 769, 772, 775, 776, 779, 780
General: Arctic, 6926; N.S., 1203; Ont., 3628, 3555; Que., 1952, 2036, 2072, 2092; Hamilton, 3839, 3869; Kingston, 4026, 4027; London, 4162; Montreal, 2267, 2272, 2306, 2453, 2473, 2578, 2600, 2653, 2672, 2700, 2708, 2713, 2734, 2736, 2738, 2748, 2753, 2757, 2770, 2771, 2848, 2867, 2879, 2894, 2923, 2935; Quebec City, 2984; Saskatoon, 5891; Sudbury, 4609; Toronto, 4746, 4778, 4898, 4900, 5066, 5121, 5231; Vancouver, 6529, 6630; Victoria, 6832; Whitehorse, 7017; Winnipeg, 5544
Specific: building, Que., 2060; Montreal, 2891; Vancouver, 6726; *companies,* Toronto, 4897, 4988; *conditions,* Toronto, 5029; *coops,* 773; Que., 1933; Toronto, 5062; *cost,* 729, 767; Winnipeg, 5091; *design,* Montreal, 2708; Vancouver, 6528; *environment,* Winnipeg, 5670, 5709; *market,* 739, 1049; Toronto, 5028; *mortgages,* 782; *planning,* 730; Vancouver, 6500; *policy,* 718, 747, 749, 756, 757, 787; Ont., 3600; Toronto, 5091; *preference,* Edmonton, 6216; *privacy,* 744; *problems,* 719, 751, 752, 754, 768, 770, 782; Vancouver, 6713; *rehabilitation and reform,* 771, 788, 838, 846; Britain and Canada, 778, 854; Ont., 3410; Toronto, 4995; *rental,* 732; *shortage,* 764; Toronto, 5203; Windsor, 5251, 5252; *social responsibilities,* 721, 724; *social status,* London, 4161; *spatial patterns,* Toronto, 5153; *types,* 696; Hamilton, 3875; *unsanitary,* 753, 759, 762, 766
Hudson's Bay Co.: West, 5362; Prairie towns,

5397; Calgary, 6049; Vancouver, 6623; Winnipeg, 5612, 5613, 5632
Hungarians: Montreal, 2766, 2896. *See also* Ethnicity
Hydro power: B.C., 6614; Man., 5437; N.S., 1189; Ont., 3408, 3457, 3484; Sask., 5796; Fort William, 4620; Hamilton, 3763; Humboldt, 5951; Montreal, 2857; Moose Jaw, 5813; St. Hyacinthe, 3254; St. Thomas, 4560; Toronto, 4647, 4683, 4931, 5159; Victoria, 6828; Winnipeg, 5550. *See also* Energy

Icelanders: Gimli, 5755; Winnipeg, 5639. *See also* Ethnicity; Immigration
Illustrated histories: 689; N.B., 1557; Niagara Peninsula, 4513; North York, 4759; Belleville, 3642; Calgary, 6010; Cobalt, 3666; Fredericton, 1593; Guelph, 3718; London, 4105; Montreal, 2298, 2329, 2337, 2347, 2598, 2621; Niagara, 3456; Ottawa, 4252; Peterborough, 4458; Quebec City, 2967, 2973, 2991, 2995; Regina, 5808; Saskatoon, 5889; Toronto, 4685, 4692, 4694, 4791, 4799, 4809; Vancouver, 6540, 6586, 6660; Vernon, 6754; Victoria, 6770, 6780, 6839; Winnipeg, 5486
Immigration: 404, 423, 426, 427, 428, 432
  General: N.S., 1180, 1182; Calgary, 6132; Edmonton, 6266; Hamilton, 3849; Kingston, 4017; Toronto, 4713, 4714, 4715, 4772, 4863, 4864, 5101; Toronto and Montreal, 5175; Vancouver, 6472; Winnipeg, 5578
  Specific: adjustment, Montreal, 2869; *American,* North, 7046; Prairies, 5563; Que., 2032; *British,* Que., 2087; Hamilton, 3849; Montreal, 2310, 2773; Port Arthur and Fort William, 4624; Toronto, 5013; *groups and group formation,* 411; Toronto, 5188; *housing,* 781; *industry,* Winnipeg, 5571; *integration,* Toronto, 5172; *interaction,* 3217; *public health,* 413, 416; *residential patterns,* Montreal, 2921; *social concern,* 414
  See also Particular ethnic and immigrant groups
Income: Canada, 477, 478; Eastern Arctic, 6972; Maritimes, 1112; Boston, Toronto, 5044; Ottawa, Quebec City, 4362; Windsor, 5255. *See also* Occupations
Incorporation: London, 4170; Montreal, 2548; Winnipeg, 5576. *See also* Municipal government
Indexes: inventory of towns, Que., 2113; Ontario Historical Assn., Ont., 3407;

sources, Prairies, 5386; township plans, Western Canada, 5391; urban and regional studies, Alta., 5995
Indians:
  General: Western Canada, 5360; B.C. 6323, 6384, 6385, 6386; Northeast Ont. town, 5332; Calgary, 6085, 6096; Churchill, 5452; Easterville, 5744; Ft. McMurray, Ft. Chipewyan, Hinton, Slave Lake, Wabasco, 6296; Toronto, 5075, 5171; Toronto, Winnipeg, Edmonton, Vancouver, 5146, 5532, 6163, 6549; Vancouver, 6493, 6506, 6562, 6612, 6730, 6747; Winnipeg, 5523, 5673, 5693, 5708; Whitehorse, 7021
  Specific: demography, 451; integration, 446, 447, 450, 452, 453, 455, 456, 457, 458; literacy, 449; migrants, 450, 458; religious concerns, 448; social services, 454; urban institutions, 445
  See also Ethnicity
Indians (Asian): Saskatoon, 5926; Vancouver, 6750. *See also* Ethnicity; Immigration
Industry: 224, 230, 232, 375, 1000, 1006, 1017
  General: Maritimes, 1099; Western Canada, 5345, 5371; Wheat frontier, 5356; B.C., 6711, 6360; N.B., 1558, 1574; Nfld., 1814; N.S., 1142, 1175; Ont., 3553, 3618, 4226; Que., 1978, 1980, 1992, 2015, 2091, 2125; Sask., 5792; Midwestern Ont., 3594; Southern Ont., 3413, 3414, 3478, 3488, 3505, 3517, 3625, 4729; Niagara Peninsula, 4522, 4546; Waterloo County, 4082; Amherst, 1205; Brandon, 5440; Calgary, 6055, 6097, 6119; Carberry, 5733; Charlottetown, 1764; Chicoutimi, 2156; Cod Cove, 1909; Drummondville, 2173, 2176; Edmonton, 6161, 6219, 6226; Emerson, 5737; Fiber, 1909; Ft. Saskatoon, 6315; Granby, 2183; Guelph, 3729; Halifax, 1256, 1414; Hamilton, 3559, 3798, 3837, 3840; Hull, 2186, 2202, 2203; Joliette, 2217, 2219, 2221; Kitchener-Waterloo, 4091; London, 4215; Merriton, 4539; Montreal, 2241, 2260, 2264, 2409, 2422, 2589, 2623, 2752, 2772, 2776, 2777, 2788, 2794, 2851, 2864, 2887, 2915, 2917, 2929; Montreal, Toronto, 5074; New Glasgow, 1488; Ore Blight, 1909; Ottawa, Hull, 4256; Pictou, 1469; Port Arthur, 4617; Portage la Prairie, 5471; Saskatoon, 5933; St. Hyacinthe, 3232, 3233; St. John, 1671; St. John's 1861; Ste. Marie, 3342; St. Thomas, 4563; Sault Ste. Marie, 4499; Schefferville, 3246; Shawinigan, 3250,

3253, 3256, 3258, 3259; Sorel, 3281, 3289, 3291; Toronto, 3466, 4741, 5073, 5104, 5111, 5130, 5131; Trois-Rivières, 3316, 3318, 3326, 3327; Vancouver, 6553, 6633, 6683, 6734; Victoria, 6816; Welland, 4503; Windsor (N.S.), 1515; Windsor (Ont.), 5248; Winkler, 5738; Winnipeg, 5644
Specific: automotive, Ont., 3428; *clothing*, Southern Ont., 3415; Montreal, 2289, 2726, 2924; Montreal and Toronto, 5217; Winnipeg, 5500, 5522, 5547; St. Croix, 1714; *farm machinery*, Toronto, 4682, 4748; *fishing*, Nfld., 1771, 1775, 1777, 1793, 1814, 1825; N.B., 1730; *furniture*, Southwestern Ont., 3437; *iron and steel*, Hamilton, 3778, 3779, 3787, 3794; N.S., 1486; St. Maurice, 3331; Schefferville, 3248; *leather and shoe*, Kingston, 3899; Montreal, 2234, 2571, 2572; *liquor*, Walkerville, 5261, 5262; *locomotive*, Kingston, 4018, 4024; *metal fabricating*, Southern Ont., 3415; Edmonton, 6143; *publishing*, Que., 2095; Kingston, 3918; *shipping*, Maritimes, 1132; N.B., 1553; Moncton, 1608; *shipbuilding*, N.B., 1553; N.S., 1165; Clifton, 1722; Quebec City, 3097, 3171; St. John, 1681, 1706; St. Martin's, 1715, 1716; Windsor (N.S.), 1516; *textile*, Eastern Townships, 2012; Montreal, 2444; *whaling*, Dartmouth, 1353

Intermunicipal bodies: 949

Irish: Maritimes, 1131; as workers on canals, 3416, 5287; Canada West, 3562; Nfld., 1802; N.S., 1201; Halifax, 1380, 1382, 1387; Hamilton, 3806A; London, 4138, 4150; Montreal, 2498, 2517, 2518, 2519, 2582, 2626; Peterborough, 4451, 4454, 4464, 4465; Quebec, 3107, 3114, 3115, 3142; St. John, 1634; Sudbury, 4608; Toronto, 4668, 4884, 4941, 4956, 4967. *See also* Ethnicity; Religion; Education; Immigration

Iron industry. *See* Industry

Irrigation: Lethbridge, 6270

Italians: Edmonton, 6173, 6174; Fort William, 4629; Guelph, 3710; Hamilton, 3858, 3865, 3884; London, 4111, 4178, 4183; Montreal, 2640, 2665, 2682, 2787, 2895; Quebec City, 3203; Sault Ste. Marie, 4492; Toronto, 4810, 4830, 4927, 4928, 4997, 5040, 5118, 5204, 5220, 5225, 5241; Vancouver, 6699. *See also* Ethnicity; Immigration; Education

Japanese: Toronto, 5154, 5229; Vancouver, 6517, 6668. *See also* Ethnicity

Jews: 410; Calgary, 6021; Fredericton, 1583; Halifax, 1252, 1253; Hamilton, 3760, 3788; Montreal, 2387, 2410, 2426, 2715, 2784, 2816, 2900, 2902, 2903, 2912, 2913; Quebec City, 3156; Regina, 5868; St. John, 1608; Saskatoon, 5899; Toronto, 4727, 4737, 4749, 4767, 4793, 5094, 5096, 5114, 5196; Vancouver, 6523; Victoria, 6801, 6826; Winnipeg, 5508, 5516, 5517, 5544, 5545, 5570, 5641, 5642, 5643. *See also* Ethnicity

Journey to work: Edmonton, 6246, 6247; Kitchener, 4081; Ottawa, 4401; Toronto, 5008

Justice: 1065; Y.T., 6928; Edmonton, 6193; Hamilton, 3795; London, 4108; Montreal, 2466; Pictou, 1474; Quebec City, 3099; Toronto, 5054. *See also* Social problems; Police

Juvenile delinquency: Montreal, 2905; Toronto, 5117; Vancouver, 6656; Whitehorse, 7015. *See also* Social problems

Keefer, T., 3549

Labour: *ethnic divisions*, Montreal, 2796; *mobility*, N.B., 1552, 1709; Southern Ont., 3608; *organization of work*, Que., 2010, 2011; Hamilton, 3838; *politics*, Que., 2093; Hamilton, 3873; Montreal, 2574; Oshawa, 4233; *relations*, 472, 475, 476; Halifax, 1290; Victoria, 6774; *working conditions*, Halifax, 1431; Montreal, 2561, 2563, 2564, 2567, 2576, 2577, 2610, 2634, 2716, 2769. *See also* Occupations

Land: *acquisition*, Saskatoon, 5922; *assignment*, 660; *bank*, 658; Montreal, 2867; Red Deer, 6292; Saskatoon, 5892; *claims*, Que., 2104; Prince Albert, 5818; *dealer*, Toronto, 5158; *development*, 640, 645; Calgary, 6011; Hamilton, 3815; Saskatoon, 5919; Toronto, 5069, 5198; *market*, 649, 650; Waterloo Township, 4057; Vancouver, 6703; Victoria, 6761; *ownership*, Lennox and Addington County, 5298; Peterborough and Victoria County, 4453; Sherbrooke and Sorel, 3277; London, 4211; *planning*, Ont., 3395; *policy*, 653; Home district, Ont., 4869; *politics*, Winnipeg, 5675; *reservation*, Calgary, 2123; *speculation*, Calgary, 6061; *value*, Montreal, 2754. *See also* Land use

Land use: 638, 647; North, 6965; Southern Ont., 3583; Niagara Peninsula, 4527; Calgary, 6015, 6129; Edmonton, 6231, 6232; Kapuskasing, 3889; Kitchener, 4094; Lethbridge, 6276; Lethbridge and Medicine Hat, 6283; London, 4117; Montreal, 2755, 2783; Ottawa, 4360, 4367, 4399; Peterborough, 4492; Pictou, 1475; Prince Albert, 5820; Regina, 5824; Revelstoke, 6893; Richmond, 6743; St. John's, 1864; Sudbury, 4580; Toronto, 3451, 4678, 4686, 5020, 5021, 5022, 5063, 5119; Vancouver, 6611; Vancouver and Seattle, Tacoma, U.S.A., 6679; Victoria, 6785; Victoria, Halifax, Saint John, 6786; Waterloo, 4079; Winnipeg, 5566, 5723. *See also* Land

Landscape architecture: Montreal, 2313, 2590; Ottawa, 4431. *See also* Planning

Latin Quarter: Montreal, 2669

Lebanese: Lac La Biche, 6294, 6295. *See also* Ethnicity

Libraries: N.S., 1168; Calgary, 6005; Hamilton, 3817; Kingston, 3917; Montreal, 2387, 2529, 2606; Quebec City, 2989, 3094; Vancouver, 6636; Victoria, 6811. *See also* Education

Liquor trade: Prairie provinces, 5366; Ont., 3466; Halifax, 1411. *See also* Social problems; Hotels

Little Italy: Fort William, 4629A. *See also* Italians

Local government. *See* Municipal government

Loyalists: N.B., 1555, 1570, 1707; Kingston, 3933; Kingston and Adolphustown, 3980; St. Andrew's, 1620; St. John, 1640, 1657, 1699. *See also* Elites

Lumbering: N.B., 1575, 1718; Nfld., 1814; Blind River, 5311; Burrard Inlet, 6629; Hull, 2198; Montreal, 2557; Ottawa, 4240, 4259, 4278, 4282, 4283, 4317, 4319, 4321, 4339, 4344; Peterborough, 4442; Vancouver, 6524, 6527

Macedonians: Toronto, 4764, 4765, 4766. *See also* Ethnicity

Machine politics: 932; Montreal, 2594. *See also* Politics; Bossism

Manufacturing. *See* Industry

Maps: 95, 112, 113, 117, 182; B.C., 6342; Man., 5436; Ont., 3452; P.E.I., 1748; Que., 1981, 2120; Sask., 5791; Wellington County, 3736; Ottawa, 4287; Montreal, 2331, 2386, 2464, 2594A, 2594B; Quebec City, 3024, 3052, 3092; Vancouver, 6563; Waterloo, 4048; Winnipeg, 5487, 5488, 5563

Markets: Kitchener, 4066, 4080; St. John, 1700

Marriage: 381, 389, 391, 400; Halifax, 1409; St. John, 1705. *See also* Family; Children

Mass transit: 282, 293, 295, 298, 299, 300, 307, 312; Calgary, 6005; Montreal, 2823; Toronto, 4804, 4805, 4916, 4918, 5060, 5123, 5168, 5181, 5223; Winnipeg, 5711. *See also* Transportation

Mayors: Drapeau (Montreal), 2723, 2875, 2930; Houde (Montreal), 2588, 2781, 2859, 2860, 2892; Crombie (Toronto), 5037; Howland (Toronto), 4965; Mackenzie (Toronto), 4881; Phillips (Toronto), 5178; Logan (Winnipeg), 5573; Farmer (Winnipeg), 5622; Queen (Winnipeg), 5682; Webb (Winnipeg), 5716

Mechanics Institutes: Goderich, 3704; London, 4163; Napanee, 5301; St. John, 1633. *See also* Libraries

Medicine: Ont., 3571; Western Ont., 3593; Calgary, 6005; Edmonton, 6194; Montreal, 2297, 2692, 2737; St. John, 1654; Toronto, 4645, 4651; Vancouver, 6620, 6621. *See also* Public health; Hospitals

Mental health: Ont., 3514; Joliette, 2224; London, 4137; Peterborough, 4437; Toronto, 4649, 4769. *See also* Social problems; Medicine

Merchants: 237, 239, 244, 250; Maritimes, 1136; Nfld., 1821, 1826; N.S., 1174, 1184; N.S. and British West Indies, 1184; Labrador, 1826; Fredericton, Marysville, Woodstock, Moncton, and Yarmouth 1136; Halifax, 1234, 1311, 1358, 1388, 1389; London, 4135; Louisbourg, 1455, 1456; Montreal, 2513, 2514, 2515, 2516, 2540, 2446; Quebec City, 3066, 3122; St. John, 1623, 1631, 1671; St. John's, 1887; Strait of Belle Isle, 1914; Sudbury, 4583; Toronto, 4660, 4855, 4937; Vancouver, 6653; Yarmouth, 1521. *See also* Commerce; Entrepreneurs; Trade

Methodology: 101, 123, 127, 131, 133, 136, 137, 139, 143, 145, 147, 153, 164, 165, 168, 187, 188; census, 103; comparative study, 155, 157; economic, 158, 160; exhibitions, 100; films, 96; geography, 102, 111, 134, 140, 144, 152, 154, 166, 167, 185; local history, 104, 105, 118, 120, 121, 122, 125, 132, 135, 149, 162, 184; oral history, 168; political science, 146; planning, 161; quantification, 130, 164A, 173; sociology, 148, 156; spatial analysis, 163; teaching, studying, 116, 129, 138, 181; urban studies, B.C., 6352; Que., 2038, 2050, 2051; Brampton, 5325;

Hamilton, 3819, 3821, 3822, 3823; Sydney, 1475; Toronto, 4648
Métis: Man., 5756; St. Paul, 6301; Winnipeg, 5561. *See also* Indians; Ethnicity
Metropolitan areas: 195, 197, 202, 355; Que., 1946, 2063, 2084; Calgary, 6098; Calgary and Edmonton, 6094, 6208; Edmonton, 6258; Halifax, 1423, 1424; Montreal, 2845, 2908; Ottawa, Hull, 4391; Quebec City, 3161; Toronto, 4933, 5055, 5079, 5085, 5106, 5162, 5205; Vancouver, 6521; Winnipeg, 5492, 5654, 5672, 5689, 5702, 5704. *See also* Metropolitanism
Metropolitan government: 860, 876, 884, 936, 971, 973, 974, 1079; B.C., 6691; Montreal, 2918, 2919; Toronto, 5014, 5033, 5050, 5095; Vancouver, 6740, 6741. *See also* Metropolitan areas; Municipal government
Metropolitanism: 209, 255, 256, 257, 258, 260, 267; Maritimes, 1114; B.C., 6380; Man., 5415; Que., 1944; Chicoutimi, 2164; Cobourg and Port Hope, 3680; Kingston, 3996; Montreal, 2944; Toronto, 4840; New Westminster, 6440. *See also* Metropolitan areas
Migration: 261, 407, 412, 422, 436, 437, 439, 440, 441, 443, 444, 479; Maritimes, 1108, 1109; N.S., 1179,; Que., 2021, 2031, 2056, 2144, 2145; Ont., 3453; Cape Breton, 1502; Canso, 1546; Edmonton, 6238, 6240; Montreal, 2768; Toronto, 5115. *See also* Immigration; Demography
Military: Que., 3056, 3079, 3108, 3123; Upper Canada, 3476, 3533, 3568; Calgary, 6005; Esquimalt, 6399, 6400, 6404; Gagetown and Oromocto, 1729; Halifax, 1277, 1349, 1354, 1359, 1386; Kingston, 3956, 3958, 3967, 3976, 4008; London, 4158, 4164; Montreal, 2549, 2550, 2551; Niagara, 4511; Quebec City, 3013, 3056, 3067, 3079; Toronto, 4674, 4872; Trois-Rivières, 3338, 3339; Vancouver, 6567. *See also* Fortifications
Mining: Nfld.; 1814; Churchill Falls, 1913; Flin Flon, 5740, 5751; Merritt, 6899; Noranda, 3219. *See also* Staples
Mining Towns: 322, 323, 325; Canadian Rockies, 5975; North, 6978; B.C., 6325; Y.T., 6953; N.S., 1203; Que., Labrador, 2014, 3366; Eastern Townships, 3386; Northern Ont., 3566; Chibougamau, 3361; Cobalt, 3665, 3671; Duparquet, 3355; Nelson, 6801. *See also* Staples
Mobile homes: Calgary, 6117, 6119; Edmonton, 6227. *See also* Housing
Mobility, urban: Calgary, 6121; Montreal, 2709; Toronto, 5077; Winnipeg, 5505, 5665
Model towns: Pine Falls, 5748; Toronto, 5102; Woodstock, 5321. *See also* New towns
Mortality: Montreal, 2782, 2790, 2791. *See also* Demography
Municipal administration: Northern Canada, 6966, 6973, 6977; N.B., 1568; Que., 1999, 2075, 2128; Calgary, 6111; Halifax, 1284; Montreal, 2367, 2624, 2650, 2676, 2880, 2890, 2927; Quebec City, 3194
Municipal amalgamation and annexation: 878; Que., 1967; Edmonton and Calgary, 6009; Montreal, 2871
Municipal boundaries: Sask., 5770; Quebec City, 3090
Municipal Corporations Act: 931; Ont., 3396
Municipal councils: Ont., 3442, 3498; Bytown, 4328; Calgary, 6057; Edmonton, 6144, 6151; Regina, 5858; St. John, 1698; Winnipeg, 5698, 5699
Municipal finance: 993, 994, 995, 996, 999, 1001, 1002, 1003, 1004, 1005, 1010, 1012, 1013, 1014, 1015, 1016, 1018, 1019, 1021, 1022, 1023, 1025, 1027, 1028, 1029, 1032, 1033, 1034, 1037, 1039, 1040, 1045, 1047, 1048, 1053, 1055, 1056; Western municipalities, 5346; Maritimes, 1139; Alta., 5968; N.B., 1564, 1565, 1566, 1571, 1800; Nfld., 1564, 1800, 1815; N.S., 1152, 1155, 1739; Ont., 3490, 3491, 3518; P.E.I., 1739; Que., 1953, 1959, 2025, 2066; Brandon, 5446; Edmonton, 6170; London, 4180; Montreal, 2730, 2817, 2821, 2850, 2853, 2861, 2926; Moose Jaw, 5813; Ottawa, 4419; Quebec City, 2998; Saskatoon, 5896; Toronto, 4910, 5041, 5139, 5219; Vancouver, 6475, 6506, 6543, 6654; Victoria, 6835; Winnipeg, 5668, 5685
Municipal government: 857, 858, 859, 862, 863, 864, 865, 866, 868, 869, 871, 872, 873, 875, 879, 881, 882, 883, 885, 886, 887, 889, 890, 891, 892, 893, 895, 896, 916, 918, 933, 934, 935, 937, 938, 941, 947, 948, 950, 952, 953, 954, 956, 957, 958, 959, 960, 961, 968, 969, 970, 981, 982, 983, 986, 988, 991; Maritimes, 1134; N.W.T., 5394; Alta., 5967, 5969, 5970, 5984A; B.C., 6361, 6392, 6688, 6689; Man., 5425, 5439; N.B., 1573; Nfld., 1776, 1779, 1798, 1807, 1816; N.S., 1141, 1156, 1157, 1195; Ont., 3441, 3446, 3458, 3464, 3480, 3492, 3511, 3524, 3563, 3587, 3597, 3598; Southern Ont., 3633; P.E.I., 1745; Que., 1962, 2017; Sask., 5794; Northwestern Ont.,

Subject Index   389

5411, 5412; County of Kent, 5335; Northumberland County, 1728; Cornerbrook, 1832; Dawson, 6988; Edmonton, 6145; Grimsby, 3789; Halifax, 1393, 1394; Kamloops, 6418; Kingston, 3977, 3979, 4014; Montreal, 2370, 2417, 2654, 2717, 2758, 2809, 2880; Ottawa, 4336, 4396, 4409, 4413, 4414, 4429; Quebec City, 3044, 3120; Regina, 5865; St. John, 1661, 1676; Toronto, 4925, 5004, 5195, 5221; Windsor, 5243; Winnipeg, 5564, 5640, 5645; Vancouver, 6578. *See also* City manager; Commission government

Municipal government and federal relations: 934, 939, 940, 942, 943, 944, 977, 1011, 1035, 1043; North, 6926; Edmonton, 6137; Montreal, 2831

Municipal government and provincial relations: 997, 1002, 1011, 1024, 1026, 1030, 1031, 1036, 1046, 1054, 1058, 1113; Alta., 5985, 5995; B.C., 6348, 6353; Man., 5414; N.B., 1562, 1568; N.S., 1143, 1162, 1187, 1188, 1193; Ont., 3463, 3467, 3495, 3531, 3554, 3559, 3586; P.E.I., 1746; Que., 1923, 1968, 2832

Municipal government reform: Western Canada, 5344; Manitoba, 5417; Sask., 5782; Upper Canada, 3465; Montreal, 2885; Nanaimo, 6436; Winnipeg, 5657

Municipal institutions: 880; Man., 5428; Ont., 3411, 3527; Que., 2127

Municipal organization: N.S., 1549; Nfld., 1815; Ont., 3530, 3573; Que., 1987, 2024, 2116; Cape Breton, 1487; Burnaby, 6686; Edmonton, 6147; Lévis, 3184; Montreal, 2351; St. Boniface, 5477; Winnipeg, 5686

Museums: Dawson City, 7004; Montreal, 2268, 2319, 2865; Vancouver, 6674; Yellowknife, 7038. *See also* Art

Music: N.S., 1148; Calgary, 6066; Halifax, 1288; Kingston, 3969; Montreal, 2648; Toronto, 4960; Vancouver, 6564; Windsor, 5257. *See also* Entertainment

Nativism. *See* Churches and religion; Immigration

Neighbourhoods; Calgary, 6099, 6130; Edmonton, 6162; Guelph, 3758; London, 4181; Montreal, 2597; Ottawa, 4394; St. John's, 1891; Toronto, 5034, 5110, 5143, 5199

New towns: Canada, 6975; North, 6980; Alta., 5981; B.C., 6328, 6330, 6831; Ont., 3532, 3565, 3596,; N.S., 1145; Que., 3301; Ajax, 5284; Atikokan, 5086; Elliot Lake, 3694, 3697; Fermont, Grand Rapids, 3354; Inuvik, 7050; Kipawa, 3300; Lanigan, 5945; Mackenzie, Leaf Rapids, 5745, 6883; Montreal, 2800, 2876; Ojibway, 5280; Powell River, 6880, 6890. *See also* Single enterprise towns

Nickel mining: Sudbury, 4566, 4569, 4570, 4575, 4576, 4591, 4597, 4600, 4610, 4612. *See also* Staples

Occupations: 464, 466, 468, 470, 473, 480
  General: Que., 1974, 2006, 3404; Cape Breton, 1490, 1491, 1498, 1499; Fort William, Port Arthur, 4626; London, 4129, 4149, 4190; Montreal, 2357, 2358; Ottawa, 4337; Quebec City, 3101, 3117, 3202; St. Jerome, 3227; St. John, 1680; Toronto, 4913, 4926, 4973, 4982, 5083; Vancouver, 6598, 6676; Winnipeg, 5623
  Specific: apprentices, Montreal, 2486; *carters,* Montreal, 2601; *craftsmen,* Ont., 3627; Quebec City, 3199; *dock workers,* Vancouver, 6615; *garment workers,* Winnipeg, 5656; *masons,* Montreal, 2468; *mechanics,* Kingston, 3997; *miners,* Cape Breton, 1498; *printers,* Toronto, 4981; *railway workers,* Sherbrooke, 3272; *sailors,* Maritimes, 1118; *servants,* Montreal, 2483; *shoe makers,* Montreal, 2571, 2572; *skilled,* Que., 2059; *tailors,* Toronto, 5185; *white collar,* Toronto, 4914
  Topics: class, 461, 462, 463, 464, 465, 466, 469; Ont., 3502; *ethnicity,* Montreal, 2893; London, 4140; *residence,* Hamilton, 3860; Kingston, 3962; London, 4193; Toronto, 5116
  See also Labour

Office functions and patterns: Calgary, 6125; Ottawa, 4380

Oil: Alta., 5971; B.C., 6387; Calgary, 6103, 6113, 6134, 6136; London, 4131; Montreal, 2855. *See also* Energy

Open space: Capital Region, 4427; Montreal, 2265, 2764, 2792; Regina, 5836; Toronto, 5113. *See also* Planning; Parks and playgrounds

Orphans and widows: Halifax, 1360; Kingston, 3896; Quebec City, 3115. *See also* Children; Social problems; Women

Outports: Nfld., 1782, 1812, 1825

Pakistani: Saskatoon, 5926. *See also* Ethnicity

Panama Canal: Western Canada, 5343; Vancouver, 6622

Parks and playgrounds: 790, 793, 826, 1060, 1085; Calgary, 6005, 6029; Hull, 2215; Montreal, 2437, 2632; Ottawa, 4417,

4418; Regina, 5855; Toronto, 4943; Vancouver, 6481, 6556, 6559, 6745; Winnipeg, 5498, 5501, 5567, 5568, 5569, 5652, 5730
Parliament buildings: Regina, 5879; Toronto, 4646A
Parasite towns: 251; Nfld., 1828
Perkins, Simon: Liverpool, 1531
Place names: Alta., 5974; B.C., 6322; N.S., 1158; Ont., 3401, 3541; Y.T., 6935
Planning: 29, 481, 482, 483, 486, 487, 491, 495, 496, 498, 502, 504, 505, 506, 507, 509, 510, 511, 512, 515, 516, 517, 520, 529, 533, 536, 538, 542, 544, 549, 552, 555, 557, 567, 572, 577, 583, 585, 591, 592, 597, 602, 604, 607, 609, 611, 613, 618, 625, 1086
  General: Arctic, 6958; Maritimes, 1117; North, 6970; West, 5387A; Alta., 5965, 5984A, 5989, 5990, 5991, 5993, 5994A, 5995; B.C., 6339, 6371, 6378, 6394; N.S., 1176, 1178, 1183; Nfld., 1772, 1791, 1835; Ont., 3394, 3425, 3426, 3445, 3574, 3619; Western Ont., 3503; Que., 1917, 1938, 1982A, 2016, 2085, 2108; Sask.; 5773, 5778, 5786, 5798, 5799; Upper Canada, 3609; Niagara District, 4501; Calgary, 6127; Chicoutimi, 2154; Cobalt, 3663; Edmonton, 6145, 6164, 6217, 6221, 6261; Elliot Lake, 3669, 3698, 3700; Fredericton, 1584; Granby, 2181; Guelph, 3722; Halifax, 1391, 1407, 1418, 1432; Hamilton, 3864; London, 4115; Kapuskasing, 3887; Kipawa, 3295; Kitchener, 4042, 4063, 4087; Kitchener-Waterloo, 4041, 4044, 4085; Kitimat, 6421; Mackenzie, Leaf Rapids, 6883; Montreal, 2620, 2677, 2703, 2704, 2720, 2743, 2745, 2746, 2747, 2751, 2835, 2878, 2882, 2940; Noranda, 3220; Oromocto, 1712; Oshawa, 4232; Ottawa, 4241, 4375, 4376, 4378, 4404, 4405, 4416, 4430; Ottawa South, 4372; Ottawa-Carleton, 4432; Ottawa, Hull, 4306, 4330, 4350, 4410; Ottawa-National Capital, 4364, 4369, 4371, 4384, 4385, 4403; Quebec City, 3040, 3201; Regina, Hamilton, Windsor, Peterborough, Stratford, Kenora, Terrace Bay, Etobicoke, 549; Regina, 5826, 5832, 5885; Saguenay, 2166; St. John, 1636, 1665; Sainte-Marie de Beauce, 3385; Sudbury, 4602, 4603; Thetford Mines, 3306; Toronto, 4945, 4950, 5007, 5030, 5049, 5052, 5056, 5082, 5103, 5144, 5177, 5179, 5180; Trois-Rivières, 3311; Vancouver, 6501, 6539, 6565, 6576, 6593, 6618, 6681, 6684, 6690, 6725, 6732, 6746, 6752; Victoria, 6809, 6846; Waterloo, 4086; Windsor, Sarnia, London, Waterloo-South Wellington, 3429, 4199; Winnipeg, 5489, 5574, 5664, 5701
  Topics: boards, 569; central area, 794; citizen participation, 573; civic improvement, 590, 605; conservation, 503, 603, 617; design, 510; ecological interpretation, 622; environment, 563; federalism, 596, 599; finance, 614, 1052; growth, 559, 567; hexagonal, 527, 528; housing, 485, 490, 575, 576, 594, 595, 631, 714, 715, 758, 760, 761, 763, 783, 784; industrial districts, 815, 817, 818; industrial growth, 492, 550, 612; land development, 635, 651, 656, 657, 659; and the law, 598; local area, 500, 553; metro government, 606; municipal engineer, 540, 548, 629; municipal government, 490, 535, 581, 1072, 1073, 1083, 1094; models, 556, 610, 614, 619, 621, 623; plan makers, 624; politics, 587, 921; provincial authority, 531, 584, 593, 634; public health, 485, 528, 547, 551, 554, 1074; public services, 1064; regional, 268, 508, 524, 526, 541, 560, 561, 564, 578, 589, 599; roads, 484; social life, 489; spatial, 608; suburbia, 518; for sunlight, 700; welfare, 543; zoning, 494, 522, 523, 530, 547, 566, 570, 579, 580, 616, 632
Police: West, 5385; Nfld., 1784; Calgary, 6005; Halifax, 1304; Lethbridge, 6299; Montreal, 2340, 2360; Regina, 5839, 5840; Toronto, 4917; Vancouver, 6657, 6677; Winnipeg, 5520
Polish: Montreal, 2302, 2718, 2803. *See also* Ethnicity
Political corruption: 906
Politics: 29, 899, 900, 903, 904, 905, 907, 909, 910, 911, 913, 916, 918, 919, 920, 921, 922, 923, 924, 925, 927
  General: Alta., 5966, 5984; B.C., 6365, 6368; N.B., 1551, 1567; Nfld., 1771, 1776; Ont., 3569; P.E.I., 1747; Que., 1986, 2064; Brandon, 5443; Calgary, 6100, 6118; Edmonton, 6188, 6212, 6245; Elliot Lake, 3695; Glace Bay, 1547; Halifax, 1430; Harbour Breton, 1904; Harbour Grace, 1911; Hamilton, 3806, 3830, 3856, 3871; Hamilton-Wentworth, 3857; Kitchener-Waterloo, 4078; Lakehead, 4632A; London, 4179, 4188, 4208; Montreal, 2536, 2656, 2666, 2676, 2687, 2688, 2731, 2763, 2829, 2842; Ottawa, 4310, 4338; Ottawa-Carleton, 4415; Peterborough, 4450; Port Arthur, 4632; Prince

Albert, 5816; Quebec, 3060, 3120, 3155, 3166; Regina, 5886; St. John, 1660, 1690, 1704; Sarnia, 4474; Saskatoon, 5895; St. Hyacinthe, 3243; Sherbrooke, 3276; Sudbury, 4585, 4604; Toronto, 4843, 5042, 5043, 5088, 5092, 5122, 5124, 5125, 5126, 5127, 5128, 5144A; Trois-Rivières, 3307; Winnipeg, 5557, 5565, 5622, 5648, 5651, 5700, 5716; Vancouver, 6682, 6693, 6694, 6706, 6709, 6716, 6717, 6748; Waterloo, 3655
Specific: communism, Toronto, 5200; Vancouver, 6714; Winnipeg, 5590, 5683, 5684; *minorities*, 914; *non-partisan*, 897, 898, 904; *radical*, Winnipeg, 5580, 5610, 5621, 5641, 5642, 5643; *socialism*, Canada, 4931A; Toronto, 5200; Vancouver, 6727, 6728; Winnipeg, 5681, 5682
Population size and characteristics: Canada, 2121; Prairies, 5388, 5410; Alta., 5558; B.C., 6390; Man., 5438; Man., Sask., 5426; N.W.T., Y.T., 6937; Ont., 3424, 3616; Ont., Que., 1922, 3405; Que., 2013; Nfld., 1769, 1822, 1823; Sask., 5763, 5774; Northern Sask., 5775, 5978; Southern Ont., 3439; Calgary, 6115; Dewdney, 6866; Edmonton, 6223; London, 4205; Montreal, 2670, 2805, 2928; Peterborough, 4461; Quebec City, 2026, 3103, 3172, 3182, 3195; Regina, 5871; Rimouski, 3207; Saguenay, 2150; Saskatoon, 5909; Sherbrooke, 3267; Sudbury, 4601; Toronto, 4653, 4745, 5015, 5068, 5108, 5140, 5173, 5233; Vancouver, 6497, 6550, 6742; Victoria, 6789; Winnipeg, 5513, 5724; Yellowknife, 7040
Ports: Western Canada, 6358; B.C., 6333; P.E.I., 1740; Que., 1950; Great Lakes, 3601; Lake Erie, 3561; Chicoutimi, 2163; Churchill, 5451, 5454, 5455; Port Coquitlam, 6836; Halifax, 1257, 1413; Kingston, 3949, 3950, 3971; Montreal, 2230, 2256, 2257, 2258, 2259, 2260, 2261, 2262, 2314, 2419, 2433, 2562, 2569, 2579, 2580, 2615, 2629, 2647, 2691, 2706, 2707, 2762, 2807, 2870; Port Arthur, 4634; Port Credit, 5293; Prince Rupert, 6462; Oakville, 5318; Quebec City, 2971, 2997, 3159; Rimouski, 3212; St. John, 1626, 1648, 1658, 1659, 1662, 1677, 1683, 1687, 1697; St. John's, 1853, 1859, 1888; Sept-Isles, 3379; Sorel, 3284; Toronto, 4777, 4803, 4845, 5129, 5184; Trois-Rivières, 3308, 3315, 3323; Valleyfield, 3371; Vancouver, 6483, 6492, 6495, 6513, 6545, 6555, 6558, 6596, 6597, 6615, 6640; Vancouver and Victoria, 6581, 6827; Victoria, 6838; Yarmouth, 1500, 1503. *See also* Transportation

Portuguese: Montreal, 2750; Toronto, 5010. *See also* Ethnicity

Post offices: N.S., 1192; Calgary, 6005; Halifax, 1247

Poverty: 471, 474, 1066, 1096; N.B., 1560; Ont., 3548; Cobourg, 3679; Halifax, 1363; Kingston, 3995; Montreal, 2398, 2456, 2512, 2522, 2561, 2576, 2577, 2599, 2723, 2769; St. John, 1702; Toronto, 4953, 4957, 4971; Windsor, 5270

Preservation, architecture: 664, 666, 669, 671, 674, 675, 678, 686, 692, 703, 711; Ont., 3585, 3606; Cape Breton, 1508; Annapolis Royal, 1212; Calgary, 6006, 6007; Cobourg, 3689; Halifax, 1232, 1237, 1241, 1242, 1244, 1249, 1271, 1275, 1281, 1299, 1305, 1306, 1307, 1310, 1315, 1335; Montreal, 2240, 2301, 2346, 2607, 2711, 2719, 2847; Quebec City, 2112; Saskatoon, 5894; Vancouver, 6473; Victoria, 6836, 6837; Yarmouth, 1527. *See also* Architecture; Buildings; Planning

Press: N.S., 1196; Que., 1924, 1925; Calgary, 6042; Dawson City, 6990; Edmonton, 6047, 6186; Halifax, 1292; Hamilton, 3816; Kingston, 3948, 3983; Lethbridge, 6270; London, 4126, 4166, 4168; Montreal, 2256, 2510, 2523, 2532, 2533, 2552; Ottawa, 4281, 4293, 4322; Regina, 5848, 5883; Toronto, 4851, 4856, 4902, 4904, 4926, 4952, 4954, 4956, 4974, 4991, 4998, 5100; Trois-Rivières, 3314; Vancouver, 6554; Winnipeg, 5594, 5596, 5611, 5720

Prisons: Kingston, 3906, 3907, 3960, 3997; Montreal, 2252, 2524. *See also* Police; Justice

Professionals: Montreal, 2491, 2797, 2881

Prostitution: Prairie provinces, 5365; Halifax, 1417; Montreal, 2838; Toronto, 4984; Vancouver, 6570; Winnipeg, 5591

Public health: 1059, 1968; Arctic, 6936; Ont., 3556; Upper Canada, 3422; Upper and Lower Canada, 2042, 3523; Calgary, 6076; Edmonton, 6241; Kingston, 3975; London, 4174; Montreal, 2592, 2652; Toronto, 4821, 4895, 4896, 4966A, 4978; Vancouver, 6619

Public housing: Halifax, 1432; Hull, 2185; Toronto, 5011; Vancouver, 6737. *See also* Housing

Public and private space: 831, 835

Public utilities: 1069; N.S., 1185; Cochrane,

5339; Edmonton, 6237; Rivière du Loup, 3343; Toronto, 4807; Victoria, 6818
Pulp and paper towns: 340; B.C., 6351; N.B., 1731; Badger, 1916; Baie Comeau, 3388; Espanola, 5305; Forrestville, 3373; Grand Falls, 1901, 1915, 1916; Kapuskasing, 3886; Mackenzie, 6910; Temiskaming, 3295-3301; Trois-Rivières, 3310. *See also* Single industry towns; Resource towns

Railways: 304, 850; North, 6918; Western Canada, 5369; B.C., 6346, 6432; N.B., 1552; N.S., 1150; Ont., 3603; Southern Ont., 3613; Que., 1944, 2658; Sask., 5766, 5767; Niagara Peninsula, 4521; Calgary, 6014; Calgary and Edmonton, 6047, 6186; Edmonton, 6159, 6207, 6249; Esquimalt, 6402; Hamilton, 3791, 3851; London, 4107, 4198; Minnedosa, 5465; Montreal, 2375, 2657, 2744; Ottawa, 4237; Peterborough and Cobourg, 3688; Prince Rupert, 6464; Regina, 5830; St. John, 1625, 1696; Saskatoon, 5906; Sault Ste. Marie, 4491; St. Thomas, 4563; Sudbury, 4587, 4592; Trois-Rivières, 3308; Vancouver, 6499, 6582, 6647, 6661; Victoria and Sidney, 6796; Winnipeg, 5582, 5607. *See also* Transportation
Ranching: Alta., 5957; Calgary, 6056, 6089, 6092; Swift Current, 5937. *See also* Rural
Real estate: N.S., 1142; Que., 3211A; Calgary, 6077; Montreal, 2728; Prince Rupert, 6458; Regina, 5854; Saskatoon, 5923; Toronto, 5017; Vancouver, 6651; Victoria, 6779. *See also* Land use
Recreation: 1047; London, 4201, 4207; Toronto, 5169; Winnipeg, 5499, 5507, 5667, 5669. *See also* Sport
Recreational area: 600; Ont., 3637; Southern Ont., 3626; Niagara, 4518; Ottawa, 4257; Quebec City, 3193; Toronto, 5009; Vancouver, 6477
Redevelopment: Nfld., 1825; Calgary, 6120; Charlottetown, 1767; Halifax, 1426; Montreal, 2825; Ottawa, 4273; Vancouver, 6708; Winnipeg, 5662, 5715, 5722. *See also* Development
Reform, urban: 962, 978, 987; Alta., 5980, 5983; N.B., 1550, 1556; Montreal, 2593, 2594, 2631, 2673; Ottawa, 4345; St. John's, 1838, 1870; Toronto, 4946, 5001, 5086; Vancouver, 6480, 6702; Winnipeg, 5677, 5679, 5725. *See also* Politics
Renewal, urban: 833, 834, 836, 837, 838, 839, 840, 841, 842, 843, 845, 847, 848, 851, 852, 853, 856, 895; Que., 2115; Dawson City, 6998; Drummondville, 2178; Hull, 2199, 2201; Montreal, 2711, 2719, 2732, 2799; Ottawa, 4400; Port Arthur, 4617A; Quebec City, 2954, 2965, 2968, 3004, 3083; St. John, 1674; Sault Ste. Marie, 4488; Toronto, 5076, 5132; Trail, 6889; Winnipeg, 5652, 5661. *See also* Redevelopment
Residential: *characteristics*, Edmonton, 6230; *density*, 786; *development*, Edmonton, 6239; Montreal, 2814; Ottawa, 4377; Pointe Claire, 2841; *filtering*, 5152; *growth*, Calgary, 6131; London, 4194; Montreal, 2695, 2696; *land conversion*, Winnipeg, 5653; *land use*, Edmonton, 6162; Maple Ridge, 6881; *location*, Kamloops, 6419; Kingston, 4028; *mobility*, Edmonton, 6233; Kingston, 3929, 3990; Montreal, 2774; Toronto, 4903, 5208; *neighbourhood*, Victoria, 6791; *path analysis*, London, 4185; *patterns*, 5012; Windsor, 5429; *planning*, 731; Calgary, 6109; Edmonton, 6229; *rehabilitation*, Montreal, 2909; *relocation*, Winnipeg, 5730; *segregation*, Red Deer, 6290; Vancouver, 6494; *structure*, 789, 814; St. John, 1670
Resource towns: Alta., 5986A; B.C., 6329, 6332; Fort McMurray, 6305; Gold River, 6878, 6900; Nanaimo, 6426; Vanderhoof and Mackenzie, 6888
Topics: development, 316, 317; housing, 343; immigrants, 325; internal structure, 327, 333; planning, 325, 329, 331, 336, 337, 342, 348; social activity, 324, 325, 326, 335, 337, 339, 343
See also New towns; Mining towns; Single-enterprise towns; Nickel Mining
Retailing: Calgary, 6020, 6102; Hamilton, 3880; Kitchener, 4090; Montreal, 2603, 2683; Sherbrooke, 3278; Toronto, 5207. *See also* Commerce; Trade
Riots: 4941; Halifax, 1390; Montreal, 2507; Ottawa, 4320; Regina, 5876; Toronto, 4922, 4941; Vancouver, 6667, 6669, 6670, 6676, 6687; Victoria, 6844
Rivalry: Quebec City and Montreal, 2537, 3116; Port Arthur and Fort William, 4614. *See also* Boosterism
Roads and highways: Hull, 2210; London, 4200; Que., 1941; Regina, 5838; Toronto, 4852
Rural: *development*, P.E.I., 1743; *economy, wheat belt*, 5376; *farm land loss*, 488, 537; *fringe*, 568, 630; London, 4184; London, Kitchener, Waterloo, Sarnia, 4083; Niagara, 4526; Thunder Bay, 4636; *land use*, Niagara escarpment, 3444; Edmonton, 6232; Montreal, 2815; *population change*,

350, 405, 406, 415, 417, 435; Maritimes, 1116; Alta., 5953; Ont., 3620; Southern Ont., 3509, 3629; Que., 2008, 2018; Brandon and Winnipeg, 5447; Wellington County, 3725; *roads,* Upper Canada, 3528; *society,* 244; Maritimes, 1115; Nfld., 1774; *urban relationships,* 274; Sask., 5762; Beauport, 3181; Kingston, 4020; Montreal, 2826
Russians: Vancouver, 6599, 6600. *See also* Ethnicity

Scots: Nfld., 1780; Cape Breton, 1497; Wellington County, 3730. *See also* Ethnicity
Seaway: Great Lake Ports, 3409; Cornwall area, 3520, 5340, 5341; Montreal, 2858, 2922. *See also* Ports; Transportation
Segregation. *See* Ethnicity
Seigneury: Montreal, 2235, 2323, 2445, 2476, 2478; Sorel, 3288
Separate schools. *See* Education
Settlement patterns: Arctic, 6917, 6963; North, 6924, 6942, 6967, 6976; Western Canada, 5392; Maritimes, 1107, 1128, 1129; B.C., 6355, 6367; Man., 5419; N.B., 1555, 1559; Nfld., 1777, 1778, 1793, 1801, 1805, 1825; N.W.T., 6943; N.S., 1161; Eastern Ont., 3577; Southern Ont., 3501, 3513; Southwestern Ont., 3507; Que., 1998; Sask., 5772; Y.T., 6938, 6939; Upper Canada, 3403, 3636, 3438; Lincoln County, Ont., 5300; Waterloo County, 4062; Niagara Township, 4504; Lower Fraser Valley, 6363; Vancouver Island, 6476; Buckingham, 3392; Burrard Inlet, 6639; Elizabethtown, 5313; Guelph, 3713; Hay River, 7054; Heberville, 3390; Kootenay, 6916; London District, 4139; Lloydminster, 5805, 5806, 5807; Montreal, 2443, 2462; Moose Jaw, 5808; Peterborough and County, 4441, 4444, 4446; Pictou, 1475; Portage la Prairie, 5472; Quebec City, 3085; Victoria, 6848; Walhachin, 6897, 6898
Service centres: 269; Man., 5431; Brandon, 5449; Calgary, 6108; Regina, 5850; Saskatoon, 5900. *See also* Commerce; Trade; Trading centres
Sewage: 1082, 1087; Toronto, 4987, 5235, 5238. *See also* Public health
Shipping: N.B., 1553; Nfld., 1783; P.E.I., 1741; Que., 2503; Burrard Inlet, 6638. *See also* Water transportation; Ports
Shopping centres: 709, 816; Prairie provinces, 5377; Ont., 3521, 3575; Calgary, 6114, 6133; Edmonton, 6215; Hull, 4395; London, 4177; Montreal, 2849; Ottawa, 4395; Winnipeg, 5690, 5712
Sikhs: Vancouver, 6487. *See also* Ethnicity
Simcoe, John Graves: 3522, 3533, 3599
Single enterprise towns: 313, 344; North Eastern Ont., 3469; Elliot Lake, 3691; Flin Flon, 5732; Marysville, 1724; Pinawa, 5735; Wawa and Algoma, 5342. *See also* New towns; Mining towns; Nickel mining; Resource towns
Single tax: Western Canada, 5405; Alta., 5987; Vancouver, 6637, 6671. *See also* Municipal finance
Skid row: Winnipeg, 5707
Slavs: Montreal, 2846. *See also* Ethnicity
Slovacks: Canada, 3436; Montreal, 2698. *See also* Ethnicity
Slums: 774, 833; Montreal, 2894; Toronto, 5036, 5155, 5191, 5192. *See also* Housing
Social area: Montreal, 2779
Social bonds: Sudbury, 4567
Social change: N.B., 1552, 1709; Nfld., 1806, 1814; Lindsay, 5281; Toronto, 4967
Social characteristics: 383, 384, 386, 392, 394, 397; Calgary, 6105; Montreal, 2804; Toronto, 4867
Social class and structure: 685, 908, 1079; Maritimes, 1135; B.C., 6329; Lower Canada, 2070; N.S., 1377; Que., 1971, 2033, 2039, 2071, 2101; Cape Breton, 1490, 1491; Calgary, 6117; Edmonton, 6225; Fleetwood, 6868; Halifax, 1430; Hamilton, 3811, 3800; Louisbourg, 1457; Montreal, 2492, 2525, 2575, 2627, 2793, 2796, 2830, 2891; Ottawa and Hull, 4392; Regina, 5851, 5866; St. Jerome, 3229; St. John, 1682; Schefferville, 3245, 3247; Toronto, 4949, 5024; Vancouver, 6701; Winnipeg, 5698. *See also* Ethnicity; Labour; Occupation; Elite
Society: 364
General: Ont., 3640; Que., 1977, 1984; Abitibi-Temiskaming, 3299; Atikokan, 5286; Nanaimo, 6435; Montreal, 2320, 2481, 2482, 2554, 2616; Placentia Bay, 1902; Vancouver, 6710
Specific: social beliefs, Vancouver, 6516; *social comment,* Montreal, 2561, 2573, 2644; Toronto, 4744, 4808, 4907; *social control,* Montreal, 2813; *social geography,* Joliette, 2220; Montreal, 2756; Quebec City, 3164; *social interactions,* St. John's, 1890; *social life,* Arctic, 6944; Western Canada, 5354; Nfld., 1827; Ont., 3479; Halifax, 1255, 1259, 1331; *social mobility,* 466; Toronto, 4999; *social orga-*

nization, 1090; Kingston, 3915; St. Martin's, 1716; Surrey, 6498; Toronto, 4935, 5064; *social planning,* Edmonton, 6259; Halifax, 1238; *social problems,* 1077; N.B., 1709; Calgary, 6067; Elliot Lake, 3693; St. John's, 1899; *social reform,* Calgary, 6060; *social space,* Winnipeg, 5718
Spaniards: Montreal, 2749. *See also* Ethnicity
Spatial organization: Ottawa, 4408; Shawinigan, 3252A. *See also* Central business district; Civic centre; Development; Suburbs
Sport:
 General: Calgary, 6005; Edmonton, 6213, 6218; London, 4151; Montreal, 2627, 2628; Windsor, 5274
 Specific: athletic clubs, Halifax, 1286; *basketball,* Halifax, 1425; *cricket, skating, curling,* Toronto, 4699; *curling,* 1903; *lacrosse,* Souris, 5749; *yacht clubs,* Vancouver, 6496
 See also Recreation; Entertainment
Squatters: Northern settlement, 6956; Whitehorse, 7010, 7023, 7024, 7025, 7027
Stage coach: N.S., 1153; Cobourg, 3683. *See also* Transportation
Stampede: Calgary, 6017, 6051, 6093. *See also* Recreation
Staples: 224, 247; Halifax, 1414; Vancouver, 6643. *See also* Fur trade; Lumbering; Mining; New towns; Single enterprise towns; Pulp and paper towns
Steel industry: N.S., 1506; St. John, 1701; Sault Ste. Marie, 4493, 4496. *See also* Industry
Stock exchanges: Montreal, 2334; Toronto, 4820
Street cars and electric railways: 287, 291, 297, 302, 305; Grand River Valley, 3544; Calgary, 6018, 6027; Hamilton, 3766, 3807; London, 4127; Montreal, 2565, 2568, 2645, 2872; Ottawa, 4426; Regina, 5845; St. John, 1624; St. John's, 1895; Sudbury, 4588; Toronto, 4698, 4889, 4891, 4975, 5026, 5027; Winnipeg, 5494, 5511, 5600, 5631; Vancouver, 6583, 6584, 6665, 6666. *See also* Transportation
Streets: 519, 525, 1089; Ont., 3567; London, 4130; Montreal, 2378, 2435, 2602, 2836; Ottawa, 4289, 4424, 4425; Quebec City, 2970, 2985, 3020, 3021, 3180; Saskatoon, 5924; Toronto, 4755, 4798, 4847, 4875, 4879, 4882, 4885, 5120; Vancouver, 6511; Winnipeg, 5549, 5604. *See also* Transportation; Planning
Strikes: N.B., 1552; Que., 1955, 2133, 2135, 2136, 2137, 2139, 2140; Cape Breton, 1499; Amherst, 1206; Cobalt, 3672; Drumheller, 6321; Edmonton, 6179, 6254;

Hamilton, 3841, 3876, 3881; Kirkland Lake, 4035; Lachute, 3357; Lakehead, 4628; Montreal, 2601; Sorel, 3287; Toronto, 4842, 4985, 5151; Wellington and Steveston, 6903; Winnipeg, 5580, 5584, 5596, 5598, 5615, 5620, 5626, 5637, 5697. *See also* Labour; Occupations; Riots
Subdivisions: 654; Vancouver, 6744, 6751
Suburbs: 636, 646, 661, 803, 804, 823, 824; Hamilton, 3800, 3861; Kitchener-Waterloo, 4052; Montreal, 2312, 2364, 2405, 2470, 2801; Ottawa, 4284; Quebec City, 3153, 3162, 3170; Shawinigan, 3251; Sherbrooke, 3274; Thompson, 5742; Toronto, 5202, 5222; Vancouver, 6509, 6738; Winnipeg, 5518
Swedes: Vancouver, 6530. *See also* Ethnicity

Talbot, Col. Thomas: London, 4114, 4157
Taxation and taxes: 1042
 General: Western Canada, 5400; Man., 5421, 5422; N.B., 1565, 1566, 1571; N.S., 1146; Ont., 3468; Edmonton, 6169, 6267; Halifax, 1224, 1262; Hamilton, 3383; Vancouver, 6552
 Specific types: business, 1008; income, 1007, 1050; land, 998, 1038, 1041; property, 1009, 1010, 1020; sales, 1044
 See also Municipal finance
Taxis: Kingston, 3955. *See also* Transportation
Teachers. *See* Education
Technology: 225, 229
Theatre: Barkerville, 6859; Charlottetown, 1766; Dawson City, 6993, 6994; Edmonton, 6201; Halifax, 1225, 1228, 1246, 1342, 1343, 1366, 1374, 1375, 1395; Hull, 2190; Montreal, 2388, 2496, 2511, 2566; Ottawa, 4295; Quebec City, 3029; Regina, 5862; St. John, 1645, 1691; Saskatoon, 5932; Toronto, 4760, 4846, 4877, 4887, 4930, 5000; Vancouver, 6673; Victoria, 6760, 6778; Winnipeg, 5393, 5635. *See also* Entertainment
Tourism: Kingston, 4006; Montreal, 2811; Victoria, 6810, 6825
Tornado: Regina, 5823
Townsite: North, 7049; Canadian and American West, 5381; Nfld., 1818; Ont., 3579, 3588; Sask., 5779; Calgary, 6062; Hamilton, 3804; Moose Jaw, 5809
Trade: Nfld., 1799; Que., 2058; Halifax, 1298; Quebec City, 3068, 3074; St. John's, Nfld., 1861. *See also* Merchants; Commerce; Entrepreneurs
Trading centres: Western Canada, 5409; Alta.,

5954; Sask., 5781; Alberni Valley, Nanaimo, Comox, Duncan, Courtney, Campbell River, Victoria, 6875; Camrose and Wetaskiwin, 6310; Okotoks, 6319. *See also* Service centres

Transportation: 283, 285, 288, 289, 294, 296, 306, 309, 1102, 1132, 1137
  General: B.C., 6324; N.S., 1200; Ont., Que., 3537; Southern Ont., 3623; Y.T., 6920; Niagara Peninsula, 4544; Halifax, 1386; Hamilton, 3853; Kingston, Ogdensburg, U.S.A., 3920; Montreal, 2565, 2568, 2645, 2684, 2701, 2754, 2778, 2907; Regina, 5878; Sudbury, 4578; Toronto, 4805, 5018, 5047, 5084, 5186, 5212; Vancouver, 6520, 6722; Victoria, 6823; Winnipeg, 5496
  Specific: communication, N.B., 1553; N.S., 1154, 1516; *philosophy,* 284, 301, 303, 3549; *public,* Montreal, 2345, 2391; Windsor and London, 5265

Tuberculosis: Quebec, 2081. *See also* Hospitals; Public health; Disease

Typhoid: Ottawa, 4355; Winnipeg, 5616. *See also* Hospitals; Public health; Disease

Ukrainians: 421; Kingston, 3935; London, 4178; Montreal, 2665, 2718, 2943; Regina, 5849, 5877; Sudbury, 4582, 4594; Winnipeg, 5526, 5659, 5662. *See also* Ethnicity

Unemployment: 1061; Maritimes, 1119; Prairie provinces, 5361; Ont., 3434; Brandon, 5441; Burnaby, North Vancouver City, North Vancouver District, West Vancouver, 6685; Halifax, 1400; Hamilton, 3863; Regina, 5829; Saskatoon, 5890; Vancouver, 6587. *See also* Strikes; Unionism; Labour

Unicity: Winnipeg, 5647, 5676, 5696, 5726

Union of Municipalities: 963; N.S., 1172; Que., 2124

Union Station, Toronto: 4959, 5098

Unionism: 472; Ont., 3440, 3602; Abitibi-Temiskaming, 3215A; Calgary, 6088; Hamilton, 3846, 3855, 3862; Hull, 2205; Montreal, 2477, 2808, 2852; Quebec City, 2962; Sherbrooke, 3261; Stratford, 4554; Sudbury, 4590, 4596; Toronto, 4808, 4829, 4921, 4926, 4938, 4979, 5006; Vancouver, 6664; Windsor, 5245, 5258, 5276; Winnipeg, 5633. *See also* Labour; Occupations; Strikes

Universities. *See* Education

University settlement: Toronto, 5230

Urban government. *See* Municipal government

Urban growth. *See* Growth, urban

Urban system: 252, 253, 254, 259, 262, 264, 266, 270, 271, 272, 273, 275, 276, 277, 278, 279; Prairie, 5389, 5413; Western Canada, 5382; Man., 5434; Nfld., 1810; Ont., Que., 3481; P.E.I., 1744; Que., 2062

Urbanization: 227, 245, 246, 249, 356, 359, 360, 363, 365, 367, 368, 369, 371, 372, 373, 374, 377, 378, 379; Prairies, 5404; Alta., 5982, 5992; B.C., 6377, 6379; Ont., 3431; Que., 1982, 1993, 2028, 2037, 2043, 2079; Fraser Valley, 6356; Strait of Georgia Region, 6347; Niagara Fruit Belt, 3510; Pictou County, 1164

Victorian City: 44, 186, 237, 646, 704, 808, 905; Cobourg, 3686; Hamilton, 3815; Toronto, 4923; Victoria, 6769

Villages: Ont., 3632; Que., 1934, 3346; Wellington County, 3723, 3726; Montreal, 2911; Winnipeg, 5656

Voting franchise: 966; Edmonton, 6139; Montreal, 2808; Vancouver, 6733; Victoria, 6843. *See also* Elections

Walking tours: Calgary, 6005; Dundas, 3796; Guelph, 3719; Kingston, 3913; Paris and Wolverton, 5322; Toronto, 4681; Victoria, 6808, 6831. *See also* Guides

War, impact of: 1062, 1072; Edmonton, 6260, 6265; Halifax, 1243; Prince Albert, 6463

Warehousing: Winnipeg, 5546, 5559

Water supply: 1071, 1081, 1087, 1092; Alta., 5972; Southwest Ont., 3584; Grand River Basin, 3529; Edmonton, 6235; Fort William, 4620A; Halifax, 1278; Hamilton, 3781, 3785; Montreal, 2604; Ottawa, 4301, 4361; Regina, 5835; Saskatoon, 5921; Toronto, 4726, 4888, 5097; Winnipeg, 5537, 5624; Vancouver, 6486. *See also* Public health

Water transportation: 239, 248, 292, 308, 310, 311; Maritimes, 1118, 1132; N.B., 1732; Nfld., 1783; N.S., 1165; P.E.I., 1704, 1741; Halifax, 1223, 1257, 1276, 1297, 1302, 1303, 1309, 1311, 1312, 1313, 1386; Moncton, 1608; Port Arthur, Fort William, 4616; Quebec City, 3149; St. John, 1625, 1662, 1681, 1692, 1706; St. Martin's, 1716. *See also* Transportation

Waterfront land development: 811; Halifax, 1408; Kingston, 3914; Ottawa, 4274; Peterborough, 4473; Prince Albert 5819; Quebec City, 2974; St. John, 1639, 1692;

Toronto, 4903, 5087, 5093, 5148, 5174, 5206; Vancouver, 6696
Welfare: 1067, 1075, 1078, 1080, 1090, 1091, 1093, 1097; Urban West, 5402; N.W.T., 6962; Ont., 3631; Sask., 5776; Brockville, 3652; Calgary, 6124; Halifax, 1341; London, 4123; Moncton, 1605; Montreal, 2512, 2659, 2680, 2916; Quebec City, 3163; Saskatoon, 5907; Toronto, 4664, 4768, 4992, 5194, 5215; Vancouver, 6655, 6657, 6692, 6695; Victoria, 6783; Winnipeg, 5491, 5586. *See also* Public health
West Indians: Hamilton and London, 3882; London, 4209; Montreal, 2785. *See also* Ethnicity
Wholesaling: 250; Edmonton and Northern communities, 6171; Toronto, 5035, 5038, 5039; Winnipeg, 5553, 5606; Windsor, 5277
Women: Calgary, 6082; Montreal, 2583, 2611, 2637; Peterborough, 4445; Port Arthur and Fort William, 4635; Trois-Rivières, 3321. *See also* Family; Marriage
Women's organizations: Calgary, 6006; Montreal, 2280, 2303; Regina, 5853; St. Catharines, 4502
Women, working: 398; Montreal, 2639, 2685, 2819, 2899; Toronto, 4944, 4990, 5214; Vancouver, 6664. *See also* Labour
Working class:
General: Algoma, 4490; Calgary, 6068; Halifax, 1289; Hamilton, 3847; Lakehead, 4626A; Montreal, 2411, 2585, 2617, 2820; Quebec City, 3055; Toronto, 4739, 4939, 4940, 4942; Vancouver, 6544
Specific: attitudes of, Canso, 1546; *education of,* Hamilton, 3810; *formation of,* Montreal, 2553
See also Labour; Occupations
Working class housing: 725, 727, 735, 736, 737, 740, 777, 785; Hamilton, 3814; Toronto, 4994; Montreal, 2753; Quebec City, 2067, 3087; Vancouver, 6630. *See also* Housing

Youth: Prince Rupert, 6457; Vancouver, 6715
YMCA: Kingston, 3931; Montreal, 2286, 2290; Toronto, 4781A. *See also* Youth

Zones: built-up, Quebec City, 3173; transition, London, 4113
Zoning: 494, 522, 523, 530, 547, 566, 570, 579, 580, 616, 632, 642; Alta., 5979; London, 4206; Mount Royal, 2827; Ottawa, 4373, 4390, 4407; Prince Albert, 5821; Saskatoon, 5925; Toronto, 5164, 5165; Vancouver, 6698. *See also* Planning

Ref
Z
7165
C 2
A 77

FEB 8 1982